Frommer's®
San Francisco 2002

POSTCARDS FROM

Pine

KEEP OFF
TRACK LANE

Bush

PINE

POWELL
AND
MARKET

2

BAY - TAYLOR
FISHERMANS
WHARF

"Meet me
at the
St. Francis"

D0040682

The quintessential San Francisco transportation, the cable car. See chapter 7.
© *John Elk III Photography.*

A room with no view—one stop on the cellblock tour of Alcatraz. See chapter 7.
© *John Elk III Photography.*

Some of the residents of Pier 39 soak up some rays. See chapter 7. © *John Elk III Photography.*

Strolling through the Strybing Arboretum in Golden Gate Park. See chapter 7.
© John Elk III Photography.

The view from Alamo Square offers a fantastic juxtaposition of San Francisco—sharp-edged Financial District skyscrapers behind a row of Victorian "Painted Ladies." See chapter 7.
© Alan Kearney/Viesti Collection, Inc.

Shooting for the pin at Lincoln Park Municipal Golf Course. See chapter 7.
© John Elk III Photography.

Redwood Canyon Walk at The Muir Woods National Monument, home to the magnificent California Redwoods and located only several miles outside of San Francisco. See chapter 11.
© Richard Cummins Photography.

The Japanese Tea Garden in Golden Gate Park. See chapter 7. © *Robert Holmes Photography.*

Left, an overview of the neighborhood of North Beach, home to the City Lights Bookstore and an assortment of funky cafes.
Photo opposite © Catherine Karnow; both photos on this page © Robert Holmes Photography.

San Francisco's art scene is not limited to traditional museums—colorful murals abound in the Mission District (above), and can be found elsewhere throughout the city, such as this one (below) in the interior of the Coit Tower. See chapter 7. *Top photo © Catherine Karnow Photography; bottom photo © John Elk III Photography.*

The Age of Aquarius, updated for the millennium—this friendly local sells eggs at the Farmer's Market on the Embarcadero. See chapter 9. © Wolfgang Kaehler Photography.

Chinatown is a bustling neighborhood filled with restaurants, shops, and markets—perfect for the urban explorer. See chapter 7. *Top photo © John Elk III Photography; bottom photo © Catherine Karnow Photography.*

Cars descending Lombard Street, the "crookedest street in the world." See chapter 7.
© *Jim Corwin/Tony Stone Images.*

Night falls over the San Francisco skyline. © *Catherine Karnow Photography.*

Touristy Fisherman's Wharf attracts millions of visitors every year. See chapter 7.
© Tom Tracy/The Stock Market.

Located in the Marina District, the Palace of Fine Arts is home to the Exploratorium. See chapter 7. © *John Elk III Photography.*

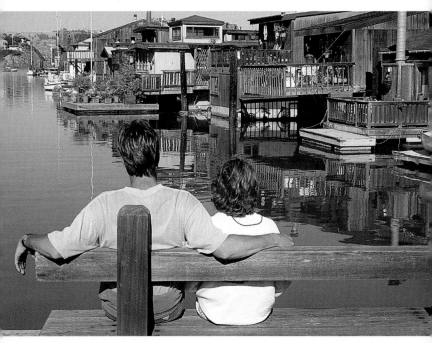

Just north of Golden Gate Bridge, Sausalito makes for a relaxing day trip from the city. See chapter 11. © *Robert Holmes Photography.*

A quick jaunt to the wineries of Napa and Sonoma offers a different taste of Northern California, just about an hour from San Francisco. See chapter 12. *Left and both photos opposite © John Elk III Photography; bottom © Jerry Alexander/Tony Stone Images.*

The Golden Gate Bridge is one of the most spectacular sites in the United States. See chapter 7. © *Wolfgang Kaehler Photography.*

When should I travel to get the best airfare?
Where do I go for answers to my travel questions?
What's the best and easiest way to plan and book my trip?

frommers.travelocity.com

Frommer's, the travel guide leader, has teamed up with **Travelocity.com**, the leader in online travel, to bring you an in-depth, easy-to-use resource designed to help you plan and book your trip online.

At **frommers.travelocity.com**, you'll find free online updates about your destination from the experts at Frommer's plus the outstanding travel planning and purchasing features of Travelocity.com. Travelocity.com provides reservations capabilities for 95 percent of all airline seats sold, more than 47,000 hotels, and over 50 car rental companies. In addition, Travelocity.com offers more than 2,000 exciting vacation and cruise packages. Travelocity.com puts you in complete control of your travel planning with these and other great features:

Expert travel guidance from Frommer's - over 150 writers reporting from around the world!

Best Fare Finder - an interactive calendar tells you when to travel to get the best airfare

Fare Watcher - we'll track airfare changes to your favorite destinations

Dream Maps - a mapping feature that suggests travel opportunities based on your budget

Shop Safe Guarantee - 24 hours a day / 7 days a week live customer service, and more!

Whether traveling on a tight budget, looking for a quick weekend getaway, or planning the trip of a lifetime, Frommer's guides and Travelocity.com will make your travel dreams a reality. You've bought the book, now book the trip!

A New Star-Rating System & Other Exciting News from Frommer's!

In our continuing effort to publish the savviest, most up-to-date, and most appealing travel guides available, we've added some great new features.

Frommer's guides now include a new **star-rating system.** Every hotel, restaurant, and attraction is rated from 0 to 3 stars to help you set priorities and organize your time.

We've also added **seven brand-new features** that point you to the great deals, in-the-know advice, and unique experiences that separate travelers from tourists. Throughout the guide look for:

Finds	Special finds—those places only insiders know about
Fun Fact	Fun facts—details that make travelers more informed and their trips more fun
Kids	Best bets for kids—advice for the whole family
Moments	Special moments—those experiences that memories are made of
Overrated	Places or experiences not worth your time or money
Tips	Insider tips—some great ways to save time and money
Value	Great values—where to get the best deals

We've also added a **"What's New"** section in every guide—a timely crash course in what's hot and what's not in every destination we cover.

Other Great Guides for Your Trip:

Frommer's San Francisco from $60 a Day
Frommer's Portable San Franciso
Frommer's Irreverent Guide to San Francisco
Frommer's Memorable Walks in San Francisco
Wonderful Weekends from San Francisco
Frommer's Portable Wine Country
Frommer's California
Frommer's California from $60 a Day

San Francisco
2002

by Erika Lenkert

Here's what the critics say about Frommer's:

"Amazingly easy to use. Very portable, very complete."

—Booklist

"The only mainstream guide to list specific prices. The Walter Cronkite of guidebooks—with all that implies."

—Travel & Leisure

"Complete, concise, and filled with useful information."

—New York Daily News

"Hotel information is close to encyclopedic."

—Des Moines Sunday Register

Hungry Minds™

Best-Selling Books • Digital Downloads • e-Books • Answer Networks •
e-Newsletters • Branded Web Sites • e-Learning

New York, NY • Cleveland, OH • Indianapolis, IN

About the Author

A native San Franciscan, **Erika Lenkert** spends half her time in Napa Valley and the other half traveling to San Francisco and the world. She's currently a columnist for *San Francisco Magazine,* co-author of several guides to California, and has contributed to *InStyle, Travel & Leisure, Brides, Appellation, Los Angeles Magazine,* and *Time Out.* Erika is pleased that she actually gets paid to force her opinions onto others—something she'd done pro bono for years.

Published by:

Hungry Minds, Inc.

909 Third Avenue
New York, NY 10022

ISBN 0-7645-6486-2
ISSN 1090-5480

Editor: Kitty Wilson Jarrett
Production Editor: Tammy Ahrens
Photo Editor: Richard Fox
Cartographer: Nick Trotter
Production by Hungry Minds Indianapolis Production Services

Front cover photo: View atop the Golden Gate Bridge
Back cover photo: San Francisco's famous Victorian houses or "Painted Ladies" in historic Alamo Square

Special Sales

For general information on Hungry Minds' products and services, please contact our Customer Care department; within the U.S. at 800-762-2974, outside the U.S. at 317-572-3993, or fax 317-572-4002. For sales inquiries and reseller information, including discounts, bulk sales, customized editions, and premium sales, please contact our Customer Care department at 800-434-3422.

Manufactured in the United States of America

5   4   3   2   1

Contents

List of Maps   viii

What's New in San Francisco   1

1 The Best of San Francisco   3

1 Frommer's Favorite San Francisco
Experiences 3

2 Best Hotel Bets 5

Politics of the City Today 6

3 Best Dining Bets 8

2 Planning Your Trip to San Francisco   10

1 Visitor Information 10

2 Money 10

3 When to Go 11

*San Francisco Calendar
of Events* 12

4 Tips for Travelers with
Special Needs 16

5 Getting There 19

*Flying for Less: Getting the
Best Airfare* 22

6 Planning Your Trip Online 23

*Frommers.com: The Complete
Travel Resource* 25

3 For Foreign Visitors   27

1 Preparing for Your Trip 27

2 Getting to the U.S. 31

3 Getting Around the U.S. 31

*Fast Facts: For the Foreign
Traveler* 32

4 Getting to Know San Francisco   38

1 Orientation 38

Neighborhoods in Brief 39

2 Getting Around 44

Fast Facts: San Francisco 51

5 Where to Stay   55

1 Union Square 56

2 The Financial District 75

Sleeping Seaside 76

3 Nob Hill 77

*Free Parking: Pass GO,
Do Not Pay $200* 80

4 North Beach/Fisherman's
Wharf 81

5 The Marina/Pacific Heights/
Cow Hollow 85

6 Japantown & Environs 88

7 Civic Center 90

8 SoMa 91

9 The Castro 93

10 Haight-Ashbury 94

11 Near the Airport 95

6 Where to Dine   97

1 Restaurants by Cuisine 98
2 Union Square 101
3 The Financial District 108
  The Sun on Your Face at Belden Place 111
4 Nob Hill/Russian Hill 113
5 Chinatown 116
  The Best Family-Friendly Restaurants 117
6 North Beach/Telegraph Hill . . .117
7 Fisherman's Wharf 124
8 The Marina/Pacific Heights/ Cow Hollow 125
9 Civic Center 131
10 SoMa 133
11 The Mission District 138
  Hidden Treasures 139
12 The Castro 142
13 Haight-Ashbury 144
14 Richmond/Sunset Districts 145
  Lunching Near Golden Gate Park 147

7 Exploring San Francisco   149

1 Famous San Francisco Sights 149
  Funky Favorites at Fisherman's Wharf 153
2 Museums 157
3 Neighborhoods Worth a Visit 161
4 Golden Gate Park 166
5 The Presidio & Golden Gate National Recreation Area 169
6 Here's the Church & Here's the Steeple 173
7 Architectural Highlights 174
  Especially for Kids 177
8 Self-Guided & Organized Tours 177
9 Outdoor Pursuits 180
10 Spectator Sports 184

8 City Strolls   186

Walking Tour 1: Chinatown: History, Culture, Dim Sum & Then Some 186
Walking Tour 2: Getting to Know North Beach 191

9 Shopping   198

1 The Shopping Scene 198
2 Shopping A to Z 199

10 San Francisco After Dark   214

1 The Performing Arts 214
2 Comedy & Cabaret 219
3 The Club & Music Scene 220
4 The Bar Scene 224
  Midnight (or Midday) Mochas 227
5 Gay & Lesbian Bars & Clubs 229
6 Film 230

11 Side Trips from San Francisco   232

1 Berkeley 232
*People's Park/
People's Power* 236
2 Oakland 239
3 Angel Island & Tiburon 242
4 Sausalito 245
5 Muir Woods & Mount
Tamalpais 248

6 Point Reyes National
Seashore 249
Johnson's Oyster Farm 251
7 Half Moon Bay 254
*Dinner at Duarte's & a Stop at
Phipps Ranch* 259

12 The Wine Country   260

1 Napa Valley 260
*The Ins & Outs of Shipping
Wine Home* 270
Enjoying Art & Nature 274
*Where to Stock Up for a
Gourmet Picnic* 285

2 Sonoma Valley 289
*Touring the Sonoma Valley
by Bike* 293
The Super Spa 297

Appendix A: San Francisco in Depth   304

Dateline 304

Appendix B: Useful Toll-Free
Numbers & Websites   315

Index   317

List of Maps

San Francisco Neighborhoods   42

San Francisco Mass Transit   46

Accommodations Near
   Union Square & Nob Hill   58

Accommodations Around Town   82

Union Square & Financial District
   Dining   102

Dining Around Town   114

Dining Near North Beach &
   Chinatown   119

Major San Francisco Sights   150

Fisherman's Wharf & Vicinity   155

Yerba Buena Gardens   161

The Castro & the Haight   165

Golden Gate Park   167

Golden Gate National
   Recreation Area   170

The Civic Center   175

Walking Tour: Chinatown   187

Walking Tour: North Beach   193

San Francisco Shopping   200

San Francisco After Dark   216

The Bay Area   233

Berkeley   235

Marin County   243

The Wine Country   261

An Invitation to the Reader

In researching this book, we discovered many wonderful places—hotels, restaurants, shops, and more. We're sure you'll find others. Please tell us about them, so we can share the information with your fellow travelers in upcoming editions. If you were disappointed with a recommendation, we'd love to know that, too. Please write to:

Frommer's San Francisco 2002
Hungry Minds, Inc. • 909 Third Avenue • New York, NY 10022

An Additional Note

Please be advised that travel information is subject to change at any time—and this is especially true of prices. We therefore suggest that you write or call ahead for confirmation when making your travel plans. The authors, editors, and publisher cannot be held responsible for the experiences of readers while traveling. Your safety is important to us, however, so we encourage you to stay alert and be aware of your surroundings. Keep a close eye on cameras, purses, and wallets, all favorite targets of thieves and pickpockets.

New! Frommer's Star Ratings & Icons

Every hotel, restaurant, and attraction listing in this guide has been ranked for quality, value, service, amenities, and special features using a star-rating scale. In country, state, and regional guides, we also rate towns and regions to help you narrow down your choices and budget your time accordingly. Hotels and restaurants in the Very Expensive and Expensive categories are rated on a scale of one (highly recommended) to three stars (exceptional). Those in the Moderate and Inexpensive categories rate from zero (recommended) to two stars (very highly recommended). Attractions, towns, and regions are rated according to the following scale: zero stars (recommended), one star (highly recommended), two stars (very highly recommended), and three stars (must-see).

In addition to the rating system, we also use seven icons to highlight insider information, useful tips, special bargains, hidden gems, memorable experiences, kid-friendly venues, places to avoid, and other useful information:

Finds   *Fun Fact*   *Kids*   *Moments*   *Overrated*   *Tips*   *Value*

The following abbreviations are used for credit cards:

AE	American Express	DISC	Discover	V	Visa
DC	Diners Club	MC	MasterCard		

FROMMERS.COM

Now that you have the guidebook to a great trip, visit our website at **www.frommers. com** for travel information on nearly 2,000 destinations. With features updated regularly, we give you instant access to the most current trip-planning information available. At Frommers.com, you'll also find the best prices on air fares, accommodations, and car rentals—and you can even book travel online through our travel booking partners. At Frommers.com, you'll also find the following:

- Daily Newsletter highlighting the best travel deals
- Hot Spot of the Month/Vacation Sweepstakes & Travel Photo Contest
- More than 200 Travel Message Boards
- Outspoken Newsletters and Feature Articles on travel bargains, vacation ideas, tips & resources, and more!

What's New in San Francisco

Almost everywhere you look in San Francisco, new construction or renovation is under way. Despite the downturn in the stock market, The City by the Bay has reaped the rewards of the past several high-rolling years, and its profits are evident in everything from freshly painted homes to new high-end shops and restaurants.

ACCOMMODATIONS San Francisco has never had enough rooms to accommodate its annual visitors, but new hotel openings in recent years have proven that there's an effort under way to change that. After **Campton Place Hotel's** (340 Stockton St. © **800/235-4300**) $10 million renovation, the hotel actually has fewer rooms, but man, oh man, are they posh. Ian Schrager debuts his revamp of the historic **Clift Hotel,** 495 Geary St. (© **800/652-5438**). **The Juliana Hotel,** 590 Bush St. (© **800/328-3880**) barely had time to get scuffed after its 1996 overhaul before its latest renovation, which closed the hotel until mid-2001, premiered an even better boutique hotel. Already bargain-beautiful, The **Clarion Bedford Hotel,** 761 Post St. (© **800/252-7466** or 415/673-6040) spruced up half its rooms in 2001. Others to receive facelifts include **Hyatt Regency San Francisco,** 5 Embarcadero Center (© **800/233-1234** or 415/788-1234) and the fabulous **Fairmont Hotel & Tower,** 950 Mason St. (© **800/527-4727** or 415/772-5000), which gussied to the tune of $85 million. Chic home-away-from-home **The Huntington Hotel,** 1075 California St. (© **800/227-4683** or 415/474-5400) now beckons with a full spa. **Hotel Del Sol,** 3100 Webster St. (© **877/433-5765** or 415/921-5520), is one of The Marina's newer and cheerier motels. **The Hotel Majestic,** 1500 Sutter St. (© **800/869-8966** or 415/441-1100) revamped its tranquil restaurant, Perlot. There's also a new eatery at **The Radisson Miyako Hotel,** 1625 Post St. (© **800/533-4557** or 415/922-3200), which is owned by underwear designer Joe Boxer. For complete details on each, see chapter 5.

DINING Food is still the focus in the city surrounded on all sides by edible wonders from the land, sea, and vineyards. New additions include Vietnamese oasis **Ana Mandara,** 891 Beach St. (© **415/771-6800**), which gives even locals a reason to head to the Fisherman's Wharf area. **Ella's,** 500 Presidio Ave. (© **415/441-5669**) encourages breakfast lovers to venture to lower Pacific Heights. Jazz supper club **Butterfly,** 1710 Mission St. (© **415/864-5575**), spreads its wings in The Mission District. **MoMo's,** 760 Second St., at King St. (© **415/227-8660**), has been hitting home runs with crowds since it opened near the Giants's new home Pacific Bell Park. **bacar,** 448 Brannan St. (© **415/904-4100**), the hottest new restaurant of 2001 pours on the charm with industrial-chic surroundings and the ultimate wine-drinking experience.

SHOPPING The boom-and-bust lifestyle of San Francisco is optimized downtown, where many new upscale chains have set up shop in the past year. Elsewhere around town, there's also evidence of heightened retail therapy. **Nest** is now nesting with its fantastic French interior accouterments and must-have slippers and sleepwear at its new digs on 340 Presidio Ave. (© **415/776-7289**). Italian designer Alberto Alessi's flagship home accessories store **Alessi**, 424 Sutter St. (© **415/434-0403**), features all the whimsical suspects. **Boulangerie**, 2325 Pine St (© **415/440-0356,** ext. 204) brings Paris to your picnic basket. **Artisan Cheese,** 2413 California St. (© **415/929-8610**) exemplifies why San Franciscans are fanatical about the delicious dairy.

AFTER DARK Despite all the changes San Francisco faces, few of them have to do with nightlife beyond the restaurant scene. One especially noteworthy exception is **The Top of the Mark** in the Mark Hopkins Intercontinental Hotel, 1 Nob Hill (© **800/327-0200** or 415/392-3434). The famous cocktail lounge underwent renovation and now has dinner service a few days per week.

SIDE TRIPS FROM SAN FRANCISCO Alice Waters's famed restaurant Chez Panisse isn't the only reason foodies should flock to the East Bay. **Scharffen Berger Chocolate Maker,** 914 Heinz Ave, Berkeley (© **510/981-4051**) launched a factory and retail shop that's sure to lure chocoholics from around the world.

WINE COUNTRY Accommodations in the city of Napa took a step up in quality with the opening of **Napa River Inn** (500 Main St, Napa, CA 94599. © **877/251-8500** or 707/251-8500).

The Best of San Francisco

From an outsider's perspective, San Francisco is still very much the city it's reputed to be. The restaurant scene is booming, boutiques abound, The Castro is The Castro, liberalism is hip, and all the goings-on in the unique neighborhoods take place against picture-perfect backdrops of famous bridges, bay vistas, cable cars, and colorful only-in-San-Francisco city life. But from an insider's view, the historic City by the Bay is striving to maintain its identity while embracing an evolution spawned by a burgeoning new economy, dot-commercialization, the slew of new residents who just don't want to live anywhere else. The result? Out-of-this-universe housing prices, a growing community of 20-something millionaires, and commercial and residential expansion to make room for the deep-pocketed masses. Even the sting of mass layoffs in the high-tech industry and stock-market correction hasn't put a damper on the growing pains that resulted from a 7.3% population growth over 10 years of the already crowded city.

But that's nothing for you to worry about—so long as you're prepared to pay the high hotel and restaurant prices that come along with San Francisco's status as the nation's favorite city destination and epicenter of cutting-edge technology. In fact, it makes a visit here even more exciting (minus the traffic, of course).

You'll still encounter classic San Francisco. You'll feel the cool blast of salt air as you stroll across the Golden Gate Bridge, stuff yourself on dim sum, browse the Haight for incense and crystals, and walk along the beach. But on the flip side, much is new. These days, it is impossible to drive up, down, or around the streets of San Francisco without stumbling on a new happening spot, extensive construction, or whisperings of yet another insider stock tip.

So, what can you expect from the country's most romantic European-style city, which was founded on—and still revels in—the pioneers' boom-or-bust lifestyle? Despite the thick fog bank that blocks out the sun most every summer, the city's stature and future indeed look bright. Like an eternal world's fair, it's all happening in San Francisco, and everyone's invited.

1 Frommer's Favorite San Francisco Experiences

- **Cafe Hopping in North Beach:** One of the most pleasurable smells of San Francisco is the aroma of roasted coffee beans wafting down Columbus Avenue. Start the day with a cup of Viennese at Caffé Trieste (a haven for true San Francisco characters), followed by a walk in and around Washington Square. Continue with lunch at Mario's Bohemian Cigar Store (a la focaccia sandwiches), book browsing at City Lights, more coffee at Caffé Greco, and dinner at L'Osteria del Forno or Moose's. Finish the day with a nightcap as Enrico Caruso plays on the jukebox at Tosca.

- **A Walk Along the Coastal Trail:** Stroll the forested coastal trail from the Cliff House to the Golden Gate Bridge, and you'll see why San Franciscans put up with living on a fault line. Start at the parking lot just above Cliff House and head north. On a clear day you'll have incredible views of the Marin Headlands, but even on foggy days, it's worth the trek to scamper over old bunkers and relish the crisp, cool air. Dress warmly.

- **A Drive to Muir Woods, Stinson Beach & Point Reyes:** If you have wheels, reserve a day for a trip across the Golden Gate Bridge. Take the Stinson Beach exit off Highway 101 and spend a few hours gawking at the monolithic redwoods at Muir Woods (people, I'm telling you, this place is amazing). Continue to Stinson Beach for lunch at the Parkside Café, then head up the coast to the spectacular Point Reyes National Seashore. Rain or shine, it's a day trip you'll never forget.

- **An Adventure at Alcatraz:** Even if you loathe tourist attractions, you'll like Alcatraz. The rangers have done a fantastic job of preserving The Rock—just looking at it is enough to give you the heebie-jeebies—and they give excellent guided tours (highly recommended). Heck, even the boat ride across the bay is worth the price, so don't miss this one.

- **A Stroll Through Chinatown:** Chinatown is a trip. We've been through it at least 100 times, and it has never failed to entertain us. Skip the crummy camera and luggage stores and head straight for the outdoor markets, where a cornucopia of the bizarre, unbelievable, and just plain weird sits in boxes for you to scrutinize (one day we saw an armadillo for sale, and it wasn't meant to be a pet). Better yet, take one of Shirley Fong-Torres's Wok Wiz tours of Chinatown.

- **A Date in the Haight:** Although the flowers of power have wilted, the Haight is still, more or less, the Haight: aging hippies, dazed Dead-heads, skate punks, and an assortment of young panhandlers mix with chi-chi stores that accommodate the new, wealthier alternative residents. Think of it as visiting a people zoo as you walk down the rows of used clothing stores and leather shops, trying hard not to stare at that girl (at least we *think* it's a girl) with the pierced eyebrows and shaved head. End the mystery tour with a plate of mussels at Cha Cha Cha, one of San Francisco's most festive restaurants.

- **An Afternoon at the Marin Headlands:** San Francisco's backyard of sorts, the Marin Headlands are just across the Golden Gate Bridge to the west. They offer not only the best views of the city but also a wealth of outdoor activities. Bird watching, hiking, mountain biking, horseback riding—the list goes on—are all fair game at this glorious national recreation area. Don't miss the Marine Mammal Center, a ward for injured or abandoned seals (cute little buggers) and sea lions.

- **A Walk Across the Golden Gate Bridge:** Don your windbreaker and walking shoes and prepare for a wind-blasted, exhilarating journey across San Francisco's most famous landmark. It's simply one of those things you have to do at least once in your life.

- **A Cruise Through the Castro:** The most populated and festive street in the city is not just for gays and lesbians (although the best cruising in town is right here). While there are some great shops and cafes, it's the people-watching that makes the trip a must. If you have time, catch a flick at the beautiful 1930s Spanish colonial movie palace, the Castro Theatre.

- **A Day in Golden Gate Park:** Golden Gate Park is a crucial—and relaxing—part of the San Francisco experience. Its arboreal paths stretch from the Haight all the way to Ocean Beach, offering dozens of fun things to do along the way. Top sights are the Conservatory of Flowers, Japanese Tea Garden, Asian Art Museum, and Steinhart Aquarium. The best time to go is Sunday, when portions of the park are closed to traffic (rent skates or a bike for the full effect). Toward the end of the day, head west to the beach and watch the sunset.

- **A Soul-Stirring Sunday Morning Service at Glide:** Preacher Cecil Williams turns churchgoing into a spiritual party that leaves you feeling elated, hopeful, and unified with the world. All walks of life attend the service, which focuses not on any particular religion, but on what we have in common as people. It's great fun, with plenty of singing and hand clapping.

- **An Early-Morning Cable Car Ride:** Skip the boring California line and take the Powell-Hyde cable car down to Fisherman's Wharf—the ride is worth the wait. When you reach the top of Nob Hill, grab the rail in one hand and hold the camera with the other, because you're about to see a view of the bay that'll make you a believer. Oh, and don't call it a trolley.

- **A Visit to MOMA & Yerba Buena:** Ever since the new Museum of Modern Art opened in 1995, it's been the best place to go for a quick dose of culture. Start by touring the museum, then head straight for the gift shop (oftentimes more entertaining than the rotating exhibits). Have a light lunch at Caffé Museo, where the food is a vast improvement over most museums' mush. Finish the trip with a stroll through the Yerba Buena Gardens and its slew of new attractions across from the museum.

2 Best Hotel Bets

See chapter 5 for complete hotel reviews.

- **Best for Families:** Kids like the **Westin St. Francis,** 335 Powell St. (© **800/228-3000** or 415/397-7000), because upon arrival, children under 12 get a Kids Club hat and a special sport bottle that includes complimentary refills in the restaurants. Those ages 3 to 7 also get coloring books and dinosaur soaps and sponges.

- **Best for Romance:** At the **Sherman House,** 2160 Green St. (© **800/424-5777** or 415/563-3600), secure a garden suite with French doors leading out onto a sunken garden terrace with gazebo and pond, or the Paderewski suite, with a fireplace in the bathroom. Honorable mentions include **The Archbishop's Mansion,** 1000 Fulton St. (© **800/543-5820** or 415/563-7872), **The Hotel Bohème,** 444 Columbus St. (© **415/433-9111**), and **The Hotel Majestic,** 1500 Sutter St. (© **800/869-8966** or 415/441-1100).

- **Best Public Space in a Historic Hotel: The Palace Hotel,** 2 New Montgomery St. (© **800/325-3535** or 415/392-8600), the extravagant creation of banker Bonanza King Will Ralston in 1875, has one of the grandest

Politics of the City Today

Shaken but not stirred by the Loma Prieta earthquake in 1989, San Francisco witnessed a spectacular rebound during the following decade. But the real shakedown originates in the modern gold rush of the Internet industry, which continues to change the face of the city. The seaside Embarcadero, once plagued by a horrendously ugly freeway overpass, has been revitalized by a multimillion-dollar face-lift, complete with palm trees, a new cable car line, wide cobblestone walkways, new restaurants, and a skating, biking, and walking promenade. SoMa, the once-shady neighborhood south of Market Street, has exploded with new development. It's home to the world-class Museum of Modern Art, the beautiful and attraction-packed Yerba Buena Gardens, a slew of hip new clubs, cafes, and condos, the new baseball stadium, and, most influential, the wake of thriving-now-failed dot-commerce companies. In short, even though San Francisco may be bearing the brunt of the recent economic hiccup, San Francisco is still hot these days.

Of course, the city has typical big-city problems—and then some. Homelessness and panhandling have gone largely ignored. Those with enough funds to buy a spacious home in most parts of the U.S. can't afford a one-bedroom condo here. Rental units are practically impossible to find and outrageously expensive, which is quickly changing the city's demographics. Artists, gays, and others seeking an alternative lifestyle can no longer afford to move here and sustain their lifestyle—unless they also happen to have a tech background or an MBA and are willing to join the new corporate forces. Parking is beyond a nightmare, even in the outer neighborhoods. Congestion and impatient drivers make cruising the town an anxiety-ridden and very slow ride. And Union Square is looking particularly shabby. (It is, however, slated for renovation.) Thanks to

rooms in the city: the Garden Court. Running a close second is the magnificent lobby at Nob Hill's **The Fairmont Hotel & Tower,** 950 Mason St. (© **800/527-4727** or 415/772-5000).

- **Best Old World Hotel:** Those who appreciate comfort, beautiful surroundings, absolute privacy, and unobtrusive service choose **The Huntington Hotel,** 1075 California St. (© **800/227-4683** or 415/474-5400).

- **Best for Your Budget:** Sure, the rooms at **The San Remo Hotel,** 2237 Mason St. (© **800/352-REMO** or 415/776-8688), are small, but the North Beach location, friendly staff, and low prices can't be beaten. Besides, you're here to see the city, not your hotel room. For overall extra perks, my vote is for the adorable and super-cheap **Marina Inn,** 3110 Octavia St. (© **800/274-1420** or 415/928-1000).

- **Best Moderately Priced Hotel:** **The Laurel,** 444 Presidio Ave. © **415/567-8467,** may be off the beaten track, but it's the newest affordable and fashionable hotel in the city—and it has free parking. If you prefer more classically San Francisco surroundings, try the blessing/curse of the high-tech boom and an influx of new residents, the city's just too darn crowded for its own good.

Some credit mayor Willie Brown, the legendary ex-speaker of the house in California's State Assembly, for the changes, both good and bad. On some levels, since he was voted into office—and reelected after an interestingly close run-off against openly gay Board of Supervisors president and activist Tom Ammiano—things have been looking up for the city. During his first term, Brown gave just about every member of former mayor Frank Jordan's administration the boot. Then he administered steady doses of shock therapy to his proud but oft-troubled city. But has he been effective? Public transportation, always a thorny issue, is still beleaguered, but it's on the slow road to improvement. Homelessness is no longer a crime, and shelters and work programs are on the rise, although it's hard to stomach the lack of care for street dwellers when so much money is flowing through the city. Meanwhile, in this highly political town, critics still insist that the mayor is nothing more than a show-boater with too many big-business connections who's turning the city into a Hollywood caricature of itself.

But as a whole, San Francisco is doing just fine. Its symphony is in the black, its convention halls are fully booked, and though many of the newly rich residents lost it all in the stock market, many argue it's a good thing for the city. We needed a little reality, not to mention elbow room for those making under six figures.

Anyone who knows the old, liberal, truly progressive, and funky San Francisco knows those days are long behind us. But even without the alternative edge, San Francisco rightfully retains its title as Americans' favorite city destination.

the quaint **White Swan Inn,** 845 Bush St. (© **800/999-9570** or 415/775-1755).

- **Best Bed-and-Breakfast:** Attention to detail and darned cute rooms along a prime stretch of Union Street shopping make The **Union Street Inn,** 2229 Union St. (© **415/346-0424**) an excellent way to experience true San Francisco–style living.

- **Best Funky Hotel: The Phoenix Hotel,** 601 Eddy St. (© **800/248-9466** or 415/776-1380), wouldn't look out of place in Palm Springs. A favorite with the rock and movie set, including Sinead O'Connor, k.d. lang, and the Red Hot Chili

Peppers, it has one of the bluest and most bizarre restaurant/bars in town. It's also one of the only hotels in San Francisco with an outdoor pool.

- **Best Trendy-Chic Hotel:** Check into the **W San Francisco Hotel,** 181 Third St. (© **800/877-WHOTEL** or 415/777-5300), and you'll be less than a block from the Museum of Modern Art. But the real visuals are here, where the hottest hotel scene means lots of lookers, fun bar action, and modern surroundings.

- **Best Views:** From the rooms in **The Mandarin Oriental,** 222 Sansome St. (© **800/622-0404** or 415/276-9888), all of which are on the 38th to the 48th floors, you'll have a great view of the city and the entire Bay Area, although you'll pay dearly for the vista.

- **Best Service:** The small, luxurious **Campton Place Hotel,** 340 Stockton St. (© **800/235-4300** or 415/781-5555); the historic, eager-to-please **Ritz-Carlton,** 600 Stockton St. (© **800/241-3333** or 415/296-7465); and the modern, pampering **Mandarin Oriental** (see above) are all tops for service.

- **Best Hotel Dining Room:** George Morrone's Modern French food is just as fancy and decadent as the sexy setting at **Fifth Floor Restaurant** in the swank **Hotel Palomar,** 12 Fourth St. (© **415/ 348-1111).**

3 Best Dining Bets

See chapter 6 for complete restaurant reviews.

- **Best for Impressing Clients:** Show your business associates you've got class—and deep pockets—by reserving a table at the Financial District's **Aqua,** 252 California St. (© **415/956-9662**). It pairs power lunching with excellent seafood and wine.

- **Best Romantic Spot:** Anyone could be seduced at **Fleur de Lys,** 777 Sutter St. (© **415/673-7779**), under the rich burgundy-tented canopy that swathes the elegant room in romance. Lots of question-popping here, too.

- **Best for a Celebration:** Great food, a full bar, and a lively atmosphere are the key ingredients that make **Boulevard,** 1 Mission St. (© **415/543-6084**), the place to celebrate. Care less about fancy food and more about festive surroundings? Go to **Gordon's House of Fine Eats,** 500 Florida St. (© **415/861-8900**), where the menu matches the fun surroundings.

- **Best Decor:** Celeb restaurant designer Pat Kuleto spent a week sketching sea life at the Monterey Bay Aquarium before applying his Midas touch to **Farallon,** 450 Post St. (© **415/956-6969**). The result is an orgy of oceanic artwork, from jellyfish lamps to sea urchin chandeliers. It's truly a spectacular achievement in restaurant design.

- **Best Wine List:** Thanks to renowned master sommelier Larry Stone **Rubicon,** 558 Sacramento St. (© **415/434-4100**), is known to have one of the best lists in the country.

- **Best Pizza:** Has **Pauline's,** 260 Valencia St. (© **415/552-2050**), perfected the pizza? Quite possibly. At least it's the best we've ever had. Pauline's does only two things—pizza and salad—and it does them better than any other restaurant in the city.

- **Best Desserts:** What a decision! Sweet tooths can be satisfied in a number of spots around town, including **Restaurant Gary Danko,** 800 North Point St. (© **415/ 749-2060**), and **Absinthe,** 398 Hayes St. (© **415/551-1590**).

- **Best Value:** No other place in town serves up heaping plates of fresh pasta at penny-pinching prices the way **Pasta Pomodoro,** 655 Union St. (© **415/399-0300**), does. It has other locations at 2027 Chestnut St. (© **415/474-3400**), 2304 Market St. (© **415/558-8123**), 3611 California St. (© **415/ 831-0900**), and 816 Irving St. (© **415/566-0900**). Want a little more atmosphere and more sophisticated cooking? Head to **Delfina,**

3621 18th St. (© **415/552-4055**), or **The Slanted Door,** 584 Valencia St. (© **415/861-8032**).

- **Best Brunch:** The Sunday spread at the **Terrace Restaurant** in the **Ritz-Carlton,** 600 Stockton St. (© **415/296-7465**), will set your eyes popping and your feet tapping. Strut around to the lavish buffets featuring sushi, caviar, freshly made blinis, and traditional egg dishes. A jazz trio brings even more joy to it all.

- **Best Bistro:** Casual and comfortable, **Fringale Restaurant,** 570 Fourth St. (© **415/543-0573**), offers the best moderately priced French food in the city. Start with a scrumptious galette and finish with the vanilla bean crème brûlée. The middle part is up to you.

- **Best Dim Sum:** Downtown and Chinatown dim sum restaurants may be more centrally located, but that's all they've got on **Ton Kiang,** 5821 Geary Blvd. (© **415/387-8273**). Carts bring the freshest and most delicious Chinese dumplings and other dim sum delicacies to your table.

- **Best Vegetarian:** For the food, the view of the Golden Gate, and the redwood booths, go to **Greens Restaurant,** Building A, Fort Mason Center (© **415/771-6222**). If you want to experience how rich and varied vegetables can taste, sample the extraordinary five-course tasting menu.

- **Best Party Scene:** Throw back a few glasses of sangria with your tapas at **Cha Cha Cha,** 1801 Haight St. (© **415/386-5758**), and you'll quickly be swinging with the rest of the crowd.

- **Best Coffee Shop or Cafe:** With all the wonderful coffee shops throughout this cafe town, there can be no one winner. We do, however, love the authentic atmosphere at **Mario's Bohemian Cigar Store,** 566 Columbus Ave. (© **415/362-0536**), and **Caffè Trieste,** 601 Vallejo Ave. (© **415/392-6739;** see chapter 8, "City Strolls"). If you see one you like, pull up a chair. Just do San Francisco one favor: Stay away from Starbucks and support our unique coffee culture.

Planning Your Trip to San Francisco

Regardless of whether you map out your vacation months in advance or travel on a whim, you need to do a little planning to make the most of your stay. This chapter will help you with all the logistics.

1 Visitor Information

Visitors from outside the United States should also see chapter 3 for entry requirements and other pertinent information.

The **San Francisco Convention and Visitors Bureau,** 900 Market St. (at Powell Street), Hallidie Plaza, Lower Level, San Francisco, CA 94102 (② **415/283-0177;** www.sfvisitor. org), is the best source for specialized information about the city. Even if you don't have a specific question, you might want to send $3 for the 100-page *The San Francisco Book.* It includes a 3-month calendar of events, city history, shopping and dining information, and several good, clear maps, plus a 50-page lodging guide. It's free if you drop by to pick it up. If you simply need specific information faxed to you, you can call ② **800/ 220-5747;** follow the prompts to receive information by fax only. The bureau highlights only members' establishments, so if it doesn't have what you're looking for, that doesn't mean it's nonexistent.

You can also get the latest on San Francisco at the following online addresses:

- The *Bay Guardian,* the city's free weekly page: **www.sfbaguardian. com**
- Hotel reservations: **www.hotelres. com**
- *QSF,* for gays and lesbians: **www.qsanfrancisco.com**
- The *SF Gate,* the city's combined *Chronicle* and *Examiner* newspapers: **www.sfgate.com**
- Channel 7, ABC, and KGO's city guide: **www.citysearch7.com**

2 Money

Foreign visitors should also see chapter 3 for more information.

All over San Francisco, you'll find **ATMs** linked to a national network that most likely includes your bank at home. Withdrawing cash as you need it is the easiest way to deal with money while you're on the road. **Cirrus** (② **800/424-7787;** www.mastercard. com/atm) and **PLUS** (② **800/ 843-7587;** www.visa.com/atms) are the two most popular networks. Use the toll-free numbers or websites to locate ATMs in your destination. Be sure to check your daily withdrawal limit before you depart, and be prepared for withdrawal fees of $1 to $3 if you use another network.

Traveler's checks are something of an anachronism from the days before the ATM made cash accessible at any time. These days, traveler's checks seem less necessary, but you might still prefer the security of knowing you can get a refund or replacement if they're lost or stolen. You can get traveler's checks at almost any bank. **American Express** offers denominations of $10, $20, $50, $100, $500, and $1,000. You'll pay a service charge ranging from 1% to 4%. You can also order American Express traveler's checks over the phone by calling ℂ **800/ 221-7282;** by using this number, Amex gold and platinum cardholders are exempt from the 1% service fee. AAA members can get checks without a fee at most AAA offices. **Visa** offers traveler's checks at Citibank locations nationwide, as well as at several other banks. The service charge is 1.5% to 2%; checks come in denominations of $20, $50, $100, $500, and $1,000. If you opt to carry traveler's checks, be sure to keep a record of their serial numbers, separately from the checks, so you're ensured a refund or replacement in case of an emergency.

Credit cards are invaluable when traveling. They are a safe way to carry money and keep a convenient record of your expenses. You can also withdraw cash advances against your credit cards at any bank (although you start paying hefty interest on the advance the moment you get the cash, and you won't get frequent-flyer miles on an airline credit card). At most banks, you don't even need to go to a teller; you can get a cash advance at the ATM if you know your PIN (personal identification number).

Almost every credit-card company has an emergency toll-free number that you can call if your wallet or purse is stolen. The company may be able to wire you a cash advance off your credit card immediately and, in many places, can deliver an emergency credit card in a day or two. **Citicorp Visa**'s U.S. emergency number is ℂ **800/336-8472. American Express** cardholders and traveler's check holders should call ℂ **800/221-7282** for all money emergencies. **MasterCard** holders should call ℂ **800/307-7309.** Odds are that if your wallet is gone, the police won't be able to recover it for you. However, after you realize that it's gone and you cancel your credit cards, it is still worth informing them. Your credit-card company or insurer might require a police-report number.

3 When to Go

If you're dreaming of convertibles, Frisbee on the beach, and tank-topped evenings, change your reservations and head to Los Angeles. Contrary to California's sunshine-and-bikini image, San Francisco's weather is "mild" (to put it nicely) and can often be downright bone-chilling because of the common wet, foggy air and cool winds—it's nothing like that of southern California. Summer, the most popular time to visit, is often characterized by damp, foggy days, cold, windy nights, and crowded tourist destinations. A good bet is to visit in spring or, better yet, autumn. Every September, right about the time San Franciscans mourn being cheated (or fogged) out of another summer, something wonderful happens: The thermometer rises, the skies clear, and the locals call in sick to work and head for the beach. It's what residents call "Indian summer." The city is also delightful during winter, when the opera and ballet seasons are in full swing; there are fewer tourists, many hotel prices are lower, and downtown bustles with holiday cheer.

San Francisco's Average Temperatures (°F) & Rainfall (in.)

	Jan	Feb	Mar	Apr	May	June	July	Aug	Sept	Oct	Nov	Dec
High	56	59	60	61	63	64	64	65	69	68	63	57
Low	46	48	49	49	51	53	53	54	56	55	52	47
Rain	4.5	2.8	2.6	1.5	0.4	0.2	0.1	0.1	0.2	1.1	2.5	3.5

CLIMATE

San Francisco's temperate, marine climate usually means relatively mild weather year-round. In summer, chilling fog rolls in most mornings and evenings, and if temperatures top 70°F, we're ready to throw an all-city celebration. Even when autumn's heat occasionally stretches into the 80s and 90s, you should still dress in layers, or by early evening you'll learn firsthand why sweatshirt sales are a great business at Fisherman's Wharf. In winter, the mercury seldom falls below freezing and snow is almost unheard of, but that doesn't mean you won't be whimpering if you forget your coat. Still, compared to most of the states' varied weather conditions, San Francisco is consistently pleasant.

That beautifully fluffy, chilly, wet, heavy, sweeping fog makes the city's weather so precarious. A rare combination of water, wind, and topography creates northern California's summer fog bank. It lies off the coast, and rising air currents pull it in when the land heats up. Held back by coastal mountains along a 600-mile front, the low clouds seek out any passage they can find. The easiest access is the slot where the Pacific Ocean penetrates the continental wall—the Golden Gate.

SAN FRANCISCO CALENDAR OF EVENTS

January

San Francisco Sports and Boat Show, Cow Palace. Draws thousands of boat enthusiasts over a 9-day period. Call the **Cow Palace Box Office** (℗ **415/469-6065**) for details. Mid-January.

February

Chinese New Year, Chinatown. In 2002, the year of the horse, public celebrations will again spill onto every street in Chinatown. Festivities begin with the "Miss Chinatown USA" pageant parade and climax a week later, with a celebratory parade of marching bands, rolling floats, barrages of fireworks, and a block-long dragon writhing in and out of the crowds. The revelry runs for several weeks and wraps up with a memorable parade through Chinatown. Arrive early for a good viewing spot on Grant Avenue. Make your hotel reservations early. For dates and information, call ℗ **415/982-3000** or visit www.chineseparade.com.

March

St. Patrick's Day Parade. Almost everyone's honorarily Irish at this festive affair, which starts at 12:45pm at Market and Second streets and continues to City Hall. But the party doesn't stop there. Head down to the Civic Center for the post-party, or venture to Embarcadero's Harrington's bar and celebrate with hundreds of the Irish-for-a-day yuppies as they gallivant around the closed-off streets and numerous pubs. Call ℗ **510/644-1164** for details. Sunday before March 17.

April

Cherry Blossom Festival, Japantown. Meander through the arts-and-crafts and food booths lining the blocked-off streets; watch traditional drumming, flower arranging, origami, or a parade celebrating the

> **Tips** **Travel Attire**
>
> Even if it's sunny out, don't forget to bring a jacket; the weather can change almost instantly from sunny and warm to windy and cold.

cherry blossom and Japanese culture. Call ✆ **415/563-2313** for information. Mid- to late April.

San Francisco International Film Festival, with screenings at the AMC Kabuki 8 Cinemas, Fillmore and Post streets, and many other locations. Started 45 years ago, this is America's oldest film festival. It features more than 200 films and videos from more than 50 countries, and awards ceremonies where renowned honorees join the festivities. Tickets are relatively inexpensive, and screenings are accessible to the public. Entries include new films by beginning and established directors. For a schedule or information, call ✆ **415/931-FILM.** Mid-April to early May.

May

Cinco de Mayo Celebration, Mission District. The Latino community celebrates the victory of the Mexicans over the French at Puebla in 1862. Mariachi bands, dancers, food, and a parade fill the streets of The Mission. The parade starts at 10am at 24th and Bryant streets and ends at the Civic Center. Sunday before May 5.

Bay to Breakers Foot Race, Golden Gate Park. Even if you don't participate, you can't avoid this run from downtown to Ocean Beach, which stops morning traffic throughout the city. Around 80,000 entrants gather—many dressed in wacky, innovative, and sometimes X-rated costumes—for the approximately 7½-mile run. If you're feeling lazy, join the throng of spectators who line the route.

Sidewalk parties, bands, and cheerleaders of all ages provide a good dose of true San Francisco fun. The *San Francisco Examiner* (✆ **415/777-7770**) sponsors the event. Third Sunday of May.

Carnival, Mission Street between 14th and 24th streets, and Harrison Street between 16th and 21st streets. The Mission District's largest annual event is a day of festivities that culminates with a parade on Mission Street. For one of San Franciscans' favorite events, more than half a million spectators line the route, and samba musicians and dancers continue to entertain on 14th Street, near Harrison, at the end of the march. Just show up, or call the **Mission Economic and Cultural Association** (✆ **415/826-1401**) for complete information. The Sunday of Memorial Day weekend

June

Union Street Art Festival, along Union Street from Fillmore to Gough streets. With a new promotion company leading the way, the Union Street Fair is now the Union Street Art Festival, which celebrates San Francisco with themes, gourmet food booths, music, entertainment, and a juried show with more than 350 artists. No doubt the change won't deter the great-looking yuppie cocktailers from packing every bar and spilling out into the street. Call the **Union Street Association** (✆ **415/441-7055**) or the **Union Street Art Festival** promoters (✆ **510/970-3217**) for more information. First weekend of June.

Haight Street Fair. This fair features alternative crafts, ethnic foods, rock bands, and a healthy number of hippies and street kids whooping it up and slamming beers in front of the blaring rock 'n' roll stage. The fair usually extends along Haight between Stanyan and Ashbury streets. For details and the exact date, call ✆ **415/661-8025.**

North Beach Festival, Grant Avenue, North Beach. In 1999, this party celebrated its 45th anniversary; organizers claim it's the oldest urban street fair in the country. Close to 100,000 city folk meander along Grant Avenue, between Vallejo and Union streets, to eat, drink, and browse the arts-and-crafts booths, poetry readings, swing dancing venue, and *arte di gesso* (sidewalk chalk art). But the most enjoyable part of the event is listening to music and people-watching. Call ✆ **415/989-2220** for details. Usually Father's Day weekend, but call to confirm.

San Francisco Lesbian, Gay, Bisexual, Transgender Pride Parade & Celebration, Market Street. A prideful event that draws up to half a million participants who celebrate all of the above—and then some. The parade's start and finish have been moved around in recent years to accommodate road construction. Regardless of its path, the parade ends with hundreds of food, art, and information booths and soundstages. Call ✆ **415/864-3733** for information and location. Usually the third or last weekend of June.

Stern Grove Midsummer Music Festival. Pack a picnic and head out early to join the thousands who come here to lie in the grass and enjoy classical, jazz, and ethnic music and dance in the Grove, at 19th Avenue and Sloat Boulevard.

The free concerts take place every Sunday at 2pm. Show up with a lawn chair or blanket. There are food booths if you forget snacks, but you'll be dying to leave if you don't bring warm clothes—the Sunset District can be one of the coldest parts of the city. Call ✆ **415/252-6252** for listings. Mid-June through August.

July

Jazz and All That Art on Fillmore. July starts with a bang, when the upscale portion of Fillmore closes to traffic and several blocks of arts and crafts, gourmet food, and live jazz fill the street. (The blocked-off section is changing, so call for details.) Call ✆ **510/970-3217** for more information. First weekend in July, 10am to 6pm.

Fourth of July Celebration and Fireworks. This event can be somewhat of a joke—more often than not, fog, like everyone else, comes into the city to join in the festivities. Sometimes it's almost impossible to view the million-dollar pyrotechnics from Pier 39 on the northern waterfront. Still, it's a party, and if the skies are clear, it's a darn good show.

San Francisco Marathon. This is one of the largest marathons in the world. For entry information, contact West End Management, the event organizer (✆ **800/698-8699**). Usually the second weekend in July.

August

Renaissance Pleasure Faire. An expensive, but enjoyable, festival takes place north of San Francisco and takes you back to Renaissance times—with games, plays, and arts-and-crafts and food booths. In the past the fair was in Black Point Forest, just east of Novato, but there's talk of a new location. For more information, call ✆ **800/52-FAIRE.** Six to eight weekends late in summer.

September

A La Carte, A La Park, usually at Sharon Meadow, Golden Gate Park. You probably won't get to go to all the restaurants you'd like while you're visiting the city, but you can get a good sampling at this annual event. More than 40 of the town's favorite restaurants, accompanied by 20 microbreweries and 20 wineries, offer tastings in San Francisco's favorite park. There's entertainment as well, and proceeds benefit the Friends of Recreation & Parks. Admission in 2001 was $9 adults in advance and $10 on site, $7 seniors, free for children under 12. Prices for 2002 were not determined at press time. Call ✆ **415/458-1988** for details. Labor Day weekend.

Sausalito Art Festival, Sausalito. A juried exhibit of more than 180 artists. It includes music—provided by Bay Area jazz, rock, and blues performers—and international cuisine, enhanced by wines from some 50 Napa and Sonoma producers. Parking is impossible; take the **Blue & Gold Fleet ferry** (✆ **415/705-5555**) from Fisherman's Wharf to the festival site. For more information, call ✆ **415/332-3555.** Labor Day weekend.

Opera in the Park. Each year the San Francisco Opera launches its season with a free concert featuring a selection of arias. Usually in Sharon Meadow, Golden Gate Park, on the Sunday after Labor Day; call ✆ **415/861-4008** to confirm the date.

San Francisco Blues Festival, on the grounds of Fort Mason. The largest outdoor blues music event on the West Coast will be 30 years old in 2002 and will again feature local and national musicians performing back-to-back during the 3-day extravaganza. You can charge tickets by phone through **BASS** Ticketmaster (✆ **510/762-2277**). For schedule information, call ✆ **415/826-6837** or www.sfblues. com. Usually in late September.

October

Castro Street Fair. Celebrates life in the city's most famous gay neighborhood. Call ✆ **415/467-3354** or visit www.castrostreetfair.org for information. First Sunday in October.

Reggae in the Park, usually in Sharon Meadow, Golden Gate Park. Going into its 12th year, this event draws thousands to the park to dance and celebrate the soulful sounds. Big-name reggae and world-beat bands play all weekend, and ethnic arts-and-crafts and food booths line the stage's periphery. Tickets are around $15 in advance, $20 on site. Two-day discounted passes are available. Free for children under 12. Call ✆ **415/458-1988** for more details. First weekend in October.

Italian Heritage Parade. The city's Italian community leads the festivities around Fisherman's Wharf, celebrating Columbus's landing in America. The festival includes a parade along Columbus Avenue and sporting events, but for the most part, it's just a great excuse to hang out in North Beach and people-watch. For information, call ✆ **415/434-1492.** Sunday closest to October 12.

Exotic Erotic Halloween Ball. Thousands come dressed in costume, lingerie, and sometimes even less than that. It's a wild fantasy affair with bands, dancing, and costume contests. Beware: It can be somewhat cheesy. Tickets cost approximately $35 per person. For information, call ✆ **415/567-BALL;** for tickets, call ✆ **510/762-BASS.** Friday or Saturday night before Halloween.

Halloween. A huge night in San Francisco. A fantastic parade is organized at Market and Castro streets, and a mixed gay/straight crowd revels in costumes of extraordinary imagination. October 31.

San Francisco Jazz Festival. This festival presents eclectic programming in an array of fabulous jazz venues throughout the city. With close to 2 weeks of nightly entertainment and dozens of performers, the jazz festival is a hot ticket. Past events have featured Herbie Hancock, Dave Brubeck, the Modern Jazz Quartet, Wayne Shorter, and Bill Frisell. For information, call © 800/850-SFJF or 415/398-5655. Late October and early November.

December

The Nutcracker, War Memorial Opera House. The San Francisco Ballet (© 415/865-2000) performs this holiday classic annually. Order tickets to this Tchaikovsky tradition well in advance.

4 Tips for Travelers with Special Needs

FOR PEOPLE WITH DISABILITIES

A disability shouldn't stop anyone from traveling. There are more resources out there than ever before.

You can join the Society for Accessible Travel & Hospitality (SATH), 347 Fifth Ave., Suite 610, New York, NY 10016 (© 212/ 447-7284; fax 212/725-8253; www. sath.org), for $45 annually, $30 for seniors and students. Membership includes access to the society's vast network of connections in the travel industry. It provides information sheets on travel destinations along with referrals to tour operators who specialize in travelers with disabilities. Its quarterly magazine, *Open World for Disability and Mature Travel,* is full of good information and resources. A year's subscription is $13 ($21 outside the U.S.).

Most of San Francisco's major museums and tourist attractions have wheelchair ramps. Many hotels offer special accommodations and services for wheelchair users and other visitors with disabilities. They include extra-large bathrooms, wheelchair ramps, and telecommunication devices for hearing-impaired travelers. The San Francisco Convention and Visitors Bureau (see "Visitor Information," above) has the most up-to-date information.

Travelers in wheelchairs can request special ramped taxis by calling **Yellow Cab** (© 415/626-2345), which charges regular rates for the service. Travelers with disabilities can also get a free copy of the *Muni Access Guide,* published by the San Francisco Municipal Railway, Accessible Services Program, Municipal Railway, 949 Presidio Ave., San Francisco, CA 94115 (© 415/923-6142), staffed weekdays 8am to 5pm. Many of the major car-rental companies offer hand-controlled cars for drivers with disabilities. **Avis** can provide a vehicle at any of its U.S. locations with 48 hours advance notice; **Hertz** requires between 24 and 72 hours of advance reservation at most locations.

Travelers with disabilities might also want to consider joining a tour that caters specifically to them. One of the best operators is **Flying Wheels Travel,** 143 West Bridge (P.O. Box 382), Owatonna, MN 55060 (© 800/535-6790; www.flyingwheelstravel.com). It offers escorted tours and cruises, as well as private tours in minivans with lifts.

Vision-impaired travelers should contact the **American Foundation for the Blind,** 11 Penn Plaza, Suite 300, New York, NY 10001 (© 800/ 232-5463), for information on traveling with guide dogs.

FOR GAYS & LESBIANS

If you head down to the Castro—an area surrounding Castro Street near Market Street—you'll understand why the city is a mecca for gay and lesbian travelers. Since the 1970s, this unique part of town has remained a colorfully festive neighborhood, teeming with "outed" city folk who meander the streets shopping, eating, partying, or cruising. If anyone feels like an outsider in this part of town, its heterosexuals, who, although warmly welcomed in the community, may feel uncomfortable or downright threatened if they harbor any homophobia or aversion to being "cruised." For many San Franciscans, it's just a fun area (especially on Halloween) with some wonderful shops.

It is estimated that gays and lesbians form one-fourth to one-third of the population of San Francisco, so it's no surprise that clubs and bars all over town cater to them. Although lesbian interests are concentrated primarily in the East Bay (especially Oakland), a significant community resides in the Mission District, around 16th Street and Valencia.

Several local publications concentrate on in-depth coverage of news, information, and listings of goings-on around town for gays and lesbians. The *Bay Area Reporter* has the most comprehensive listings, including a weekly calendar of events. Distributed free on Thursdays, it can be found stacked at the corner of 18th and Castro streets and at Ninth and Harrison streets, as well as in bars, bookshops, and stores around town. It may also be available in gay and lesbian bookstores elsewhere in the country.

GUIDES & PUBLICATIONS For accommodations, check the international guides *Odysseus* ($29) and *Inn Places* ($19.95). These books and others are available by mail from **Giovanni's Room,** 345 S. 12th St., Philadelphia, PA 19107 (✆ **215/ 923-2960;** giophilp@netaxs.com), and **A Different Light Bookstore,** 489 Castro St., San Francisco, CA 94114 (✆ **415/431-0891;** www. adlbooks.com). Another location is in Los Angeles (✆ **310/854-6601**).

Our World, 1104 N. Nova Rd., Suite 251, Daytona Beach, FL 32117 (✆ **904/441-5367;** www.ourworld mag.com), is a magazine devoted to gay and lesbian travel worldwide. It costs $35 for 10 issues. *Out & About,* 8 W. 19th St., Suite 401, New York, NY 10011 (✆ **800/929-2268;** www. outandabout.com), has been hailed for its "straight" reporting about gay travel. It profiles the best gay or gay-friendly hotels, restaurants, clubs, and other places, with coverage of destinations throughout the world. It costs $49 a year for 10 information-packed issues plus a monthly calendar. Both of these publications are available at most gay and lesbian bookstores.

ORGANIZATIONS The **International Gay & Lesbian Travel Association (IGLTA),** 4331 N. Federal Hwy., Suite 304, Fort Lauderdale, FL 33308 (✆ **800/448-8550** for a voice mailbox, or 954/776-2626; www. iglta.org), encourages gay and lesbian travel worldwide. It has around 1,100 travel-professional members and offers monthly newsletters, marketing mailings, and a membership directory that is updated annually. Travel agents who are IGLTA members are tied into the organization's vast information resources.

TRAVEL AGENCIES In California, a leading gay-friendly option is **Now Voyager,** 4406 18th St., San Francisco, CA 94114 (✆ **800/ 255-6951** or 415/626-1169).

Also in California is **Skylink Women's Travel,** 1006 Mendocino Ave., Santa Rosa, CA 95401 (✆ **800/ 225-5759** or 707/546-9888).

Tips Healthy Travel

If you suffer from a chronic illness, consult your doctor before your departure. For conditions like epilepsy, diabetes, or heart problems, wear a **Medic Alert Identification Tag** (© 800/825-3785; www.medicalert.org), which immediately alerts doctors to your condition and gives them access to your records through Medic Alert's 24-hour hotline. Membership is $35, plus a $20 annual fee after the first year.

Pack prescription medications in your carry-on luggage. Carry written prescriptions in generic, not brand-name form, and dispense all prescription medications from their original labeled vials. Also bring along copies of your prescriptions in case you lose or run out of your medication.

General gay and lesbian travel agencies include **Above and Beyond Tours** (© 800/397-2681).

FOR WOMEN

Women's services are often lumped together in the lesbian category, but some resources assist women without regard to sexuality. The **Bay Area Women's and Children's Center,** 318 Leavenworth St. (© 415/474-2400), offers specialized services and city information to women and families. The **Women's Building,** 3543 18th St. (© 415/431-1180), is a Mission-area space housing feminist art shows and political events. It offers classes in yoga, aerobics, movement, and tai chi chuan.

FOR SENIORS

If you're a senior, don't be shy about asking for discounts—you're entitled to them on public transportation and at many attractions. Always carry some kind of identification, such as a driver's license, that shows your date of birth.

Also, mention that you're a senior citizen when you make your travel reservations. For example, both **Amtrak** (© 800/USA-RAIL; www. amtrak.com) and **Greyhound** (© 800/ 752-4841; www.greyhound.com) offer discounts to people over 62, as do most airlines. And many hotels offer senior discounts; **Choice Hotels** (Clarion Hotels, Quality Inns, Comfort Inns,

Sleep Inns, Econo-Lodges, Friendship Inns, and Rodeway Inns), for example, give 30% off their published rates to anyone over 50, provided you book your room through their nationwide toll-free reservation numbers (that is, not directly with the hotels or through a travel agent). See appendix B, "Useful Toll-Free Numbers & Websites," for a handy list of national numbers.

When making airline reservations, ask about senior discounts, but find out if there's a cheaper promotional fare before committing yourself.

The **Senior Citizen Information Line** (© 415/626-1033) offers advice, referrals, and information on city services. The **Friendship Line for the Elderly** (© 415/752-3778) is a support, referral, and crisis-intervention service.

Members of the **American Association of Retired Persons (AARP),** 601 E St. NW, Washington, DC 20049 (© 800/424-3410 or 202/ 434-2277; www.aarp.org), get discounts on hotels, airfares, and car rentals. AARP offers members a wide range of special benefits, including *Modern Maturity* magazine and a monthly newsletter.

The Mature Traveler, a monthly 12-page newsletter, is a valuable resource. It is available by subscription ($30 a year) from publisher John Stickler at P.O. Box 15791, Sacramento, CA 95852. *The Book of Deals,* a collection of more than 1,000 senior discounts on airlines, lodging, tours, and attractions around the country; it's available for $9.95 (or free with subscription) by calling ℂ **800/460-6676.** Another helpful publication is *101 Tips for the Mature Traveler,* available from **Grand Circle Travel,** 347 Congress St., Suite 3A, Boston, MA 02210 (ℂ **800/221-2610** or 617/350-7500; www.gct.com). Grand Circle Travel is also one of the hundreds of travel agencies specializing in vacations for seniors. Many of these packages, however, are of the tour-bus variety, with free trips thrown in for those who organize groups of 10 or more. Seniors seeking more independent travel should probably consult a regular travel agent. **SAGA International Holidays,** 222 Berkeley St., Boston, MA 02116 (ℂ **800/343-0273;** www.sagaholidays.com), offers inclusive tours and cruises for those 50 and older. SAGA also sponsors the more substantial "Road Scholar Tours" (ℂ **800/621-2151**), which are fun-loving but with an educational bent.

You might also want to peruse *The 50+ Traveler's Guidebook* (St. Martin's Press) or *The Seasoned Traveler* (Country Roads Press). Also check your newsstand for the quarterly magazine *Travel 50 & Beyond.*

FOR FAMILIES

San Francisco is full of sightseeing opportunities and special activities geared toward children. See "Especially for Kids," in chapter 7 for information and ideas for families.

Several books offer tips on travel with kids. *How to Take Great Trips with Your Kids* (The Harvard Common Press) is full of good general advice that can apply to travel anywhere. Another reliable book with a worldwide focus is *Adventuring with Children* (Foghorn Press).

The Unofficial Guide to California with Kids (Hungry Minds) is an excellent resource covering the entire state. It rates and ranks attractions for each age group, lists dozens of family-friendly accommodations and restaurants, and suggests lots of beaches and adventures that are great for the whole clan.

5 Getting There

BY PLANE
AIRPORTS
The Bay Area has two major airports: San Francisco International and Oakland International.

SAN FRANCISCO INTERNATIONAL AIRPORT Almost four dozen major scheduled carriers serve **San Francisco International Airport** (ℂ **650/877-0118;** www.flysfo.com), 14 miles directly south of downtown on U.S. 101. Travel time to downtown during commuter rush hour is about 40 minutes; at other times, it's about 20 to 25 minutes.

The airport offers a toll-free **hotline** (ℂ **800/736-2008**) for information on ground transportation. It's available

weekdays from 7am to 5pm local time. During operating hours, a real person answers the line and gives you a rundown of all your options for getting into the city from the airport. Each of the three main terminals has a desk where you can get the same information.

A **cab** from the airport to downtown costs $28 to $32, plus tip.

SFO Airporter buses (ℂ **650/624-0500;** www.sfoairporter.com) depart from outside the lower-level baggage-claim area to downtown San Francisco every 15 to 30 minutes from 6:15am to midnight. They stop at several Union Square–area hotels, including the Grand Hyatt, San

Francisco Hilton, San Francisco Marriott, Westin St. Francis, Parc Fifty-Five, Hyatt Regency, and Sheraton Palace. No reservations are needed. For the return trip, SFO Airporter picks up at hotels as early as 5:30am; make a reservation 24 hours in advance if possible. The cost is $12 per person each way, and children under 2 ride free.

Other private shuttle companies offer door-to-door airport service, in which you share a van with a few other passengers. **SuperShuttle** (© 415/ 558-8500; www.supershuttle.com) takes you anywhere in the city, charging $14.50 to a residence or business. Add $8 for each additional person. It costs $40 to charter an entire van for up to seven passengers. The shuttle stops every 20 minutes or so and picks up passengers from the marked areas outside the terminals' upper level. Reservations are required for the return trip to the airport only and should be made 1 day before departure. Keep in mind that these shuttles demand they pick you up 2 hours before your domestic flight and 3 hours before international flights and during holidays.

The San Mateo County Transit system, **SamTrans** (© 800/660-4287 within northern California, or 650/ 508-6200; www.samtrans.com), runs two buses between the airport and the Transbay Terminal at First and Mission streets. The 292 bus costs $2.20 and makes the trip in about 55 minutes. The KX bus costs $3 and takes just 35 minutes but permits only one carry-on bag. Both buses run daily. The 292 starts at 5:27am and the KX starts at 6:03am. Both run frequently until 8pm and then hourly until about midnight.

OAKLAND INTERNATIONAL AIRPORT About 5 miles south of downtown Oakland, at the Hagenberger Road exit of Calif. 17 (U.S.

880), **Oakland International Airport** (© 510/577-4000; www.oakland airport.com) primarily serves passengers with East Bay destinations. Some San Franciscans prefer this less crowded, accessible airport during busy periods—especially because by car it takes around half an hour to get there from downtown San Francisco (traffic permitting) and is accessible by **BART,** which is not influenced by traffic because it travels on its own tracks.

Taxis from the airport to downtown San Francisco are expensive— approximately $45, plus tip.

Bayporter Express (© 877-467-1800 in the Bay Area, 415/ 467-1800 elsewhere; www.bayporter. com) is a shuttle service that charges $23 for the first person and $10 for each additional person to downtown San Francisco. The fare for outer areas of town is higher. The service accepts advance reservations. To the right of the airport exit, there are usually shuttles that take you to the city for around $20 per person. The shuttles in this fleet are independently owned, and prices vary.

The cheapest way to reach downtown San Francisco is to take the shuttle bus from the airport to BART. (Bay Area Rapid Transit; © 510/ 464-6000; www.bart.org). The Air-BART shuttle bus runs about every 15 minutes Monday to Saturday 6am to 11:30pm and Sunday 8:30am to 11:30pm. It stops in front of Terminals 1 and 2 near the ground transportation signs. Tickets must be purchased at the airport's vending machines prior to boarding. The cost is $2 for the 10-minute ride to BART's Coliseum terminal. BART fares vary, depending on your destination; the trip to downtown San Francisco costs $2.75 and takes 20 minutes once onboard. The entire excursion should take around 45 minutes.

AIRLINES

Dozens of carriers serve San Francisco International Airport and Oakland International Airport, including the following major domestic airlines: **Alaska Airlines** (© 800/426-0333; www.alaskaair.com), **America West Airlines** (© 800/235-9292; www. americawest.com), **American Airlines** (© 800/433-7300; www.im.aa.com), **Continental Airlines** (© 800/ 525-0280; www.continental.com), **Delta Air Lines** (© 800/221-1212; www.delta.com), **Hawaiian Airlines** (© 800/367-5320; www.hawaiianair. com), **Northwest Airlines** (© 800/ 225-2525; www.nwa.com); **Southwest Airlines** (© 800/I-FLY-SWA; www.southwest.com), **TWA** (© 800/ 221-2000; www.twa.com), **United Airlines** (© 800/241-6522; www. ual.com), and **US Airways** (© 800/ 428-4322; www.usairways.com). **National Airlines** (© 888/757-JETS; www.nationalairlines.com) offers flights to San Francisco from Chicago, New York, Dallas, Philadelphia, and Los Angeles through Las Vegas. All passengers can take a free stopover in Las Vegas.

If you're coming from outside the United States, refer to chapter 3, which lists the major international carriers.

BY TRAIN

Traveling by train takes a long time and usually costs as much as, or more than, flying. Still, if you want to take a leisurely ride across America, rail may be a good option.

San Francisco–bound **Amtrak** (© 800/872-7245 or 800/USA-RAIL; www.amtrak.com) trains leave from New York and cross the country via Chicago. The journey takes about 3½ days and seats sell quickly. At this writing, the lowest round-trip fare costs $381 to $600 from New York and $355 to $570 from Chicago. These heavily restricted tickets are good for 45 to 180 days and allow up to three stops along the way, depending on your ticket.

Round-trip tickets from Los Angeles can cost as little as $88 or as much as $148. Trains arrive in Emeryville, just north of Oakland, and connect with regularly scheduled buses to San Francisco's Ferry Building and Cal-Train station in downtown San Francisco.

CalTrain (© 800/660-4287 or 415/546-4461) operates train service between San Francisco and the towns of the peninsula. The city depot is at 700 Fourth St., at Townsend Street.

BY CAR

San Francisco is easily accessible by major highways: **Interstate 5,** from the north, and **U.S. 101,** which cuts south-north through the peninsula from San Jose and across the Golden Gate Bridge to points north. If you drive from Los Angeles, you can take the longer coastal route (437 miles and 11 hours) or the inland route (389 miles and 8 hours). From Mendocino, it's 156 miles and 4 hours; from Sacramento, 88 miles and 1½ hours; from Yosemite, 210 miles and 4 hours.

If you are driving and aren't already a member, it's worth joining the **American Automobile Association (AAA)** (© 800/922-8228). It charges $40 to $60 per year (with an additional one-time joining fee), depending on where you join, and provides

Car Rentals

All major car-rental agencies have locations at both airports. You don't need a car to explore San Francisco if you stay in a city hotel. If you decide you need one, look for tips on car rentals in chapter 4.

> **_Tips_ Flying for Less: Getting the Best Airfare**
>
> - Keep checking the newspaper for **sales.** You almost never see a sale during the peak summer vacation months of July and August or during the Thanksgiving or Christmas holidays, but at slower times, airlines may slash their fares dramatically.
> - If your schedule is flexible, ask if you can get a cheaper fare by staying an extra day or by flying midweek. If you stay over a Saturday night, you can usually save. Many airlines won't volunteer this information, so ask lots of questions.
> - Formerly known as "bucket shops," **consolidators** (wholesalers who buy tickets in bulk at a discount) today are legitimate and offer some of the best deals around. You can get virtually any flight, on any airline, from them; sometimes their fare is identical to the airline's, but often it's discounted 15% to 50%. The tickets carry the same restrictions the airline imposes on advance and discount fares. Their ads usually run in the Sunday travel section, and many have followed the lead of the major airlines and travel agencies by setting up online reservations systems.
>
>   There are lots of fly-by-night consolidators, though, and problems can range from disputing tickets you never received to finding that you have no seat booked when you get to the airport. Play it safe by going with a reputable business. Here are some suggestions: **1-800-FLY-CHEAP** (www. flycheap.com); **Cheap Seats** (✆ 800/451-7200; www.cheapseatstravel.com); and our favorite, **Cheap Tickets** (✆ 800/377-1000; www.cheaptickets.com). **Council Travel**

roadside and other services to motorists. **Amoco Motor Club** (✆ 800/334-3300) is another recommended choice.

PACKAGE DEALS

Packages combining airfare, accommodations, and perhaps even car rentals or airport transfers are sometimes a good way to go. Although some companies offer escorted tours, others simply buy airline tickets and hotel rooms in bulk, passing on some of the discount to you (you travel independently). Often you pay much less than if you had organized the same trip by booking each component separately. To find out what tours and packages are available, check the ads in the travel section of your newspaper or visit your travel agent.

For information on independent fly-drive packages (no escorted tour groups, just a bulk rate on your airfare, hotel, and possibly rental car), contact **American Airlines Fly AAway Vacations** (✆ 800/321-2121; www.im.aa.com), **Continental Airlines Vacations** (✆ 800/634-5555; www.continental.com), **Delta Vacations** (✆ 800/872-7786; www.delta.com), **TWA Getaway Vacations** (✆ 800/438-2929; www.twa.com), **Southwest Airlines** (✆ 800/I-FLY-SWA; www.southwest.com), or **United Vacations** (✆ 800/328-6877; www.ua.com). Availability varies widely based on season and demand, but it always pays to investigate what the major air carriers are offering.

One of the biggest packagers in the Northeast, **Liberty Travel** (✆ 888/

(© 800/ 226-8624; www.counciltravel.com) and **STA Travel** (© 800/ 781-4040; www.sta.travel.com) cater especially to young travelers, but their bargain prices are available to people of all ages; **Travel Bargains** (© 800/AIR-FARE; www.1800airfare.com) was formerly owned by TWA but now offers the deepest discounts on many other airlines as well, with a 4-day advance purchase.

- Surf the Net for bargains. Start out by consulting "Planning Your Trip Online," below. Among the best sites for finding great deals are **Arthur Frommer's Budget Travel** (www. frommers.com), **Microsoft Expedia** (www.expedia.com), and **Travelocity** (www.travelocity.com). The **Internet Travel Network** (www. itn.net) provides a one-stop shopping destination for air, car, and hotel bookings. Its "Fare Mail" keeps you informed of low-cost deals to any of six locations you request; you can eliminate unwanted messages by specifying, for example, that you want to be notified only when flights from New York to San Francisco drop below $350. **Smarter Living** (www. smarterliving.com) offers a customized weekly e-mail summarizing the discount fares available from your departure city.

- Several major airlines offer a free e-mail service known as **E-Savers,** which allows them to send you their best bargain airfares on a regular basis. It's a service for the spontaneously inclined and travelers looking for a quick getaway. But the fares are cheap, so it's worth a look. Check directly with the individual airlines' websites (see above, or the appendix at the end of this book).

271-1584;   www.libertytravel.com) boasts a full-page ad in many Sunday papers. You won't get much in the way of service, but you get a good deal.

For one-stop shopping on the Web, go to **www.vacationpackager.com**, a search engine that links you to many different package-tour operators offering California vacations, often with a company profile summarizing the basic booking and cancellation terms.

6 Planning Your Trip Online

With a mouse, a modem, and a certain do-it-yourself determination, Internet users can tap into the same travel-planning databases that were once accessible only to travel agents. Sites such as **Travelocity, Expedia,** and **Orbitz** allow consumers to comparison shop for airfares, book flights, learn of last-minute bargains, and reserve hotel rooms and rental cars.

But don't fire your travel agent just yet. Although online booking sites offer tips and information to help you bargain shop, they cannot endow you with the hard-earned experience that makes a seasoned, reliable travel agent an invaluable resource, even in the Internet age. And for consumers with a complex itinerary, a trusty travel agent is still the best way to arrange the most direct flights to and from the best airports.

Still, there's no denying the Internet's emergence as a powerful tool in researching and plotting travel time. The benefits of researching your trip online can be well worth the effort:

- **Last-minute specials,** known as **E-Savers,** such as weekend deals or Internet-only fares, are offered by airlines to fill empty seats. Most of these are announced on Tuesday or Wednesday and must be purchased online. They are only valid for travel that weekend, but some can be booked weeks or months in advance. Sign up for weekly e-mail alerts at airline websites (see appendix B) or check mega-sites that compile comprehensive lists of E-savers, such as Smarter Living (www.smarterliving.com) or Web-Flyer (www.webflyer.com).

- Some sites will send you **e-mail notification** when a cheap fare to your favorite destination becomes available. Some will also tell you when fares to a particular destination are lowest.

- The best of the travel planning sites are now **highly personalized;** they track your frequent-flier miles, and store your seating and meal preferences, tentative itineraries, and credit-card information, letting you plan trips or check agendas quickly.

- All major airlines offer **incentives**—bonus frequent-flier miles, Internet-only discounts, sometimes even free cell phone rentals—when you purchase online or buy an e-ticket.

- Advances in mobile technology provide business travelers and other frequent travelers with **the ability to check flight status, change plans, or get specific directions** from handheld computing devices, mobile phones, and pagers. Some sites will e-mail or page a passenger if a flight is delayed.

TRAVEL PLANNING & BOOKING SITES

The best travel planning and booking websites cast a wide net, offering domestic and international flights, hotel and rental-car bookings, plus news, destination information, and deals on cruises and vacation packages. Keep in mind that free (one-time) registration is often required for booking. Because several airlines are no longer willing to pay commissions on tickets sold by online travel agencies, be aware that these online agencies will either charge a $10 surcharge if you book a ticket on that carrier—or neglect to offer those air carriers' offerings.

The sites in this section are not intended to be a comprehensive list, but rather a discriminating selection to get you started. Recognition is given to sites based on their content value and ease of use and is not paid for—unlike some website rankings, which are based on payment. Remember: This is a press-time snapshot of leading websites—some undoubtedly will have evolved or moved by the time you read this.

- **Travelocity** (www.travelocity.com or www.frommers.travelocity.com) and **Expedia** (www.expedia.com) are the most longstanding and reputable sites, each offering excellent selections and searches for complete vacation packages. Travelers search by destination and dates coupled with how much they are willing to spend.

- The latest buzz in the online travel world is about **Orbitz** (www.orbitz.com), a site launched by United, Delta, Northwest, American, and Continental airlines. It shows all possible fares for your desired trip, offering fares lower than those available through travel agents. (Stay tuned: At press time,

Frommers.com: The Complete Travel Resource

For an excellent travel planning resource, we highly recommend **Arthur Frommer's Budget Travel Online** (www.frommers.com). We're a little biased, of course, but we guarantee you'll find the travel tips, reviews, monthly vacation giveaways, and online-booking capabilities thoroughly indispensable. Among the special features are: **"Ask the Expert"** bulletin boards, where Frommer's authors answer your questions via online postings; **Arthur Frommer's Daily Newsletter**, for the latest travel bargains and inside travel secrets; and Frommer's **Destinations archive**, where you'll get expert travel tips, hotel and dining recommendations, and advice on the sights to see for more than 200 destinations around the globe. Once your research is complete, the **Online Reservation System** (www.frommers.com/booktravelnow) takes you to Frommer's favorite sites for booking your vacation at affordable prices.

travel-agency associations were waging an antitrust battle against this site.)

- **Qixo** (www.qixo.com) is another powerful search engine that allows you to search for flights and hotel rooms on 20 other travel-planning sites (such as Travelocity) at once. Qixo sorts results by price, after which you can book your travel directly through the site.

SMART E-SHOPPING

The savvy traveler is one who is armed with good information. Here are a few tips to help you navigate the Internet successfully and safely:

- **Know when sales start.** Last-minute deals may vanish in minutes. If you have a favorite booking site or airline, find out when last-minute deals are released to the public. (For example, Southwest's specials are posted every Tuesday at 12:01a.m. central time.)
- **Shop around.** Compare results from different sites and airlines—and against a travel agent's best

fare, if you can. If possible, try a range of times and alternate airports before you make a purchase.

- **Follow the rules of the trade.** Book in advance, and choose an off-peak time and date if possible. Some sites will tell you when fares to a particular destination tend to be cheapest.
- **Stay secure.** Book only through secure sites (some airline sites are not secure). Look for a key icon (Netscape) or a padlock (Internet Explorer) at the bottom of your web browser before you enter credit card information or other personal data.
- **Avoid online auctions.** Sites that auction airline tickets and frequent-flier miles are the number-one perpetrators of Internet fraud, according to the National Consumers League.
- **Maintain a paper trail.** If you purchase an e-ticket, print out a confirmation, or write down your confirmation number, and keep it safe and accessible—or your trip could be a virtual one!

ONLINE TRAVELER'S TOOLBOX

Veteran travelers usually carry some essential items to make their trips easier. Following is a selection of online tools to bookmark and use:

- **Visa ATM Locator** (www.visa. com/pd/atm) or **MasterCard ATM Locator** (www.mastercard. com/atm). Find ATMs in hundreds of cities in the U.S. and around the world.
- **Foreign Languages for Travelers** (www.travlang.com). Here you can learn basic terms in more than 70 languages and click on any underlined phrase to hear what it sounds like. *Note:* To use this site, you must have speakers and downloadable free audio software.
- **Intellicast** (www.intellicast.com). Get weather forecasts for all 50 states and cities around the world. *Note:* Temperatures are in Celsius for many international destinations.

- **Mapquest** (www.mapquest.com). This best of the mapping sites lets you choose a specific address or destination, and in seconds, it returns a map and detailed directions.
- **Cybercafes.com** (www.cybercafes. com) or **Net Café Guide** (www. netcafeguide.com). Locate Internet cafes at hundreds of locations around the globe. Catch up on your e-mail and log onto the Web for a few dollars per hour.
- **Universal Currency Converter** (www.xe.com). See what your dollar or pound is worth in more than 100 other countries.
- **U.S. State Department Travel Warnings** (www.travel.state.gov/ travel_warnings.html). Reports on places where health concerns or unrest might threaten U.S. travelers. It also lists the locations of U.S. embassies around the world.

For Foreign Visitors

The pervasiveness of U.S. culture around the world may make you feel that you know the USA pretty well, but leaving your own country for the United States still requires an additional degree of planning. This chapter will help prepare you for the most common problems (expected and unexpected) you might encounter during your trip to San Francisco.

1 Preparing for Your Trip

ENTRY REQUIREMENTS

Immigration laws are a hot political issue in the United States, and the requirements outlined here may have changed somewhat by the time you plan your trip. Check at any U.S. embassy or consulate for current information and requirements.

DOCUMENT REGULATIONS The U.S. State Department has a **Visa Waiver Pilot Program** that allows citizens of certain countries to enter the United States without a visa for stays of up to 90 days. At press time, these countries included Andorra, Argentina, Austria, Australia, Belgium, Brunei, Denmark, Finland, France, Germany, Iceland, Ireland, Italy, Japan, Liechtenstein, Luxembourg, Monaco, The Netherlands, New Zealand, Norway, Portugal, San Marino, Singapore, Slovenia, Spain, Sweden, Switzerland, the United Kingdom, and Uruguay. Citizens of these countries need only a valid passport and a round-trip air or cruise ticket in their possession upon arrival. If they first enter the United States, they can then visit Mexico, Canada, Bermuda, and the Caribbean islands and return to the United States without needing a visa. Further information is available from any U.S. embassy or consulate. Canadian citizens can enter the United

States without visas; they need only proof of residence.

Citizens of all other countries must have (1) a valid **passport** with an expiration date at least 6 months later than the scheduled end of the visit to the United States; and (2) a **tourist visa,** which can be obtained without charge from the nearest U.S. consulate.

To get a visa, the traveler must submit a completed application form (either in person or by mail) with a 1½-inch-square photo, and must demonstrate binding ties to a residence abroad. Usually you can get a visa at once or within 24 hours, but it might take longer during the summer rush, from June through August. If you cannot apply for a visa in person, contact the nearest U.S. embassy or consulate for directions on applying by mail.

MEDICAL REQUIREMENTS Unless you're arriving from an area known to be suffering from an epidemic (particularly cholera or yellow fever), no inoculations or vaccinations are required to enter the United States. If you have a disease requiring treatment with medications containing narcotics or drugs requiring a syringe, carry a valid signed prescription from your physician to allay suspicions that you may be smuggling drugs.

Tips Travel Information

If you have questions about U.S. Immigration policies or laws, call the **Federal Information Center (800/375-5283)** or the **Immigration and Naturalization Service (INS) Office** at the San Francisco International Airport (✆ **650/837-2876**; www.ins.gov). Otherwise, call San Francisco's **INS Ask Immigration System** (✆ **800/375-5283**). Your travel agent or airline office might also be able to give you visa applications and instructions. The U.S. consulate or embassy that issues your visa determines whether you receive a multiple- or single-entry visa and any restrictions on the length of your stay.

British subjects can get up-to-date passport and visa information by calling the **U.S. Embassy Visa Information Line** (✆ **0891/200-290**) or the **London Passport Office** (✆ **0990/210-410** for recorded information).

Foreign driver's licenses are recognized in San Francisco, although you might want to get an international driver's license if your home license is not written in English.

For HIV-positive visitors, requirements for entering the United States are somewhat vague and change frequently. According to the latest publication of *HIV and Immigrants: A Manual for AIDS Service Providers,* "although INS doesn't require a medical exam for everyone trying to come into the United States, INS officials may keep out people who they suspect are HIV positive. INS may stop people because they look sick or because they are carrying AIDS/HIV medicine."

It's a confusing situation, so if you're HIV-positive and need advice, contact an AIDS center in your area.

CUSTOMS REQUIREMENTS

Every visitor over 21 years of age can bring in, free of duty, the following: (1) 1 liter of wine or hard liquor; (2) 200 cigarettes (if not U.S.-made), 100 cigars (but none from Cuba), or 4.25 pounds of smoking tobacco; and (3) $100 worth of gifts. These exemptions are offered to travelers who spend at least 72 hours in the United States and who have not claimed them within the preceding 6 months. It is altogether forbidden to bring into the country foodstuffs (particularly fruit, cooked meats, and canned goods) and plants (vegetables, seeds, tropical plants, and

the like). Foreign tourists can bring in or take out up to $10,000 in U.S. or foreign currency with no formalities; larger sums must be declared to U.S. Customs on entering or leaving, which includes filing Form CF 4790. For more specific information on U.S. Customs, call your nearest U.S. embassy or consulate.

INSURANCE

Insurance policies can cover everything from the loss or theft of your baggage and trip cancellation to the guarantee of bail in case you're arrested. Good policies also cover costs due to an accident, repatriation, or death. Automobile clubs, insurance companies, and travel agents sell such packages.

Although it's not required of travelers, health insurance is highly recommended. Unlike many European countries, the United States does not usually offer free or low-cost medical care to its citizens or visitors. Doctors and hospitals are expensive and in most cases require advance payment or proof of coverage before they render their services.Although lack of health insurance might prevent you from being admitted to a hospital in non-emergencies, don't worry about being left on a street corner to die: The

American way is to fix you now and bill the living daylights out of you later.

FOR BRITISH TRAVELERS   Most big travel agents offer their own insurance, and will probably try to sell you their package when you book a holiday. Think before you sign. Britain's Consumers' Association recommends that you insist on seeing the policy and reading the fine print before buying travel insurance. **The Association of British Insurers** (© 020/7600-3333) gives advice by phone and publishes the free *Holiday Insurance,* a guide to policy provisions and prices. You might also shop around for better deals: Try **Columbus Travel Insurance Ltd.** (© 020/7375-0011) or, for students, **Campus Travel** (© 0870/240-1010).

MONEY

CURRENCY   The U.S. monetary system is painfully simple: The most common bills (all ugly, all green) are the $1 (colloquially, a "buck"), $5, $10, and $20 denominations. There are also $2 bills (seldom encountered), $50 bills, and $100 bills (the last two are usually not welcome when paying for small purchases). Note that redesigned bills of denominations over $1 are now in circulation, along with the old-style stuff. Despite rumors to the contrary, the old-style bills are still legal tender.

There are six denominations of coins: 1¢ (1 cent, or a penny); 5¢ (5 cents, or a nickel); 10¢ (10 cents, or a dime); 25¢ (25 cents, or a quarter); 50¢ (50 cents, or a half dollar); and $1. A gold-colored $1 piece entered circulation in 2000; other versions are the rare silver dollar, prized by collectors, and the quarter-sized Susan B. Anthony coin.

Note: The foreign-exchange bureaus so common in Europe are rare even at airports in the United States, and they're nonexistent outside major cities. It's best not to change foreign money (or traveler's checks denominated in a currency other than U.S. dollars) at a small-town bank or even a branch in a big city; in fact, leave any currency other than U.S. dollars at home—it might prove a greater nuisance than it's worth.

TRAVELER'S CHECKS   Although traveler's checks are widely accepted, make sure they're denominated in U.S. dollars. Foreign-currency checks are often difficult to exchange. The three brands that are most widely recognized—and least likely to be denied—are Visa, American Express, and Thomas Cook. Be sure to record the numbers of the checks, and keep that information separate should they get lost or stolen. San Francisco businesses are pretty good about taking traveler's checks, but you're better off cashing them in at a bank (in small amounts, of course) and paying in cash. *Remember:* You'll need identification, such as a driver's license or passport, to change a traveler's check. Please see "Money" in chapter 2 for more information about traveler's checks.

CREDIT CARDS & ATMS   You can use Visa and MasterCard almost everywhere in San Francisco, and you can use most of the major credit cards at the larger hotels. A handful of stores and restaurants, however, do not take credit cards, so be sure to ask in advance. Most businesses display stickers near their entrance to let you know which cards they accept. (*Note:* Often businesses require a minimum purchase price, usually around $10, to use a credit card.)

It's strongly recommended that you carry at least one major credit card. Hotels, car-rental companies, and airlines usually require a credit-card imprint as a deposit against expenses. In an emergency, a credit card can be priceless. Plus, the exchange rate you get on credit card purchases is often better than what you'd get at a currency exchange.

Tips   Keeping Copies

Be sure to keep a copy of all your travel papers separate from your wallet or purse, and leave a copy with someone at home should you need it faxed in an emergency.

You can find an automated teller machine (ATM) on just about every block in downtown San Francisco. Most accept Visa, MasterCard, and American Express, as well as ATM cards from other U.S. banks. Expect to be charged up to $3 per transaction if you're not using your own bank's ATM. *Tip:* One way around this is to ask for cash back at stores (for example, Safeway) that accept ATM cards and don't charge usage fees. Of course, you have to buy something first.

SAFETY

GENERAL SAFETY TIPS   While most San Francisco tourist areas are generally safe, there are a few neighborhoods you should leave out of your itinerary, such as the Tenderloin (just west of Union Square) and Hunter's Point areas.

Avoid deserted areas, especially at night, and don't go into any of the parks at night unless there's a concert or similar occasion that attracts crowds.

Avoid carrying valuables with you on the street, and don't display expensive cameras or electronic equipment. Hold on to your pocketbook, and place your billfold in an inside pocket. In theaters, restaurants, and other public places, keep your possessions in sight.

Remember also that hotels are open to the public, and in a large hotel security might not be able to screen everyone entering. Always lock your hotel room door—don't assume that once inside your room you are automatically safe and no longer need to be aware of your surroundings.

See "Fast Facts: San Francisco" in chapter 4 for more city-specific safety tips.

DRIVING SAFETY   Driving safety is important, too, especially given the highly publicized carjackings of foreign tourists in Florida. Question your car rental agency about personal safety and ask for a brochure describing safety tips when you pick up your car. Get written directions—or a map with the route clearly marked—from the agency showing how to get to your destination. And, if possible, arrive and depart during daylight hours.

Recently, more and more crime has involved cars and drivers. If you drive off a highway into a doubtful neighborhood, leave the area as quickly as possible. If you have an accident, even on the highway, stay in your car with the doors locked until you assess the situation or until the police arrive. If your car is bumped from behind or you are involved in a minor accident with no injuries and the situation appears to be suspicious, motion to the other driver to follow you. *Never* get out of your car in such situations. Go directly to the nearest police precinct, well-lit service station, or 24-hour store.

Always try to park in well-lit and well-traveled areas if possible. If you leave your rental car unlocked and empty of your valuables, you're probably safer than if you lock your car with valuables in plain view. Never leave any packages or valuables in sight. If someone attempts to rob you or steal your car, don't try to resist—report the incident to the police department immediately.

2 Getting to the U.S.

Traveling overseas on a budget is something of an oxymoron, but there are ways to reduce the cost of a plane ticket by several hundred dollars if you take the time to shop around. For example, travelers from overseas can take advantage of the APEX (Advance Purchase Excursion) reduced fares offered by all major U.S. and European carriers. For more money-saving airline advice, see "Getting There" in chapter 2.

In addition to the domestic U.S. airlines listed under "Getting There" in chapter 2, a number of international carriers also serve the Bay Area airports. They include **Aer Lingus** (© 01/886-8888 in Dublin; www.aerlingus.ie), **Air Canada** (© 800/776-3000; www.aircanada.ca), **British Airways** (© 0845/77 33-377 in the U.K.; www.british-airways.com), **Japan Airlines** (© 0354/89-1111 in Tokyo; www.jal.co.jp), **Qantas** (© 13-13-13 in Australia; www.qantas.com.au), and **Virgin Atlantic** (© 01293/747-747 in the U.K.; www.virgin-atlantic.com). British Airways and Virgin Atlantic offer direct flights to San Francisco from London. **Air New Zealand** (© 73-7000 in New Zealand; www.airnewzealand.co.nz) flies to Los Angeles and will book you straight through to San Francisco on a partner airline.

Major U.S. carriers, such as **Continental** (© 01293/776-464 in the U.K.; www.continental.com), **TWA** (© 800/892-4141 in the U.K.; www.twa.com), **United** (© 084/ 584-44777 in the U.K.; www.ual.com), **American** (© 0345-789-789 in the U.K.; www.aa.com), and **Delta** (© 0800/414-767 in the U.K.; www.delta.com), have service from Europe to the United States. **United** (© 61/131-777 from within Australia) flies from Sydney to San Francisco.

Visitors arriving by air, no matter what the port of entry, should cultivate patience and resignation before setting foot on U.S. soil. Getting through immigration control can take as long as 2 hours on some days, especially on summer weekends, so be sure to have this guidebook or something else to read. Add the time it takes to clear customs, and you'll see that you should allow plenty of time for making connections between international and domestic flights—figure on 2 to 3 hours at least.

In contrast, for the traveler arriving by car or rail from Canada, the border-crossing formalities have been streamlined to the vanishing point. Travelers by air from Canada, Bermuda, and some places in the Caribbean can sometimes go through customs and immigration at the point of departure, which is much quicker.

3 Getting Around the U.S.

BY PLANE

Some large airlines offer travelers on their transatlantic or transpacific flights special discount tickets under the name **Visit USA.** They allow travel between any U.S. destinations at minimum rates. *These discount tickets are not on sale in the United States and must be purchased abroad with your international ticket.* This system is the best, easiest, and fastest way to see

the United States at a low cost. You should get information well in advance from your travel agent or from the airline concerned, because the conditions attached to these discount tickets can change without advance notice.

BY TRAIN

International visitors can buy a **USA Railpass,** good for 15 or 30 days of unlimited travel on Amtrak (© **800/ USA-RAIL**; www.amtrak.com). The pass is available through many foreign travel agents. Prices in 2001 for a 15-day pass were $295 off-peak adults and half price for children 2 to 15, $385 peak; for a 30-day pass, $440 off-peak, $550 peak. With a foreign passport, you can also buy passes at some Amtrak offices in the United States, including locations in San Francisco, Los Angeles, Chicago, New York, Miami, Boston, and Washington, D.C. Reservations are generally required and should be made for each part of your trip as early as possible.

BY BUS

For short hops between cities, the bus is often the most economical form of public transit. However, bus travel in the United States can be both slow and uncomfortable, so this option isn't for everyone—particularly when Amtrak, which is far more luxurious, offers similar rates. **Greyhound/Trailways** (© **800/231-2222**; www.greyhound.com), the sole nationwide bus line, offers an **Ameripass** (© **888/ 454-7277**) for unlimited travel for 7 days at $209, 15 days at $319, 30 days at $429, and 60 days at $599. Passes must be purchased at a Greyhound terminal or over the Internet.

BY CAR

The most cost-effective, convenient, and comfortable way to travel around the United States—especially California—is by car. (In the city of San Francisco, though, you may find a car more of a hassle than a help.) The interstate highway system connects cities and towns all over the country. In addition to these high-speed, limited-access roadways, there's an extensive network of federal, state, and local highways and roads. The national car-rental companies that have offices in San Francisco include **Alamo** (© **800/ 327-9633**; www.goalamo.com), **Avis** (© **800/331-1212**; www.avis.com), **Budget** (© **800/527-0700**; www. drivebudget.com), **Dollar** (© **800/ 800-4000**; www.dollar.com), **Enterprise** (© **800/325-8007**; www. enterprise.com); **Hertz** (© **800/ 654-3131**; www.hertz.com), **National** (© **800/227-7368**; www.national car.com), and **Thrifty** (© **800/ 367-2277**; www.thrifty.com).

If you plan to rent a car in the United States, you probably won't need the services of an automobile organization. If you plan to buy or borrow a car, automobile-association membership is recommended. The **American Automobile Association (AAA),** 150 Van Ness Ave., San Francisco, CA 94102 (© **800/922-8228**; www.aaa.com), is the country's largest auto club. It has reciprocal arrangements with many foreign auto clubs. Check with your local club to find out if you have access to free AAA service in America. For more information on traveling by car, see "Getting There" in chapter 2.

 FAST FACTS: **For the Foreign Traveler**

Business Hours See "Fast Facts: San Francisco," in chapter 4.

Climate See "When to Go," in chapter 2.

Currency Exchange Foreign-exchange bureaus are rare in the United States, and most banks are not equipped to handle currency exchange. San Francisco's money-changing offices include **Bank of America,** 345 Montgomery St. (© **415/622-2451**), open Monday to Friday 9am to 6pm, and **Thomas Cook,** 75 Geary St. (℗ **415/362-3452;** www.us.thomas cook.com), open Monday to Friday 9am to 5pm and Saturday 10am to 4pm.

Drinking Laws   The legal age for purchase and consumption of alcoholic beverages is 21. Proof of age is required and often requested at bars, nightclubs, and restaurants, so it's always a good idea to bring identification when you go out. In San Francisco, supermarkets and grocery and liquor stores sell liquor daily from 6am to 2am. Licensed restaurants are permitted to sell alcohol during the same hours. Note that many restaurants are licensed only for beer and wine.

A big no-no is having an open container of alcohol in your car or in any public area that isn't zoned for alcohol consumption. The police can, and probably will, fine you on the spot. And nothing will ruin your trip faster than getting a citation for DUI (driving under the influence), so don't even think about driving while intoxicated.

Electricity   U.S. wall outlets give power at 110 to 115 volts, 60 cycles, compared with 220 volts, 50 cycles in most of Europe. In addition to a 100-volt transformer, small foreign appliances, such as hair dryers and shavers, require a plug adapter (available at most hardware stores) with two flat, parallel pins.

Embassies & Consulates   All embassies are located in Washington, D.C. In addition, several major English-speaking countries have consulates in either San Francisco or Los Angeles.

The embassy of **Australia** is at 1601 Massachusetts Ave. NW, Washington, DC 20036 (℗ **202/797-3000**); a consulate-general is at 601 Market St., Suite 200, San Francisco, CA 94104 (℗ **415/536-1970**). The embassy of **Canada** is at 501 Pennsylvania Ave. NW, Washington, DC 20001 (℗ **202/ 682-1740**); the nearest consulate is at 550 Hope St, 9th Floor, Los Angeles, CA 90071 (℗ **213/346-2700**). The embassy of the **Republic of Ireland** is at 2234 Massachusetts Ave. NW, Washington, DC 20008 (℗ **202/462-3939**); a consulate is at 44 Montgomery St., Suite 3830, San Francisco, CA 94104 (℗ **415/392-4214**). The embassy of **New Zealand** is at 37 Observatory Circle NW, Washington, DC 20008 (℗ **202/328-4800**); the nearest consulate is at 12400 Wilshire Blvd., Suite 1150, Los Angeles, CA 90025 (℗ **310/ 207-1605**). The embassy of the **United Kingdom** is at 3100 Massachusetts Ave. NW, Washington, DC 20008 (℗ **202/462-1340**); the nearest consulate is at 1 Sansome St., Suite 850, San Francisco, CA 94104 (℗ **415/617-1300**). The embassy of **Japan** is at 2520 Massachusetts Ave. NW, Washington, DC 20008 (℗ **202/238-6700**); the consulate-general of Japan is at 50 Fremont St., 23rd Floor, San Francisco, CA 94105 (℗ **415/777-3533**).

If you are from another country, you can get the telephone number of your embassy by calling information (directory assistance) in Washington, D.C. (℗ **202/555-1212**).

Emergencies   You can call the police, an ambulance, or the fire department through the single emergency telephone number ℗ **911** from any phone or pay phone (no coins needed). If that doesn't work, another useful way of reporting an emergency is to call the telephone company operator by dialing 0 (zero, not the letter *O*).

Gasoline (Petrol)   Prices vary, but expect to pay anywhere between $1.70 and $2 for 1 U.S. gallon (about 3.8 liters) of "regular" unleaded gasoline (petrol). Higher-octane fuels are also available at most gas stations for slightly higher prices. The displayed price includes taxes.

Holidays   On the following legal national holidays, banks, government offices, post offices, and many stores, restaurants, and museums are closed: New Year's Day (January 1), Martin Luther King Day (third Monday in January), Presidents' Day (third Monday in February), Memorial Day (last Monday in May), Independence Day (July 4), Labor Day (first Monday in September), Columbus Day (second Monday in October), Veterans Day (November 11), Thanksgiving Day (fourth Thursday in November), and Christmas Day (December 25). Election Day, for national elections, falls on the Tuesday following the first Monday in November. It's a legal national holiday during a presidential election, which occurs every fourth year (next in 2004).

Internet Connectivity   See "Fast Facts: San Francisco," in chapter 4.

Mail   If you want to receive mail but aren't sure where you'll be, have it sent to you, in your name, c/o **General Delivery** (Poste Restante) at the main post office of the city or region you're visiting. Call ℂ **800/275-8777** for information on the nearest post office. The addressee must pick it up in person and produce proof of identity (such as a driver's license, credit card, or passport). Most post offices will hold your mail up to 1 month and are open Monday to Saturday from 8am to 6pm. The local address is **Civic Center Post Office Box Unit,** P.O. Box 429991, San Francisco, CA 94142-9991 (ℂ **800/275-8777**). The street address is 101 Hyde St.

Generally found at street intersections, mailboxes are blue and carry the inscription U.S. MAIL. If your mail is addressed to a U.S. destination, don't forget to add the five-digit ZIP code after the two-letter abbreviation of the state to which the mail is addressed (CA for California).

For overseas mail, **postal rates** are as follows: A first-class letter of up to one-half ounce costs 80¢ to Europe (50¢ to Canada and Mexico); a first-class postcard costs 70¢ to Europe (50¢ to Canada and Mexico).

Medical Emergencies   To call an ambulance, dial ℂ **911** from any phone—no coins are needed in pay phones. For hospitals and other emergency information, see "Fast Facts: San Francisco" in chapter 4.

Newspapers & Magazines   Many of San Francisco's newsstands offer a selection of foreign periodicals and newspapers, such as *The Economist, Le Monde,* and *Der Spiegel.* For information on local literature and specific newsstand locations, see "Fast Facts: San Francisco," in chapter 4.

Post Office   See "Mail," above.

Radio & Television   There are seven national broadcast television networks: ABC (Channel 7), CBS (Channel 5), NBC (Channel 4), PBS (Channel 9), Fox (Channel 2), UPN (Channel 44), and WB (Channel 20). Cable television encompasses the national networks and 50 or so other stations, including the Cable News Network (CNN), ESPN (sports), and MTV. Most hotels offer a dozen cable stations and pay-per-view movies. You'll also find a wide choice of local radio stations. Each broadcasts particular kinds of talk shows, music—classical, country, jazz, rock, pop, gospel—or both, punctuated by news broadcasts and frequent commercials.

Smoking   Heavy smokers are in for a tough time in San Francisco. No smoking is permitted in public buildings, sports arenas, elevators, theaters, banks, lobbies, restaurants, offices, stores, bed-and-breakfasts, most small hotels, or bars. That's right—as of January 1, 1998, you can't even smoke in a bar in California. The only exception is a bar in which drinks are served solely by the owner. You will find, however, that many neighborhood bars turn the other cheek and pass you an ashtray.

Taxes   In the United States there's no value-added tax (VAT) or other direct tax at a national level. Every state, as well as every city, is allowed to levy its own local sales tax on all purchases, including hotel and restaurant checks and airline tickets. Taxes are included in the price of certain goods and services, such as public transportation, cab fares, phone calls, and gasoline. The amount of sales tax varies from 4% to 10%, depending on the state and city, so when you are making major purchases, such as photographic equipment, clothing, or high-fidelity components, it can be a significant part of the cost. In addition, many cities charge a separate "bed" or room tax on accommodations, above and beyond sales tax.

For information on sales and room taxes in San Francisco, see "Fast Facts: San Francisco," in chapter 4.

Telephone & Fax   Pay phones can be found almost everywhere—at street corners, in bars and restaurants, and in hotels. Outside the metropolitan area, however, public telephones are more difficult to find; stores and gas stations are your best bet.

Phones do not accept pennies, and few will take anything larger than a quarter. Some public phones, especially those in airports and large hotels, accept credit cards, such as MasterCard, Visa, and American Express. Credit cards are especially handy for international calls; instructions are printed on the phone.

In San Francisco, **local calls** cost 35¢. To make a local call, dial the seven-digit local number. For domestic long-distance calls or international calls, stock up with a supply of quarters; after you dial the number, a recorded voice instructs you when and in what quantity you should put the coins into the slot. For **domestic long-distance calls,** first dial 1 (the long-distance access code), then the three-digit area code and seven-digit local number. For **direct overseas calls,** dial 011 (the international access code), then the country code (Australia, 61; Republic of Ireland, 353; New Zealand, 64; United Kingdom, 44), followed by the city code, then the local number. To place a call to Canada or the Caribbean, just dial 1, the area code, and the local number.

Before calling from a hotel room, always ask the hotel phone operator if there are any telephone surcharges. They can sometimes be reduced by calling collect or by using a telephone charge card. Hotel phone surcharges, which can be exorbitant, can be avoided altogether by using a pay phone in the lobby.

Note that almost all calls to phone numbers in area codes 800, 888, and 877 are **toll-free,** but your hotel might still charge a fee for making the call.

For **local directory assistance** ("information"), dial © **411;** for **long-distance information** in the United States and Canada, dial **1,** then the appropriate area code and **555-1212.**

For "collect" (reversed-charge) calls and for "person-to-person" calls, dial 0 (zero, not the letter O) followed by the area code and the number; an operator or recording then comes on the line. You should specify that you are calling collect or person-to-person, or both. If your operator-assisted call is international, just dial 00 and wait for the operator.

Like the telephone system, **telegraph** services are provided by private corporations, such as ITT, MCI, and above all, **Western Union.** You can bring your telegram to a Western Union office or dictate it over the phone (© **800/325-6000**). You can also telegraph money, or have it telegraphed to you, very quickly. In San Francisco, there are several locations around town; call © **800/325-6000** for the one nearest you.

Fax facilities are widely available. They can be found in most hotels and many other establishments. Try Mail Boxes Etc. or any photocopying shop.

Telephone Directory   Two kinds of telephone directories are available in the United States. The general directory is the so-called **White Pages,** which lists private and business subscribers in alphabetical order. The inside front cover lists the emergency number for police, fire, and ambulance, and other vital numbers (like the Coast Guard, poison-control center, crime-victims hotline, and so on). The first few pages are devoted to community-service numbers, including a guide to long-distance and international calling, complete with country codes and area codes.

The second directory, printed on yellow paper (hence its name, the **Yellow Pages**), lists local services, businesses, and industries by type of activity, with an index at the back. The listings cover not only such obvious items as automobile repairs by make of car and drugstores (pharmacies), often by geographical location, but also restaurants by type of cuisine and geographical location, bookstores by special subject or language, places of worship by religious denomination, and other information that the tourist might otherwise not readily find. The Yellow Pages also include city plans or detailed maps, and often show postal ZIP codes and public-transportation routes.

Time   The continental United States is divided into four time zones. From east to west, they are eastern time (ET), central time (CT), mountain time (MT), and Pacific time (PT). There are also Alaska time (AT) and Hawaii time (HT). San Francisco is on Pacific standard time, which is 8 hours behind Greenwich mean time. Noon in New York City (ET) is 11am in Chicago (CT), 10am in Denver (MT), 9am in San Francisco (PT), 8am in Anchorage (AT), and 7am in Honolulu (HT).

Daylight saving time is in effect from the first Sunday in April until 2am on the last Sunday in October, except in Arizona, Hawaii, part of Indiana, and Puerto Rico. Daylight saving time moves the clock 1 hour ahead of standard time.

Tipping   Service in America is some of the best in the world and is rarely included in the price of anything. It's part of the American way of life to tip, on the principle that you must expect to pay for any service you get. Many employees receive little direct salary and must depend on tips for their income. In fact, the U.S. federal government imposes income taxes on service personnel based on an estimate of how much they should have earned in tips in relation to their employer's total receipts. In other words, they might have to pay taxes on a tip you didn't give them!

Here are some rules of thumb:

• In **hotels,** tip bellhops at least $1 per piece of luggage ($2 to $3 if you have a lot of bags) and tip the chamber staff at least $1 per day (the more expensive the hotel, the bigger the tip). Tip the doorman or concierge only if he or she has provided you with some specific service (for example, calling a cab for you or obtaining difficult-to-get theater tickets). Tip the valet parking attendant at least $2 every time you get your car.

• In **restaurants, bars, and nightclubs,** tip service staff 15% to 20% of the check, tip bartenders 10% to 15%, tip checkroom attendants $1 per garment, and tip valet-parking attendants at least $2 per vehicle. Tip the doorman only if he has provided you with some specific service (such as calling a cab for you). Tipping is not expected in cafeterias and fast-food restaurants.

• Tip **cab drivers** 15% of the fare.

• For **other service personnel,** tip skycaps at airports at least $1 per piece ($2 to $3 if you have a lot of luggage), and tip hairdressers and barbers 15% to 20%.

• Tipping gas-station attendants and ushers at movies and theaters is not expected.

Toilets   Public toilets can be hard to find in San Francisco. A handful of fancy new French stalls have been strategically placed on high-volume streets and a few small stores allow you access to their facilities. You can almost always find a toilet in restaurants and bars; note, however, a growing practice in some restaurants and bars of displaying a notice that toilets are for the use of patrons only. You can ignore this sign or, better yet, avoid arguments by paying for a cup of coffee or soft drink, which qualifies you as a patron. Large hotels and fast-food restaurants are probably the best bet for good, clean facilities. Museums, department stores, shopping malls, and, in a pinch, gas stations all have public toilets. If possible, avoid the toilets at parks and beaches, which are a real crap shoot (pun intended) when it comes to cleanliness.

4

Getting to Know San Francisco

Half the fun of becoming familiar with San Francisco is wandering around and haphazardly stumbling upon great shops, restaurants, and viewpoints that even locals might not know about. You'll find that, although it's metropolitan, San Francisco is a small town, and you won't feel like a stranger for long. If you get disoriented, just remember that downtown is east and the Golden Gate Bridge is north—and even if you do get lost, you probably won't go too far, since water surrounds three sides of the city. The most difficult challenge you'll have, if you're traveling by car, is mastering the maze of one-way streets. This chapter offers useful information on how to become better acquainted with the city.

1 Orientation

VISITOR INFORMATION

Once in the city, visit the **San Francisco Visitor Information Center,** on the lower level of Hallidie Plaza, 900 Market St., at Powell Street (© 415/283-0177; fax 415/362-7323). Information, brochures, discount coupons, and advice on restaurants, sights, and events in the city are available. The staff can provide answers in German, Japanese, French, Italian, and Spanish (as well as English, of course). To find the office, descend the escalator at the cable-car turnaround.

Dial © 415/283-0177 anytime, day or night, for a recorded message about current cultural events, theater, music, sports, and other special happenings. This information is also available in German, French, Japanese, and Spanish. Keep in mind that this service supports only members of the Convention and Visitors Bureau and is very tourist oriented. While there's tons of information, it's not representative of all that the city has to offer. The office is open Monday to Friday 9am to 5pm, Saturday 9am to 3pm, and Sunday 10am to 2pm. It's closed on January 1, Thanksgiving Day, and December 25. You can get a fax with information anytime from the bureau's automated service if you call © 800/220-5747 and follow the prompts.

Pick up a copy of the *Bay Guardian.* The city's free alternative paper lists all city happenings. You'll find it in kiosks throughout the city and in most coffee shops.

For specialized information on Chinatown's shops and services, and on the city's Chinese community in general, contact the **Chinese Chamber of Commerce,** 730 Sacramento St., San Francisco, CA 94108 (© 415/982-3000), open daily 9am to 5pm.

The **Visitors Information Center of the Redwood Empire Association,** located at the California Welcome Center at Pier 39 (© 800/200-8334 or 510/536-8808; www.redwoodempire.com), offers informative brochures and has a knowledgeable desk staff who can plan tours in San Francisco and north of the city. Its annual 48-page *Redwood Empire Visitors' Guide* is available free in person or by mail. Priority mail in the U.S. costs $5 (check, cash, or money order); international mail, $5.50. The center offers information on everything from San Francisco hotels and walking tours to museums in northern California. The office is open daily 10am to 6pm.

CITY LAYOUT

San Francisco occupies the tip of a 32-mile-long peninsula between San Francisco Bay and the Pacific Ocean. Its land area measures about 46 square miles. Twin Peaks, in the geographic center of the city, is more than 900 feet high.

San Francisco might seem confusing at first, but it quickly becomes easy to negotiate. The city's downtown streets are arranged in a simple grid pattern, with the exception of Market Street and Columbus Avenue, which cut across the grid at right angles to each other. Hills appear to distort this pattern, however, and can be disorienting. As you learn your way around, the hills will become your landmarks and reference points.

MAIN ARTERIES & STREETS   Market Street is San Francisco's main thoroughfare. Most of the city's buses travel this route on their way to the Financial District from the outer neighborhoods to the west and south. The tall office buildings clustered downtown are at the northeast end of Market; 1 block beyond lies the Embarcadero and the bay.

The Embarcadero ⨁—an excellent strolling, skating, and biking route (thanks to recent renovations)—curves along San Francisco Bay from south of the Bay Bridge to the northeast perimeter of the city. It terminates at Fisherman's Wharf, the famous tourist-oriented pier. Aquatic Park, Fort Mason, and the Golden Gate National Recreation area are on the northernmost point of the peninsula.

From the eastern perimeter of Fort Mason, **Van Ness Avenue** runs due south, back to Market Street. The area just described forms a rough triangle, with Market Street as its southeastern boundary, the waterfront as its northern boundary, and Van Ness Avenue as its western boundary. Within this triangle lie most of the city's main tourist sights.

**FINDING AN ADDRESS   Since most of the city's streets are laid out in a grid pattern, finding an address is easy when you know the nearest cross street. Numbers start with 1 at the beginning of the street and proceed at the rate of 100 per block. When asking for directions, find out the nearest cross street and the neighborhood where your destination is located, but be careful not to confuse numerical avenues with numerical streets. Numerical avenues (Third Avenue and so on) are in the Richmond and Sunset districts in the western part of the city. Numerical (Third Street and so on) are south of Market in the east and south parts of town.

NEIGHBORHOODS IN BRIEF

Union Square Union Square is the commercial hub of the city. Most major hotels and department stores are crammed into the area surrounding the actual square, which was named for a series of violent pro-Union mass demonstrations staged here on the eve of the Civil War. A plethora of upscale boutiques, restaurants, and galleries occupy the spaces tucked between the larger buildings. A few blocks west is the **Tenderloin,** a patch of poverty and blight where you should keep your wits about you. The **Theater District** is 3 blocks west of Union Square.

The Financial District   East of Union Square, this area bordered by the Embarcadero, Market, Third, Kearny, and Washington streets is the city's business district and the stomping grounds for many major corporations. The pointy TransAmerica Pyramid, at Montgomery and Clay streets, is one of the district's most conspicuous architectural features. To its east stands the sprawling Embarcadero Center, an 8½-acre complex housing offices, shops, and restaurants. Farther east still is the World Trade Center, adjacent to the old Ferry Building, the city's pre-bridge transportation hub. Ferries to Sausalito and Larkspur still leave from this point.

Nob Hill & Russian Hill Bounded by Bush, Larkin, Pacific, and Stockton streets, Nob Hill is a genteel, well-heeled district, still occupied by the major power brokers and the neighborhood businesses they frequent. Russian Hill extends from Pacific to Bay and from Polk to Mason. It contains steep streets, lush gardens, and high-rises occupied by both the moneyed and the more bohemian.

Chinatown   A large red-and-green gate on Grant Avenue at Bush Street marks the official entrance to Chinatown. Beyond lies a 24-block labyrinth, bordered by Broadway, Bush, Kearny, and Stockton streets, filled with restaurants, markets, temples, shops—and, of course, a substantial percentage of San Francisco's Chinese residents. Chinatown is a great place for exploration all along Stockton, Grant, and Portsmouth Square and the alleys that lead off them, like Ross and Waverly. This area is jam-packed, so don't even think about driving here.

North Beach   The Italian quarter, which stretches from Montgomery and Jackson to Bay Street, is one of the best places in the city to grab a coffee, pull up a cafe chair, and do some serious people-watching. Nightlife is equally happening; restaurants, bars, and clubs along Columbus and Grant avenues attract folks from all over the Bay Area, who fight for a parking place and romp through the festive neighborhood. Down Columbus toward the Financial District are the remains of the city's Beat Generation landmarks, including Ferlinghetti's City Lights Bookstore and Vesuvio's Bar. Broadway—a short strip of sex joints—cuts through the heart of the district. **Telegraph Hill** looms over the east side of North Beach, topped by Coit Tower, one of San Francisco's best vantage points.

Fisherman's Wharf   North Beach runs into Fisherman's Wharf, which was once the busy heart of the city's great harbor and waterfront industries. Today, it is a tacky but interesting tourist area with little, if any, authentic waterfront life, except for recreational boating and some friendly sea lions.

The Marina District   Created on landfill for the Pan Pacific Exposition of 1915, the Marina boasts some of the best views of the Golden Gate, as well as plenty of grassy fields alongside San Francisco Bay. Elegant Mediterranean-style homes and apartments, inhabited by the city's well-to-do singles and wealthy families, line the streets. Here, too, are the Palace of Fine Arts, the Exploratorium, and Fort Mason Center. The main street is Chestnut between Franklin and Lyon, which abounds with shops, cafes, and boutiques. Because of its landfill foundation, the Marina was one of the hardest-hit districts in the 1989 quake.

Cow Hollow Located west of Van Ness Avenue, between Russian Hill and the Presidio, this flat, grazable area supported 30 dairy farms in 1861. Today, Cow Hollow is largely residential and largely yuppie. Its two primary commercial thoroughfares are Lombard Street, known for its many relatively inexpensive motels, and Union Street, a flourishing shopping sector filled with restaurants, pubs, cafes, and shops.

Pacific Heights The ultra-elite, such as the Gettys and Danielle Steele—and those lucky enough to buy before the real-estate boom—reside in the mansions and homes here. When the rich meander out of their fortresses, they wander down to Union Street, a long stretch of boutiques, restaurants, cafes, and bars.

Japantown Bounded by Octavia, Fillmore, California, and Geary, Japantown shelters only about 4% of the city's Japanese population, but exploring these few square blocks and the shops and restaurants within them is still a cultural experience.

Civic Center Although millions of dollars have gone toward brick sidewalks, ornate lampposts, and elaborate street plantings, the southwestern section of Market Street remains downright dilapidated. The Civic Center, at the "bottom" of Market Street, is an exception. This large complex of buildings includes the domed and newly dapper City Hall, the Opera House, Davies Symphony Hall, and the city's main library. The landscaped plaza connecting the buildings is the staging area for San Francisco's frequent demonstrations for or against just about everything.

SoMa No part of San Francisco has been more affected by recent development than South of Market (dubbed "SoMa"). The area—until recently, a district of old warehouses and industrial spaces, with a few scattered underground nightclubs, restaurants, and shoddy residential areas—is the hub of dot-commercialization and half-million-dollar-plus lofts. It also houses urban entertainment a la the Museum of Modern Art and Yerba Buena Gardens. The official boundaries are the Embarcadero, Highway 101, and Market Street, with the greatest concentrations of interest around Yerba Buena Center, along Folsom and Harrison streets between Steuart and 6th, and Brannan and Market. Along the waterfront are an array of restaurants and the new and absolutely fab Pacific Bell Park. Farther west, around Folsom between 7th and 11th streets, much of the city's nightclubbing occurs.

Mission District This is another area greatly affected by the city's new wealth. The Mexican and Latin American populations with their cuisine, traditions, and art, make the Mission District a vibrant area to visit. Some parts of the neighborhood are still poor and sprinkled with the homeless, gangs, and drug addicts, but more and more young urbanites are infiltrating, moving into the "reasonably" (a relative term) priced rentals and forging the endless oh-so-hot restaurants and bars that stretch from 16th Street and Valencia to 25th and Mission Street. Less adventurous tourists still duck into Mission Dolores, cruise by a few of the 200-plus amazing murals, and head back downtown. But if there ever was a sign that things are a-changin', it's gotta be that President Clinton was spotted dining in a Mission Street restaurant (The Slanted Door) with Chelsea and friends. Don't be afraid to visit this area, but do use caution at night.

San Francisco Neighborhoods

San Francisco Bay

Pier 41
(Ferries to
Alcatraz)

Fisherman's
Wharf

Pier 39

Fort
Mason

Aquatic
Park

FISHERMAN'S WHARF

Jefferson St.

Beach St.

Marina Blvd.

Ghirardelli
Square

NORTH BEACH

Bay St.

**MARINA
DISTRICT**

RUSSIAN HILL

Columbus Ave.

Coit Tower

The Embarcadero

Chestnut St.

Lombard St.

101

"Crookedest Street"

**TELEGRAPH
HILL**

COW HOLLOW

Union St.

Gough St.

Van Ness Ave.

Polk St.

Hyde St.

Taylor St.

Grant Ave.

Kearny St.

Battery St.

Blvd.

PACIFIC HEIGHTS

Broadway

CHINATOWN

**FINANCIAL
DISTRICT**

Presidio Ave.

Lyon St.

Washington St.

Powell St.

NOB HILL

**Trans-Bay
Transit■
Terminal**

1st St.

Divisadero St.

Sacramento St.

California St.

Fillmore St.

Franklin St.

101

Sutter St.

Post St.

Geary St.

*Yerba
Buena
Gardens*

**Moscone
Convention
◆ Center**

**UNION
SQUARE**

Geary Blvd.

JAPANTOWN

Mission St.

Howard St.

Folsom St.

Harrison St.

3rd St.

**WESTERN
ADDITION**

Turk St.

Golden Gate Ave.

CIVIC CENTER

SOMA

4th St.

Masonic St.

Fulton St.

**Alamo
Square**

Fell St.

8th St.

9th St.

Bryant St.

5th St.

6th St.

Oak St.

Market St.

10th St.

7th St.

Ashbury St.

Haight St.

**HAIGHT-
ASHBURY**

101

Cole St.

14th St.

280

17th St.

17th St.

THE CASTRO

Castro St.

Church St.

Dolores St.

Mission St.

South Van Ness Ave.

**MISSION
DISTRICT**

Potrero Ave.

**POTRERO
HILL**

edon Ave.

Deharo St.

Connecticut St.

Twin
Peaks

Portola Dr.

24th St.

Clipper St.

101

The Castro   One of the liveliest streets in town, Castro is practically synonymous with San Francisco's gay community (even though technically it is only a street in the Noe Valley district). Located at the very end of Market Street, between 17th and 18th streets, the Castro supports dozens of shops, restaurants, and bars catering to the gay community. Open-minded straight people are welcome, too.

Haight-Ashbury   Part trendy, part nostalgic, part funky, the Haight, as it's most commonly known, was the soul of the psychedelic, free-loving 1960s and the center of the counterculture movement. Today, the neighborhood straddling upper Haight Street on the eastern border of Golden Gate Park is more gentrified, but the commercial area still harbors all walks of life. Leftover aging hippies mingle with grungy, begging street kids outside Ben and Jerry's ice cream shop (where they might still be talking about Jerry Garcia), nondescript marijuana dealers whisper "Buds" as shoppers pass, and many people walking down the street have Day-Glo hair. But you don't need to be a freak or wear tie-dye to enjoy the Haight—the food, shops, and bars cover all tastes. From Haight, walk south on Cole Street for a more peaceful and quaint neighborhood experience.

Richmond & Sunset Districts   San Francisco's suburbs of sorts, these are the city's largest and most populous neighborhoods, consisting mainly of small (but expensive) homes, shops, and neighborhood restaurants. Although it borders Golden Gate Park and Ocean Beach, few tourists venture into "The Avenues," as this area is referred to locally.

2 Getting Around

BY PUBLIC TRANSPORTATION

The **San Francisco Municipal Railway,** 949 Presidio Ave., better known as "Muni" (© **415/673-6864;** www.sfmuni.com), operates the city's cable cars, buses, and Metro streetcars. Together, these three services crisscross the entire city. Buses and Metro streetcars cost $1 for adults, 35¢ for seniors over 65 and children 5 to 17. Cable cars, which run 6:30am to 12:30am, cost a whopping $2 for all people over 5 ($1 for seniors 6:30 to 7am and 9pm to midnight). Needless to say, they're packed primarily with tourists. Exact change is required on all vehicles except cable cars. Fares are subject to change.

For detailed route information, phone Muni or consult the bus map at the front of the San Francisco Yellow Pages. If you plan to use public transportation extensively, you might want to invest in a comprehensive route map ($2), sold at the San Francisco Visitor Information Center (see "Visitor Information" in "Orientation," above) and many downtown retail outlets. Also see "Muni Discounts," below.

BY CABLE CAR   San Francisco's cable cars might not be the most practical means of transport, but the rolling historic landmarks sure are a fun ride. The three lines are all condensed in the downtown area. The most scenic, and exciting, is the **Powell-Hyde line,** which follows a zigzag route from the corner of Powell and Market streets, over both Nob Hill and Russian Hill, to a turntable at gaslit Victorian Square in front of Aquatic Park. The **Powell-Mason line** starts at the same intersection and climbs over Nob Hill before descending to Bay Street, just three blocks from Fisherman's Wharf. The least scenic is the

Value **Muni Discounts**

Muni discount passes, called **Passports,** entitle holders to unlimited rides on buses, Metro streetcars, and cable cars. A Passport costs $6 for 1 day, and $10 or $15 for 3 or 7 consecutive days. Muni's **City Pass,** which costs $33.25 for adults, $26.25 for seniors 65 and older, and $24.25 for kids 5 to 17, entitles you to unlimited rides for 7 days, plus 50% off admission at 24 of the city's major attractions, including the M. H. De Young Memorial Museum, the Asian Art Museum, the California Academy of Sciences, and the Japanese Tea Garden (all in Golden Gate Park); the Museum of Modern Art; Coit Tower; the Exploratorium; the zoo; and the National Maritime Museum and Historic Ships (where you can visit the USS *Pampanito* and the SS *Jeremiah O'Brien*). You can buy a Passport or City Pass at the San Francisco Visitor Information Center, the Holiday Inn Civic Center, and the TIX Bay Area booth at Union Square, among other outlets.

California Street line, which begins at the foot of Market Street and runs a straight course through Chinatown and over Nob Hill to Van Ness Avenue. All riders must exit at the last stop and wait in line for the return trip. The cable-car system operates approximately 6:30am to 12:30am, and each ride costs $2.

BY BUS   Buses reach almost every corner of San Francisco and beyond—they travel over the bridges to Marin County and Oakland. Overhead electric cables power some buses; others use conventional gas engines. All are numbered and display their destinations on the front. Signs, curb markings, and yellow bands on adjacent utility poles designate stops, and most bus shelters exhibit Muni's transportation map and schedule. Many buses travel along Market Street or pass near Union Square and run from about 6am to midnight. After midnight, there is infrequent all-night "Owl" service. If you can help it, for safety purposes, avoid taking buses late at night.

Popular tourist routes include bus nos. 5, 7, and 71, all of which run to Golden Gate Park; 41 and 45, which travel along Union Street; and 30, which runs between Union Square and Ghirardelli Square. A bus rides costs $1 for adults and 35¢ for seniors over 65 and children 5 to 17.

BY METRO STREETCAR   Five of Muni's six Metro streetcar lines, designated J, K, L, M, and N, run underground downtown and on the street in the outer neighborhoods. The sleek railcars make the same stops as BART (see below) along Market Street, including Embarcadero Station (in the Financial District), Montgomery and Powell streets (both near Union Square), and the Civic Center (near City Hall). Past the Civic Center, the routes branch off: The J line takes you to Mission Dolores; the K, L, and M lines run to Castro Street; and the N line parallels Golden Gate Park and extends all the way to the Embarcadero. Metros run about every 15 minutes, more frequently during rush hours. They operate Monday to Friday 5am to 12:30am, Saturday 6am to 12:20am, and Sunday 8am to 12:20am. The L and N lines operate 24-7 (all day, all night). Because the operation is part of Muni, the fares are the same as for buses, and passes are accepted.

The most recent addition to this system is not a newcomer at all, but is, in fact, San Francisco's beloved rejuvenated 1930s streetcars. The beautiful multicolored F-Market line runs from 17th Street and Castro Street to Beach and

San Francisco Mass Transit

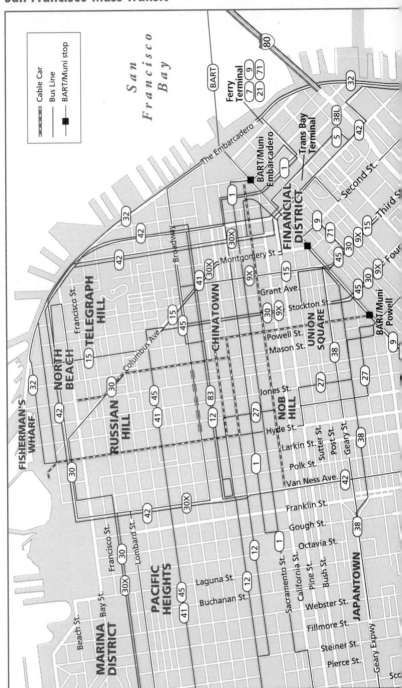

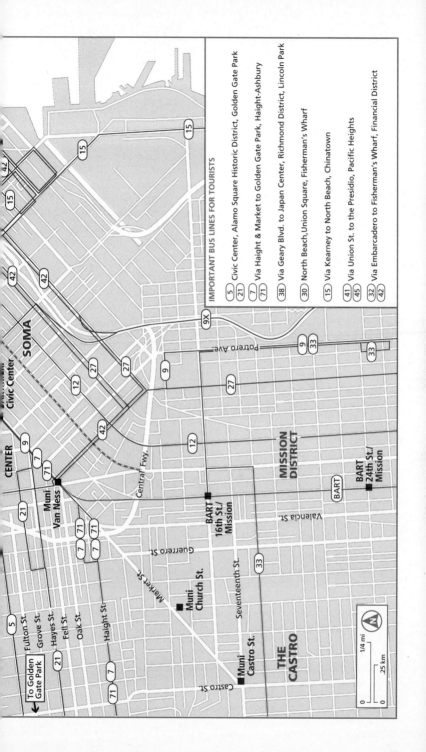

IMPORTANT BUS LINES FOR TOURISTS

⑤ Civic Center, Alamo Square Historic District, Golden Gate Park
㉑

⑦ Via Haight & Market to Golden Gate Park, Haight-Ashbury
㉛

㊳ Via Geary Blvd. to Japan Center, Richmond District, Lincoln Park

㉚ North Beach, Union Square, Fisherman's Wharf

⑮ Via Kearney to North Beach, Chinatown

㊶ Via Union St. to the Presidio, Pacific Heights
㊺

㉜ Via Embarcadero to Fisherman's Wharf, Financial District
㊷

SOMA

Civic Center

CENTER

Muni
Van Ness

Central Fwy.

Potrero Ave.

BART
16th St./
Mission

MISSION
DISTRICT

BART

BART
24th St./
Mission

Valencia St.

Guerrero St.

Market St.

Muni
Church St.

Seventeenth St.

Muni
Castro St.

THE
CASTRO

Castro St.

Haight St.

Oak St.

Fell St.

Hayes St.

Grove St.

Fulton St.

To Golden
Gate Park

0   1/4 mi
0   .25 km

47

Jones streets; every other car continues to Jones and Beach streets in Fisherman's Wharf. It's a quick and charming way to get up- and downtown without any hassle.

BY BART   BART, an acronym for **Bay Area Rapid Transit** (© 415/989-2278; www.bart.org), is a futuristic-looking, high-speed rail network that connects San Francisco with the East Bay—Oakland, Richmond, Concord, and Fremont. Four stations are on Market Street (see "By Metro Streetcar," above). Fares range from $1.10 to $4.30, depending on how far you go. Machines in the stations dispense tickets that are magnetically encoded with a dollar amount. Computerized exits automatically deduct the correct fare. Children 4 and under ride free. Trains run every 15 to 20 minutes, Monday to Friday 4am to midnight, Saturday 6am to midnight, and Sunday 8am to midnight.

A $2.5-billion, 33-mile BART extension, currently under construction, includes a southern line that will extend all the way to San Francisco International Airport. It will open, presumably, around the beginning of 2005.

BY TAXI

This isn't New York, so don't expect a taxi to appear whenever you need one—or even close. If you're downtown during rush hour or leaving a major hotel, it won't be hard to hail a cab; just look for the lighted sign on the roof that indicates the vehicle is free. Otherwise, it's a good idea to call one of the following companies to arrange a ride; even then I've had more than one situation when the cab never came. What to do? Call back if your cab is late and insist on attention, but don't expect prompt results on weekends, no matter how nicely you ask. The companies: **Veteran's Cab** (© 415/552-1300), **Luxor Cabs** (© 415/282-4141), and **Yellow Cab** (© 415/626-2345). Rates are approximately $2.50 for the first mile and $1.80 for each mile thereafter.

BY CAR

You don't need a car to explore downtown San Francisco. In fact, with the city becoming more crowded by the minute, a car can be your worst nightmare—you're likely to end up stuck in traffic with lots of aggressive and frustrated drivers, pay upward of $25 a day to park, and spend a good portion of your vacation looking for a parking space. If you want to venture outside the city, driving is the best way to go.

Before heading outside the city, especially in winter, call for California **road conditions** (© 800/427-7623).

CAR RENTALS   All the major rental companies operate in the city and have desks at the airports. When we last checked, you could get a compact car for a week for about $170, including all taxes and other charges, but prices change dramatically on a daily basis and depend on which company you rent from.

Some of the national car-rental companies operating in San Francisco include **Alamo** (© 800/327-9633), **Avis** (© 800/331-1212), **Budget** (© 800/527-0700), **Dollar** (© 800/800-4000), **Hertz** (© 800/654-3131), **National** (© 800/227-7368), and **Thrifty** (© 800/367-2277).

Car rental rates vary even more than airline fares. Prices depend on the size of the car, where and when you pick it up and drop it off, the length of the rental period, where and how far you drive it, whether you buy insurance, and a host of other factors. A few key questions could save you hundreds of dollars, but you have to ask—reservations agents don't often volunteer money-saving information:

> ## (Tips) Safe Driving
>
> Keep in mind the following handy driving tips:
>
> - California law requires that both drivers and passengers wear seat belts.
> - You can turn right at a red light (unless otherwise indicated), after yielding to traffic and pedestrians, and after coming to a complete stop.
> - Cable cars always have the right-of-way, as do pedestrians at intersections and crosswalks.
> - Pay attention to signs and arrows on the streets and roadways, or you might suddenly find yourself in a lane that requires exiting or turning when you want to go straight. What's more, San Francisco's many one-way streets can drive you in circles, but most road maps of the city indicate which way traffic flows.

- Are weekend rates lower than weekday rates? Ask if the rate is the same for pickup Friday morning, for instance, as it is for Thursday night. Reservations agents won't volunteer this information, so don't be shy about asking lots of questions.
- Does the agency assess a drop-off charge if you don't return the car to the same location where you picked it up?
- Are special promotional rates available? If you see an advertised price in your local newspaper, be sure to ask for that specific rate; otherwise, you could be charged the standard cost. Terms change constantly.
- Are discounts available for members of AARP, AAA, frequent-flyer programs, or trade unions? If you belong to any of these organizations, you may be entitled to discounts of up to 30%.
- How much tax will be added to the rental bill? Will there be local tax and state use tax?
- How much does the rental company charge to refill your gas tank if you return with the tank less than full? Most rental companies claim their prices are "competitive," but fuel is almost always cheaper in town. Try to allow enough time to refuel the car before returning it.

Some companies offer "refueling packages," in which you pay for an entire tank of gas up front. The cost is usually fairly competitive with local prices, but you don't get credit for any gas remaining in the tank. If a stop at a gas station on the way to the airport will make you miss your plane, then by all means take advantage of the fuel purchase option. Otherwise, skip it.

Most agencies enforce a minimum-age requirement—usually 25. Some also have a maximum-age limit. If you're concerned that these limits might affect you, ask about rental requirements at the time of booking to avoid problems later.

Make sure you're insured. Hasty assumptions about your personal auto insurance or a rental agency's additional coverage could end up costing you tens of thousands of dollars, even if you are involved in an accident that was clearly the fault of another driver.

If you already have your own car insurance, you are most likely covered in the United States for loss of or damage to a rental car and liability in case of injury to any other party involved in an accident. Be sure to check your policy before you spend extra money (usually $10 per day) on the **collision damage waiver (CDW),** which all agencies offer.

Most major credit cards (especially gold and platinum cards) provide some degree of coverage as well—if they were used to pay for the rental. Terms vary widely, however, so be sure to call your credit-card company directly before you rent and rely on the card for coverage. If you are uninsured, your credit card may provide primary coverage as long as you decline the rental agency's insurance. If you already have insurance, your credit card may provide secondary coverage, which basically covers your deductible. However, note that *credit cards will not cover liability,* which is the cost of injury to an outside party and/or damage to an outside party's vehicle. If you do not hold an insurance policy, you should seriously consider buying additional liability insurance from your rental company, even if you decline the CDW.

PARKING   If you want to have a relaxing vacation, don't even attempt to find street parking in Nob Hill, North Beach, Chinatown, by Fisherman's Wharf, or on Telegraph Hill. Park in a garage or take a cab or a bus. If you do find street parking, pay attention to street signs that explain when you can park and for how long. Be especially careful not to park in zones that are tow areas during rush hours.

Curb colors also indicate parking regulations. *Red* means no stopping or parking; *blue* is reserved for drivers with disabilities who have a California-issued disabled plate or a placard; *white* means there's a 5-minute limit; *green* indicates a 10-minute limit; and *yellow* and *yellow-and-black* curbs are for commercial vehicles only. Also, don't park at a bus stop or in front of a fire hydrant, and watch out for street-cleaning signs. If you violate the law, you might get a hefty ticket or your car might be towed; to get your car back, you'll have to get a release from the nearest district police department and then go to the towing company to pick up the vehicle.

When parking on a hill, apply the hand brake, put the car in gear, and *curb your wheels*—toward the curb when facing downhill, away from the curb when facing uphill. Curbing your wheels not only prevents a possible "runaway" but also keeps you from getting a ticket—an expensive fine that is aggressively enforced.

BY FERRY

TO/FROM SAUSALITO   The **Golden Gate Ferry Service** fleet (✆ 415/923-2000) shuttles passengers daily between the San Francisco Ferry Building, at the foot of Market Street, and downtown Sausalito. Service is frequent, departing at reasonable intervals every day of the year except January 1, Thanksgiving Day, and December 25. Phone for an exact schedule. The ride takes half an hour, and one-way fares are $5 for adults and $3.75 for kids 6 to 12. Senior and disabled passengers ride for $2.50; children under 6 ride free. Family rates are available on weekends.

Ferries of the **Blue & Gold Fleet** (✆ 415/773-1188 for recorded info; ✆ 415/705-5555 for tickets) also provide round-trip service to downtown Sausalito, leaving from Fisherman's Wharf at Pier 41. The cost is $12 round-trip, half-price for kids 5 to 11. Boats run on a seasonal schedule; phone for departure information.

TO/FROM LARKSPUR   The **Golden Gate Ferry Service** fleet (✆ 415/923-2000) shuttles passengers daily between the San Francisco Ferry Building, at the foot of Market Street, and downtown Larkspur. The Larkspur ferry is primarily a weekday commuter service, with frequent departures around rush hours and limited service on weekends. Boats make the 13-mile trip in about 45 minutes and costs $2.95 for adults, $2.25 for kids 6 to 12, and $1.45 for seniors and passengers with disabilities; on weekends, prices rise to $5, $3.75, and $2.50, respectively.

TO/FROM ANGEL ISLAND & TIBURON   Ferries of the **Blue & Gold Fleet** (© 415/773-1188 for recorded info; © 415/705-5555 for tickets) leave from Pier 43½ (Fisherman's Wharf) and travel to both Angel Island and Tiburon. Boats run on a seasonal schedule; phone for departure information. The round-trip fare is $12 to Angel Island, $11 to Tiburon; half-price for kids 5 to 11.

 FAST FACTS: **San Francisco**

Airport   See "Orientation," earlier in chapter.

American Express   For travel arrangements, traveler's checks, currency exchange, and other member services, offices are located at 560 California St., at Battery Street (© **415/536-2686**), open Monday to Friday 8:30am to 5:30pm, and at 455 Market St., at First Street (© **415/536-2600**), in the Financial District, open Monday to Friday 8:30am to 5:30pm and Saturday 9am to 3:30pm. To report lost or stolen traveler's checks, call © **800/221-7282**. For American Express Global Assist, call © **800/554-2639**.

Area Code   The area code for San Francisco is 415; for Oakland, Berkeley, and much of the East Bay, 510; for the peninsula, generally 650. Most phone numbers in this book are in San Francisco's 415 area code, but there's no need to dial it if you're within city limits.

Baby-sitters   Hotels can often recommend a baby-sitter or child-care service. If yours can't, try **Temporary Tot Tending** (© **650/355-7377**, or 650/871-5790 after 6pm), which offers child care by licensed teachers for children 3 to 12. It charges $6.50 an hour, $51 for an entire day, and $150 to $180 for a week, depending on the age of the child. It's open Monday to Friday 6:30am to 6:30pm; weekend service is available only during convention times.

Business Hours   Most banks are open Monday to Friday 9am to 3pm. Several stay open until about 5pm at least 1 day a week. Many banks also have ATMs for 24-hour banking (see "Money," in chapter 2).

Most stores are open Monday to Saturday from 10 or 11am to at least 6pm, with shorter hours on Sunday. But there are exceptions: Stores in Chinatown, Ghirardelli Square, and Pier 39 stay open much later during the tourist season, and large department stores, including Macy's and Nordstrom, keep late hours.

Most restaurants serve lunch from about 11:30am to 2:30pm and dinner from 5:30 to 10pm. They sometimes serve later on weekends. Nightclubs and bars are usually open daily until 2am, when they are legally bound to stop serving alcohol.

Car Rentals   See "Getting Around," earlier in this chapter.

Climate   See "When to Go," in chapter 2.

Dentist In the event of a dental emergency, see your hotel concierge or contact the **San Francisco Dental Society** (© 415/421-1435) for a referral to a specialist. The **San Francisco Dental Office,** 131 Steuart St. (© 415/777-5115), between Mission and Howard streets, offers emergency service and comprehensive dental care Monday, Tuesday, and Friday 8am to 4:30pm, Wednesday and Thursday 10:30am to 6:30pm.

Doctor **Saint Francis Memorial Hospital,** 900 Hyde St., between Bush and Pine streets on Nob Hill (© 415/353-6000), provides emergency service 24 hours a day; no appointment is necessary. The hospital also operates a **physician-referral service** (© 800/333-1355).

Driving Rules See "Getting Around," earlier in this chapter.

Drugstores **Walgreens** pharmacies are all over town, including one at 135 Powell St. (© 415/391-4433). The store is open Monday to Saturday 8am to midnight and Sunday 9am to 10pm; the pharmacy is open Monday to Saturday 8am to 8:30pm, Saturday 9am to 5pm, and Sunday 10am to 6pm. The branch on Divisadero Street at Lombard (© 415/931-6415) has a 24-hour pharmacy. **Merrill's** pharmacy, 805 Market St. (© 415/431-5466), is open Monday to Friday 8:30am to 6:30pm, Saturday 9:30am to 5:30pm; the rest of the drugstore is open Monday to Friday 7am to 9pm, Saturday 8am to 7pm, and Sunday 9:30am to 6pm. Both chains accept MasterCard and Visa.

Earthquakes There will always be earthquakes in California, most of which you'll never notice. However, in case of a significant shaker, there are a few basic precautionary measures you should know. When you are inside a building, seek cover; do not run outside. Stand under a doorway or against a wall, and stay away from windows. If you exit a building after a substantial quake, use stairwells, not elevators. If you are in your car, pull over to the side of the road and stop—but not until you are away from bridges, overpasses, telephone poles, and power lines. Stay in your car. If you're out walking, stay outside and away from trees, power lines, and the sides of buildings. If you're in an area with tall buildings, find a doorway in which to stand.

Emergencies Dial © 911 for police, an ambulance, or the fire department; no coins are needed from a public phone. Emergency hotlines include the **Poison Control Center** (© 800/523-2222) and **Rape Crisis** (© 415/647-7273).

Information See "Visitor Information," at the beginning of this chapter.

Internet Connectivity Surprisingly, San Francisco has very few Internet cafes. However, there are locations around town where you can get online access, perhaps with a sandwich and a cup o' joe. The most fun and oh-so-San Francisco place to reach out and touch someone is **Chat Café,** The Castro's vibrant meeting house where access to the web and a colorful and friendly clientele is free with a food (pastries and sandwiches) or beverage purchase. It's open Mon–Fri 6:45am–7pm, and Saturday and Sunday 8am–7pm; hours vary in winter. 498 Sanchez St., at 18th St., © 415/626-4700. You can do your laundry, listen to music, dine, and check your stocks online at **SoMa's Brainwash** (1122 Folsom St, between 7th and 8th Sts. © 415/861-FOOD; daily 7am–11pm; rates are $1 per 5 minutes.) For access without the ambiance, try **Copy Central** (110 Sutter St., at Montgomery St. © 415/392-6470), which provides access for $12 per hour (or 20¢ a minute), as does **Kinko's** (1967 Market St, near Gough St. © **415/252-0864**). Both of these companies have numerous locations around town.

Liquor Laws   Liquor stores and grocery stores, as well as some drugstores, can sell packaged alcoholic beverages between 6am and 2am. Most restaurants, nightclubs, and bars are licensed to serve alcoholic beverages during the same hours. The legal age for purchase and consumption is 21; proof of age is required.

Maps   See "City Layout," earlier in this chapter.

Newspapers & Magazines   The city's two main dailies are the *San Francisco Chronicle* and the *San Francisco Examiner;* both are distributed throughout the city. The two papers combine for a massive Sunday edition that includes a pink "Datebook" section—an excellent preview of the week's upcoming events. The free weekly *San Francisco Bay Guardian,* a tabloid of news and listings, is indispensable for nightlife information; it's widely distributed through street-corner kiosks and at city cafes and restaurants.

Of the many free tourist-oriented publications, the most widely read are *Key* and *San Francisco Guide*. Both handbook-sized weeklies contain maps and information on current events. You can find them in most hotels, shops, and restaurants in the major tourist areas.

Pharmacies   See "Drugstores," above.

Police   For emergencies, dial © **911** from any phone; no coins are needed. For other matters, call © **415/553-0123.**

Post Office   Dozens of post offices are located around the city. The closest to Union Square is inside Macy's department store, 170 O'Farrell St. (© **800/275-8777**). You can pick up mail addressed to you and marked "General Delivery" (Poste Restante) at the **Civic Center Post Office Box Unit,** P.O. Box 429991, San Francisco, CA 94142-9991 (© **800/275-8777**). The street address is 101 Hyde St.

Safety   San Francisco, like any other large city, has its fair share of crime, but most folks don't have firsthand horror stories. In some areas you need to exercise extra caution, particularly at night—notably the Tenderloin, the Western Addition (south of Japantown), the Mission District (especially around 16th and Mission streets), the lower Fillmore area (also south of Japantown), around lower Haight Street, and around the Civic Center. In addition, there are a substantial number of homeless people throughout the city with concentrations in and around Union Square, the Theater District (3 blocks west of Union Square), the Tenderloin, and Haight Street, so don't be alarmed if you're approached for spare change. Basically, just use common sense.

For additional crime-prevention information, phone **San Francisco SAFE** (© **415/553-1984**).

Smoking   If San Francisco is the state's most European city in looks and style, the comparison stops when it comes to smoking in public. Each year smoking laws become stricter. As of January 1, 1998, smoking is prohibited in restaurants and bars. Although there have been arguments against it, so far the law has been enforced in most establishments. Hotels are also offering more nonsmoking rooms, which often leaves those who like to puff out in the cold—sometimes literally.

Taxes   An 8.5% sales tax is added at the register for all goods and services purchased in San Francisco. The city hotel tax is a whopping 14%. There is no airport tax.

Taxis   See "Getting Around," earlier in this chapter.

Television   In addition to cable stations, available in most hotels, all the major networks and several independent stations are represented. They include Channel 2, KTVU (Fox); Channel 4, KRON (NBC); Channel 5, KPIX (CBS); Channel 7, KGO (ABC); Channel 9, KQED (PBS); Channel 20, KBWB (WB); and Channel 44, KBHK (UPN).

Time Zone   San Francisco is in the Pacific standard time zone, which is 8 hours behind Greenwich mean time and 3 hours behind eastern time. To find out what time it is, call ✆ **415/767-8900.**

Transit Information   The San Francisco Municipal Railway, better known as **Muni,** operates the city's cable cars, buses, and Metro streetcars. For customer service, call ✆ **415/673-6864** weekdays 7am to 5pm, weekends 9am to 5pm. At other times, you can call this number to get recorded information.

Useful Telephone Numbers   The following are some telephone numbers that you might find useful: **Tourist information** (✆ **415/283-0177**); **highway conditions** (✆ **800/427-7623**); **Movie Phone Line** (✆ **415/777-FILM**); and **Grateful Dead Hotline** (✆ **415/457-6388**).

Weather   Call the National Weather Service (✆ **831/656-1725**; www.nws. noaa.gov) to find out when the next fog bank is rolling in.

5

Where to Stay

Whether you want a room with a view or just a room, San Francisco is more than accommodating to its 11 million annual guests. Most of the city's 200-plus hotels cluster near Union Square, but some smaller independent gems are scattered around town.

When reading over your options, keep in mind that prices listed are "rack" (published) rates. Especially at big, upscale hotels, almost no one actually pays them. Always ask for special discounts or, even better, vacation packages. It's often possible to get the room you want for $100 less than what is quoted here, except in summer, when the hotels are packed and bargaining is close to impossible. Use the rates listed here for the big hotels as guidelines for comparison only; prices for inexpensive choices and smaller B&Bs are closer to reality, though.

Hunting for hotels in San Francisco can be a tricky business, particularly if you're not a seasoned traveler. What you don't know—and the reservation agent may not tell you—could very well ruin your vacation, so keep the following pointers in mind when it comes time to book a room:

- Prices listed below do not include state and city taxes, which total 14%. Other hidden extras include parking fees, which can be up to $30, and hefty surcharges—up to $1 per local call—for telephone use.
- San Francisco is Convention City, so if you want a room at a particular hotel during high season, book well in advance.

- Be sure to have a credit card in hand when making a reservation, and know that you may be asked to pay for at least 1 night in advance (this doesn't happen often, though).
- Hotels usually hold reservations until 6pm. If you don't tell the staff you're arriving late, you might lose your room.
- Almost every hotel in San Francisco requires a credit-card imprint for "incidentals" (and to prevent walkouts). If you don't have a credit card, be sure to make special arrangements with the management before you hang up the phone, and make a note of the name of the person you spoke with.

The accommodations listed below are classified first by area, then by price, using the following categories: **Very Expensive,** more than $250 per night; **Expensive,** $200 to $250 per night; **Moderate,** $150 to $200 per night; and **Inexpensive,** less than $150 per night. These categories reflect the rack rates for an average double room during the high season, which runs approximately from April through September.

Read the entries carefully: Many hotels also offer rooms at rates above and below the price category that applies to most of the units. If you like the sound of a place that's a bit over your budget, it never hurts to call and ask a few questions. Also note that we do not list single rates. Some hotels, particularly more affordable choices,

---

Value **Dial Direct**

When booking a room in a chain hotel, call the hotel's local line and the toll-free number and see where you get the best deal. A hotel makes nothing on a room that stays empty. The clerk who runs the place is more likely to know about vacancies and will often grant deep discounts in order to fill up rooms.

---

do charge lower rates for singles, so inquire about them if you are traveling alone.

In general, hotel rates in San Francisco don't vary much because the city is so popular year-round. Still, you should always ask about weekend discounts, corporate rates, and family plans; most larger hotels, and many smaller ones, offer them, but many reservations agents don't mention them unless you ask specifically.

You'll find nonsmoking rooms available in all larger hotels and many smaller hotels; reviews indicate establishments that are entirely nonsmoking. Nowadays, the best advice for smokers is to confirm a smoking-permitted room in advance.

While you'll find most accommodations have an abundance of amenities (including phones, unless otherwise noted), don't be alarmed by the lack of air-conditioned guest rooms. San Francisco weather is so mild you'll never miss it.

Most larger hotels can accommodate guests who use wheelchairs and those who have other special needs. Ask when you make a reservation to ensure that your hotel can accommodate your needs, especially if you are interested in a bed-and-breakfast.

HELPING HANDS   Having reservations about your reservations? Leave it up to the pros:

Bed-and-Breakfast California, 12711 McCartysville Place, Saratoga, CA 95070 (℗ **800/872-4500** or 408/867-9662; fax 408/867-0907; www.bbintl. com), offers a selection of B&Bs that cost $60 to $140 per night, with a 2-night minimum. Accommodations range from simple rooms in private homes to luxurious, full-service carriage houses, houseboats, and Victorian homes.

San Francisco Reservations, 360 22nd Street, Suite 300, Oakland, CA 94612; 510/628-4498 (℗ **800/677-1500** or 415/227-1500; www.hotelres. com), arranges reservations for more than 300 of San Francisco's hotels and often offers discounted rates. Their nifty Web site allows Internet users to make reservations online.

1 Union Square

VERY EXPENSIVE

Campton Place Hotel ✦✦✦   With a $10 million room renovation completed at the end of 2000, this already fabulous luxury boutique hotel offers some of the best accommodations in town—not to mention the most expensive. Along with gutting the rooms and replacing the furnishings with limestone, pear wood, and more Italian-modern and Asian-influenced decor, management changed the rooms' layout for the better. By eliminating 17 rooms, they made the new 110 units more spacious—a smart move, because the old rooms were cramped. The two executive suites and one luxury suite push the haute envelope to even more luxurious heights. Discriminating returning guests will still find superlative service, extra-large beds, exquisite bathrooms, bathrobes, top-notch toiletries, slippers, and every other necessity and extra that's made Campton Place a favored temporary address.

Revered chef Laurent Manrique delights diners at the excellent Campton Place Restaurant.

340 Stockton St. (between Post and Sutter sts.), San Francisco, CA 94108. © **800/235-4300** or 415/781-5555. Fax 415/955-5536. www.camptonplace.com. 110 units. $335–$460 double; from $550–$2,000 suite. American breakfast $19. AE, DC, MC, V. Valet parking $32. Cable car: Powell-Hyde and Powell-Mason lines (1 block west). Bus: 2, 3, 4, 30, or 45. **Amenities:** Access to nearby health club; concierge; courtesy car; secretarial services; 24-hour room service; in-room massage; babysitting; laundry service, same-day dry cleaning. *In room:* A/C, TV w/ movie rentals, fax, dataport, minibar, hair dryer, iron, safe.

The Clift Hotel 🐿🐿   Ian Schrager, king of such ultra-hip hotels as New York's Royalton and Paramount, L.A.'s Mondrian, and Miami's Delano, renovated this classic old luxury property in 2001, erasing virtually every trace of its original integrity and replacing it with trendy hipness. Although the hotel is not complete as this book goes to press, I can promise that this is no longer the spot for the older clientele who used to book rooms to relive San Francisco's favorite classic-hotel memories. The Clift is now for young trendsetters who aren't hung up on the fact that Schrager shirked the hotel's historic nature for modern-day glamour. Situated in the city's Theater District, 2 blocks from Union Square, location is still key. The Redwood Room underwent renovation and will be noticeably different, although word has it they're keeping the redwood walls. The French Room is gone (replaced by hip restaurant Asia de Cuba), as is the majority of the staff, many of whom had worked for the hotel for over 20 years. Schrager's hotel will surely be fab, but longtime locals can't help but grieve that the hotelier gave the city veteran complete plastic surgery rather than a far classier nip and tuck.

As this book goes to press, management is tight-lipped about what the rooms will look like when they debut in late summer 2001. But you can anticipate that extras will include individual climate control, two-line telephones, and windows that open—a nice touch for guests who appreciate fresh air.

495 Geary St. (at Taylor St., 2 blocks west of Union Square), San Francisco, CA 94102. © **800/652-5438** in the U.S., or 415/775-4700. Fax 415/441-4621. www.clifthotel.com. 326 units. $255–$350 double; from $360 petite suite; from $405 executive suite. Continental breakfast $12.50. AE, DC, MC, V. Parking $30. Cable car: Powell-Hyde and Powell-Mason lines (2 blocks east). Bus: 2, 3, 4, 30, 38, or 45. **Amenities:** 1 Asian-inspired restaurant, 1 bar; exercise room; concierge; room service, same-day laundry service and dry cleaning. *In room:* TV, minibar, hair dryer, iron.

The Donatello 🐿   If you're not looking for trendy lodgings or an anonymous business hotel, but want Old World elegance, book a room here. The Donatello is, in a word, dignified. The lobby is classy, with Italian marble and a serious staff. The rooms, which are some of the largest in the city (an average of 425 square feet!), are airy and decorated with traditional dark-wood antiques, tapestries, and original art. Unfortunately, most of the extra-large windows lack great views, and some of the furnishings need to be updated. Still, each room comes

---

Fun Fact **Inflation at the Clift**

The Clift Hotel charged a mere $2 per night when it first opened in 1915. The price for a room now? More than $250.

Accommodations Near Union Square & Nob Hill

The Adelaide Inn **8**	The Fairmont Hotel & Tower **14**	Hotel Beresford **30**
The Andrews Hotel **6**	The Fitzgerald **7**	Hotel Beresford Arms **5**
The Argent Hotel **52**	The Golden Gate Hotel **24**	Hotel Diva **39**
Campton Place Hotel **33**	Grand Hyatt San Francisco	Hotel Milano **49**
The Cartwright Hotel **29**	on Union Square **32**	Hotel Monaco **11**
The Clarion Bedford Hotel **4**	Grant Plaza Hotel **20**	Hotel Nikko **47**
The Clift Hotel **12**	Handlery Union Square Hotel **43**	Hotel Palomar **50**
The Commodore Hotel **3**	Hilton San Francisco **46**	Hotel Rex **28**
The Cornell Hotel de France **25**	Hostelling International	Hotel Triton **26**
The Donatello **38**	San Francisco—Downtown **45**	Hotel Vintage Court **21**

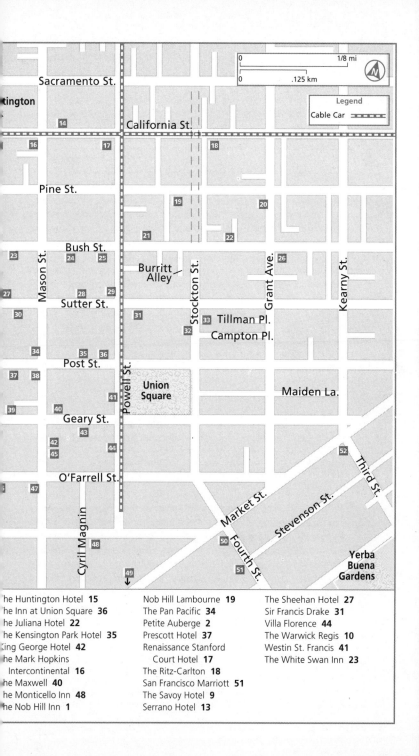

Sacramento St.

tington

14

California St.

16   **17**   **18**

Pine St.

19   **20**

21   **22**

Bush St.

23   Mason St.   **24**   **25**

Burritt
Alley

Stockton St.

Grant Ave.   **26**

Kearny St.

27   **28**   **29**

Sutter St.

30   **31**

32   **33** Tillman Pl.

Campton Pl.

34   **35**   **36**

Post St.

37   **38**

Powell St.

41   Union
Square

Maiden La.

39   **40**

Geary St.

42   **43**

45   **44**

52   Third St.

O'Farrell St.

47

Cyril Magnin

Market St.

Stevenson St.

48

50   Fourth St.

49

51   Yerba
Buena
Gardens

he Huntington Hotel **15**
he Inn at Union Square **36**
he Juliana Hotel **22**
he Kensington Park Hotel **35**
ing George Hotel **42**
he Mark Hopkins
   Intercontinental **16**
he Maxwell **40**
he Monticello Inn **48**
he Nob Hill Inn **1**

Nob Hill Lambourne **19**
The Pan Pacific **34**
Petite Auberge **2**
Prescott Hotel **37**
Renaissance Stanford
   Court Hotel **17**
The Ritz-Carlton **18**
San Francisco Marriott **51**
The Savoy Hotel **9**
Serrano Hotel **13**

The Sheehan Hotel **27**
Sir Francis Drake **31**
Villa Florence **44**
The Warwick Regis **10**
Westin St. Francis **41**
The White Swan Inn **23**

with a dish of hard candies and bottled Italian water, as well as guaranteed service from an attentive (though sometimes stuffy) staff. Rooms include voicemail, hair dryers, dataports, and terry bathrobes.

501 Post St. (at Mason St.), San Francisco, CA 94102. ℂ **800/227-3184** or 415/441-7100. Fax 415/885-8842. 94 units. $270 double; from $695 suite. Extra person $25. Children under 12 free in parents' room. Continental breakfast $9.95. AE, DC, DISC, MC, V. Valet parking $25. Cable car: Powell-Hyde and Powell-Mason lines (2 blocks west). Bus: 2, 3, 4, 30, or 45. **Amenities:** 1 Italian restaurant, 1 bar; exercise room; concierge; limited room service; same-day laundry service and dry cleaning. *In room:* A/C, TV w/ pay movies, dataport, hair dryer, iron.

Grand Hyatt San Francisco on Union Square ✦ If the thought of a 10-second walk to Saks Fifth Avenue makes your pulse race, this high-rise luxury hotel is the place for you. The Grand Hyatt sits amid all the downtown shopping, while it also boasts some of the best views in the area. The lobby is indeed grand, with Chinese artifacts and enormous ceramic vases. Thankfully, the well-kept rooms were recently renovated; they're even more luxurious than they used to be, and they still have an upscale corporate vibe. Each room has new mattresses, bed frames, shower tiles, lounge chairs, desk chairs, and textiles, as well as elbow room, a small desk and sitting area. Views from most of the 36 floors are truly spectacular. Accommodations include such amenities as TVs in the bathrooms, first-run movies, and telephones with computer-connection capability.

Rates for Regency Club rooms include continental breakfast and evening hors d'oeuvres. Three floors hold business plan rooms, each of which has a private fax, telephone with computer hookup, coffeemaker, iron and ironing board, and hair dryer. These rooms also include special services; for the extra $45 cost of the room, you get 24-hour access to a printer, a photocopier, and office supplies; free local calls and credit-card phone access; and a daily newspaper.

345 Stockton St. (between Post and Sutter sts.), San Francisco, CA 94108. ℂ **800/233-1234** or 415/398-1234. Fax 415/391-1780. www.sanfrancisco.grand.hyatt.com. 685 units. $424 double; $464 Regency Club rm. AE, DC, DISC, MC, V. Valet parking $34. Cable car: Powell-Hyde and Powell-Mason lines (2 blocks west). Bus: 2, 3, 4, 30, 38, or 45. **Amenities:** 1 restaurant; 1 bar; health club; concierge; business center; secretarial services; room service (6am–midnight); laundry service, same-day dry cleaning. *In room:* A/C, TV w/ pay movies, dataport, minibar, coffeemaker, hair dryer, iron, safe.

Hotel Monaco ✦✦ This remodeled 1910 beaux arts building made its debut in June 1995 and instantly claimed title as one of the divas among Union Square's luxury hotels. For $24 million, the Kimpton Group did this place right—from the cozy main lobby with a two-story French inglenook fireplace to the guest rooms with canopy beds, Chinese-inspired armoires, bamboo writing desks, bold stripes, and vibrant color. Everything is fresh, in the best of taste, and as playful as it is serious, with nifty extras like WebTV and two-line phones. The decor, combined with the breathtaking neighboring restaurant, makes this my favorite luxury hotel in the city. The only downside is that many rooms are way too small (especially for the price).

The adjoining Grand Cafe restaurant is a grand space with sky-high ceilings, elaborate 1920s and 1930s style, an amazing collection of local art, and okay French-inspired cuisine.

501 Geary Blvd. (at Taylor St.), San Francisco, CA 94102. ℂ **800/214-4220** or 415/292-0100. Fax 415/ 292-0111. www.monaco-sf.com. 201 units. $259–$319 double; from $369–$479 suite. Rates include evening wine hour. Call for discounted rates. AE, DC, DISC, MC, V. Valet parking $28. Bus: 2, 3, 4, 27, or 38. **Amenities:** 1 restaurant; exercise room; Jacuzzi; sauna; concierge; courtesy car; business center; room service (6:30am–11pm); in-room massage; laundry service; dry cleaning. *In room:* A/C, TV, fax, dataport, minibar, hair dryer, iron, safe. Pets accepted.

Hotel Nikko ★★★ Part of Japan Airlines' international fleet of super-luxury hotels, the 25-story Hotel Nikko combines the luxuries of Eastern and Western cultures with heavenly results. Work out in the fitness center; take a few laps in the glass-enclosed indoor swimming pool; rest in the Jacuzzi, Japanese sauna, or soaking tub; and top off the morning with a shiatsu massage, and drop by the concierge to rent PDAs listing the city's top restaurants and attractions. What more could you ask for?

Ideally located near Union Square and the Theater District, the Nikko has a penchant for pampering that extends to the guest rooms. They feature top-of-the-line amenities such as two-line speakerphones with modem ports, blackout curtains, large windows with city views, and huge marble bathrooms with separate tubs and showers. Suites contain separate sitting areas, stereos with CD players, and entry halls (a Japanese tradition). Although the hotel's decor might be a bit too staid for Western tastes—simple furnishings and beige tones predominate—luxury ultimately prevails—even in the hotel's prime beef and sushi restaurant, Anzu.

222 Mason St. (at O'Farrell St.), San Francisco, CA 94102. ✆ **800/645-5687** or 415/394-1111. Fax 415/394-1106. www.nikkohotels.com/americas/sanfran.html. 532 units. $315–$355 double; $475–$2,000 suite. AE, DISC, DC, MC, V. Valet parking $27. Cable car: Powell-Hyde and Powell-Mason lines. Bus: 2, 3, 4, 30, 38, or 45. **Amenities:** 1 restaurant (w/ sushi bar), 1 bar; large indoor heated pool; health club ($6); spa; Jacuzzi, sauna; concierge; business center; secretarial services; car-rental desk; 24-hour room service; in-room massage; laundry service; same-day dry cleaning. *In room:* A/C, TV w/ pay movies, fax, dataport, minibar, coffeemaker, hair dryer, iron. Dogs under 20 pounds welcome.

Hotel Rex ★★ Joie de Vivre, the most creative hotel group in the city, is the brilliance behind this restored historic building, which is near several fine galleries, theaters, and restaurants. The group kept some of the imported furnishings and the European boutique hotel ambience, but gave the lobby and rooms a $2 million face-lift, adding the decorative flair that makes its hotels among the most popular in town. The clublike lobby lounge is modeled after a 1920s library and is, like all the group's properties, cleverly stylish. Joie de Vivre is positioning the Rex as a hotel for the arts and literary community (not unlike the Algonquin Hotel in New York City); in that spirit, an antiquarian bookstore adjoins the lobby.

The renovated rooms, which are above average in size, feature CD players and two-line telephones. If you have one of the rooms in the back, you'll look out over a shady, peaceful courtyard (that's something you won't get in New York). Attention to the details makes Hotel Rex one of the better choices in this price range downtown.

562 Sutter St. (between Powell and Mason sts.), San Francisco, CA 94102. ✆ **800/433-4434** or 415/433-4434. Fax 415/433-3695. www.thehotelrex.com. 94 units. $245–$255 double; $275–$675 suite. AE, DC, MC, V. Valet parking $25. Cable car: Powell-Hyde and Powell-Mason lines (1 block east). Bus: 2, 3, 4, 30, 38, or 45. **Amenities:** Access to nearby health club; concierge; limited room service; same-day laundry and dry cleaning service. *In room:* TV, dataport, minibar, hair dryer, iron.

Hotel Triton ★★ Hotel magnate Bill Kimpton requisitioned a cadre of local artists and designers to "do their thing" to the Hotel Triton. The result was San Francisco's first three-star hotel to break the boring barrier. Described as vogue, chic, retro-futuristic, and even neo-baroque, the Triton begs for attention, from the Dalí-esque lobby to the sumptuous designer suites a la Jerry Garcia, Wyland (the ocean artist), and Joe Boxer. Two dozen environmentally sensitive "Eco-Rooms"—with biodegradable soaps, filtered water and air, and all-natural linens—were also installed to please the tree-hugger in all of us. A mild caveat:

Don't expect perfection; many of the rooms could use a little touching up here and there (stained curtains, chipped furniture), and service isn't as snappy as it could be. If you can live with the imperfections and want to inject a little fun and style into your stay, then join Dorothy and Toto for a trip far from Kansas.

The hotel serves coffee each morning and wine each evening (included in the room rate) in the lobby. Café de la Presse, a European-style newsstand and outdoor cafe, serves breakfast, lunch, and dinner.

342 Grant Ave. (at Bush St.), San Francisco, CA 94108. © **800/433-6611** or 415/394-0500. Fax 415/394-0555. www.hotel-tritonsf.com. 140 units. $219–$269 double; $329 suite. AE, DC, DISC, MC, V. Parking $28. Cable car: Powell-Hyde and Powell-Mason lines (2 blocks west). Pets accepted; $50 charge. **Amenities:** 1 cafe; exercise room; business center; room service 7am–11pm; same-day laundry service and dry cleaning. *In room:* A/C, TV, fax, dataport, minibar, hair dryer, coffeemaker, iron.

The Pan Pacific ⭐⭐ The Pan Pacific is artistically glitzy, enormous, and somehow romantic, all at the same time. If this were a Hollywood set, James Bond might hoodwink a villain here, magically drop down from the sky-rise's atrium, and disappear into the night. But all is quiet and intimate in the third-floor lobby, even though the skylight ceiling is another 18 floors up. The lobby's marble fountain with four dancing figures and its player piano set the mood for guests relaxing in front of the fireplace. The rooms underwent a $1.4 million touch-up in 1999 and now are decorated in a swirl of sage and browns in various patterns. Each room is rather large, immaculate, and well equipped with luxurious extras, including a lavish marble bathroom with a mini-TV at the sink, and bathrobes. The hotel is conveniently located close to Union Square.

500 Post St. (at Mason St.), San Francisco, CA 94102. © **800/533-6465** or 415/771-8600. Fax 415/398-0267. www.panpac.com. 329 units. $390–$490 double; from $545 suite. AE, DC, DISC, MC, V. Valet parking $34. Cable car: Powell-Hyde and Powell-Mason lines. Bus: 2, 3, 4, 30, 38, or 45. **Amenities:** 1 restaurant (California/Asian/French), bar; exercise room; concierge; business center; 24-hour room service; in-room massage; laundry service; same-day dry cleaning. *In room:* A/C, TV, fax, dataport, minibar, hair dryer, iron, safe. Dogs under 25 pounds welcome for additional $75 fee.

Prescott Hotel ⭐⭐ It may be small, but boutique Prescott has some big things going for it. The staff treats you like royalty, rooms are attractively unfrilly and masculine, the location (just a block from Union Square) is perfect, and limited room service is provided by one of the most popular restaurants in the city, Postrio (see chapter 6). Dark tones of green, plum, and burgundy blend well with the cherrywood furnishings in each of the soundproofed rooms; the view, alas, isn't so pleasant. The very small bathrooms contain terry robes, and the suites have Jacuzzi bathtubs. Concierge-level guests are pampered with free continental breakfast, evening cocktails, and even head-and-shoulders massages.

545 Post St. (between Mason and Taylor sts.), San Francisco, CA 94102. © **800/283-7322** or 415/563-0303. Fax 415/563-6831. www.kimptongroup.com/prescotthotel.com. 164 units. $270–$325 double; $300 concierge-level double (including breakfast and evening cocktail reception); from $365 suite. AE, DC, DISC, MC, V. Valet parking $30. Cable car: Powell-Hyde and Powell-Mason lines (1 block east). Bus: 2, 3, 4, 30, 38, or 45. **Amenities:** 1 restaurant/bar; small exercise room; concierge; limited courtesy car; limited room service. *In room:* TV w/ pay movies, minibar, hair dryer, iron, safe.

Westin St. Francis ⭐⭐ *Kids* At the turn of the 20th century, Charles T. Crocker and a few of his wealthy buddies decided that San Francisco needed a world-class hotel, and up went the St. Francis. Since then, hordes of VIPs have hung their hats and hosiery here, including Emperor Hirohito, Queen Elizabeth II, Mother Teresa, King Juan Carlos of Spain, the Shah of Iran, and all the U.S. presidents since Taft. In 1972, the hotel gained the 32-story Tower, doubling its capacity and adding banquet and conference centers. The older rooms of the main

> **Fun Fact   Hotel Rendezvous**
>
> For nearly a century, the most popular place for visitors to rendezvous in San Francisco has been under the magnificent hand-carved grandfather clock in the lobby of the Westin St. Francis hotel.

building vary in size and have more Old World charm than the newer rooms, but the Tower is remarkable for its great views of the city from above the 18th floor.

Although the St. Francis is too massive to offer the personal service you get at the smaller deluxe hotels on Nob Hill, few other hotels in San Francisco can match its majestic aura. It sounds corny, but the St. Francis is so intertwined with the city's past that it truly *is* San Francisco: Stroll through the vast, ornate lobby, and you can feel 100 years of history oozing from its hand-carved redwood paneling. The hotel did a massive $50 million renovation in 1996 and threw in another $60 million in 1999, replacing the carpeting, furniture, and bedding in every main building guest room, gussying up the lobby, and restoring the facade.

The Westin makes kids feel right at home, with a goodie bag upon check-in. Today the Tower Rooms, which were renovated in 2001, evoke a contemporary design along the lines of the W Hotel. The historic main building accentuates its history with traditional, more elegant ambiance, high ceilings, and crown molding. Even if you stay elsewhere, it's worth a visit if only to partake in high tea at the Compass Rose, one of San Francisco's most enduring and enjoyable traditions.

335 Powell St. (between Geary and Post sts.), San Francisco, CA 94102. © 800/WESTIN-1 or 415/397-7000. Fax 415/774-0124. www.westin.com. 1,194 units. Main building: $249–$499 double; from $650 suite. Tower: $389–$549 double; from $850 suite. Extra person $30. Continental breakfast $15–$18. AE, DC, DISC, MC, V. Valet parking $40. Cable car: Powell-Hyde and Powell-Mason lines (direct stop). Bus: 2, 3, 4, 30, 38, 45, or 76. Pets accepted for $30 fee. **Amenities:** 3 American/Californian restaurants, 1 bar; elaborate health club & spa; gifts for children upon check in; concierge; car-rental desk; business center; 24-hour room service. *In room:* A/C, TV, dataport, minibar, fridge, hair dryer.

EXPENSIVE

Handlery Union Square Hotel ⚐   A mere half-block from Union Square, the Handlery covers all bets by offering every amenity you could possibly need, plus lots of extras, to make up for the rather homely rooms. Some rooms (especially in the back of the hotel) are rather grim, some mattresses are hard, and furnishings are scuffed and reminiscent of a tired motel. "Club" status is your safest bet since these rooms have been renovated in recent years and perks include a complimentary morning newspaper, turndown service, an extra dressing room, bathroom scale, robes, two phones, and—here's the clincher—an electric shoe polisher. Hipsters can skip this one; the Handlery caters to families and older folks. I recommend the Clarion Bedford over this place; better rooms make it worth the extra blocks to Union Square.

351 Geary St. (between Mason and Powell sts.), San Francisco, CA 94102. © 800/843-4343 or 415/781-7800. Fax 415/781-0269. www.handlery.com. 377 units. $195 double. Club section: from $225 double; from $245 suite. Extra person $10. AE, DC, DISC, MC, V. Parking $23.50. Cable car: Powell-Hyde and Powell-Mason lines (direct stop). Bus: 2, 3, 4, 30, 38, or 45. **Amenities:** 1 restaurant (California); heated outdoor swimming pool; access to nearby health club ($10 per day); sauna; barber shop; limited room service; babysitting; same-day laundry. *In room:* A/C, TV w/ Nintendo & movie channels, dataport, some with kitchenette, hair dryer, iron, safe.

Hilton San Francisco ⚐   Complete with bustling conventioneers and a line to register that resembles airport check-in, the Hilton's lobby is so enormous and

---

Fun Fact **Coin Cleaning**

The Westin St. Francis operates the world's only legal money-laundering operation. In 1938, the hotel's manager ordered that all coinage be sorted, scrubbed, polished, and dried to keep ladies' white gloves from getting dirty, and today the tradition continues.

---

busy that it feels more like a convention hall than a hotel. The three connecting buildings (the original 19-story main structure, a 46-story tower topped by a panoramic restaurant and a 23-story landmark with 386 luxurious rooms and suites) bring swarms of visitors. Even during quieter times, the sheer enormity of the place makes the Hilton somewhat overwhelming.

After you get past the sweeping grand lobby, jump on an elevator, and wind through endless corridors to your room, you'll find the mystique ends with run-of-the-mill corporate accommodations. Some of the views from the floor-to-ceiling windows in the main tower's rooms might be memorable, but the decor definitely is not. Room size is standard. Unless you're staying in one of the more luxurious units, the feel and decor are impersonal and plain—perfect for conventioneers, but not for a romantic weekend. Towers-level accommodations offer upgraded services, including a separate registration lounge with complimentary breakfast and hors d'oeuvres and daily newspaper. One bonus: The Hilton is always upgrading somewhere on the property.

The Hilton has two restaurants: Cityscape, on the 46th floor, offers classic American cuisine and a breathtaking 360-degree view, and Intermezzo serves Italian-style food.

333 O'Farrell St. (between Mason and Taylor sts.), San Francisco, CA 94102. ⒸⒸ **800/HILTONS** or 415/771-1400. Fax 415/771-6807. www.hilton.com. 1,900 units. $169–$309 double; from $425 suite. Children free in parents' room. AE, DC, DISC, MC, V. Parking $30. Cable car: Powell-Hyde and Powell-Mason lines (1 block east). Bus: 2, 3, 4, 7, 9, 21, 27, 30, 38, 45, or 71. **Amenities:** 2 restaurants, 1 coffee shop; outdoor pool; health club; sauna; concierge; tour desk; car-rental desk; business center; secretarial services; room service (6am–midnight); babysitting; laundry service, dry cleaning. *In room:* A/C, TV, dataport, minibar, coffeemaker, hair dryer, iron.

Hotel Diva Ⓕ The Diva is the prima donna of San Francisco's affordable modern hotels. A showbiz darling when it opened in 1985, the sleek, ultra-modern Diva won "Best Hotel Design" from *Interiors* magazine. A profusion of curvaceous glass, marble, and steel marks the Euro-tech lobby; the minimalist rooms, spotless and neat, are softened with utterly fashionable "Italian modern" furnishings of monochromatic colors, silver, and wood. The enormous headboards, for example, are made of polished stainless steel meant to evoke the bow of a ship. Personally, I find the hotel a little on the cold side (figuratively speaking). Toys and services abound, and fitness and business centers complete the package. *Insider tip:* Reserve one of the rooms ending in 09 because they have extra-large bathrooms with vanity mirrors and makeup tables. The downside is that these rooms have views that make you want to keep the chic curtains closed.

440 Geary St. (between Mason and Taylor sts.), San Francisco, CA 94102. ⒸⒸ **800/553-1900** or 415/885-0200. Fax 415/346-6613. www.hoteldiva.com. 111 units. $189 double; $229 junior suite; $550 suite. Rates include continental breakfast. AE, DC, DISC, MC, V. Valet parking $27. Cable car: Powell-Mason line. Bus: 38 or 38L. **Amenities:** Exercise room; concierge; secretarial services; limited room service from nearby California Pizza Kitchen; laundry service, dry cleaning. *In room:* A/C, TV/VCR, fax, dataport, CD player, minibar, hair dryer, iron, safe.

Hotel Milano ✦   Contemporary Italian design, elegantly streamlined rooms, and its central location make Hotel Milano a popular choice for tourists and businesspeople alike. The hotel also has a film-production facility and private screening room to entice media types. Corporate travelers come for the spacious guest rooms, which feature everything an executive could want, from fax/computer modem hookups to a Nintendo game system. Other features include sound-proofed windows and some rooms have spa tubs, bidets, and double lavatories.

55 Fifth St. (between Market and Mission sts.), San Francisco, CA 94103. ☎ **800/398-7555** in the U.S., or 415/543-8555. Fax 415/543-5885. 108 units. $195–$279 double. Extra person $20. AE, DC, DISC, MC, V. Valet parking $24. Bus: All Market St. buses. **Amenities:** 1 restaurant (w/ sushi bar); concierge, room service, laundry and valet, health club and spa with steam and sauna. *In room:* A/C, TV, fax, dataport, minibar, coffeemaker, hair dryer, iron.

Hotel Vintage Court ✦✦ *Value*   Consistent personal service and great value attract a loyal clientele at this European-style hotel 2 blocks north of Union Square. The lobby, accented with dark wood, and deep green and rose colors, is welcoming enough to actually spend a little time in, especially when California wines are being poured each evening from 5pm to 6pm free of charge.

But the varietals don't stop at ground level. Each tidy room, renovated from 1995 to mid-2000, is named after a winery. While the decor used to mimic an old fashioned wine-country excursion, today the style's a more modern country look (think Pottery Barn meets Napa Valley). Earth tones reign supreme, with cream duvets, wrought-iron accents, and lovely mahogany-slat blinds. Niebaum-Coppola (named after the winery owned by the movie maverick), the deluxe two-room penthouse suite, has an original 1912 stained-glass skylight, wood-burning fireplace, whirlpool tub, complete entertainment center, and panoramic views of the city.

Masa's restaurant serves fantastic contemporary French fare (see chapter 6 for complete information).

650 Bush St. (between Powell and Stockton sts.), San Francisco, CA 94108. ☎ **800/654-1100** or 415/392-4666. Fax 415/392-1889. www.vintagecourt.com. 107 units. $179–$239 double; $350 penthouse suite. Rates include evening wine service. AE, DC, DISC, MC, V. Valet parking $28; self-parking $20. Cable car: Powell-Hyde and Powell-Mason lines (direct stop). Bus: 2, 3, 4, 30, 45, or 76. **Amenities:** 1 restaurant; access to off-premises health club ($10 per day); concierge; same-day laundry service and dry cleaning; room service (breakfast only); in-room massage. *In room:* A/C, TV, dataport, minibar, coffeemaker, hair dryer, iron.

The Inn at Union Square ✦✦   As narrow as an Amsterdam canal house, the Inn at Union Square is the antithesis of the big, impersonal hotels that surround Union Square. If you need plenty of elbow room, skip this one. But if you're looking for an inn whose staff knows each guest's name, read on. A half-block west of the square, the seven-story inn makes up for its small stature by spoiling guests with a pile of perks. Mornings start with breakfast served in lounges stocked with the *New York Times,* and evening hors d'oeuvres are served in sweet little fireplace lounges at the end of each hall. The handsome rooms, which were renovated in 1999, are individually decorated with Georgian reproductions and floral fabrics, and they are smaller than average but infinitely more appreciable than the cookie-cutter rooms of most larger hotels. Smoking is not allowed in the rooms.

440 Post St. (between Mason and Powell sts.), San Francisco, CA 94102. ☎ **800/288-4346** or 415/397-3510. Fax 415/989-0529. www.unionsquare.com. 30 units. $165–$350 double. Rates include continental breakfast, afternoon tea, and evening wine and hors d'oeuvres. AE, DC, DISC, MC, V. Valet parking $23. Cable car: Powell-Hyde and Powell-Mason lines. Bus: 2, 3, 4, 30, 38, or 45; all Market Street buses. **Amenities:** Access to nearby health club; concierge; secretarial services; limited room service; laundry service. *In room:* TV, hair dryer, iron.

The Juliana Hotel ★★ (Value) A European-style boutique hotel in the best possible way, the Juliana is hard not to like. Completely renovated in 1996, rooms are trendy-bright, with yellow and pale-blue–striped wallpaper, candy-striped yellow and red upholstered chairs, floral patterned bedspreads with matching curtains, and blue carpeting. It's vibrant and cheery, for sure, but not the kind of place where you'd want to nurse a wicked hangover. With the coffee available in the lobby by day and wine by night (included in the room rate), there's no real reason to leave. Each bathroom, most of which are rather small, contains a large, well-lit mirror and a basket of soap and other toiletries. Rooms can be on the small side, but the junior suites have plenty of space and lovely homey touches. *Note:* The entire hotel is undergoing renovation as this book goes to press and will have a more modernized, fresh look upon its completion in late 2001. Call for more information.

The Oritalia restaurant (see chapter 6 for complete review) blends Asian and Italian influences.

590 Bush St. (at Stockton St.), San Francisco, CA 94108. (C) **800/328-3880** or 415/392-2540. Fax 415/391-8447. www.julianahotel.com. 107 units. $169–$199 double; $199–$245 junior suite; $199–$239 executive suite; $359–$559 2-bedroom suite. Continental breakfast $7.95. Special winter packages available. AE, DC, MC, V. Valet parking $25; self-parking $18. Cable car: Powell-Hyde and Powell-Mason lines (1 block west). Bus: 2, 3, 4, 30, 38, or 45. **Amenities:** 1 restaurant; access to nearby health club; limited room service; same-day laundry service and dry cleaning. *In room:* A/C, TV, fax, dataport, minibar, coffeemaker, hair dryer, iron.

The Kensington Park Hotel ★★ The Kensington is a spiffed-up fairly old hotel with a cheery, eager-to-please (albeit sometimes shorthanded) staff, tasteful accommodations, and extra efforts that show the hotel really cares about its guests. Large, recently upgraded rooms on the 5th through 12th floors have handsome furnishings, and the bathrooms, though small, are sweetly appointed in brass and marble. As for the views, ask for an upper corner room, and you'll get far more than your money's worth. Coffee and croissants are available on each floor every morning; tea, sherry, and cookies are served every afternoon; and there's a complimentary wine hour with piano accompaniment on Thursdays and weekends. If you want the full treatment, book the Royal Suite, which contains a canopy bed, fireplace, Jacuzzi, and wet bar.

450 Post St. (between Powell and Mason sts.), San Francisco, CA 94102. (C) **800/553-1900** or 415/788-6400. Fax 415/399-9484. www.kensingtonparkhotel.com. 89 units. $175–$205 double; $550 suite. Extra person $10. Rates include continental breakfast; afternoon tea, sherry, and cookies; and Thursday/weekend wine hour. AE, DC, DISC, MC, V. Valet parking $28. Cable car: Powell-Hyde and Powell-Mason lines (½ block east). **Amenities:** 1 adjoining restaurant (Farallon; see chapter 6 for details); access to nearby health club; concierge; business center; babysitting; room service (limited); laundry service and same-day dry cleaning. *In room:* TV, fax, dataport, fridge, hair dryer, iron.

The Maxwell ★ What was once an old, somewhat run-down hotel in an excellent location (1 block from Union Square) is now an incredibly chic-boutique experience that was created in 1997. Rooms blend velvets, brocades, stripes, plaids, rich color, and handcrafted artistic accents into what the management calls "Theatre Deco," fused with Victorian decor (a sort of smoking club/study atmosphere). Rooms come with upholstered chairs, hand-painted bedside lamps, luxurious pillows, writing desks, and boldly tiled sinks. The suites, which are like personal penthouse apartments, are some of the most stunning in town; unfortunately, from their location you can hear the old elevator kick into gear every time it's beckoned. Swank Max's on the Square serves American cuisine.

386 Geary St. (at Mason St.), San Francisco, CA 94102. 𝒞 **888/734-6299** or 415/986-2000. Fax 415/397-2447. www.maxwellhotel.com. 153 units. $185–$235 double; $295–$595 suite. Extra person $15. Corporate discounts available. AE, DC, DISC, MC, V. Parking $22. Cable car: Powell-Hyde and Powell-Mason lines (1 block east). Bus: 2, 3, 4, 30, 38, or 45. **Amenities:** 1 restaurant; limited room service; concierge; meeting facilities; laundry service and dry cleaning. *In room:* A/C, TV w/ pay movies, dataport, hair dryer, iron.

Serrano Hotel ★★   Everything old is new again at the Kimpton Group's landmark hostelry. Los Angeles designer Cheryl Rowley (who also designed the Hotel Monaco) swathed the 17-story 1920s hotel in her trademark vibrant color and added a dash of Moroccan flair while preserving the building's Spanish revival integrity. Original architectural elements dot the living room–like lobby, with its intricately painted beams, high ceilings, large, ornate fireplace, and dramatic colonnade. Equally colorful guest rooms have oversized windows and high ceilings, cherrywood headboards on new beds, terry robes, and theater-themed artwork. The hotel is in the heart of the Theater District, right off Union Square.

405 Taylor St. (at O'Farrell St.), San Francisco, CA 94102. 𝒞 **877/294-9709** or 415/885-2500. Fax 415-474-4879. www.serranohotel.com. 236 units. From $199 double; from $299 suite. Rates include morning coffee and tea service and afternoon beverages. AE, DC, DISC, MC, V. Valet parking $27. Cable car: Powell and Market. Bus: 2, 3, 4, 27, or 38. **Amenities:** 1 restaurant/bar (Japanese); exercise room; sauna; courtesy car; concierge; business center; limited room service; babysitting; same-day laundry service and dry cleaning. *In room:* A/C, TV w/ pay movies, fax, dataport, minibar, hair dryer, iron, safe in most rooms.

Sir Francis Drake ★★   It took a change of ownership and a multimillion-dollar restoration to save the Sir Francis Drake from becoming a Starbucks, but the stately old queen is again housing guests. Granted, the venerable septuagenarian is still showing signs of age—the owners admitted there was more work to be done and threw another $5 million into room renovations in early 1999. But the price of imperfection certainly shows in the room rate: a good $100 less per night than its Nob Hill cousins. The new Sir Francis Drake is a hotel for people who are willing to trade a chipped bathroom tile or oddly matched furniture for the opportunity to vacation in pseudo-grand fashion. Allow Tom Sweeny, the ebullient (and legendary) Beefeater doorman, to handle your bags as you enter the elegant, captivating lobby. Here you can live like the king or queen of Union Square without all the pomp, circumstance, and credit-card bills.

Scala's Bistro, one of the hottest restaurants downtown, serves good Italian cuisine in a stylish setting (see chapter 6); the Parisian-style Café Expresso does an equally commendable job serving coffees, pastries, and sandwiches daily. The superchic Starlight Lounge on the 21st floor offers cocktails, entertainment, and dancing nightly with a panoramic view of the city.

450 Powell St. (at Sutter St.), San Francisco, CA 94102. 𝒞 **800/227-5480** or 415/392-7755. Fax 415/391-8719. www.sirfrancisdrake.com. 417 units. $235–$269 double; $500–$700 suite. AE, DC, DISC, MC, V. Valet parking $24. Cable car: Powell-Hyde and Powell-Mason lines (direct stop). Bus: 2, 3, 4, 45, or 76. **Amenities:** 2 restaurants, 1 bar; exercise room; concierge; limited room service; same-day laundry and dry cleaning. *In room:* A/C, TV w/ pay movies, dataport, minibar, hair dryer, iron on request.

Fun Fact **A Living Legend**

Tom Sweeny, the head doorman at the Sir Francis Drake hotel, is San Francisco's living historical monument. Dressed in traditional Beefeaters attire (you can't miss those $1,400 duds), he's been the subject of countless snapshots—an average 200 per day for the past 20 years—and has shaken hands with every president since Jerry Ford.

MODERATE

A few worthy hotel companies operate many properties throughout the city. **Holiday Inn** (© **800/465-4329;** www.basshotels.com/holiday-inn) has several strategic locations. **Personality Hotels** (© **800/553-1900;** www.personality hotels.com) spiffs up older buildings in central locales, and **Joie de Vivre** (© **800/ SF-TRIPS**) has lots of festive options scattered around town.

The Andrews Hotel ★ Two blocks west of Union Square, the Andrews was a Turkish bath before its conversion in 1981. As is typical in Euro-style hotels, the rooms are small but well maintained and comfortable, with nice touches like white lace curtains and fresh flowers. Bathrooms tend to be tiny, but for the location and price, the Andrews is a safe bet for an enjoyable stay. A bonus is the adjoining Fino Bar and Ristorante, which offers wine to hotel guests in the evening.

624 Post St. (between Jones and Taylor sts.), San Francisco, CA 94109. © **800/926-3739** or 415/563-6877. Fax 415/928-6919. www.andrewshotel.com. 48 units (some with shower only). $99–$145 double; $139–$175 superior rooms. Rates include continental breakfast and evening wine. AE, DC, MC, V. Self-parking $20. Cable car: Powell-Hyde and Powell-Mason lines (3 blocks east). Bus: 2, 3, 4, 30, 38, or 45. **Amenities:** Access to nearby health club; concierge; room service (5:30–9:30pm); babysitting; self-service laundromat, laundry service, dry cleaning. *In room:* TV, hair dryer on request, iron.

The Cartwright Hotel ★★ Diametrically opposed to the hip-hop, happenin' Hotel Triton down the street, the Cartwright Hotel is geared toward the "older, mature traveler" (as hotel marketers like to put it). Management takes pride in its reputation for offering comfortable rooms at fair prices, which explains why most guests have been repeat customers for a long time. Remarkably quiet despite its convenient location near one of the busiest downtown corners, the eight-story hotel looks not unlike it did when it opened some 80 years ago. High-quality antiques collected during its decades of faithful service furnish the lobby and the individually decorated rooms, all of which were blessed with new carpets, mattresses, wallpaper, phones, and window treatments in 2001. A nice perk usually reserved for fancier hotels is the fully equipped bathrooms, all of which have tubs, massaging showers, terry robes, and thick, fluffy towels. *Tip:* Request a room with a view of the backyard; they're the quietest. Complimentary wine is served in the small library Friday and Saturday evenings, and afternoon tea and cookies are a daily treat, as are the apples and hot beverages in the lobby.

524 Sutter St. (at Powell St.), San Francisco, CA 94102. © **800/919-9779** or 415/421-2865. Fax 415/ 398-6345. www.kimptongroup.com/cartwrighthotel.com. 114 units. $129–$269 double; $199–$399 family suite (sleeps 4). Rates include wine on Friday and Saturday evenings and afternoon tea and cookies. AE, DC, DISC, MC, V. Valet parking $30; self-parking $26. Cable car: Powell-Hyde and Powell-Mason lines (direct stop). Bus: 2, 3, 4, 30, or 45. **Amenities:** Access to nearby health club; concierge. *In room:* TV, minibar, dataport, hair dryer, iron.

The Clarion Bedford Hotel ★★ *Value* Even before the hotel began renovations to half its rooms in 2001, the price and location (3 blocks from Union Square) of the 17-story Bedford offered a darn good deal. Your hard-earned dollars will get you a large, spotless room with flowery decor that's not exactly *en vogue* but definitely in fine taste, as well as service from an enthusiastic, attentive, and professional staff. Each unit is well furnished with king, queen, or two double beds, writing desk, armchair, and well-stocked honor bar with plenty of munchies. Although closets are big, bathrooms are small. Most rooms are sunny and bright, with priceless views of the city (the higher the floor, the better the view).

The hotel's bistro, Crushed Tomato's, which is virtually in the lobby, has a small, beautiful mahogany bar opposite the registration desk.

761 Post St. (between Leavenworth and Jones sts.), San Francisco, CA 94109. (✆) 800/252-7466 or 415/673-6040. Fax 415/563-6739. www.hotelbedford.com. 144 units. $159–$199 double; from $209 suite. Continental breakfast $8.50. AE, DC, DISC, MC, V. Valet parking $25. Cable car: Powell-Hyde and Powell-Mason lines (4 blocks east). Bus: 2, 3, 4, or 27. **Amenities:** 1 restaurant/bar; secretarial services; room service (breakfast only); laundry service, dry cleaning. *In room:* TV w/ pay movies & Nintendo, dataport, minibar, coffeemaker, hair dryer, iron. Pets under 25 pounds welcome for a $50 deposit.

The Commodore Hotel 👯
If you're looking to pump a little fun and fantasy into your vacation, this six-story downtown Art Deco building is the place. Before its new owners revamped the aging Commodore from top to bottom, it . . . well, okay, it sucked. Then along came San Francisco hotelier Chip Conley, who instantly recognized the dilapidated eyesore's potential, added it to his collection, and let his hip-hop designers do their magic. The result? One groovy hotel frequented by an eclectic mix of gen-Xers and everyday folks in search of reasonably priced accommodations. Stealing the show is the Red Room, a Big Apple–style bar and lounge that reflects no other color of the spectrum but ruby red (you gotta see this one). The stylish lobby, which was renovated in 2000, comes in a close second, followed by the adjoining Titanic Café, a cute little diner that serves griddle cakes, Vietnamese tofu sandwiches, and dragon-fire salads. The "Neo-Deco" rooms, all of which have been undergoing continued upgrades through 2001, feature bright colors, whimsical furnishings, pretty artwork, and recently refurbished bathrooms.

825 Sutter St. (at Jones St.), San Francisco, CA 94109. (✆) 800/338-6848 or 415/923-6800. Fax 415/923-6804. www.thecommodorehotel.com. 113 units. $125–$169 double. AE, DC, MC, V. Parking $22. Bus: 2, 3, 4, 27, or 76. **Amenities:** 1 diner, 1 bar; access to nearby health club ($15 per day); concierge; laundry service and same-day dry cleaning. *In room:* TV, dataport, fridge on request; coffeemaker, hair dryer.

The Cornell Hotel de France 👯
Its quirks make this hotel more charming than many others in its price range. Regretfully, return visitors will find that beloved Rameau, the house golden retriever, passed away in 2001. However, a new puppy now greets you when you enter the small French-style hotel. Pass the office, where a few faces will glance in your direction and smile, and embark on a ride in the old-fashioned elevator to get to your room. Each floor is dedicated to a French painter and decorated with reproductions. Rooms are all plain and comfortable, with a desk and chairs, and individually decorated in simple, modern style. No smoking is allowed. Breakfast is served in the cavernlike provincial basement dining room, Jeanne d'Arc. Union Square is a few blocks away.

715 Bush St. (between Powell and Mason sts.), San Francisco, CA 94108. (✆) 800/232-9698 or 415/421-3154. Fax 415/399-1442. www.cornellhotel.com. 58 units. $120–$155 double. Rates include full breakfast. Package including 7 breakfasts and 5 dinners, $1,050 double per week. AE, DC, DISC, MC, V. Parking across street $16. Cable car: Powell-Hyde and Powell-Mason lines. Bus: 2, 3, 4, 30, or 45. **Amenities:** 1 restaurant. *In room:* TV, dataport, hair dryer.

The Fitzgerald 👯
If you think the guy at the front desk looks cramped in his nook of the lobby, wait until you get to your room. The Fitzgerald's guest accommodations may be outfitted with newish furniture, accented with bright bedspreads and patterned carpet, but some of the rooms are really small. (One that I saw had a dresser less than a foot from the bed.) Ask for a larger room. If you can live without a sizable closet, you'll find that the price, breakfast (home-baked breads, scones, muffins, juice, tea, and coffee), and cleanliness of this hotel make it a good value. Take heed: The view of the Golden Gate that's printed on the brochure is not actually visible from the hotel.

620 Post St. (between Jones and Taylor sts.), San Francisco, CA 94109. © **800/334-6835** or 415/775-8100. Fax 415/775-1278. www.fitzgeraldhotel.com. 39 units. $79–$189 double. Extra person $10. Rates include continental breakfast. Lower rates in winter. AE, DC, DISC, MC, V. Self-parking $18. Cable car: Powell-Hyde and Powell-Mason lines. Bus: 2, 3, 4, or 27. **Amenities:** Access to a nearby indoor pool and health club; concierge; in-room massage; dry cleaning, laundry service. *In room:* TV, dataport, hair dryer.

Hotel Beresford ★★ The small and friendly sister property of the Hotel Beresford Arms, the seven-floor Hotel Beresford is another good moderately priced choice near Union Square. Perks are the same: $5 video rentals for the VCR, clock radios, a mishmash of furniture and stocked fridges. To block out street noise, management recently installed soundproof windows. Everything's well kept, but don't expect much more than a clean place to rest. The White Horse Tavern, an attractive replica of an old English pub, serves breakfast, lunch, and dinner.

635 Sutter St. (near Mason St.), San Francisco, CA 94102. © **800/533-6533** or 415/673-9900. Fax 415/474-0449. 114 units. www.beresford.com. $135–$155 double. Extra person $10. Rates include continental breakfast. Children under 12 free in parents' room. Senior-citizen and AAA discounts available. Ask for special rates. AE, DC, DISC, MC, V. Self-parking $20. Cable car: Powell-Hyde line (1 block east). Bus: 2, 3, 4, 30, 38, or 45. **Amenities:** 1 restaurant/bar; access to nearby health club ($10 per day); babysitting; laundry service. *In room:* TV/VCR, dataport, minibar, hair dryer, iron.

Hotel Beresford Arms ★★ *Value* The bargain prices are the main reason I recommend this dependable, though slightly unfashionable, hotel. On the plus side, many rooms have Jacuzzi whirlpool bathtubs and bidets. You also have the choice of a wet bar or fully-equipped kitchen—an advantage for families—and continental breakfast is included in the rock-bottom price. All accommodations include plenty of in-room perks, including clock radios and $5 video rentals for the VCR, and there's a "Manager's Social Hour" (included in the room rates) with wine, tea, and snacks. The downsides are minimal: frighteningly red carpeting (adored by the owner's wife) in the common areas and the occasional old mattress. The location, between the Theater District and Union Square in a quieter section of San Francisco, is ideal for visitors without cars, and the price for what you get is hard to beat. *Tip:* Rooms that face Post Street might be a bit noisier than others, but they're also larger and sunnier, and some have window seats.

701 Post St. (at Jones St.), San Francisco, CA 94109. © **800/533-6533** or 415/673-2600. Fax 415/929-1535. www.beresford.com. 95 units. $145 double; $169 Jacuzzi suite; $199 parlor suite. Extra person $10. Rates include continental breakfast and afternoon wine and tea. Children under 12 free in parents' room. Senior-citizen and AAA discounts available. AE, DC, DISC, MC, V. Valet parking $20. Cable car: Powell-Hyde line (3 blocks east). Bus: 2, 3, 4, 27, or 38. **Amenities:** Access to nearby health club ($10 per day); babysitting; laundry service. *In room:* TV/VCR, dataport, minibar, hair dryer, iron.

King George Hotel ★★ *Value* Built in 1914 for the Panama-Pacific Exhibition (when rooms went for $1 per night), the delightful boutique King George has fared well over the years with its mostly European clientele. The location—surrounded by cable-car lines, the Theater District, Union Square, and dozens of restaurants—is superb, and the rooms, all of which were renovated in 1999, are surprisingly quiet for such a busy spot. Although rooms can be small, the hotel makes the most of the space; and truth be told, with affordable prices, a spiffy bathroom, new mattresses, desks, and a handsome studylike ambience, the smaller quarters come off pretty darned good. All units contain hair dryers and lovely amenities. A big hit since it started a few years back is the hotel's English afternoon tea, served above the lobby in the Windsor Tea Room Wednesday to Sunday from 3 to 6:30pm.

334 Mason St. (between Geary and O'Farrell sts.), San Francisco, CA 94102. ℭ **800/288-6005** or 415/781-5050. Fax 415/835-5991. www.kinggeorge.com. 141 units. $160 double; $240 suite. Breakfast $6.50–$8. Special-value packages available seasonally. AE, DC, DISC, MC, V. Self-parking $18. Cable car: Powell-Hyde and Powell-Mason lines (1 block west). Bus: 2, 3, 4, 30, 38, or 45. **Amenities:** Access to health club ½ block away; concierge; secretarial services; 24-hour room service; same-day laundry service and dry cleaning. *In room:* TV w/ pay movies & Nintendo, dataport, hair dryer, iron, safe.

The Monticello Inn 🐀

Federal-style decor, Chippendale furnishings, grandfather clocks, Revolutionary War paintings, a brass-mantled fireplace, and other old stuff scattered around the lobby attempt to create a colonial milieu. Although it makes for a pleasant entrance, the period effect, unfortunately, doesn't quite follow through to the rooms, although they were updated in 2000 with new textiles. They're comfortable, spacious, and reasonably attractive, but the stark blue carpets and floral upholstery don't have the same faux-Federal theme (and the homely air conditioners recessed into the walls certainly don't help). If you can live with this, however, you'll be quite content here, especially considering the extras—umbrellas, voicemail, and a morning ride to the Financial District. The service is wonderful and the downtown location is primo. The adjoining Puccini & Pinetti restaurant features modern Italian cuisine.

127 Ellis St. (between Mason and Powell sts.), San Francisco, CA 94102. ℭ **800/669-7777** or 415/392-8800. Fax 415/398-2650. www.kimptongroup.com/monticelloinn.com. 91 units. $149–$179 double; $169–$249 suite. Extra person $15. Rates include continental breakfast, coffee and tea in the lobby, and evening wine. AE, DC, DISC, MC, V. Valet parking $26. Cable car: Powell-Hyde and Powell-Mason lines (direct stop). Muni Metro: All Market St. metros. Bus: All Market St. buses. **Amenities:** Access to great nearby health club ($15 per day); concierge; limited room service; laundry service, dry cleaning. *In room:* A/C, TV w/ pay movies & Nintendo, dataport, minibar, fridge, hair dryer, iron.

Petite Auberge 🐀🐀

The Petite Auberge is so pathetically cute I can't stand it. I want to say it's overdone, that any hotel that's filled with teddy bears is absurd, but I can't. Bribed each year with fresh-baked cookies from the never-empty platter, I make rounds through the rooms and ruefully admit that I'm just going to have to use that word I loathe to hear: adorable.

Nobody does French country like the Petite Auberge. Handcrafted armoires, delicate lace curtains, cozy little fireplaces, adorable (there's that word again) little antiques and knickknacks—no hotel in Provence ever had it this good. Honeymooners should splurge on the petite suite, which has a private entrance, deck, and spa tub. The breakfast room, with its mural of a country market scene, terra-cotta tile floors, and gold-yellow tablecloths, opens onto a small garden. California wines, tea, and hors d'oeuvres (included in the room rates) are served each afternoon.

863 Bush St. (between Taylor and Mason sts.), San Francisco, CA 94108. ℭ **415/928-6000**. Fax 415/775-5717. www.foursisters.com. 26 units. $145–$245 double; $245 petite suite. Rates include full breakfast and afternoon tea. AE, DC, MC, V. Parking $25. Cable car: Powell-Hyde and Powell-Mason lines. Bus: 2, 3, 4, 30, 38, or 45. **Amenities:** Access to small exercise room next door; concierge; babysitting; same-day laundry service and dry cleaning. *In room:* TV dataport, fridge with soft drinks; coffeemaker, hair dryer on request.

The Savoy Hotel 🐀

A European-style hotel through and through. The Savoy is no longer the darling it was upon its 1989 debut, but it is a lovely and affordable option downtown. A few years ago it was clear that the hotel hasn't kept up with the wear and tear associated with brisk business. However, rooms have been renovated and, while they are still cozy French provincial, with some 18th-century period furnishings, featherbeds, and goose-down pillows, they now incorporate contemporary designs and upgraded textiles. Not all rooms are alike—they can be small, but each has beautiful patterned draperies, triple sheets, full-length mirrors, and two-line telephones. Guests also enjoy concierge service and free overnight shoeshines. Rates include late-afternoon cookies, sherry, and tea, served in the Brasserie Savoy, a dependable seafood restaurant (see chapter 6 for complete details).

580 Geary St. (between Taylor and Jones sts.), San Francisco, CA 94102. ℂ **800/227-4223** or 415/441-2700. Fax 415/441-0124. www.thesavoyhotel.com. 83 units. $149–$189 double; from $205 suite. Rates include late-afternoon cookies, sherry, and tea. Ask about package, government, senior, and corporate rates. AE, DC, DISC, MC, V. Parking $18. Bus: 2, 3, 4, 27, or 38. **Amenities:** 1 restaurant (seafood); concierge; laundry service, dry cleaning. *In room:* TV, dataport, hair dryer, iron.

Villa Florence ★★   Located half a block south of Union Square, fronting the Powell Street cable-car line, the seven-story Villa Florence is in one of the liveliest sections of the city (no need to drive, 'cause you're already here). A sorely needed renovation completed in 2000 brightened up the remarkably affordable rooms considerably. Essentially, Villa Florence offers a lower-end rendition of the spectacular rooms at the Hotel Monaco (owned by the same company), with lots of bold stripes and vibrant colors. You'll like the large, comfortable bed, CD player, and cable TV. Amenities lovers like me are thrilled by such frivolities as Aveda bath products, Frette bathrobes, and umbrellas. But never mind the rooms: The restaurant is what makes it a worthy contender among Union Square's medium-priced inns—as if the location alone weren't reason enough to book a room. Adjoining the hotel is Kuleto's, one of San Francisco's most popular and stylish Italian restaurants (you'll want to make a reservation for dinner when you book your room). See chapter 6 for complete information.

225 Powell St. (between Geary and O'Farrell sts.), San Francisco, CA 94102. ℂ **800/553-4411** or 415/397-7700. Fax 415/397-1006. www.villaflorence.com. 183 units. $159–$219 double; $259 executive king. Rates include evening wine. AE, DC, DISC, MC, V. Valet parking $25. Cable car: Powell-Hyde and Powell-Mason lines (direct stop). Bus: 2, 3, 4, 30, 38, or 45. **Amenities:** Access to nearby health club ($15 per day); concierge; courtesy car; business center; secretarial services; babysitting; same-day laundry service and dry cleaning. *In room:* A/C, TV w/ pay movies, dataport, minibar, fridge, coffeemaker, hair dryer, iron.

The Warwick Regis ★ *Value*   Louis XVI might have been a rotten monarch, but he certainly had taste. Fashioned in the style of pre-Revolutionary France, the Warwick is awash with pristine French and English antiques, Italian marble, chandeliers, four-poster beds, hand-carved headboards, and the like. The result is an expensive-looking hotel that, for all its pleasantries and perks, is surprisingly affordable when compared to its Union Square contemporaries. Honeymooners should splurge on the fireplace rooms with canopy beds—ooh la la! Adjoining the lobby is La Scene Café, a fashionable place to start your day with a latte and end it with a nightcap.

490 Geary St. (between Mason and Taylor sts.), San Francisco, CA 94102. ℂ **800/827-3447** or 415/ 928-7900. Fax 415/441-8788. www.warwickregis.com. 80 units. $159–$215 double; $199–$289 suite. Rates include continental breakfast. AE, DC, DISC, MC, V. Parking $23. Cable car: Powell-Hyde and Powell-Mason lines. Bus: 2, 3, 4, 27, or 38. **Amenities:** 1 restaurant; access to nearby health club ($10 per day); concierge; business center; secretarial services; 24-hour room service; babysitting; laundry service, dry cleaning. *In room:* TV, dataport, minibar, hair dryer, iron, safe.

The White Swan Inn ★★ *Value*   From the moment you're buzzed into this well-secured great-value inn, you'll know you're not in a generic bed-and-breakfast. If the nearly 50 teddy bears gracing the lobby doesn't cure homesickness, homemade cookies, tea, and coffee will. The romantically homey rooms are warm and cozy—the perfect place to snuggle up with a good book. They're

also quite big, with hardwood entryways, rich dark-wood furniture, working fireplaces, and an assortment of books tucked in nooks. The decor is English elegance at its best, if not to excess, with floral prints almost everywhere. Continental breakfast, wine, and hors d'oeuvres are served daily. The luxury king suites are not much better than regular rooms, just a little bigger and feature perks like chocolates, champagne, and a VCR. Each morning a generous breakfast is served in a common room just off a tiny garden. Afternoon tea, consisting of hors d'oeuvres, sherry, wine, and home-baked pastries, can be enjoyed in front of the fireplace while you browse through the books in the library.

The inn's location—2½ blocks from Union Square—makes this no-smoking 1900s building a charming and serene choice, with service and style that will please even the most discriminating traveler.

845 Bush St. (between Taylor and Mason sts.), San Francisco, CA 94108. (℃ 800/999-9570 or 415/775-1755. Fax 415/775-5717. www.foursisters.com. 26 units. $180–$190 double; $220 luxury king suite; $275 2-room suite. Extra person $15. Rates include full breakfast and afternoon wine and hors d'oeuvres. AE, DC, MC, V. Valent parking (from 7:30am–10:30pm) $25. Cable car: California St. line (1 block north). Bus: 1, 2, 3, 4, 27, or 45. **Amenities:** Concierge; laundry service; small exercise room. *In room:* A/C, dataport, fridge, coffeemaker, hair dryer, iron.

INEXPENSIVE

The Adelaide Inn   San Francisco reputedly is America's most European city, and if you're into the facade, the Adelaide will definitely complete the illusion. The last of the true old-style pensiones, this three-level building tucked in a surprisingly quiet cul-de-sac is bright, cheery, and decorated in long-forgotten style (remember textured wallpaper?). Colors and furniture hark back to the 1960s, not because the owner has gone retro, but probably because he hasn't changed the furnishings since then. But in an inexplicably quaint way, the atmosphere works. Perhaps it's the sunny, funky rooms; the small, bright breakfast room; the stairway skylight; or the shared fridge in the kitchen. It certainly isn't the spongy mattresses or tiny bathrooms or old, wet-smelling showers. Whatever it is, this place does feel a lot like someone's home. Services include morning coffee and rolls and on-the-premises pay phones (there are no phones in the rooms). *Note:* This place is not for anyone with mobility issues—it has steep stairs and no elevators.

5 Isadora Duncan Court (formerly Adelaide Place, off Taylor St., between Post and Geary sts.), San Francisco, CA 94102. (℃ 415/441-2261. Fax 415/441-0161. 18 units, all with shared bathroom. $64 double with shared bathroom. Rates include continental breakfast. AE, MC, V. Bus: 2, 3, 4, 27, 38, 76. *In room:* TV, no phone.

Hostelling International San Francisco-Downtown   For just over $20 per night (with a notarized ID), you can relive college-dorm life in an old San Francisco–style building right in the heart of Union Square. Occupying five sparsely-decorated floors, rooms here are simple and clean. Each has two or three bunk beds (4 to 6 beds), its own sink, a closet, and lockers (bring your own lock or buy one at the front desk). Although private rooms share hallway bathrooms, a few have private facilities. Suite rooms are reserved for families. Laminated posters adorn the freshly-painted hallways, and there are several common rooms, including a reading room, a smoking room, and a large kitchen with lots of tables, chairs, and refrigerator space. There are laundry facilities nearby and a helpful information desk where you can book tour reservations and sightseeing trips. The hostel is open 24 hours, and reservations are essential, especially during the summer. Persons under 18 may not stay without a parent unless they have a notarized letter, and then they must pay the adult rate.

312 Mason St. (between Geary and O'Farrell sts.), San Francisco, CA 94102. ℂ 800/909-4667, access code 02, or 415/788-5604. www.norcalhostels.org. Fax 415/788-3023. 260 beds. Hosteling members $22–$24; nonmembers $25–$27. Children under 12 half-price when accompanied by a parent. Maximum stay 14 nights per year. MC, V. Cable car: Powell-Mason line. Bus: 7B or 38. **Amenities:** Children's room; TV lounge; kitchen; Internet access; tour desk; free walking tours; free nightly movie. *In room:* Linens.

The Golden Gate Hotel ★★   San Francisco's stock of small hotels in historic turn-of-the-century buildings includes some real gems, and the Golden Gate Hotel is one of them. It's 2 blocks north of Union Square and 2 blocks down (literally) from the crest of Nob Hill, with cable-car stops at the corner for easy access to Fisherman's Wharf and Chinatown. The city's theaters and best restaurants are also within walking distance. But the best thing about the 1913 Edwardian hotel is that it's family run: John and Renate Kenaston are hospitable innkeepers who take obvious pleasure in making their guests comfortable. Each individually decorated room has handsome antique furnishings (plenty of wicker) from the early 1900s, quilted bedspreads, fresh flowers, and recently-updated carpeting. Request a room with a claw-foot tub if you enjoy a good, hot soak. Continental breakfast includes coffee, tea, juice, and croissants, afternoon tea is served daily from 4 to 7pm, and guests are welcome to use the house fax and computer free of charge.

775 Bush St. (between Powell and Mason sts.), San Francisco, CA 94108. ℂ **800/835-1118** or 415/392-3702. Fax 415/392-6202. www.goldengatehotel.com. 23 units, 14 with bathroom. $85 double without bathroom, $130 double with bathroom. Rates include continental breakfast and afternoon tea. AE, DC, MC, V. Self-parking $15. Cable car: Powell-Hyde and Powell-Mason lines (1 block east). Bus: 2, 3, 4, 30, 38, or 45. Powell & Market BART. **Amenities:** Access to health club 1 block away; laundry service and dry cleaning next door. *In room:* TV, dataport, hair dryer upon request.

Grant Plaza Hotel   You won't find any free little bottles of shampoo here. What you will find are cheap rates and basic—and I mean basic—rooms right in the middle of the Union Square–Chinatown action. Many of the small, well-kept abodes in the six-story building overlook Chinatown's main street; all gained new bedspreads, draperies, and hair dryers in 1997. The downsides are minuscule bathrooms with small showers. Corner rooms on higher floors are both larger and brighter. Ask for a room on the top floor—they're the newest, and they are substantially nicer than the older rooms.

465 Grant Ave. (at Pine St.), San Francisco, CA 94108. ℂ **800/472-6899** or 415/434-3883. Fax 415/434-3886. www.grantplaza.com. 72 units (most with shower only). $67–$95 double. AE, DC, MC, V. Nearby parking $17.50. Cable car: Powell-Hyde and Powell-Mason lines (2 blocks west). **Amenities:** Access to nearby health club ($8 per day); concierge; laundry service. *In room:* Dataport, hair dryer.

The Sheehan Hotel ★   Formerly a YWCA hotel, the Sheehan is dirt-cheap, considering its location 2 blocks from Union Square. Of course, this isn't the Ritz—some walls could use a little paint, and plenty of areas would benefit from a little TLC. Ask for one of the remodeled rooms, and you'll do just fine. Rooms are simply furnished, and bathrooms are brand-new and contain hair dryers. The hotel has a pleasant lobby and an indoor, heated lap pool and workout area.

620 Sutter St. (near Mason St.), San Francisco, CA 94102. ℂ **800/848-1529** or 415/775-6500. Fax 415/775-3271. www.sheehanhotel.com. 65 units, 62 with bathroom. $119 double without bathroom; $119–$129 double with bathroom. Rates include continental breakfast. AE, DISC, MC, V. Parking $18. Cable car: Powell-Hyde and Powell-Mason lines (2 blocks east). Bus: 2, 3, 4, 30, 38, or 45. **Amenities:** Indoor heated pool; exercise room. *In room:* TV.

2 The Financial District

VERY EXPENSIVE

Hyatt Regency San Francisco ⚹   The Hyatt Regency, a convention favorite, rises from the edge of the Embarcadero Center at the foot of Market Street. The gray concrete structure, with a 1970s, bunkerlike facade, is shaped like a vertical triangle, serrated with long rows of jutting balconies. The 17-story atrium lobby, illuminated by museum-quality theater lighting, features flowing water and a simulated environment of California grasslands and wildflowers.

Rooms, most of which were part of an $8 million renovation in 2000, are comfortably furnished in "contemporary decor" a la corporate hotel fashion. Bonuses include new makeup mirrors, ergonomic workstation chairs, and all new textiles in shades of gold, charcoal gray, and celadon. Upgraded digs for Gold Passport members, which, along with the suites, underwent a soft-goods renovation in 1999, have extra perks like tea- and coffee-making facilities and private fax machines on request. The hotel's 16th and 17th floors house the Regency Club, with 102 larger guest rooms, complimentary continental breakfast, and after-dinner cordials.

The Eclipse Café serves breakfast and lunch daily; Thirteen-Views Bar is open for morning coffee and evening cocktails; and The Equinox, a revolving rooftop restaurant and bar, has 360-degree city views.

5 Embarcadero Center, San Francisco, CA 94111. ✆ **800/233-1234** or 415/788-1234. Fax 415/398-2567. www.hyatt.com. 805 units. $199–$375 double; $450–$525 suite. Continental breakfast $14. AE, DC, DISC, MC, V. Valet parking $38. Muni Metro: All Market St. trams. Bus: All Market St. buses. **Amenities:** 1 restaurant, 1 cafe, 1 bar; access to health club; concierge; laundry and dry cleaning; business center. *In room:* A/C, TV/VCR, dataport.

The Mandarin Oriental ⚹⚹⚹ *Finds*   No hotel boasts better ultra-luxury digs with incredible views as this gem. The only reason to pause in the lobby or mezzanine is for the recommended Japanese-style tea service (complete with bento box of incredible bite-sized delicacies), cocktails, or dinner at luxe Silks, which serves delicious contemporary California cuisine. Otherwise, heaven begins after a rocketing ride on the elevators to the rooms, all of which are located between the 38th and 48th floors of a high-rise. Each of the very roomy accommodations offers extraordinary panoramic views of the bay and city. Not all rooms have tub-side views (incredible and standard with the signature rooms!), but every one does have a luxurious marble bathroom stocked with a natural loofah, a large selection of English toiletries, terry and cotton cloth robes, a makeup mirror, and silk slippers. Rooms are equally opulent, with beautiful Asian-influenced decor, handsome furnishings, and all-around comfort and accoutrements that make it difficult to find reason to leave your room. But if you muster enough gumption to make it to the hotel's formal Asian-influenced restaurant, Silks, you are in for a very good meal at the hands of chef Chris Floyd.

222 Sansome St. (between Pine and California sts.), San Francisco, CA 94104. ✆ **800/622-0404** or 415/276-9888. Fax 415/433-0289. www.mandarinoriental.com. 158 units. $475–$495 double; $675–$700 signature rooms; from $1,400 suite. Continental breakfast $18. AE, DC, DISC, MC, V. Valet parking $34. Muni Metro: J, K, L, or M to Montgomery. Bus: All Market St. buses. **Amenities:** 1 restaurant, 1 bar; fitness center; concierge; car-rental; business center; 24-hour room service; in-room massage; laundry service; same-day dry cleaning. *In room:* A/C, TV w/ pay movies, CD player, fax, dataport, minibar, hair dryer, iron, safe.

The Palace Hotel ⚹   The original 1875 Palace was one of the world's largest and most luxurious hotels, and every time you walk through the doors, you'll be

Sleeping Seaside

You would think that a city surrounded on three sides by water would have a slew of seaside hotels. Oddly enough, it has only one: the **Seal Rock Inn.** It's about as far from Union Square and Fisherman's Wharf as you can place a hotel in San Francisco, but that just makes it all the more unique. The hotel fronts Sutro Heights park, which faces Ocean Beach. Most rooms in the four-story structure have at least partial views of the ocean; at night, the sound of the surf and distant foghorns lulls guests to sleep. The rooms, although large and spotless, obviously haven't been redecorated since the Nixon administration; a monotone scheme of beige, brown, and gray makes you feel as though you're color-blind. Options range from kitchenettes to two-room suites with wood-burning fireplaces; phones, TVs, covered parking, and use of the enclosed patio and pool area are standard. Adjacent to the inn is a small cafe serving breakfast and lunch. Golden Gate Park and the Presidio are both nearby, and the Geary bus—which snails its way to Union Square and Market Street—stops right out front.

The Seal Rock Inn (© **888/SEALROCK** or 415/752-8000; fax 415/752-6034; www.sealrockinn.com) is at 545 Point Lobos Ave. (at 48th Avenue), San Francisco, CA 94121. Double rooms range from $110 to $138. **Amenities:** Outdoor pool (heated in summer only). *In room:* TV, dataport, fridge, coffeemaker, hair dryer, iron.

reminded how incredibly majestic old luxury really is. The hotel was rebuilt after the 1906 quake and most recently renovated in 1991. Its most spectacular attributes remain the regal lobby and the Garden Court, a San Francisco landmark that has been restored to its original 1909 grandeur. A double row of massive Italian-marble Ionic columns flank the court, and 10 huge chandeliers dangle above. The real heart-stopper, however, is the 80,000-pane stained-glass ceiling (good special effects made Mike Douglas look like he fell through it in the movie *The Game*). Regrettably, the rooms have that standardized, chain-hotel appearance.

Garden Court is famous for its $75 brunch on special holidays and a scaled-down version on regular weekends. Maxfield's Restaurant, a traditional San Francisco grill, serves lunch and dinner. Kyo-ya, an authentic Japanese restaurant, is highly regarded, and The Pied Piper Bar is named after the $2.5 million Maxfield Parrish mural that dominates the room.

2 New Montgomery St. (at Market St.), San Francisco, CA 94105. © **800/325-3535** or 415/512-1111. Fax 415/543-0671. www.sfpalace.com. 551 units. $300–$560 double; from $550 suite. Extra person $40. Continental breakfast $16; deluxe continental $18. Children under 18 sharing existing bedding free in parents' room. Weekend rates and packages available. AE, DC, DISC, MC, V. Parking $30. Muni Metro: All Market St. trams. Bus: All Market St. buses. **Amenities:** 4 restaurants; health club with a skylight-covered heated lap pool; whirlpool; sauna; concierge; business center; lobby-level shops; 24-hour room service; laundry and dry cleaning. *In room:* A/C, TV w/ pay movies, dataport, minibar, hair dryer, iron, safe.

The Park Hyatt San Francisco 🏵🏵   If you're looking for a small luxury business hotel in the heart of the Financial District—especially if you're billing it to the boss—stay at the Park Hyatt San Francisco. About half the size of Hyatt's typical mega-hotels, the 26-story Park Hyatt has a rather plain exterior, but it is a pleasure to behold from within. The lobby is lavishly appointed with Australian lacewood paneling, polished Italian granite, handmade custom carpets from China, and opalescent Spanish alabaster chandeliers. A magnificent spiral staircase, encircling a rather phallic bronze sculpture by Italian sculptor Arnaldo Pomodoro, leads to the upper-level restaurant, The Park Grill. Guest rooms are more understated, with Italian wood furnishings, large bathrooms, and exceedingly comfortable beds. They have extraordinary views of the city, particularly from the corner suites on the upper floors, which also come with outdoor balconies or a Jacuzzi tub (a tough choice). Ten executive suites have separate offices with all the business fixings.

333 Battery St. (at Clay St.), San Francisco, CA 94111. ⓒ 800/HYATT-CA or 415/392-1234. Fax 415/421-2433. www.hyatt.com. 360 units. $465–$555 double; $595–$4,400 suite. AE, DC, MC, V. Parking $33. Cable car: California line. Bus: 12, 15, 41, 42, or 83. **Amenities:** 2 restaurants, 1 bar; fitness center; concierge; courtesy car; business center; secretarial services; 24-hour room service; in-room massage; babysitting; laundry service and same-day dry cleaning. *In room:* A/C, TV w/ pay movies, fax (in suites), dataport, minibar, hair dryer, iron, safe.

3 Nob Hill

VERY EXPENSIVE

The Fairmont Hotel & Tower ✯✯   The granddaddy of Nob Hill's elite cadre of ritzy hotels, the Fairmont wins high honors for an incredibly jaw-dropping lobby. Even if you're not a guest, it's worth a side trip to gape at its massive, marble Corinthian columns, vaulted ceilings, velvet chairs, gilded mirrors, and spectacular wraparound staircase. In previous years, we've warned that the rooms fell short, but thanks to an $85 million renovation completed in 2001, the glamour carries to guest rooms where everything is brand-spanking new and in good taste. In addition to the expected luxuries, guests will appreciate such details as goose-down pillows, electric shoe buffers, bathroom scales, and large walk-in closets. Spectacular views from the top floors remain the showstoppers, but nuances such as 24-hour on-call dentist and doctor, high-speed Internet access, a notary public, travel agency, and in-room Playstations and dual phone lines enhance every guest's stay. Whatever you do, make a point of getting to the Tonga Room, a fantastically kitsch Disneyland-like tropical bar and restaurant where happy hour hops and rain falls every 20 minutes.

950 Mason St. (at California St.), San Francisco, CA 94108. ⓒ 800/527-4727 or 415/772-5000. Fax 415/772-5013. www.fairmont.com. 600 units. Main building $289–$409 double; from $500 suite; Tower $269–$359 double; from $800 suite. Extra person $30. Continental breakfast $14. AE, DC, DISC, MC, V. Parking $30. Cable car: California St. line (direct stop). **Amenities:** 2 restaurants, 1 bar; health club ($15 daily); concierge; tour desk; car-rental desk; business center; shopping arcade; salon; 24-hour room service, massage; babysitting; same-day laundry service and dry cleaning. *In room:* A/C, TV w/ pay movies and Playstation, fax, dataport, kitchenette in some units, minibar, coffeemaker, hair dryer, iron, safe.

The Huntington Hotel ✯✯✯   One of the kings of Nob Hill, the stately Huntington Hotel has long been a favorite retreat for Hollywood stars and political VIPs who desire privacy and security. Family-owned since 1924—an extreme rarity among large hotels—the Huntington eschews pomp and circumstance; absolute privacy and unobtrusive service are its mainstays. Although the lobby, decorated in grand 19th-century style, is rather petite, the guest rooms are quite large; they feature Brunschwig and Fils fabrics and bed coverings, antique French furnishings, and views of the city. The lavish suites, so opulent that they've been featured in *Architectural Digest,* are individually decorated with custom-made and antique furnishings. Prices are steep, as you would expect, but special offers such as a Romance Package, which includes champagne, sherry, and limousine service, make the Huntington worth considering for a special occasion.

The Big Four restaurant offers expensive contemporary American cuisine (see chapter 6 for a full description). Live piano music plays nightly in the lounge.

1075 California St. (between Mason and Taylor sts.), San Francisco, CA 94108. ℂ **800/227-4683** or 415/474-5400. Fax 415/474-6227. www.huntingtonhotel.com. 140 units. $285–$430 double; $485–$1000 suite. Continental breakfast $15. Special packages available. AE, DC, DISC, MC, V. Valet parking $19.50. Cable car: California St. line (direct stop). Bus: 1. **Amenities:** 1 restaurant, 1 lounge; indoor heated pool (for ages 16 and up); health club and new spa; steam room; sauna; concierge; massage; babysitting; same-day laundry service and dry cleaning. *In room:* A/C, TV w/ pay movies, fax, dataport, kitchenettes in some units, minibar, fridges in some units, hair dryer, iron, safe.

The Mark Hopkins Intercontinental 🐱🐱

Built in 1926 on the spot where railroad millionaire Mark Hopkins's turreted mansion once stood, the 19-story Mark Hopkins gained global fame during World War II when it was *de rigueur* for Pacific-bound servicemen to toast their good-bye to the States in the Top of the Mark cocktail lounge. Nowadays, the hotel, which renovated its rooms in 2000, caters mostly to convention-bound corporate executives who can afford the high rates. Each neoclassical room is exceedingly comfortable and comes with all the fancy amenities you'd expect from a world-class hotel, including custom furniture, plush fabrics, sumptuous bathrooms, and extraordinary views of the city. Luxury suites, added in early 2001, are twice the size of most San Francisco apartments and cost close to a month's rent per night.

The Top of the Mark, a fantastic bar/lounge, underwent a $1.5 million renovation, so dancing to live jazz or swing, enjoying afternoon tea or brunch, and dining on the newly added three-course price-fixed dinner Thursday through Saturday is done in spruced up, old-fashioned style. (Romantics, this place is for you.) A minor caveat: The hotel has only three guest elevators, making a quick trip to your room difficult during busy periods. The Top of the Mark serves afternoon tea, cocktails, and dinner Thursday through Saturday. The formal Nob Hill Restaurant offers California-French cuisine nightly and a full buffet breakfast each morning. The Nob Hill Terrace serves lunch, cocktails, and dinner daily.

1 Nob Hill (at California and Mason sts.), San Francisco, CA 94108. ℂ **800/327-0200** or 415/392-3434. Fax 415/421-3302. www.markhopkins.net. 382 units. $380–$500 double; from $610 suite; from $2500 luxury suite. Breakfast buffet $24. AE, DC, DISC, MC, V. Valet parking $27. Cable car: California St. line (direct stop). Bus: 1. **Amenities:** 3 restaurants, 2 bars; exercise room; concierge; car-rental desk; business center; secretarial services; 24-hour room service; massage; babysitting; laundry service and dry cleaning. *In room:* A/C, TV, dataport, minibar, coffeemaker, hair dryer, iron, safe.

Renaissance Stanford Court Hotel 🐱🐱

The Stanford Court has maintained a long and discreet reputation as one of San Francisco's most exclusive hotels. Keeping company with the Ritz, Fairmont, Mark Hopkins, and Huntington hotels atop Nob Hill, it's frequented mostly by corporate execs. The building was originally the mansion of Leland Stanford, whose legacy lives on in the many portraits and biographies that adorn the rooms. At first, the guest rooms come across as austere and antiquated compared to those at most other top-dollar business hotels, but the quality and comfort of the furnishings are so superior that you're forced to admit there's simply no room for improvement. The Stanford Court also prides itself on its impeccable service; a nice touch is the complimentary tray of tea or coffee placed outside your door on request. The lobby, furnished in 19th-century style with Baccarat chandeliers, French antiques, and a gorgeous stained-glass dome, makes for a grand entrance.

Many of the guest rooms have partially canopied beds; all have writing desks, extremely comfortable beds, and oak armoires that conceal new television sets. Bathrooms contain mini-TVs, telephones, heated towel racks, overhead heat lamps, and makeup mirrors.

Fournou's Ovens features contemporary American-Mediterranean cuisine in a romantic multilevel setting.

905 California St. (at Powell St.), San Francisco, CA 94108. © **800/468-3571,** 800/622-0957 in CA, or 415/989-3500. Fax 415/391-0513. www.renaissancehotels.com. 393 units. $329 double; from $775 suite. Continental breakfast $15; American breakfast $22.50. AE, DC, DISC, MC, V. Valet parking $30. Cable car: Powell-Hyde and Powell-Mason lines (direct stop). Bus: 1. **Amenities:** 1 restaurant; concierge; 24-hour room service; fitness center; business center; babysitting; complimentary car to downtown destinations; same-day 24-hour laundry and dry cleaning. *In room:* A/C, TV w/ pay movies and video games, dataport, hair dryer, iron on request.

The Ritz-Carlton 🎔🎔🎔   Ranked among the top hotels in the world (as well as the top hotel in the city) by readers of *Condé Nast Traveler,* the Ritz-Carlton has been the benchmark for San Francisco's luxury hotels since it opened in 1991. A Nob Hill landmark, the former Metropolitan Insurance headquarters stood vacant for years until the Ritz-Carlton company acquired it and embarked on a $4.5 million, four-year renovation. The interior was completely gutted and restored with fine furnishings, fabrics, and artwork, including a pair of Louis XVI blue marble-covered urns with gilt mounts, and 19th-century Waterford candelabras. The guest rooms offer every possible amenity: Italian-marble bathrooms with double sinks, telephone, and name-brand toiletries; plush terry robes; and an in-room safe. The more expensive rooms take advantage of the hotel's location—the south slope of Nob Hill—and have good views of the city. Club rooms, on the seventh, eighth, and ninth floors, have a dedicated concierge, separate elevator-key access, and complimentary meals throughout the day. No restaurant in town has more formal service than this hotel's Dining Room, which is a fine place, but not included in chapter 6 because others in its price range are more exciting. The less formal Terrace Restaurant offers contemporary Mediterranean cuisine and the city's best Sunday brunch. The lobby lounge serves afternoon tea, cocktails, and sushi daily, with low-key live entertainment from 3pm to 1am.

600 Stockton St. (between Pine and California sts.), San Francisco, CA 94108. © **800/241-3333** or 415/296-7465. Fax 415/986-1268. www.ritzcarlton.com. 336 units. $475–$575 double; $595–$695 club-level double; from $700 suite. Buffet breakfast $18; Sun brunch $55. Weekend discounts and packages available. AE, DC, DISC, MC, V. Parking $45. Cable car: Powell-Hyde and Powell-Mason lines (direct stop). **Amenities:** 2 restaurants, 1 bar; indoor heated pool; outstanding health club; jacuzzi; sauna; concierge; courtesy car; business center; secretarial services; 24-hour room service; in-room massage & manicure; babysitting; same-day laundry service and dry cleaning. *In room:* A/C, TV w/ pay movies, dataport, minibar, hair dryer, iron, safe.

EXPENSIVE

Nob Hill Lambourne 🎔🎔   One of San Francisco's top "business boutique" hotels, the Nob Hill Lambourne bills itself as an urban health spa, offering

---

(*Fun Fact* **I'll Have a Scotch**

The Ritz-Carlton's bar holds claim to one of the country's largest collection of single-malt scotches. Prices range from $7.25 to $66 per glass.

Value **Free Parking: Pass GO, Do Not Pay $200**

With parking fees averaging $20 a night at most hotels (talk about a monopoly), you might want to consider staying at one of the lodgings listed below if you're crazy enough to drive the sinister streets of San Francisco. (As one seasoned driver put it, "We separate pedestrians between the quick and the dead.") All offer free parking—some even offer free covered parking—and are moderate- to low-priced:

- **Beck's Motor Lodge,** 2222 Market St. (at 15th Street); ℂ **800/227-4360** or 415/621-8212. See p. 94.
- **Cow Hollow Motor Inn & Suites,** 2190 Lombard St. (between Steiner and Fillmore streets); ℂ **415/921-5800.** See p. 87.
- **Fort Mason Youth Hostel,** Building 240, Fort Mason; ℂ **415/771-7277.** See p. 88.
- **The Laurel,** 444 Presidio Ave. (at Masonic Avenue); ℂ **800/552-8735** or 415/567-8467. See p. 87.
- **The Phoenix Hotel,** 601 Eddy St. (at Larkin Street); ℂ **800/248-9466** or 415/776-1380. See p. 90.
- **The Wharf Inn,** 2601 Mason St. (at Beach Street); ℂ **800/548-9918** or 415/673-7411. See p. 84.

massages, facials, aromatherapy, and yoga lessons to ease corporate-level stress. Even without this hook, the Lambourne deserves a top-of-the-class rating. Sporting one of San Francisco's most stylish interiors, the hotel flaunts the comfort and quality of its contemporary French design. Top-quality, hand-sewn mattresses and goose-down comforters complement a host of thoughtful in-room accoutrements that include laptop computers, umbrellas, and CD player/stereos. Bathrooms have oversized tubs. Suites include an additional sitting room, plus a choice of treadmill, Lifecycle, or rowing machine. The wine hour starts at 6pm. Smokers should seek a room elsewhere: This place prohibits puffing.

725 Pine St. (between Powell and Stockton sts.), San Francisco, CA 94108. ℂ **800/274-8466** or 415/433-2287. www.nobhilllambourne.com. 20 units. From $230 double; $250 executive; $370 suite. Rates include continental breakfast, evening wine hour. AE, DC, DISC, MC, V. Valet parking $25. Cable car: California St. line (1 block north). **Amenities:** Access to nearby health club; concierge; spa treatments and in-room massage; laundry service and same-day dry cleaning. *In room:* TV/VCR, dataport, kitchenette, minibar, coffeemaker, hair dryer, iron.

MODERATE

The Nob Hill Inn ⭐⭐ *Value*   Although most of the rooms at the luxurious Nob Hill Inn are well out of budget range, the three Gramercy rooms are among the most opulent you will find in the city for under $125. Built in 1907 as a private home, the four-story inn has been masterfully refurbished with Louis XV antiques, expensive fabrics, museum-quality artwork, and a magnificent etched-glass European-style lift. Even the lowest-priced rooms receive equal attention: large bathrooms with marble sinks and claw-foot tubs, antique furnishings, faux-antique phones and discreetly placed televisions, and a comfortable full-sized bed. Granted, the Gramercy rooms are small. But they're so utterly charming that it's tough to complain, especially when you consider that rates include continental breakfast, afternoon tea and sherry, nightly turndown service, and the distinction of being among the city's most prestigious hotels.

1000 Pine St. (at Taylor St.), San Francisco, CA 94109. (© **415/673-6080.** Fax 415/673-6098. 21 units. $125–$195 double; $245–$275 suite. Rates include continental breakfast, afternoon tea, and sherry. AE, DC, DISC, MC, V. Cable car: California St. line. Bus: 1. *In room:* TV, hair dryer.

4 North Beach/Fisherman's Wharf

EXPENSIVE

Sheraton Fisherman's Wharf Hotel ✫ Built in the mid-1970s, this modern, four-story hotel offers the reliable comforts of a Sheraton in San Francisco's most popular tourist area. In other words, the clean, modern rooms, which were completely renovated in 1995, are comfortable and well-equipped but nothing unique to the city. A corporate floor caters exclusively to business travelers.

2500 Mason St. (between Beach and North Point sts.), San Francisco, CA 94133. (© **800/325-3535** or 415/362-5500. Fax 415/956-5275. www.sheratonatthewharf.com. 525 units. $165–$380 double; from $550–$1,000 suite. Extra person $20. Continental breakfast $17. AE, DC, DISC, MC, V. Valet parking $26. Cable car: Powell-Mason line (1 block east, 2 blocks south). Bus: 15, 32, or 42. **Amenities:** 1 restaurant, 1 bar; outdoor heated pool; exercise room; concierge; business center; salon; car-rental desk; room service (6am–midnight); dry cleaning and laundry. *In room:* A/C, TV, fax (in club-level rooms), dataport, coffeemaker, hair dryer.

The Tuscan Inn ✫✫ The Tuscan Inn is the best hotel at Fisherman's Wharf. Like an island of respectability in a sea of touristy schlock, it exudes a level of style and comfort far beyond its neighboring competitors. Splurge on hotel parking—which is actually cheaper than the wharf's outrageously priced garages—and then saunter toward the plush lobby, warmed by a grand fireplace. Even the rooms are a definite cut above competing Fisherman's Wharf hotels. Most have writing desks and armchairs. The only caveat is the lack of scenic views—a small price to pay for a good hotel in a great location. This hotel also offers seven wheelchair-accessible rooms. The adjoining Cafe Pescatore, which is open for breakfast, lunch, and dinner, serves standard Italian fare in an airy setting. (See chapter 6 for complete information.)

425 North Point St. (at Mason St.), San Francisco, CA 94133. (© **800/648-4626** or 415/561-1100. Fax 415/561-1199. www.tuscaninn.com. 221 units. $189–$269 double; $279–$339 suite. Rates include coffee, tea, and evening fireside wine reception. AE, DC, DISC, MC, V. Parking $22. Cable car: Powell-Mason line. Bus: 15, 32, or 42. **Amenities:** Access to nearby gym; concierge; courtesy car; secretarial services; room service (7am–9:30pm); same-day laundry and dry cleaning. *In room:* A/C, TV w/ pay movies, dataport, minibar, hair dryer, iron. Pets welcome for $50 fee.

MODERATE

The Hotel Bohème ✫✫ *Finds* North Beach romance awaits you at the Bohème. Although located on the busiest strip in the neighborhood, the hotel sports a style and demeanor reminiscent of a fine home in upscale Nob Hill. The decor recalls the Beat Generation, which flourished here in the 1950s; rooms are small but hopelessly romantic, with gauze-draped canopies and walls artistically accented with lavender, sage green, black, and pumpkin. The staff is ultra-hospitable, and bonuses include hair dryers in the rooms and sherry in the lobby each afternoon. Some of the greatest cafes, restaurants, bars, and shops in the city lie a few steps away, and Chinatown and Union Square are within walking distance. Take note: While the bathrooms, which are being renovated as this

Accommodations Around Town

The Abigail Hotel **37**
The Archbishop's Mansion **15**
The Argent Hotel **33**
Beck's Motor Lodge **18**
Bed & Breakfast Inn **8**
The Castillo Inn **16**
Cow Hollow Motor Inn & Suites **3**
Edward II Inn & Suites **2**
El Drisco **9**
The Harbor Court **31**
Hostelling International San Francisco—
    Fisherman's Wharf **1**
The Hotel Bohème **27**
Hotel Del Sol **4**
The Hotel Griffon **31**
The Hotel Majestic **12**
Hotel Palomar **35**
Hyatt Regency San Francisco **30**
Inn on Castro **19**
Jackson Court **10**
The Laurel **11**
The Mandarin Oriental **29**
The Marina Inn **5**
The Palace Hotel **32**
The Park Hyatt San Francisco **28**
The Parker House **20**
The Phoenix Hotel **36**
The Queen Anne Hotel **12**
The Radisson Miyako Hotel **13**
The San Remo Hotel **25**
Seal Rock Inn **14**
Sheraton Fisherman's Wharf Hotel **23**
Sherman House **7**
Stanyan Park Hotel **21**
The Tuscan Inn **24**
24 Henry **16**
Union Street Inn **6**
W San Francisco Hotel **34**
The Washington Square Inn **26**
The Wharf Inn **22**
The Willows Inn **17**

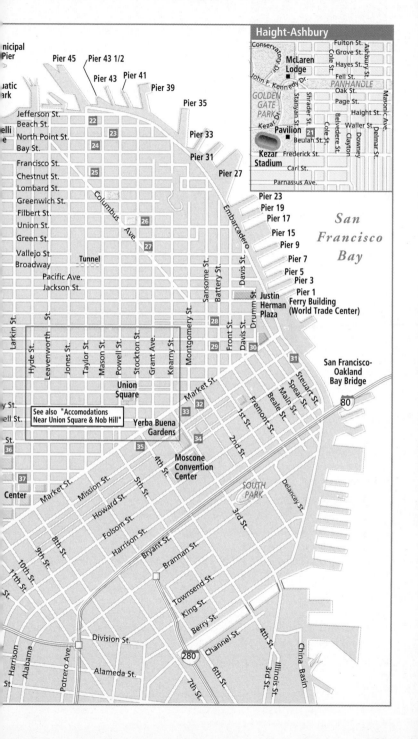

Haight-Ashbury

Conservatory Dr.
Fulton St.
Grove St.
Ashbury St.
McLaren Lodge
Cole St.
Hayes St.
John F. Kennedy Dr.
Fell St.
PANHANDLE
GOLDEN GATE PARK
Oak St.
Page St.
Masonic Ave.
Stanyan St.
Shrader St.
Haight St.
Belvedere St.
Waller St.
Delmar St.
Kezar
Pavilion
Clayton
Downey
Cole St.
Beulah
Kezar Stadium
Frederick St.
Carl St.
Parnassus Ave.

Municipal Pier

Aquatic Park

Pier 45
Pier 43 1/2
Pier 43
Pier 41
Pier 39
Pier 35

Jefferson St.
Beach St.
North Point St.
Bay St.

Francisco St.
Chestnut St.
Lombard St.
Greenwich St.
Filbert St.
Union St.
Green St.
Vallejo St.
Broadway
Pacific Ave.
Jackson St.

22
23
24
25

Columbus Ave.

Tunnel

26
27

Pier 33
Pier 31
Pier 27

Embarcadero

Pier 23
Pier 19
Pier 17
Pier 15
Pier 9
Pier 7
Pier 5
Pier 3
Pier 1

San Francisco Bay

Justin Herman Plaza
Ferry Building (World Trade Center)

Larkin St.
Hyde St.
Leavenworth St.
Jones St.
Taylor St.
Mason St.
Powell St.
Stockton St.
Grant Ave.
Kearny St.
Montgomery St.
Sansome St.
Battery St.
Davis St.
Front St.
Davis St.
Drumm St.

28
29
30
31

Union Square

See also "Accomodations Near Union Square & Nob Hill"

Yerba Buena Gardens

Market St.

32
33
34
35

San Francisco-Oakland Bay Bridge

Steuart St.
Spear St.
Main St.
Beale St.
Fremont St.
1st St.

80

y St.
ell St.

St.

36
37

Center

Market St.
Mission St.
Howard St.
Folsom St.
Harrison St.

5th St.
4th St.
3rd St.
2nd St.

Moscone Convention Center

SOUTH PARK

Delancey St.

8th St.
9th St.
10th St.
11th St.

St.

Bryant St.
Brannan St.
Townsend St.
King St.
Berry St.
Channel St.

4th St.
3rd St.
Illinois St.

China Basin

Division St.

280

6th St.
7th St.

Harrison
Alabama
Potrero Ave.
Alameda St.

St.

83

book goes to press, are sweet, they're also absolutely tiny. *Tip:* Request a room off the street side; these rooms are quieter.

444 Columbus Ave. (between Vallejo and Green sts.), San Francisco, CA 94133. ✆ **415/433-9111.** Fax 415/362-6292. www.hotelboheme.com. 15 units. $164–$174 double. Rates include afternoon sherry. AE, CB, DISC, DC, MC, V. Parking $27.50 at nearby public garage. Cable car: Powell-Mason line. Bus: 12, 15, 30, 41, 45, or 83. **Amenities:** Concierge. *In room:* TV, dataport, hair dryer.

The Washington Square Inn 🐾   Reminiscent of a traditional English inn— right down to the cucumber sandwiches served during the afternoon tea, wine, and cheese hour—this small, comely bed-and-breakfast is ideal for older couples who prefer a quieter, more subdued environment than the commotion of downtown San Francisco. It's across from Washington Square in North Beach— a coffee-craver's haven—and within walking distance of Fisherman's Wharf and Chinatown. Each room is decorated in English floral fabrics with quality European antique furnishings and plenty of fresh flowers. Faxes and VCRs are available upon request.

1660 Stockton St. (between Filbert and Union sts.), San Francisco, CA 94133. ✆ **800/388-0220** or 415/981-4220. Fax 415/397-7242. www.wsisf.com. 15 units, 2 with bathroom across the hall. $145–$245 double. Rates include continental breakfast and afternoon tea, wine, and hors d'oeuvres. AE, DC, DISC, MC, V. Valet parking $25. Bus: 15, 30, 41, or 45. **Amenities:** Limited room service. *In room:* TV, dataport, hair dryer, iron on request.

The Wharf Inn 🐾🐾 *Value*   My top choice for good-value lodging at Fisher- man's Wharf, the Wharf Inn offers above-average accommodations at one of the most popular tourist attractions in the world. The recently refurbished rooms, done in handsome tones of forest green, burgundy, and pale yellow, come well- stocked. But more importantly, they are well-situated smack-dab in the middle of the wharf, 2 blocks from Pier 39 and the cable-car turnaround, and they're within walking distance of the Embarcadero and North Beach. The inn is ideal for car-bound families because parking is free (that saves $25 a day right off the bat).

2601 Mason St. (at Beach St.), San Francisco, CA 94133. ✆ **800/548-9918** or 415/673-7411. Fax 415/ 776-2181. www.wharfinn.com. 51 units. $99–$199 double; penthouse $270–$399. AE, DC, DISC, MC, V. Free parking. Cable car: Powell-Mason line. Bus: 15, 32, or 42. Metro: F. **Amenities:** Access to nearby health club ($10 per day); concierge; tour desk. *In room:* TV, hair dryer on request.

INEXPENSIVE

The San Remo Hotel 🐾🐾 *Value*   This small, European-style pensione is one of the best budget hotels in San Francisco. In a quiet North Beach neighbor- hood, within walking distance of Fisherman's Wharf, the San Remo originally served as a boardinghouse for dock workers displaced by the great fire of 1906. As a result, the rooms are small and bathrooms are shared, but all is forgiven when it comes time to pay the bill. Rooms are decorated in cozy country style, with brass and iron beds; oak, maple, or pine armoires; and wicker furnishings. All have ceiling fans. The immaculate shared bathrooms feature claw-foot tubs and brass pull-chain toilets with oak tanks and brass fixtures. If the penthouse is available, book it: You won't find a more romantic place to stay in San Francisco for so little money. It has its own bathroom, TV, fridge, and patio.

2237 Mason St. (at Chestnut St.), San Francisco, CA 94133. ✆ **800/352-REMO** or 415/776-8688. Fax 415/776-2811. www.sanremohotel.com. 62 units, 61 with shared bathroom. $60–$90 double; $150 suite. AE, DC, MC, V. Parking $10–$12. Cable car: Powell-Mason line. Bus: 15, 22, 30, or 42. **Amenities:** Access to nearby health club; tour desk; self-service Laundromat. *In room:* Ceiling fan.

5 The Marina/Pacific Heights/Cow Hollow

VERY EXPENSIVE

El Drisco ★★ *Finds*   Perched on one of the most coveted blocks of residential property in all of San Francisco, the El Drisco is one of the finest small hotels in the city. The stately six-story structure was built in 1903 as a boardinghouse for the servants who worked in Pacific Heights. After some major refinements by interior designer Glenn Texeira (who also did the Ritz-Carlton in Manila), it now caters to a far more affluent clientele. The guest rooms—swathed in soothing shades of alabaster, celadon, and buttercup yellow—boast superior fabrics, quality antiques, and exceedingly comfortable mattresses. Each suite has a couch that unfolds into a bed (although you would never guess from the looks of it), an additional phone and TV, and superior views. The marble-laden bathrooms are quite spacious, and they're equipped with hair dryers and plush robes. My favorite room is 304A, a corner suite with an extraordinary view of the Pacific Heights mansions and surrounding bay. Guests eat breakfast in one of the hotel's three quiet, comfortable common rooms, where you can find 24-hour coffee and tea service. The only things that prevent a top ranking are the service, which is nowhere near the level of that at the Ritz-Carlton, and the lack of parking.

2901 Pacific Ave. (at Broderick St.), San Francisco, CA 94115. © **800/634-7277** or 415/346-2880. Fax 415/567-5537. www.eldriscohotel.com. 48 units (some with shower only). $245 double; $395–$650 suite. Rates include buffet breakfast and evening wine hour. AE, DC, DISC, MC, V. No parking available. Bus: 3 or 24. **Amenities:** Exercise room; concierge; limited room service; same-day laundry service and dry cleaning. *In room:* TV/VCR, CD player, dataport, minibar, fridge, coffeemaker, hair dryer, iron, safe.

Sherman House ★★★ *Finds*   How expensive is a night at the Sherman House? Put it this way: If you have to ask, you can't afford it. Built in 1876 by philanthropist and music publisher Leander Sherman, this magnificent Pacific Heights Victorian doubled as his home and playhouse for such guest stars as Enrico Caruso, Lillian Russell, and Victor Herbert. After years of neglect, it took 4 years and a small fortune to restore the estate to its original splendor. Today the Sherman House sets the standard in San Francisco for privacy, personal service, and sumptuous furnishings. All rooms are individually decorated with authentic French Second Empire, Biedermeier, or English Jacobean antiques, and all but one boasts a wood-burning fireplace. Rooms contain queen-sized canopy featherbeds, ultra-rich tapestry fabrics, and down comforters; 13 rooms have fireplaces. Along with expected amenities, rooms also have stereos and beautiful recently renovated black granite bathrooms with bathrobes and whirlpool bathtubs. The English-style Hyde Park room offers a fine bay view from its cushioned window seat. The Jacobean-style Paderewski suite offers dark wainscoting and a beamed ceiling. The least expensive room (no. 203) contains a king bed and English antiques, but it lacks a fireplace. The most expensive suite is the Thomas Church Garden suite, which consists of two rooms with 1½ bathrooms, with an adjoining sunken garden terrace with gazebo and pond.

The dining room has a fine reputation, but because of a zoning dispute, it lost its license to serve food to nonguests. Main courses, which can be customized to diet requirements, run about $40. Meals are served daily (except there's no dinner on Wednesday).

2160 Green St. (between Webster and Fillmore sts.), San Francisco, CA 94123. © **800/424-5777** or 415/563-3600. Fax 415/563-1882. www.theshermanhouse.com. 14 units. $460–$545 double; $775–$1,200 suite. Rates include full breakfast and valet parking. AE, DC, DISC, MC, V. Cable car: Powell-Hyde line. Bus: 22, 41, or 45. **Amenities:** 1 restaurant (California-French); access to nearby health club; concierge; butler (who will discreetly unpack luggage), business center; secretarial services; 24-hour room service; babysitting; laundry service and same-day dry cleaning. *In room:* TV/VCR, hair dryer, iron on request, safe.

EXPENSIVE

Union Street Inn ★★   Who would have guessed that one of the most delightful B&Bs in California would be in San Francisco? This two-story Edwardian fronts perpetually busy (and trendy) Union Street, but it's quiet as a church on the inside. The individually decorated rooms are comfortably furnished, and most have canopied or brass beds with down comforters, fresh flowers, and bay windows (beg for one with a view of the garden). A few even have Jacuzzi tubs. An extended continental breakfast is served in the parlor, in your room, or on an outdoor terrace overlooking a lovely English garden. The ultimate honeymoon retreat is the private carriage house behind the inn, but any room at this warm, friendly inn is guaranteed to please.

2229 Union St. (between Fillmore and Steiner sts.), San Francisco, CA 94123. © **415/346-0424.** Fax 415/922-8046. www.unionstreetinn.com. 5 units, 1 cottage. $159–$239 standard double; $255 cottage. Rates include breakfast, hors d'oeuvres, and evening beverages. AE, MC, V. Parking $15. Bus: 22, 28, 41, 45, or 47. *In room:* TV.

MODERATE

Bed & Breakfast Inn ★   San Francisco's first bed-and-breakfast consists of a trio of Victorian houses all gussied up in English country style, hidden in a cul-de-sac just off Union Street. While it doesn't have quite the casual ambience of neighboring Union Street Inn, the Bed & Breakfast Inn is a good deal in an expensive town. Be prepared for majorly worn furnishings and dated carpets in conjunction with family antiques and original art. The funky Garden Suite—highly recommended for families or groups of four—lacks in the interior design department, but it comes with a fully stocked kitchen, a living room, two bedrooms, two bathrooms (one with a Jacuzzi tub), a study, and French doors leading to the sunroom and garden. Breakfast (freshly baked croissants, fresh fruit, orange juice, and coffee, tea, or cocoa) is either brought to your room with a morning newspaper or served in a sunny Victorian breakfast room.

4 Charlton Court (off Union St., between Buchanan and Laguna sts.), San Francisco, CA 94123. © **415/921-9784.** Fax 415/921-0544. www.thebandb.com. 13 units, 9 with shared bathroom. $90–$135 double without bathroom; $175–$185 double with bathroom; $280–$390 suite. Rates include continental breakfast. MC, V. Parking $11 at nearby garage. Bus: 41 or 45.

Hotel Del Sol ★★ *Kids* *Value*   The cheeriest motel in town is located just two blocks off Marina's bustling section of Lombard. Two-level Hotel del Sol is all about festive flare. The sunshine theme extends through the Miami-Beach–style use of vibrant color, as in the yellow, red, orange, and blue exterior, to the heated courtyard pool, which beckons the youngish clientele as they head to their cars parked (for free!) in cabanalike spaces. (This great pool could keep the tots busy all day.) Fair weather fun doesn't stop at the front door of the 54 spacious rooms, which boast equally cheery interior decor (read: loud and very colorful) to the unexpected extras like a CD player and tips to the town's happenings and shopping meccas.

3100 Webster St., at Greenwich St., San Francisco, CA 94123.©**877/433-5765** or 415/921-5520. Fax 415/931-4137. www.thehoteldelsol.com. 57 units, including 10 one-bedroom suites. $119–$165 double; $160–$235 suite. AE, DC, DIS, MC, V. Bus: 22, 28, 41, 43, 45, or 76. **Amenities:** Heated outdoor pool; sauna. *In room:* TV, dataport,kitchenettes in some rooms, coffeemaker, iron.

Jackson Court ★★   The Jackson Court, a stately three-story brownstone Victorian mansion, is in one of San Francisco's most exclusive neighborhoods,

Pacific Heights. Its only fault—that it's far from the action—is also its blessing: If you crave a blissfully quiet vacation in elegant surroundings, this is the place. Each recently renovated room is individually furnished with superior-quality antique furnishings; two have wood-burning fireplaces (whose use is *de rigueur* in the winter). The Blue Room features an inviting window seat; the Garden Suite has handcrafted wood paneling and a large picture window looking out on the private garden patio. After breakfast, spend the day browsing the shops along nearby Union and Fillmore streets, and return in time for afternoon tea. Continental breakfast includes muffins, scones, croissants, oatmeal, juice, and fruit.

2198 Jackson St. (at Buchanan St.), San Francisco, CA 94115. **415/929-7670.** Fax 415/929-1405. www.sftrips.com. 10 units. $150–$215 double. Rates include continental breakfast. AE, MC, V. Parking on street only. Bus: 1, 12, or 22. **Amenities:** Concierge; room service; laundry service and dry cleaning. *In room:* TV, dataport, hair dryer, some rooms with iron.

The Laurel *Value*   If you don't mind being out of the downtown area, this lovely hotel, renovated in 1999, is one of the most tranquil, affordable places to rest your head. Tucked just beyond the southernmost tip of the Presidio and Pacific Heights, the outside is nothing impressive—just another motor inn. And that's what it was until the hotel group Joie de Vivre bought it and breathed new life into the place. Now it serves as a sophisticated spot for the budget-minded traveler. Decor is tres chic and modern, with Zen-like influences (think W Hotel at half the price). Some rooms have excellent city views; all have CD players, voicemail, and spiffy bathrooms. The continental breakfast is fine, but why bother when you're across the street from Ella's, San Francisco's best breakfast? Other thoughtful touches: 24-hour coffee and tea service, pet-friendly rooms, and free parking! Chalk up the great shopping one block away at Sacramento Street and the new and very hip bar, G, which serves cocktail food and libations, and there's plenty of reason to stay here.

444 Presidio Ave. (at Masonic Ave.), San Francisco, CA 94115. **800/552-8735** or 415/567-8467. Fax 415/928-1866. www.thelaurelinn.com. 49 units. $135–$165 double. Rates include continental breakfast, afternoon lemonade and cookies. AE, DC, DISC, MC, V. Free parking. Muni Metro: 1, 3, 4, 43. **Amenities:** 1 bar; access to health club across the street; concierge; self-service Laundromat; iron. *In room:* TV/VCR, dataport, kitchenette in some rooms, hair dryer. Pets accepted.

INEXPENSIVE

Cow Hollow Motor Inn & Suites   If you're less interested in being downtown than in playing in and around the beautiful bayfront Marina, check out this modest brick hotel on busy Lombard Street. There's no fancy theme, but each room has cable TV, free local phone calls, free covered parking, and a coffeemaker. All the rooms were renovated in 1996, so you'll be sure to sleep on a relatively firm mattress surrounded by clean carpeting and drapes. Families will appreciate the one- and two-bedroom suites, which have full kitchens and dining areas.

2190 Lombard St. (between Steiner and Fillmore sts.), San Francisco, CA 94123. **415/921-5800.** Fax 415/922-8515. www.cowhollowmotorinn.com. 130 units. $115 double; from $205 suite. Extra person $10. AE, DC, MC, V. Free parking. Bus: 28, 43, or 76. **Amenities:** Access to nearby health club ($10 per day); car-rental desk; laundry and dry cleaning within a block. *In room:* A/C, TV, dataport, kitchenettes in suites only; coffeemaker, hair dryer.

Edward II Inn & Suites   This three-story "English country" inn has a room for almost anyone's budget, ranging from pensione units with shared bathrooms to luxuriously appointed suites and cottages with living rooms, kitchens, and whirlpool bathtubs. Originally built to house guests who attended the 1915 Pan-Pacific Exposition, it's now run by innkeepers Denise and Bob Holland, who have done a fantastic job maintaining its worldly charm. Regardless of price, all rooms are spotless, comfortably appointed with cozy antique furnishings and plenty of fresh flowers. Their price includes a standard continental breakfast. The only caveat is that its Lombard Street location is usually congested with traffic. Nearby Chestnut and Union Streets offer some of the best shopping and dining in the city. The adjoining pub serves evening drinks.

3155 Scott St. (at Lombard St.), San Francisco, CA 94123. ℂ 800/473-2846 or 415/922-3000. Fax 415/931-5784. www.edwardii.com. 32 units, 21 with bathroom. $77–$85 double with shared bathroom; $110 double with private bathroom; $185–$235 suite or cottage. Rates include continental breakfast and evening sherry. AE, MC, V. Self-parking $10 across the street. Bus: 28, 43, or 76. **Amenities:** 1 bar (open Thurs–Sat). *In room:* TV, hair dryer and iron available on request.

Hostelling International San Francisco—Fisherman's Wharf ⭐ *(Finds)* Unbelievable but true—you can get front-row bay views for a mere $21 nightly. The hostel, on national park property, provides dorm-style accommodations and offers easy access to the Marina's shops and restaurants. Rooms sleep 2 to 12 people; communal space includes a fireplace, pool table, kitchen, dining room, and coffee bar. The breakfast alone practically makes it worth the price. Make reservations well in advance.

Fort Mason, Building 240, San Francisco, CA 94123. ℂ 800/909-4776, ext. 03, or 415/771-7277. Fax 415/771-1468. www.norcalhostels.org. 170 beds. $21–$22.50 per night. Rates include breakfast. MC, V. Limited parking. Bus: 28, 30, 42, 47, or 49. **Amenities:** Self-service Laundromat.

The Marina Inn ⭐⭐ *(Value)*   The Marina Inn is one of the best low-priced hotels in San Francisco. How it offers so much for so little is mystifying. Each guest room in the 1924 four-story Victorian looks like something from a country furnishings catalog, complete with rustic pine-wood furniture, a four-poster bed with silk-soft comforter and new mattress, pretty wallpaper, and soothing tones of rose, hunter green, and pale yellow. You also get new remote-control televisions, discreetly hidden in pine cabinetry, and nightly turndown service with chocolates on your pillow—all for as little as *$65 a night!* Combine that with continental breakfast, afternoon sherry, friendly service, and an armada of shops and restaurants within easy walking distance, and there you have it: the top choice for Best Overall Value. (*Note:* Traffic can be a bit noisy so the hotel is planning to add double-paned windows.)

3110 Octavia St. (at Lombard St.), San Francisco, CA 94123. ℂ 800/274-1420 or 415/928-1000. Fax 415/928-5909. www.marinainn.com. 40 units. Nov–Feb $65–$105 double; Mar–May $75–$125 double; June–Oct $85–$135 double. Rates include continental breakfast and afternoon sherry. AE, MC, V. Bus: 28, 30, 43, or 76. *In room:* TV, hair dryer and iron on request.

6 Japantown & Environs

EXPENSIVE

The Archbishop's Mansion ⭐⭐ *(Finds)*   One thing is certain, the archbishop who built this 1904 Belle Époque beauty was no Puritan. Drippingly romantic, the Archbishop's Mansion, tucked away in a very residential but central neighborhood, is one of the most opulent and fabulously adorned B&Bs you could possibly imagine. Here, within the uniquely adorned rooms, it's all about whimsy and drama. The Don Giovanni suite—larger than many San Francisco houses—holds a huge, cherub-encrusted four-poster bed imported from a French castle, a palatial fireplace, elaborately embroidered linens, and a seven-head shower that you'll never want to leave. Slightly closer to earth is the Carmen suite, which has a deadly romantic combination of a claw-foot bathtub fronting a wood-burning fireplace. In the morning, breakfast is delivered to the guest rooms, and in the evening, wine is served in the elegant parlor, which also serves as the 24-hour coffee and tea pit stop. With CD players in every room and a video and CD library accessible to every guest, this is one hotel that is enticing enough to make you want to linger in your room.

1000 Fulton St. (at Steiner St.), San Francisco, CA 94117. © **800/543-5820** or 415/563-7872. Fax 415/885-3193. www.archbishopsmansion.com. 15 units. $195–$425 double. Rates include continental breakfast and evening wine. AE, DC, MC, V. Limited free parking. Bus: 5 or 22. **Amenities:** Access to nearby gym ($20 daily); concierge; room service; same-day laundry and dry cleaning. *In room:* TV/VCR, dataport, fridge (in suite only), hair dryer, iron.

The Hotel Majestic ★★
Both tourists and business travelers adore The Majestic because it covers every professional need while retaining the ambience of a luxurious Old World hotel. It was built in 1902, and the lobby alone sweeps guests into another era, with an overabundance of tapestries, tasseled brocades, Corinthian columns, and intricate, lavish detail. Rooms are just as opulent, with French and English antiques; the centerpiece of many rooms is a large four-poster canopy bed. You'll also find custom-made, mirrored armoires and antique reproductions. All drapes, fabrics, carpet, and bedspreads were replaced in 1997, and half the bathrooms and guest rooms underwent a $2 million renovation in 1999. But they're still sprucing, and in early 2002 The Majestic plans to add new coats of paint and change the wallpaper.

Perks go beyond the usual. Along with bathrobes, two phones (one of which is portable), and umbrellas are complimentary faxes sent and received by the office (a nice touch!), fresh-baked cookies with turndown service, and a well-lit desk. Some rooms have fireplaces. The quiet Perlot restaurant serves delicious California-Asian fare in a romantic setting, complete with live piano music most nights. Avalon, a quaint French mahogany marble-topped bar, boasts a collection of African butterflies.

1500 Sutter St. (between Octavia and Gough sts.), San Francisco, CA 94109. © **800/869-8966** or 415/441-1100. Fax 415/673-7331. www.thehotelmajestic.com. 58 units. $175–$285 double; from $350 suite. Continental breakfast $8.50. Rates include complimentary coffee in lobby 6:30–9am and wine and appetizers 4–6pm. Group, government, corporate, and relocation rates available. AE, DC, DISC, MC, V. Valet parking $23. Bus: 2, 4, 42, 47, or 49. **Amenities:** 1 restaurant, 1 bar; access to nearby health club ($10 per day); concierge; 24-hour room service; same-day dry cleaning and laundry service; in-room massage; babysitting. *In room:* A/C, TV, dataport, honor basket; fridges in some rooms; hair dryer, iron.

The Radisson Miyako Hotel ★
Japantown's Miyako is a tranquil alternative to staying downtown, and it's only about a mile away from downtown. The 16-story tower and 5-story Garden Wing overlook the Japan Center, which is home to the city's largest complex of Japanese shops and restaurants and a huge movie complex. The hotel manages to maintain a feeling of peace and quiet you'd expect somewhere much more remote. Rooms are Zen-like with East-meets-West decor. The Western-style (don't think cowboy) rooms are fine, but romantics and adventurers should opt for the traditional-style Japanese rooms with tatami mats and futons, a *tokonoma* (alcove for displaying art), and shoji screens that slide away to frame views of the city. Two futon luxury suites have Japanese rock gardens and deep-tub Japanese bathrooms. A bonus: Fillmore Street's upscale boutiques are a few blocks away. Dot is a trendy restaurant/bar owned by Joe Boxer.

1625 Post St. (at Laguna St.), San Francisco, CA 94115. © **800/533-4557** or 415/922-3200. Fax 415/921-0417. www.radisson.com. 218 units. $209–$229 double; from $299 suite. Children under 13 free in parents' room. AE, DC, DISC, MC, V. Valet parking $20; self-parking $10. Bus: 2, 3, 4, or 38. **Amenities:** 1 restaurant, 1 bar; limited exercise room; business center; room service (6:30–10:30pm); in-room massage; same-day laundry service and dry cleaning. *In room:* TV w/ pay movies, dataport, minibar, coffeemaker on request; hair dryer, iron, safe.

MODERATE

The Queen Anne Hotel ★★   The majestic 1890 Victorian, which was once a grooming school for upper-class young women, is today a stunning hotel. Restored in 1981 and renovated in 1995, the four-story building recalls San Francisco's golden days. Walk under rich, red draperies to the lavish "grand salon" lobby, complete with English oak paneling and period antiques. Rooms also contain antiques—armoires, marble-top dressers, and other Victorian pieces. Some have corner turret bay windows that look out on tree-lined streets, as well as separate parlor areas and wet bars; others have cozy reading nooks and fireplaces. All rooms have a telephone in the bathroom. Guests can relax in the parlor, with an impressive floor-to-ceiling fireplace, or in the hotel library. If you don't mind staying outside the downtown area, this hotel is highly recommended and very San Francisco.

1590 Sutter St. (between Gough and Octavia sts.), San Francisco, CA 94109. ☎ **800/227-3970** or 415/441-2828. Fax 415/775-5212. www.queenanne.com. 48 units. $139–$199 double; $199–$315 suite. Extra person $10. Rates include continental breakfast and afternoon tea and sherry. AE, DC, DISC, MC, V. Parking $14. Bus: 2, 3, or 4. **Amenities:** Access to nearby health club; 24-hour concierge; business center; same-day dry cleaning. *In room:* TV, dataport, hair dryer, iron, safe.

7 Civic Center

MODERATE

The Phoenix Hotel ★★   If you'd like to tell your friends back home that you've stayed in the same hotel as Linda Ronstadt, Arlo Guthrie, and the Red Hot Chili Peppers, this is the place. *People* described it as the hippest hotel in town. On the fringes of San Francisco's less-than-pleasant Tenderloin District, the retro 1950s-style hotel is a gathering place for visiting rock musicians, writers, and filmmakers who crave a dose of southern California—hence the palm trees and pastel colors. The focal point of the Palm Springs–style hotel is a small, heated outdoor pool adorned with a mural by artist Francis Forlenza and ensconced in a modern-sculpture garden.

   The rooms, while more pop than plus, were upgraded in 1998 and are comfortably equipped with bright, festive furnishings, potted plants, and original local art. In addition to the usual amenities, the hotel offers VCRs and movies on request and a party vibe that's not part of the package at most city hotels. A big bonus: free parking. Adjoining the hotel is Backflip (☎ **415/771-3135**), an oh-so-blue cocktail lounge where grooving tunes are served with tapas, Caribbean-style appetizers, and an alternative dose of San Francisco attitude.

601 Eddy St. (at Larkin St.), San Francisco, CA 94109. ☎ **800/248-9466** or 415/776-1380. Fax 415/885-3109. www.sftrips.com. 44 units. $125–$145 double; $175–$195 suite. Rates include continental breakfast. AE, DC, MC, V. Free parking. Bus: 19, 31, 38, 42, or 47. **Amenities:** 1 restaurant, 1 bar; heated outdoor pool; concierge; tour desk; limited room service; in-room massage; same-day laundry and dry cleaning. *In room:* TV, dataport, hair dryer and iron available on request.

INEXPENSIVE

The Abigail Hotel ★★ *Value*   The Abigail is one of San Francisco's rare sleeper hotels: Although it doesn't get much press, it's one of the better, affordable lodgings in the city. Built in 1925 to house celebrities performing at the world-renowned Fox Theater, the Abigail more than makes up in charm what it lacks in luxury. The rooms, while on the small side, are cute and comfortably furnished with cozy antiques and down comforters. Morning coffee, pastries, and complimentary newspapers greet you in the beautiful faux-marble lobby designed by Shawn Hall. The vegan restaurant, Millennium (see chapter 6 for complete information), serves dinner.

246 McAllister St. (between Hyde and Larkin sts.), San Francisco, CA 94102. ℰ **800/243-6510** or 415/ 626-6500. Fax 415/626-6580. www.abigailhotel.com. 61 units. $115–$159 standard double; $125–$189 deluxe double; $350 suite. Extra person $10. Rates include continental breakfast. AE, DC, DISC, MC, V. Valet parking $20. Muni Metro: All Market St. trams. Bus: All Market St. buses. **Amenities:** 1 restaurant, 1 bar; access to nearby health club; concierge. *In room:* TV, dataport, fridge upon request; hair dryer, iron.

8 SoMa

VERY EXPENSIVE

The Argent Hotel 🟊🟊   The large number of rooms and fine location—just a block south of Market Street, and a block from the Moscone Convention Center—make the Argent attractive to both groups and business travelers. Rooms, which are decorated in warm, modern, and surprisingly attractive furnishings (surprising considering what a corporate hotel it is) and textiles, have floor-to-ceiling windows and are well-outfitted with three telephones (with voicemail). Corner suites look across the Bay Bridge and to 3Com (old Candlestick) Park. But then again, so long as you're on an upper story, you're bound to get a good view of the city. Rates for executive level rooms include continental breakfast and evening hors d'oeuvres.

50 Third St. (between Market and Mission sts.), San Francisco, CA 94103. ℰ **800/505-9039** or 415/974-6400. Fax 415/495-6152. www.argenthotel.com. 667 units. $245–$265 double; from $420 suite. AE, DC, DISC, MC, V. Valet parking $32. Muni Metro: All Market St. trams. Bus: All Market St. buses. **Amenities:** 1 restaurant, 1 bar; fitness center; concierge; business center; secretarial services; 24-hour room service; in-room massage; babysitting; same-day laundry and dry cleaning. *In room:* A/C, TV w/ pay movies, dataport, kitchenettes in some rooms; minibar, coffeemaker, hair dryer, iron, safe.

The Harbor Court 🟊🟊🟊   When the Embarcadero Freeway was torn down after the Big One in 1989, one of the major benefactors was the Harbor Court hotel: The 1926 landmark building's backyard view went from a wall of cement to a dazzling vista of the Bay Bridge (be sure to request a bay-view room, for an extra fee). Located just off the Embarcadero at the edge of the Financial District, this former YMCA books a lot of corporate travelers, but anyone who seeks stylish, high-quality accommodations—half-canopy beds, large armoires, writing desks, soundproofed windows—with a superb view and lively scene will be perfectly content here. A major bonus for health nuts is the free use of the adjoining fitness club, a top-quality facility with an indoor Olympic-size swimming pool. And for the lounger in all of us, there's an evening wine reception and ever-available coffee, tea, and apples.

165 Steuart St. (between Mission and Howard sts.), San Francisco, CA 94105. ℰ **800/346-0555** or 415/ 882-1300. Fax 415/882-1313. www.harborcourthotel.com. 131 units. $165–$399 double. Continental breakfast $12. AE, DC, MC, V. Parking $28. Muni Metro: Embarcadero. Bus: 14, 32, or 80X. **Amenities:** Access to adjoining health club and large, heated indoor pool; coutesy car; room service (breakfast only); same-day laundry service and dry cleaning. *In room:* A/C, TV, fax, dataport, minibar, hair dryer, iron, safe. Pets accepted.

The Hotel Griffon 🟊🟊   After pumping a cool $10 million into a complete rehab in 1989, the Hotel Griffon emerged as a top contender among San Francisco's small hotels. Ideally situated on the historic waterfront and steps from the heart of the Financial District, the Griffon is impeccably outfitted with a masculine design sensibility. It boasts contemporary features such as whitewashed brick walls, lofty ceilings, marble vanities, window seats, cherrywood furniture, and art-deco-style lamps (really, this place is smooth). Be sure to request a bay-view room overlooking the Bay Bridge—the added perks and view make it well worth the extra cost.

155 Steuart St. (between Mission and Howard sts.), San Francisco, CA 94105. (📞 800/321-2201 or 415/495-2100. Fax 415/495-3522. www.hotelgriffon.com. 62 units. $230–$300 double; $375–$415 suite. Rates include continental breakfast and newspaper. AE, DC, DISC, MC, V. Parking $24. All Market St. buses, BART, and ferries. **Amenities:** 1 restaurant; access to large neighboring health club; concierge; secretarial services; room service (11:30am–10pm); in-room massage; laundry service, dry cleaning. *In room:* TV, dataport, minibar, hair dryer, iron.

Hotel Palomar ★★ The Kimpton Group's latest—and most luxurious—downtown property occupies the top five floors of a refurbished 1907 landmark office building. As the group's most refined boutique property, the French-inspired interior designed by Cheryl Rowley features rooms with an updated twist of 1930s modern design, with artful, understated textural elements such as emerald-tone velvets, fine woods, and raffia. Tailored lines and rich textures throughout lend a sophisticated, fresh aspect to the overall air of elegance. You'll also find homey luxuries like CD players and 27-inch televisions. The dining room, The Fifth Floor, is considered one of the hottest (and most expensive) restaurants in town (see chapter 6 for a complete review).

12 Fourth St. (at Market St.) San Francisco, CA., 94103. (📞 877/294-9711 or 415/348-1111. Fax 415-348 0302. www.hotelpalomar.com. 198 units. From $335 double; from $475 suite. Continental breakfast $23. AE, DC, DISC, MC, V. Parking $32. Metro: I5, 30, 8, and all underground Muni and BART. **Amenities:** 1 restaurant; exercise room; courtesy car; concierge; business center; secretarial services; room service; in-room massage; babysitting; same-day laundry service and dry cleaning. *In room:* A/C, TV, CD player, fax, dataport, printer, photocopier, minibar, fridge, hair dryer, iron, safe. Dogs welcome for $50 fee and $250 deposit.

W San Francisco Hotel ★★★ Starwood Hotels & Resorts' 31-story property is as modern and hip as its fashionable clientele. Sophisticated, sleek, and stylish, it suits its neighbors, which include the Museum of Modern Art, the Moscone Center, and the Metreon Sony entertainment center. The striking gray granite facade, piped with polished black stone, complements the octagonal three-story glass entrance and lobby. The hip, urban style extends to the guest rooms, which have a residential feel. Each contains a "luxury" bed with a pillow-top mattress, goose-down comforter and pillows, an oversized dark wood desk, upholstered chaise lounge, and louvered blinds that open to (usually) great city views. Each room contains a compact media wall complete with a Sony CD and videocassette player, an extensive CD library, a 27-inch color TV with Internet service (and an infrared keyboard). The bath? Supersleek and stocked with Aveda products. All in all, since 2000 this has been the place to be.

181 Third St. (between Mission and Howard sts), San Francisco, CA 94103. (📞 800/877-WHOTEL or 415/777-5300. Fax 415/817-7800. www.whotels.com. 423 units. From $399 double; from $900 suite. AE, DC, DISC, MC, V. Valet parking $33. Muni Metro: J, K, L, or M to Montgomery. Bus: 15, 30, or 45. **Amenities:** 1 restaurant, 2 bars; heated atrium pool and whirlpool; fitness center; sundeck; 24-hour concierge; business center; secretarial services; 24-hour room service; same-day laundry and dry cleaning. *In room:* A/C, TV/VCR w/ pay movies and Internet access; fax, dataport, minibar, coffeemaker, hair dryer, iron, safe; portable two-line phone with conference calling and voicemail.

EXPENSIVE

San Francisco Marriott ★★ Some call it a masterpiece; others liken it to the world's biggest parking meter. In either case, the Marriott is one of the largest buildings in the city, making it a popular stop for convention-goers and those looking for a room with a view. Fortunately, the controversy does not extend to the recently renovated rooms; expect pleasant accommodations, floral patterns, large bathrooms and beds, and exceptional city vistas. Upon arrival, enter from

Fourth Street, between Market and Mission, to avoid a long trek to the registration area.

Kinoko, a Japanese teppanyaki restaurant and sushi bar, serves dinner only; the Garden Terrace serves breakfast, lunch, and dinner; the View Lounge serves a light lunch menu with a panoramic view of the Bay Bridge and Golden Gate Bridge (fog permitting); there's also a sports bar.

55 Fourth St. (between Market and Mission sts.), San Francisco, CA 94103. ✆ **800/228-9290** or 415/896-1600. Fax 415/777-2799. www.marriott.com. 1,500 units. $199–$279 double; $320–$2,700 suite. AE, CB, DC, MC, V. Parking $27. Cable car: Powell-Hyde and Powell-Mason lines (3 blocks west). Muni Metro: All Market St. trams. Bus: All Market St. buses. **Amenities:** 3 restaurants, 1 bar; indoor pool and health club; business center; tour desk; car rental; laundry service, dry cleaning. *In room:* A/C, TV w/ pay movies, dataport, minibar, hair dryer, iron.

9 The Castro

Everyone is welcome, but most hotels in the Castro cater to a gay and lesbian clientele. Unfortunately, there are few choices, and their amenities don't really compare to those at most of the better hotels in the city.

MODERATE

Inn on Castro ⭑   One of the better choices in the Castro, half a block from all the action, is this Edwardian-style inn decorated with contemporary furnishings, original modern art, and fresh flowers throughout. Most rooms share a small back patio, and the suite has a private outdoor sitting area. There's also a two-bedroom apartment ($155 to $250).

321 Castro St. (at Market St.), San Francisco, CA 94114. ✆ **415/861-0321.** Fax 415/861-0321. www.innoncastro2.com. 8 units (2 with bathroom across the hall). $110–$185 double; $125–$155 suite. Rates include full breakfast and evening brandy. AE, MC, V. Muni Metro: Castro. *In room:* TV, dataport, hair dryer.

The Parker House ⭑⭑   This is the best B&B option in the Castro, and one of the best in the entire city. In fact, even some of the better hotels could learn a thing or two from this fashionable, gay-friendly 5,000-square-foot, 1909 beautifully restored Edwardian home a few blocks from the heart of Castro's action. Within the bright, cheery urban compound, period antiques abound. But thankfully, the spacious guest rooms are wonderfully updated with smart, patterned furnishings, voicemail, robes, and a spotless private bath (plus amenities) en suite or across the hall. A fire burns nightly in the cozy living room, and guests are welcome to make themselves at home in the wood-paneled common library (with fireplace and piano), sunny breakfast room overlooking the garden, formal dining room, and spacious garden with fountains and a steam room. Animal lovers will appreciate the companionship of the house pug named Parker. As this book goes to press, the owners of The Parker House are in the process of completing renovation on an adjoining sister property.

520 Church St. (between 17th and 18th sts.), San Francisco, CA 94114. ✆ **888/520-PARK** or 415/621-3222. Fax 415/621-4139. www.parkerguesthouse.com. 10 units. $120–$180 double; $200 junior suite. Rates include extended continental breakfast. AE, DISC, MC, V. Muni Metro: J Church. Bus: 22, 33. Self-parking $15. **Amenities:** Access to nearby health club; steam room; concierge. *In room:* TV, dataport, hair dryer.

INEXPENSIVE

24 Henry   Its Castro location is not the only thing that makes 24 Henry a good choice for gay travelers. The building, an 1870s Victorian on a serene side street, is quite charming. The five guest rooms have high ceilings, period furniture, and voicemail. Guests tired of tromping around the neighborhood can watch TV or read in the double parlor (where breakfast is served). The apartment suite sleeps three comfortably and has a separate entrance and TV. All rooms are nonsmoking. Under the same management, a house a few blocks away, at 18th Street between Castro and Hartford streets, also offers five rooms, two of which have bathrooms.

24 Henry St. (near Sanchez St.), San Francisco, CA 94114. © **800/900-5686** or 415/864-5686. Fax 415/864-0406. www.24henry.com. 6 units, 2 with bathroom. $80–$95 double; $95 suite. Extra person $25. Rates include continental breakfast. AE, MC, V. Muni Metro: F, J, K, L, M, or N. Bus: 8, 22, or 37.

Beck's Motor Lodge ✦   In a town where DINK (double income, no kids) tourists happily spend fistfuls of money, you'd think someone would create a gay luxury hotel—or even a moderate hotel, for that matter. But absurdly, the most commercial and modern accommodation in the touristy Castro is this run-of-the-mill motel. Standard but contemporary, the ultra-tidy rooms include standard motel furnishings, a sundeck overlooking upper Market Street's action, and free parking. Unless you're into homey B&Bs, this is really your only choice in the area—fortunately, it's very well maintained.

2222 Market St. (at 15th St.), San Francisco, CA 94114. © **800/227-4360** in the U.S., except CA, or 415/621-8212 (from CA, call collect to make reservations). Fax 415/241-0435. 58 units. $119–$145 double. AE, DC, DISC, MC, V. Free parking. Metro: F. Bus: 8 or 37. **Amenities:** Coin-operated washing machines. *In room:* TV, dataport, fridge, coffeemaker.

The Castillo Inn ✦   Just 2 minutes from the heart of the Castro, this charming little house provides a safe, quiet environment. Catering mostly to gay men (although anyone is welcome), The Castillo makes its clientele feel at home. Hardwood floors decorated with throw rugs aid in the warmth. Rooms are small yet cozy, and the front desk uses voicemail to collect phone messages. The Castillo also offers the shared use of a large refrigerator and microwave oven in the kitchen.

48 Henry St., San Francisco, CA 94114. © **800/865-5112** or 415/864-5111. Fax 415/641-1321. 5 units, none with bathroom. $80 double. Rates include continental breakfast. Suite rate negotiable depending on season and number of guests. AE, MC, V. Muni Metro: F, K, L, or M. Bus: 8, 22, 24, or 37.

The Willows Inn ✦   Right in the heart of the Castro, the Willows Inn employs a staff eager to greet and attend to visitors. The country and antique willow furnishings don't strictly suit a 1903 Edwardian home, but everything's quite comfortable—especially considering the extras, which include an expanded continental breakfast (fresh fruit, yogurt, baked goods, gourmet coffee, assorted teas, and fresh orange juice), the morning paper, and nightly cocktails, a sitting room, and a pantry with limited kitchen facilities. The homey rooms vary in size from large (queen bed) to smaller (double bed) and are priced accordingly. Each room has a vanity sink, and all the rooms share eight water closets and shower rooms.

710 14th St. (near Church and Market sts.), San Francisco, CA 94114. © **415/431-4770.** Fax 415/431-5295. www.willowssf.com. 12 units with shared bathrooms. $90–$120 double; $130 suite. Rates include continental breakfast. AE, DISC, MC, V. Limited off-street parking. Muni Metro: Church St. Station (across the street) or F. Bus: 22 or 37. *In room:* TV in some rooms.

10 Haight-Ashbury

MODERATE

Stanyan Park Hotel ✦✦ *(Value)*   The only real hotel on the east end of Golden Gate Park and the west end of funky-chic Haight Street, this small inn offers classic San Francisco-style living at a very affordable price. The Victorian structure, which has operated as a hotel under a variety of names since 1904 and is on the National Register of Historic Places, offers good-size rooms all done in period decor. Its three stories are decorated with antique furnishings, Victorian wallpaper, and pastel quilts, curtains, and carpets, much of which—including mattresses—was updated in 2001. Bathrooms come complete with massaging showerhead, shampoos, and fancy soaps. Families appreciate the six one- and two-bedroom suites, each of which has a full kitchen and formal dining and living rooms and can sleep up to six comfortably. Tea is served each afternoon and evening. Continental breakfast is served in a pleasant room off the lobby. All rooms are nonsmoking.

750 Stanyan St. (at Waller St.), San Francisco, CA 94117. (C) 415/751-1000. Fax 415/668-5454. www. stanyanpark.com. 36 units. $135–$190 double; $270–$325 suite. Rates include continental breakfast and afternoon tea service. Rollaway $20; cribs free. AE, DC, DISC, MC, V. Off-site parking $12. Muni Metro: N. Bus: 7, 33, 43, 66, or 71. **Amenities:** Bike rental; concierge. *In room:* TV, dataport, kitchenette (in suites), hair dryer.

11 Near the Airport

Comfort Suites   Two miles north of the airport, well outside the heart of the city, Comfort Suites is a well-appointed option for travelers on the way into or out of town. Each studio-suite has a king bed, queen sleeper sofa (great for the kids), and all the basic amenities for the weary traveler. There are enough pay-cable channels to keep you glued to your TV set for an entire day, although you'll have to fight the kids over whether it's the HBO special or another round of Nintendo. Rooms are fine, but the freebies are most attractive: continental breakfast, evening soup-and-bread bar, airport shuttle, and use of the outdoor hot tub.

121 E. Grand Ave., South San Francisco, CA 94080. (C) 800/228-5150 or 650/589-7100. Fax 650/589-7796. www.comfortsuites.com. 168 units. $139 double. Rates include continental breakfast and evening soup-and-bread bar. AE, DC, DISC, MC, V. **Amenities:** Outdoor Jacuzzi; airport shuttle. *In room:* A/C, TV, fridge, microwave; coffeemaker, hair dryer; iron.

Embassy Suites ⋆   Your best pick of the airport chain hotels—and the most expensive—is Embassy Suites, which does its darnedest to make you forget you're in the middle of drab South San Francisco. The property has an indoor pool, whirlpool, sauna, courtyard with a fountain, palm plants, and bar/restaurant. Each tastefully decorated two-room suite has a wet bar, two TVs, and two phones. A complimentary, cooked-to-order breakfast comes before you're whisked to the airport on the free shuttle.

250 Gateway Blvd., South San Francisco, CA 94080. (C) 800/362-2779 or 650/589-3400. Fax 650/876-0305. www.embassysuites.com. 312 units. $119–$209 double. Rates include breakfast. AE, DC, MC, V. **Amenities:** 1 restaurant, 1 bar; indoor pool; Jacuzzi; sauna; airport shuttle. *In room:* A/C, TV, fridge, microwave; coffeemaker, hair dryer, iron.

Holiday Inn   Considering all the free amenities—movie channels, 24-hour airport shuttle, free guest parking—a room at this Holiday Inn is surprisingly reasonable. Granted, there's nary a thing to see or do within a 10-mile radius, but as a stop before a morning flight, the Holiday Inn is always a safe bet: The airport is a mere 5 minutes away on the hotel's complimentary shuttle. The rooms are classic Holiday Inn: large, clean, and inoffensively dull, with the usual amenities.

San Francisco International Airport North, 275 S. Airport Blvd. (off Hwy. 101), South San Francisco, CA 94080. (C) 800/HOLIDAY or 650/873-3550. Fax 650/873-4524. www.holiday-inn.com. 224 units. $85–$189 double. Free parking and shuttle service. AE, DC, DISC, MC, V. **Amenities:** 2 restaurants; exercise room; secretarial services; airport shuttle. *In room:* A/C, TV w/ pay movies, dataport, minibar, fridge, coffeemaker, hair dryer, iron.

San Francisco Airport North Travelodge *(Kids)*   The Travelodge is a good choice for families, mainly because of the hotel's large heated pool, which allows the kids to let off some steam while the parents bask in South San Francisco's typically balmy weather. Although new carpets and bedspreads were added in 2001, the rooms are as ordinary as you'd expect from a Travelodge. Still they're comfortable and come with plenty of perks like Showtime and free toll-free and credit-card calls. Each junior suite has a microwave and refrigerator. The clincher is the 24-hour complimentary shuttle, which makes the 2-mile trip to SFO in 5 minutes.

326 S. Airport Blvd. (off Hwy. 101), South San Francisco, CA 94080. © **800/578-7878** or 650/583-9600. Fax 650/873-9392. www.sfotravelodge.com. 197 units. $89–$139 double. AE, DC, DISC, MC, V. **Amenities:** 1 restaurant; heated outdoor pool; fax and copier services; courtesy car to airport. *In room:* A/C, TV, coffeemaker, hair dryer, safe.

6

Where to Dine

San Francisco's restaurants are so renowned that many people visit just to eat—and with good reason. The city's brilliant chefs, combined with California's abundance of organic produce, seafood, and free-range meats, guarantee some of the world's finest dining, and fierce competition means slackers need not apply to any local kitchen.

Unfortunately, kitchen talent and quality ingredients are costing more and more. Combine that with the onslaught of new millionaire residents to whom foie gras and sweetbreads are as common as bread and butter, and the results are clear: The price of dining in the average San Francisco restaurant has gone up by 30% to 50% in the past 6 years! But there are still bargains to be found, and plenty of places are so good, you might not mind spending $25 to $35 per entree.

But it's not only about chi-chi fare. As one of the world's cultural crossroads, the city is blessed with a cornucopia of cuisines. Afghan, Cajun, Burmese, Jewish, Moroccan, Persian, Cambodian, vegan—whatever you're in the mood for, this town has it covered. So book your reservations and break out the credit cards, because half the fun of visiting San Francisco is the rare opportunity to sample the flavors of the world in one fell swoop.

As you join the locals in their most beloved pastime, there are a few things you should keep in mind:

- If you want a table at the expensive restaurants with the best reputations, you probably need to book 6 to 8 weeks ahead for weekends, and a couple of weeks ahead for weekdays.
- If there's a long wait for a table, ask if you can order at the bar, which is often faster and more fun.
- Don't leave *anything* valuable in your car while dining, particularly in or near high-crime areas such as the Mission, Downtown, or—believe it or not—Fisherman's Wharf (thieves know tourists with nice cameras and a trunk full of mementos are headed there!). Not that I'm paranoid, but it's best to give the parking valet only the key to your car, *not* your hotel room or house key.
- Remember: It is against the law to smoke in any restaurant in San Francisco, even if it has a separate bar or lounge area. You're welcome to smoke outside, however.
- This ain't New York: plan on dining early. Most restaurants close the kitchen around 10pm.

The restaurants listed below are classified first by area, then by price,

---

Tips **Technological Tip**

Want to book your reservations online? Go to **www.opentable.com**, where you can save seats in San Francisco and the rest of the Bay Area in real time.

using the following categories: **Expensive,** dinner from $50 per person; **Moderate,** dinner from $35 per person; and **Inexpensive,** dinner from $20 per person. These categories reflect prices for an appetizer, main course, dessert, and glass of wine.

1 Restaurants by Cuisine

AMERICAN

Beach Chalet Brewery & Restaurant ✦ (Richmond District, $$, p. 145)

The Big Four ✦ (Nob Hill, $$$, p. 113)

Bix ✦✦ (North Beach, $$$, p. 117)

Boulevard ✦✦✦ (SoMa, $$$, p. 133)

Carnelian Room ✦✦ (The Financial District, $$$, p. 109)

Chow ✦ (The Castro, $, p. 143)

Doidge's ✦✦ (Pacific Heights, $$, p. 127)

Dottie's True Blue Café ✦ (Union Square, $, p. 107)

Ella's ✦✦ (Pacific Heights, $$, p. 127)

Firewood Café ✦✦ (The Castro, $, p. 143)

Fog City Diner ✦ (Telegraph Hill, $$, p. 120)

Gordon's House of Fine Eats ✦✦ (The Mission District, $$, p. 139)

Hard Rock Cafe (Russian Hill, $, p. 113)

Mecca ✦✦ (The Castro, $$$, p. 142)

Mel's Diner ✦✦ (The Marina, $, p. 130)

MoMo's ✦ (SoMa, $$, p. 135)

Mo's Gourmet Burgers ✦✦ (North Beach, $, p. 123)

Postrio ✦✦ (Union Square, $$$, p. 105)

Sears Fine Foods ✦✦ (Union Square, $, p. 108)

The Waterfront Restaurant & Cafe ✦ (The Financial District, $$, p. 112)

Universal Café ✦✦✦ (The Mission District, $$, p. 140)

AMERICAN BRASSERIE

bacar ✦✦ (SoMa, $$$, p. 133)

Johnfrank ✦✦ (The Castro, $$, p. 143)

ARGENTINEAN

Il Pollaio ✦ (North Beach, $, p. 122)

ASIAN

AsiaSF ✦ (SoMa, $, p. 137)

Azie ✦✦✦ (SoMa, $$$, p. 133)

Oritalia ✦✦ (Union Square, $$, p. 106)

BREAKFAST

Doidge's ✦✦ (Pacific Heights, $, p. 127)

Dottie's True Blue Café ✦ (Union Square, $, p. 107)

Ella's ✦✦ (Pacific Heights, $$, p. 127)

CAJUN/CREOLE

The Elite Café ✦ (Pacific Heights, $$, p. 127)

CALIFORNIA

2223 Restaurant & Bar ✦✦ (The Castro, $$, p. 142)

AsiaSF ✦ (SoMa, $, p. 137)

Bix ✦✦ (North Beach, $$$, p. 117)

Brasserie Savoy ✦ (Union Square, $$, p. 105)

Cafe Kati ✦✦ (Pacific Heights, $$$, p. 125)

Cliff House ✦ (Richmond District, $$, p. 145)

Gordon Biersch Brewery Restaurant (SoMa, $$, p. 135)

Hawthorne Lane ✦✦ (SoMa, $$$, p. 134)

Jardinière ✦✦ (Civic Center, $$$, p. 131)

Moose's ✦✦ (North Beach, $$$, p. 118)

One Market ✦✦ (The Financial
District, $$$, p. 109)

PlumpJack Café ✦✦ (Cow
Hollow, $$, p. 128)

Pluto's ✦✦ (The Marina, $,
p. 130)

CARIBBEAN

Cha Cha Cha ✦✦ (Haight-
Ashbury, $, p. 144)

CHINESE

Brandy Ho's Hunan Food ✦✦
(Chinatown, $, p. 116)

Eliza's ✦✦✦ (Pacific Heights, $,
p. 130)

House of Nanking ✦ (Chinatown,
$, p. 116)

The Mandarin ✦✦ (Fisherman's
Wharf, $$$, p. 124)

R&G Lounge ✦✦ (Chinatown, $,
p. 116)

Tommy Toy's ✦✦ (The Financial
District, $$$, p. 110)

CHINESE/DIM SUM

Harbor Village ✦ (The Financial
District, $$$, p. 109)

Ton Kiang ✦✦✦ (Richmond
District, $, p. 147)

Yank Sing ✦✦ (The Financial
District, $$, p. 112)

CRÊPES

Ti Couz ✦✦ (The Mission
District, $, p. 141)

EAST-WEST FUSION

Cafe Kati ✦✦ (Pacific Heights,
$$$, p. 125)

Eos ✦✦ (Haight-Ashbury, $$$,
p. 144)

FRENCH

Absinthe ✦✦ (Civic Center, $$,
p. 131)

Azie ✦✦✦ (SoMa, $$$, p. 133)

Brasserie Savoy ✦ (Union Square,
$$, p. 105)

Café Claude ✦✦ (Union Square,
$, p. 107)

Fifth Floor Restaurant ✦✦✦
(SoMa, $$$, p. 134)

Fleur de Lys ✦✦✦ (Union Square,
$$$, p. 104)

Florio ✦✦ (Pacific Heights, $$,
p. 127)

Flying Saucer (The Mission
District, $$$, p. 138)

Fringale Restaurant ✦✦ (SoMa,
$$, p. 135)

Jardinière ✦✦ (Civic Center, $$$,
p. 131)

La Folie ✦✦ (Pacific Heights, $$$,
p. 126)

Masa's ✦✦✦ (Union Square, $$$,
p. 105)

PlumpJack Café ✦✦ (The Marina,
$$, p. 128)

Restaurant Lulu ✦ (SoMa, $$,
p. 136)

Rubicon ✦✦✦ (The Financial
District, $$$, p. 110)

Scala's Bistro ✦✦ (Union Square,
$$, p. 107)

South Park Café ✦ (SoMa, $$,
p. 136)

Universal Café ✦✦✦ (The
Mission District, $$, p. 140)

FRENCH BISTRO

Foreign Cinema ✦✦ (The Mission
District, $$, p. 138)

Grand Café ✦ (Union Square,
$$$, p. 104)

GREEK

Kokkari ✦✦✦ (The Financial
District, $$, p. 111)

INTERNATIONAL

World Wrapps ✦✦ (The Marina,
$, p. 130)

ITALIAN

Cafe Pescatore ✦ (Fisherman's
Wharf, $$$, p. 125)

Caffè Luna Piena ✦ (The Castro,
$$, p. 142)

Caffè Macaroni ✦✦ (North Beach,
$, p. 121)

Caffè Sport ✦ (North Beach, $$$,
p. 118)

Capp's Corner ✦ (North Beach, $,
p. 122)

Delfina ★★★ (The Mission District, $, p. 140)

Emporio Armani Cafe ★ (Union Square, $, p. 108)

Firewood Café ★★ (The Castro, $, p. 143)

Florio ★★ (Pacific Heights, $$, p. 127)

Il Fornaio ★★ (Telegraph Hill, $$, p. 120)

Il Pollaio ★ (North Beach, $, p. 122)

Kuleto's ★★ (Union Square, $$, p. 106)

L'Osteria del Forno ★★ (North Beach, $, p. 122)

Mario's Bohemian Cigar Store ★ (North Beach, $, p. 122)

Oritalia ★★ (Union Square, $$, p. 106)

Pane e Vino ★★ (Pacific Heights, $$, p. 128)

Pasta Pomodoro ★★ (North Beach, $, p. 123)

Prego ★ (Pacific Heights, $$, p. 129)

Rose Pistola ★ (North Beach, $$, p. 121)

Scala's Bistro ★★ (Union Square, $$, p. 107)

The Stinking Rose ★ (North Beach, $$, p. 121)

Tommaso's ★★ (North Beach, $, p. 123)

Zinzino ★ (The Marina, $$, p. 129)

JAPANESE

Ace Wasabi's Rock 'n' Roll Sushi ★★ (The Marina, $$, p. 126)

Kabuto Sushi ★★ (Richmond District, $$, p. 146)

Kyo-Ya ★★ (The Financial District, $$$, p. 109)

MEDITERRANEAN

42 Degrees ★★★ (China Basin, $$$, p. 139)

Enrico's ★ (North Beach, $$, p. 118)

Moose's ★★ (North Beach, $$$, p. 118)

PlumpJack Café ★★ (The Marina, $$, p. 128)

Zuni Café ★★★ (Civic Center, $$, p. 132)

MEXICAN

Andalé Taqueria ★★ (The Marina, $, p. 129)

Sweet Heat ★ (Haight-Ashbury, $, p. 145)

Taquerias La Cumbre ★★ (The Mission District, $, p. 141)

Zona Rosa ★ (Haight-Ashbury, $, p. 145)

MODERN CLASSIC

Restaurant Gary Danko ★★★ (Fisherman's Wharf, $$$, p. 124)

NOODLES

Long Life Noodle Company & Jook Joint ★ (SoMa, $, p. 137)

PACIFIC RIM

Butterfly (The Mission District, $$, p. 138)

PERSIAN/MIDDLE EASTERN

Maykedah ★ (North Beach, $$, p. 120)

PIZZA

Marcello's Pizza ★ (The Castro, $, p. 144)

Pauline's ★★ (The Mission District, $, p. 141)

SEAFOOD

A. Sabella's ★★ (Fisherman's Wharf, $$$, p. 124)

Alioto's ★ (Fisherman's Wharf, $$$, p. 124)

Aqua ★★★ (The Financial District, $$$ p. 108)

Cliff House ★ (Richmond District, $$, p. 145)

Farallon ★ (Union Square, $$$, p. 101)

Hayes Street Grill ★★ (Civic Center, $$, p. 132)

Sam's Grill & Seafood Restaurant
☆ (The Financial District, $$,
p. 111)

Swan Oyster Depot ☆☆☆
(Russian Hill, $$, p. 113)

Tadich Grill ☆☆ (The Financial
District, $$, p. 112)

SINGAPOREAN
Straits Café ☆ (Richmond District,
$$, p. 147)

SPANISH
Thirsty Bear Brewing Company ☆
(SoMa, $$, p. 136)

STEAK HOUSE
Harris' ☆☆ (Pacific Heights, $$$,
p. 126)

SUSHI
Ace Wasabi's Rock 'n' Roll Sushi
☆☆ (The Marina, $$, p. 126)

Kabuto Sushi ☆☆ (Richmond
District, $$, p. 146)

Kyo-Ya ☆☆ (The Financial
District, $$$, p. 109)

THAI
Khan Toke Thai House ☆☆
(Richmond District, $$, p. 146)

Manora's ☆ (SoMa, $, p. 137)

Thep Phanom ☆☆☆ (Haight-
Ashbury, $, p. 145)

VEGAN
Millennium ☆ (Civic Center, $$,
p. 136)

VEGETARIAN
Greens Restaurant, Fort Mason
☆☆ (The Marina, $$, p. 128)

VIETNAMESE
Ana Mandara ☆☆ (Fisherman's
Wharf, $$$, p. 125)

The Golden Turtle ☆ (Russian
Hill, $, p. 116)

Le Colonial ☆☆ (Union Square,
$$, p. 106)

The Slanted Door ☆☆☆ (The
Mission District, $$, p. 140)

Tú Lan ☆ (SoMa, $, p. 137)

2 Union Square

EXPENSIVE

Farallon ☆ *Overrated* COASTAL CUISINE/SEAFOOD   While this seafood restaurant is hands-down the most whimsical in its stunning oceanic decor, the high price tag and fine, but not mind blowing, food make it a better cocktail and appetizer or lunch stop than dinner choice. The multimillion-dollar attraction and outrageous decor follows the "coastal" cuisine theme; hand-blown jellyfish lamps, kelp bed–like backlit columns, glass clamshells, sea-urchin light fixtures, a sea-life mosaic floor, and a tentacle-encircled bar set the scene. (Thankfully, designer Pat Kuleto's impressive renovation of the 1924 building left the original Gothic arches intact.)

Executive chef Mark Franz, who opened Stars with Jeremiah Tower, orchestrates the cuisine. He offers starters ranging from the expected (very expensive oysters, at $14.50) to the more ambitious, like bay scallops and lobster indulgence (a cornucopia of oysters, clams, crayfish, prawns, mussels, and scallops with horseradish mignonette, for $21.50 per person). While most main

---

Tips Multicourse Dining

Ordering a "fixed-price," "prix fixe," or "tasting" menu can be a good bargain as well as a great way to sample lots of dishes at one sitting. Many dining rooms in town offer these multicourse menus, which tend to cost around $75 for four courses, including dessert.

Union Square & Financial District Dining

Aqua **17**
Belden Place **23**
The Big Four **1**
Brasserie Savoy **5**
Cafe Bastille **23**
Café Claude **25**
Cafe Tiramisu **23**
Carnelian Room **21**

Dottie's True Blue Café **6**
Emporio Armani Cafe **27**
Farallon **9**
Fifth Floor Restaurant **28**
Fleur de Lys **3**
Grand Café **7**
Harbor Village **16**
Kokkari **13**

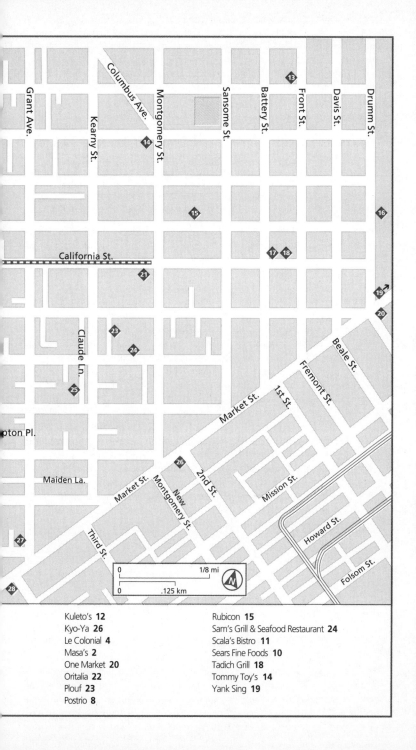

Kuleto's **12**
Kyo-Ya **26**
Le Colonial **4**
Masa's **2**
One Market **20**
Oritalia **22**
Plouf **23**
Postrio **8**

Rubicon **15**
Sam's Grill & Seafood Restaurant **24**
Scala's Bistro **11**
Sears Fine Foods **10**
Tadich Grill **18**
Tommy Toy's **14**
Yank Sing **19**

courses—such as sautéed black bass with wild mushroom ragout, leek risotto, and pesto or grilled monkfish loin with truffled cauliflower puree, saffron jus, and lobster aioli—stick with the seaside theme, meat and game eaters have at least one option. The whimsy-meets-sophistication extends only as far as the food—the service and wine list (more than 300 by the bottle; 24 by the glass) are seriously professional. This place has been quite the scene since it opened in mid-1997, so reserve well in advance. I suggest stopping by for lunch. The food is good, but on my last visit, it was not outstanding. Besides, for seafood, Aqua is worlds better.

450 Post St. (between Mason and Powell sts., adjoining the Kensington Park Hotel). ✆ **415/956-6969.** www.farallonrestaurant.com. Reservations recommended. Lunch main courses $10.50–$16.25; dinner main courses $22–$32. AE, DC, DISC, MC, V. Tues–Sat 11:30am–2:30pm; Tues–Sat 2:30–5pm (bistro menu); Mon–Wed 5:30–10:30pm; Thurs–Sat 5:30–11pm; Sun 5–10pm. Valet parking $12. Bus: 2, 3, 4, or 38.

Fleur de Lys ★★★ FRENCH   Fleur de Lys is a classic French, elegant, affair amidst 700 yards of rich red-patterned fabric, dim French candelabras, an extraordinary sculptural floral centerpiece, and well-dressed diners. Just as romantic as the ambiance is the cuisine of chef Hubert Keller (who was President Clinton's first guest chef at the White House). Unlike lots of celebrity chefs, Keller is usually in the kitchen preparing the menus, which range from a la carte to a five-course tasting menu and four-course vegetarian menu. Fans of bite-size samplings appreciate the "Symphony" appetizer, which may include Hudson Valley foie gras terrine, sea scallop cake, and lobster gelée. Even better are crispy veal sweetbreads atop artichokes and leeks and truffle vinaigrette, or my personal favorite, salmon on a fluffy corn pancake with American sturgeon caviar and watercress sauce. The best main course of late was choucroute-crusted veal loin wrapped in applewood-smoked bacon with whole-grain mustard and Riesling sauce. I was less crazy about the Maine lobster tail, which came cozied in a tartelette and was too sweet, with its Pinot Noir sauce with vanilla oil. Desserts are artistic creations and might feature chocolate tartelette with mandarin oranges and walnuts. The selection of 300 French and California wines is impressive, but the by-the-glass options are woefully weak.

777 Sutter St. (at Jones St.). ✆ **415/673-7779.** Reservations required. Main courses $29–$35; 5-course tasting menu $72; 4-course vegetarian menu $60. AE, DC, MC, V. Mon–Thurs 6–9:30pm; Fri–Sat 5:30–10:30pm. Bus: 2, 3, 4, 27, or 38.

Grand Café ★ FRENCH BISTRO   If you aren't interested in exploring restaurants beyond those in Union Square, Grand Café is one of your best bets. It has the most, well, *grand* dining room in San Francisco; the cocktail area is festive, but the pièce de résistance is the enormous turn-of-the-century grand ballroom/dining room, a magnificent combination of old Europe and Art Nouveau. No matter where you sit while enjoying chef Victor Scargle's French-inspired, California-based cuisine you'll see playful sculptures, original murals, and a cadre of dazzling deco chandeliers.

   Rising-star chef Victor Scargle stepped out of Aqua's sister restaurant Pisces and into the Grand Café to introduce his bistro menu in early 2001. The fare, which was hit-and-miss upon his initial arrival, changes seasonally; winter welcomed a rich polenta souffle with wild mushroom ragout and cambozola fondue, pan-seared Hudson Valley foie gras with sweet onion cranberry relish and brioche toast, tournedo of petrale sole with braised leeks and fennel batons and verjus, and braised beef shortribs Bourguinonne with herb barley and winter veggies. *Note:* The bar area has its own exhibition kitchen and menu, offering similar dishes for about half the price. Desserts, such as devil's food chocolate pudding gateau with coffee caramel sauce and cashew toffee ice cream, are opulent, and pizzas from the wood-burning oven make for a fine light dinner or cocktail snack.

501 Geary St. (at Taylor St., adjacent to the Hotel Monaco). ℂ 415/292-0101. Reservations recommended. Main courses $15–$25. AE, DC, DISC, MC, V. Mon–Sun 8–10:30am; daily 11:30am–2:30pm; Mon–Sat 5:30–11pm; Sun 5:30–10pm. Valet parking $7 for 3 hr., $3 each additional half hour. Bus: 2, 3, 4, 27, or 38.

Masa's 🏵🏵🏵 FRENCH   One of the city's veteran contenders for best French restaurant underwent major changes in early 2001, including a new chef and updated interior. Executive Chef Ron Siegel, who presided over Charles Nob Hill until Masa's made an offer he couldn't refuse (great money and a customized kitchen), deftly designs three-, six-, and nine-course tasting menus within an almost startlingly trendy (think hip hotelier Ian Schrager) room. Fortunately, beyond the small, minimalist bar and illuminated white curtains one thing has remained the same: a dedication to culinary excellence. Amuse bouches abound the minute the attentive French waiter appears, and the treats continue, in the form of delicate seared scallops elevated both literally and figuratively by microgreens and a dab of decadent uni (sea urchin) and savory skate balanced atop a short rib ravioli, all of which is bathed in a mushroom jus. Desserts are too precious and are far better to look at than they are to eat. But the candy cart, which is wheeled by so you may select lollipops, chocolates, and mini cookies, almost makes up for it.

In the Hotel Vintage Court, 648 Bush St. (at Stockton St.). ℂ 800/258-7694 or 415/989-7154. Reservations required; accepted up to 3 weeks in advance. Fixed-price dinner $60–$105. AE, DC, DISC, MC, V. Tues–Sat 5:30–9:30pm. Closed first 2 weeks in Jan, first week in July. Cable car: Powell-Mason and Powell-Hyde lines. Valet parking: $9. Bus: 2, 3, 4, 30, or 45.

Postrio 🏵🏵 AMERICAN   Over 10 years after Wolfgang Puck launched the trend for large, glamorous downtown dining rooms, it's still a rare night when brother chefs Mitchell and Steven Rosenthal don't perform to a full house. Eating, however, is only half the reason one comes to Postrio. After squeezing through the perpetually swinging bar—which dishes out excellent pizzas from a wood-burning oven in the corner—guests are forced to make a grand entrance down the antebellum staircase to the cavernous dining room below (it's everyone's 15 seconds of fame, so make sure your fly is zipped). Pure Hollywood, for sure, but it's fun.

The menu combines Italian, Asian, French, and California styles with mixed results. When I last visited Postrio, I had a stellar meal. The time before I was not as lucky. Regardless, the fare's way above par. The menu changes nightly; you might find grilled chicken breast with caramelized onion purée, morels, fava beans, and natural chicken juice, or roasted salmon with porcini mushrooms, artichoke fritters, and garlic aïoli. The desserts, artistically sculpted by pastry chef Christine Law, are memorable.

In the Prescott Hotel, 545 Post St. (between Mason and Taylor sts.). ℂ 415/776-7825. Reservations recommended. Main courses $6–$16 breakfast; $12–$16 lunch; $24–$36 dinner. AE, DC, DISC, MC, V. Mon–Fri 7–10am; Mon–Sat 11:30am–2pm; Sun brunch 11am–2pm; Sun–Wed 5:30–10pm; Thurs–Sat 5:30–10:30pm. Bar menu daily 11:30am–11:30pm, open till 2am. Cable car: Powell-Mason and Powell-Hyde lines. Bus: 2, 3, 4, or 38.

MODERATE
Brasserie Savoy 🏵 CALIFORNIA/FRENCH   If you're headed to the theater or are just looking for a good meal and cheery atmosphere downtown,

Brasserie Savoy is an excellent option. The atmosphere is French bistro, with a bright, busy dining room and black-and-white marble floors. The food is consistent, affordable, and delicious. Among the appetizers, preferred choices are oysters with champagne sauce, leeks, and Osetra caviar; mussels marinière with shallots, muscadet, and parsley; and freshly made salad. Main-course choices might include bouillabaisse with local seafood and roasted bread, grilled salmon and halibut with veggies and dry vermouth sauce, or grilled rib-eye with pommes frites, watercress, and bordelaise sauce. To finish, try the innovative crème brûlée.

In the Savoy Hotel, 580 Geary St. (at Jones St.). 🕐 **415/441-2700**. Reservations recommended. Main courses $16–$22. AE, DC, DISC, MC, V. Daily 7am–10:30pm, Tues–Sun 5:30–10pm. Bus: 2, 3, 4, 27, or 38.

Kuleto's ★★ ITALIAN   Kuleto's is a beautiful place filled with beautiful people who are here to see and be seen (don't come underdressed or overdressed). The best plan of action is to skip the wait for a table, muscle a seat at the antipasto bar, and fill up on appetizers, which are often better than the entrees. For a main course, try penne pasta drenched in tangy lamb-sausage marinara sauce, clam linguini (generously overloaded with fresh clams), or any of the fresh-fish specials grilled over hardwoods. If you don't arrive by 6pm, expect to wait—this place fills up fast.

In the Villa Florence Hotel, 221 Powell St. (between Geary and O'Farrell sts.). 🕐 **415/397-7720**. Reservations recommended. Breakfast $5–$10; main courses $10–$20. AE, DC, MC, V. Mon–Fri 7–10:30am; Sat–Sun 8–10:30am; daily 11:30am–11pm. Cable car: Powell-Mason and Powell-Hyde lines. Muni Metro: Powell. Bus: 2, 3, 4, or 38.

Le Colonial ★★ *Finds* VIETNAMESE   Sexy, French-Vietnamese plantation environs and delicious—albeit pricey—Vietnamese food make this an excellent choice for an all-around fun experience. One of my favorite reasons to enter the long dining room and beautiful front patio is the sea bass. Wrapped in banana leaf with glass noodles, ginger, scallions, and cilantro, the buttery fish is genuine bliss. Then again, the vibrant flavors of tender wok-seared beef tenderloin with watercress onion salad are outstanding as well. More nods of approval go to the crispy Vietnamese spring rolls (which I would praise more if Tú Lan hadn't jaded me for life) and delicate steamed Vietnamese rice crêpes with chicken, wood-ear mushrooms, and bean sprouts (although the sauce needed a bit more oomph). The spicy duck rolls bored me and I'm not a fan of the fried rice with chicken, shrimp, egg, onion, and chile. But I can't say enough about the upstairs lounge, where romance reigns, with cozy couches, seductive surroundings (and, often, live jazz), and a kicked-back cocktail crowd of swank professionals.

20 Cosmo Place (off Taylor St., between Post and Sutter sts). 🕐 **415/931-3600**. Reservations recommended. Main courses $14–$33. AE, DC, DISC, MC, V. Sun–Wed 5:30–10pm; Thurs–Sat 5:30–11pm. Valet parking $5 first hour, $2 each additional half hour. Bus: 2, 3, 4, or 27.

Oritalia ★★ ASIAN/ITALIAN   If you can't decide between Italian and Asian food, try both. Oritalia (from *Oriental* and *Italian*) blends the flavors of Italy, China, Korea, and Southeast Asia to create unique dishes that can be over-the-top or just right. Previously a favorite on upper Fillmore Street, Oritalia moved into bigger and better digs and swapped chefs, but it still serves the creative Asian-Italian cuisine that made it famous as a food-forward restaurant. The colorful room—with a 19-foot bar, Fortuny silk chandeliers, Oriental rugs, and some booths with curtains for privacy—is in the best of taste, but the real attraction is executive chef Jon Nelson's food. Expect unusual combos like seared day boat scallops with black sesame and sweet dumplings, and Meyer lemon risotto

Impressions

[San Francisco is] the city that knows how.

—Pres. William Howard Taft

[San Francisco is] the city that knows chow.

—Trader Vic, restaurateur

with shao-xing sauce. Pastry chef Francisco Amlaguer's creative desserts may include Valhrona chocolate and raspberry pyramid with primrose sorbet.

In the Juliana Hotel, 586 Bush St. (at Stockton St.). ℂ **415/782-8122**. Reservations recommended. Main courses $17.25–$26.50. AE, DC, MC, V. Daily 5:15–11pm. Bus: 2, 3, 4, 30, 38, or 45.

Scala's Bistro ✦✦ FRENCH/ITALIAN   Firmly entrenched at the base of the refurbished Sir Francis Drake Hotel, this latest venture by husband-and-wife team Giovanni and Donna Scala blends Parisian-bistro and Old World atmosphere with jovial and bustling results. With just the right balance of elegance and informality, it's a perfect place to have some fun (and apparently most people do).

Drawing from her success at incredible Bistro Don Giovanni in Napa, Donna put together a fantastic array of Italian and French dishes. Start with the "Earth and Surf" calamari appetizer or grilled portabello mushrooms. Golden beet salad and Anchor Steam mussels are also good bets. Generous portions of moist, rich duck-leg confit will satisfy hungry appetites, but if you can order only one thing, make it Scala's signature dish: seared salmon. Resting on a bed of creamy buttermilk mashed potatoes and accented with a tomato, chive, and white-wine sauce, it's downright delicious. Finish with creamy Bostini cream pie, a dreamy combo of vanilla custard and orange chiffon cake with a warm chocolate glaze.

In the Sir Francis Drake hotel, 432 Powell St. (at Sutter St.). ℂ **415/395-8555**. Reservations recommended. Breakfast $7–$10; lunch and dinner main courses $12–$24. AE, DC, DISC, MC, V. Daily 8am–midnight. Cable car: Powell-Hyde line. Bus: 2, 3, 4, 30, 45, or 76.

INEXPENSIVE

Café Claude ✦✦ FRENCH   Euro transplants love Café Claude, a crowded and lively restaurant tucked into a narrow lane near Union Square. Seemingly everything—every table, spoon, salt shaker, and waiter—is imported from France. With prices topping out at about $12 for main courses such as *poussin rôti* (roast Cornish hen with potatoes and aïoli), French shepherd's pie, or *poisson du jour* (fish of the day), Café Claude is a good value. There is live jazz Thursday and Friday from 8pm to 11pm and Saturday from 7 to 10pm. Outdoor seating is available when the weather permits.

7 Claude Lane (off Sutter St.). ℂ **415/392-3515**. www.cafeclaude.com. Reservations recommended. Main courses $7–$13. AE, DC, DISC, MC, V. Mon 11:30am–2:30pm, Tues–Wed 11:30am–10pm, Thurs–Fri 11:30am–10:30pm Sat 11:30am–11:30pm. Cable car: Powell-Mason and Powell-Hyde lines.

Dottie's True Blue Café ✦ *Kids* AMERICAN/BREAKFAST   This family-owned breakfast restaurant is one of my favorite downtown diners. It's the kind of place you'd expect to see off Route 66, where most customers are on a first-name basis with the staff and everyone is welcomed with a hearty hello and steaming mug of coffee. Dottie's serves above-average American morning fare (big portions of French toast, pancakes, bacon and eggs, omelets, and the like) delivered to blue-and-white checkerboard tablecloths on rugged, diner-quality plates. Whatever you order arrives with delicious homemade bread, muffins, or scones, as well as homemade jelly. There are also daily specials and vegetarian dishes.

In the Pacific Bay Inn, 522 Jones St. (at O'Farrell St.). ℂ 415/885-2767. Reservations not accepted. Breakfast $5–$9. DISC, MC, V. Thurs–Mon 7:30am–3pm. Cable car: Powell-Mason line. Bus: 2, 3, 4, 27, or 38.

Emporio Armani Cafe ✮ ITALIAN All the hobnobbing of an elite dining club comes at a moderate price at the Armani Cafe. It's nothing more than a circular counter in the middle of Armani's ever-fashionable (and expensive) clothing store, a few newer tables on a mezzanine, and a few sidewalk seats when the weather's right. But the fare and upscale casual atmosphere are enough to lure folks who have only lunch, not a new designer suit, on their minds. Local favorites include the homemade antipasto misto, panini, salads, and daily pizza specials. There's also a nice variety of pricey lunch entrees—such as spaghetti al croccio in parchment paper and grilled chicken breast with wild mushroom crostini and greens—and when you're seated inside, a large dose of attitude.

1 Grant Ave. (at O'Farrell St., off Market St.). ℂ 415/677-9010. Reservations not accepted. Main courses $9–$17. AE, DC, DISC, MC, V. Mon–Sat 11:30am–4:30pm; Sun noon–4:30pm. Bus: All Union Square buses.

Sears Fine Foods ✮✮ *Kids* AMERICAN Sears is not just another pink-tabled diner run by motherly matrons—it's an institution, famous for its crispy, dark-brown waffles, light sourdough French toast, and silver dollar–sized Swedish pancakes served in funky old-fashioned surroundings. As the story goes, Ben Sears, a retired clown, founded the diner in 1938. His Swedish wife, Hilbur, was responsible for the legendary pancakes, which are still whipped up according to her family's secret recipe. Sears also offers a "healthy-heart menu," classic lunch fare, and big slices of pie for dessert.

439 Powell St. (between Post and Sutter sts.). ℂ 415/986-1160. Reservations accepted for parties of 6 or more. Breakfast $3–$8; salads and soups $3–$8; main courses $6–$10. No credit cards. Daily 6:30am–2:30pm. Cable car: Powell-Mason and Powell-Hyde lines. Bus: 2, 3, 4, or 38.

3 The Financial District

EXPENSIVE

Aqua ✮✮✮ SEAFOOD Without question, Aqua remains San Francisco's finest seafood restaurant, light years beyond the genre of shrimp cocktails and lemon-butter sauce. Heralded chef Michael Mina dazzles his customers with a bewildering juxtaposition of earth and sea in his seasonally changing menus. The ahi tartare, my favorite all-time rendition, period, is mixed tableside with pears, pine nuts, quail egg, and spices. The roasted spot prawn with crab stuffing, citrus hollandaise, and hot-and-sour vinaigrette is deliciously creative. Miso-marinated Chilean sea bass and grilled medallions of ahi tuna with foie gras in Pinot sauce is addictive, extravagant, and sculptural in its presentation. Desserts are equally impressive. The large dining room with high ceilings, one big floral arrangement, and otherwise stark decor can be quite loud, but that doesn't stop power-lunchers from pow-wowing by day and well-dressed gourmands from feasting in style at night. Steep prices prevent most people from making a regular appearance, but for special occasions or billable lunches, Aqua is on my top-ten list. Keep in mind that there's no valet or street parking at lunch, so you'll have to pull into one of the Embarcadero lots two blocks away.

252 California St. (near Battery). ℂ 415/956-9662. Reservations required. Main courses $26–$45; 5-course tasting menu $75; 8-course tasting menu $95; vegetarian tasting menu $55. AE, DC, MC, V. Mon–Fri 11:30am–2pm; Mon–Sat 5:30–10:30pm. Bus: All Market St. buses.

Carnelian Room ★★ *Moments* CONTEMPORARY AMERICAN   Soaring 52 stories above the Financial District on the top floor of the Bank of America building, the Carnelian Room is a definite contender for "Best View," as well as "Top Pick for Old-School Luxury Diners." Dark oak paneling, brass railings, and huge picture windows positively reek of romance, particularly if you're fortunate enough to get a window table. The upscale menu used to cater to old-style bankers' tastes—expensive meat dishes with rich, thick sauces—but the recent trend toward healthier eating has rounded out the menu considerably. You can find numerous fish, fowl, and pasta dishes, along with such Carnelian classics as prime rib and thick-cut New York steak, lobster Thermidor, and herb-mustard crusted rack of lamb. A wine cellar of some 36,000 bottles and the restaurant's accomplished sommelier all but guarantee the proper vintage to accompany your meal.

555 California St. (at Montgomery St.). ✆ 415/433-7500. Reservations recommended. Main courses $28–$48; Sun brunch $30 adults, $15 children. AE, DC, DISC, MC, V. Daily 6–11pm; Sun brunch 10am–1:30pm. Self-parking $7. Cable car: California St. line. Bus: 1, 9, 15, or 42.

Harbor Village ★ CHINESE/DIM SUM   This is one of the city's most upscale Chinese restaurants, serving primarily Cantonese dishes, spicy Szechwan specials, and, during the lunch rush, great dim sum. The courteous staff will guide you through the extensive menu, which includes some 30 seafood dishes, such as striped bass steamed with ginger and scallions. If you've never had shark-fin soup, this is the place to try it. Unique appetizers include shredded spicy chicken and minced squab in lettuce cups. Stir-fried garlic prawns, beggar's chicken cooked in a clay pot, and sizzling beef in black-pepper sauce are excellent main-course choices. Dim sum lunch, served daily, is definitely worth trying. The waitstaff brings trays full of steaming-hot appetizers (and will happily explain what they are), and you choose what you like. Try Shanghai-style steamed pork dumplings flavored with ginger and scallions, rice-paper dumplings filled with sweet shrimp, taro cake, or curried beef wonton.

The restaurant offers validated parking at all the Embarcadero Center garages (at the foot of Clay Street). It'll cost you a few dollars weekdays, but it's free after 5pm Monday to Friday and all day on weekends and holidays.

4 Embarcadero Center, lobby level (at Drumm St. between Sacramento and Clay sts.). ✆ 415/781-8833. Reservations required for dinner. Main courses $10–$35. AE, DC, DISC, MC, V. Mon–Fri 11am–2:30pm; Sat 10:30am–2:30pm; Sun 10am–2:30pm; daily 5:30–9:30pm. Bus: 15, 45, or 76.

Kyo-Ya ★★ JAPANESE/SUSHI   It's anything but cheap, but this restaurant offers an authentic Japanese experience, from the decor to the service to (most assuredly) the stellar food. Specialties feature the freshest sushi and sashimi, as well as grilled and *nabemono* dishes (kettle dishes cooked at the table). To start, try any of the appetizers, and move on to the grilled butter fish with miso sauce. Complete dinners include kobachi, soup, rice, pickles, and dessert. Many consider this—along with Kabuto—among the top five sushi restaurants in the city. (Unfortunately—and surprisingly—San Francisco is dreadfully lacking in truly great sushi spots.)

In the Sheraton Palace Hotel, 2 New Montgomery St. (at Market St.). ✆ 415/546-5090. Reservations recommended. Sushi $4–$16; main courses $25–$30; fixed-price menu $50. AE, DC, DISC, MC, V. Tues–Fri 11:30am–2pm; Tues–Sat 6–10pm. Muni Metro: All Market St. trams. Bus: All Market St. buses.

One Market ★★ CALIFORNIA   If you don't mind enormous restaurants, this one, which features a farm-fresh menu, is particularly good, especially since the recent arrival of executive chef Adrian Hoffman. Amid tapestry, banquettes, mahogany, slate floors, seating for 220, and a bar that displays a prominent colorful mural of a market scene, a sea of diners feast on delights from the ever-changing menu of fresh salads, fish, meat, and game. A corporate crowd convenes from 4:30 to 6pm weeknights for $2.50 pints and three specially priced daily specials. The room picks up with live jazz nightly.

1 Market St. (at Steuart St., across from Justin Herman Plaza). ☎ 415/777-5577. Reservations recommended. Main courses $19–$31. AE, DC, MC, V. Mon–Fri 11:30am–2pm; Mon–Thurs 5:30–9:30pm; Fri 5:30–10pm; Sat 5–10pm. Valet parking $8. Bus: All Market St. buses.

Rubicon ✫✫✫ FRENCH CONTEMPORARY Despite a rather stiff atmosphere, Rubicon remains one of the very best restaurants in San Francisco. Why? The prices are great for what you get, the wine list is world renowned, and the food is outstanding. Opened in 1994, Rubicon won instant publicity because of its celebrity backers, which include Robin Williams, Francis Ford Coppola, and Robert De Niro. Almost a decade later the place still deserves celebrity status. Named for Coppola's Napa Valley wine, Rubicon has never shaken its contemporary and somewhat staid dining scene or its loyal clientele of big-business power lunchers and an upscale, middle-aged crowd.

Executive Chef Dennis Leary presides over the menu, which changes monthly and features 10 or so appetizers that might include ahi tuna tartare with soy vinaigrette, out-of-this-world foie gras with caramelized rhubarb compote, and delicate seared scallops with braised endive, sweet onion puree, and truffles. About eight main courses are available daily, and they might include an outstanding butter-poached Alaskan Halibut with asparagus, ham hocks, and green onion broth or pot au feu of beef with braised turnips, pearl onions, and horseradish jus. Not surprisingly, a stellar wine list—in fact one of the best in the country—accompanies the excellent food.

558 Sacramento St. (between Sansome and Montgomery sts.). ☎ 415/434-4100. Reservations recommended. Main courses $22–$33. AE, DC, MC, V. Mon–Fri 11:30am–2:30pm; Mon–Thurs 5:30–10:30pm; Fri–Sat 5:30–11pm. Bus: 15 or 41.

Tommy Toy's ✫✫ *Finds* CHINESE If you want romantic, superfancy Chinese, Tommy's is all you: It's opulent, dark, unmistakably Asian, and perhaps the only Chinese restaurant where dressing up is apropos. Dimly lit candelabras and ancient paintings accent the $1.5-million dining room, patterned on the 19th-century empress dowager's reading room. Most evenings, the restaurant is crowded with tourists and some locals who come for the six-course fixed-price meal. Not much changes on the French-influenced Chinese menu, but that's fine for the loyalists who return year after year for a taste of classic Tommy Toy's. Expect beautifully presented minced squab in lettuce leaves, creamy lobster bisque served in a coconut and topped with puff pastry, a delicious whole lobster sautéed with mushrooms, chives, and angelhair crystal noodles, Peking duck carved tableside and served with lotus buns and plum sauce, medallions of beef, and a dessert of fluffy peach mousse. The a la carte menu flaunts vanilla prawns and other delicacies. I've been here twice; once the food was very good, and the next time it was fine, and both times the portions were substantial and the environment memorable.

655 Montgomery St. (at Columbus Ave. and Washington St.). ☎ 415/397-4888. Reservations recommended. Main courses $17–$22.50; fixed-price dinner $46.50–$57.50. AE, DC, DISC, MC, V. Mon–Fri 11:30am–2:30pm; daily 5:30–9:30pm. Valet parking (dinner only) $3.50. Bus: 9AX, 9BX, 12, 15, or 41.

Finds **The Sun on Your Face at Belden Place**

San Francisco has always been woefully lacking in the alfresco dining department. One exception is **Belden Place,** an adorable little brick alley in the heart of the Financial District that is open only to foot traffic. When the weather is agreeable, the restaurants that line the alley break out the big umbrellas, tables, and chairs, and voilà—a bit of Paris just off Pine Street.

A handful of adorable cafes line Belden Place and offer a variety of cuisine. There's **Cafe Bastille,** 22 Belden Place (*☎* 415/986-5673), a classic French bistro and fun speakeasy basement serving excellent crêpes, mussels, and French onion soup; it schedules live jazz on weekends. **Cafe Tiramisu,** 28 Belden Place (*☎* **415/421-7044**), is a stylish Italian hot spot serving addictive risottos and gnocchi. **Plouf,** 40 Belden Place (*☎* **415/986-6491**), specializes in big bowls of mussels slathered in a choice of seven sauces, as well as fresh seafood.

MODERATE

Kokkari ★★★ *Finds* GREEK   It figures that it would take a French chef to make Greek food fabulous, and executive chef Jean Alberti, the mastermind behind the moussaka, does exactly that. In truth, there are few restaurants I continually like as much as Kokkari ("Ko-car-ee"). The love affair begins with the setting: a beautifully rustic living room–like dining area with a commanding fireplace and oversized furnishings. Past the bar, generally two-deep with yuppies, the other main room is pure rustic romance with exposed wood beams, pretty standing lamps, and a view of the glass-enclosed private dining room. Then there are chef Alberti's traditional Aegean dishes, which are stunning, fresh, and flavorful. Start with *Pikilia,* a sampling of traditional Greek spreads served with *dolmathes.* There are excellent soups and salads, too, but try not to overindulge before the main courses, which include to-die-for moussaka (eggplant, lamb, potato, and béchamel) and phenomenal quail stuffed with wintergreens served on oven-roasted leeks, orzo, and wild rice *pilafi.* Take my advice and don't leave without sinking your fork into an order of *Kalithopita,* the most velvety chocolate cake you'll ever eat.

200 Jackson St. (at Front St.). *☎* 415/981-0983. Reservations recommended. Main courses $16.50–$32.50. www.kokkari.com. AE, DC, MC, V. Mon–Fri lunch 11:30am–2:30pm; bar menu 2:30–5:30pm; dinner Mon–Thurs 5:30–10pm; Fri 5:30–11pm and Sat 5–11pm. Closed Sunday. Valet parking (dinner only) $8. Bus: 12, 15, 41, 42, or 83.

Sam's Grill & Seafood Restaurant ★ *Finds* SEAFOOD   Power lunching at Sam's is a San Francisco tradition, and Sam's has done a brisk business with Financial District suits since 1967. Even if you're not carrying a briefcase, this is the place to come for time-capsule dining at its most classically San Francisco. Pass the crowded entrance and small bar to the main dining room, packed with virtually all men, kick back, and watch yesteryear happen today. (Or conversely, slither into a curtained booth and see nothing but your dining companion.) Tuxedo-clad waiters race around, doling out big crusty cuts of sourdough bread and distributing salads overflowing with fresh crab and Roquefort vinaigrette, towering plates of seafood pasta with marinara, charbroiled fish, roasted chicken, and old-school standbys like calf's liver with bacon or onions or Salisbury steak. Don't worry—they didn't forget the delicious creamed spinach. There's good argument for yesterday's food to stay in the past—such as overcooked pasta and fish. Then again, it's hard not to like any fettuccini in buttery, garlicky sauce—or the mildly salty service and restaurant's good old-fashioned character, which make everything on the menu taste that much better.

374 Bush St. (between Montgomery and Kearny sts). ✆ 415/421-0594. Reservations recommended for dinner and for 5 or more at lunch. Main courses $9–$24. AE, DC, MC, V. Mon–Fri 11am–9pm. Bus: 15, 45, or 76.

Tadich Grill ☆☆ *Finds* SEAFOOD   Not that the veteran restaurant needed more reason to be beloved, but the city's ongoing loss of local institutions makes 153-year-old Tadich the last of a long-revered dying breed. This business began as a coffee stand during the 1849 gold rush and claims to be the very first to broil seafood over mesquite charcoal, in the early 1920s. An old-fashioned power-dining restaurant to the core, Tadich boasts its original mahogany bar, which extends the length of the restaurant, and seven curtained booths for private pow-wows. Big plates of sourdough bread top the tables, which are draped in no-nonsense white linen.

You won't find fancy California cuisine here. The novellalike menu features a slew of classic salads, such as sliced tomato with Dungeness crab or prawn Louis, daily specials, meats and fish from the charcoal broiler, grilled items, and casseroles. Hot dishes include baked avocado with shrimp diablo, baked casserole of stuffed turbot with crab and shrimp à la Newburg, and charcoal-broiled steaks petrale sole with butter sauce, a local favorite. Almost everyone orders a side order of big, tasty french fries.

240 California St. (between Battery and Front sts.). ✆ 415/391-1849. Reservations not accepted. Main courses $12–$18. MC, V. Mon–Fri 11am–9:30pm; Sat 11:30am–9:30pm. Muni Metro: All Market St. trams. BART: Embarcadero Station. Bus: All Market St. buses.

The Waterfront Restaurant & Cafe ☆ AMERICAN   Bay Bridge views, a sunny patio, a sleek industrial-chic dining room, and great food have made the Waterfront a hit since its renovation and reopening in late '97. Unfortunately, the parade of chefs in and out of the kitchen recently has made a sure thing more like an interesting gamble. Still, the atmosphere alone (refined in the restaurant upstairs, nautical in the café downstairs) can induce idyllic San Francisco memories. For now my vote is with the café, which in my experience has served great (and more affordable) food, while upstairs has been ambitious to its own detriment. The café lunch menu includes appetizers such as Dungeness blue crab cakes (yum) and grilled apricot-glazed quail, plus excellent salads, pizzas, wood-fired grill items, and "house favorites," such as falafel-crusted sea bass and sautéed chicken breast with herbed polenta and rosemary pan sauce. The restaurant is more exotic—and in my mind too pricey—with abalone "Amandine" with wild mushroom-Arugula ragout and beef tenderloin with red wine braised lentils, stilton butter, and Merlot demi-glace. The wine list is fine and includes many selections starting at $18.

Pier 7 (on the Embarcadero near Broadway). ✆ 415/391-2696. Reservations recommended. Café main courses $15–$30; dining room main courses $26–$33. AE, DC, DISC, MC, V. Café daily 11:30am–3pm and 5:30–10pm; dining room daily 5:30–10pm. Free valet parking. Muni Metro: F.

Yank Sing ☆☆ CHINESE/DIM SUM   Loosely translated as "a delight of the heart," Yank Sing is the best dim sum restaurant in the downtown area. Poor quality of ingredients has always been the shortcoming of all but the most expensive Chinese restaurants, but Yank Sing manages to be both affordable and excellent. Confident, experienced servers take the nervousness out of novices—they're good at guessing your gastric threshold. Most dishes are dumplings, filled with tasty concoctions of pork, beef, fish, or vegetables. *Congees* (porridges), spare ribs, stuffed crab claws, scallion pancakes, shrimp balls, pork buns, and other palate-pleasers complete the menu. As at most good dim sum places, you choose the small dishes from a cart continually wheeled around the dining room. While the food is delicious, the location makes this the most popular tourist spot; locals generally head to Ton Kiang (see p. 147). A second location is at 49 Stevenson St., off First Street (© **415/541-4949**). Returning diners take note: The Battery Street location is closed.

101 Spear St (at Mission St at Rincon Center). © **415/957-9300.** Dim sum $2.65–$3.40 for 3 to 4 pieces. AE, DC, MC, V. Mon–Fri 11am–3pm; closed Sat; Sun 11am–2:30pm. Cable car: California St. line. Bus: 1 or 42.

4 Nob Hill/Russian Hill

EXPENSIVE

The Big Four ✿ CONTEMPORARY AMERICAN   Shining brass, historic California photographs, forest-green leather banquettes, and ram's-horn sconces establish the clubby, upscale atmosphere at this Nob Hill restaurant where an older clientele returns for well-prepared hearty American entrees. At dinner, you might find a lovely Caesar salad, then roasted rack of lamb with rosemary crust, gingered pear chutney, gruyere potato crisp, and cracked pepper-zinfandel sauce.

In the Huntington Hotel, 1075 California St. (between Mason and Taylor sts.). © **415/771-1140.** Reservations recommended. Breakfast from $10; lunch main courses $10–$19; dinner main courses $20–$35. AE, DC, DISC, MC, V. Mon–Fri 7–10am; Sat–Sun 7–11am; Mon–Fri 11:30am–3pm; daily 5:30–10pm. Valet parking $7. Cable car: California St. line (direct stop). Bus: 1.

MODERATE

Swan Oyster Depot ✿✿✿ *(Finds* SEAFOOD   Facing 90 years of faithful service to Bay Area chowder-heads, the Swan Oyster Depot is classic San Francisco, a unique dining experience you shouldn't miss. Opened in 1912, this tiny hole-in-the-wall run by the city's friendliest servers is little more than a narrow fish market that decided to slap down some bar stools. There are only 20 or so seats, jammed cheek-by-jowl along a long marble bar. Most patrons come for a quick cup of chowder or a plate of oysters on the half-shell that arrive chilling on crushed ice. The menu is limited to fresh crab, shrimp, oyster, and clam cocktails, Maine lobster, and Boston-style clam chowder, all of which are exceedingly fresh. *Note:* Don't let the lunchtime line dissuade you—it moves fast.

1517 Polk St. (between California and Sacramento sts.). © **415/673-1101.** Reservations not accepted. Seafood cocktails $5–$8; clams and oysters on the half shell $6–$7.50 per half dozen. No credit cards. Mon–Sat 8am–5:30pm. Bus: 27.

INEXPENSIVE

Hard Rock Cafe *(Kids* AMERICAN   I hate to plug chains, and this loud, rock-nostalgia-laden place would be no exception if 1) I knew tourists were no longer interested in it and 2) it didn't serve a fine burger and overall decent heaping plates of food at such moderate prices. For many, the real draw—almost 20 years past the time when it was hip to wear their logo—is the merchandise shop, but a shopper's gotta eat, thus the friendly menu offers burgers, fajitas, baby-back

Dining Around Town

2223 Restaurant & Bar **33**
42 Degrees **68**
A. Sabella's **43**
Absinthe **22**
Ace Wasabi's Rock 'n' Roll Sushi **6**
Alioto's **42**
Ana Mandara **39**
Andalé Taqueria **5**
AsiaSF **64**
Avenue 9 **19**
Azie **54**
bacar **62**
Beach Chalet Brewery & Restaurant **18**
Boulevard **57**
Butterfly **29**
Cafe Kati **15**
Cafe Pescatore **44**
Caffè Luna Piena **31**
Cha Cha Cha **69**
Chow **26**
Cliff House **16**
Delfina **34**
Doidge's **10**
Ebisu **19**
The Elite Café **13**
Eliza's **12**
Ella's **12**
Eos **71**
Firewood Café **30**
Florio **14**
Flying Saucer **35**
Fog City Diner **45**
Foreign Cinema **38**
Fringale Restaurant **61**
The Golden Turtle **48**
Gordon Biersch Brewery Restaurant **59**
Gordon's House of Fine Eats **66**
Greens Restaurant, Fort Mason **1**
Hard Rock Cafe **50**
Harris' **49**

Hawthorne Lane **56**
Hayes Street Grill **23**
Il Fornaio **46**
Jardinière **21**
Johnfrank **25**
Kabuto Sushi **17**
Khan Toke Thai House **17**
La Folie **47**
Long Life Noodle Company & Jook Joint **58**
The Mandarin **40**
Manora's **65**
Marcello's Pizza **32**
Mecca **27**
Mel's Diner **7**
Millennium **52**
MoMo's **63**
Pane e Vino **9**
Park Chow **19**
Pauline's **33**
PlumpJack Café **8**
Pluto's **3**
Prego **11**
Restaurant Gary Danko **41**
Restaurant Lulu **54**
South Park Café **60**
Straits Café **17**
Swan Oyster Depot **51**
Sweet Heat **70**
Taquerias La Cumbre **37**
The Slanted Door **37**
Thep Phanom **20**
Thirsty Bear Brewing Company **55**
Ti Couz **36**
Ton Kiang **17**
Tú Lan **53**
Universal Café **67**
World Wrapps **4**
Zinzino **2**
Zona Rosa **69**
Zuni Café **24**

114

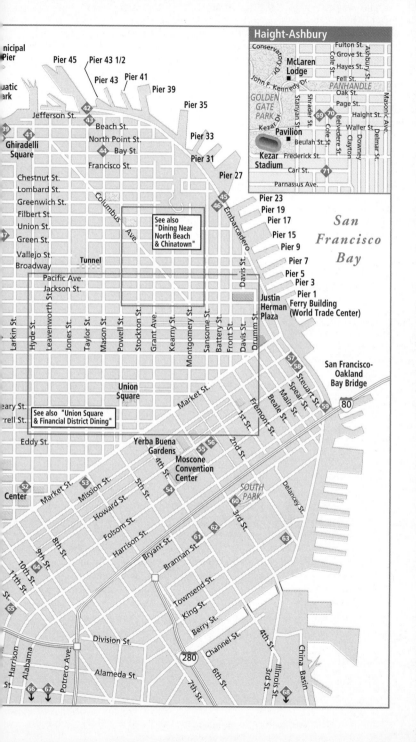

Conservatory

Fulton St.
Grove St.
Hayes St.
Fell St.
Oak St.
Page St.
Haight St.
Waller St.

McLaren Lodge

John F. Kennedy Dr.

GOLDEN GATE PARK

Kezar

Pavilion

Beulah St.

Kezar Stadium

Frederick St.

Carl St.

Parnassus Ave.

Ashbury St.
Cole St.
Stanyan St.
Shrader St.
Masonic Ave.
Belvedere St.
Clayton
Downey
Delmar St.

PANHANDLE

69
70
71

nicipal Pier

Pier 45
Pier 43 1/2
Pier 43
Pier 41
Pier 39
Pier 35
Pier 33
Pier 31
Pier 27

uatic ark

39
41
42
43
44

Ghirardelli Square

Jefferson St.
Beach St.
North Point St.
Bay St.
Francisco St.
Chestnut St.
Lombard St.
Greenwich St.
Filbert St.
Union St.
Green St.
Vallejo St.
Broadway
Pacific Ave.
Jackson St.

Columbus Ave.

Tunnel

See also "Dining Near North Beach & Chinatown"

San Francisco Bay

Pier 23
Pier 19
Pier 17
Pier 15
Pier 9
Pier 7
Pier 5
Pier 3
Pier 1

45
46

Embarcadero

Davis St.

Justin Herman Plaza

Ferry Building (World Trade Center)

Larkin St.
Hyde St.
Leavenworth St.
Jones St.
Taylor St.
Mason St.
Powell St.
Stockton St.
Grant Ave.
Kearny St.
Montgomery St.
Sansome St.
Battery St.
Front St.
Davis St.
Drumm St.

Union Square

Market St.

57
58
59

80

San Francisco-Oakland Bay Bridge

Steuart St.
Spear St.
Main St.
Beale St.
Fremont St.
1st St.

eary St.
rell St.

See also "Union Square & Financial District Dining"

Eddy St.

52

Center

Market St.

53

Mission St.

Howard St.

Folsom St.

Harrison St.

8th St.
9th St.
10th St.
11th St.

64

65

Yerba Buena Gardens

Moscone Convention Center

4th St.
5th St.

54

55
56

2nd St.

SOUTH PARK

60

Delancey St.

3rd St.

61
62
63

Bryant St.
Brannan St.
Townsend St.
King St.
Berry St.

Division St.

Alameda St.

Harrison
Alabama
Potrero Ave.

66
67

280

Channel St.

4th St.
6th St.
7th St.

China Basin

Illinois St.
3rd St.

68

ribs, grilled fish, chicken, salads, and sandwiches, the munching of which are muffled by blaring music. Although it's nothing unique to San Francisco, the Hard Rock is a fine place to bring the kids and grab a bite.

1699 Van Ness Ave. (at Sacramento St.). ℂ **415/885-1699.** Reservations accepted for groups of 15 or more. Main courses $6–$16. AE, DC, DISC, MC, V. Sun–Thurs 11:30am–11pm; Fri–Sat 11:30am–midnight. Valet parking $6 for 2 hr. Cable car: California St. line. Bus: 1.

The Golden Turtle 𝒢 VIETNAMESE The Golden Turtle is widely regarded as one of the city's finest Vietnamese restaurants, a far cry better than the typical *pho* noodle houses that have recently sprung up all over the place. In a converted Victorian home on a busy stretch of Van Ness, the restaurant's elaborate carved-wood paneling creates a soothing, romantic ambience. Recommended dishes are five-spice roasted chicken; marinated barbecued quail; imperial rolls with minced pork, prawn, and crab; and any of the seasonal crab dishes.

2211 Van Ness Ave. (between Broadway and Vallejo St.). ℂ **415/441-4419.** Reservations recommended. Main courses $8–$21. AE, DISC, MC, V. Tues–Sun 5–11pm. Bus: 38 or 45.

5 Chinatown

INEXPENSIVE

Brandy Ho's Hunan Food 𝒢𝒢 *Kids* CHINESE Fancy black-and-white granite tabletops and a large, open kitchen give you the first clue that the food at this casual and fun restaurant is a cut above the usual Hunan fare. Take my advice and start immediately with fried dumplings (in sweet-and-sour sauce) or cold chicken salad. Move on to fish-ball soup with spinach, bamboo shoots, noodles, and other goodies. The best main course is Three Delicacies, a combination of scallops, shrimp, and chicken with onion, bell pepper, and bamboo shoots, seasoned with ginger, garlic, and wine, and served with black-bean sauce. Most dishes are quite hot and spicy, but the kitchen will adjust the level to meet your specifications. There is a small selection of wines and beers, including plum wine and sake.

217 Columbus Ave. (at Pacific Ave.). ℂ **415/788-7527.** Reservations recommended. Main courses $8–$13. AE, DC, DISC, MC, V. Sun–Thurs 11–11pm; Fri–Sat 11am–midnight. Bus: 15 or 41.

House of Nanking 𝒢 CHINESE To the unknowing passerby, the House of Nanking has "greasy dive" written all over it. To its legion of fans, however, the wait—sometimes up to an hour—is worth what's on the plate. On the edge of Chinatown, just off Columbus Avenue, this inconspicuous little diner is one of San Francisco's worst-kept secrets. When the line is reasonable, I drop by for a plate of pot stickers and chef-owner Peter Fang's signature shrimp-and-green-onion pancake, served with peanut sauce. You can select from a good number of pork, rice, beef, seafood, chicken, or vegetable dishes, but I suggest you trust the waiter when he recommends a special, or simply point to what looks good on someone else's table. Even with an expansion that doubled the space, seating is tight, so prepare to be bumped around a bit and don't expect good service—it's all part of the Nanking experience.

919 Kearny St. (at Columbus Ave.). ℂ **415/421-1429.** Reservations not accepted. Main courses $6–$12. MC, V. Mon–Fri 11am–10pm; Sat noon–10pm; Sun 4–10pm. Bus: 9, 12, 15, or 30.

R&G Lounge 𝒢𝒢 CHINESE It's tempting to take your chances and duck into any of the exotic Chinese restaurants in Chinatown, but if you want a sure thing, go directly to two-story R&G Lounge. During lunch, both plainly decorated floors are packed with hungry neighborhood workers who go straight to the $5 rice plate specials. But even then you can order from the dinner menu,

---

(Kids) **The Best Family-Friendly Restaurants**

Cliff House *(see p. 145)*   The folks at this oceanfront multiplex of restaurants are used to churning out fast meals for tourists with kids in tow. The best part? If the young-uns get anxious, you can hand over a couple of bucks and send them to the adjoining Musée Mechanique, an authentic old-fashioned arcade with 150 coin-operated amusement machines.

Eliza's *(see p. 130)*   Colorful surroundings and a reasonable amount of quiet allow families to gather 'round the table for some of the best Chinese food around. Just don't come starving, because there's usually a wait.

Hard Rock Cafe *(see p. 113)*   Like its affiliates around the world, this loud, nostalgia-laden place offers big portions of decent food, moderate prices, and plenty of blaring music to an almost exclusively tourist clientele.

Mel's Diner *(see p. 130)*   This retro-style burger-slinging joint is not only neat to look at (it was the diner that starred in the movie *American Graffiti*), it also caters to kids. Youngsters get their own color-in menu (crayons are already on the table), and some meals are served in boxes shaped like classic American cars. Jukeboxes at each table will keep the whole family busy figuring out which oldie to select.

Mo's Gourmet Burgers *(see p. 123)*   Head to the second location, near the Metreon, and kill two birds with one stone: Get one of the best burgers in town, then shimmy over to the space-age Metreon shopping and entertainment center for some fun for everyone. If burgers aren't your thing, the Metreon's food court offers affordable gourmet versions of fast food and has plenty of seating.

Pasta Pomodoro *(see p. 123)*   Pasta, pasta, more pasta, plenty of other dishes, plenty of locations, cheery atmosphere, and rock-bottom prices mean you can take the whole family here and let 'em splurge.

---

which features legendary (and very greasy and rich) deep-fried salt and pepper crab. A personal favorite is R&G Special Beef, which melts in your mouth and explodes with the tangy flavor of the accompanying sauce. I was less excited by the tired chicken salad, house specialty noodles, and bland spring rolls. But that was just fine since it saved room for generous and savory seafood in a clay pot, delicious classic roast duck, and the adzuki bean pudding finale.

631B Kearny St. (at Clay St.). ✆ **415/982-7877.** Reservations recommended. Main courses $7–$25. AE, MC, V. Mon–Fri 11am–10pm; Sat 11:30am–10:30pm; Sun 11:30am–9:30pm. Bus: 1, 9AX, 9BX, 12, 15.

6 North Beach/Telegraph Hill
EXPENSIVE
Bix 𝒜𝒜 (Moments) CLASSIC AMERICAN/CALIFORNIA   The martini lifestyle may now be en vogue, but it was never out of style in this sexy and glamorous dining room. Modeled after a 1920s supper club, Bix is utterly stylish, with curving Honduran mahogany, massive silver columns, and Art-Deco-style

lighting, all of which sets the stage for live music and plenty of hobnobbing. While the ultra-sleek setting far overshadows the expensive—and, on one recent occasion, skimpy—food, the legions of diners entranced by the Bix experience don't seem to care. Chicken hash has been a menu favorite for the past 13 years, but newer dishes—such as crisp potato pancake with smoked salmon with caviar, classic steak tartare prepared tableside, prime New York steak grilled and served with Parmesan mashed potatoes with walnut and green peppercorn butter or pan-sautéed sea bass with roasted fingerling potatoes and spicy onion marmalade—are developing their own fan clubs.

56 Gold St. (between Sansome and Montgomery sts.). © 415/433-6300. Reservations recommended. Main courses $13–$20 lunch; $14–$26 dinner. AE, DC, DISC, MC, V. Mon–Fri 11:30am–3:30pm and 5:30–11pm; Sat 5:30–11pm; Sun 6–10pm. Bus: 15, 30, 41, or 45.

Caffè Sport ☞ ITALIAN   People either love or hate this stodgy Sicilian eatery. Cluttered with hanging hams, fishnets, decorative plates, dolls, mirrors, and over 2 decades' worth of dust, Caffè Sport was once a culinary landmark. Now it's better known for its surly staff and eclectic ambience than for its good, but cream- and butter-heavy, food. Owner-chef-artiste Antonio Latona serves up hearty portions of attitude along with garlic-laden pasta dishes and is happy to report that this is Senator Dianne Feinstein's favorite North Beach hangout. Lunch is tame in comparison to dinner, when the Sport is mobbed and lively, and strangers might be packed together family-style. Disregard the framed menu that sits on each table and accept the waiter's "suggestions." Whatever arrives— whether calamari, mussels, and shrimp in tomato-garlic sauce, or pasta in pesto sauce—it's bound to be *bene*. Bring a huge appetite, but above all, don't be late if you have a reservation.

574 Green St. (between Grant and Columbus aves.). © 415/981-1251. Reservations accepted only for parties of 2 or more. Main courses $15–$24. No credit cards. Tues–Sat noon–2:30pm and 5–10:30pm. Bus: 15, 30, 41, or 45.

Moose's ☞☞ *Value* MEDITERRANEAN/CALIFORNIA   A big blue neon moose marks your arrival to North Beach's most schmoozy restaurant, where Nob Hill socialites and local politicians come to dine and be seen. But convivial Moose's is not just an image. The food on recent visits has been very, very good. Appetizers are innovative, fresh, and well balanced (thank goodness for a truly good Caesar salad and perfect Dungeness crab cake with apple salad and Meyer lemon aioli). Main courses (especially meats) tend to be lovingly prepared. Try the commendable center-cut pork loin chop with creamy yellow grits and apple and onion compote; grilled Arctic char with baby artichokes, black trumpet mushrooms, and lobster sauce; or oven roasted chicken with a wild mushroom tart, baby carrots, and cippolini onions. Another reason to love Moose's: They make a darned good hamburger.

The bar, separated from the main dining room by a low, frosted-glass partition, remains busy long after the kitchen closes. There's excellent jazz piano nightly and during Sunday brunch.

1652 Stockton St. (between Filbert and Union sts.). © 800/28-MOOSE or 415/989-7800. www.mooses.com. Reservations recommended. Main courses $13–$26. AE, DC, MC, V. Mon–Wed 5:30–10pm; Thurs 11:30am–10pm; Fri 11:30am–11:30pm; Sat 11:30am–11:30pm (bar menu 2:30–5:30pm); Sun 10am–10pm (bar menu 2:30–5pm). Valet parking $6 lunch, $9 dinner for 3 hr. Bus: 15, 30, 41, or 45.

MODERATE

Enrico's ☞ MEDITERRANEAN   Enrico's is the most fun sidewalk restaurant/supper club destination on this North Beach strip. Families might want to

...glers, dancers and an assortment of acrobats fill the street.

...e shoots you a wide-eyed look as a seven-foot cartoon character approaches.

...at brought you here was wanting the kids

...ee something magical while they still believed in magic.

...erica Online Keyword: Travel

...n 700 airlines, 50,000 hotels and over 5,000 cruise and vaca-

...h getaways, you can now go places you've always dreamed of.

Travelocity.com
A Sabre Company
Go Virtually Anywhere.

...RLD'S LEADING TRAVEL WEB SITE, 5 YEARS IN A ROW" WORLD TRAVEL AWARDS

I HAVE TO CALL THE TRAVEL AGENC
AGAIN. DARN, OUT TO LUNCH. NOW
HAVE TO CALL THE AIRLINE. I HAT
CALLING THE AIRLINES. I GOT PUT O
HOLD AGAIN. "INSTRUMENTAL TOI
40" … LOVELY. I HATE GETTING PUT O
HOLD. TICKET PRICES ARE ALL OVE
THE MAP. HOW DO I DIAL INTERNA
TIONALLY? OH SHOOT, FORGOT TH
RENTAL CAR. I'M STILL ON HOLD. TH
MUSIC IS GIVING ME A HEADACHE.
WONDER IF SOMEONE ELSE HA
CHEAPER FLIGHTS. FORGET IT, CAN
TAKE IT ANYMORE … I'M HANGING U

YAHOO! TRAVEL
100% MUZAK-FREE

Booking your trip online at Yahoo! Travel is simple. You
compare the best prices. You click. You go have fun.
Tickets, hotels, rental cars, cruises & more. Sorry, no muzak.

Dining Near North Beach & Chinatown

Bix **17**
Brandy Ho's Hunan Food **14**
Caffè Macaroni **16**
Caffè Sport **8**
Capp's Corner **6**
Enrico's **12**
House of Nanking **15**
Il Pollaio **5**
L'Osteria del Forno **7**

Mario's Bohemian Cigar Store **3**
Maykedeh **9**
Mo's Gourmet Burgers **10**
Moose's **1**
Pasta Pomodoro **2**
R & G Lounge **18**
Rose Pistola **4**
The Stinking Rose **11**
Tommaso's **13**

skip this one, but anyone with an appreciation for live jazz (played nightly), late-night noshing, and people-watching from the outdoor patio would be quite content spending an alfresco evening under the heat lamps. (However, the best view of the band is from inside.) Chewy brick-oven pizza, a handful of pastas, zesty tapas, and thick steaks are hot items on the menu, which changes monthly. The best part? No cover charge.

504 Broadway (at Kearny St.). © **415/982-6223.** Reservations recommended. Main courses $8–$13 lunch, $13–$19 dinner. AE, DC, DISC, MC, V. Sun–Thurs 11:30am–11:30pm; Fri–Sat 11:30am–12:30am; bar daily 11:30am–1:30am or earlier depending on patronage. Valet parking $7 lunch, $10 dinner. Bus: 12, 15, 30, or 83.

Fog City Diner ✿ AMERICAN   More popular because of its Visa commercial than its food, Fog City is a tourist destination, with locals straggling in for business lunches. But that may change now that Bruce Hill, who brought fame to the renovated Waterfront Restaurant, came onboard in late 2000. The restaurant looks like a genuine American metallic diner—but only from the outside. Inside, dark polished woods, inspired lighting, and a well-stocked raw bar tell you this is no hash-slinger. Here dressed-up diner dishes include gourmet burgers, salads, "warm breads," soups, sandwiches, cioppino, macaroni and gouda cheese, and pot roast. Fancier fish and meat meals include grilled catches of the day and thick-cut steaks. Lighter eaters can make a meal out of the long list of "small plates," which include crab cakes and quesadillas with asparagus and leek. The food is fine, but if your heart is set on coming here, do so at lunch—you'll be better off elsewhere if you want a special dinner.

1300 Battery St. (at Lombard St.). © **415/982-2000.** Reservations recommended. Main courses $10.50–$22. DC, DISC, MC, V. Sun–Thurs 11:30am–11pm; Fri–Sat 11:30am–midnight. Bus: 42.

Il Fornaio ✿✿ *Kids* ITALIAN   This trattoria is one of my favorite standbys, producing consistently good Italian fare at decent prices. The large split dining room in Levi Plaza, a few minutes from Pier 39, has a lively atmosphere and smart decor. By day it buzzes with Financial District types and socialites; by night, with couples and gathering friends.

If you don't have a reservation and can't wait to eat, pull up a stool at the marble-topped bar, with its unobstructed view of the open kitchen and dining room. On a sunny day, grab a patio table that looks onto Levi Plaza's fountain. Once you're situated, the first of many delights is the basket of fresh-baked breads, breadsticks, and a dipping dish of olive oil. Complement them with any of the delicious salads or the daily soup (especially if it's carrot), then venture to any of the pastas, pizzas, or main courses. My favorite is rotisserie duck in balsamic vinegar, which Il Fornaio somehow serves without all the fat you'd expect from duck and all the crispy skin you could wish for. Parents especially appreciate the "bambini" menu, which features pint-size fare for under $6. Desserts are decadent and wonderful. Try tiramisu and a glass of rose grappa—a perfect way to end the meal.

Try Il Fornaio for breakfast, too. You'll find a nice selection of Italian-inspired egg dishes and great crisped and seasoned home fries.

Levi Plaza, 1265 Battery St. (between Sansome, Battery, Union, and Greenwich sts.). © **415/986-0100.** Reservations recommended. Main courses $10–$25. AE, DC, MC, V. Mon–Thurs 7am–10pm; Fri 7am–11pm; Sat 9am–11pm; Sun 9am–10pm. Valet parking $5. Bus: 12, 32, or 42.

Maykedah ✿ PERSIAN/MIDDLE EASTERN   If you're looking to add a little exotic adventure to your dinner plans, this is the place. Surrounded by a sea of Italian bistros, Maykedah is one of San Francisco's best and most elegant Persian restaurants. The Middle East might no longer be the culinary capital of the world, but at Maykedah you can still sample the exotic flavors that characterize Persian cuisine. Of the dozen or so appetizers, some of the best are eggplant with mint garlic sauce, stuffed grape leaves, and lamb tongue with lime juice, sour cream, and saffron (c'mon, live a little). About eight mesquite-grilled items are on the menu, including filet of lamb marinated in lime, homemade yogurt, saffron, and onions. House specialties include half a dozen vegetarian dishes, including eggplant braised with saffron, fresh tomato, and dried lime.

470 Green St. (between Kearny St. and Grant Ave.). ✆ **415/362-8286.** Reservations recommended. Main courses $10–$22. MC, V. Mon–Thurs 5–10:30pm; Fri–Sat 11:45am–11pm; Sun 11:45am–10pm. Valet parking $6 lunch, $7 dinner. Bus: 15 or 41.

Rose Pistola ✦ ITALIAN The hottest restaurant of 1997 is still going strong under the watchful eye of restaurateur extraordinaire Reed Hearon. The smart, bustling bistro offers divided dining areas, cramped bar tables, and sidewalk tables on sunny afternoons. Inside, there's plenty to see as chefs crank out the eclectic food from the open kitchen. The appetizer list features a barrage of hot and cold antipasti such as fried artichokes with aioli, roasted chili and garlic shrimp, and chopped salad with bleu cheese vinaigrette, which are reasonably priced at $6 to $11.50. Unfortunately, portions tend to be small. Along with meats and fowl, the menu includes a variety of fish selections. My party tried mussels in rich tomato broth, and it was so flavorful we kept it around to soak up with bread long after the shellfish had been devoured. Our favorite dish was the whole Arctic char, which came crispy, perfectly seasoned, and bathed in fennel and tapenade in a big iron skillet.

532 Columbus Ave. (between Union and Green sts.). ✆ **415/399-0499.** Reservations recommended. Main courses $7–$18.50 lunch; most dishes $9–$24 dinner. AE, DC, MC, V. Sun–Thurs 11:30am–11pm; Fri–Sat 11:30am–midnight. Valet parking $10. Bus: 15, 30, 41, or 45

The Stinking Rose ✦ ITALIAN Garlic is the "flower" from which this restaurant gets its name. From soup to ice cream, the supposedly healthful herb is a star ingredient in most every dish. ("We season our garlic with food," exclaims the menu.) From a strictly gourmet point of view, The Stinking Rose is unremarkable. Pizzas, pastas, and meats smothered in simple, overpowering sauces are tasty, but they're memorable only for their singular garlicky intensity. That said, this is a fun place; the restaurant's lively atmosphere and odoriferous aroma combine for good entertainment. Black-and-white floors, gray marble tables, and large windows overlooking the street help maintain the high energy. The best dishes include iron-skillet-roasted mussels with garlic sauce, smoked mozzarella, garlic, and tomato pizza, salt-roasted tiger prawns with garlic parsley glaze, and 40-clove garlic chicken (served with garlic mashed potatoes, of course).

325 Columbus Ave. (between Vallejo and Broadway). ✆ **415/781-7673.** www.thestinkingrose.com. Reservations recommended. Main courses $13–$30. AE, DC, MC, V. Sun–Thurs 11am–11pm; Fri–Sat 11am–midnight. Bus: 15, 30, 41, or 45.

INEXPENSIVE

Caffè Macaroni ✦✦ ITALIAN You wouldn't know it from the looks (or name) of it, but this tiny, funky restaurant on busy Columbus Avenue is one of the best southern Italian restaurants in the city. It looks as though it can hold only two customers at a time, and if you don't duck your head when entering the upstairs dining room, you might as well ask for one lump or two. Fortunately, the kitchen also packs a wallop, dishing out a large variety of antipasti and excellent pastas. The spinach-and-cheese ravioli with wild-mushroom sauce is outstanding, and the gnocchi is probably the best you'll find outside Italy. The owners and staff are always vivacious and friendly, and young ladies in particular will enjoy the attentions of the charming Italian men manning the counter.

59 Columbus Ave. (at Jackson St.). © **415/956-9737.** Reservations accepted on weekdays—not on weekends. Main courses $9–$18. No credit cards. Mon–Sat 5–10pm. Bus: 15 or 41.

Capp's Corner ⭐ *Value* *Kids* ITALIAN   Capp's is a place of givens: It's a given that some high-spirited regulars are hunched over the bar, that Frank Sinatra's singing on the jukebox, and that you'll be served huge portions of straightforward Italian fare at low prices in a raucous atmosphere that prevails until closing. The waitresses are usually brusque and bossy, but always with a wink. Long tables are set up for family-style dining: bread, soup, salad, choice of around 20 classic main dishes (herb-roasted leg of lamb, spaghetti with meatballs, osso buco with fresh polenta, fettuccine with rock shrimp), and dessert—all for $15 to $17 or so per person, around $10 for kids. You might have to wait an hour for a table, but you won't get bored if the old cronies at the bar take a liking to you.

1600 Powell St. (at Green St.). © **415/989-2589.** www.cappscorner.com. Reservations recommended. Main courses $14.50–$17.50. AE, DISC, MC, V. Sun–Fri 4:30–10:30pm; Sat 4:30–11pm. Bus: 15. 30, or 41.

Il Pollaio ⭐ *Value* ITALIAN/ARGENTINEAN   Simple, affordable, and consistently delicious is a winning combination at super-basic Il Pollaio. Order at the counter, be seated in the tiny room, and wait for the fresh-from-the-grill chicken, which is so moist it practically falls off the bone. Each meal comes with a choice of salads and fries, and if you're not in the mood for chicken, you can opt for rabbit, lamb, pork chop, or Italian sausage.

555 Columbus Ave. (between Green and Union sts.). © **415/362-7727.** Reservations not accepted. Main courses $7–$15. AE, MC, V. Mon–Sat 11:30am–9pm. Cable car: Powell-Mason line. Bus: 15, 30, 39, or 41.

L'Osteria del Forno ⭐⭐ ITALIAN   L'Osteria del Forno might be only slightly larger than a walk-in closet, but it's one of the top three authentic Italian restaurants in North Beach. Peer in the window facing Columbus Avenue, and you'll probably see two Italian women with their hair up, sweating from the heat of the brick-lined oven, which cranks out the best focaccia (and focaccia sandwiches) in the city. There's no pomp or circumstance: Locals come here strictly to eat. The menu features a variety of superb pizzas, salads, soups, and fresh pastas, plus a good selection of daily specials (pray for the roast pork braised in milk), which includes a roast of the day, pasta, and ravioli. Small baskets of warm focaccia keep you going until the arrival of the entrees, which should always be accompanied by a glass of Italian red. Good news for folks on the go: You can get pizza by the slice.

519 Columbus Ave. (between Green and Union sts.). © **415/982-1124.** Reservations not accepted. Sandwiches $5.50–$6.50; pizzas $10–$17; main courses $6–$11. No credit cards. Sun–Mon, Wed–Thurs 11:30am–10pm; Fri–Sat 11:30am–10:30pm. Closed Tuesday. Bus: 15 or 41.

Mario's Bohemian Cigar Store ⭐ *Finds* ITALIAN   Across the street from Washington Square is one of North Beach's most popular neighborhood hangouts. The century-old bar—small, well worn, and perpetually busy—is best known for its focaccia sandwiches, including meatball and eggplant. Wash it all down with an excellent cappuccino or a house Campari as you watch the tourists stroll by. And yes, they do sell cigars (although you can't smoke 'em inside).

566 Columbus Ave. (at Union St.). © **415/362-0536.** Sandwiches $6.75–$7.25. No credit cards. Daily 10am–11pm. Closed Dec 24–Jan 1. Bus: 15, 30, 41, or 45.

Mo's Gourmet Burgers ★★ *(Kids)* AMERICAN/BURGERS   Some of the best—and juiciest—burgers in town are at this simple North Beach diner. Mo's offers a straightforward but winning combination: big, thick grilled patties of fresh-ground, best-quality, center-cut chuck; fresh french fries; cabbage slaw, sautéed garlic mushrooms, or beans and rice. Voilà! You've got the city's burger of choice (Zuni Café's is a contender, but at almost twice the price). The other food—spicy chicken sandwich; steak with veggies, garlic bread, and potatoes; and token veggie dishes—is also up to snuff, but it's that messy, memorable burger that keeps the carnivores captivated (the sinisterly sweet shakes are fantastic, too). Bargain-diners will appreciate prices, with burgers ranging from $4.95 for a classic to $8.95 for an "Alpine" burger with cheese, sautéed mushrooms, and fries; entrees start at $7.95 for a roasted half chicken with three sides and top out at $13.95 for New York steak. The classic breakfast menu is also a bargain. A second location at SoMa's Yerba Buena Gardens, 772 Folsom St., between 3rd and 4th streets (✆ **415/957-3779**), is open Tuesday through Sunday 11am to 9pm, Sunday and Monday 11am to 5pm.

1322 Grant Ave. (between Vallejo and Green sts.). ✆ **415/788-3779.** Main courses $5–$14. MC, V. Sun–Thur 11am–10:30pm; Fri–Sat 11am–11:30pm; breakfast Sat–Sun 9am–2pm. Bus: 9X, 15, 30, 39, 41, or 45.

Pasta Pomodoro ★★ *(Value)* *(Kids)* ITALIAN   If you're looking for a good, cheap meal in North Beach—or anywhere else in town, for that matter—this San Francisco chain can't be beat. There's usually a 20-minute wait for a table, but after you're seated, you'll be surprised at how promptly you're served. Every dish is fresh and sizable, and, best of all, costs a third of what you'd pay elsewhere. Winners include spaghetti *frutti di mare* made with calamari, mussels, scallops, tomato, garlic, and wine; and *cavatappi pollo,* with roast chicken, sun-dried tomatoes, cream, mushrooms, and Parmesan—both under $7. When I don't feel like cooking, I often stop by here for angel hair pasta with tomato and basil and a decadent spinach salad with candied walnuts and bleu cheese. The tiramisu is huge, delicious, and cheap, too.

655 Union St. (at Columbus Ave.). ✆ **415/399-0300.** Reservations not accepted. Main courses $4.60–$10.50. MC, V. Mon–Thurs 11am–11pm; Fri 11am–midnight; Sat noon–midnight; Sun noon–11pm. Cable car: Powell-Mason line. Bus: 15, 30, 41, or 45. There are 12 other locations, including 2027 Chestnut St., at Fillmore Street (✆ **415/474-3400**); 2304 Market St., at 16th Street (✆ **415/558-8123**); 3611 California St. (✆ **415/831-0900**); and 816 Irving St., between 9th and 10th streets (✆ **415/566-0900**).

Tommaso's ★★ *(Kids)* ITALIAN   From the street, Tommaso's looks wholly unappealing—a drab, windowless brown facade sandwiched between sex shops. Then why are people always waiting in line to get in? Because everyone knows that Tommaso's bakes one of San Francisco's best traditional-style pizzas and has been doing so for decades. The center of attention in the downstairs dining room is the chef, who continuously tosses huge hunks of garlic and mozzarella onto pizzas before sliding them into the oak-burning brick oven. Nineteen different toppings make pizza the dish of choice, even though Italian classics such as veal Marsala, chicken cacciatore, superb lasagna, and wonderful calzones are also available. Tommaso's also offers half-bottles of house wines, homemade cannoli, and good Italian coffee. If you can overlook the seedy surroundings, this fun, boisterous restaurant is a great place to take the family.

1042 Kearny St. (at Broadway). ✆ **415/398-9696.** Reservations not accepted. Pasta and pizza $9–$22; main courses $9–$17. AE, DC, MC, V. Tues–Sat 5–10:30pm; Sun 4–9:30pm. Closed Dec 15–Jan 15. Bus: 15 or 41.

7 Fisherman's Wharf

EXPENSIVE

A. Sabella's ★★ *Finds* SEAFOOD   The Sabella family has been serving seafood in San Francisco since the turn of the century and has operated A. Sabella's restaurant on the wharf continuously since 1920, catering heavily to the tourist trade. The menu offers something for everyone—steak, lamb, seafood, chicken, and pasta, all made from scratch with fresh local ingredients. Where A. Sabella's really shines, however, is in the shellfish department. Its 1,000-gallon saltwater tank allows for fresh crab, abalone, and lobster year-round, which means no restaurant in the city can touch A. Sabella's when it comes to feasting on fresh Dungeness crab and abalone out of season. Of course, such luxuries are anything but cheap. An added bonus: The restaurant overlooks the wharf.

Fisherman's Wharf, 2766 Taylor St. (at Jefferson St.), 3rd floor. ✆ 415/771-6775. Reservations recommended. Main courses $12–$47. AE, DC, DISC, MC, V. Daily 11am–10:30pm. Cable car: Powell-Mason line. 2-hr. validated parking at the Wharf Garage, 350 Beach St.

Alioto's ★ SEAFOOD   One of San Francisco's oldest restaurants, run by one of the city's most prominent families, the Aliotos, this Fisherman's Wharf landmark has a long-standing reputation for serving the Bay Area's best cioppino. The curbside crab stand, Oysteria Deli, the Steam Kettle Bar, and the new Nonna Rose restaurant are great for a quick, inexpensive dose of San Francisco's finest; for more formal and fancy selections, continue up the carpeted stairs to the multilevel, harbor-view dining room. Don't mess around with the menu: You're after Dungeness crab. Cracked, caked, stuffed, or stewed, it's impossible to get your fill, so bring plenty of money—particularly if you intend to order from Alioto's prodigious (and pricey) wine list. If you don't care for cracked crab (I can't imagine that!), try the griddle-fried sand dabs and rex sole served with tartar sauce.

Fisherman's Wharf (at Taylor St.). ✆ 415/673-0183. Reservations recommended. Main courses $12–$24 lunch, most main courses $18–$25 dinner. AE, DC, DISC, MC, V. Daily 11am–11pm. Cable car: Powell-Hyde line. Bus: 30 or 42.

The Mandarin ★★ CHINESE   Created by Madame Cecilia Chiang in 1968, The Mandarin is meant to feel like a cultured, northern Chinese home; fine furnishings, silk-covered walls, and good-quality Asian art create one of the most elegant Chinese restaurants in the city. Tables are spaced comfortably apart, and the better of two softly lit dining rooms offers matchless views of the bay.

True to its name, The Mandarin offers exceptional northern Chinese cuisine. Take my advice and start with sesame prawns or minced squab. Follow with smoked tea duck (the house version of Beijing duck, but smoked over burning tea leaves until crispy) or—if you have a party of two or more and call a day in advance—Beggar's Chicken, encased in clay and slowly cooked to perfection.

At Ghirardelli Square, 900 North Point St. ✆ 415/673-8812. Reservations recommended. Main courses $16–$25. AE, DC, MC, V. Daily 11:30am–10pm. Cable car: Powell-Hyde line. Bus: 19, 30, 42, 47, or 49.

Restaurant Gary Danko ★★★ *Finds* MODERN CLASSIC   James Beard award–winning chef Gary Danko presides over the city's modernized four-star dining experience. Eschewing the white-glove formality of yesteryear's fine dining, Danko offers impeccable cuisine and perfectly orchestrated service in an untraditionally unstuffy environment of wooden paneling and shutters and well-spaced tables. The three- to six-course fixed-price seasonal menu is freestyle, so whether you want a sampling of appetizers or a flight of meat courses, you need only ask. I am a devoted fan of his trademark buttery-smooth glazed oysters with leeks, salsify, and Osetra caviar; seared foie gras with peaches, caramelized onions, and verjus sauce; and adventurous Moroccan spiced squab with chermoula and orange-cumin carrots. But truthfully, I've never had a dish here that wasn't precious. And wine? It's a stellar, albeit expensive, list. If after dinner you have the will to pass on the glorious cheese cart or flambeed dessert of the day, a plate of petit fours reminds you that Gary Danko is one sweet and memorable meal. *Tip:* If you can't get a reservation and are set on dining here, slip in and grab a seat at the very small bar where you can also order a la carte.

800 North Point St. (at Hyde St.). © **415/749-2060.** www.garydanko.com. Reservations required. 3- to 5-course fixed-price menu $55–$74. AE, DC, MC, V. Sun–Wed 5:30–9:30pm, Thur–Sat 5:30–10pm. Bus: 42.

MODERATE

Ana Mandara ★★ *(Kids)* VIETNAMESE   Yes, Don Johnson is part owner. But more importantly, this Fisherman's Wharf favorite serves fine Vietnamese food in an outstandingly beautiful setting. Amid a shuttered room with mood lighting, palm trees, and Vietnamese-inspired decor, diners (mostly tourists) splurge on crisp spring rolls; Dungeness crab with zesty lemon sauce; buttery Chilean sea bass, lovingly wrapped and steamed in banana leaf with shiitake mushrooms and miso sauce; a sculptural "lobster tower" with rice, avocado, and daikon sprouts; and wok-charred tournedos of beef tenderloin with sweet onions and peppercress. There is no more expensive Vietnamese dining room in town. But along with the enjoyable fare, diners are paying for the atmosphere, which, if they're in the neighborhood and want something more exotic than the standby seafood dinner, is worth the price.

891 Beach St. (at Polk St.). © **415/771-6800.** Reservations recommended. Main courses $18–$28. AE, DISC, MC, V. Mon–Fri 11:30am–2pm; Sun–Thurs 5:30–9:30pm; Fri–Sat 5:30–10:30pm. Valet parking $8. Bus: 19, 30, 32, or 42.

Cafe Pescatore ★ ITALIAN   This cozy trattoria is one of the better bets in Fisherman's Wharf. Two walls of sliding glass doors offer pseudo-sidewalk seating when the weather's warm, although heavy vehicular traffic can detract from the alfresco experience. All the classics are well represented here: crisp Caesar salad, fried calamari, bruschetta, cioppino, pastas, chicken marsala, and veal medallions with mushrooms, caramelized onions, sage, and veal sauce. The consensus is to order anything that's cooked in the open kitchen's wood-fired oven, such as pizzas (margarita) or roasts (sea bass with pinenut crust, sundried tomato pesto, and roasted veggies), or panino (lunch only; grilled chicken or grilled eggplant).

2455 Mason St. (at North Point St., adjoining the Tuscan Inn). © **415/561-1111.** Reservations recommended. Main courses $4–$9 breakfast, $8.50–$16.50 lunch and dinner. AE, DC, DISC, MC, V. Sun–Thurs 7am–10pm; Fri–Sat 7am–11pm; Sat–Sun 7am–3pm brunch, 3–5pm cafe menu. Cable car: Powell-Mason line. Bus: 15, 39, or 42.

8 The Marina/Pacific Heights/Cow Hollow

EXPENSIVE

Cafe Kati ★★ *(Finds)* CALIFORNIA/EAST-WEST FUSION   Chef Kirk Webber works small wonders in an even smaller kitchen at this diminutive yet distinctive restaurant off Fillmore Street. The menu highlights California-style dishes spiced with a dash of the Orient and Italy, presented in high form, such as the signature Caesar salad sculpted into a towering monument of romaine. The seasonally changing menu offers such cross-cultural creations as miso-marinated Chilean sea bass saddled with tempura kabocha squash and chanterelle mushrooms; and sesame-crusted hamachi with a shiitake mushroom dumpling. When making a reservation, request a table in the front room.

1963 Sutter St. (between Fillmore and Webster sts.). ✆ **415/775-7313.** Reservations recommended. Main courses $24–$29. MC, V. Tues–Sun 5:30–10pm. Bus: 2, 3, or 4.

Harris' ★★ STEAK HOUSE   Every big city has a great steak restaurant, and in San Francisco it's Harris'—a comfortably elegant establishment where the handsome wood-paneled dining room has curving banquettes and stately waiters. Proprietor Ann Lee Harris knows steaks; she grew up on a cattle ranch and married the owner of the largest feedlot in California. In 1976, the couple opened the Harris Ranch Restaurant on Interstate 5 in central California, where they built a rock-solid reputation up and down the coast.

Here, the point, of course, are the steaks, which can be seen hanging in a glass-windowed aging room off Pacific Avenue, and are cut thick—New York style or T-bone—and are served with a baked potato and seasonal vegetables. You'll find classic spinach or Caesar salads, and sides of delicious creamed spinach, sautéed shiitake mushrooms, or caramelized onions. Harris' also offers lamb chops, fresh fish, lobster, and roast duckling, as well as venison, buffalo (on occasion), and other seasonal game.

2100 Van Ness Ave. (at Pacific Ave.). ✆ **415/673-1888.** Reservations recommended. Main courses $22–$34. AE, DC, DISC, MC, V. Mon–Thurs 5:30–9:30pm; Fri 5:30–10pm; Sat–Sun 5–10pm. Closed January 1, July 4, and December 25. Valet $6. Bus: 12, 42, 47, 49, or 83.

La Folie ★★ *Finds* FRENCH   My mother and I call this unintimidating, cozy intimate French restaurant "the house of foie gras." Why? Because on our first visit, virtually every dish overflowed with the ultrarich delicacy. But in truth, there's more to chef Roland Passot's fantastic menu. Like what? Melt-in-your-mouth starters such as roast quail and—drum roll, please—foie gras with salad, wild mushrooms, and roasted garlic. Generous main courses include rôti of quail and squab stuffed with wild mushrooms and wrapped in crispy potato strings, and roast venison with vegetables, quince, and huckleberry sauce. The country French decor is tasteful but not too serious, with whimsical chandeliers and a cloudy sky painted overhead. The staff is friendly, knowledgeable, and accommodating, and the food is outstanding. Best of all, the environment is relaxed and comfortable. Finish with any of the delectable desserts, and when you're done, you're sure to loosen your belt a few notches.

2316 Polk St. (between Green and Union sts.). ✆ **415/776-5577.** Reservations recommended. Main courses $32–$48; 4-course tasting menu $75; 10-course chef's tasting menu (order in advance for whole table; $120 per person); vegetarian tasting menu $55. AE, DC, DISC, MC, V. Mon–Sat 5:30–10pm. Bus: 19, 41, 45, 47, 49, or 76.

MODERATE

Ace Wasabi's Rock 'n' Roll Sushi ★★ JAPANESE/SUSHI   What differentiates this Marina hot spot (formerly known as Flying Kamikazes) from the usual sushi spots around town are the unique combinations, the varied menu, and the young, hip atmosphere. The innovative rolls are a nice change for those bored with traditional styles. But don't worry if someone in your party isn't a fish fan. There are plenty of non-seafood and cooked items on the menu. Don't miss the rainbow "Three Amigos" roll or the "Rock and Roll," with cooked eel, avocado, and cucumber. Buckwheat-noodle-and-julienne-vegetable salad is also a treat. The service could be improved—on busy nights you'll wait forever for your server to pour your Sapporo—but the staff is friendly and the atmosphere fun, so nobody seems to mind.

3339 Steiner St. (at Chestnut St.). ℂ **415/567-4903**. Reservations not accepted. Sushi $4–$9. AE, MC, V.
Mon–Thurs 5:30–10:30pm; Fri–Sat 5:30–11pm; Sun 5–10pm. Closed Thanksgiving, Christmas Eve, Christmas,
and New Year's Day. Bus: 30.

Doidge's ✩✩ AMERICAN/BREAKFAST   Sweet, small, and always packed,
Doidge's has served one of the better breakfasts in San Francisco since 1971. The
restaurant's fame rests on eggs Benedict; eggs Florentine, prepared with thinly
sliced Motherlode ham, runs a close second. Invariably, the menu includes a
gourmet omelet packed with luscious combinations; to delight the kid in you,
hot chocolate comes in your very own teapot. Lunch also puts a gourmet spin
on such favorites as Cobb salad, a lean ground chuck burger, and the good ol'
BLT. Locals covet the six seats at the original mahogany counter.

2217 Union St. (between Fillmore and Steiner sts.). ℂ **415/921-2149**. Reservations essential on weekends.
Breakfast $6–$10; lunch $5.25–$10. MC, V. Mon–Thurs 8am–12:30pm; Fri 8am–1:30; Sat–Sun 8am–2:30pm.
Bus: 22 or 45.

Ella's ✩✩ (Kids) AMERICAN/BREAKFAST   Although this homey American
restaurant serves dinner on weeknights, it's well known throughout town as the
undisputed king of breakfasts. Unfortunately, its acclaim means you're likely to
wait up to an hour on weekends. But midweek and in the wee hours of morning, it's possible to slide into a counter or table seat in the colorful split dining
room and lose yourself in outstanding and obscenely generous servings of
chicken hash, crisped to perfection and served with eggs any way you like them,
with fluffy buttermilk biscuits. Pancakes, omelets, and the short list of other
breakfast essentials are equally revered. Alas, service can be woefully slow, but at
least the busboys are quick to fill coffee cups. Come lunchtime and the far more
mellow dinner, solid entrees like salads or grilled salmon with mashed potatoes
remind you what's great about good old American cooking.

500 Presidio Ave. (at California St.). ℂ **415/441-5669**. For parties of 8 or more reservations are accepted
for breakfast and are always accepted for lunch and dinner. Main courses breakfast $2.75–$8.25; main
courses dinner $9–$17. AE, MC, V. Mon–Fri 7am–9pm; Sat–Sun 8:30am–2pm. Bus: 1, 5, or 43.

The Elite Café ✩ CAJUN/CREOLE   Some habits do indeed die hard, and the
Elite is one of them. This place is always bustling with Pacific Heights's beautiful
people, who come for fresh oysters, blackened beef filet with Cajun butter, jamba-
laya, Granddad's chicken and dumplings, and other well-spiced Cajun dishes. The
high-backed booths provide more intimate dining than the crowded tables and bar.
Brunch here is good, too, and it includes all kinds of egg dishes—Benedict, sardou,
and many more—and such goodies as cornbread, bagels, and lox.

2049 Fillmore St. (between Pine and California sts.). ℂ **415/346-8668**. Reservations not accepted. Main
courses $16.50–$26. AE, DC, DISC, MC, V. Sun 10am–3pm and 5–10pm; Mon–Sat 5–11pm. Bus: 22, 41, or 45.

Florio ✩✩ FRENCH/ITALIAN BISTRO   When I'm in the mood for a good
meal without hoopla, I head directly to bistrolike Florio. Not only because the
staff is friendly, or because since they don't take reservations it's almost always
painless to get a table or dine at the bar, and not even because the place is small
enough to make me feel that I'm in a restaurant whose number-one goal is not
to get as many consumers as possible in and out. The real reason is that I'm
addicted to the soft polenta with mushrooms, shrimp and white bean salad,
steak frites, and virtually every other little comfort dish that makes its way to the
table. The wines by the glass (and by the bottle) always disappoint, but I don't
care. I pull up a chair, make myself at home, and enjoy casual and cozy surroundings and consistently satisfying food. I suggest you do the same.

1915 Fillmore St. (between Pine and Bush sts.). ℂ **415/775-4300.** Reservations recommended. Most main courses $17–$20. AE, MC, V. Sun–Thurs 5:30–10pm; Fri–Sat 5:30–11pm. Bus: 22, 41, or 45.

Greens Restaurant, Fort Mason ★★ *Finds* VEGETARIAN In an old warehouse, with enormous windows overlooking the bridge and the bay, the vegetarian restaurant is a pioneer and a legend. Renowned vegetarian cook and executive chef Annie Somerville (author of *Fields of Greens*) cooks with the seasons, using produce from local organic farms. A weeknight dinner might feature such appetizers as tomato lentil soup with spinach and Parmesan cheese or ricotta and white corn griddlecakes with asiago, smoked mozzarella, and scallions. Follow with spring-vegetable risotto with asparagus, peas, shiitake and cremini mushrooms, and Parmesan cheese; or Sri Lankan curry of new potatoes, cauliflower, carrots, peppers, and snap peas stewed with tomatoes, coconut milk, ginger, and spices. A special four-course dinner is served on Saturday only. A recent example began with yellow finn potato and goat cheese griddlecakes with chives, crème fraiche, and apple-quince compote or cannellini bean vegetable soup. Desserts are equally adventuresome—try chocolate pave with mint crème anglaise or espresso ice cream with chocolate sauce. Lunch and brunch are somewhat simpler, but they're equally inventive.

The adjacent Greens To Go sells homemade breads, sandwiches, soups, salads, and pastries.

Building A, Fort Mason Center (enter Fort Mason opposite the Safeway at Buchanan and Marina sts.). ℂ 415/771-6222. Reservations recommended 2 weeks in advance. Main courses $8–$13 lunch, $13–$18 dinner; fixed-priced dinner $45; brunch $8–$12. DISC, MC, V. Tues–Fri 11:30am–2pm; Sat 11:30am–2:30pm; Sun 10am–2pm; Mon–Fri 5:30–9:30pm; Sat 5:30–9pm. Greens To Go Mon–Fri 8am–9:30pm; Sat 8am–4:30pm; Sun 9am–3:30pm. Bus: 28 or 30.

Pane e Vino ★★ *Kids* ITALIAN Pane e Vino is one of San Francisco's most authentic Italian restaurants. The food is consistently good—be careful not to fill up on the outstanding breads—the prices reasonable, and the mostly Italian-accented staff always smooth and efficient under pressure (you'll see). The two small dining rooms, separated by an open kitchen that emanates heavenly aromas, offer only limited seating, so expect a wait even if you have a reservation. The menu offers a wide selection of appetizers, including a fine carpaccio, *vitello tonnato* (sliced roasted veal and capers in lemony tuna sauce), and the hugely popular chilled artichoke stuffed with bread and tomatoes and served with vinaigrette. The antipasti of mixed grilled vegetables always spurs a fork fight. The broad selection of pastas includes flavorful *pennette alla boscaiola* with porcini mushrooms and pancetta in tomato cream sauce. Other specialties are grilled fish and meat dishes, including chicken breast marinated in lime juice and herbs. Top dessert picks are any of the Italian ice creams, crème caramel, and (but of course) creamy tiramisu.

3011 Steiner St. (at Union St.). ℂ 415/346-2111. Reservations recommended. Main courses $8.50–$20. AE, MC, V. Mon–Thurs 11:30am–3pm and 5–10pm; Fri–Sat 11:30am–10pm; Sun 5–10pm. Valet parking (Mon–Sat evenings only) $8. Bus: 41 or 45.

PlumpJack Café ★★ CALIFORNIA/FRENCH/MEDITERRANEAN Wildly popular among San Francisco's style-setters, this small Cow Hollow restaurant is one of the neighborhood's most "in" places to dine. That's partly because it's affiliated with the Gettys clan (as in J. Paul) and sweetheart supervisor Gavin Newsom, and because everything old is new again since chef Keith Luce took over the kitchen.

Appetizers might include crispy duckling confit on shallot marmalade with frisée and banyula vinaigrette. Main dishes might include Parmesan breaded breast of capon stuffed with basil and prosciutto and drizzled with crushed tomato-almond sauce. Top it off with lime-leaf-scented panna cotta with fresh strawberries and rhubarb syrup. The extraordinarily extensive California wine list—gleaned from the PlumpJack wine shop down the street—is sold at next to retail, with many wines available by the glass.

3127 Fillmore St. (between Filbert and Greenwich sts.). © **415/563-4755.** www.plumpjack.com. Reservations recommended. Main courses $15–$25. AE, DC, DISC, MC, V. Mon–Fri 11:30am–2pm; Mon–Sat 5:30–10pm. Valet parking $9.50 for three hours. Bus: 41 or 45.

Prego ⭐ ITALIAN   A light and airy trattoria with an upscale clientele, Prego is a place to be seen or to people-watch as you dine behind the windows facing Union Street. Specialties include thin-crust, oak-fired pizzas, pasta, and grilled fish and meats. Spit-roasted, free-range chicken is prepared on a rotisserie and served with potatoes and vegetables. A good selection of wine is available by the glass or bottle.

2000 Union St. (at Buchanan St.). © **415/563-3305.** Reservations recommended. Pasta and pizza $10–$13; main courses $13–$24. AE, DC, MC, V. Daily 11am–midnight. Bus: 22, 41, or 45.

Zinzino ⭐ ITALIAN   Zinzino might look like a tiny trattoria from the outside, but you could fit a small nuclear sub in the space from the sun-drenched facade to the shaded back patio of this former laundromat. And it's a good thing because lots of people know this affordable spot is one of the city's better and more festive Italian restaurants.

The seasonal menu is refreshingly compact, focusing on starters and salads, fewer than a dozen main courses, and a handful of wood-fired pizzas. Salad takes on new dimensions; the apple-smoked chicken salad comes ornamented with gorgonzola, toasted walnuts, and champagne-white raisin vinaigrette. Comfort is yours with the double-cut pork chop stuffed with Swiss chard and goat cheese, accompanied by winter veggies. Zinzino gives Zuni Café a run for its money with its version of roasted half chicken. Pizzas are a thin-crust lover's dream— made with fresh cow's milk mozzarella and sprinkled with the likes of pear and gorgonzola, classic pepperoni, or prosciutto and arugula.

2355 Chestnut St. (at Divisadero St.). © **415/346-6623.** Reservations recommended. Main courses $13.50–$21.50. AE, DC, MC, V. Mon–Thurs 6–10pm; Fri–Sat 5:30–11pm; Sun 5:30–9:30pm. Bus: 22, 30, 43, or 45.

INEXPENSIVE

Andalé Taqueria ⭐⭐ (Value) (Kids) MEXICAN   I love this place. Andalé (Spanish for "hurry up") offers incredible high-end fast food for the health-conscious and the just plain hungry. As the long menu explains, this small California chain prides itself on its fresh ingredients and low-cal options. Lard, preservatives, or canned items are eschewed; Andalé Taqueria favors salad dressings made with double virgin olive oil; whole vegetarian beans (not refried); skinless chicken; salsas and aguas frescas made from fresh fruits and veggies; and mesquite-grilled meats. Add the location (on a sunny shopping stretch), sophisticated decor, full bar, and check-me-out patio seating (complete with corner fireplace), and it's no wonder the good-looking, fitness-fanatic Marina District considers this place home. Cafeteria-style service keeps prices low. *Bargain tips:* No one can complain about a quarter of a mesquite-roasted chicken with potatoes, salsa, and tortillas for $6.25. If you want to go traditional, stick with the giant burritos or the fantastic $2.95 tacos—a nibbler's dream.

2150 Chestnut St. (between Steiner and Pierce sts.). ℂ 415/749-0506. Reservations not accepted. Most dishes $5.25–$9.50. AE, MC, V. Mon–Thurs and Sun 11am–10pm; Fri–Sat 11am–11pm. Bus: 22, 28, 30, 30X, 43, 76, or 82X.

Eliza's ★★★ (Value (Kids CHINESE   Eliza's is one of my very favorite restaurants—I eat here at least once a week. Despite the humorous train-wreck-like design of modern architecture, glass art, and color, this perennially packed neighborhood haunt serves some of the freshest, best-tasting, cheap Chinese in town. Unlike most comparable options, here the atmosphere (albeit unintentionally funky) and presentation parallel the food. The fantastically fresh soups, salads, seafood, pork, chicken, duck, and such specials as spicy eggplant are outstanding and served on beautiful Italian plates. (Get the sea bass with black bean sauce and go straight to heaven!) I often come at midday and order the wonderful kung-pao chicken lunch special: a mixture of tender chicken, peanuts, chili peppers, subtly hot sauce, and perfectly crunchy vegetables. It's one of 21 main-course choices that come with rice and soup for around $5. The place is also jumping at night, so prepare to stand in line.

2877 California St. (at Broderick St.). ℂ 415/621-4819. Reservations not accepted. Main courses $4.50–$5.15 lunch, $5.25–$9 dinner. MC, V ($10 minimum). Mon–Fri 11am–3pm and 5–9:45pm; Sat 11am–9:45pm. Bus: 6, 7, 21, 66, or 71.

Mel's Diner ★★ (Kids AMERICAN   Sure, it's contrived, touristy, and nowhere near healthy, but when you get that urge for a chocolate shake and banana cream pie at the stroke of midnight—or when you want to entertain the kids—no other place in the city comes through like Mel's Diner. Modeled after a classic 1950s diner, right down to the nickel jukebox at each table, Mel's harks back to the halcyon days when cholesterol and fried foods didn't jab your guilty conscience with every greasy, wonderful bite. Too bad the prices don't reflect the '50s; a burger with fries and a Coke runs about $8.

There's another Mel's at 3355 Geary St., at Stanyan Street (ℂ **415/387-2244**); it's open 6am to 3am Thursday through Saturday.

2165 Lombard St. (at Fillmore St.). ℂ 415/921-3039. Reservations accepted. Main courses $4–$5.50 breakfast, $6–$8 lunch, $8–$12 dinner. No credit cards. Sun–Wed 6am–2am; Thurs 6am–3am; Fri–Sat 24-hr. Bus: 22, 30, or 43.

Pluto's ★★ (Value CALIFORNIA   Catering to the Marina District's DINKs (double income, no kids) crowd, Pluto's combines assembly-line efficiency with high quality. The result is cheap, fresh fare: huge salads with a dozen choices of toppings, oven-roasted poultry and grilled meats (the flank steak is great), sandwiches, and a wide array of sides like crispy garlic potato rings, seasonal veggies, and barbecued chicken wings. Pluto's serves cappuccinos, teas, sodas, bottled brews, and Napa wines, as well as homemade desserts. The ordering system is bewildering to newcomers; grab a checklist, then hand it to the servers who check off your order and relay it to the cashier. Seating is limited during the rush, but the turnover is fairly fast. A second location is at 627 Irving St., at 7th Avenue (ℂ **415/753-8867**).

3258 Scott St. (at Chestnut St.). ℂ 415/7-PLUTOS. Reservations not accepted. Main courses $3.50–$5.75. MC, V. Mon–Thurs 11:30am–10pm; Fri 11:30am–11pm; Sat 9:30am–11pm; Sun 9:30am–10pm. Bus: 28, 30, 42, or 76.

World Wrapps ★★ INTERNATIONAL   There are hardly any tables here and plenty of other eateries nearby, so what's the big deal? It's yet another version of San Franciscans' beloved burrito, only this time it's not Mexican-influenced. These are tortillas filled with your choice of cuisine from around the world (hence the name). Fresh ingredients, cheap prices, and the love affair Marina residents have with hanging out on this street make World Wrapps a grand place to grab a bite.

2257 Chestnut St. (between Pierce and Scott sts.). ℭ **415/563-9727.** Reservations not accepted. Wraps $3–$7. MC, V. Daily 11am–9pm. Bus: 22, 28, 30, 43, or 76.

9 Civic Center

EXPENSIVE

Jardinière ✰✰ FRENCH/CALIFORNIA   Jardinière is a pre- and post-symphony favorite, and it also happens to be the perfect setting for a cocktail. A culinary dream team runs the sexy dining room: owner-chef Traci Des Jardins, who packed up her pots and pans at Rubicon to go solo; owner-designer Pat Kuleto, who created the swank ambience; and general manager Doug Washington, whose good looks and unswerving charm have won him local fame in the restaurant circuit. On most evenings the two-story brick structure is abuzz with an older crowd (including Mayor Brown, a regular) that sips cocktails at the centerpiece mahogany bar or watches the scene discreetly from the circular balcony. The restaurant's champagne theme extends to twinkling lights and fun ice buckets built into the balcony railing, making the atmosphere conducive to throwing back a few in the best of style—especially when there's live jazz (at 7pm nightly).

Actually, cocktailing is my preferred reason to visit Jardinière. True, the daily changing menu is lovely; it might include seared scallops with truffled potatoes and truffle reduction, the famed truffled chicken pot pie, or venison with celery root, red wine, braised cabbage, and juniper sauce. But the atmosphere just doesn't have enough warmth for me. Still, anyone in search of a quality meal will not be disappointed. I also have to give kudos to the great wine selection—many by the glass, and over 300 bottles.

300 Grove St. (at Franklin St.). ℭ **415/861-5555.** Reservations recommended. Main courses $21–$29; 6 course tasting menu $75. AE, DC, DISC, MC, V. Daily 5–10:30pm. Valet parking $10. Bus: 19 or 21.

MODERATE

Absinthe ✰✰ (Value SOUTHERN FRENCH   This Hayes Valley hot spot is a sexy, fun, *and* reasonably priced restaurant preferred by everyone from the theatergoing crowd to the young and chic. Decor is scrumptious brasserie, with French rattan cafe chairs, copper-topped tables, a pressed-tin ceiling, soft lighting, period art, and a rich use of color and fabric, including leather and mohair banquettes. Fare is fun—from the specialty cocktails (ever had a "Ginger Rogers," made with gin, mint, lemon juice, ginger ale, and a squeeze of lime?) and good wine list to the slew of seafood starters, including oysters and cold seafood platters. Appetizers range from classic (Caesar salad, French onion soup) to modern luxe (perhaps grilled asparagus with black-truffled mayonnaise, or lamb's lettuce with pickled beets and walnuts). Main courses are equally satisfying, from coq au vin to grilled salmon with beet vinaigrette, dried fig and walnut crostini, and grilled vegetables to an excellent burger to inventive vegetarian dishes. Don't forget the fine cheese menu or the noteworthy desserts. Stopping for breakfast? Anticipate creamy polenta with mascarpone, maple syrup, bananas, and toasted walnuts; soft-boiled eggs with sage croutons; and the usual suspects.

398 Hayes St. (at Gough St.). ℭ **415/551-1590.** Reservations recommended. Breakfast $6–$12; most main courses $8.50–$18 lunch, $9–$20 dinner. AE, DC, DISC, MC, V. Tues–Fri 7:30am–1am (bar menu 3pm–1am); Sat 11am–1am (brunch until 3pm, bar menu 3pm–1am); Sun 11am–10:30pm (brunch until 3pm, bar menu 3pm–10:30pm). Valet parking (Tues–Sat) $6 with dinner, $18 without. Bus: 21.

Hayes Street Grill ★★ SEAFOOD   For well over a decade this small, no-nonsense seafood restaurant owned and operated by revered food writer and chef Patricia Unterman has maintained a solid reputation among San Francisco's picky epicureans, for its impeccably fresh and straightforwardly prepared fish. The concise menu offers a dozen first courses—most of which are fresh and lively salads—a half dozen grilled fish selections cooked to perfection and matched with your sauce of choice (Szechwan peanut, tomatillo salsa, herb-shallot butter) and a side of signature fries. Fancier seafood specials, which change with the seasons and range from braised skate with roasted winter vegetables and salsa verde to Peekytoe crab cakes with beurre blanc, are balanced by a few meat-driven dishes, which may include Niman Ranch (organic and wonderful) rib-eye steak with mustard butter and balsamic onions. Finish with the outstanding crème brûlée.

320 Hayes St. (near Franklin St.). ℰ 415/863-5545. Reservations recommended. Main courses $14.50–$25. AE, DC, DISC, MC, V. Mon–Fri 11:30am–2pm; Mon–Thurs 5–9:30pm; Fri 5–10:30pm; Sat 5:30–10:30pm; Sun 5–8:30pm. Bus: 19, 31, or 38.

Millennium ★ VEGAN   Banking on the trend toward lighter, healthier cooking, chef Eric Tucker and his band of merry waiters set out to prove that a meatless menu doesn't mean you have to sacrifice taste. In a narrow, handsome Parisian-style dining room with checkered tile flooring, French windows, and sponge-painted walls, Millennium has had nothing but favorable reviews for its egg-, butter-, and dairy-free creations since the day it opened. Granted, it can be a hit-or-miss experience for nonvegans like me, but I've also had some fantastic dishes (particularly soups). Favorites include sweet and spicy plantain torte served over a wonderful papaya and black-bean salsa appetizer, and main courses such as the filo purse filled with a ragout of wild mushrooms, leeks, and butternut squash, or the warm Yukon Gold potato salad with sautéed portabello mushrooms. Even the wine-and-beer list has a good selection of organic labels.

In the Abigail Hotel, 246 McAllister St. (between Hyde and Larkin sts.). ℰ 415/487-9800. Reservations recommended. Main courses $13–$19. DC, MC, V. Daily 5–9:30pm. Bus: 5, 9, or 71.

Zuni Café ★★★ *Finds* MEDITERRANEAN   Even factoring in the sometimes-snotty waitstaff, delicious Zuni Café is, and probably always will be, a local favorite. Its expanse of windows and prime Market Street location guarantee good people-watching, but even better is the action within: attractive thirty- and fortysomethings crowding in for the flavors of chef Judy Rodgers's incredibly satisfying Mediterranean-influenced menu. For the full effect, stand at the bustling, copper-topped bar, order a glass of wine and a few oysters from the oyster menu (a dozen or so varieties are on hand at all times). Then, since *of course* you made advance reservations, take your seat in the stylish exposed-brick two-level maze of little dining rooms or on the outdoor patio. Although the changing menu always includes meat (such as New York steak with Belgian endive gratin) and fish (grilled or braised in the kitchen's brick oven), the proven winners are Rodgers's brick-oven-roasted chicken for two with Tuscan-style bread salad, the polenta with mascarpone, and the hamburger on grilled rosemary focaccia bread (a strong contender for the city's best burger). Whatever you decide, be sure to order a stack of shoestring potatoes.

1658 Market St. (at Franklin St.). ℰ 415/552-2522. Reservations recommended. Main courses $15–$24. AE, MC, V. Tues–Sat 11:30am–midnight; Sun 11am–11pm. Valet parking $7. Muni Metro: All Market St. trams. Bus: 6, 7, 71, or 75.

10 SoMa

EXPENSIVE

Azie ★★★ ASIAN-INSPIRED FRENCH Eschewing the same old same old, this ultraswank SoMa spot is a breath of fresh, hip, sexy air—in both food and atmosphere. Fashionable from the salt and pepper shakers to the DJ who spins unobtrusive jazzy grooves on the first-floor turntable, this deliciously dim dining room celebrates a "modernist interpretation of Pacific Rim." The rich red-and-brown split-level room contains fun light fixtures, 22-foot ceilings intimated by columns, translucent paneling, curtained booths (on the first floor), and an exhibition kitchen. Equally sexy is executive chef and partner Jody Denton's innovative and beautifully presented cuisine. Denton, one of the city's recently heralded talents, offers various must-try dishes: "nine bites," a slew of adorable mini appetizers I order every time I set foot in the door; and tuna sashimi roll—especially if you like truffle oil, because the truffle ponzu dipping sauce scents the entire table. Main courses are delightful—inventive, generous, and, following the recent trend, luxurious with the likes of lobster and sweetbread pot au feu with truffles, fingerling potatoes, turnips, and fennel. My favorite? Whole crispy fish. If you can't decide, follow the chef's lead with the five-course tasting menus, one of which is vegetarian. The ambitious wine list features 300 to 400 selections. Desserts include cheeses, perhaps triple chocolate cream napoleon, and almond cardamom panna cotta.

826 Folsom St (at 4th St.). ✆ **415/538-0918.** Reservations recommended. Lunch main courses $11–$18; dinner main courses $24–$34; tasting menu $55–$62. AE, DC, MC, V. Mon–Fri 11:30am–2pm; Sun 5–10:30pm, Mon–Wed 5:30–11:30pm; Thur–Fri 5:30–11:30pm; Sat 5–11:30pm Valet parking $10. Bus: 15, 30, 32, 42, or 45.

bacar ★★ AMERICAN BRASSERIE No other dining room makes wine as integral to the meal as popular new bacar. Up to 250 eclectic, fashionable diners pack into the warehouse-restaurant's three distinct areas—the casual (loud) downstairs salon, the bustling bar and loud mezzanine, or the more quiet upstairs, which looks down on the mezzanine's action—for chef Arnold Eric Wong's "American Brasserie" (that is, French Bistro with a California twist) cuisine. During a recent visit, cod cakes and roasted mussels were lovely, while fried smelt was bland. Skate atop picholine olives and roasted peppers and osso bucco were outstanding. Just as much fun is the wine selection, which gives you 1,000 choices. Around 100 come by the glass, 2-ounce pour, or 250- or 500-milliliter decanter, and Wine Director Debbie Zachareas is almost always available to introduce you to new and exciting options. Vibrant in both energy and design, bacar is definitely the hot-spot right now, so don't be surprised if even with a reservation you have to wait for a table.

448 Brannan St., at Third St. ✆ **415/904-4100.** Reservations recommended. Main courses $12–$29. AE, MC, V. Daily 5:30pm–1am. Valet parking (dinner only) $9. Bus: 15, 30, 45, 76, 81.

Boulevard ★★★ *Finds* AMERICAN Master restaurant designer Pat Kuleto and chef Nancy Oaks teamed up to create one of San Francisco's most exciting restaurants, and although it made its debut in 1993, it's still one of my—and the city's—all-time favorites.

The dramatically artistic belle époque interior, with vaulted brick ceilings, floral banquettes, a mosaic floor, and tulip-shaped lamps, is the setting for Oaks's equally impressive sculptural and mouth-watering dishes. Starters alone could make a perfect meal, especially if you indulge in sweetbreads wrapped in prosciutto on watercress and Lola Rose lettuce, with garlic croutons and whole-grain mustard vinaigrette; Sonoma foie gras with elderberry syrup, toast, and Bosc pear salad; or Maine sea scallops on garlic mashed potato croustade with truffle and portabello mushroom relish. The nine or so main courses are equally creative and might include pan-roasted miso-glazed sea bass with asparagus salad, Japanese rice, and shiitake mushroom broth, or spit-roasted cider-cured pork loin with sweet potato-swirled mashed potatoes and sautéed baby red chard. Vegetarian items, such as wild-mushroom risotto with fresh chanterelles and Parmesan, are also offered. Three levels of formality—bar, open kitchen, and main dining room—keep things from getting too snobby. Although steep prices prevent most from making Boulevard a regular gig, you'd be hard-pressed to find a better place for a special, fun-filled occasion. Cocktailers: Do ask the bartender about the special martinis—they're some of the best in town.

1 Mission St. (between Embarcadero and Steuart sts.). ℂ **415/543-6084.** Reservations recommended. Main courses $19–$30. AE, DC, DISC, MC, V. Mon–Fri 11:30am–2pm; Sun–Wed 5:30–10pm; Thurs–Sat 5:30–10:30pm. Valet parking $10. Bus: 15, 30, 32, 42, or 45.

Fifth Floor Restaurant 𝒶𝒶𝒶 MODERN FRENCH

Two white-hot restaurants opened in late 1999, and this is one of them (Restaurant Gary Danko is the other). For a brief moment, skeptics wondered whether locals would head downtown to the fifth floor of a hotel and pay more than $30 per entree. It's no mystery now. Since The Fifth Floor's opening, executive chef George Morrone (who opened Aqua and has reigned at L.A.'s Hotel Bel-Air and San Francisco's Campton Place), has enjoyed a month-long waiting list. Like the decor—rich colors and fabrics, red leather and velvet banquettes, Frette linens, zebra-striped carpeting, and a clublike atmosphere—his menu features all things luxurious. You'll see Kobe beef, foie gras, sea urchin (accompanied by salmon paillard, Belon oyster, and diver scallop), caviar, the signature "tuna foie gras," suckling pig à l'orange, milk-fed veal steak with Madeira-glazed sweetbreads, curry oil, and jasmine rice—the list goes on. While giving a nod to the classics, the kitchen goes one step further, into a world of pure modern indulgence. Sommelier Rajat Parr is big on little wineries and specialties from Burgundy; the outstanding wine list offers 250-plus selections.

In the Hotel Palomar, 12 Fourth St. (at Market St). ℂ 415/348-1555. Reservations required. Main courses: $24–$39. AE, DC, DISC, MC, V. Mon–Thurs 5:30–10pm; Fri–Sat 5:30–11pm. Valet parking $10. Bus: All Market St. buses.

Hawthorne Lane 𝒶𝒶 CALIFORNIA

Even with the departure of Anne, owner David Gingrass's then-wife who with him launched the famed Postrio and this highly regarded restaurant, Hawthorne Lane remains in good hands with newly promoted executive chef Bridget Batson. Menus continue to change with the seasons and reflect the eastern and western influences that made the Gingrasses famous under Wolfgang Puck. The bar area is spacious, comfortable, and inviting, with both cocktail tables and bar seating. In the dining room, earthquake reinforcement beams divide the space in a way that is not only functional but also decorative. The room is not too fancy or pretentious, but it's well lit and adorned with bright artwork, fresh floral arrangements, and a leaf motif throughout.

Each dish is beautifully presented and well balanced. I've personally found that accompaniments are often more exciting than the main course. My all-time favorite: Miso-glazed black cod with sesame spinach rolls and soy-lime vinaigrette. Others kill two cravings with one dish: fried calamari salad with chili sauce and lime cilantro crème fraiche. Main courses might include grilled venison loin with sweet potato charlotte and madeira currant sauce, Chinese style roasted duck, rice-noodle stuffed yellowfin tuna, and roasted chicken filled with sage sausage. Desserts are as good to look at as they are to eat.

22 Hawthorne Street (at Howard St. between Second and Third sts.). ✆ 415/777-9779. www. hawthornelane.com. Reservations recommended. Jacket appropriate but not required. Main courses $11–$16.50 lunch, $26–$34 dinner. DC, DISC, MC, V. Mon–Fri 11:30am–2pm; Sun–Thurs 5:30–10pm; Fri–Sat 5:30–10:30pm. Bar menu Mon–Thurs 2:30–10pm; Fri–Sat 5:30–10:30pm; Sun 5:30–10pm. BART: Montgomery Station. Muni Metro: F, J, K, L, M, or N. Bus: 12, 30, 45, or 76.

MODERATE

Fringale Restaurant ★★ *Value* FRENCH   Still one of San Francisco's better restaurants for the money a decade after opening, Fringale—colloquial French for "sudden urge to eat"—has enjoyed a waiting list since the day chef and co-owner Gerald Hirigoyen opened this small bistro. Sponged, eggshell-blue walls and other muted sand and earth tones provide a serene dining environment, which is all but shattered when the 18-table room fills with Hirigoyen's fans. For starters, try steamed mussels with fried garlic vinaigrette, or roasted quail with apple risotto and foie gras. Among the 10 courses on the seasonally changing menu, you might find rack of lamb with potato gratin or pork tenderloin confit with cabbage and onion and apple marmalade. Desserts are worth savoring, too, particularly the Gateau Basque (which has won me many culinary friends since I began preparing it myself, with the help of Hirigoyen's cookbook). The mostly French waiters provide charming service, and prices are surprisingly reasonable for such high-quality cuisine.

570 Fourth St. (between Brannan and Bryant sts.). ✆ 415/543-0573. Reservations recommended. Main courses $4–$12 lunch; $11–$21 dinner. AE, MC, V. Mon–Fri 11:30am–3pm; Mon–Sat 5:30–10:30pm. Bus: 30 or 45.

Gordon Biersch Brewery Restaurant CALIFORNIA   Popular with the young Republican crowd (loose ties and tight skirts predominate), this modern, two-tiered brewery and restaurant eschews traditional brew-pub fare—no spicy chicken wings on this menu—in an attempt to attract a more upscale clientele. And it works. The baby-back ribs with garlic fries are the best seller, followed by the lemon-roasted half chicken with garlic mashed potatoes. Start with the delicate and crunchy calamari fritti appetizer or, if you're a garlic hound, the tangy Caesar salad. Most dishes can be paired with one of the brewery's lagers. Couples bent on a quiet, romantic dinner can skip this one; when the lower-level bar fills up, you practically have to shout to be heard. But beer-lovers who want to pair their suds with decent grub will be quite content.

2 Harrison St. (on the Embarcadero). ✆ 415/243-8246. Reservations recommended. Main courses $9.50–$20. AE, DC, DISC, MC, V. Mon–Fri 11am–3pm; Sat–Sun 11am–4pm; Sun–Mon 5–9pm; Tues–Thurs 5–10pm; Fri–Sat 5–10:30pm (bar closes later). Bus: 32.

MoMo's AMERICAN   With an abundance of patio seating, a huge swank-yet-casual dining room, and proximity to Pacific Bell Park baseball stadium, festive MoMo's was a hit the second it opened. Good weather accompanied by some wine (the bottle selection is far better than the by-the-glass selection) and decent snack foods like greasy-good thin-sliced onion rings, refreshing seared ahi salad, good old french fries, a-okay thin-crust pizza, and awesome burgers are what get me excited to dine here. Come sundown, there are dozens of other restaurants where I'd prefer to spend my money. But from the looks of the crowds, locals feel otherwise, and when you've got a seat under the outdoor heat lamps and a glass of wine in hand, almost anything tastes good. Singles appreciate the bar after work, and the dining room welcomes an eclectic mix of sports fans (midseason) and white-collar workers, many of whom are likely to start their lunch or dinner with a martini before indulging in braised short ribs or New York steak. If you're headed here on game day, make a reservation or arrive early, because party people form a line around the block to get in.

760 Second St. (at King St.). ℭ **415/227-8660.** Reservations recommended. Main courses $16–$26. EA, MC, V. Mon–Fri 11:30am–10pm; Sat 11am–3pm and 5–11pm;. Sun 11am–3pm and 5–10pm. Valet parking $6 lunch, $9 dinner. Bus: 15, 30, 42, 45, 80x.

Restaurant Lulu ⭐ FRENCH PROVINÇAL   Famed chef Reed Hearon put this place on the map, but long after his departure, Lulu is still a fun place to eat. Energy radiates throughout the enormous dining room as the cadre of cooks, communicating with headsets, slide bubbling plates of pizza and shellfish in and out of the open kitchen's wood-fired ovens. Watching the carefully orchestrated chaos makes dining here something of an event. The main room seats 170 and has a crowded bar that overlooks the cavernous room, but even amid a sea of stylish diners, the room somehow feels warm and convivial. Then there's the food, which is consistently good. Locals return again and again for roasted mussels piled high on an iron skillet; pork loin with fennel, garlic, and olive oil; and any of the other wonderful dishes. Unfortunately, the last time I had risotto here, it was one of the grimmest dishes I could recall. Everything is served family style and is meant to be shared. Save room for dessert, and try the gooey, oozing chocolate cake with melting ice cream.

816 Folsom St. (at Fourth St.). ℭ **415/495-5775.** Reservations recommended. Main courses $9–$18 lunch; $12–$23 dinner. AE, DC, MC, V. Sun–Thurs 11:30am–10:30pm; Fri–Sat 11:30am–11:30pm. Valet parking $10. Bus: 15, 30, 32, 42, or 45.

South Park Café ⭐ FRENCH   Want to immerse yourself in the dot-community? Head to lunch at casual-chic South Park Café, where the chat is less about IPOs, ISPs, and B-to-B and C-to-C than it is lost fortunes and worthless stock options in between bites of white-wine mussels or roasted duck breast with lavender sauce. The restaurant is in one of the most cutting-edge parts of town. On a sunny day, you can watch the young and the hopelessly hip lunch at the adjoining park.

108 South Park (between Second and Third sts. and Brannan and Bryant sts.). ℭ **415/495-7275.** Reservations recommended for dinner. Main courses $14–$22. AE, MC, V. Mon–Fri 11:30am–10pm; Sat 6–10pm. Closed Sun. Bus: 15, 30, 32, 42, 45, or 76.

Thirsty Bear Brewing Company ⭐ SPANISH   Despite the dumb name, the Thirsty Bear Brewing Company is a favorite of the Financial District/SoMa crowd, who come for the excellent house-made brews and Spanish food. Paella Valenciana—a sizzling combo of chicken, shrimp, sausage, shellfish, and saffron-laden rice served in a cast-iron skillet—is a must. Upscale pub grub includes a variety of hot and cold tapas, a few winners being *escalivada* (roasted vegetables—the spicy caramelized onions are outstanding—served at room temperature) and *espinacas à la catalana* (spinach sautéed with garlic, pine nuts, and raisins). Ask the waiter which brews best accompany the dishes. The house's signature dessert is La Sagrada Familia—twin towers of sugar cones (fans of Gaudí will recognize them immediately) filled with chocolate mousse that rest on a bed of Chantilly cream and fresh berries. Almost as impressive as the food is the costly conversion from a high-ceilinged brick warehouse to a two-level industrial-chic brewpub complete with pool tables and dartboards.

661 Howard St. (1 block east of the Moscone Center). ✆ **415/974-0905.** Reservations recommended. Main courses $12–$18. AE, DC, MC, V. Mon–Thurs 11:30am–10:30pm; Fri–Sat 11:30am–11pm; Sun 5–11pm. Bus: 12, 15, 30, 45, or 76.

INEXPENSIVE

AsiaSF ⋆ CALIFORNIA/ASIAN   At AsiaSF you'll be entertained by Asian men—dressed as women—who lip-sync show tunes as they dish out an excellent grilled shrimp and herb salad, Asian-influenced hamburger, pot stickers, duck quesadillas, and chicken sate. Fortunately, the food and the atmosphere are as colorful as the staff, which means a night here is more than a meal—it's a very happening event.

201 9th St. (at Howard St.). ✆ **415/255-8889.** Reservations recommended. Main courses $7–$18. AE, DC, MC, V ($20 minimum). Daily 5–10pm. Bus: 9, 12, 42, or 47.

Long Life Noodle Company & Jook Joint ⋆ NOODLES   The concept at sleek Long Life is to offer a wide range of unfamiliar noodle dishes from China, Korea, Japan, and other Asian lands and serve them in a familiar Westernized setting (in this case, a super-modern space with lots of neon and Plexiglas). The problem is choosing from the 30 or so noodle dishes, all of which are wildly different. Do you go with Buddha's Bliss (ramen noodles in miso broth with smoked trout, tofu, and enoki mushrooms) or Enchanted Heat (a "Chinese hangover cure" composed of whole-wheat noodles, lily pods, tree ears, and secret healing ginseng herbs)? I recommend the Ghengis' Buns, crisp sesame biscuits filled with Chinese roast beef, cucumber, cilantro, and hoisin sauce; wash it all down with Cool Cucumber Juice or Ginseng Ginger Ale.

139 Steuart St. (near Mission St.). ✆ **415/281-3818.** Reservations recommended. Main courses $6.50–$8.50. MC, V. Mon–Thurs 11:30am–10pm; Fri 11:30am–11pm. Bus: 15, 30, 32, 42, or 45.

Manora's ⋆ THAI   Manora's cranks out some of the best Thai in town and is well worth a jaunt to SoMa. But this is no relaxed affair. It's perpetually packed (unless you come early), and you'll be seated sardinelike at one of the cramped but well-appointed tables. During the dinner rush, the noise level can make conversation among larger parties almost impossible, but the food is so darn good, you'll probably prefer to turn toward your plate and stuff your face. Start with a Thai iced tea or coffee and tangy soup or chicken satay, which comes with decadent peanut sauce. Follow with any of the wonderful dinner dishes—which should be shared—and a side of rice. There are endless options, including a vast array of vegetarian plates. Every remarkably flavorful dish arrives seemingly seconds after you order it, which is great if you're hungry, a bummer if you were planning a long, leisurely dinner. *Tip:* Come before 7pm or after 9pm if you don't want a loud, rushed meal.

1600 Folsom St. (at 12th St.). ✆ **415/861-6224.** Reservations recommended for 4 or more. Main courses $7–$12. MC, V. Mon–Fri 11:30am–2:30pm; Mon–Sat 5:30–10:30pm; Sun 5–10pm. Bus: 9, 12, or 47.

Tú Lan ⋆ VIETNAMESE   Only adventurous foodies interested in a cheap, midday snack need read this review. You'll have to brave the winos, weirdos, and street stench to get to this total dive bordering Union Square and SoMa, but I do it happily to get my hands on the best imperial rolls on the planet. Daily crowds and even Julia Child (whose face once graced the greasy old menus) have been known to pull up a chair at this down-and-dirty shack of a restaurant. They feast on such goodies as out-of-this-world imperial rolls on a bed of rice noodles, lettuce, peanuts, and mint (under $5), and other regional dishes. But don't think the scene is any prettier inside than out. You'll feel brave just eating here, where I have on one occasion shared my table with a cockroach.

8 Sixth St. (at Market St.). ✆ **415/626-0927.** Reservations not accepted. Main courses $3.50–$7. No credit cards. Mon–Sat 11am–9pm. Bus: 6, 7, 27, 31, 66, or 71. Cable car: Powell-Mason and Powell-Hyde lines. Muni Metro: F, J, K, L, M,or N.

11 The Mission District

EXPENSIVE

Flying Saucer FRENCH   Outrageously yet artfully presented food is the hallmark of this Mission District fixture. Peering into the glass-walled kitchen, diners can catch the kitchen staff leaning over plates, carefully standing a jumbo prawn on its head atop a baked column of potato polenta. Fish, beef, and fowl dishes are competently grilled, baked, or flamed before being surrounded by a flurry of sauces and garnishes. While the pricey food is certainly intense and most recently not so great, the overwhelming sensation at this bistro is visual. The party extends from the plate to the decor, where plastic flying saucers mingle with colorful murals and creative lighting. The menu changes frequently, and there are almost always specials. If you ask your waiter to bring you the chef's most flamboyant-looking offering, chances are you won't be disappointed. Reservations are essential, as is a blind eye to the sometimes infuriatingly snotty service.

1000 Guerrero St. (at 22nd St.). ✆ **415/641-9955.** Reservations recommended. Main courses $19–$36. AE, MC, V. Tues–Sat 5:30–10pm. BART: 24th St. Station. Bus: 14 or 26.

MODERATE

Butterfly 👤 *Finds* PACIFIC RIM   The gloomy streets don't affect the cocoon of chicdom at oh-so-hip butterfly, a sexy 3,500-square-foot supper club that's aflutter with good times and an impressively multicultural mix of San Franciscans. The spacious, dim, brick-walled warehouse restaurant/bar manages to be all things to most all San Francisco people. To some it's a good, albeit very noisy bar (which overlooks the open dining room and jazz band that performs after prime dining hours). To others it's a fine dining destination (equally noisy) where the eclectic mix of Pacific Rim foods range from huge plates of chunky tuna tartar, which is best enjoyed when scooped up with a wonton chip, mahi mahi and lobster mushu fish tacos, guava and sake–marinated pork loin, or crab and rock shrimp ravioli. But to everyone it's a place to hear live music—like it or not since the band plays loudly in hopes of being heard over the chatter of thirtysomething revelers.

1710 Mission St. (at Duboce St.). ✆415/864-5575. www.butterflysf.com. Reservations recommended. Main courses $9–$22. AE, MC, V. Tues–Sat 6pm–2am. Muni Metro: 14, 14L, 26, 49, or 53.

Foreign Cinema 👤👤 FRENCH BISTRO   This place is so chic that it's hard to believe it's a San Francisco restaurant, and it's so well hidden on Mission Street that it eludes me every time I seek the valet. The ultratrendy vibe carries through the long, mysterious entry hall and alternative-cool hosts at the end of it to the doorway and beyond. An indoor seat is a lovely place to watch San Francisco's most fashionable; outdoors (heated, partially covered, but still chilly), the enormous foreign film showing on the side of an adjoining building steals the show. (Although the purpose is not to actually watch the film, it's still a bummer for those facing away from it.) Thing is, the food has been uneven. But that's not surprising since this newbie seats and serves up to 200. Still, it's a

Finds **Hidden Treasures**

Okay, so I couldn't find a neat category in which to place this restaurant, but since it's among the city's best, it would be a crime to leave it out. If you're not familiar with the streets of San Francisco, be sure to call first to get directions; otherwise, you'll spend more time driving than dining.

42 Degrees ★★★, tucked behind the Esprit Outlet in an industrial area, is an oh-so-chic supper club. A jazz trio sets the mood in the warehouselike, velvet-soft two-story dining room. Sleek cocktailers crowd the dark bar area, which specializes in Scotches, cognacs, and a selection of small vintners' wines. The dining mezzanine has a men's smoking-club feel; downstairs is all 1940s sophistication, from the velvet curtains that frame 22-foot windows right down to the waitstaff and clientele. There's also a dining patio that's a perfect spot for a sunny luncheon. The Mediterranean-influenced menu is rather expensive, but portions are large, and the food and atmosphere are exceptionally good. The very concise menu changes weekly but usually includes house favorites such as hearts of romaine with Caesar dressing, marrow bones with toast, blood sausage, great fish dishes, and Niman meats. (The slow-braised Sonoma lamb shank with polenta, kale, and dates is amazing.) It's easier to book a table at lunch, but the time to come is for dinner, when the chi-chi vibe is full-force; reservations are definitely recommended.

235 16th St., at Illinois Street, 1 block off Third Street (© 415/777-5558). Prices for main courses run $22 to $28. Open Wednesday to Sunday 6 to 10:30pm. AE, MC, V. Muni Metro: 22.

drag when sweetbreads or foie gras appetizers come tired and cold. On occasions that they don't, the food surpasses "good enough" and even can be classified as enjoyable. It might also include asparagus salad with truffle vinaigrette, frogs' legs, herb-crusted chicken breast with garlic mashed potatoes, roasted duck breast with black mission figs, rosemary marinated lamb loin with potato gratin, and lobster and monkfish bouillabaisse with coral aïoli. But truth be told, even if the food sucked, I'd come here. It's just that cool. By the way, if you have to wait for your table, consider stepping next door to the new adjoining bar, Lazslo's.

2534 Mission St. (between 21st and 22nd sts.). © 415/648-7600. www.foreigncinema.com. Reservations recommended. Main courses $12–$19. MC, V. Sun–Wed 5:30–10pm; Thurs–Sat 5:30–11pm; late-night menu until 1am. Valet parking $6. Bus: 14, 14L, 49.

Gordon's House of Fine Eats ★★ AMERICAN   This is one of my favorite spots for a fun night out with friends. The food is fine—not noteworthy on the serious foodie scale—and everything is good once you submerge yourself in the jovial scene. In the 110-seat color-and-concrete warehouse space, San Francisco's funky-fashionable and everyday dot-commers cluster around mahogany tables beneath a 20-foot open-beam ceiling. Eclectic live music drifts through the room almost nightly from the band quietly jamming on the understated mezzanine. At least partial credit for the festive vibe must go to owner-chef Gordon

Drysdale, who bounces through the dining room almost every evening. The menu sections include the likes of "healthful," "comfort," "local showcase," and "luxury." The ultra-rich appetizer coquille St. Jacques—scallop shells bubbling with mushroom cream sauce beneath seared scallops—is luxurious. Moist and decadent pork osso buco towering over a heap of brown butter spaetzle is indeed comfort at its most comfortable. Grilled king salmon with salt-roasted beet vinaigrette might be one of the night's tributes to "local showcase." Healthful? A selection ranging from a veggie burger to fava bean ravioli with morels and artichoke chips. Do what you will, but don't skip dessert: Donuts rule.

500 Florida St. (at 18th St). ℂ 415/861-8900. Reservations recommended. Main courses $8.25–$28. AE, MC, V. Mon–Fri 11:30am–4:30pm; nightly 5:30–11pm. Bus: 27.

The Slanted Door ★★★ *Finds* VIETNAMESE   This place is so popular that Mick Jagger and President Clinton made stopovers last time they hit town. Why? Despite the sometimes can't-be-bothered staff, the colorful industrial-chic warehouse of a dining room serves incredibly fresh and flavorful Vietnamese food. Pull up a modern, color-washed chair and order anything from clay-pot catfish or amazing green papaya salad to one of the inexpensive lunch rice dishes, which come in a large ceramic bowl and are topped with such options as grilled shrimp and stir-fried eggplant. Dinner items, which change seasonally, might include steamed chicken with black-bean sauce, long beans with shrimp, or vegetarian noodles sautéed with mushrooms, lily buds, tofu, bamboo, and shiitake mushrooms. Whatever you order, it's bound to be wholesome, flavorful, and outstanding. There's also an eclectic collection of teas, which come by the pot for $3 to $5.

584 Valencia St. (at 17th St.). ℂ **415/861-8032.** Reservations recommended. Lunch main courses $6.50–$15.50; most dinner dishes $7–$20. MC, V. Tues–Sun 11:30am–3pm; Sun–Thurs 5:30–10pm; Fri–Sat 5:30–10:30pm. Valet parking (dinner only) $7. Bus: 22, 26, 33, 49, or 53. BART: 16th St. Station.

Universal Café ★★★ *Finds* AMERICAN/FRENCH   For me it was love at first sight (and bite) at this small restaurant in the middle of an up-and-coming part of inner Mission. Not only does the intimate, rather cramped place look good—suave and stylish, with thick floor-to-ceiling windows and a row of tables running the length of the restaurant and paralleling the bar and open kitchen— it also attracts a nightly gaggle of locals. They come for phenomenal focaccia sandwiches (such as moist and memorable salmon), huge leafy salads, and inventive thin-crust pizzas at lunch. Superb dinner dishes include braised duck leg on a bed of creamy polenta; sea bass served with risotto, spinach, and caramelized onions; and hearty pot roast with lumpy mashed potatoes and fresh veggies. Granted, it's on the way to nowhere, but if you want an authentic small-restaurant charming San Francisco experience, it's well worth the detour.

2814 19th St. (at Bryant St.). ℂ 415/821-4608. Reservations recommended for dinner. Main courses $2–$8 breakfast (full on weekends, continental on weekdays); $7–$15 lunch; $11–$24 dinner. AE, MC, V. Tues–Fri 11:30am–2:30pm; Sat–Sun 9am–2:30pm; Tues–Thurs 6–10pm; Fri–Sat 6–11pm; Sun 5:30–10pm. Bus: 27.

INEXPENSIVE

Delfina ★★★ *Value* SEASONAL ITALIAN   Delfina avoids the bells, whistles, big-time design, and fancy preparations for something that used to be utterly San Francisco: straightforward simplicity and a small-business feel. Unpretentious atmosphere, unreasonably reasonable prices, and chef and co-owner Craig Stoll's ultrafresh seasonal Italian cuisine mean you're in for a price-painless and delicious experience from the minute you're seated by Craig's fiancée Ann Spencer to the time you receive your surprisingly low (by local standards) bill. The recipe for success has been so rewarding for Delfina that it was forced to expand to accommodate frustrated diners begging for reservations. The menu changes, but may feature Niman Ranch flat-iron steak with French fries; roasted chicken with Yukon gold mashed potatoes and shiitake mushrooms; and Alaskan halibut roasted on a fig leaf with yellow wax beans and tarragon butter. The only downside: It's impossible to find parking—literally—and there's no valet.

3621 18th St. (between Dolores and Guererro sts.). ✆ 415/552-4055. Reservations required. Main courses $9–$18.25. MC, V. Mon–Thurs 5:30–10pm; Fri–Sat 5:30–11pm. Bus: 26, 33; Metro: J.

Pauline's ✿✿ PIZZA   Housed in a cheery, yellow double-decker building that stands out like a beacon in a somewhat seedy neighborhood, Pauline's does only two things—pizzas and salads—but does them better than most restaurants in the city. It's worth running the gauntlet of panhandlers for a slice of Italian sausage pizza on handmade thin-crust dough. The eclectic toppings include house-spiced chicken, French goat cheese, roasted eggplant, Danish fontina cheese, and tasso (spiced pork shoulder). The salads are equally amazing: certified organic, handpicked by California growers, and topped with fresh and dried herbs (including edible flowers) from Pauline's own gardens in Berkeley. The wine list offers a smart selection of low-priced wines, and it's slated to expand to include a wine-tasting room in 2002, where Star Canyon Vineyards, yet another of the owners' pursuits, will be showcased. Yes, prices are a bit steep (small pizzas start at $11.75), but what a paltry price to pay for perfection.

260 Valencia St. (between 14th St. and Duboce Ave.). ✆ 415/552-2050. Main courses $10.50–$21.50. MC, V. Tues–Sat 5–10pm. Bus: 14, 26, or 49.

Taquerias La Cumbre ✿✿ MEXICAN   If San Francisco commissioned a flag honoring its favorite food, we'd probably all be waving a banner of the Golden Gate Bridge bolstering a giant burrito—that's how much we love the mammoth tortilla-wrapped meals. And while most restaurants gussy up their gastronomic goods with million-dollar decor and glamorous gimmicks, the burrito needs only to be craftily constructed, use fresh pork, steak, chicken, or vegetables, plus cheese, beans, rice, salsa, and maybe a dash of guacamole or sour cream, and practically the whole town will drive to the remotest corners to taste it. In this case, the fact that it's served in a cafeterialike brick-lined room with overly shellacked tables and chairs is all the better: There's no mistaking the attraction here.

515 Valencia St. (between 16th and 17th sts.). ✆ 415/863-8205. Reservations not accepted. Tacos and burritos $2.50–$5.50; dinner plates $5–$7. DISC, MC, V. Mon–Sat 11am–10pm; Sun noon–9pm. BART: Mission. Bus: 14, 22, 33, 49, or 53.

Ti Couz ✿✿ CRÊPES   At Ti Couz (say "Tee Cooz"), one of the most architecturally stylish and popular restaurants in the Mission, the headliner is simple: the delicate, paper-thin crêpe. While the fillings aren't exactly original, they're well executed and infinite in their combinations. The menu advises how to enjoy these wraps: Order a light crêpe as an appetizer, a heftier one as a main course, and a drippingly sweet one for dessert. Recommended combinations are listed, but you can build your own from the 15 main-course selections (such as smoked salmon, mushrooms, sausage, ham, scallops, and onions) and 19 dessert options (caramel, fruit, chocolate, Nutella, and more). Soups and salads are equally stellar; the sensational seafood salad, for example, is a compilation of shrimp, scallops, and ahi tuna with veggies and five kinds of lettuce. Ciders and beer complement the cuisine.

3108 16th St. (at Valencia St.). © 415/252-7373. Reservations not accepted. Crê[af]pes $2–$9.25. MC, V. Mon–Wed 11am–11pm; Thur–Fri 11am–midnight; Sat 10am–midnight; Sun 10am–11pm. BART: 16th & Mission. Bus: 14, 22, 33, 49, or 53.

12 The Castro

Although you see gay and lesbian singles and couples at almost any restaurant in San Francisco, the following spots cater particularly to the gay community—but being gay is certainly not a requirement for enjoying them.

EXPENSIVE

Mecca ★★ *Finds* AMERICAN   In 1996, Mecca entered the scene in a decadent swirl of chocolate-brown velvet, stainless steel, cement, and brown Naugahyde. It's an industrial-chic supper club that makes you want to order a martini just so you'll match the ambience. The eclectic city clientele (with a heavy dash of same-sex couples) mingles at the oval centerpiece bar. A night here promises a live DJ spinning hot grooves (or live entertainment on Mondays) and a fine American meal, served at tables tucked into several nooks. Menu options include such classic starters as Osetra caviar, oysters on the half shell, and Caesar salad, as well as more creative dishes, such as stir-fried clams with garlic and minced pork in black-bean sauce. Main courses include shrimp and lemongrass-crusted Chilean sea bass, rosemary-grilled rack of lamb, and soft-shell crabs with white-corn salsa and Creole mustard vinaigrette. The food is very good, but it's that only-in-San Francisco vibe that makes this place the smokin' hot spot in the Castro.

2029 Market St. (by 14th and Church sts.). © 415/621-7000. www.sfmecca.com. Reservations recommended. Main courses $16–$32. AE, DC, MC, V. Mon–Thurs 5–11pm; Fri–Sat 5pm–midnight; Sun 4–10pm. Valet parking $8. Muni Metro: F, K, L, or M. Bus: 8, 22, 24, or 37.

MODERATE

2223 Restaurant & Bar ★★ CALIFORNIA   Surrounded by hardwood floors, candles, streamlined modern light fixtures, and loud music, festive gays and straights come here for heavy-handed specialty drinks and grilled pork chops or ever-popular roasted chicken with garlic mashed potatoes. Along with Mecca, this is one of the top dining and schmoozing spots in the area—and definitely one of the better Sunday brunch spots.

2223 Market St. (between Sanchez and Noe sts.). © 415/431-0692. Reservations recommended. Main courses $7–$15 brunch; $13–$21.50 dinner. AE, DC, MC, V. Sun 11am–2:45pm and 5–10pm; Mon–Thurs 5:30–10pm; Fri–Sat 5–11pm. Muni Metro: F, L, K, or M. Bus: 8, 22, 24, or 37.

Caffè Luna Piena ★ ITALIAN   This is one of the Castro's warmest dining environments, complete with rich yellow walls adorned with local artwork. The room stretches back to the outdoor dining patio (yes, there are heat lamps) and a lush Japanese garden. The fare is contemporary American with Italian and Mediterranean influences. Lunch options include soups, salads, and sandwiches (with a choice of garlic fries or a green salad), such as grilled eggplant with roasted red pepper and smoked mozzarella on *pane integrale*. Main lunch courses might include blanched vegetables and lemon-caper vinaigrette. Dinner features such dishes as grilled black-pepper filet mignon with herb bleu cheese-cabernet butter and caramelized red onions, and roasted vegetable lasagna with sweet-potato sauce. Counter diners can watch chefs at work in the partially open kitchen. If you come for Saturday or Sunday brunch, reserve in advance or be prepared to wait in a long line. The menu includes salmon hash with poached eggs and tomato coulis, almond French toast with fruit compote and mascarpone cream, and other breakfast treats.

558 Castro St. (between 18th and 19th sts.). ℂ 415/621-2566. Reservations recommended for brunch. Main courses $6–$14 brunch; $11–$21 dinner. AE, DC, DISC, MC, V. Mon–Fri 11am–3pm; Tues–Sun 5:30–10pm, brunch Sat–Sun 9am–3pm. Muni Metro: F, K, L, or M. Bus: 24, 35, or 37.

Johnfrank ★★ *Value* MODERN AMERICAN BRASSERIE   This sleek, bustling hot spot has upped the dining-quality ante in the ever-vibrant Castro. All walks of San Francisco life happily crowd the long bar, in a rather loud room with low ceilings and modern artwork. Sure, they're here because it's a top contender in the Castro, but they're also here to enjoy the culinary consequences of a partnership between local restaurant veterans Frank Everett and John Hurley. What's on the menu? Organic beets, Fuji apple chips, fromage blanc, and verjus vinaigrette; hearts of romaine salad; a lovely potato gnocchi with rabbit sugo and cream; and pan-steamed P.E.I. mussels with pearl barley, romensco, and scallions. And that's just a few of the appetizers! Dinner might include salt-baked steelhead salmon with cucumber salad and fennel-smoked bacon sauce; a rich slow-simmered lamb shank with soft polenta and zinfandel sauce, and classic country chicken with fried cream. The wine list is both affordable and approachable. If they're offering the 3-course prix fixe menu, consider it—at $25 it's a bargain.

2100 Market St. (at 14th St). ℂ 415/503-0333. Reservations recommended. Main courses $16–$24. AE, MC, V. Sat–Sun 11am–3pm; Sun–Thurs 6–10pm; Fri–Sat 6pm–11pm. Limited parking. Muni Metro: F, J, K, L, or M. Bus: 8, 22, 24, or 37.

INEXPENSIVE

Chow ★ *Value* AMERICAN   Chow claims to serve American cuisine, but the management must be thinking of today's America, because the menu is not exactly baseball and apple pie. And that's just fine for eclectic and cost-conscious diners. After all, what's not to like about starting with a cobb salad ($5.50 for a half order) before moving on to Thai-style noodles with steak, chicken, peanuts, and spicy lime-chili garlic broth or pasta with duck bolognese. Better yet, everything except pot-roasted beef short ribs is under $10. More traditional are the budget-wise daily sandwich specials, which range from meatball with mozzarella (Sunday) to fresh sea bass (Monday); both come with salad, soup, or fries, for less than $7. While the food and prices alone would be a good argument for coming here, beer on tap, a great inexpensive wine selection, and the fun, tavernlike environment clinch the deal. A second location, **Park Chow,** is at 1240 Ninth Ave. (ℂ **415/665-9912**).

215 Church St. (near Market St.). ℂ 415/552-2469. Reservations not accepted. Main courses $5–$11. MC, V. Daily 11am–11pm. Muni Metro: F, J, K, L, or M. Bus: 8 or 37.

Firewood Café ★★ *Value* ITALIAN/AMERICAN   One of the sharpest rooms in the neighborhood, the colorful Firewood put its money in the essentials and eliminated extra overhead. There are no waiters or waitresses; everyone orders at the counter and then relaxes at the single family-style table, one of the small tables facing the huge street-side windows, or in the cheery back dining room. Management didn't skimp on the cozy-chic atmosphere and inspired but limited menu: The fresh salads ($6.75) come with a choice of three "fixin's" ranging from caramelized onions to spiced walnuts, and three gourmet dressing options. Then there are the pastas—three tortellini selections, such as roasted chicken and mortadella—and gourmet pizzas; calamari with lemon-garlic aïoli is a winner. Or how about herb-roasted half or whole chicken ($6.25 or $12.50, respectively) with roasted new potatoes? Wines cost $3.95 to $4.95 by the glass and a reasonable $16.95 to $19.95 per bottle. Draft and bottled beers are also available, and desserts top off at $2.95. (Thank goodness someone realized that $7 for an after-dinner treat is bordering on ridiculous.)

4248 18th St. (at Diamond St.). ✆ 415/252-0999. Reservations not accepted. Main courses $6.25–$9. MC, V. Daily 11am–11pm. Muni Metro: F, K, L, or M. Bus: 8, 33, 35, or 37.

Marcello's Pizza ✿ PIZZA   Marcello's isn't a fancy place, just a traditional pizza joint with a couple of tables, tasty pizza by the slice, and a few other basic dishes. Weekend nights there's a line out the door of drunk and/or stoned Castro Street partiers with the late-night munchies.

420 Castro St. (at Market St.). ✆ 415/863-3900. Reservations not accepted. Pizza slices $2.25–$2.85; pies $10.20–$25. No credit cards. Sun–Thurs 11am–1am; Fri–Sat 11am–2am. Muni Metro: L, M, or N to Castro St. Station.

13 Haight-Ashbury

EXPENSIVE

Eos ✿✿ EAST-WEST FUSION   Named after the Greek goddess of dawn, Eos put Cole Valley on the culinary map, thanks to chef-proprietor Arnold Wong, a master of texture and taste who perfected his craft while working at Masa's and Silks and also heads up one of the city's hottest new restaurants, bacar. With a twinge of guilt, you dig in and mar the artistic presentation of each dish, such as the albacore tuna tetaki tower, which comes seared with cracked black pepper, sprouts, white miso sauce, and black tobiko caviar. For starters, try tea-smoked salmon and mango spring rolls with wasabi–honey mustard dipping sauce. Unfortunately, the stark, industrial-deco decor does little to dampen the decibels, making a romantic outing nearly impossible unless you're into shouting. Around the corner is a less noisy, casual wine bar (with the same name) that stocks more than 400 vintages from around the globe.

901 Cole (at Carl St.). ✆ 415/566-3063. Reservations recommended. Main courses $19–$28. AE, MC, V. Mon–Sat 5:30–11pm; Sun 5–11pm. Muni Metro: N. Bus: 6, 33, or 43.

INEXPENSIVE

Cha Cha Cha ✿✿ _Value_ CARIBBEAN   This is one of my all-time favorite places to get festive, but it's not for everybody. Cha Cha Cha is not a meal; it's an experience. Put your name on the mile-long list, crowd into the minuscule bar, and sip sangria while you wait (try not to spill when you get bumped by all the young, attractive patrons who are also waiting). When you do finally get seated (it usually takes at least an hour), you'll dine in a loud—and I mean _loud_—dining room with Santeria altars, banana trees, and plastic tropical tablecloths. The best thing to do is order from the tapas menu and share the dishes family-style. Fried calamari, fried new potatoes, Cajun shrimp, and mussels in saffron broth are all bursting with flavor and accompanied by rich, luscious sauces—but whatever you choose, you can't go wrong. This is the kind of place where you take friends in a partying mood, let your hair down, and make an evening of it. If you want all the flavor without the festivities, come during lunch. There's a second, larger location in The Mission District, at 2327 Mission St., between 19th and 20th streets (✆ 415/648-0504).

1801 Haight St. (at Shrader St.). ⒸⒸ **415/386-5758.** Reservations not accepted. Tapas $4.50–$8.75; main courses $9–$15. MC, V. Daily 11:30am–4pm; Sun–Thurs 5–11pm; Fri–Sat 5–11:30pm. Muni Metro: N. Bus: 6, 7, 66, 71, or 73.

Sweet Heat Ⓕ MEXICAN   If you're looking for a flavorful light lunch or a cheap, festive dinner, check out this casual place, offering "healthy Mexican food to die for." Far from traditional Mexican food, Sweet Heat has capitalized on California's love affair with old-style food prepared in new ways, and the results are addictive. Prices are low—$6.25 for a veggie burrito with grilled zucchini, red pepper, and roasted corn; and $6.75 for two swordfish tacos. A dining room expansion and renovation, which includes a vibrant new mosaic, and the expanded cocktail menu featuring more tequilas than one could possibly taste, as well as a number of South American cocktails, adds more spice to the already whimsical Haight Street haunt. As of April 2001, there is happy hour from 4pm to 7pm.

1725 Haight St. ⒸⒸ **415/387-8845.** Reservations accepted. All entrees under $9. MC, V. Sun–Thurs 11:30am–10pm; Fri–Sat 11:30am–11pm.

Thep Phanom ⒻⒻⒻ THAI   By successfully incorporating flavors from India, China, Burma, Malaysia, and more recently the West, Thep Phanom has risen through the ranks to become one of the best Thai restaurants in San Francisco. (The line out the front door proves it's no secret.) Start with the signature dish, *ped swan*—boneless duck in a light honey sauce served on a bed of spinach. *Larb ped* (minced duck salad), velvety basil-spiked seafood curry served on banana leaves, and spicy *yum plamuk* (calamari salad) are also recommended. The Haight location attracts an eclectic crowd; the atmosphere is informal, and the decor quite tasteful. Don't leave anything even remotely valuable in your car.

400 Waller St. (at Fillmore St.). ⒸⒸ **415/431-2526.** Reservations recommended. Main courses $8–$12. AE, DC, DISC, MC, V. Daily 5:30–10:30pm. Bus: 6, 7, 22, 66, or 71.

Zona Rosa Ⓕ MEXICAN   This is a great place to stop and get a cheap (and healthful) bite. The most popular items are the burritos, which are made to order and include your choice of beans (refried, whole pinto, or black), meats, or vegetarian ingredients. You can sit on a stool at the window and watch the Haight Street freaks strolling by, relax at one of five colorful interior tables, or take it to go and head to Golden Gate Park (just 2 blocks away). Zona Rosa is one of the best burrito stores around.

1797 Haight St. (at Shrader St.). ⒸⒸ **415/668-7717.** Reservations not accepted. Burritos $4.50–$5.75. No credit cards. Daily 11am–10pm. Muni Metro: N. Bus: 6, 7, 66, 71, or 73.

14 Richmond/Sunset Districts

MODERATE

Beach Chalet Brewery & Restaurant ⒦ᵢ𝒹ₛ AMERICAN   While Cliff House has historic character worth exploration, this is the most modern ocean-side restaurant, with commanding views of the Pacific Ocean (fog permitting). The Chalet occupies the upper floor of a historic public lounge that originally opened in 1900, was renovated, closed, and was reopened in 1997. Today, the main floor's wonderful restored WPA frescoes and historical displays on the area are enough to lure tourists and locals, but there's nothing historic about the bright and cheery restaurant, which does the trick when you're in the 'hood, but is not a destination in itself. In fact, a great beer selection and live music have been the primary nighttime draw of late.

Dinner is pricey, and the view disappears with the sun, so come for breakfast or lunch when you can eat your Niman Ranch hamburger, rock shrimp nachos, or salmon-stuffed rainbow trout with one of the best vistas around. After dinner, it's a more local thing, especially on select evenings when live bands accompany the cocktails and house-made English-style ales and root beer. (Call for schedules.) *Note:* Be careful getting into the parking lot (accessible only from the northbound side of the highway); it's a quick, sandy turn.

1000 Great Hwy. (at west end of Golden Gate Park, near Fulton St.). ℂ 415/386-8439. Reservations accepted. Main courses $8–$20 lunch; $12.50–$20 dinner. MC, V. Daily 8am–5pm; Sun–Thur 5:30–10pm; Fri–Sat 5:30–11pm. Muni Metro: N. Bus: 18, 31, or 38.

Cliff House ⭐ *Finds* *Kids* SEAFOOD/CALIFORNIA   In the old days (we're talking way back), the Cliff House was the place to go for a romantic night on the town. Nowadays, the aging San Francisco landmark caters mostly to tourists who arrive by the busload to gander at the Sutro Bath remains next door.

Three restaurants in the main two-story building give diners a choice of how much they want to spend. **Phineas T. Barnacle** is the least expensive; it serves sandwiches, salads, soups, and such Hofbrau-style across from the elaborate saloon-style bar. Afterward, you can seat yourself at the window-side tables overlooking the shore, or beside the fireplace if you're chilled. A step up from the P.T.B. (literally) is **Upstairs at the Cliff House,** a slightly more formal setting that's best known for its breakfast omelets. The main room, known as the **Seafood and Beverage Co.,** is the fanciest of the lot. Refurbished to recall its glory days near the turn of the century, it offers superb ocean views, particularly at sunset, when the fog lets up; unfortunately, the food is a distant second to the scenery. Arrive before dusk, request a window seat, order a few appetizers and cocktails, and enjoy the view. Or follow my family's lead: We make the elaborate Sunday brunch served from 10am to 3pm in the newly renovated Terrace Room a much anticipated annual event.

1090 Point Lobos (at Merrie Way). ℂ 415/386-3330. Reservations recommended for upstairs and brunch only. Upstairs main courses $7–$12 breakfast; $7–$16 lunch; $15–$29 dinner. Main room main courses $9–$22 lunch; $17–$25 dinner. AE, DC, MC, V. Upstairs Mon–Fri 9am–3:30pm; Sat–Sun 8:30am–4pm; daily 5–10pm. Main room Mon–Thurs 11am–10:30pm; Fri–Sat 11am–11pm; Sun 9am–2pm and 3:30–10:30pm. Bus: 18 or 38.

Kabuto Sushi ⭐⭐ JAPANESE/SUSHI   In a town overflowing with seafood and pretentious taste buds, you'd think it would be easier than it is to find great sushi. But the truth is, finding an outstanding sushi restaurant in San Francisco is more challenging than spotting a parking space in Nob Hill. Still, chop-sticking these fish-and-rice delicacies is one of the most joyous and adventurous ways to dine, and Kabuto is one of the best (and most expensive) places to do it. Chef Sachio Kojima, who presides over the small, crowded sushi bar, constructs each dish with smooth, lightning-fast movements known only to master chefs. If you're big on wasabi, ask for the stronger stuff Kojima serves on request.

5116 Geary Blvd. (at 15th Ave.). ℂ 415/752-5652. Reservations recommended. Sushi $3–$10; main courses $11–$18. MC, V. Tues–Sat 5:30–11pm; Sun 5:30–10pm; closed Mon. Bus: 2, 28, or 38.

Khan Toke Thai House ⭐⭐ *Value* THAI   Khan Toke Thai is so traditional, you're asked to remove your shoes before being seated. Popular for special occasions, this Richmond Distinct fixture is easily the prettiest Thai restaurant in the city; lavishly carved teak interiors evoke the ambience of a Thai temple.

To start, order the *tom yam gong* soup of lemongrass, shrimp, mushroom, tomato, and cilantro. Follow with such well-flavored dishes as ground pork with

Lunching Near Golden Gate Park

Curiously (and happily), there are no restaurants other than museum cafes in Golden Gate Park, but that doesn't mean your choices are limited to the hot dog cart. The newly chic neighborhood of Inner Sunset boasts a handful of excellent moderately priced restaurants. All serve lunch and are a block outside the park along Ninth Avenue.

Bare-bones traditional **Ebisu**, 1283 Ninth Ave., between Lincoln and Irving (✆ **415/566-1770**), a neighborhood favorite for 17 years, serves some of the city's best sushi, sashimi, and other Japanese fare. The absolutely delightful **Avenue 9** ⚘, 1243 Ninth Ave. (✆ **415/664-6999**), is a colorful retro-modern setting for the creative kitchen. It cooks fabulous gourmet cheeseburgers, flat-iron steaks, insanely good fries, spinach and prawn salad, Yukon gold potato latkes with house-cured salmon, and poached eggs with hollandaise sauce. Brunch is offered on Saturday and Sunday from 11am to 3pm.

fresh ginger, green onion, peanuts, and lemon juice; prawns with hot chiles, mint leaves, lime juice, lemongrass, and onions; or chicken with cashews, crispy chiles, and onions. For a real treat, have the deep-fried pompano topped with sautéed ginger, onions, peppers, pickled garlic, and yellow-bean sauce, or deep-fried red snapper with "three-flavors" sauce and hot basil leaves. A complete dinner, including appetizer, soup, salad, two main courses, dessert, and coffee is a great value.

5937 Geary Blvd. ✆ **415/668-6654**. Reservations recommended. Main courses $6–$12; fixed-price dinner $18. AE, MC, V. Daily 5–10pm. Bus: 38.

Straits Café ⚘ SINGAPOREAN   Straits Café is what I like to call "adventure dining," because you never know quite what foods you're going to get. Burlap palm trees, pastel-painted trompe l'oeil houses, faux balconies, and clotheslines strung across the walls evoke a surreal image of a Singaporean village in the Richmond District. The cuisine, however, is the real thing. Among chef Chris Yeo's spicy Malaysian-Indian-Chinese offerings are *murtabak* (stuffed Indian bread), chili crab, basil chicken, *nonya daging rendang* (beef simmered in lime leaves), *ikan pangang* (fish stuffed with chili paste), and, hottest of all, *sambal udang* (prawns sautéed in chili-shallot sambal sauce). For dessert, try the sago pudding.

3300 Geary Blvd. (at Parker St.). ✆ **415/668-1783**. Reservations recommended. Main courses $8.25–$22. AE, DC, MC, V. Mon–Thurs 11:30am–3pm and 5–10pm; Fri–Sat 11:30am–11pm; Sun 11:30–10pm. Bus: 2, 3, 4, or 38.

INEXPENSIVE

Ton Kiang ⚘⚘⚘ *Finds* *Kids* CHINESE/DIM SUM   Ton Kiang is the number-one place in the city to do dim sum. Wait in line (which is out the door anytime between 11am and 1:30pm), get a table on the first or second floor, and get ready to say yes to dozens of delicacies, which are brought to the table for your approval. From stuffed crab claws, roast Peking duck, and a gazillion dumpling selections (including scallop and vegetable, shrimp, and beef) to the delicious and hard-to-find *doa miu* (snow pea sprouts flash-sautéed with garlic and peanut oil), shark-fin soup, and a mesmerizing mango pudding, every tray of morsels coming from the kitchen is an absolute delight. Though it's hard to get past the dim sum, which is served all day everyday, the full menu of Hakka cuisine is worth investigation as well—fresh and flavorful soups, an array of seafood, beef, and chicken, and clay pot specialties await. This is definitely one of my favorite places to do lunch, and it happens to have an unusually friendly staff.

5821 Geary Blvd. (between 22nd and 23rd aves.). ℂ 415/387-8273. Reservations accepted for parties of 8 or more. Dim sum $2–$5.50. AE, MC, V. Mon–Sat 10:30am–10pm; Sun 9am–10pm. Bus: 38.

7

Exploring San Francisco

San Francisco's parks, museums, tours, and landmarks are favorites for travelers the world over and offer an array of activities to suit every visitor. But no particular activity or place makes the city one of the most popular destinations in the world. It's San Francisco itself—its charm, its atmosphere, its perfect blend of big metropolis with small-town hospitality. No matter what you do while you're here—whether you spend all your time in central areas like Union Square or North Beach, or explore the outer neighborhoods—you're bound to collect a treasure trove of vacation memories that can only be found in this culturally rich, strikingly beautiful City by the Bay.

1 Famous San Francisco Sights

Alcatraz Island ★★★ *Finds*   Visible from Fisherman's Wharf, Alcatraz Island (a.k.a. "The Rock") has seen a checkered history. Juan Manuel Ayala discovered it in 1775 and named it after the many pelicans that nested on the island. From the 1850s to 1933, when the army vacated the island, it served as a military post, protecting the bay shoreline. In 1934, the government converted the buildings of the military outpost into a maximum-security prison. Given the sheer cliffs, treacherous tides and currents, and frigid water temperatures, it was believed to be a totally escape-proof prison. Among the famous gangsters who occupied cell blocks A through D were Al Capone, Robert Stroud, the so-called Birdman of Alcatraz (because he was an expert in ornithological diseases), Machine Gun Kelly, and Alvin Karpis. It cost a fortune to keep them imprisoned here because all supplies, including water, had to be shipped in. In 1963, after an apparent escape in which no bodies were recovered, the government closed the prison, and in 1972 it became part of the Golden Gate National Recreation Area. The wildlife that was driven away during the military and prison years has begun to return—the black-crested night heron and other seabirds are nesting here again—and a new trail passes through the island's nature areas. Tours, including an audio tour of the prison block and a slide show, are given by the park's rangers, who entertain their guests with interesting anecdotes.

Allow about 2½ hours for the round-trip and the tour. Wear comfortable shoes and take a heavy sweater or windbreaker, because even when the sun's out, it's cold. The National Park Service also notes that there are a lot of hills to climb on the tour. It's a popular excursion and space is limited, so purchase tickets as far in advance as possible. **Blue & Gold Fleet** (*C* **415/705-5555;** www.blueandgold fleet.com) operates the tour; they accept American Express, MasterCard, and Visa, and there's a $2.25 per ticket service charge on phone orders. You can also buy tickets in advance from the Blue & Gold ticket office on Pier 41.

For those who want to get a closer look at Alcatraz without going ashore, two boat-tour operators offer short circumnavigations of the island (see "Self-Guided & Organized Tours," below, for complete information).

Major San Francisco Sights

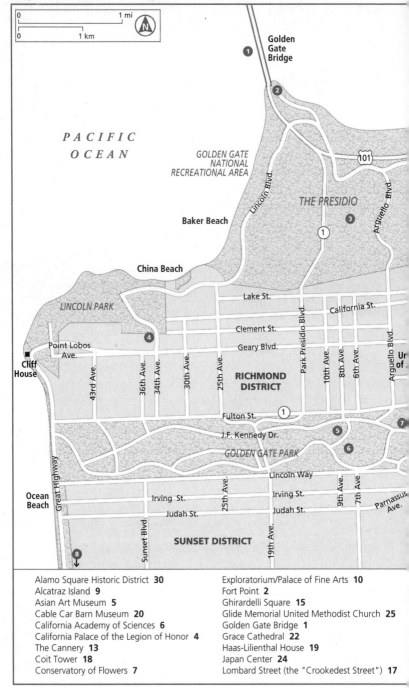

Alamo Square Historic District **30**
Alcatraz Island **9**
Asian Art Museum **5**
Cable Car Barn Museum **20**
California Academy of Sciences **6**
California Palace of the Legion of Honor **4**
The Cannery **13**
Coit Tower **18**
Conservatory of Flowers **7**

Exploratorium/Palace of Fine Arts **10**
Fort Point **2**
Ghirardelli Square **15**
Glide Memorial United Methodist Church **25**
Golden Gate Bridge **1**
Grace Cathedral **22**
Haas-Lilienthal House **19**
Japan Center **24**
Lombard Street (the "Crookedest Street") **17**

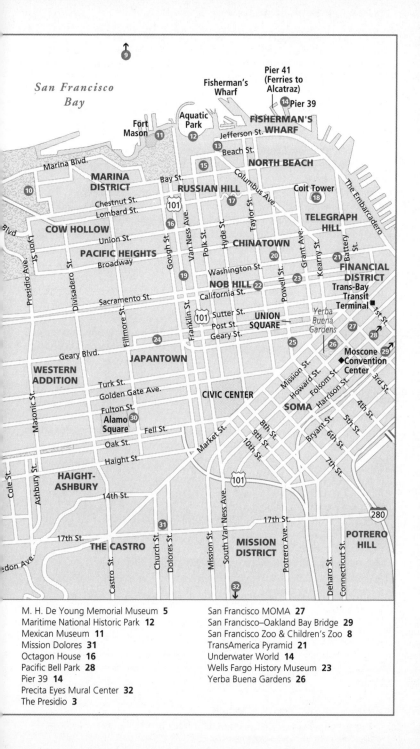

San Francisco Bay

↑
9

San Francisco
Bay

10

Fort
Mason **11**

Aquatic
Park **12**

Fisherman's
Wharf

Pier 41
(Ferries to
Alcatraz)

14 Pier 39

**FISHERMAN'S
WHARF**

Jefferson St.

13 Beach St.

15

Marina Blvd.

**MARINA
DISTRICT**

Bay St.

RUSSIAN HILL

Columbus Ave.

NORTH BEACH

Coit Tower **18**

The Embarcadero

Chestnut St.

Lombard St.

101

16

17

COW HOLLOW

Union St.

PACIFIC HEIGHTS

Broadway

Lyon St.

Presidio Ave.

Divisadero St.

Gough St.

Van Ness Ave.

Polk St.

Hyde St.

Taylor St.

CHINATOWN

20

Grant Ave.

Kearny St.

Battery St.

**TELEGRAPH
HILL**

21

**FINANCIAL
DISTRICT**

Washington St.

19

NOB HILL **22**

California St.

Powell St.

23

Trans-Bay
Transit
Terminal ■

Sacramento St.

Fillmore St.

Franklin St.

101

Sutter St.

Post St.

Geary St.

**UNION
SQUARE**

25

*Yerba
Buena
Gardens*

26

27

1st St.

28

24

Geary Blvd.

JAPANTOWN

**WESTERN
ADDITION**

Masonic St.

Turk St.

Golden Gate Ave.

Fulton St.

Alamo
Square **30**

Fell St.

Oak St.

Haight St.

CIVIC CENTER

Market St.

8th St.

9th St.

10th St.

Mission St.

Howard St.

Folsom St.

Harrison St.

Bryant St.

SOMA

4th St.

5th St.

6th St.

7th St.

3rd St.

♦ Moscone
Convention
Center **29**

**HAIGHT-
ASHBURY**

Cole St.

Ashbury St.

14th St.

101

17th St.

31

THE CASTRO

Castro St.

Church St.

Dolores St.

Mission St.

South Van Ness Ave.

17th St.

**MISSION
DISTRICT**

32

Potrero Ave.

Deharo St.

Connecticut St.

280

**POTRERO
HILL**

edon Ave.

M. H. De Young Memorial Museum **5**
Maritime National Historic Park **12**
Mexican Museum **11**
Mission Dolores **31**
Octagon House **16**
Pacific Bell Park **28**
Pier 39 **14**
Precita Eyes Mural Center **32**
The Presidio **3**

San Francisco MOMA **27**
San Francisco–Oakland Bay Bridge **29**
San Francisco Zoo & Children's Zoo **8**
TransAmerica Pyramid **21**
Underwater World **14**
Wells Fargo History Museum **23**
Yerba Buena Gardens **26**

Pier 41, near Fisherman's Wharf. ℂ 415/773-1188 (info only). Admission (includes ferry trip and audio tour) $13.25 adults with headset, $9.25 without; $11.50 seniors 62 and older with headset, $7.50 without; $8 children 5–11 with headset, $6 without. Winter daily 9:30am–2:15pm; summer daily 9:15am–4:15pm. Advance purchase advised; evening tours are available; call for information. Ferries depart at 15 and 45 min. after the hour. Arrive at least 20 min. before sailing time.

Fisherman's Wharf *(Overrated*   Few cities in America are as adept at wholesaling their historical sites as San Francisco, which has converted Fisherman's Wharf into one of the most popular tourist attractions in the world. Unless you come really early in the morning, you won't find any traces of the traditional waterfront life that once existed here; the only fishing going on around here is for tourists' dollars.

Originally called Meigg's Wharf, this bustling strip of waterfront got its present moniker from generations of fishers who used to base their boats here. Today, the bay has become so polluted with toxins that bright yellow placards warn against eating fish from the waters. A small fleet of fewer than 30 boats still operates from here, but basically Fisherman's Wharf has been converted into one long shopping mall that stretches from Ghirardelli Square at the west end to Pier 39 at the east.

Accommodating a total of 350 boats, two marinas flank Pier 39 and house the **Blue & Gold bay sightseeing fleet.** In recent years, some 600 California **sea lions** have taken up residence on the adjacent floating docks. Until they abandon their new playground, which seems more and more unlikely, these playful, noisy creatures (some nights you can hear them all the way from Washington Square) create one of the best free attractions on the wharf. Docent-led programs, offered at Pier 39 on weekends from 11am to 5pm, teach visitors about the range, habitat, and adaptability of the California sea lion.

Some people love Fisherman's Wharf, others can't get far enough away from it, but most agree that Fisherman's Wharf, for better or for worse, has to be seen at least once in your life.

To reach the area by cable car, take the Powell-Mason line to the last stop and walk to the wharf; by bus, take no. 15, 30, 32, 39, 42, or 82X of the F-line. If you're arriving by car, park on adjacent streets or on the wharf between Taylor and Jones streets.

Ghirardelli Square ⭐   Ghirardelli Square dates from 1864, when it served as a factory making Civil War uniforms. It's best known as the former chocolate and spice factory of Domingo Ghirardelli (pronounced "Gear-a-deli"). The factory has been converted into a 10-level mall containing 50-plus stores and 11 dining establishments. Scheduled street performers entertain regularly in the West Plaza. Incidentally, the Ghirardelli Chocolate Company still makes chocolate, but its factory is in a lower-rent district in the East Bay.

900 North Point St. (between Polk and Larkin sts.). ℂ **415/775-5500.** Stores generally open 10am–9pm in the summer and until 6 or 7pm in the winter.

Pier 39 *(Overrated*   Pier 39 is a 4½-acre, multilevel waterfront complex a few blocks east of Fisherman's Wharf. Constructed on an abandoned cargo pier, it is, ostensibly, a re-creation of a turn-of-the-century street scene, but don't expect a slice of old-time maritime life. This is the busiest mall of the lot and, according to the *London Observer,* the third most visited attraction in the world, behind Disney World and Disneyland. It has more than 100 stores, 10 bay-view restaurants, a two-tiered Venetian carousel, and a big-screen Cinemax Theater showing the *Great San Francisco Adventure.*

On the waterfront at the Embarcadero and Beach St. ℂ **415/705-5500.** Shops open daily 10:30am–8:30pm, with extended weekend hours during the summer.

(Kids) Funky Favorites at Fisherman's Wharf

The following sights clustered on or near Fisherman's Wharf are great fun for kids and the kid in adults. To reach the area by cable car, take the Powell-Mason line to the last stop and walk to the wharf; by bus, take no. 15, 30, 32, 39, 42, or 82X. If you're arriving by car, park on adjacent streets or on the wharf between Taylor and Jones streets.

The popular battle-scarred World War II fleet submarine **USS Pampanito,** Pier 45, Fisherman's Wharf (© **415/775-1943**), saw plenty of action in the Pacific. It has been completely restored, and visitors are free to crawl around inside. Admission includes an audio tour. It runs $7 for adults 13 to 61, $4 for children 6 to 12, $5 for seniors, and free for children under 6; the family pass (two adults, up to four kids) costs $20. The *Pampanito* is open Monday through Thursday 9am to 8 pm, Friday through Sunday 9 am to 8 pm.

Ripley's Believe It or Not! Museum, 175 Jefferson St. (© **415/771-6188;** www.ripleysf.com), has drawn curious spectators through its doors for over 30 years. Inside, you'll experience the extraordinary world of improbabilities: a one-third-scale matchstick cable car, a shrunken human torso once owned by Ernest Hemingway, a dinosaur made from car bumpers, a walk through a kaleidoscope tunnel, and video displays and illusions. Robert LeRoy Ripley's infamous arsenal may lead you to ponder whether truth is, in fact, stranger than fiction. Admission is $9.95 for adults, $7.50 for seniors over 60, $6.95 for children 5 to 12, free for children under 5. Open every day of the year, Sunday to Thursday 10 am to 10 pm, until midnight on Friday and Saturday.

Conceived and executed in the Madame Tussaud mold, San Francisco's **Wax Museum,** 145 Jefferson St. (© **415/202-0400**), has long been a kitschy harborside tourist trap. In 1999, with the closing of the adjoining Haunted Goldmine, the museum underwent a $15-million tear-down, renovation, and expansion. It opened in June 2000 as a huge complex that includes Rainforest Café with walk-through aquariums. (Not any less of a tourist trap, mind you—only a newer, slicker one.) The overhaul spiffed up the museum's 280 life-like figures, including singer Michael Jackson, Marilyn Monroe, John Wayne, former president George Bush, and "Feared Leaders," such as Fidel Castro. The Chamber of Horrors, which features Dracula, Frankenstein, and a werewolf, along with bloody victims hanging from meat hooks, will reopen. But the clinchers will be the addition of pop icons such as Leonardo DiCaprio and Will Smith. Admission is $12.95 for adults, $10.55 for seniors 62 and older, $6.95 for children 5 to 17 years, and free for children under 5. Discount group rates are available and are arranged via telephone call or the website, **www.waxmuseum.com**.

Aquarium of the Bay   The latest major addition to Fisherman's Wharf is Aquarium of the Bay, a $38 million, 707,000-gallon marine attraction filled with sharks, stingrays, and more. A moving footpath transports visitors through clear acrylic tunnels.

Embarcadero at Beach St. © **415-623-5328**. www.aquariumofthebay.com. Aquarium admission $12.95 adults, $6.50 seniors and children 3–17, free for children under 3. A family of 2 adults and 2 children can purchase a family package for $29.95. A behind-the-scenes tour is available for $25 per person, including admission to the aquarium.

Cable Cars ★★★ *Moments*   Although they may not be San Francisco's most practical means of transportation, cable cars are certainly the best loved and are a must-experience when visiting the city. Designated official historic landmarks by the National Park Service in 1964, they clank up and down the city's steep hills like mobile museum pieces, tirelessly hauling thousands of tourists each day to nowhere in particular.

London-born engineer Andrew Hallidie invented San Francisco's cable cars in 1869. He got the idea by way of serendipity. As the story goes, Hallidie was watching a team of overworked horses haul a heavily laden carriage up a steep San Francisco slope. As he watched, one horse slipped and the car rolled back, dragging the other tired beasts with it. At that moment Hallidie resolved that he would invent a mechanical contraption to replace such horses, and just 4 years later, in 1873, the first cable car made its maiden run from the top of Clay Street. Promptly ridiculed as "Hallidie's Folly," the cars were slow to gain acceptance. One early onlooker voiced the general opinion by exclaiming, "I don't believe it—the damned thing works!"

Even today, many visitors have difficulty believing that these vehicles, which have no engines, actually work. The cars, each weighing about 6 tons, run along a steel cable, enclosed under the street in a center rail. You can't see the cable unless you peer straight down into the crack, but you'll hear its characteristic clickity-clanking sound whenever you're nearby. The cars move when the gripper (not the driver) pulls back a lever that closes a pincerlike "grip" on the cable. The speed of the car, therefore, is determined by the speed of the cable, which is a constant 9½ miles per hour—never more, never less.

The two types of cable cars in use hold a maximum of 90 and 100 passengers, and the limits are rigidly enforced. The best views are from the outer running boards, where you have to hold on tightly when taking curves. Everyone, it seems, prefers to ride on the running boards.

Hallidie's cable cars have been imitated and used throughout the world, but all have been replaced by more efficient means of transportation. San Francisco planned to do so, too, but the proposal met with so much opposition that the cable cars' perpetuation was actually written into the city charter in 1955. The mandate cannot be revoked without the approval of a majority of the city's voters—a distant and doubtful prospect.

San Francisco's three existing lines form the world's only surviving system of cable cars, which you can experience for yourself should you choose to wait in the endless boarding line (up to a 2-hour wait in summer). For more information on riding them, see "Getting Around" in chapter 4.

Powell-Hyde and Powell-Mason lines begin at the base of Powell and Market sts.; California St. line begins at the foot of Market St. $2 per ride.

The Cannery ★   The Cannery was built in 1894 as a fruit-canning plant and converted into a mall in the 1960s. It contains 50-plus shops, a paint-it-yourself ceramic studio, a comedy club, and several restaurants and galleries, including **Jack's Cannery Bar** (© **415/931-6400**), which features 110 beers on tap (the most anywhere in the country). Vendors' stalls and sidewalk cafes occupy the

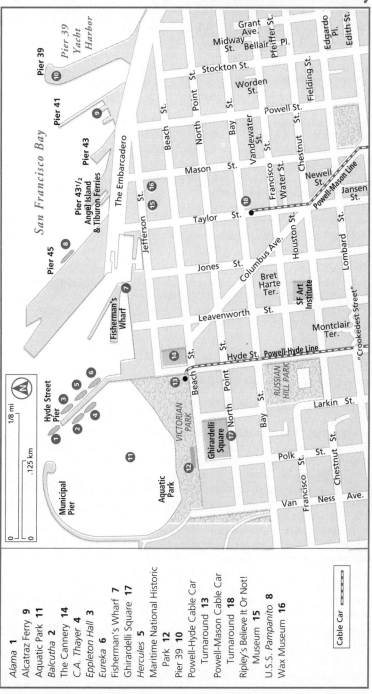

Fisherman's Wharf & Vicinity

San Francisco Bay

Pier 39 Yacht Harbor

Pier 39

Pier 41

Pier 43

Pier 43½
Angel Island
& Tiburon Ferries

Pier 45

The Embarcadero

Fisherman's Wharf

Grant Ave.
Midway St.
Bellair Pl.
Pfeiffer St.
Edgardo Pl.
Edith St.

Stockton St.
Worden St.
Fielding St.

Powell St.
Beach St.
North Point St.
Bay St.
Vandewater St.
Chestnut St.
Newell St.
Jansen St.
Powell-Mason Line

Mason St.
Francisco St.
Water St.

Taylor St.
Houston St.

Columbus Ave.
Jones St.
Bret Harte Ter.
SF Art Institute
Lombard St.

Jefferson St.

Leavenworth St.
Montclair Ter.
"Crookedest Street"

Hyde St. Powell-Hyde Line

Beach St.
North Point St.
RUSSIAN HILL PARK

Hyde Street Pier

VICTORIAN PARK

Municipal Pier

Aquatic Park

Ghirardelli Square

Larkin St.

North Point St.

Bay St.

Polk St.

Chestnut St.

Francisco St.

Van Ness Ave.

1/8 mi

.125 km

N

Alama **1**
Alcatraz Ferry **9**
Aquatic Park **11**
Balcutha **2**
The Cannery **14**
C.A. Thayer **4**
Eppleton Hall **3**
Eureka **6**
Fisherman's Wharf **7**
Ghirardelli Square **17**
Hercules **5**
Maritime National Historic Park **12**
Pier 39 **10**
Powell-Hyde Cable Car Turnaround **13**
Powell-Mason Cable Car Turnaround **18**
Ripley's Believe It Or Not! Museum **15**
U.S.S. Pampanito **8**
Wax Museum **16**

Cable Car

155

courtyard amid a grove of century-old olive trees, and on summer weekends, street performers are out in force, entertaining tourists.

2801 Leavenworth St. (between Beach and Jefferson sts.). © 415/771-3112. www.thecannery.com.

Coit Tower ★★ In a city known for its great views and vantage points, Coit Tower is tops. Located atop Telegraph Hill, just east of North Beach, the round, stone tower offers panoramic views of the city and the bay.

Completed in 1933, the tower is the legacy of Lillie Hitchcock Coit, a wealthy eccentric who left San Francisco a $125,000 bequest "for the purpose of adding beauty to the city I have always loved" and as a memorial to its volunteer firemen. She had been saved from a fire as a child and held the city's firefighters in particularly high esteem.

Inside the base of the tower are impressive **murals** titled *Life in California,* and *1934,* which were completed under the WPA during the New Deal. They are the work of more than 25 artists, many of whom had studied under Mexican muralist Diego Rivera.

Telegraph Hill. © 415/362-0808. Admission to the top $3.75 adults, $2.50 seniors, $1.50 children 6–12. Daily 10am–6pm. Bus: 39 ("Coit").

Farmers' Market ★★ Every Saturday from 8am to 1:30pm, northern California fruit, vegetable, bread, and dairy vendors join local restaurateurs in selling fresh, delicious edibles to throngs of resident chefs, gourmands, and tourists. There's no better way to enjoy a bright San Francisco morning than strolling this gourmet street market and snacking your way through breakfast. You can also pick up locally made vinegars and oils—they make wonderful gifts. There's another market every Tuesday at Justin Herman Plaza (Market Street and Embarcadero) from 10:30am to 2:30pm.

Embarcadero, at Green St. © 415/353-5650. Saturday 8am–1:30pm.

Golden Gate Bridge ★★★ The year 2001 marked the 65th birthday of possibly the most beautiful, and certainly the most photographed, bridge in the world. Often half-veiled by the city's trademark rolling fog, San Francisco's Golden Gate Bridge spans tidal currents, ocean waves, and battering winds to connect the City by the Bay with the Redwood Empire to the north.

With its gracefully swung single span, spidery bracing cables, and zooming twin towers, the bridge looks more like a work of abstract art than one of the 20th century's greatest practical engineering feats. Construction began in May 1937 and was completed at the then-colossal cost of $35 million.

The mile-long steel link (longer if you factor in the approach), which reaches a height of 746 feet above the water, is an awesome bridge to cross. Traffic usually moves quickly, so crossing by car won't give you too much time to see the sights. If you drive from the city, park in the lot at the foot of the bridge on the city side and make the crossing by foot. Back in your car, continue to Marin's Vista Point, at the bridge's northern end. Look back, and you'll be rewarded with one of the greatest views of San Francisco.

Millions of pedestrians walk or bike across each year, gazing up at the tall red towers, out at the vistas of San Francisco and Marin County, and down into the stacks of oceangoing liners. You can walk out onto the span from either end, but be prepared—it's usually windy and cold, and the bridge vibrates. Still, walking even a short distance is one of the best ways to experience the immense scale of the structure.

Highway 101 North. www.goldengatebridge.org. $3 toll collected when driving south. Bridge-bound Golden Gate Transit buses (𝄐 **415/923-2000**) depart every 30 to 60 min. during the day for Marin County, starting from the Transbay Terminal (Mission and First sts.) and stopping at Market and Seventh sts., at the Civic Center, and along Van Ness Ave. and Lombard St.

Lombard Street ★ *Overrated*   Known (erroneously) as the "crookedest street in the world," this whimsically winding block of Lombard Street draws thousands of visitors each year (much to the chagrin of neighborhood residents, most of whom would prefer to block off the street to tourists). The angle of the street is so steep that the road has to snake back and forth to make a descent possible. The brick-lined street zigzags around the residences' bright flower gardens, which explode with color during warmer months. This short stretch of Lombard Street is one way, downhill, and fun to drive. Take the curves slowly and in low gear, and expect a wait during the weekend. Save your film for the bottom, where, if you're lucky, you can find a parking space and take a few snapshots of the silly spectacle. You can also take staircases (without curves) up or down on either side of the street. In truth, most locals don't understand what the fuss is all about. I'm guessing the draw is the combination of a classic unusually steep San Francisco street and a great photo op.

Between Hyde and Leavenworth sts.

2 Museums

For information on museums in Golden Gate Park, see "Golden Gate Park," later in this chapter.

Cable Car Barn Museum *Value*   If you've ever wondered how cable cars work, this nifty museum explains (and demonstrates!) it all. Yes, this is a museum, but the Cable Car Barn is no stuffed shirt. It's the living powerhouse, repair shop, and storage place of the cable-car system and is in full operation. Built for the Ferries and Cliff House Railway in 1887, the building underwent an $18 million reconstruction to restore its original gaslight-era look, install an amazing spectators' gallery, and add a museum of San Francisco transit history.

The exposed machinery, which pulls the cables under San Francisco's streets, looks like a Rube Goldberg invention. Stand in the mezzanine gallery and become mesmerized by the massive groaning and vibrating winches as they thread the cable that hauls the cars through a huge figure-eight and back into the system using slack-absorbing tension wheels. For a better view, move to the lower-level viewing room, where you can see the massive pulleys and gears operating underground.

Also on display here is one of the first grip cars developed by Andrew S. Hallidie, operated for the first time on Clay Street on August 2, 1873. Other displays include an antique grip car and trailer that operated on Pacific Avenue until 1929, and dozens of exact-scale models of cars used on the various city lines. There's also a shop where you can buy a variety of cable-car gifts. You can see the whole museum in about 45 minutes.

Washington and Mason sts. 𝄐 **415/474-1887**. Free admission. Apr–Oct daily 10am–6pm; Nov–Mar daily 10am–5pm. Cable car: Both Powell St. lines.

California Palace of the Legion of Honor ★★   Designed as a memorial to California's World War I casualties, the neoclassical structure is an exact replica of the Legion of Honor Palace in Paris, right down to the inscription HONNEUR ET PATRIE above the portal.

The Legion of Honor reopened in late 1995, after a 2-year, $34.6 million renovation and seismic upgrading that was stalled by the discovery of almost 300 turn-of-the-century coffins. The exterior's grassy expanses, cliff-side paths, and incredible view of the Golden Gate make this an absolute must-visit attraction before you even get in the door. But the inside is equally impressive. The museum's permanent collection covers 4,000 years of art and includes paintings, sculpture, and decorative arts from Europe, as well as international tapestries, prints, and drawings. The chronological display of more than 800 years of European art includes one of the world's finest collections of Rodin's sculptures. Plan to spend 2 or 3 hours here.

In Lincoln Park (34th Ave. and Clement St.). ℂ **415/750-3600** or 415/863-3330 (recorded information). Admission (including the Asian Art Museum and M. H. De Young Memorial Museum) $8 adults, $6 seniors 65 and over, $5 youths 12–17, free for children under 12. Fees may be higher for special exhibitions. Free to all second Wed. of each month (9:30am–8:45pm). Tues–Sun 9:30am–5pm. Bus: 18 or 38.

The Exploratorium ✯ (Kids) *Scientific American* magazine rated the Exploratorium as "the best science museum in the world"—pretty heady stuff for this exciting hands-on science fair. It contains more than 650 permanent exhibits that explore everything from giant bubble blowing to Einstein's theory of relativity. It's like a mad scientist's penny arcade, an educational fun house, and an experimental laboratory, all rolled into one. Touch a tornado, shape a glowing electrical current, finger-paint using a computer, or take a sensory journey in total darkness in the Tactile Dome—you could spend all day here and still not see everything. Every exhibit at the Exploratorium is designed to be interactive, educational, safe, and, most important, fun. And don't think it's just for kids; parents inevitably end up being the most reluctant to leave. On the way out, be sure to stop in the wonderful gift store, which is chock-full of affordable brain candy.

The museum is in the Marina District at the beautiful **Palace of Fine Arts** ✯, the only building left standing from the Panama-Pacific Exposition of 1915. The adjoining park and lagoon—the perfect place for an afternoon picnic—is home to ducks, swans, seagulls, and grouchy geese, so bring bread.

3601 Lyon St., in the Palace of Fine Arts (at Marina Blvd.). ℂ **415/563-7337** or 415/561-0360 (recorded information). www.exploratorium.edu. Admission $9 adults, $7 seniors and college students with ID, $5 children 6–17, $2.50 children 3–5, free for children under 3. Free to all first Wed. of each month. AE, MC, V. Summer (Memorial Day–Labor Day) and holidays, Mon–Tues and Thurs–Sun 10am–6pm; Wed 10am–9pm. Rest of the year Tues and Thurs–Sun 10am–5pm; Wed 10am–9pm. Closed Thanksgiving, Dec 25. Free parking. Bus: 30 from Stockton St. to the Marina stop.

Haas-Lilienthal House Of the city's many gingerbread Victorians, this handsome Queen Anne house is one of the most flamboyant. The 1886 structure features all the architectural frills of the period, including dormer windows, flying cupolas, ornate trim, and winsome turrets. The elaborately styled house is now a museum, its rooms fully furnished with period pieces. The Foundation for San Francisco's Architectural Heritage maintains the house and offers docent-led tours. The 1-hour tours (the only way to see the house) start every 20 to 30 minutes. A new Costume Exhibit features such themes as Ragtime-era costumes, artifacts, and accessories.

2007 Franklin St. (at Washington St.). ℂ **415/441-3004.** Guided tour $5 adults, $3 seniors and children 6–12. Wed noon–3pm; Sun 11am–4pm. Cable car: California St. line. Bus: 1, 12, 19, 27, 42, 47, 49, or 83.

Octagon House This unusual, eight-sided, cupola-topped house of interest to architecture buffs dates from 1861 and is maintained by the National Society of Colonial Dames of America. The architectural features are extraordinary, and from the second floor it is possible to look up into the cupola, which is illuminated at night. In the small museum, you'll find Early American furniture, portraits, silver, pewter, looking glasses, and English and Chinese ceramics. There are also some historic documents, including signatures of 54 of the 56 signers of the Declaration of Independence. Even if you're not able to visit the inside, this strange structure is worth a look.

2645 Gough St. (at Union St.). ℭ 415/441-7512. Free admission; donation suggested. Feb–Dec second Sun and second and second and fourth Thurs of each month noon–3pm. Closed Jan and holidays. Bus: 41 or 45.

San Francisco Maritime National Historical Park   Shaped like an Art Deco ship, the Maritime Museum is filled with sailing, whaling, and fishing lore. Remarkably good exhibits include intricate model craft and scrimshaw. The collection of shipwreck photographs and historic marine scenes includes an 1851 snapshot of hundreds of abandoned ships, deserted en masse by crews dashing off to participate in the gold rush. Beautifully carved, brightly painted wooden figureheads from old windjammers line the walls. Two blocks east, at the park's Hyde Street Pier, are several historic ships, now moored and open to the public.

The *Balclutha,* one of the last surviving square-riggers and the handsomest vessel in San Francisco Bay, was built in Glasgow, Scotland, in 1886 and used to carry grain from California at a near-record speed of 300 miles a day. The ship is now completely restored. Kids can climb into the bunking quarters, visit the "slop chest" ("galley" to you, matey), and read the sea chanteys (clean ones only) that decorate the walls.

The 1890 *Eureka* still carries a cargo of nostalgia for San Franciscans. It was the last of 50 paddle-wheel ferries that regularly plied the bay; it made its final trip in 1957. Restored to its original splendor at the height of the ferryboat era, the side-wheeler is loaded with deck cargo, including antique cars and trucks.

The black-hulled, three-masted *C.A. Thayer,* built in 1895, was crafted for the lumber trade and carried logs felled in the Pacific Northwest to the carpentry shops of California.

Other historic ships docked here include the tiny two-masted *Alma,* one of the last scow schooners to bring hay to the horses of San Francisco; the *Hercules,* a huge 1907 oceangoing steam tug; and the *Eppleton Hall,* a side-wheel tugboat built in England in 1914 to operate on London's River Thames.

At the pier's small-boat shop, visitors can follow the restoration progress of historic boats from the museum's collection. It's behind the maritime bookstore on your right as you approach the ships.

At the foot of Polk St. (near Fisherman's Wharf). ℭ 415/556-3002. Museum free; ships $5 adults, $2 seniors over 62 and youths 12–17, free for children under 12. Museum daily 10am–5pm. Ships on Hyde St. Pier May 15–Sept 15 daily 9:30am–5:30pm; Sept 16–May 14 daily 9:30am–5pm. Closed Jan 1, Thanksgiving, Dec 25. Cable car: Powell-Hyde St. line to the last stop. Bus: 19, 30, 32, 42, or 47.

San Francisco Museum of Modern Art (MOMA) ✯   Swiss architect Mario Botta, in association with Hellmuth, Obata, and Kassabaum, designed the $62 million museum, which has made SoMa one of the more popular areas to visit, for tourists and residents alike. The museum's collection consists of more than 15,000 works, including close to 5,000 paintings and sculptures by artists such as Henri Matisse, Jackson Pollock, and Willem de Kooning. Other artists represented include Diego Rivera, Georgia O'Keeffe, Paul Klee, the Fauvists, and exceptional holdings of Richard Diebenkorn. MOMA was also one of the first to recognize photography as a major art form; its extensive collection includes more than 9,000 photographs by such notables as Ansel Adams, Alfred Stieglitz, Edward Weston, and Henri Cartier-Bresson. Not surprisingly considering its surroundings, media arts and architecture and design are also celebrated. Docent-led tours take place daily. Times are posted at the admission desk. Phone for current details of upcoming special events or check MOMA's website.

The **CaffèMuseo,** to the right of the museum entrance, sets a new precedent for museum food, with flavorful and fresh soups, sandwiches, and salads as respectable as those served in many local restaurants.

No matter what, don't miss the **MuseumStore,** which carries a wonderful array of architectural gifts, books, and trinkets. It's one of the best shops in town.

151 Third St. (2 blocks south of Market St., across from Yerba Buena Gardens). ℂ 415/357-4000. www. sfmoma.org. Admission $9 adults, $6 seniors, $5 students over 12 with ID, free for children 12 and under. Half-price for all Thurs 6–9pm; free to all first Tues of each month. Thurs 10am–9pm; Fri–Tues 10am–6pm. Closed Wed and major holidays. Muni Metro: J, K, L, or M to Montgomery Station. Bus: 15, 30, or 45.

Wells Fargo History Museum

Wells Fargo, one of California's largest banks, got its start in the Wild West. Its history museum, at the bank's head office, houses hundreds of genuine relics from the company's whip-and-six-shooter days, including pistols, photographs, early banking articles, posters, and mining equipment.

420 Montgomery St. (at California St.). ℂ 415/396-2619. Free admission. Mon–Fri 9am–5pm. Closed bank holidays. Muni Metro: Montgomery St. Bus: Any to Market St. Cable car: California St. line.

Yerba Buena Center for the Arts/Yerba Buena Gardens ★★ Finds Kids

The Yerba Buena Center, which opened in 1993, is the city's cultural facility, similar to New York's Lincoln Center but far more fun on the outside. It stands on top of the northern extension of the underground Moscone Convention Center. The center's two buildings present music, theater, dance, and visual arts. James Stewart Polshek designed the 755-seat theater, and Fumihiko Maki designed by the Galleries and Arts Forum, which features three galleries and a space designed especially for dance.

Cutting-edge computer art, multimedia shows, traditional exhibitions, and performances occupy the center's high-tech galleries. A recent exhibition, "Surf Trip: Surf Culture Art and Artifacts," featured a colorful look at the sport and the most influential surf films, including *The Endless Summer* and *Free Ride.*

The 5-acre **Yerba Buena Gardens** is a great place to relax in the grass on a sunny day and check out several artworks. The most dramatic outdoor piece is an emotional mixed-media memorial to Martin Luther King, Jr. Created by sculptor Houston Conwill, poet Estella Majozo, and architect Joseph de Pace, it features 12 panels, each inscribed with quotations from King, sheltered behind a 50-foot-high waterfall.

In the Children's Center, **Zeum** (ℂ 415/777-2800), includes a cafe, interactive cultural center, ice-skating rink, fabulous 1906 carousel, and interactive play and learning garden. Sony's new **Metreon Entertainment Center** (ℂ 415/ 537-3400) is a 350,000-square-foot complex housing movie theaters, an IMAX Theatre, great fast-food and more formal restaurants (**Montage;** ℂ 415/ 369-6111 is your best bet), interactive attractions (including one that features Maurice Sendak's *Where the Wild Things Are*), and shops. Also in the Yerba Buena Center are a bowling alley, child-care center, and ice-skating rink. As part of the plan to develop this area as the city's cultural hub, the **California Historical Society** opened at 678 Mission St. in 1995, and the **Mexican Museum** is relocating in the area in late 2001.

Yerba Buena Gardens

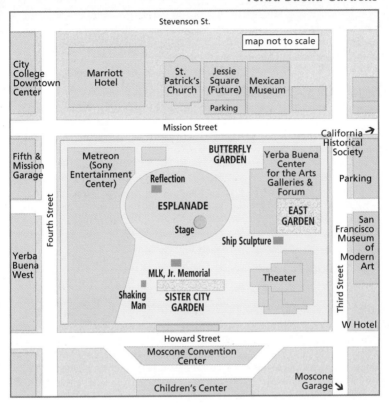

701 Mission St. ℂ **415/978-2700** or 415/978-ARTS (box office). www.yerbabuenaarts.org. Admission $6 adults, $3 seniors and students. Free to all first Thurs of each month 5–8pm. Tues–Wed and Sat–Sun 11am–6pm; Thurs–Fri 11am–8pm. Muni Metro: Powell or Montgomery. Bus: 30, 45, or 9X.

3 Neighborhoods Worth a Visit

To really get to know San Francisco, break out of the downtown and Fisherman's Wharf areas to explore the ethnically and culturally diverse neighborhoods. Walk the streets, browse the shops, grab a bite at a local restaurant—you'll find that San Francisco's beauty and charm is around every corner, not just at the popular tourist destinations.

Note: For information on Fisherman's Wharf, see "Famous San Francisco Sights," earlier in this chapter. For information on other San Francisco neighborhoods and districts that aren't discussed here, see "Neighborhoods in Brief" in chapter 4.

NOB HILL

When the cable car started operating in 1873, this hill became the city's exclusive residential area. The "Big Four" and the "Comstock Bonanza kings" built their mansions here, but they were all destroyed by the earthquake and fire in 1906. The only two surviving buildings were the Flood Mansion, which serves today as the **Pacific Union Club,** and the **Fairmont Hotel,** which was under construction when the earthquake struck. Today the burned-out sites of former mansions hold the city's luxury hotels—the **Mark Hopkins,** the **Stanford Court,** the **Fairmont,** and the **Huntington**—as well as spectacular **Grace Cathedral,** which stands on the Crocker mansion site. Nob Hill is worth a visit if only to stroll around **Huntington Park,** attend a Sunday service at the cathedral, or ooh and aah your way around the Fairmont's spectacular lobby.

SOUTH OF MARKET (SOMA)

From Market Street to Townsend and the Embarcadero to Division Street, SoMa has become the city's newest cultural and multimedia center. The process started when alternative clubs began opening in the old warehouses in the area nearly a decade ago. A wave of entrepreneurs followed, seeking to start new businesses in what was once an extremely low-rent area compared to the neighboring Financial District. Today, gentrification and high rents hold sway, spurred by a building boom that started with the **Moscone Convention Center** and continued with the **Center for the Arts at Yerba Buena Gardens** and the **San Francisco Museum of Modern Art.** Other institutions, businesses, and museums move into the area on an ongoing basis. A substantial portion of the city's nightlife takes place in warehouse spaces throughout the district.

NORTH BEACH 𝒜𝒜𝒜

In the late 1800s, an enormous influx of Italian immigrants to North Beach firmly established this aromatic area as San Francisco's "Little Italy." Dozens of Italian restaurants and coffeehouses continue to flourish in what is still the center of the city's Italian community. Walk down **Columbus Avenue** on any given morning, and you're bound to be bombarded with the wonderful aromas of roasting coffee and savory pasta sauces. Although there are some interesting shops and bookstores in the area, it's the dozens of eclectic little cafes, delis, bakeries, and coffee shops that give North Beach its Italian-bohemian character.

For a proper perspective, follow the detailed walking tour in chapter 8 or sign up for a guided Javawalk with coffee nut Elaine Sosa (see "Walking Tours," later in this chapter).

CHINATOWN 𝒜𝒜

The first of the Chinese emigrants came to San Francisco in the early 1800s to work as servants. By 1851, 25,000 Chinese people were working in California, and most had settled in San Francisco's Chinatown. Fleeing famine and the Opium Wars, they had come seeking the promise of good fortune in the "Gold Mountain" of California, hoping to return with wealth to their families in China. For the majority, the reality of life in California did not live up to the promise. First employed as workers in the gold mines during the gold rush, they later built the railroads, working as little more than slaves and facing constant prejudice. Yet the community, segregated in the Chinatown ghetto, thrived. Growing prejudice led to the Chinese Exclusion Act of 1882, which halted all Chinese immigration for 10 years and severely limited it thereafter; the Chinese Exclusion Act was not repealed until 1943. Chinese people were also denied the opportunity to buy homes outside the Chinatown ghetto until the 1950s.

Today, San Francisco has the second-largest community of Chinese people in the United States (about 33% of the city's population is Chinese). More than 80,000 people live in Chinatown, but the majority of Chinese people have moved out into newer areas like the Richmond and Sunset districts. Although frequented by tourists, the area continues to cater to Chinese shoppers, who crowd the vegetable and herb markets, restaurants, and shops. Tradition runs deep here, and if you're lucky, through an open window you might hear women mixing mah-jongg tiles as they play the centuries-old game.

The gateway at Grant Avenue and Bush Street marks the entry to Chinatown. The heart of the neighborhood is at Portsmouth Square, where you'll find locals playing board games (often gambling) or just sitting quietly.

On Waverly Place, a street where the Chinese celebratory colors of red, yellow, and green are much in evidence, you'll find three **temples:** Jeng Sen at no. 146, Tien Hou at no. 125, and Norras at no. 109.

A block west of Grant Avenue, **Stockton Street** from 1000 to 1200 is the community's main shopping street, lined with grocers, fishmongers, tea sellers, herbalists, noodle parlors, and restaurants. Here, too, is the Kon Chow Temple, at no. 855, above the Chinatown post office. Explore at your leisure. A Chinatown walking tour is outlined in chapter 8.

JAPANTOWN

More than 12,000 citizens of Japanese descent live in San Francisco, or Soko, as it is often called by the Japanese who first emigrated here. Initially, they settled in Chinatown and south of Market along Stevenson and Jessie streets from Fourth to Seventh. After the earthquake in 1906, SoMa became a light industrial and warehouse area, and the largest Japanese concentration took root in the Western Addition between Van Ness Avenue and Fillmore Street, the site of today's Japantown. By 1940 it covered 30 blocks.

In 1913, the Alien Land Law was passed, depriving Japanese Americans of the right to buy land. From 1924 to 1952 the United States banned Japanese immigration. During World War II, the U.S. government froze Japanese bank accounts, interned community leaders, and removed 112,000 Japanese Americans—two-thirds of them citizens—to camps in California, Utah, and Idaho. Japantown was emptied of Japanese people, and war workers took their place. Upon their release in 1945, the Japanese found their old neighborhood occupied. Most of them resettled in the Richmond and Sunset districts; some did return to Japantown, but it had shrunk to a mere 6 or so blocks. Among the community's notable sights are the **Buddhist Church of San Francisco,** 1881 Pine St. (at Octavia Street); the **Konko Church of San Francisco,** 1909 Bush St. (at Laguna Street); the **Sokoji-Soto Zen Buddhist Temple,** 1691 Laguna St. (at Sutter Street); **Nihonmachi Mall,** 1700 block of Buchanan Street between Sutter and Post streets, which contains two steel fountains by Ruth Asawa; and the **Japan Center.** The Japan Center is an Asian-oriented shopping mall occupying 3 square blocks bounded by Post, Geary, Laguna, and Fillmore streets. At its center stands the five-tiered **Peace Pagoda,** designed by world-famous Japanese architect Yoshiro Taniguchi "to convey the friendship and goodwill of the Japanese to the people of the United States." Surrounding the pagoda, in a network of arcades, squares, and bridges, are dozens of shops and showrooms featuring everything from TVs and tansu chests to pearls, bonsai (dwarf trees), and kimonos. When it opened in 1968, the complex seemed as modern as a jumbo jet. Today, the concrete structure seems less impressive, but it still holds some interesting surprises. The **Kabuki Springs & Spa** (see box, "Urban Renewal") is the center's most famous tenant. The Japan Center houses numerous restaurants, teahouses, and shops, and the Asian-inspired 14-story **Radisson Miyako Hotel** (see chapter 5, "Where to Stay," for complete information).

There is often live entertainment on summer weekends, including Japanese music and dance performances, tea ceremonies, flower-arranging demonstrations,

---

Finds **Urban Renewal**

The **Kabuki Springs & Spa,** 1750 Geary Blvd. (© **415/922-6002**), the Japan Center's most famous tenant, was once an authentic, traditional Japanese bathhouse. The Joie de Vivre hotel group bought and renovated it, and it's now more of a pan-Asian spa with a focus on wellness. The deep ceramic communal tubs, private baths, and shiatsu massages remain; joining them are an array of massages and ayurvedic treatments, body scrubs, wraps, and facials.

Spa Radiance, 3061 Fillmore St. (© **415/346-6281**; www.sparadiance. com), is an utterly San Francisco spa experience. No, I'm not talking groovy, hippielike treatments. This is an unassuming Victorian where Sharon Stone reportedly has come for rejuvenation, from wonderfully luxurious treatments such as facials (14 kinds!), body treatments, massages, manicures, pedicures, and waxing.

---

martial-arts presentations, and other cultural events. The Japan Center is open Monday to Friday 10am to 10pm, and Saturday and Sunday 9am to 10pm. To get there, take bus no. 2, 3, or 4 (exit at Buchanan and Sutter streets), or no. 22 or 38 (exit at the northeast corner of Geary Boulevard and Fillmore Street).

HAIGHT-ASHBURY
Few of San Francisco's neighborhoods are as varied—or as famous—as Haight-Ashbury. Walk along Haight Street, and you'll encounter everything from drug-dazed drifters begging for change to an armada of the city's funky-trendy shops, clubs, and cafes. Yet, turn anywhere off Haight, and instantly you're among the clean-cut, young urban professionals who are the only ones who can afford the steep rents in this hip 'hood. The result is an interesting mix of well-to-do and we'll-screw-you aging flower children, former Dead-heads, homeless people, and throngs of tourists who try not to stare as they wander through this most human of zoos. Some find it depressing, others find it fascinating, but everyone agrees that it ain't what it was in the free-lovin' psychedelic Summer of Love. Is it still worth a visit? Not if you are here for a day or two, but certainly worth an excursion on longer trips, if only to enjoy a cone of Cherry Garcia at the now-famous Ben & Jerry's ice cream shop on the corner of Haight and Ashbury streets, then wander and gawk at the area's intentional freaks.

THE CASTRO
Castro Street, between Market and 18th, is the center of the city's gay community, as well as a lovely neighborhood teeming with shops, restaurants, bars, and other institutions that cater to the area's colorful residents. Among the landmarks are **Harvey Milk Plaza** and the **Castro Theatre,** a 1930s movie palace with a Wurlitzer. The gay community began to move here in the late 1960s and early 1970s from a neighborhood called Polk Gulch, which still has a number of gay-oriented bars and stores. Castro is one of the liveliest streets in the city and the perfect place to shop for gifts and revel in how free-spirited this town is.

THE MISSION DISTRICT
Once inhabited almost entirely by Irish immigrants, the Mission District is now the center of the city's Latino community. It's an oblong area stretching roughly from 14th to 30th streets between Potrero Avenue on the east and Dolores on the

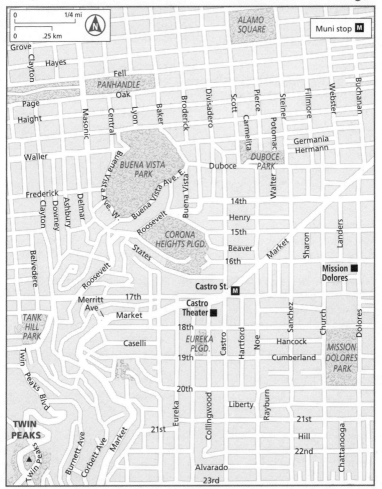

west. In the outer areas many of the city's finest Victorians still stand, although many seem strangely out of place in the mostly lower-income neighborhoods. The heart of the community lies along 24th Street between Van Ness and Potrero, where dozens of excellent ethnic restaurants, bakeries, bars, and specialty stores attract people from all over the city. The area surrounding 16th Street and Valencia is a hotbed for impressive—and impressively cheap—restaurants and bars catering to the city's hip crowd. The Mission District at night isn't exactly the safest place, and walking around the area should be done with caution, but it's usually quite safe during the day, and highly recommended.

For an even better insight into the community, go to the **Precita Eyes Mural Arts Center,** 2981 24th St., between Harrison and Alabama streets (© **415/ 285-2287**), and take one of the 1¾-hour tours conducted on Saturdays at 11am and 1:30pm and Sundays at 1:30pm. They cost $10 for adults, $8 for students with ID, $5 for seniors, $2 for children under 18. You'll see 85 murals in an 8-block walk. Every year during Mural Awareness Month (usually May), tours are given daily. All but the Saturday morning tour (call for information) leave from the center's 24th St. location (☎ **415/285-2287**). Other signs of cultural life include a number of progressive theaters—Eureka, Theater Rhinoceros, and Theater Artaud, to name only a few.

At 16th and Dolores is the **Mission San Francisco de Assisi,** better known as Mission Dolores. It's the city's oldest surviving building (see the separate listing in the section "Here's the Church & Here's the Steeple . . .," below) and the district's namesake.

4 Golden Gate Park ★★★

Everybody loves **Golden Gate Park**—people, dogs, birds, frogs, turtles, bison, trees, bushes, and flowers. Literally everything feels unified here in San Francisco's enormous arboreal front yard, but this great city landmark wasn't always a favorite place to convene. It was conceived in the 1860s and 1870s, and took its current shape in the 1880s and 1890s, thanks to the skill and effort of John McLaren, a Scot who arrived in 1887 and began landscaping the park. Totaling 1,017 acres, the park is a narrow strip that stretches from the Pacific coast inland. No one had thought about the challenge the sand dunes and wind would present to any landscape artist. McLaren developed a new strain of grass called "sea bent," which he had planted to hold the sandy soil along the Firth of Forth, and he used it to anchor the soil here, too. He also built the two windmills that stand on the western edge of the park to pump water for irrigation. Every year the ocean eroded the western fringe of the park, and ultimately he solved this problem, too. It took him 40 years to build a natural wall, putting out bundles of sticks that the tides covered with sand. Under his brilliant eye, the park took shape.

Today's Golden Gate Park is a truly magical place. Spend one sunny day stretched out on the grass along JFK Drive, have a good read in Shakespeare Garden, or stroll around Stow Lake and you too will understand the allure. It's an interactive botanical symphony, and everyone is invited to play in the orchestra.

The park consists of hundreds of gardens and attractions attached by wooded paths and paved roads. While many worthy sites are clearly visible, there are infinite hidden treasures, so pick up information if you want to find the more obscure, quaint spots. For information on the park, head first to the **McLaren Lodge and Park Headquarters** (☎ **415/831-2700**), which is open daily. Of the dozens of special gardens in the park, most recognized are the **McLaren Memorial Rhododendron Dell,** the **Rose Garden,** the **Strybing Arboretum,** and, at the western edge of the park, a springtime array of thousands of tulips and daffodils around the **Dutch windmill.**

In addition to the highlights described in this section, the park contains lots of recreational facilities: tennis courts; baseball, soccer, and polo fields; a golf course; riding stables; and fly-casting pools. The Strawberry Hill boathouse handles boat rentals. The park is also the home of three major museums: the M. H. De Young Memorial Museum, the Asian Art Museum, and the California Academy of Sciences (see separate listings below). *Note:* There's talk of moving the De Young Museum to an undetermined location, and the Asian Art Museum is moving to the old Main Library site in the Civic Center sometime in 2002.

For further information, call the San Francisco Visitor Information Center, at ☎ **415/283-0177.** Enter the park at Kezar Drive, an extension of Fell Street. Bus: 5, 6, 7, 16AX, BX, 66, or 71.

Golden Gate Park

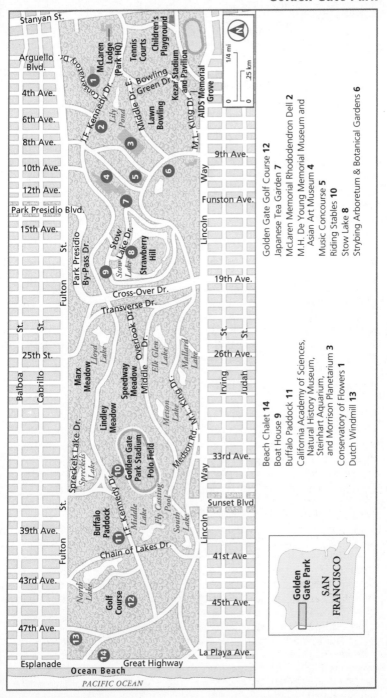

Golden Gate Golf Course **12**
Japanese Tea Garden **7**
McLaren Memorial Rhododendron Dell **2**
M.H. De Young Memorial Museum and
  Asian Art Museum **4**
Music Concourse **5**
Riding Stables **10**
Stow Lake **8**
Strybing Arboretum & Botanical Gardens **6**

Beach Chalet **14**
Boat House **9**
Buffalo Paddock **11**
California Academy of Sciences,
  Natural History Museum,
  Steinhart Aquarium,
  and Morrison Planetarium **3**
Conservatory of Flowers **1**
Dutch Windmill **13**

Value **Saving with the Culture Pass**

If you plan to visit all the park's attractions, consider buying the Culture Pass, which enables you to visit lots of San Francisco museums plus the park's museums. The cost is $33.75 for adults, $26.75 for seniors, and $24.75 for youths. Passes are available at each site and at the **San Francisco Visitor Information Center,** on the lower level of Hallidie Plaza, 900 Market St., at Powell Street (© **415/283-0177;** fax 415/362-7323).

MUSEUMS INSIDE THE PARK

Asian Art Museum   The Asian's current location in Golden Gate Park is closing October 7, 2001, but the museum is scheduled to reopen in its new Civic Center digs toward the end of 2002. It will continue to display selections from the museum's vast collection of 12,000 items. Details about the new facilities and its hours are not out as this book goes to press. However, there's no question that the museum will still have Chinese and Korean galleries, which include world-class sculptures, paintings, bronzes, ceramics, jades, and decorative objects spanning 6,000 years of history, as well as a wide range of exhibits from Pakistan, India, Tibet, Japan, and Southeast Asia. Call for more information or visit the website.

In Golden Gate Park, near 10th Ave. and Fulton St. © **415/379-8800** or 415/752-2635 for the hearing impaired. www.asianart.org. Admission (including the M. H. De Young Memorial Museum and California Palace of the Legion of Honor) $7 adults, $5 seniors 65 and over, $4 youths 12–17, free for children under 12. Fees may be higher for special exhibitions. Free to all first Wed of each month. Tues–Sun 9:30am–4:45pm; first Wed of each month 9:30am–8:45pm. Bus: 5, 21, 44, or 71.

California Academy of Sciences *Kids*   Clustered around the Music Concourse in Golden Gate Park are three outstanding museums and exhibitions guaranteed to entertain every member of the family. You could quite easily spend a whole day here. The **Steinhart Aquarium** is the most diverse aquarium in the world, housing some 14,000 specimens, including amphibians, reptiles, marine mammals, penguins, and much more, in 189 displays. A huge hit with the youngsters is the California tide pool and a "hands-on" area where children can touch starfish and sea urchins. The living coral reef is the largest display of its kind in the country and the only one in the West. In the Fish Roundabout, fast-swimming schools of fish swim in a 100,000-gallon tank that surrounds visitors.

The **Morrison Planetarium** presents sky shows as well as laser-light shows. Sky shows offer guided tours through the universe projected onto a 65-foot domed ceiling. Approximately four major exhibits, with titles such as "Star Death: The Birth of Black Holes" and "The Universe Unveiled," are presented each year. Related cosmos exhibits are in the adjacent Earth and Space Hall. Sky shows begin at 2pm on weekdays and hourly every weekend and holiday (call © **415/750-7141** for more information).

The **Natural History Museum** includes several halls displaying classic dioramas of fauna in their habitats. The Wattis Hall of Human Cultures traces the evolution of different human cultures and the way they adapted to their natural environment. The "Wild California" exhibition in Meyer Hall includes a 14,000-gallon aquarium and seabird rookery, life-sized battling elephant seals, and two larger-than-life views of microscopic life forms. In McBean-Peterson Hall, visitors can walk through an exhibit tracing the course of 3½ billion years of evolution, from the earliest life forms to the present day. The Hohfeld Earth and Space Hall allows visitors to experience a simulation of two of San Francisco's biggest earthquakes, determine what their weight would be on other planets, see a real moon rock, and learn about the rotation of the planet at a replica of Foucault's pendulum (the real one is in Paris).

On the Music Concourse of Golden Gate Park. ✆ **415/750-7145** for recorded information. Admission (aquarium, Natural History Museum, and Planetarium) $8.50 adults, $5.50 seniors 65 and over and students 12–17, $2 children 4–11, free for children under 4. Free to all first Wed of each month. Planetarium shows $2.50 adults, $1.25 seniors 65 and over and children under 18. Labor Day–Memorial Day daily 10am–5pm; Memorial Day–Labor Day daily 9am–6pm; first Wed of each month 10am–9pm. Muni Metro: N to Golden Gate Park. Bus: 5, 44, or 71.

OTHER HIGHLIGHTS

CONSERVATORY OF FLOWERS (1878)   Built for the 1894 Midwinter Exposition, this striking assemblage of glass architecture usually exhibits a rotating display of plants and shrubs at all times of the year. Unfortunately, in recent years rough weather has damaged the already delicate structure. Renovations aren't scheduled to be finished until 2004. Still, the exterior, which is modeled on the famous glass house at Kew Gardens in London, is indeed grand. The Dahlia Garden to the right of the entrance in the center of what was once a carriage roundabout is an explosion of color from spring through fall.

JAPANESE TEA GARDEN (1894)   McLaren hired the Hagiwara family to care for this garden developed for the 1894 Midwinter Exposition. It's a quiet place with cherry trees, shrubs, and bonsai crisscrossed by winding paths and high-arched bridges crossing over pools of water. Focal points and places for contemplation include the massive bronze Buddha (cast in Japan in 1790 and donated by the Gump family), the Shinto wooden pagoda, and the Wishing Bridge, which, reflected in the water, looks as though it completes a circle. The garden is open daily November through February 8:30am to 5pm (teahouse 10am to 4:30pm), March through October 8:30am to 6pm (teahouse 10am to 5:30pm). For **information** on admission, call ✆ **415/752-4227.** For the **teahouse,** call ✆ **415/752-1171.**

STRAWBERRY HILL/STOW LAKE   Rent a paddleboat, rowboat, or motorboat and cruise around the circular lake as painters create still lifes and joggers pass along the grassy shoreline. Ducks waddle around waiting to be fed, and turtles bathe on rocks and logs. Strawberry Hill, the 430-foot-high artificial island that lies at the center of Stow Lake, is a perfect picnic spot and boasts a bird's-eye view of San Francisco and the bay. It also has a waterfall and peace pagoda. For the **boathouse,** call ✆ **415/752-0347.** Boat rentals are available daily from 9am to 4pm.

STRYBING ARBORETUM & BOTANICAL GARDENS   Six thousand plant species grow here, among them some ancient plants in a special "primitive garden," rare species, and a grove of California redwoods. Docent tours begin at 1pm daily. Open Monday to Friday 8am to 4:30pm, and Saturday and Sunday 10am to 5pm. For more information, call ✆ **415/753-7090.**

5 The Presidio & Golden Gate National Recreation Area

THE PRESIDIO

In October 1994, the Presidio passed from the U.S. Army to the National Park Service and became one of a handful of urban national parks that combines historical, architectural, and natural elements into one giant arboreal expanse. (It also contains a previously private golf course and a home for George Lucas's

Golden Gate National Recreation Area

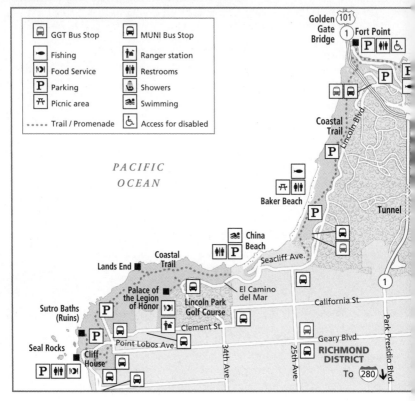

production company.) The 1,480-acre area incorporates a variety of terrain—coastal scrub, dunes, and prairie grasslands that shelter many rare plants and more than 150 species of birds, some of which nest here.

This military outpost has a 220-year history, from its founding in September 1776 by the Spanish under José Joaquin Moraga to its closure in 1995. From 1822 to 1835, the property was in Mexican hands.

During the war with Mexico, U.S. forces occupied the fort, and in 1848, when California became part of the Union, it was formally transferred to the United States. When San Francisco suddenly became an important urban area during the gold rush, the U.S. government installed battalions of soldiers and built Fort Point to protect the entry to the harbor. It expanded the post during the Civil War and during the Indian Wars of the 1870s and 1880s. By the 1890s, it was no longer a frontier post but a major base for U.S. expansion into the Pacific. During the war with Spain in 1898, thousands of troops camped in tent cities awaiting shipment to the Philippines, and the Army General Hospital treated the sick and wounded. By 1905, 12 coastal defense batteries were built along the headlands. In 1914, troops under the command of Gen. John Pershing left here to pursue Pancho Villa and his men. The Presidio expanded during the 1920s, when Crissy Army Airfield (the first airfield on the West Coast) was established, but the major action was seen during World War II, after the attack on Pearl Harbor. Soldiers dug foxholes along nearby beaches, and the Presidio became the headquarters for the Western Defense Command. Some

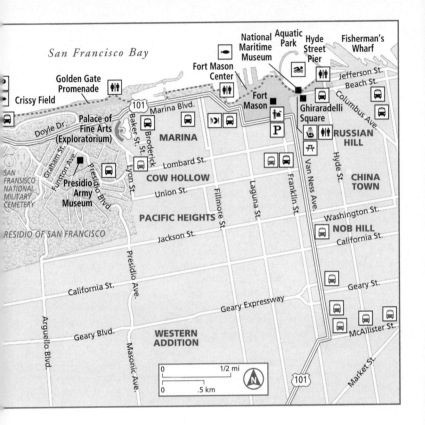

1.6 million men were shipped out from nearby Fort Mason to fight in the Pacific; many returned to the hospital, whose capacity peaked one year at 72,000 patients. In the 1950s, the Presidio served as the headquarters for the Sixth U.S. Army and a missile defense post, but its role slowly shrank. In 1972, it was included in new legislation establishing the Golden Gate National Recreation Area; in 1989, the Pentagon decided to close the post and transfer it to the National Park Service.

Today, the area encompasses more than 510 historic buildings, a scenic golf course, a national cemetery, and a variety of terrain and natural habitats. The National Park Service offers a variety of walking and biking tours around the Presidio; reservations are suggested. At press time the **Presidio Museum** was scheduled to move to new digs at 102 Montgomery St. on the parade grounds. For more information, call the **Visitor Information Center** at © **415/561-4323.** Take the 28, 76, or 82X bus.

San Francisco Zoo & Children's Zoo (Kids)

Located between the Pacific Ocean and Lake Merced, in the southwest corner of the city, the San Francisco Zoo is not remotely as fantastic as, say, the San Diego Zoo. But it is a fun place to take the kids—especially if you make it to the hands-on Children's Zoo. Begun in 1889 with a grizzly bear named Monarch donated by the *San Francisco Examiner,* the zoo now sprawls over 65 acres and is growing. It attracts up to a million visitors each year. Most of the 1,000-plus inhabitants are in landscaped enclosures guarded by concealed moats. The innovative Primate Discovery Center is particularly noteworthy for its many rare and endangered species. Expansive outdoor atriums, sprawling meadows, and a midnight world for exotic nocturnal primates house such species as the owl-faced macaque, ruffed-tailed lemur, black-and-white colobus monkeys, patas monkeys, and emperor tamarins—pint-sized primates distinguished by their long, majestic mustaches.

Other highlights include Koala Crossing, which connects to the Australian Walk About exhibit with its kangaroos, emus, and wallaroos; Gorilla World, one of the world's largest exhibits of the gentle giants; and Penguin Island, home to a large breeding colony of Magellanic penguins. The new Feline Conservation Center is a wooded sanctuary and breeding facility for the zoo's endangered snow leopards, Persian leopards, and other jungle cats. Musk Ox Meadow is a 2½-acre habitat for a herd of rare white-fronted musk oxen brought from Alaska. The Otter River exhibit features waterfalls, logs, and boulders for North American otters to climb. And the Lion House is home to rare Sumatran and Siberian tigers, Prince Charles (a rare white Bengal tiger), and the African lions (you can watch them being fed at 2pm Tuesday to Sunday).

The **Children's Zoo,** adjacent to the main park, allows both kids and adults to get close to animals. The barnyard is alive with strokable domestic animals, such as sheep, goats, ponies, and a llama. Also of interest is the Insect Zoo, which showcases a multitude of species, including the hissing cockroach and walking sticks.

A free, informal walking tour of the zoo is available on weekends at 11am. The Zebra Zephyr train tour takes visitors on a 30-minute "safari" daily (only on weekends in winter). The tour is $2.50 for adults, $1.50 for seniors and children under 18.

Sloat Blvd. and 45th Ave. (€ **415/753-7080.** www.sfzoo.org. Admission to main zoo and children's zoo $10 adults, $7 seniors and youths 12–17, $4 children 3–11, free for children under 3 accompanied by an adult. Free to all first Wed of each month, except $2 fee for children's zoo. Carousel $2. Main zoo daily 10am–5pm. Children's Zoo Mon–Fri 11am–4pm; Sat–Sun 10:30am–4:30pm. Muni Metro: L from downtown Market St. to the end of the line.

GOLDEN GATE NATIONAL RECREATION AREA

The largest urban park in the world, the GGNRA makes New York's Central Park look like a putting green, covering three counties along 28 miles of stunning, condo-free shoreline. Run by the National Park Service, the Recreation Area wraps around the northern and western edges of the city, and just about all of it is open to the public with no access fees. The Muni bus system provides transportation to the more popular sites, including Aquatic Park, the Cliff House, Fort Mason, and Ocean Beach. For more information, contact the **National Park Service** (€ **415/556-0560**). For more detailed information on particular sites, see the "Outdoor Pursuits" section near the end of this chapter.

Here is a brief rundown of the salient features of the park's peninsula section, starting at the northern section and moving westward around the coastline:

Aquatic Park, adjacent to the Hyde Street Pier, has a small swimming beach, although it's not that appealing (and darn cold). Far more entertaining is a visit to the ship-shaped museum across the lawn that's part of the San Francisco Maritime National Historical Park (see "Museums," above, for more information).

Fort Mason Center, from Bay Street to the shoreline, consists of several buildings and piers used during World War II. Today they hold a variety of museums, theaters, and organizations, and Greens vegetarian restaurant, which affords views of the Golden Gate Bridge (see chapter 6 for more information). For information about Fort Mason events, call € **415/441-5706.** The park headquarters is also at Fort Mason.

Farther west along the bay at the northern end of Laguna Street is **Marina Green,** a favorite local spot for kite-flying, jogging, and walking along the Promenade. The St. Francis Yacht Club is also here.

Next comes the 3½-mile paved **Golden Gate Promenade** ✪, San Francisco's best and most scenic biking, jogging, and walking path. It runs along the shore past Crissy Field (be sure to stop and watch the gonzo windsurfers) and ends at Fort Point under the Golden Gate Bridge.

Fort Point ✪ (✆ **415/556-1693**) was built in 1853 to protect the narrow entrance to the harbor. It was designed to house 500 soldiers manning 126 muzzle-loading cannons. By 1900, the fort's soldiers and obsolete guns had been removed, but the formidable brick edifice remains. Fort Point is open daily from 10am to 5pm, and guided tours and cannon demonstrations are given at the site once or twice daily, depending on the time of year.

Lincoln Boulevard sweeps around the western edge of the bay to **Baker Beach,** where the waves roll ashore—a fine spot for sunbathing, walking, or fishing. Hikers can follow the **Coastal Trail** from Fort Point along this part of the coastline all the way to Lands End.

A short distance from Baker Beach, **China Beach** is a small cove where swimming is permitted. Changing rooms, showers, a sundeck, and rest rooms are available.

A little farther around the coast is **Lands End** ✪, looking out to Pyramid Rock. A lower and an upper trail offer hiking amid windswept cypresses and pines on the cliffs above the Pacific.

Still farther along the coast lie **Point Lobos,** the **Sutro Baths,** and the **Cliff House** ✪. The Cliff House has been serving refreshments to visitors since 1863 and providing views of Seal Rocks, home to a colony of sea lions and many marine birds. There's an **information center** (open daily from 10am to 5pm; ✆ **415/556-8642**) as well as the incredible **Musée Mecanique** ✪, an authentic old-fashioned arcade with 150 coin-operated amusement machines. Northeast of the Cliff House, only traces of the Sutro Baths remain. The swimming facility, a major summer attraction that could accommodate up to 24,000 people, burned down in 1966.

A little farther inland at the western end of California Street is **Lincoln Park,** which contains a golf course and the spectacular Palace of the Legion of Honor museum.

At the southern end of Ocean Beach, 4 miles down the coast, is another area of the park around Fort Funston, where there's an easy loop trail across the cliffs (ranger office: ✆ **415/239-2366**). Here you can watch hang gliders taking advantage of the high cliffs and strong winds.

Farther south along route 280, **Sweeney Ridge,** accessible only by car, affords sweeping views of the coastline from the many trails that crisscross its 1,000 acres. From here the expedition led by Don Gaspar de Portolá first saw San Francisco Bay in 1769. It's in Pacifica; take Sneath Lane off Route 35 (Skyline Boulevard) in San Bruno.

The GGNRA extends into Marin County, where it encompasses the Marin Headlands, Muir Woods National Monument, and the Olema Valley behind the Point Reyes National Seashore. See chapter 11 for information on these areas.

6 Here's the Church & Here's the Steeple . . .

Some of San Francisco's churches and other religious buildings are worth checking out.

Glide Memorial United Methodist Church 🎭 *Moments*   There would be nothing special about this Tenderloin-area church if it weren't for its exhilarating pastor, Cecil Williams. Reverend Williams's enthusiastic and uplifting preaching and singing with homeless and poor people of the neighborhood has attracted nationwide fame. In 1994, during the pastor's 30th-anniversary celebration, singers Angela Bofill and Bobby McFerrin joined comedian Robin Williams, author Maya Angelou, and talk-show queen Oprah Winfrey to honor him publicly. Williams's nondogmatic, fun Sunday services attract a diverse audience that crosses all socioeconomic boundaries. Go for an uplifting experience.

330 Ellis St. (west of Union Square.). ℂ **415/771-6300.** Services Sun at 9 and 11am. Muni Metro: Powell. Bus: 37.

Grace Cathedral   Although this Nob Hill cathedral, designed by architect Lewis P. Hobart, appears to be made of stone, it is in fact constructed of reinforced concrete, beaten to achieve a stonelike effect. Construction began on the site of the Crocker mansion in 1928 but was not completed until 1964. Among the more interesting features of the building are its stained-glass windows, particularly those by the French Loire studios, depicting such modern figures as Thurgood Marshall, Robert Frost, and Albert Einstein; the replicas of Ghiberti's bronze *Doors of Paradise* at the east end; the series of religious frescoes completed in the 1940s by Polish artist John de Rosen; and the 44-bell carillon. Along with its magical ambiance, Grace lifts spirits with services, musical performances, and their weekly Forum, which runs every Sunday from 9:30 to 10:30am, where guests lead discussions about spirituality in modern times.

California St. (between Taylor and Jones sts.). ℂ **415/749-6300.**

Mission Dolores   San Francisco's oldest standing structure, the Mission San Francisco de Assisi (a.k.a. Mission Dolores) has withstood the test of time, as well as two major earthquakes, relatively intact. In 1776, at the behest of Franciscan missionary Junípero Serra, Father Francisco Palou came to the Bay Area to found the sixth in a series of missions that dotted the California coastline. From these humble beginnings grew what was to become the city of San Francisco. The mission's small, simple chapel, built solidly by Native Americans who were converted to Christianity, is a curious mixture of native construction methods and Spanish-colonial style. A statue of Father Serra stands in the mission garden, although the portrait looks somewhat more contemplative, and less energetic, than he must have been in real life. A 45-minute audio tour costs $5 for adults, $4 for children; otherwise the rate is $3 for adults and $2 for children.

16th St. (at Dolores St.). ℂ **415/621-8203.** Donations appreciated. May–Oct daily 9am–4:30pm; Nov–Apr daily 9am–4pm; Good Friday 9am–noon. Closed Thanksgiving, Dec 25. Muni Metro: J. Bus: 14, 22, 26, or 53 to the corner of Church and 16th sts.

7 Architectural Highlights

MUST-SEES FOR ARCHITECTURE BUFFS

ALAMO SQUARE HISTORIC DISTRICT   San Francisco's collection of Victorian houses, known as **Painted Ladies,** is one of the city's most famous assets. Most of the 14,000 extant structures date from the second half of the 19th century and are private residences. Spread throughout the city, many have been beautifully restored and ornately painted. The small area bordered by Divisadero Street on the west, Golden Gate Avenue on the north, Webster Street on the east, and Fell Street on the south—about 10 blocks west of the Civic

Center—has one of the city's greatest concentrations of Painted Ladies. One of the most famous views of San Francisco—seen on postcards and posters all around the city—depicts sharp-edged Financial District skyscrapers behind a row of Victorians. This fantastic juxtaposition can be seen from Alamo Square, in the center of the historic district, at Fulton and Steiner streets.

CITY HALL & CIVIC CENTER   Built in 1881 to a design by Brown and Bakewell, it is part of this "City Beautiful" complex done in the beaux arts style. The dome rises to a height of 308 feet on the exterior and is ornamented with occuli and topped by a lantern. The interior rotunda soars 112 feet and is finished in oak, marble, and limestone, with a monumental marble staircase leading to the second floor.

OTHER ARCHITECTURAL HIGHLIGHTS

San Francisco is a center of many architecturally striking sights. This section concentrates on a few highlights.

Around Union Square and the Financial District is the former **Circle Gallery,** 140 Maiden Lane. Now a gallery housing Folk Art International, Xanadu Tribal Arts, and Boretti Amber & Design, it's the only building in the city designed by Frank Lloyd Wright (in 1948). The gallery was the prototype for the Guggenheim's seashell-shaped circular gallery space, even though it was meant to serve as a retail space for V. C. Morris, a purveyor of glass and crystal. Note the arresting exterior, a solid wall with a circular entryway to the left. Maiden Lane is just off Union Square between Geary and Post streets.

The **Hallidie Building,** 130–150 Sutter St., designed by Willis Polk in 1917, is an ideal example of a glass-curtain building. The vast glass facade is miraculously suspended between the two cast-iron cornices. The fire escapes that course down each side of the building complete the prosceniumlike theatrical effect.

Two prominent pieces of San Francisco's skyline are in the Financial District. The **TransAmerica Pyramid,** 600 Montgomery St., between Clay and Washington streets, is one of the tallest structures in San Francisco. This corporate headquarters was completed in 1972, stands 48 stories tall, and is capped by a 212-foot spire. The former **Bank of America World Headquarters,** 555 California St., was designed by Wurster, Bernardi, and Emmons with Skidmore, Owings, and Merrill. This carnelian-marble–covered building dates from 1969. Its 52 stories are topped by a panoramic restaurant and bar, the Carnelian Room (see chapter 10, "San Francisco After Dark," for complete information). The focal point of the building's formal plaza is an abstract black granite sculpture, known locally as the "Banker's Heart," designed by Japanese architect Masayuki Nagare.

The **Medical Dental Building,** 450 Sutter St., is a steel-frame structure beautifully clad in terra-cotta. It was designed by Miller and Pflueger in 1929. The entrance and the window frames are elaborately ornamented with Mayan relief work; the lobby ceiling is similarly decorated with gilding. Note the ornate elevators, too.

At the foot of Market Street you will find the **Ferry Building.** Built between 1895 and 1903, it served as the city's major transportation hub before the Golden Gate and Bay bridges were built; some 170 ferries docked here daily unloading Bay Area commuters until the 1930s. The tower that soars above the building was inspired by the Campanile of Venice and the Cathedral Tower in Seville. Plans are afoot to restore the building to its former glory, opening up the soaring galleries to the sky again. If you stop by the Ferry Building, you might also want to go to **Rincon Center,** 99 Mission St., to see the WPA murals painted by the Russian artist Refregier in the post office.

Several important buildings are on or near Nob Hill. The **Flood Mansion,** 1000 California St., at Mason Street, was built between 1885 and 1886 for James Clair Flood. Thanks to the Comstock Lode, Flood rose from being a bartender to being one of the city's wealthiest men. He established the Nevada bank that later merged with Wells Fargo. The house cost $1.5 million; the fence alone cost $30,000. It was designed by Augustus Laver and modified by Willis Polk after the earthquake to accommodate the Pacific Union Club.

Built by George Applegarth in 1913 for the sugar magnate Adolph Spreckels, the **Spreckels Mansion,** 2080 Washington St., is currently home to romance novelist Danielle Steele (don't even try to get in to see her!). The extraordinary building has rounded-arch French doors on the first and second floors and curved balconies on the second floor. Inside, the original house featured an indoor pool in the basement, Adamesque fireplaces, and a circular Pompeian room with fountain.

Finally, one of San Francisco's most ingenious architectural accomplishments is the **San Francisco–Oakland Bay Bridge.** Although it's visually less appealing than the nearby Golden Gate Bridge, the Bay Bridge is in many ways more spectacular. The silvery giant that links San Francisco with Oakland is one of the world's longest steel bridges (8¼ miles). It opened in 1936, 6 months before the

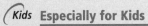

Especially for Kids

The following San Francisco attractions have major appeal to kids of all ages:

- Alcatraz Island (see p. 149)
- Cable cars (see p. 154)
- Cable Car Barn Museum (see p. 157)
- California Academy of Sciences, including Steinhart Aquarium (see p. 168)
- The Exploratorium (see p. 158)
- Golden Gate Bridge (see p. 156)
- Golden Gate Park, including the Children's Playground, Bison Paddock, and Japanese Tea Garden (see p. 166)
- National Maritime Museum and the historic ships anchored at Hyde Pier (see p. 159)
- The Metreon Entertainment Center (see p. 160)
- The San Francisco Zoo (see p. 171)

In addition to the sights listed above, a number of playgrounds are of particular interest to kids. One of the most enormous, fun playgrounds for kids is in **Golden Gate Park** (see above). Apartment buildings surround the **Cow Hollow Playground,** Baker Street between Greenwich and Filbert streets, on three of four sides. The landscaped playground features a bilevel play area fitted with well-conceived, colorful play structures, including a tunnel, slides, swings, and a miniature cable car. **Huntington Park,** Taylor Street between Sacramento and California streets, sits atop Nob Hill. This tiny play area contains several small structures particularly well-suited to children under 5. **Julius Kahn Playground,** West Pacific Avenue at Spruce Street, is a popular playground inside San Francisco's great Presidio Park. Larger play structures and forested surroundings make this area attractive to children and adults alike.

Golden Gate. Each of its two decks contains five automobile lanes. The Bay Bridge is not a single bridge at all, but a superbly dovetailed series of spans joined in midbay, at Yerba Buena Island, by one of the world's largest (in diameter) tunnels. To the west of Yerba Buena, the bridge is actually two separate suspension bridges, joined at a central anchorage. East of the island is a 1,400-foot cantilever span, followed by a succession of truss bridges. And it looks even more complex than it sounds. You can drive across the bridge (the toll is $2, paid westbound), or you can catch a bus at the Transbay Terminal (Mission at First Street) and ride to downtown Oakland.

8 Self-Guided & Organized Tours

THE 49-MILE SCENIC DRIVE

The self-guided, 49-mile drive is one easy way to orient yourself and to grasp the beauty of San Francisco and its extraordinary location. Beginning in the city, it follows a rough circle around the bay and passes virtually all the best-known sights from Chinatown to the Golden Gate Bridge, Ocean Beach, Seal Rocks, Golden Gate Park, and Twin Peaks. Originally designed for the benefit of visitors to San Francisco's 1939 and 1940 Golden Gate International Exposition, the route is marked with blue-and-white seagull signs. Although it makes an excellent half-day tour, this mini-excursion can easily take longer if you decide, for example, to stop to walk across the Golden Gate Bridge or to have tea in Golden Gate Park's Japanese Tea Garden.

The San Francisco **Visitor Information Center,** at Powell and Market streets (see "Visitor Information" in chapter 4), distributes free route maps. A few of the Scenic Drive marker signs are missing, so the map comes in handy. Try to avoid the downtown area during the weekday rush hours from 7 to 9am and 4 to 6pm.

A BART TOUR

One of the world's best commuter systems, **Bay Area Rapid Transit (BART)** runs along 71 miles of rail, linking eight San Francisco stations with Daly City to the south and 25 stations in the East Bay. Under the bay, BART runs through one of the longest underwater transit tubes in the world. This link opened in September 1974, 2 years behind schedule and 6 months after the general manager resigned under fire. The train cars are 70 feet long and designed to represent the last word in public transport luxury. Twenty years later, they no longer seem futuristic, but they're still attractively modern, with carpeted floors, tinted picture windows, air-conditioning, and recessed lighting. The trains can hit a top speed of 80 mph; a computerized control system monitors and adjusts their speed.

The people who run BART think so highly of their trains and stations that they sell a $3.80 **"Excursion Ticket,"** which allows you, in effect, to "sightsee" the BART system. Tour the entire system as much as you like for up to 3 hours; you must exit at the station where you entered (if you get out anywhere along the line, the gate instantly computes the normal fare). For more information, call © **650/992-BART** or 650/992-2278.

BOAT TOURS

One of the best ways to look at San Francisco is from a boat bobbing on the bay. There are several cruises to choose from, and many of them start from Fisherman's Wharf.

Blue & Gold Fleet, Pier 39, Fisherman's Wharf (© **415/773-1188**) tours the bay year-round in a sleek, 400-passenger sightseeing boat, complete with food and beverage facilities. The fully narrated, 1¼-hour cruise passes beneath the Golden Gate and Bay bridges and comes within yards of Alcatraz Island. Frequent daily departures from Pier 39's West Marina begin at 10am during summer and 11am in winter. Tickets cost $17 for adults, $13 for seniors over 62 and juniors 12 to 17, $9 for children 5 to 11, free for children under 5. There's a $2.25 charge for ordering tickets by phone.

The **Red & White Fleet,** Pier 43½ (© **415/447-0597;** www.redandwhite. com) offers daily Bay Cruises tours that leave from Pier 43½ and cruise under the Golden Gate Bridge, past the Marin Headlands, Sausalito, Tiburon, Angel Island, and Alcatraz. Prices are $17 for adults, $13 for seniors and teens 12 to 18, $9 for children 5 to 11.

BUS TOURS

Gray Line, with offices in the Transbay Terminal, First and Mission streets, Pier 39, and Union Square (© **800/826-0202** or 415/558-9400), is San Francisco's largest bus-tour operator. It offers several itineraries daily. Free pickup and return service is available between centrally located hotels and departure locations. Reservations are required for most tours, which are available in several foreign languages, including French, German, Spanish, Italian, Japanese, and Korean.

WALKING TOURS

Javawalk is a 2-hour walking tour by self-described "coffeehouse lizard" Elaine Sosa. As the name suggests, it's loosely a coffee walking tour through North Beach, but there's a lot more going on than drinking cups of brew. Javawalk also serves up a good share of historical and architectural trivia, offering something for everyone. The best part of the tour, however, may be the camaraderie that develops among the participants. Sosa keeps the excursion interactive and fun, and it's obvious she knows a profusion of tales and trivia about the history of coffee and its North Beach roots. It's a guaranteed good time, particularly if you're addicted to caffeine. Javawalk is offered Tuesday to Saturday at 10am. The price is $20 per person, $19 for kids under 13. For information and reservations, call © **415/673-WALK** or 415/673-9255.

Cruisin' the Castro (© **415/550-8110;** www.webcastro.com/castrotour) is an informative historical tour of San Francisco's most famous gay quarter. It gives you new insight into the contribution of the gay community to the city's political maturity, growth, and beauty. Trevor Hailey, who was involved in the development of the Castro in the 1970s, conducts the tours. She knew Harvey Milk, the first openly gay politician elected to office in the United States. You'll learn about Milk's rise from shopkeeper to city supervisor and visit Harvey Milk Plaza, where marches, rallies, and protests begin. In addition, you'll explore the Castro Theatre and side streets lined with beautifully restored Victorians, as well as the plethora of community-oriented stores in the Castro whose owners Hailey knows personally. Tours run Tuesday to Saturday from 10am to 2pm, and begin at Harvey Milk Plaza, atop the Castro Street Muni station. The cost includes lunch at a Castro area restaurant. Reservations are required. The tour, with lunch, costs $40 for adults, $35 for seniors 62 and over and for children 16 and under.

On the **Haight-Ashbury Walking Tour** (© **415/863-1621**), you explore hippie haunts with Pam and Bruce Brennan. You'll revisit in 2-1/2 short hours the Grateful Dead's crash pad, Janis Joplin's house, and other reminders of the Summer of Love. Tours begin at 9:30am Tuesday and Saturday. The cost is $15 per person. Reservations are required.

San Francisco's Chinatown is always fascinating, but for many visitors with limited time it's hard to know where to search out the "non-touristy" shops, restaurants, and historical spots in this microcosm of Chinese culture. **Wok Wiz Chinatown Walking Tours & Cooking Center,** 654 Commercial St., between Kearny and Montgomery streets (© **415/981-8989;** www.wokwiz.com), founded over a decade ago by author and cooking instructor Shirley Fong-Torres, is the answer. The Wok Wiz tours take you into nooks and crannies. Most guides are Chinese, speak fluent Cantonese or Mandarin, and are intimately acquainted with the neighborhood's alleys and small enterprises, as well as Chinatown's history, folklore, culture, and food. Tours are conducted daily 10am to 1:30pm and include dim sum (Chinese lunch). There's also a less expensive tour that does not include lunch. It's an easy walk, fun and fascinating, and you're bound to make new friends. Groups are generally held to a maximum of 15, and reservations are essential. Prices (including lunch) are $39 for adults, $35 for seniors 62 and older, and $37 for children under 12.

The NAMES Project AIDS Memorial Quilt

The NAMES Project began in 1987 in San Francisco as a memorial for people who have died from AIDS. The idea was to direct grief into positive action and help the world understand the devastating impact of the disease. Organizers invited the public to make coffin-sized panels for a giant memorial quilt. More than 40,000 individual panels now commemorate the lives of those who have died of complications related to AIDS. Each unique design was sewn by the victims' friends, lovers, and family members.

The **AIDS Memorial Quilt,** which would cover more than 24 football fields if laid out end to end, was first displayed on the Capitol Mall in Washington, D.C., during a 1987 national march for lesbian and gay rights. Although sections of the quilt are often on tour throughout the world, portions of the largest community art project in the world are on display at The NAMES Project, which recently moved to Atlanta. To find out more, contact **www.aidsquilt.org** or ✆ **404/688-5500.**

Shirley Fong-Torres also operates an **I Can't Believe I Ate My Way Through Chinatown** tour. It starts with breakfast in a noodle house, moves to a wok shop, and stops for nibbles at a vegetarian restaurant, a rice-noodle factory, and a supermarket before taking a break for a sumptuous luncheon. It's offered on most Saturdays and costs $65 per person. The **Walk & Wok** tour includes shopping for food in Chinatown, then cooking (and eating) it together at Shirley's Cooking Center (most Saturdays; $75 per person).

Jay Gifford, founder of the **Victorian Homes Historical Walking Tour** (✆ **415/252-9485;** www.victorianwalk.com) and a San Francisco resident for 2 decades, communicates his enthusiasm and love of San Francisco throughout this highly entertaining walking tour. The 2½-hour tour, at a very leisurely pace, incorporates a wealth of knowledge about San Francisco's Victorian architecture and the city's history—particularly the periods before and after the great earthquake and fire of 1906. You'll stroll through Japantown, the Western Addition (where you can take a break to cruise the trendy shops on Fillmore Street), and onward to Pacific Heights and Cow Hollow. In the process you'll see more than 200 meticulously restored Victorians, including the one where *Mrs. Doubtfire* was filmed. Jay's guests often find that they are the only ones on the quiet neighborhood streets, where tour buses are forbidden. The tour ends with a trolley bus ride back to Union Square, passing through North Beach and Chinatown. Tours, which start at Union Square at 11am, are offered daily year-round and cost $20 per person. Reservations are required.

9 Outdoor Pursuits

Half the fun in San Francisco takes place outdoors. If you're not in the mood to trek it, there are other things to do that allow you to enjoy the surroundings.

BALLOONING   Although you must drive 1 hour to get to the tour site, hot-air ballooning is an ethereal and silent flight over the Wine Country. **Adventures Aloft,** P.O. Box 2500, Vintage 1870, Yountville, CA 94599 (✆ **800/944-4408** or 707/944-4408; www.nvaloft.com), is the Napa Valley's oldest hot-air balloon company, staffed with full-time professional pilots. Groups are small, and each flight lasts about an hour. The cost of $195 per person ($160 ages 6 to 16) includes a post-adventure champagne brunch and a framed "first-flight" certificate. Flights are daily 6 to 7am (weather permitting).

BEACHES   For beach information, call the San Francisco Visitor Information Center, at © **415/283-0177.** Most days it's too chilly to hang out at the beach, but when the fog evaporates and the wind dies down, one of the best ways to spend the day is oceanside in the city. On any truly hot day, thousands flock to worship the sun, build sandcastles, and throw the ball around. Without a wet suit, swimming is a fiercely cold endeavor. Only two beaches are considered safe for swimming: **Aquatic Park,** adjacent to the Hyde Park Pier, and **China Beach,** a small cove on the western edge of the South Bay. But dip at your own risk—there are never lifeguards on duty. Also on the South Bay, **Baker Beach** is ideal for picnicking, sunning, walking, or fishing against the backdrop of the Golden Gate.

Ocean Beach, at the end of Golden Gate Park, on the westernmost side of the city, is San Francisco's largest beach—4 miles long. Just offshore, at the northern end of the beach in front of Cliff House, are the jagged Seal Rocks, inhabited by various shore birds and a large colony of barking sea lions (bring binoculars for a close-up view). To the left, Kelly's Cove is one of the more challenging surf spots in town. Ocean Beach is ideal for strolling or sunning, but don't swim here—tides are tricky, and each year bathers drown in the rough surf.

Stop by Ocean Beach bus terminal at the corner of Cabrillo and La Playa to learn about San Francisco's playful history in local artist Ray Beldner's whimsically historical sculpture garden. Then hike up the hill to explore the Cliff House and the ruins of Sutro Baths. These baths, able to accommodate 24,000 bathers, were lost to fire in 1966.

BIKING   The Parks and Recreations department maintains two city-designated bike routes. One winds 7½ miles through Golden Gate Park to Lake Merced; the other traverses the city, starting in the south, and continues over the Golden Gate Bridge. These routes are not dedicated to bicyclists, who must exercise caution to avoid crashing into pedestrians. Helmets are recommended for adults and required by law for kids under 18. A bike map is available from the San Francisco Visitor Information Center, at Powell and Mason streets (see "Visitor Information" in chapter 4), and from bicycle shops all around town.

Ocean Beach has a public walk- and bikeway that stretches along 5 waterfront blocks of the Great Highway between Noriega and Santiago streets. It's an easy ride from Cliff House or Golden Gate Park.

Avenue Cyclery, 756 Stanyan Street, at Page Street (© **415/668-8016**), rents bikes for $5 per hour or $25 per day and is open daily April through September from 10am to 7pm and October through March from 10am to 6pm.

BOATING   At the **Golden Gate Park Boat House** (© **415/752-0347**) on Stow Lake, the park's largest body of water, you can rent a rowboat or pedal boat by the hour and steer over to Strawberry Hill, a large, round island in the middle of the lake, for lunch. There's usually a line on weekends. The boathouse is open daily, June to September 9am to 5pm, the rest of the year 9am to 4pm.

Cass Marina, 1702 Bridgeway, Sausalito (© **800/472-4595** or 415/332-6789; www.cassmarina.com), is a certified sailing school that rents sailboats measuring 22 to 101 feet. Sail to the Golden Gate Bridge on your own or with a licensed skipper. In addition, large sailing yachts leave from San Francisco and Sausalito on a regularly scheduled basis. Call or check the Web site for schedules, prices, and availability of sailboats. The marina is open daily from 9am to sunset.

CITY STAIR CLIMBING   Many health clubs have stair-climbing machines and step classes, but in San Francisco, you need only to go outside. The following city stair climbs will give you not only a good workout, but great sightseeing, too.

Filbert Street Steps, between Sansome Street and Telegraph Hill, are a particular challenge. Scaling the sheer eastern face of Telegraph Hill, this 377-step climb winds through verdant flower gardens and charming 19th-century cottages. Napier Lane, a narrow wooden plank walkway, leads to Montgomery Street. Turn right, and follow the path to the end of the cul-de-sac where another stairway continues to Telegraph's panoramic summit.

The **Lyon Street Steps,** between Green Street and Broadway, were built in 1916. This historic stairway street contains four steep sets of stairs totaling 288 steps. Begin at Green Street and climb all the way up, past manicured hedges and flower gardens, to an iron gate that opens into the Presidio. A block east, on Baker Street, another set of 369 steps descends to Green Street.

FISHING   **New Easy Rider Sport Fishing,** 225 University Ave., Berkeley (© **510/849-2727**), makes daily trips for ling cod, rock fish, and many other types of game fish all year, and it makes trips for salmon runs from April through October. Fishing equipment is available; the cost, including boat ride and bait, is $62 per person, $72 during winter when it's a crab and fish combo. Reservations are required, as are licenses for adults. One-day licenses can be purchased before departure. Find out the latest on the season by contacting their hotline (©**510/486-8300**). Excursions run daily 6am to 4pm. Fish are cleaned, filleted, and bagged on the return trip for a small fee.

GOLF   San Francisco has a few beautiful golf courses. One of the most lavish is the **Presidio Golf Course** (© **415/561-4664**). Greens fees are $42 Monday to Thursday, $52 Friday, $72 Saturday and Sunday; carts cost extra. There are also two decent municipal courses in town.

The 9-hole **Golden Gate Park Course,** 47th Ave. and Fulton St. (© **415/751-8987**), charges greens fees of $10 per person weekdays, $13 weekends. The 1,357-yard course is par 27. All holes are par 3, tightly set, and well trapped with small greens. The course is a little weathered in spots, but it's casual, fun, and inexpensive. Open daily at 6am.

The 18-hole **Lincoln Park Golf Course,** 34th Ave. and Clement St. (© **415/221-9911**), charges greens fees of $23 per person weekdays, $27 weekends, with rates decreasing as the evening draws near. It's San Francisco's prettiest municipal course, with terrific views and fairways lined with Monterey cypress trees. The 5,081-yard layout plays to par 68, and the 17th hole has a glistening ocean view. This is the oldest course in the city and one of the oldest in the West. Open daily at 6:30am.

A good place for a tune-up is the **Mission Bay Golf Center,** Sixth St. at Channel St. (© **415/431-7888**). San Francisco's most popular driving range is an impeccably maintained 7-acre facility that consists of a double-decker steel and concrete arc containing 66 covered practice bays. The grass landing area extends 300 yards, has nine target greens, and is lit for evening use. There's a putting green and a chipping and bunker practice area. The center is open Monday 11:30am to 11pm, Tuesday to Sunday 7am to 11pm. A bucket of balls costs $8, and the last bucket is sold at 10pm. To get there from downtown San Francisco, take Fourth Street south to Channel Street and turn right.

HANDBALL   The city's best handball courts are in Golden Gate Park, opposite Seventh Avenue, south of Middle Drive East. Courts are available free, on a first-come, first-served basis.

PARKS   In addition to **Golden Gate Park** and the **Golden Gate National Recreation Area** (discussed above), San Francisco boasts more than 2,000 additional acres of parkland, most of which is perfect for picnicking or throwing around a Frisbee.

Smaller city parks include **Buena Vista Park** (Haight Street between Baker and Central streets), which affords fine views of the Golden Gate and is also a favored lounging ground for gay lovers; **Ina Coolbrith Park** (Taylor Street between Vallejo and Green streets), offering views of the Bay Bridge and Alcatraz; and **Sigmund Stern Grove** (19th Avenue and Sloat Boulevard) in the Sunset District, which is the site of the famous free summer music festival.

One of our personal favorites is **Lincoln Park,** a 270-acre green on the northwestern side of the city at Clement Street and 34th Avenue. The California Palace of the Legion of Honor is here (see "Museums," earlier in this chapter), as is a scenic 18-hole municipal golf course (see "Golf," above). But the best things about this park are the 200-foot cliffs that overlook the Golden Gate Bridge and San Francisco Bay. To get to the park, take bus no. 38 from Union Square to 33rd and Geary streets, and walk a few blocks to the park.

RUNNING   The **Bay to Breakers Foot Race** ✸ (© 415/777-7770; www.bay tobreakers.com) is an annual 7½-mile run from downtown to Ocean Beach. About 80,000 entrants take part in one of San Francisco's trademark events. Costumed participants and hordes of spectators add to the fun. The event, sponsored by the *San Francisco Examiner,* is held on the third Sunday of May.

The San Francisco Chronicle Marathon takes place annually in the middle of July. For more information, contact **West End Management** (© 415/284-9492).

SKATING (CONVENTIONAL & IN-LINE)   Although people skate in Golden Gate Park all week long, Sunday is best because on Sundays, John F. Kennedy Drive between Kezar Drive and Transverse Road is closed to automobiles. A smooth "skate pad" is on your right, just past the Conservatory. Another hot skating, biking, and walking spot is the newly renovated **Embarcadero promenade,** which stretches from the new Pacific Bell Park (Townsend Street and Embarcadero) to Fisherman's Wharf. **Skates on Haight,** 1818 Haight St. (© 415/752-8376), 1 block from the park, is the best place to rent in-line or conventional skates. The cost of $6 per hour, $24 per day, includes protective wrist guards and knee pads. Major credit card and ID deposit are required. The shop is open Monday to Friday 11am to 7pm, Saturday and Sunday 10am to 6pm.

TENNIS   The **San Francisco Parks and Recreations Department** (© 415/753-7001) maintains more than 100 courts throughout the city. Almost all are available free, on a first-come, first-served basis. The exceptions are the 21 courts in **Golden Gate Park,** which cost $4 to $6. Courts must be reserved for weekend play by calling © 415/753-7101 on Wednesday from 4 to 6pm or anytime Thursday or Friday.

WALKING & HIKING   The **Golden Gate National Recreation Area** offers plenty of opportunities. One pleasant walk (or bike ride) is along the Golden Gate Promenade, from Aquatic Park to the Golden Gate Bridge. The 3½-mile paved trail heads along the northern edge of the Presidio, out to Fort Point. You can also hike along the Coastal Trail all the way from near Fort Point to the Cliff House. The park service maintains several other trails in the city. For more information or to pick up a map of the Golden Gate National Recreation Area, stop by the park service headquarters at Fort Mason at the north end of Laguna Street (© 415/556-0560).

Although most drive to this spectacular vantage point, a more rejuvenating way to experience **Twin Peaks** is to walk up from the back roads of U.C. Medical Center (off Parnassus) or from either of the two roads that lead to the top (off Woodside or Clarendon avenues). The best time to trek is early morning, when the city is quiet, the air is crisp, and the sightseers haven't crowded the parking lot. Keep an eye out for cars, because there's no real hiking trail, and be sure to walk beyond the lot and up to the highest vantage point.

10 Spectator Sports

The Bay Area's sports scene includes several major professional franchises. Check the local newspapers' sports sections for daily listings of local events.

MAJOR LEAGUE BASEBALL

The **San Francisco Giants** ✿ play at the new and absolutely stunning **Pacific Bell Park,** Third and King streets (✆ **415/972-2000;** www.sfgiants.com), in the China Basin section of SoMa. From April through October, 40,800 fans root for the National League Giants. The unobstructed bay vistas take in bobbing boats beyond the outfield at the recently completed $319 million "Pac Bell Park." Tickets are hard to come by; you can try to track them down through **BASS Ticketmaster** (✆ **510/762-2277**). Special express bus service is available from Market Street on game days; call **Muni** (✆ **415/673-6864**) for pickup points and schedule information.

The American League's **Oakland Athletics** play across the bay at the Oakland Coliseum Complex, at the Hegenberger Road exit from I-880, Oakland (✆ **510/430-8020**). The stadium holds close to 50,000 spectators and is accessible through BART's Coliseum station. Tickets are available from the Coliseum Box Office or by phone through **BASS Ticketmaster** (✆ **510/762-2277**).

PRO BASKETBALL

The **Golden State Warriors** of the NBA play at the Oakland Coliseum Complex, at the Hegenberger Road exit from I-880, Oakland (✆ **510/986-2200**). The Warriors play in the 15,025-seat Oakland Coliseum Arena. The season runs from November through April, and most games start at 7:30pm. Tickets are available at the arena and by phone through **BASS Ticketmaster** (✆ **510/ 762-2277**).

PRO FOOTBALL

The **San Francisco 49ers** play at 3Com/Candlestick Park, Giants Drive and Gilman Avenue (✆ **415/468-2249**), on Sundays from August through December; kickoff is usually at 1pm. Tickets sell out early in the season, but are available at higher prices through ticket agents beforehand and from "scalpers." (illegal ticket-sellers who are usually at the gates). Ask your hotel concierge or visit **City Box Office,** 153 Kearny St., Suite 302 (✆ **415/392-4400**). Special express bus service is available from Market Street on game days; call **Muni** (✆ **415/673-6864**) for pickup points and schedule information.

The 49ers' archenemies, the **Oakland Raiders,** play at the Oakland Alameda County Coliseum, off the 880 freeway (Nimitz). Call ✆ **800/949-2626** for ticket information.

COLLEGE FOOTBALL

The **University of California Golden Bears** play at Memorial Stadium, 61 Harmon Gym, University of California, Berkeley (✆ **800/GO-BEARS** or

510/642-3277), on the university campus across the bay. Tickets usually are available at game time. Phone for schedules and information.

HORSE RACING

Ten miles northeast of San Francisco is scenic **Golden Gate Fields,** Gilman Street off I-80, Albany (© **510/559-7300;** www.ggfields.com). It schedules thoroughbred racing from November 15 to December 31. The track is on the seashore. Call for admission prices and post times.

Bay Meadows, 2600 S. Delaware St., off U.S. 101, San Mateo (© **650/574-7223;** www.baymeadows.com), is a thoroughbred track on the peninsula about 20 miles south of downtown San Francisco. Call for admission prices and post times.

8

City Strolls

Despite a handful of killer hills, San Francisco is best explored on foot. In this chapter, you'll find suggestions for introductory walks in two of the city's many great neighborhoods. For more extensive city walks, check out Frommer's Memorable Walks in San Francisco.

WALKING TOUR 1	CHINATOWN: HISTORY, CULTURE, DIM SUM & THEN SOME
Start	Corner of Grant Avenue and Bush Street.
Public Transportation	2, 3, 4, 9X, 15, 30, 38, 45, or 76 bus.
Finish	Kearny Street, between Washington and Merchant streets.
Time	2 hours, not including museum or shopping stops.
Best Times	Daylight hours, when there's the most action.
Worst Times	Too early or too late, because shops are closed and no one is milling around.
Hills That Could Kill	None.

This tiny section of San Francisco, bounded loosely by Broadway and Stockton, Kearny, and Bush streets, is said to harbor one of the largest Chinese populations outside Asia. Daily proof is the crowds of Chinese residents who flock to the herbal stores, vegetable markets, restaurants, and businesses. Chinatown also marks the spot where the city began its development in the mid-1800s. On this walk you'll learn why Chinatown remains intriguing to all who wind through its narrow, crowded streets and how its origins are responsible for the town as we know it.

To begin the tour, make your way to the corner of Bush Street and Grant Avenue, where you can't miss the Chinatown Gateway Arch.

① Chinatown Gateway Arch.
Traditional Chinese villages have ceremonial gates like this one. This gate is a lot less formal than those in China, built here more for the benefit of the tourist industry than anything else.

Once you cross the threshold, you'll be at the beginning of Chinatown's portion of Grant Avenue.

② Grant Avenue.
This is a mecca for tourists who wander in and out of gift shops that offer a variety of unnecessary junk interspersed with quality imports. You'll also find decent restaurants and grocery stores frequented by Chinese residents, ranging from children to the oldest living people you've ever seen.

Tear yourself away from the shops and go right at the corner of Pine Street. Cross to the other side of Pine, and on your left you'll come to St. Mary's Square.

Walking Tour: Chinatown

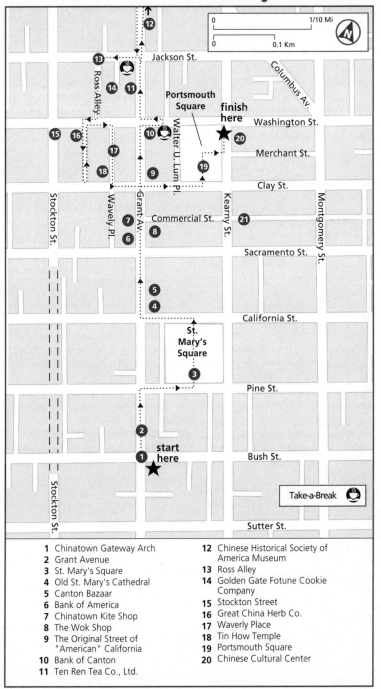

1 Chinatown Gateway Arch
2 Grant Avenue
3 St. Mary's Square
4 Old St. Mary's Cathedral
5 Canton Bazaar
6 Bank of America
7 Chinatown Kite Shop
8 The Wok Shop
9 The Original Street of "American" California
10 Bank of Canton
11 Ten Ren Tea Co., Ltd.
12 Chinese Historical Society of America Museum
13 Ross Alley
14 Golden Gate Fotune Cookie Company
15 Stockton Street
16 Great China Herb Co.
17 Waverly Place
18 Tin How Temple
19 Portsmouth Square
20 Chinese Cultural Center

❸ St. Mary's Square.

Here's where you'll find a huge metal-and-granite statue of Dr. Sun Yat-sen, the founder of the Republic of China. A native of Guandong (Canton) Province, Sun Yat-sen led the rebellion that ended the reign of the Qing Dynasty.

Note also the second monument in the square, which honors Chinese-American victims of both world wars. (A pay toilet is strategically placed here, too.)

Walk to the other end of the square, toward California Street, turn left, cross California Street at Grant Street, and you'll be standing in front of Old St. Mary's Cathedral.

❹ Old St. Mary's Cathedral.

The first Catholic cathedral in San Francisco and the site of the Chinese community's first English-language school, St. Mary's was built primarily by Chinese laborers and dedicated on Christmas Day 1854.

Step inside to find a written history of the church and turn-of-the-century photos of San Francisco. Stop in on a Tuesday or Thursday at 12:30 pm for a free half-hour classical music performance.

Upon leaving the church, take a right and walk to the corner of Grant Avenue and California Street, then go right on Grant. Here you'll find a shop called Canton Bazaar.

❺ Canton Bazaar.

Of the knickknack and import shops lining Grant Avenue, this is one of the most popular; it's located at 616 Grant Ave.

Continue in the same direction on Grant Avenue, and cross Sacramento Street, to arrive at the northwest corner of Sacramento Street and Grant Avenue, at the doorstep of the Bank of America.

❻ Bank of America.

This bank is an example of the traditional Chinese architectural style. Notice dragons subtly portrayed on many parts of the building.

Head in the same direction (north) on Grant, and a few doors down is the Chinatown Kite Shop.

❼ Chinatown Kite Shop.

This store, located at 717 Grant Ave., has an assortment of flying objects, including attractive fish kites, nylon or cotton windsock kites, hand-painted Chinese paper kites, wood-and-paper biplanes, and pentagonal kites.

Cross Grant, and you'll arrive at The Wok Shop.

❽ The Wok Shop.

Here's where you can purchase just about any cleaver, wok, cookbook, or vessel you might need for Chinese-style cooking in your own kitchen. It's located at 718 Grant Ave.

When you come out of the Wok Shop, go right. Walk past Commercial Street, and you'll arrive at the corner of Grant Avenue and Clay Street; cross Clay, and you'll be standing on the original street of "American" California.

❾ Original street of "American" California.

Here an English seaman named William Richardson set up the first tent in 1835.

Continue north on Grant to Washington Street. Go right, and at 743 Washington St. you will be standing in front of the Bank of Canton.

❿ Bank of Canton.

This building boasts the oldest (from 1909) Asian-style edifice in Chinatown. This three-tiered temple-style building once housed the China Telephone Exchange, known as "China-5" until 1945.

You're probably getting thirsty by now, so follow Washington Street a few doors down (east); on your right-hand side you will come upon Washington Bakery & Restaurant.

Go back to Grant Avenue, cross Washington Street, cross Grant, and follow the west side of Grant 1 block to Ten Ren Tea Co., Ltd.

⓫ Ten Ren Tea Co., Ltd.

In this amazing shop at 949 Grant Ave, you can sample a freshly brewed tea variety and check out the dozens of drawers and canisters labeled with more than 40 kinds of tea.

TAKE A BREAK
Washington Bakery & Restaurant, 733 Washington St. No need to have a full meal here—the service can be abrupt, and the food's mediocre. Do stop in, however, for a little potable adventure: snow red beans with ice cream. The sugary-sweet drink mixed with whole beans and ice cream is not something you're likely to have tried elsewhere, and it happens to be quite tasty. Whatever you do, don't fill up—a few blocks away some wonderfully fresh dim sum awaits you.

Leave Ten Ren, make a left, and when you reach Jackson Street, make another left. On the left side, at 735 Jackson St., through the storefront window you'll notice stacks of steaming wooden baskets and a Chinese cook. You've reached your snacking destination.

TAKE A BREAK
It's the **House of Dim Sum**—nothing fancy, for sure, but the dumplings are fresh, cheap, and delicious, and the staff is friendly. Order at the counter: pork, chive and shrimp, and shark-fin dumplings; sweet buns; turnip cake; or sweet rice with chicken wrapped in a lotus leaf. Unless they're taken, it's best to sit at one of the two tables to enjoy your feast.

As you leave the House of Dim Sum, return to Grant Avenue, and take a left so you're heading north on Grant, until you hit Broadway. Take a left on Broadway and follow it until you reach 644 Broadway. Go to the fourth floor. (Make sure you're arriving Monday through Friday between 10:30am and 4pm, or just skip this detour and go to the next attraction.) You've arrived at the Chinese Historical Society of America Museum.

⑫ Chinese Historical Society of America Museum.
Founded in 1963, the Chinese Historical Society of America Museum has a small but fascinating collection that illuminates the role of Chinese immigrants in U.S. history, particularly in San Francisco and the rest of California.

Admission is free, but the museum appreciates any donation you can give.

Retrace your steps back to the House of Dim Sum on Jackson Street. Continue past it and make another left on Ross Alley.

⑬ Ross Alley.
As you walk along the narrow street, just one of the many alleyways that crisscrossed Chinatown to accommodate the many immigrants who jammed into the neighborhood, it's not difficult to imagine that this block once was rife with gambling dens.

As you follow the alley south, on the left side of the street you'll encounter Golden Gate Fortune Cookie Company.

⑭ Golden Gate Fortune Cookie Company.
Located at 56 Ross Alley, this store is little more than a tiny place where one woman sits at a conveyer belt, folding messages into warm cookies as the manager invariably calls out to tourists, beckoning them to buy a big bag of the fortune-telling treats.

You can purchase regular fortunes or "sexy" ones (which are their specialty), or, of course, you can just take a peek and move on.

As you exit the alley, take a right on Washington and follow it up to Stockton Street.

⑮ Stockton Street.
From Broadway to Sacramento Street, Stockton is where most of the residents of Chinatown do their daily shopping. Come virtually anytime to see live fowl, fish, and various exotic cooking ingredients being purchased during an ever-fascinating flurry of commerce.

One noteworthy facet of this street's history is a place called **Cameron House** (2 blocks south at the corner of Stockton and Sacramento streets), which was named after a woman by the name of Donaldina Cameron (1869–1968). Called Lo Mo, or "the Mother," by the Chinese, she spent her life trying to free Chinese women who had come to America in hopes of marrying well but had found themselves forced into prostitution and slavery. Today, the house is still a place that helps women to free themselves from domestic violence.

Once you've had your fill of Stockton Street, double back to Stockton and Washington, turn right down Washington. On the right side of the street, you will stumble upon the Great China Herb Co.

⑯ Great China Herb Co.

For centuries, the Chinese have come to shops like this one at 857 Washington Street—full of exotic herbs, roots, and other natural substances—to buy what they believe will cure all types of ailments and ensure good health and long life.

Continue on Washinton Street back toward Grant Avenue, and take a right on Waverly Place.

⑰ Waverly Place.

This street is also known as "The Street of Painted Balconies." This is probably Chinatown's most popular side street or alleyway because of its painted balconies and colorful architectural details—a sort of Chinese-style New Orleans street. You can admire the architecture only from the ground because most of the buildings are private family associations or temples.

One temple you can visit (but make sure it's open before you go climbing up the long narrow stairway) is on the right, at 125 Waverly Place.

⑱ Tin How Temple.

Four floors up, this incense-laden sanctuary decorated in traditional black, red, and gold lacquered wood is a house of worship for Chinese Buddhists, who come here to pray, meditate, and send offerings to their ancestors and to Tin How, the Queen of the Heavens and Goddess of the Seven Seas. There are no scheduled services, but you are welcome to visit.

Just remember to quietly respect those who are here to pray, and try to be as unobtrusive as possible. It is customary to give a donation or buy a bundle of incense during your visit.

Once you've finished exploring Waverly Place, turn left on Clay Street and walk past Grant Avenue and continue until on your left you see the block-wide urban playground that also is the most important site in San Francisco's history: Portsmouth Square.

⑲ Portsmouth Square.

This very spot was the center of the region's first township, which was called Yerba Buena before it was renamed San Francisco in 1847. Around 1846, before any semblance of a city had taken shape, this plaza was at the foot of the eastern shoreline of the bay. There were fewer than 50 non–Native American residents in the settlement, there were no substantial buildings to speak of, and the few boats that pulled into the cove did so less than a block from where you're sitting.

In 1846, when California was claimed as U.S. territory, the marines who landed here named the square after their ship, the USS *Portsmouth*. (Today, a bronze plaque marks the spot where they raised the U.S. flag.)

Yerba Buena remained a modest township until the gold rush of 1849, when over the next two years the population grew from under 1,000 to over 19,000 as gold seekers from around the world made their way here.

When the square became too crowded, long wharves were constructed to support new buildings above the bay. Eventually the entire area became landfill. That was almost 150 years ago, but today the square still serves as an important meeting place for neighborhood Chinese—a sort of communal outdoor living room.

Throughout the day, the square is heavily trafficked by children and—in large part—elderly men, who gamble over Chinese cards. If you arrive early in the morning, you might come across people practicing tai chi.

It is said that Robert Louis Stevenson used to love to sit on a bench here and watch life go by. (At the northeast corner of the square, you'll find a monument to his memory, consisting of a model of the *Hispañola*, the ship in Stevenson's novel *Treasure Island*, and an excerpt from his "Christmas Sermon.")

When you've had your fill of the square, exit to the east, at Kearny Street. Across the street, at 750 Kearny, is the Holiday Inn.

Cross the street, enter the hotel, and take the elevator to the third floor, where you'll find the Chinese Cultural Center.

㉚ Chinese Cultural Center.
This center is oriented toward both the community and tourists, offering interesting display cases housing Chinese art and a gallery with rotating exhibits of Asian art and writings.

From here you might consider backtracking to Grant, taking a right (north), and following it to the end. You'll be at Broadway and Columbus, the beginning of North Beach, where you'll find an abundance of cafes or where you can venture onward for the North Beach tour, described next in this chapter.

WALKING TOUR 2   GETTING TO KNOW NORTH BEACH

Start	Intersection of Montgomery Street, Columbus Avenue, and Washington Street.
Public Transportation	15, 30X, 41, or 42 bus.
Finish	Washington Square.
Time	3 hours, including a stop for lunch.
Best Times	Start the tour Monday to Saturday anytime between 11am and 4pm.
Worst Times	Sunday, when shops are closed.
Hills That Could Kill	The Montgomery Street hill from Broadway to Vallejo Street; otherwise, this is an easy walk.

Along with Chinatown, North Beach is one of the city's oldest neighborhoods. Originally the Latin Quarter, it became the city's Italian district when Italian immigrants moved "uphill" in the early 1870s, crossing Broadway from the Jackson Square area and settling in. They quickly established restaurants, cafes, bakeries, and other businesses familiar to them from their homeland. The "Beat Generation" helped put North Beach on the map, with the likes of Jack Kerouac and Allen Ginsberg holding court in the area's cafes during the 1950s. Although most of the original beat poets are gone, their spirit lives on in North Beach, which is still a haven for bohemian artists and writers. The neighborhood, thankfully, retains its Italian village feel, where residents from all walks of life enjoy taking time for conversation over a pastry and a frothy cappuccino.

If there's one landmark you can't miss, it's the familiar building on the corner of Montgomery Street and Columbus Avenue, the TransAmerica Pyramid.

❶ TransAmerica Pyramid.
Noted for its spire (which rises 212 feet above the top floor) and its "wings" (which begin at the 29th floor

and stop at the spire), the pyramid is San Francisco's tallest building and a hallmark of the skyline. You might want to take a peek at one of the rotating art exhibits in the lobby, or go around to the right and into half-acre Redwood Park, which is part of the TransAmerica Center.

Finds **Do-It-Yourself Excursions**

The Convention & Visitors Bureau distributes a brochure detailing self-guided walking tours of North Beach, Union Square, Fisherman's Wharf, and Chinatown. Send a request plus a self-addressed business-size envelope to the San Francisco Convention & Visitors Bureau, P.O. Box 429097, San Francisco, CA 94142-9097, or visit **www.sfvisitor.org/visitorinfo/html/walkpdfs.html**.

The TransAmerica Pyramid occupies part of the 600 block of Montgomery Street, which once held a historic building called the Montgomery Block.

❷ The Montgomery Block.

Originally four stories high, the Montgomery Block was the tallest building in the West when it was built in 1853. San Franciscans called it "Halleck's Folly" because it was built on a raft of redwood logs that had been bolted together and floated at the edge of the ocean (which was right at Montgomery Street at that time). The building was demolished in 1959 but is fondly remembered for its historic importance as the power center of the city. Its tenants included artists and writers of all kinds, among them Jack London, George Sterling, Ambrose Bierce, Bret Harte, and Mark Twain.

From the southeast corner of Montgomery and Washington streets, look across Washington to the corner of Columbus Avenue, and you'll see the original TransAmerica Building, located at 4 Columbus Ave.

❸ Original TransAmerica Building.

Now Sanwa Bank, the original TransAmerica Building is a beaux arts flat-iron building covered in white terra-cotta; it was also the home of the old Fugazi Bank. Built for the Banco Populare Italiano Operaia Fugazi in 1909, it was originally a two-story building and gained a third floor in 1916. In 1928, Fugazi merged his bank with the Bank of America, which was started by A. P. Giannini, who also created the TransAmerica Corporation.

Cross Washington Street and continue north on Montgomery Street to no. 730, the Golden Era Building.

❹ Golden Era Building.

Erected in about 1852, this building is named after the literary magazine the *Golden Era,* which was published here. Some of the young writers who worked on the magazine were known as the Bohemians; they included Samuel Clemens (a.k.a. Mark Twain) and Bret Harte (who began as a typesetter here). Backtrack a few dozen feet and stop for a minute to admire the annex, at no. 722 (marked by a faded black-and-white-striped awning). The Belli Annex, as it is currently known, is registered as a historic landmark.

Continue north on Washington Street, and take the first right onto Jackson Street. Continue until you hit the 400 block of Jackson Square.

❺ 400 block of Jackson Square.

Here's where you'll find some of the only commercial buildings to survive the 1906 earthquake and fire. 415 Jackson (ca. 1853) served as the headquarters for the Ghirardelli Chocolate Company from 1855 to 1894. The Hotaling Building (no. 451) was built in 1866. At no. 472 is another of the buildings that survived the disaster of 1906.

Cross the street, and backtrack on Jackson Street. Continue toward the intersection of Columbus Avenue and Jackson Street. Turn right on Columbus and look across the street for the small triangular building at the junction of Kearny Street and Columbus Avenue, Columbus Tower (a.k.a. the Sentinel Building).

Walking Tour: North Beach

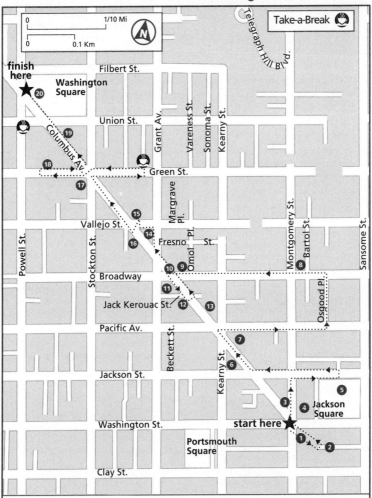

0   1/10 Mi
0   0.1 Km

Take-a-Break

finish here

Washington Square

Filbert St.

Union St.

Green St.

Vallejo St.

Fresno   St.

Broadway

Jack Kerouac St.

Pacific Av.

Jackson St.

Washington St.

Clay St.

Portsmouth Square

start here

Jackson Square

Telegraph Hill Blvd.

Columbus Av.

Grant Av.
Vareness St.
Sonoma St.
Kearny St.
Margrave Pl.
Omol Pl.
Montgomery St.
Bartol St.
Sansome St.
Osgood Pl.
Powell St.
Stockton St.
Beckett St.
Kearny St.

1	TransAmerica Pyramid	11	City Lights Bookstore
2	The Montgomery Block	12	Vesuvio
3	Original TransAmerica Building	13	Spec's Adler Museum Café
4	Golden Era Building	14	Caffe Trieste
5	400 block of Jackson Square	15	Biordi Art Imports
6	Columbus Tower	16	Molinari Delicatessen
7	140 Columbus Avenue	17	North Beach Museum
8	1010 Montgomery Street	18	Club Fugazi
9	hungry i	19	Mario's Bohemian Cigar Store
10	Former Site of the Condor Club	20	Washington Square

193

❻ Columbus Tower.

If you walk a little farther, then turn around and look back down Columbus, you'll be able to get a better look at Columbus Tower. The flat-iron beauty—a building shaped to a triangular site—went up between 1905 and 1907. Movie director and producer Francis Ford Coppola bought and restored it in the mid-1970s; it is now home to his film production company, American Zoetrope Studios. The cafe showcases all things Niebaum-Coppola (as in Francis Ford Coppola and his winery)—including olive oil, Parmesan cheese, and wine. It's a great place to stop for a glass of wine, an espresso, or a thin-crusted pizza snack. This is one of the few pre-1906 earthquake buildings in the city center.

Across the street from the Tower on Columbus Avenue is 140 Columbus Avenue.

❼ 140 Columbus Avenue.

Once home to the Purple Onion, many famous headliners have played here, often before they were famous. Phyllis Diller, who's now so big that she's famous for something as simple as her laugh, was still struggling when she played a 2-week engagement here in the late 1950s.

Continue north on Columbus, and then turn right on Pacific Avenue. After you cross Montgomery Street, you'll find brick-lined Osgood Place on the left. A registered historic landmark, it is one of the few quiet—and car-free—little alleyways left in the city. Stroll up Osgood and go left on Broadway to 1010 Montgomery Street (at Broadway).

❽ 1010 Montgomery Street.

This is where Allen Ginsberg lived during the time he wrote his legendary poem "Howl," first performed on October 13, 1955, in a converted auto-repair shop at the corner of Fillmore and Union streets. By the time Ginsberg finished reading, he was crying and the audience was going wild. Jack Kerouac proclaimed, "Ginsberg, this poem will make you famous in San Francisco." Continue along Broadway toward Columbus Avenue. This stretch of Broadway is San Francisco's answer to New York's Times Square, complete with strip clubs and peep shows that are being pushed aside by restaurants, clubs, and an endless crowd of visitors. It's among the most sought-after locations in the city as more and more profitable restaurants and clubs spring up.

Keep walking west on Broadway, and on the right side of the street, you'll come to Columbus Books, 540 Broadway. It sells new and used discount books and is worth a quick trip inside for a good, cheap read. A few dozen yards farther up, Broadway is the current location of the hungry i.

❾ hungry i.

Now a seedy strip club (at 546 Broadway), the original hungry i (at 599 Jackson St.) was owned and operated by the vociferous "Big Daddy" Nordstrom. If you had been here while Enrico Banducci (also of Enrico's restaurant) was in charge, you would have found only a plain room with an exposed brick wall and director's chairs around small tables. A who's who of nightclub entertainers fortified their careers at the original hungry i, including Lenny Bruce, Billie Holiday (who first sang "Strange Fruit" there), Bill Cosby, Richard Pryor, Woody Allen, and Barbra Streisand.

At the corner of Broadway and Columbus Avenue, you will see the former site of the Condor Club.

❿ Former site of the Condor Club.

The Condor Club was located at 300 Columbus Ave.; this is where Carol Doda scandalously bared her breasts and danced topless for the first time in 1964. Note the bronze plaque claiming the Condor Club as BIRTHPLACE OF THE WORLD'S FIRST TOPLESS & BOTTOMLESS ENTERTAINMENT. Go inside what is now the Condor Sports Bar and have a look at the framed newspaper clippings that hang around the dining room. From the elevated back room you can see Doda's old dressing room and, on the floor below, an outline of the piano that would descend from the second floor with her atop it.

When you leave the Condor Sports Bar, cross to the south side of Broadway. Note the mural of jazz musicians painted on the entire side of the building directly across Columbus Avenue. Diagonally across the intersection from the Condor Bistro is City Lights Bookstore.

⓫ City Lights Bookstore.

Owned by one of the first Beat poets to arrive in San Francisco, Lawrence Ferlinghetti, City Lights is now a city landmark and literary mecca. Located at 261 Columbus Ave., it's one of the last of the Beat-era hangouts in operation. An active participant in the Beat movement, Ferlinghetti established his shop as a meeting place where writers and bibliophiles could (and still do) attend poetry readings and other events. It's still a vibrant part of the literary scene; the well-stocked bookshop prides itself on its collection of art, poetry, and political paperbacks.

Upon exiting City Lights Bookstore, turn right, cross aptly named Jack Kerouac Street, and stop by the bar on your right that's named Vesuvio.

⓬ Vesuvio.

Because of its proximity to City Lights Bookstore, Vesuvio became a favorite hangout of the Beats. Dylan Thomas used to drink here, as did Jack Kerouac, Ferlinghetti, and Ginsberg. Even today, Vesuvio, which opened in 1949, maintains its original bohemian atmosphere. The building is located at 255 Columbus Ave. (at Broadway), and dates from 1913, and is an excellent example of pressed-tin architecture.

Facing Vesuvio across Columbus Avenue is another favorite spot of the Beat Generation: Spec's Adler Museum Café.

⓭ Spec's Adler Museum Café.

Located at 12 Saroyan Place, this is one of the city's funkiest bars, a small,

dimly lit watering hole with ceiling-hung maritime flags and exposed brick walls crammed with memorabilia. Within the bar is a mini-museum that consists of a few glass cases filled with mementos brought back and dropped off by seamen who have frequented the pub.

From here, go back up Columbus across Broadway to Grant Avenue. Turn right, and walk until you come to Vallejo Street. At 606 Vallejo St. (at Grant Avenue) is Caffè Trieste.

⓮ Caffè Trieste.

Yet another favorite spot of the Beats. Founded by Gianni Giotta in 1956, Caffè Trieste is still run by family members. The quintessential San Francisco coffeehouse, Trieste features opera on the jukebox and the real thing, performed by the Giottas, on Saturday afternoons. Any day of the week is a good one to stop in for a cappuccino or espresso—the beans are roasted right next door.

Go left out of Caffè Trieste onto Vallejo Street, turn right on Columbus Avenue, and bump into the loveliest shop in all of North Beach: Biordi Art Imports, located at 412 Columbus Avenue.

⓯ Biordi Art Imports.

This store has carried imported hand-painted majolica pottery from the hill towns of central Italy for more than 50 years. Some of the colorful patterns date from the 14th century. Biordi handpicks its artisans, and its catalog includes biographies of those who are currently represented.

Across Columbus Avenue, at the corner of Vallejo Street, is Molinari Delicatessen.

⓰ Molinari Delicatessen.

This deli, located at 373 Columbus Avenue, has been selling its pungent, air-dried salamis since 1896. Ravioli and tortellini are made in the back of the shop, but it's the mouthwatering selection of cold salads, cheeses, and marinades up front that captures the attention of most folks. Each Italian sub is big enough for two hearty appetites.

Walk north to the lively intersection of Columbus, Green, and Stockton, and look for the Eureka Bank at 1435 Stockton St. On the second floor of the bank you'll find the North Beach Museum.

⑰ North Beach Museum.

North Beach Museum displays historical artifacts that tell the story of North Beach, Chinatown, and Fisherman's Wharf. Just before you enter the museum, you'll find a framed, handwritten poem by Lawrence Ferlinghetti that captures his impressions of this primarily Italian neighborhood. After you pass through the glass doors, you'll find many photographs of some of the first Chinese and Italian immigrants, as well as pictures of San Francisco after the 1906 earthquake. You can visit the museum any time the bank is open (unfortunately, it's closed on weekends), and admission is free.

Now backtrack toward Columbus Avenue and go left on Green Street to Club Fugazi, at 678 Green Street.

⑱ Club Fugazi.

It doesn't look like much from the outside, but Fugazi Hall was donated to the city (and more importantly, the North Beach area) by John Fugazi, the founder of the Italian bank that was taken over by A. P. Giannini and turned into the original TransAmerica Corporation. For many years, Fugazi Hall has been staging the zany and whimsical musical revue *Beach Blanket Babylon*. The show evolved from Steve Silver's Rent-a-Freak service, which consisted of a group of partygoers who would attend parties dressed as any number of characters in outrageous costumes. The fun caught on and soon came *Beach Blanket Babylon*.

If you love comedy, you'll love this show. We don't want to spoil it for you by telling you what it's about, but if you get tickets and they're in an unreserved section, you should arrive fairly early because you'll be seated around

small cocktail tables on a first-come, first-served basis (two sections are reserved, four aren't, and all frequently sell out weeks in advance; however, sometimes it is possible to get tickets at the last minute on weekdays). You'll want to be as close to the stage as possible. This super-charged show is definitely worth the price of admission. (See chapter 10 for details.)

TAKE A BREAK Head back the way you came on Green Street, and cross Columbus Avenue. Before you get to Grant Avenue, you'll see **O'Reilly's Irish Pub** (622 Green St.), a homey watering hole that dishes out good, hearty Irish food and a fine selection of beers (including Guinness, of course) that are best enjoyed at one of the sidewalk tables. Always a conversation piece is the mural of Irish authors peering out from the back wall. (How many can you name?)

As you come out of O'Reilly's, turn left, cross Columbus Avenue, and proceed 1 block northwest on Columbus to Mario's Bohemian Cigar Store.

⑲ Mario's Bohemian Cigar Store.

Located at 566 Columbus Ave., across the street from Washington Square, it's one of North Beach's most popular neighborhood hangouts.

Our next stop, directly across Union Street, is Washington Square.

⑳ Washington Square.

This is one of the oldest parks in the city. This land was designated a public park in 1847 and has undergone many changes since then. Its current landscaping dates from 1955. You'll notice **Saints Peter and Paul Church,** which is the religious center for this neighborhood's Italian community, on the northwest end. Take a few moments to go inside and check out the traditional Italian interior. Also note that this is the church in which baseball great Joe DiMaggio married his first wife, Dorothy Arnold. He wasn't allowed to marry Marilyn Monroe here because he had been divorced. He married Monroe at City Hall and came here for publicity photos.

Today the park is a pleasant place to soak up the sun, read a book, or chat with a retired Italian octogenarian who has seen the city grow and change.

From here you can see the famous Coit Tower at the top of Telegraph Hill to the northwest.

WINDING DOWN
On sunny days there's no better place in North Beach for a picnic lunch than Washington Square, and no cafe serves better picnic fixings than **Gira Polli** (© 415/434-4472), located at the southwest corner of the Square at 659 Union St. Order the Gira Polli Special: half of a wood-fired chicken (scrumptious), Palermo potatoes (the best in the city), a fresh garden salad, perfectly cooked vegetables, and a soft roll. Take your goodies across the street to the Square.

9

Shopping

Like its population, San Francisco's shopping is both worldly and intimate. Every persuasion, style, era, and fetish is represented, not in big, tacky shopping malls, but in hundreds of quaint, dramatically different boutiques scattered throughout the city.

Whether you're looking for Chanel or Chinese herbal medicine, San Francisco's got it. Just pick a neighborhood and break out your credit cards—you're sure to end up with at least a few take-home treasures.

1 The Shopping Scene

MAJOR SHOPPING AREAS

San Francisco has many shopping areas, but the following places are where you'll find most of the action.

UNION SQUARE & ENVIRONS San Francisco's most congested and popular shopping mecca is centered on Union Square and enclosed by Bush, Taylor, Market, and Montgomery streets. Most of the big department stores and many high-end specialty shops are here. Be sure to venture to Grant Avenue, Post and Sutter streets, and Maiden Lane. This area is a hub for public transportation; all Market Street and several other buses run here, as do the Powell-Hyde and Powell-Mason cable-car lines. You can also take Muni Metro to Powell Station.

CHINATOWN When you pass under the gate to Chinatown on Grant Avenue, say good-bye to the world of fashion and hello to a swarm of cheap tourist shops selling everything from linen and jade to plastic toys and $2 slippers. But that's not all Chinatown has to offer. The real gems are tucked away on side streets or are small, one-person shops selling Chinese herbs, original art, and jewelry. Grant Avenue is the area's main thoroughfare, and the side streets between Bush Street and Columbus Avenue are full of restaurants, markets, and eclectic shops. Stockton Street is best for grocery shopping (including live fowl and fish.) Walking is best, since traffic through this area is slow at best and parking is next to impossible. Most stores in Chinatown are open daily from 10am to 10pm. Take bus no. 9X, 15, 30, 41, or 45.

UNION STREET Union Street, from Fillmore Street to Van Ness Avenue, caters to the upper–middle-class crowd. It's a great place to stroll, window-shop the plethora of boutiques, cafes, and restaurants, and watch the beautiful people parade by. Take bus no. 22, 41, 42, or 45.

CHESTNUT STREET Parallel and a few blocks north, Chestnut is a younger version of Union Street. It holds endless shopping and dining choices, and an ever-tanned, superfit population of postgraduate singles who hang around cafes and scope each other out. Take bus no. 22, 28, 30, 41, 42, 43, or 76.

FILLMORE STREET Some of the best shopping in town is packed into 5 blocks of Fillmore Street in Pacific Heights. From Jackson to Sutter streets,

(Tips **Hours, Taxes & Shipping**

Store hours are generally Monday to Saturday 10am to 6pm and Sunday noon to 5pm. Most department stores stay open later, as do shops around Fisherman's Wharf, the most heavily visited area.

Sales tax in San Francisco is 8.5%, which is added on at the register for all goods and services purchased. If you live out of state and buy an expensive item, you might want to consider having the store ship it home for you. You have to pay for shipping, but you escape paying the sales tax.

Most of the city's shops can wrap your purchase and **ship** it anywhere in the world via United Parcel Service (UPS). If they can't, you can send it yourself, either through **UPS** (✆ **800/742-5877**) or through the U.S. mail (see "Fast Facts: San Francisco" in chapter 4).

Fillmore is the perfect place to grab a bite and peruse the high-priced boutiques, craft shops, and incredible housewares stores. Don't miss Zinc Details and Fillamento. Take bus no. 1, 2, 3, 4, 12, 22, or 24.

HAIGHT STREET   Green hair, spiked hair, no hair, or mohair—even the hippies look conservative next to Haight Street's dramatic fashion freaks. The shopping in the 6 blocks of upper Haight Street between Central Avenue and Stanyan Street reflects its clientele. It offers everything from incense and European and American street styles to furniture and antique clothing. Buses 7, 66, 71, and 73 run the length of Haight Street. The Muni Metro N line stops at Waller Street and Cole Street.

SOMA   Although this area isn't suitable for strolling, you'll find almost all the discount shopping in warehouse spaces South of Market. You can pick up a discount-shopping guide at most major hotels. Many bus lines pass through this area.

HAYES VALLEY   It's not the prettiest area in town, with some of the shadier housing projects a few blocks away. But while most neighborhoods cater to more conservative or trendy shoppers, lower Hayes Street, between Octavia and Gough, celebrates anything vintage, artistic, or downright funky. Still in its developmental stage, it's definitely the most interesting new shopping area in town, with furniture and glass stores, thrift shops, trendy shoe stores, and men's and women's clothiers. You can find lots of great antique shops south on Octavia and on nearby Market Street. Take bus no. 16AX, 16BX, or 21.

FISHERMAN'S WHARF & ENVIRONS *(Overrated*   The tourist-oriented malls run along Jefferson Street and include hundreds of shops, restaurants, and attractions. They include Ghirardelli Square, Pier 39, the Cannery, and the Anchorage (see "Shopping Centers & Complexes," below).

2 Shopping A to Z

ANTIQUES

Jackson Square, a historic district just north of the Financial District's Embarcadero Center, is the place to go for the top names in fine furniture and fine art. You can find a number of Asian-art dealers here. More than a dozen dealers on the 2 blocks between Columbus and Sansome streets specialize in European

San Francisco Shopping

Aardvark's **70**
Alabaster **11**
Alessi **40**
All American Boy **15**
The Anchorage **22**
Art of China **33**
Artisan Cheese **9**
Atelier Dore **38**
Babushka **22**
Barnes & Noble **25**
Biordi Art Imports **28**
Birkenstock **55**
The Booksmith **67**
Borders Books
 & Music **44**
Boulangerie **10**
Britex Fabrics **52**
Brooks Brothers **50**
Buffalo Exchange **70**
Bulo **13**
Butterfield & Butterfield **64**
Cable Car Clothiers **40**
The Cannery **21**
Catharine Clark
 Gallery **55**
The Canton Bazaar **37**
The Chanel Boutique **48**
Chinatown **32**
The Chinatown Kite
 Shop **35**
Citizen Clothing **15**
City Lights Booksellers
 & Publishers **29**
A Clean, Well-Lighted
 Place for Books **59**
Cost Plus Imports **25**
Crocker Galleria **51**
Dandelion **65**
De Vera Galleries **49**
Dianne's Old & New
 Estates **2**
The Disney Store **39**
Distractions
 & Euphoria **68**
Eleonore Austerer ·
 Gallery **39**
Esprit Outlet Store **66**
F.A.O. Schwarz **54**
Fillamento **8**
Fisherman's Wharf **23**
Flax **14**
Fraenkel Gallery **55**
Fumiki Fine Asian Arts **42**
Ghirardelli Square **20**
Gimme Shoes **7**
Golden Gate Fortune
 Cookies Co. **32**
Good Byes **5**
Good Vibrations **19**
Grand Women's
 Boutique **71**

Green Apple Books **6**
Gucci America **50**
Gump's **49**
Haight Street **71**
Hayes Valley **13**
Images of the North **3**
Jackson Square **30**
Jeremy's **62**
Jerusalem Shoppe **17**
Joseph Schmidt
 Confections **18**
Kenneth Cole **58**
La Rosa **69**
Limn **63**
MAC (men's) **42**
MAC (women's) **26**
Macy's **53**
The Magical Trinket **12**
Maxwell Galleries **43**
Métier **41**
Meyerovich Gallery **50**
Minis **3**
Neiman Marcus **50**
Nest **6**
The New Unique
 Company **34**
Niketown **47**
Nordstrom **58**
The North Face **60**
On the Road Again **24**
Pearl & Jade Empire **45**
Pier 39 **24**
Quantity Postcards **27**
Recycled Records **71**
San Francisco Shopping
 Centre **58**
SFMOMA
 MuseumStore **57**
Silkroute International **1**
Smile **39**
SoMa **57**
Streetlight Records **16**
Sue Fisher King **5**
Ten Ren Tea Co. **32**
Therien & Co. **64**
Thomas Bros. Maps
 & Books **31**
Three Bags Full **2**
Tiffany & Co. **46**
Union Square **53**
Union Street Goldsmith **4**
Victorian Interiors **11**
Virgin Megastore **56**
Wilkes Bashford **47**
William Stout
 Architectural Books **30**
Wine Club San
 Francisco **61**
The Wok Shop **36**
Zinc Details **10**

Haight-Ashbury

Conservatory Dr.
Fulton St.
Grove St.
McLaren
Lodge
Hayes St.
John F. Kennedy Dr.
Fell St.
Cole St.
Ashbury St.
Masonic Ave.
PANHANDLE
GOLDEN
GATE
PARK
Stanyan St.
Shrader St.
Page St.
Oak St.
68
Kezar
67
Pavilion
Waller St.
Haight St.
70
71
Beulah St.
69
Clayton St.
Belvedere St.
Downey St.
Delmar St.
Kezar
Stadium
Frederick St.
Carl St.
Parnassus Ave.

Municipal
Pier

Pier 45
Pier 43 1/2
Pier 43
Pier 41

Aquatic
Park

Pier 39

23
Jefferson St.
Beach St.
Pier 35

21
22
24

20
North Point St.
Pier 33

Ghiradelli
Square
25
Bay St.
Pier 31

Francisco St.
Pier 27

Chestnut St.

Lombard St.

Greenwich St.

Filbert St.

Union St.
Pier 23

Green St.
Pier 19
Pier 17

Vallejo St.
Tunnel
Pier 15

Broadway
26
Pier 9

Pacific Ave.
27
Pier 7

Jackson St.
28
Pier 5

29
Pier 3

30
Pier 1
Ferry Building
(World Trade Center)

31
Justin
Herman
Plaza

San
Francisco
Bay

32

33
34

35
36

37

38

39
40
41
42

43
46
47
48
49

44
50
51

45
Union
Square
52

53
54
55

56

57
Yerba Buena
Gardens

58

Moscone
Convention
Center

San Francisco-
Oakland
Bay Bridge

80

SOUTH
PARK
62

Market St.

Mission St.

Howard St.

Folsom St.

Harrison St.
61

Bryant St.

Brannan St.
63

Townsend St.

King St.

Berry St.

Division St.

Channel St.

Alameda St.

280

65

66

201

furnishings from the 17th to the 19th centuries. Most shops here are open Monday to Friday 9am to 5pm and Saturday 11am to 4pm.

Butterfield & Butterfield   This renowned auction house holds preview weekends for upcoming auctions of furnishings, silver, antiques, art, and jewelry. Call for auction schedules. 220 San Bruno Ave. (at 16th St.). ✆ **415/861-7500.**

Fumiki Fine Asian Arts   Come here for a beautiful collection of antique Japanese Imari and Korean and Japanese *tansus* (clothing chests) and Asian-style home accouterments. The extensive collection of Asian art and antiques includes Japanese baskets and Chinese artifacts and embroidery. 272 Sutter St. (at Grant St.) **415/362-6677.** A second location is at 2001 Union St. (at Buchanan St.). ✆ **415/922-0573.**

Therien & Co.   For the best in Scandinavian, French, and Eastern European antiques, head beyond SoMa's design center to this boutique where you can find the real thing or antique replicas and made-to-order furniture from their neighboring custom furniture shop. 411 Vermont St. (at 17th St.). ✆ **415/956-8850.**

ART

The San Francisco Gallery Guide, a comprehensive, bimonthly publication listing the city's current shows, is available free by mail. Send a self-addressed, stamped envelope to San Francisco Bay Area Gallery Guide, 1369 Fulton St., San Francisco, CA 94117 (✆ **415/921-1600**), or pick one up at the San Francisco Visitor Information Center at 900 Market St. Most of the city's major art galleries are clustered downtown in the Union Square area.

Atelier Dore   Atelier Dore features American and European paintings from the 19th and 20th centuries, including some WPA art. Closed Sunday; open Monday by appointment only. 771 Bush St. (between Mason and Powell sts.). ✆ **415/391-2423.**

Catharine Clark Gallery *(Value*   Catharine Clark's is a different kind of gallery experience. While many galleries focus on established artists and out-of-this world prices, Catharine's exhibits up-and-coming contemporary as well as established artists (mainly from California) and nurtures beginning collectors by offering a purchasing plan that's almost unheard of in the art business. You can buy a piece on layaway and take up to a year to pay for it—interest free! Prices here make art a realistic purchase for almost everyone for a change, but serious collectors still frequent the shows because Clark has such a keen eye for talent. Shows change every 4 to 6 weeks. 49 Geary St. (between Kearny and Grant sts.), 2nd floor. ✆ **415/399-1439.**

Eleonore Austerer Gallery   Here you'll find limited-edition graphics by modern masters like Braque, Matisse, Miró, Picasso, Calder, Chagall, and Hockney, as well as original works by European and American contemporary artists. The gallery, in a beautiful old building near Union Square, is closed on Sunday. 540 Sutter St. (between Powell and Mason sts.). ✆ **415/986-2244.**

Fraenkel Gallery   This photography gallery features works by contemporary American and European artists. Excellent shows change frequently. Closed Sunday. 49 Geary St., 4th floor (between Grant Ave. and Kearny St.). ✆ **415/981-2661.** www. fraenkelgallery.com.

Images of the North   The highlight here is one of the most extensive collections of Canadian and Alaskan Inuit art in the United States. There's also a fine collection of Native American masks and jewelry. 2036 Union St. (at Buchanan St.). ✆ **415/673-1273.**

Maxwell Galleries   The specialties at Maxwell Galleries are 19th- and 20th-century European and American sculpture and paintings, including works by Raphael and Butler. Closed Sunday. 559 Sutter St. (between Powell and Mason sts.). ✆ 415/421-5193. www.artnet.com/maxwell.html.

Meyerovich Gallery   Works on paper by modern and contemporary masters here include Chagall, Matisse, Miró, and Picasso. Meyerovich's new Contemporary Gallery, across the hall, features works by Lichtenstein, Motherwell, Dine, and Hockney. Closed Sunday. 251 Post St. (at Stockton St.), 4th floor. ✆ 415/421-7171. www.meyerovich.com.

BOOKS

In addition to the listings below, there's a **Barnes & Noble** superstore at 2550 Taylor St., between Bay and North Point streets, near Fisherman's Wharf (✆ **415/292-6762**).

The Booksmith   Haight Street's best selection of new books is in this large, well-maintained shop. It carries all the top titles, along with works from smaller presses, and more than 1,000 different magazines. 1644 Haight St. (between Clayton and Cole sts.). ✆ **800/493-7323** or 415/863-8688.

Borders Books & Music   With four stories neatly packed with books, magazines, videos, a cafe, and plenty of reading nooks, it's a good thing this megastore is open late—you could spend hours browsing the selections. Open late daily. 400 Post St., at Union Square. ✆ **415/399-1633**.

City Lights Booksellers & Publishers *Finds*   Brooding literary types browse this famous bookstore owned by Lawrence Ferlinghetti, the renowned Beat Generation poet. The three-level bookshop prides itself on a comprehensive collection of art, poetry, and political paperbacks, as well as more mainstream books. Open daily until midnight. 261 Columbus Ave. (at Broadway). ✆ **415/362-8193**. www.citylights.com.

A Clean, Well-Lighted Place for Books *Finds*   Voted best bookstore by the *San Francisco Bay Guardian,* this independent store has good new fiction and nonfiction sections, and specializes in music, art, mystery, and cookbooks. The store is well known for its author readings and events. For a calendar of events, call or check the website. 601 Van Ness Ave. (between Turk St. and Golden Gate Ave.). ✆ **415/441-6670**. www.bookstore.com.

Green Apple Books *Finds*   The local favorite for used books, Green Apple is crammed with titles—more than 60,000 new and 100,000 used books. Its extended sections in psychology, cooking, art, history; collection of modern first editions; and rare graphic comics are superseded only by the staff's superlative service. 506 Clement St. (at 6th Ave.). ✆ **415/387-2272**.

William Stout Architectural Books *Finds*   Step inside this shrine to all things architectural, and even if you think you're not interested in exquisite bathrooms, Southern California's modern homes, or great gardens, you can't help but bury yourself in the thousands of design books. And if they don't have what you're looking for, it probably doesn't exist. 804 Montgomery St. (at Gold St.). ✆ **415/989-2341**. www.stoutbooks.com.

CHINA, SILVER & GLASS

Gump's *Finds*   Founded over a century ago, Gump's offers gifts and treasures ranging from Asian antiquities to contemporary art glass and exquisite jade and pearl jewelry. Many items are made specifically for the store. Gump's also has one of the city's most revered holiday window displays. Closed Sunday. 135 Post St. (between Kearny St. and Grant Ave.). ✆ 415/982-1616.

CRAFTS

The Canton Bazaar   Amid a wide variety of handicrafts you'll find an excellent selection of rosewood and carved furniture, cloisonné enamelware, rose Canton chinaware, porcelain, carved jade, embroideries, jewelry, and antiques from mainland China. Open daily until 10pm. 616 Grant Ave. (between Sacramento and California sts.). ✆ 415/362-5750.

The New Unique Company   Primarily a calligraphy- and watercolor-supplies store, the shop also has a good assortment of books on these topics. In addition, there's a wide selection of carved stones for use as seals on letters and documents. Should you want a special design or group of initials, the store will carve seals to order. 838 Grant Ave. (between Clay and Washington sts.). ✆ 415/981-2036.

Silkroute International   Owned and operated by an Afghan who offers fascinating wares, old and new, from his native country, the shop sells Oriental and tribal rugs, kilims, dhurries, textiles, jewelry, clothing, pillows, art, and antiques. 3119 Fillmore St. (at Filbert St.). ✆ 415/563-4936.

DEPARTMENT STORES

Macy's   The seven-story Macy's West features contemporary fashions for women, juniors, and children, plus jewelry, fragrances, cosmetics, and accessories. The sixth floor offers a "hospitality suite" where visitors can leave their coats and packages, grab a cup of coffee, or find out more about the city from the concierge. The top floors contain home furnishings, and the Cellar sells kitchenware and gourmet foods. You'll even find a Boudin Cafe (great sandwiches!) and Wolfgang Puck Cafe on the premises. Across the street, Macy's East has five floors of men's fashion, the largest Men's Polo by Ralph Lauren shop in the country, and the Fresh Choice cafe. Stockton and O'Farrell sts., Union Square. ✆ 415/397-3333.

Neiman Marcus   Some call this unit of the Texas-based chain "Needless Mark-up." The men's and women's clothes, precious gems, and conservative formal wear are some of the most glamorous in town, so if you've got the cash, go for it. The Rotunda Restaurant, on the top floor, is a beautiful, relaxing place for lunch and afternoon tea. 150 Stockton St., Union Square. ✆ 415/362-3900.

Nordstrom   Renowned for its personalized service, this is the largest branch of the Seattle-based fashion department-store chain. Nordstrom occupies the top five floors of the San Francisco Shopping Centre (see "Shopping Centers & Complexes," later in this chapter) and is the mall's primary anchor. Equally devoted to women's and men's fashions, the store has one of the best shoe selections in the city and thousands of suits in stock. The City Centre Grill, on the fourth floor, has a panoramic view and is an ideal place for an inexpensive lunch or light snack. Nordstrom Spa, on the fifth floor, is the perfect place to relax after a hectic day of bargain hunting. In the San Francisco Shopping Centre, 865 Market St. ✆ 415/243-8500.

DISCOUNT SHOPPING

San Francisco's many factory-outlet stores sell overstocked and discontinued fashions at bargain prices. All of the following shops are south of Market Street, in the city's warehouse district, SoMa.

Esprit Outlet Store   All the Esprit collections are available here at 20% or more off regular prices. In addition to clothes, the store sells accessories, shoes, and assorted other items. 499 Illinois St. (at 16th St.). ℰ **415/957-2550.**

Jeremy's *Value*   This boutique offers top designer fashions, from shoes to suits, at rock-bottom prices. There are no cheap knockoffs here, just good men's and women's clothes and accessories. Jeremy's also has its own stylish clothing line. 2 South Park (between Bryant and Brannan sts. at Second St.). ℰ **415/882-4929.**

The North Face   Well known for its sporting, camping, and hiking equipment, this off-price outlet carries a limited but high-quality selection of ski wear, boots, sweaters, and goods such as tents, packs, and sleeping bags. The North Face makes heavy use of Gore-Tex, down, and other durable, lightweight materials. 1325 Howard St. (between 9th and 10th sts.). ℰ **415/626-6444.**

FABRICS

Britex Fabrics   A San Francisco institution since 1952, Britex offers an absurd amount and variety of fabrics, not to mention a selection of more than 30,000 buttons. Closed Sunday. 146 Geary St. (between Stockton and Grant sts.). ℰ **415/392-2910.**

FASHION

See also "Vintage Clothing," later in this section.

Grand Women's Boutique   Invited to an underground club and forgot your funky rave attire? Grand's North Beach shop features the latest in fashion-forward street wear by local designers. Garb comes both baggy and tight; the style is club, and the price is right. 1429 Haight St. (between Ashbury and Masonic aves.). ℰ **415/255-1214.**

Gucci America   Donning Gucci's golden Gs is not a cheap endeavor. But if you've got the cash, you'll find all the latest lines of shoes, leather goods, scarves, and pricey accessories, such as a $9,000 handmade crocodile bag. 200 Stockton St. (between Geary and Post sts.). ℰ **415/392-2808.**

Niketown   Here it's not "I can," but "I can spend." At least that's what the kings of sportswear were banking on when they opened this megastore in 1997. As you'd expect, inside the doors it's Nike's world, offering everything the merchandising team could create. 278 Post St. (at Stockton St.). ℰ **415/392-6453.**

Three Bags Full   Snuggling up in a cozy sweater can be a fashionable event if you do your shopping at this pricey boutique, which carries the gamut in handmade and one-of-a-kind playful and extravagant knitwear. Other city locations, which are both closed on Sunday, are 500 Sutter St. and 3314 Sacramento St. (also closed Monday). 2181 Union St. (at Fillmore St.). ℰ **415/567-5753.** www.threebagsfull.com.

Wilkes Bashford *Finds*   Wilkes Bashford is one of the most expensive and best-known clothing stores in the city. In its three-plus-decades in business, the boutique has garnered a reputation for stocking only the finest clothes in the world (which can often be seen on Mayor Willie Brown, who does his suit shopping here). Most fashions come from Italy and France; they include women's designer sportswear and couture and men's Kiton and Brioni suits (at $2,500 and up, they're considered the most expensive suits in the world). Closed Sunday. 375 Sutter St. (at Stockton St.). ℰ **415/986-4380.**

MEN'S FASHIONS

All American Boy   Long known for setting the mainstream style for gay men, All American Boy is the quintessential Castro clothing shop. 463 Castro St. (between Market and 18th sts.). ℰ **415/861-0444.**

Brooks Brothers   In San Francisco, this bulwark of tradition is 1 block east of Union Square. Brooks Brothers introduced the button-down collar and single-handedly changed the standard of the well-dressed businessman. The multilevel shop also sells traditional casual wear, including sportswear, sweaters, and shirts. 201 Post St. (at Grant Ave.). ℭ **415/397-4500.**

Cable Car Clothiers   Dapper men head to this beautiful landmark building for traditional attire, such as three-button suits with natural shoulders, Aquascutum coats, McGeorge sweaters, and Atkinson ties. Closed Sunday. 441 Sutter St. (between Stockton. and Powell sts.). ℭ **415/397-4740.**

Citizen Clothing   The Castro has some of America's best men's casual clothing stores, and this is one of them. Stylish (but not faddish) pants, tops, and accessories are in stock. 536 Castro St. (between 18th and 19th sts.). ℭ **415/558-9429.**

MAC *(Finds*   The more-modern-than-corporate man shops at this hip and hidden shop for imported tailored suits in new and intriguing fabrics as well as gorgeous ties, vibrant sweaters, and a few choice home accoutrements. Lines include London's Paul Smith, Belgium's SO, Italy's Alberto Biani, and New York's John Bartlett. Its equally trend-setting women's store is at 1543 Grant Ave., between Filbert and Union streets (ℭ **415/837-1604**). 5 Claude Lane (off Sutter St. between Grant Ave. and Kearny St.). ℭ **415/837-0615.**

WOMEN'S FASHIONS
The Chanel Boutique   Ever fashionable and expensive, Chanel is appropriately located on Maiden Lane, the quaint downtown side street where the most exclusive stores and spas cluster. You'll find what you'd expect from Chanel: clothing, accessories, scents, cosmetics, and jewelry. 155 Maiden Lane (between Stockton St. and Grant Ave.). ℭ **415/981-1550.**

Métier *(Finds*   Some savvy shoppers consider this the best women's clothing shop in town. Within its walls you'll find classic, sophisticated, and expensive creations. Offerings include European ready-to-wear lines and designers, Italian designer Anna Molinari, Alberto Biani, and Los Angeles designer Katayone Adeli, as well as a distinguished collection of antique-style, high-end jewelry from L.A.'s Kathie Waterman and ultrapopular custom-designed poetry jewelry by Jeanine Payer. Closed Sunday. 355 Sutter St. (between Grant and Stockton sts.). ℭ 415/989-5395.

CHILDREN'S FASHIONS
Minis   Christina Profili, a San Francisco native who used to design for Banana Republic, opened this children's clothing store to sell her own creations. Every piece, from shirts to pants and dresses, is made from cotton or organic cotton. Every outfit perfectly coordinates with everything else in the store. Minis also offers educational and creative toys and books with matching dolls, and maternity wear. 2042 Union St. (between Webster and Buchanan sts.). ℭ **415/567-9537.**

FOOD
Artisan Cheese *(Finds*   San Francisco is fanatical about cheese, and much of local enthusiasm can be contributed to the women behind Artisan Cheese, a simple little neighborhood shop carrying nothing other than excellent small-production local and imported cheeses. 2413 California St. (at Fillmore St.). ℭ **415/929-8610.** www.cowgirlcreamery.com.

Boulangerie *(Finds*   A bit of Paris on Pine Street, this true-blue bakery is authentically French, from delicious and slightly sour French country wheat bread to rustic-style desserts, including the locally famous cannele de Bordeaux, custard baked in a copper mold. 2325 Pine St. (at Fillmore St.). ℂ 415/440-0356, ext. 204.

Golden Gate Fortune Cookies Co.   This tiny, touristy factory sells fortune cookies hot off the press. You can purchase them in small bags or in bulk, and if your order is large enough, you might even be able to negotiate your own message. Even if you're not buying, stop in to see how these sugary treats are made (although the staff can get pushy for you to buy). Open daily until 7pm. 56 Ross Alley (between Washington and Jackson sts.). ℂ 415/781-3956.

Joseph Schmidt Confections *Finds*   Chocolate takes the shape of exquisite sculptural masterpieces—such as long-stemmed tulips and heart-shaped boxes—that are so beautiful, you'll be hesitant to bite the head off your adorable panda bear. Once you do, you'll know why this is the most popular—and reasonably priced—chocolatier in town. 3489 16th St. (at Sanchez St.). ℂ 800/861-8682 or 415/861-8682. www.jsc.com.

Ten Ren Tea Co. *Finds*   At the Ten Ren Tea Co. you will be offered a steaming cup of tea. In addition to a selection of almost 50 traditional and herbal teas, the company stocks related paraphernalia, such as pots, cups, and infusers. If you can't make up your mind, take home a mail-order form. Open daily to 9pm. 949 Grant Ave. (between Washington and Jackson sts.). ℂ 415/362-0656.

GIFTS
Art of China   Amid a wide variety of collectibles, this shop features exquisite, hand-carved Chinese figurines. You'll also find a lovely assortment of ivory beads, bracelets, necklaces, and earrings. Pink-quartz dogs, jade figurines, porcelain vases, cache pots, and blue-and-white barrels suitable for use as table bases are just some of the many items. 839–843 Grant Ave. (between Clay and Washington sts.). ℂ 415/981-1602.

Babushka   Located near Fisherman's Wharf, adjacent to the Anchorage Shopping Center, Babushka sells only Russian products, most of which are wooden nesting dolls. 333 Jefferson St. (at Leavenworth St.). ℂ 415/673-6740.

Cost Plus Imports   At the Fisherman's Wharf cable-car turntable, Cost Plus is a vast warehouse crammed to the rafters with Chinese baskets, Indian camel bells, Malaysian batik scarves, and innumerable other items from Algeria to Zanzibar. More than 20,000 items from 40 nations, imported directly from their country of origin, pack this well-priced warehouse. There's also a decent wine shop. Open daily to 9pm. 2552 Taylor St. (between North Point and Bay sts.). ℂ 415/928-6200.

Dandelion *Finds*   Tucked in an out-of-the-way location in SoMa is the most wonderful collection of gifts, collectibles, and furnishings. There's something for every taste and budget here, from an excellent collection of teapots, decorative dishes, and gourmet foods, to silver, books, cards, and picture frames. Don't miss the Zen-like second floor, with its variety of peaceful furnishings in Indian, Japanese, and Western styles. Closed Sunday and Monday, except November and December when it's open daily. 55 Potrero Ave. (at Alameda St.). ℂ 415/436-9500.

Distractions & Euphoria   This is the best of the Haight Street shops selling underground-rave wear, street fashion, and underground electronica CDs. You'll find pipes, toys, and stickers liberally mixed with lots of cool stuff to look at. 1552 Haight St. (between Ashbury and Clayton sts.). ℂ 415/252-8751.

Flax   If you're the type of person who goes into an art store for a special pencil and comes out $300 later, don't go near this shop. Flax has everything you can think of in art and design supplies, an amazing collection of local arts and crafts, blank bound books, children's art supplies, frames, calendars—you name it. There's a gift for every type of person here, especially you. If you can't stop by, call for a mail-order catalog. Closed Sunday. 1699 Market St. (at Valencia and Gough sts.). ℭ 415/552-2355. www.flaxart.com.

Good Vibrations   A laypersons' sex-toy, book, and video emporium, Good Vibrations is specifically (but not exclusively) designed for women. Unlike most sex shops, it's not a back-alley business, but a straightforward shop with healthy, open attitudes about human sexuality. It also has a vibrator museum. 1210 Valencia St. (at 23rd St.). ℭ 800/BUY-VIBE or 415/974-8980 (for mail order). www.goodvibes.com. A second location is at 2504 San Pablo Ave., Berkeley (ℭ 510/841-8987).

Quantity Postcards   You'll find the perfect postcard for literally everyone you know here, as well as some depictions of old San Francisco, movie stars, and Day-Glo posters featuring concert-poster artist Frank Kozik. Prices range from 35¢ to $2 per card. Even if you don't need any cards, you'll enjoy browsing the eclectic collection of mailables. Open until 11pm. 1441 Grant St. (at Green St.). ℭ 415/986-8866.

SFMOMA MuseumStore *(Finds)*   With an array of artistic cards, books, jewelry, housewares, knickknacks, and creative tokens of San Francisco, it's virtually impossible not to find something you'll consider a must-have. (Check out the Fog Dome!) Aside from being one of the locals' favorite shops, it offers far more tasteful mementos than most Fisherman's Wharf options. You can also request a catalog by e-mail (museumstore@sfmoma.org). 151 Third St. (2 blocks south of Market St., across from Yerba Buena Gardens). ℭ 415/357-4035.

Smile   Need a little humor in your life? Smile specializes in whimsical art, furniture, clothing, jewelry, and American crafts guaranteed to make you grin. Closed Sunday. 500 Sutter St. (between Powell and Mason sts.). ℭ 415/362-3436.

HOUSEWARES/FURNISHINGS

Alabaster *(Finds)*   Any interior designer who knows Biedemeier from Bauhaus knows this Hayes Valley shop sets local home accessories trends with its predominately off-white collection of must-haves. 597 Hayes St. (at Laguna St). ℭ 415/558-0482.

Alessi   Italian designer Alberto Alessi, who's known for his whimsical and colorful kitchen utensil design, such as his ever-popular spiderlike stainless steel lemon squeezer, opened a flagship store here. Drop by for everything from gorgeous stainless steel double boilers to corkscrews in the shape of a maiden. 424 Sutter St. (at Stockton St.). ℭ 415/434-0403.

Biordi Art Imports *(Finds)*   Whether you want to decorate your dinner table, color your kitchen, or liven up the living room, Biordi's Italian majolica pottery is the most exquisite and unusual way to do it. The owner has been importing these hand-painted collectibles for 54 years, and every piece is a showstopper. Call for a catalog. They'll ship anywhere. Closed Sunday. 412 Columbus Ave. (at Vallejo St.). ℭ 415/392-8096. www.biordi.com.

Fillamento *(Finds)*   The best housewares store in the city, Fillamento has three floors that are always packed with shoppers searching for classic, artistic, and refined items. Whether you're looking to set a good table or revamp your bedroom, you'll find it all here. 2185 Fillmore St. (at Sacramento St.). ℭ 415/931-2224.

Limn   For the latest in Europe's trendsetting and ultramodern furniture and lighting, go straight to local SoMa celebrity Limn, which also showcases artworks in its adjoining gallery. 290 Townsend St. (at 4th St.) ℂ 415-543-5466. www.limn.com.

Nest *(Finds)*   Don't come into Fillmore's cutest French interiors store without your credit cards. Nest carries adorable throws, handmade quilts, vintage perfume bottles, must-have slippers and sleepwear, and a number of other things you never knew you really needed until now. 340 Presidio Ave. (at California St.). ℂ 415/776-7289.

Sue Fisher King *(Finds)*   For the ultimate in everything for the table top, bedroom, and beyond, head to this exclusive neighborhood boutique known by the society set as the only place to shop. Amidst the gourmet chocolates and other sweet finds, you can get your hands on exquisite table linens, cashmere blankets, towels, china, silver flatware, and more. 3067 Sacramento St. (at Baker St.). ℂ 415/ 922-7276.

Victorian Interiors   Draped with an array of period floral wallpapers, this little store is the perfect place for any Victoriana fanatic. Along with traditional Victorian wallpapers, moldings, drapery cornices and rods, tiles, fabrics, and carpets, you'll find a great collection of old pipes and knickknacks. Closed Monday. 575 Hayes St. (at Laguna St.). ℂ 415/431-7191.

The Wok Shop   This shop has every conceivable implement for Chinese cooking, including woks, brushes, cleavers, circular chopping blocks, dishes, oyster knives, bamboo steamers, and strainers. It also sells a wide range of kitchen utensils, baskets, handmade linens from China, and aprons. 718 Grant Ave. (at Clay St.). ℂ 888/780-7171 for mail order, or 415/989-3797. www.wokshop.com.

Zinc Details *(Finds)*   One of my favorite stores in the city, Zinc Details has received accolades everywhere from *Elle Decor Japan* to *Metropolitan Home* for its amazing collection of locally handcrafted glass vases, pendant lights, ceramics, and furniture. Each piece (except vintage items) is a true work of art created specifically for the store, and the pieces are in such high demand that the store's wholesale accounts include Barneys New York and the Guggenheim Museum Store. 1905 Fillmore St. (between Bush and Pine sts.). ℂ 415/776-2100.

JEWELRY
De Vera Galleries *(Finds)*   Don't come here unless you've got money to spend. Designer Federico de Vera's unique, rough-stone jewelry collection, art glass, and vintage knickknacks are too beautiful to pass up and too expensive to be a painless purchase. Still, if you're looking for a keepsake, you'll find it here. (*Note:* The Sutter Street location, 580 Sutter St., at Mason St., ℂ 415/989-0988, has a larger glass collection and less jewelry.) 29 Maiden Ln. (at Kearny St.). ℂ 415/788-0828.

Dianne's Old & New Estates   Buy yourself a bauble and treat yourself to a trinket at this shop featuring top-of-the-line antique jewelry—pendants, diamond rings, necklaces, bracelets, and natural pearls. For a special gift, check out the collection of platinum wedding and engagement rings and vintage watches. Don't worry if you can't afford it now—the shop offers 1-year interest-free layaway. 2181A Union St. (at Fillmore St.). ℂ 888/346-7525 or 415/346-7525.

Jerusalem Shoppe   Known for its extensive collection of silver and gold gemstone jewelry by more than 300 local and international artists, this shop displays other unique treasures, from clothing and accessories to imported antique Indian quilts. 313 Noe St. (at Market St.). ℂ 415/626-7906.

The Magical Trinket Do-it-yourself jewelry makers, beware. This store, brimming with beads, baubles, and bangles, will inspire you to make your own knickknacks and kick yourself for the prices you've been paying for costume jewelry in retail stores. If you're overwhelmed by all the bead options, colors, shapes, and styles, owner Eve Blake calmly explains how to create your wearable masterpiece. She offers more extensive classes for those who are really bead-dazzled. 524 Hayes St. (between Laguna and Octavia sts.). ✆ **415/626-0764.**

Pearl & Jade Empire The Pearl & Jade Empire has been importing jewelry from all over the world since 1957. It specializes in unusual pearls and jade and offers restringing on the premises, and recently added a collection of amber from the Baltic Sea. 427 Post St. (between Powell and Mason sts.). ✆ **415/362-0606.**

Tiffany & Co. Even if you don't have lots of cash to buy an exquisite bauble that comes in Tiffany's famous light-blue box, enjoy this renowned store a la Audrey Hepburn in *Breakfast at Tiffany's.* The designer collection features Paloma Picasso, Jean Schlumberger, and Elsa Peretti in both silver and 18-karat gold, and there's an extensive gift collection in sterling, china, and crystal. 350 Post St. (at Powell St.). ✆ **415/781-7000.**

Union Street Goldsmith A showcase for Bay Area goldsmiths, this exquisite shop sells a contemporary collection of fine custom-designed jewelry in all platinum and all karats of gold. Many pieces emphasize colored stones. 1909 Union St. (at Laguna St.). ✆ **415/776-8048.**

MUSIC

Recycled Records *(Finds* Easily one of the best used-record stores in the city, this loud shop in the Haight has a good selection of promotional CDs and cases of used "classic" rock LPs. Sheet music, tour programs, and old *TV Guides* are for sale, too. Open daily until 7pm. 1377 Haight St. (between Central and Masonic sts.). ✆ **415/626-4075.**

Streetlight Records Overstuffed with used music in all three formats, this place is best known for its records and excellent CD collection. Rock music is cheap, and the money-back guarantee guards against defects. 3979 24th St. (between Noe and Sanchez sts.). ✆ **415/282-3550** and 2350 Market St., between Castro and Noe streets (✆ **415/282-8000).**

Virgin Megastore With thousands of CDs, including an impressive collection of imports, videos, DVDs, a multimedia department, a cafe, and related books, any music-lover could blow his or her entire vacation fund in this enormous Union Square store. Open until midnight, except Sunday, when it closes at 11pm. 2 Stockton St. (at Market St.). ✆ **415/397-4525.**

SHOES

Birkenstock This relaxed store is known for its earthy form-fitting sandals, clogs, and lace-ups. 42 Stockton St. (between Market and O'Farrell sts.). ✆ **415/989-2475.**

Bulo If you have a fetish for foot fashions, you must check out Bulo, which carries nothing but imported Italian shoes. The selection is small but styles run the gamut, from casual to dressy, reserved to wildly funky. New shipments come in every three to four weeks, so the selection is ever-changing, eternally hip, and unfortunately, ever-expensive, with many pairs going for close to $200. Men's store: 437A Hayes St. (at Gough St.). ✆ **415/864-3244.** The women's shoe store is across the street, at 418 Hayes St. (✆ **415/255-4939).**

Gimme Shoes   The staff is funky-fashion snobby, the prices are steep, and the European shoes and accessories are utterly chic; everyone's crazy for the Katharine Hamnett watch collection. 2358 Fillmore St. (at Washington St.). (✆ **415/441-3040.** Additional locations are at 416 Hayes St. ((✆ **415/864-0691**) and 50 Grant Ave. ((✆ **415/434-9242**).

Kenneth Cole   This trendy shop carries high-fashion footwear for men and women. There is also an innovative collection of handbags and small leather goods and accessories. 865 Market St. (in the San Francisco Shopping Centre). (✆ **415/227-4536.** Other shops are at 2078 Union St., at Webster Street ((✆ **415/346-2161**), and 166 Grant St., at Post Street ((✆ **415/981-2653**).

SHOPPING CENTERS & COMPLEXES

The Anchorage   This touristy waterfront mall has close to 55 stores that offer everything from music boxes to home furnishings; street performers entertain during open hours. 2800 Leavenworth St. (between Beach and Jefferson sts. on Fisherman's Wharf). (✆ **415/775-6000.**

The Cannery   Once a Del Monte fruit-canning plant, this attractive complex now contains a score or two of shops, restaurants, and nightspots. Shops include **Gourmet Market** ((✆ **415/673-0400**), which sells international foods, coffees, and teas; **The Print Store** ((✆ **415/771-3576**), has a well-chosen selection of fine-art prints and local original art; and the **Basic Brown Bear Factory** ((✆ **415/931-6670**), where you can stuff your own teddy bear. Vendors' stalls and sidewalk cafes occupy the courtyard, amid a grove of olive trees. On summer weekends street performers entertain. The **Museum of the City of San Francisco** ((✆ **415/928-0289**) is on the third floor. **Cobb's Comedy Club** (see chapter 10) is also here, as are several restaurants. 2801 Leavenworth St. (at Jefferson St.). (✆ **415/771-3112.**

Crocker Galleria   Modeled after Milan's Galleria Vittorio Emanuele, this glass-domed, three-level pavilion, about 3 blocks east of Union Square, features around 40 high-end shops. Fashions include Nicole Miller, Gianni Versace, and Polo/Ralph Lauren. Closed Sunday. 50 Post St. (at Kearny St.). (✆ **415/393-1505.**

Ghirardelli Square   This former chocolate factory is one of the city's quaintest shopping malls and most popular landmarks. It dates from 1864, when it served as a factory making Civil War uniforms, but it's best known as the former chocolate and spice factory of Domingo Ghirardelli (say "Gear-a-deli"). A clock tower, an exact replica of the one at France's Château de Blois, crowns the complex. Inside the tower, on the mall's plaza level, is the fun Ghirardelli soda fountain. It still makes and sells small amounts of chocolate, but the big draw is the old-fashioned ice-cream parlor. (Got a late-night craving? The place stays open until midnight on Friday and Saturday.) A free map and guide to the mall is available from the information booth in the center courtyard. Many chain stores are located here, including the women's clothier **Ann Taylor** ((✆ **415/775-2872**) and **The Sharper Image** ((✆ **415/776-1443**), for unique, upscale electronics and designs. The hottest addition, however, is restaurant Ana Mandara (see chapter 6 for more information). Main plaza shops' and restaurants' hours vary, with extended hours during the summer. (Incidentally, the Ghirardelli Chocolate Company still makes chocolate in the East Bay.) 900 North Point (at Polk St.). (✆ **415/775-5500.** www.ghirardellisq.com.

Pier 39 *(Overrated*   The automated information line reminds callers not to forget to bring their Visa cards to this bayside tourist trap, which also happens to have stunning views. To residents, that pretty much wraps up Pier 39—an expensive spot where out-of-towners go to waste money on worthless souvenirs and greasy fast food. For vacationers, though, Pier 39 does have some redeeming qualities—fresh crab (in season), playful sea lions, phenomenal views, and plenty of fun for the kids. If you want to get to know the real San Francisco, skip the cheesy T-shirt shops and limit your time here to one afternoon, if at all. Some of the most interesting stores include **Puppets on the Pier** (ⓒ 415/ 781-4435), a store that sells—you guessed it—puppets, and **Kite Flight** (ⓒ 415/956-3181), where you can buy a fanciful creation to fly in the breezes off the bay. Open daily to 8:30pm, with extended hours during the summer. Store and restaurant hours vary. Embarcadero and Beach St. (on the waterfront). ⓒ 415/ 981-PIER.

San Francisco Shopping Centre   Opened in 1988, this $140 million complex is one of the few vertical malls in the United States. Its most attractive features are the four-story spiral escalators that circle up to Nordstrom (see "Department Stores," earlier in this chapter) and the nine-story atrium covered by a retractable skylight. More than 70 specialty shops include Abercrombie & Fitch, Ann Taylor, bebe, Benetton, Footlocker, J. Crew, and Victoria's Secret. 865 Market St. (at Fifth St.). ⓒ 415/495-5656.

TOYS
The Chinatown Kite Shop   This shop's playful assortment of flying objects includes attractive fish kites, windsocks, hand-painted Chinese paper kites, wood-and-paper biplanes, pentagonal kites, and do-it-yourself kite kits, all of which make great souvenirs or decorations. Computer-designed stunt kites have two or four control lines to manipulate loops and dives. Open daily to 8:30pm. 717 Grant Ave. (between Clay and Sacramento sts.). ⓒ 415/391-8217.

The Disney Store   Capitalizing on the world's love for The Mouse and his friends, this store offers everything Disney-oriented you could possibly want— from clothes and toys to high-end commissioned art from the Disney gallery. Those looking for a simple token can fork over $3 for a plastic character, while more serious collectors can throw down $9,000 for a Yamagata Disney lithograph. Open in winter Monday to Friday 10am to 7pm, Saturday 10am to 7pm, Sunday 11am to 5pm. Hours are extended during the summer and holiday season; call for details. 400 Post St. (at Powell St.). ⓒ 415/391-6866. Another location is at Pier 39 (ⓒ 415/391-4119).

FAO Schwarz   The world's greatest—and most overpriced—toy store for both children and adults is filled with every imaginable plaything, from hand-carved, custom-painted carousel rocking horses, Barbie dolls, and stuffed animals, to gas-powered cars, train sets, and hobby supplies. At the entrance is a singing 22-foot clock tower with 1,000 moving parts. 48 Stockton St. (at O'Farrell St.). ⓒ 415/394-8700.

TRAVEL GOODS
On the Road Again   In addition to lightweight luggage, this smart shop sells toiletry kits, travel bottles, travel-sized items, and a good selection of other related goods. Open daily to 8:30pm. Embarcadero and Beach St. (in Pier 39). ⓒ 415/434-1482.

Thomas Bros. Maps & Books   The best map shop in the city, Thomas Bros. sells street, topographic, and hiking maps depicting San Francisco, California, and the world, as well as an extensive selection of travel guides and atlases.

Closed Sunday. 550 Jackson St. (at Columbus Ave.). © **800/969-3072** for mail order, or 415/981-7520.

VINTAGE CLOTHING

Aardvark's   One of San Francisco's largest secondhand clothing dealers, Aardvark's has seemingly endless racks of shirts, pants, dresses, skirts, and hats from the past 30 years. Open daily to 7pm. 1501 Haight St. (at Ashbury St.). © **415/621-3141.**

Buffalo Exchange   This large storefront on upper Haight Street is crammed with racks of antique and new fashions from the 1960s, 1970s, and 1980s. It stocks everything from suits and dresses to neckties, hats, handbags, and jewelry. Buffalo Exchange anticipates some of the hottest new street fashions. 1555 Haight St. (between Clayton and Ashbury sts.). © **415/431-7733.** A second shop is at 1800 Polk St., at Washington Street (© **415/346-5726**).

Good Byes *Finds*   One the best new- and used-clothes stores in San Francisco, Good Byes carries only high-quality clothing and accessories, including an exceptional selection of men's fashions at unbelievably low prices (for example, $350 preowned shoes for $35). Women's wear is in a separate boutique across the street. 3464 Sacramento St. and 3483 Sacramento St. (between Laurel and Walnut sts.). © **415/346-6388.**

La Rosa   On a street packed with vintage-clothing shops, this is one of the more upscale options. It features a selection of high-quality, dry-cleaned secondhand goods. Formal suits and dresses are its specialty, but you'll also find sport coats, slacks, and shoes. 1711 Haight St. (at Cole St.). © **415/668-3744.** The more moderately priced sister store, **Held Over,** is located at 1543 Haight St., near Ashbury (© **415/864-0818**).

WINE

Wine Club San Francisco *Value*   The Wine Club is a discount warehouse that offers bargain prices on more than 1,200 domestic and foreign wines. Bottles cost between $4 and $1,100. 953 Harrison St. (between Fifth and Sixth sts.). © **415/512-9086.**

10

San Francisco After Dark

For a city with fewer than a million inhabitants, San Francisco boasts an arts scene that's nothing short of phenomenal. The city's opera is justifiably world renowned, the ballet is well respected, and the theaters are high in both quantity and quality. Dozens of piano bars and top-notch lounges augment one of the best dance-club cultures this side of New York, and skyscraper lounges offer some of the most dazzling city views in the world. In short, there's always something going on, so get off your fanny and get out there.

For up-to-date nightlife information, turn to the *San Francisco Weekly* and the *San Francisco Bay Guardian,* both of which run comprehensive listings. They are available free at bars and restaurants and from street-corner boxes all around the city. *Where,* a free tourist-oriented monthly, also lists information on programs and performance times; it's available in most of the city's finer hotels. The Sunday edition of the *San Francisco Examiner* and *Chronicle* features a "Datebook" section, printed on pink paper, with information and listings on the week's events.

TICKETS

Tix Bay Area (© **415/433-7827**) sells half-price tickets to theater, dance, and music performances on the day of the show only; tickets for Sunday and Monday events, if available, are sold on Saturday. Tix Bay Area also sells advance, full-price tickets for most performance halls, sporting events, concerts, and clubs. A service charge, ranging from $1 to $3, is levied on each ticket. Only cash and traveler's checks are accepted for half-price tickets; Visa and MasterCard are accepted for full-price tickets. Tix is inside the Union Square Garage (on Geary Street at Powell Street). It's open Tuesday to Thursday 11am to 6pm, Friday and Saturday 11am to 7pm.

You can also get tickets to most theater and dance events through **City Box Office,** 153 Kearny St., Suite 402 (© **415/392-4400**). American Express, MasterCard, and Visa are accepted.

BASS Ticketmaster (© **415/478-2277** or 510/762-2277) sells computer-generated tickets to concerts, sporting events, plays, and special events, and it imposes a hefty service charge. Downtown BASS Ticketmaster offices include Warehouse stores throughout the city. The most convenient location is at 30 Powell Street.

1 The Performing Arts

Special concerts and performances take place in San Francisco year-round. **San Francisco Performances,** 500 Sutter St., Suite 710 (© **415/398-6449;** www.performances.org), has brought acclaimed artists to the Bay Area for more than 16 years. Shows run the gamut from chamber music to dance and jazz.

Performances are in several venues, including the Performing Arts Center, Herbst Theater, and the Center for the Performing Arts at Yerba Buena Center. The season runs from late September through May. Tickets cost $12 to $55 and are available through **City Box Office** (℡ 415/392-4400).

CLASSICAL MUSIC

In addition to the world-class groups described below, visitors might be interested in the **San Francisco Contemporary Music Players** (℡ 415/252-6235; www. sfcmp.org). They perform modern chamber works by international artists at the Center for the Arts at Yerba Buena Gardens. Tickets, available by phone (℡ 415/978-ARTS), cost $18 for adults, $14 for seniors, and $7 for students. Another commendable group is the **Women's Philharmonic** (℡ 415/437-0123; www. womensphil.org). For more than 16 years, the critically acclaimed orchestra has played works by historical and contemporary female composers. Most perform-ances, at least for the next season, are at Herbst Theater. Phone for dates, pro-grams, and ticket prices.

Philharmonia Baroque Orchestra   Acclaimed by the *New York Times* as "the country's leading early music orchestra," Philharmonia Baroque performs in San Francisco and all around the Bay Area. The season lasts from September through April. Performing in Herbst Theater, 401 Van Ness Ave. ℡ 415/392-4400 (box office) or 415/252-1288 (administrative offices). www.philharmonia.org. Tickets $30–$42.

San Francisco Symphony   Founded in 1911, the internationally respected San Francisco Symphony has long been an important part of the city's cultural life under such legendary conductors as Pierre Monteux and Seiji Ozawa. In 1995, Michael Tilson Thomas took over from Herbert Blomstedt; he has led the orchestra to new heights and crafted an exciting repertoire of classical and mod-ern music. The season runs from September through June. Summer symphony activities include a Composer Festival and a Summer Pops series. Performing at Davies Symphony Hall, 201 Van Ness Ave. (at Grove St.). ℡ 415/864-6000 (box office). www. sfsymphony.org. Tickets $12–$73.

OPERA

In addition to San Francisco's major opera company, you might check out the amusing **Pocket Opera,** 44 Page St., Suite 200 (℡ 415/575-1100; www.pocket opera.org). From mid-February to mid-June, the comic company stages farcical performances of well-known operas in English. The staging is intimate and informal, without lavish costumes and sets. The cast ranges from 3 to 16 play-ers, supported by a chamber orchestra. The rich repertoire includes such works as *Don Giovanni* and *The Barber of Seville.* Performances are on Friday, Satur-day, or Sunday. Call the box office (℡ 415/575-1102) for complete informa-tion and show times. Tickets cost $13 (students) to $27.

San Francisco Opera   The San Francisco Opera was the first municipal opera in the United States and is one of the city's cultural icons. Brilliantly bal-anced casts may feature celebrated stars like Frederica Von Stade and Placido Domingo, along with promising newcomers and regular members, in produc-tions that range from traditional to avant-garde. All productions have English supertitles. The season starts in September and lasts just 14 weeks. Performances are held most evenings, except Monday, with matinees on Sundays. Tickets go on sale as early as June, and the best seats sell out quickly. Unless Pavarotti or Domingo is in town, some less coveted seats are usually available until curtain time. War Memorial Opera House, 301 Van Ness Ave. (at Grove St.). ℡ 415/864-3330 (box office). www.sfopera.com. Tickets $23–$165.

San Francisco After Dark

American Conservatory Theater (A.C.T.) **46**

Backflip **54**

Bay Area Theatresports (BATS) **1**

Beach Blanket Babylon **19**

Biscuits and Blues **44**

Blue Bar **27**

Bottom of the Hill **71**

The Bubble Lounge **31**

The Café **13**

Cafe du Nord **10**

Caffè Greco **21**

Caffè Trieste **23**

The Carnelian Room **35**

Castro Theatre **13**

Center for the Arts at Yerba Buena Gardens **53**

Chalkers Billiard Club **49**

The Cinch Saloon **37**

Cityscape **47**

Club Deluxe **72**

Cobb's Comedy Club **16**

Cowell Theater **1**

Davies Symphony Hall **57**

Detour **12**

The Eagle **68**

Edinburgh Castle **40**

The Endup **59**

Eos **73**

Equinox **34**

Eureka Theater **30**

The Fillmore **4**

Fort Mason Center **1**

Geary Theater **46**

Giraffe Lounge **39**

Gordon Biersch Brewery Restaurant **50**

Grant & Green Saloon **22**

The Great Entertainer **63**

Greens Sports Bar **18**

Harry Denton's Starlight Room **43**

Hayes and Vine **5**

Herbst Theater **55**

HiBall Lounge **28**

Jazz at Pearl's **24**

Julie's Supper Club **61**

Kimo's **38**

Li Po Cocktail Lounge **29**

London Wine Bar **33**

Lone Star Saloon **65**

Lorraine Hansberry Theatre **42**

Lou's Pier 47 Club **17**

The Magic Theatre **1**

Metro **11**

The Mint Karaoke Lounge **9**

Nickie's Bar-be-cue **7**

ODC Theatre **15**

Paradise Lounge **67**

Perry's **2**

Philharmonia Baroque Orchestra **55**

Pied Piper Bar **48**

Pocket Opera **6**

Punch Line **32**

Rasselas **3**

Rawhide II **60**

The Red Room **41**

The Redwood Room **45**

Roxie **14**

The Saloon **23**

San Francisco Ballet **56**

San Francisco Brewing Company **26**

San Francisco Contemporary Music Players **53**

San Francisco Opera **56**

San Francisco Symphony **57**

The Savoy-Tivoli **20**

Slim's **66**

Sound Factory **51**

Spec's **27**

The Stud **64**

Ten 15 **58**

Theatre Artaud **70**

Theatre Rhinoceros **69**

Thirsty Bear Brewing Company **52**

Top of the Mark **36**

Toronado **8**

Tosca **26**

Twin Peaks Tavern **13**

Up & Down Club **62**

Vesuvio **24**

216

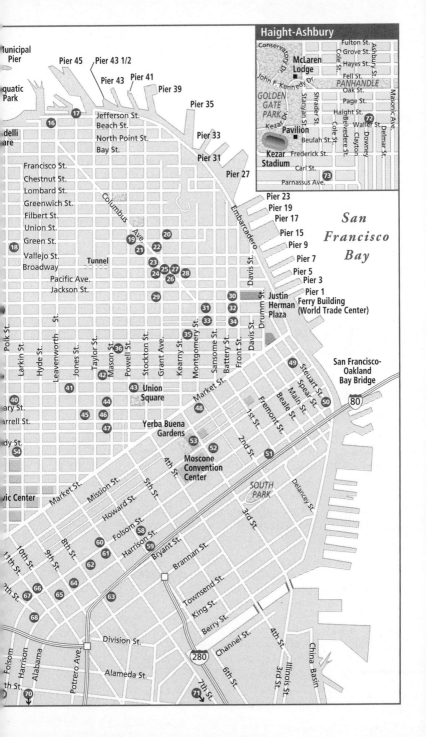

Municipal
Pier

Pier 45   Pier 43 1/2
       Pier 43   Pier 41
              Pier 39

Aquatic
Park

Pier 35

Jefferson St.
Beach St.
North Point St.
Bay St.

17
16

delli
are

Pier 33
Pier 31
Pier 27

Francisco St.
Chestnut St.
Lombard St.
Greenwich St.
Filbert St.
Union St.
Green St.
Vallejo St.
Broadway
Pacific Ave.
Jackson St.

Columbus Ave.

Tunnel

18
19 **20**
21 **22**
23
24 **25** **27** **28**
26
29

Embarcadero

Pier 23
Pier 19
Pier 17
Pier 15
Pier 9
Pier 7
Pier 5
Pier 3
Pier 1

Davis St.

*San
Francisco
Bay*

Justin
Herman
Plaza

Ferry Building
(World Trade Center)

30
31 **32**
33
34

Drumm St.

Polk St.
Larkin St.
Hyde St.
Leavenworth St.
Jones St.
Taylor St.
Mason St.
Powell St.
Stockton St.
Grant Ave.
Kearny St.
Montgomery St.
Sansome St.
Battery St.
Front St.
Davis St.

35
36
42
41
43 Union
Square

San Francisco-
Oakland
Bay Bridge

Steuart St.
Spear St.
Main St.
Beale St.
Fremont St.

49
50

80

40
ary St.
arrell St.
dy St.
54

44
45 **46**
47

48

Market St.

1st St.
2nd St.

51

Yerba Buena
Gardens

53
52

Moscone
Convention
Center

*SOUTH
PARK*

Delancey St.

ic Center

Market St.

Mission St.
Howard St.
Folsom St.
Harrison St.
Bryant St.
Brannan St.

4th St.
5th St.

3rd St.

58
60
61
62
59

10th St.
8th St.
9th St.
11th St.

66
67
68
64
65
63

7th St.

Townsend St.
King St.
Berry St.

4th St.
3rd St.

China
Basin

Division St.

Alameda St.

280

Channel St.

6th St.
7th St.
Illinois St.
3rd St.

Folsom
Harrison
Alabama
Potrero Ave.

th St.
70
71

Haight-Ashbury

Conservatory Dr.
McLaren
Lodge

Fulton St.
Grove St.
Hayes St.
Fell St.
PANHANDLE
Oak St.
Page St.
Haight St.
Waller St.

Ashbury St.
Cole St.
Masonic Ave.

John F. Kennedy Dr.

*GOLDEN
GATE
PARK*

Stanyan St.
Shrader St.

Kezar Dr.

Pavilion

Beulah St.

Kezar
Stadium

Frederick St.
Carl St.
Parnassus Ave.

Cole St.
Belvedere St.
Clayton St.
Downey St.
Delmar St.

72
73

217

THEATER

American Conservatory Theater (A.C.T.) *(Finds)*   The American Conservatory Theater made its debut in 1967 and quickly established itself as the city's premier resident theater group and one of the nation's best. The A.C.T. season runs from September through July and features both classic and experimental works. A.C.T. recently returned to its home, the fabulous **Geary Theater** (1910), a national historic landmark, after the theater sustained severe damage in the 1989 earthquake and closed for renovations. Now it's fully refurbished and modernized to such an extent that it's regarded as one of America's finest performance spaces. Performing at the Geary Theater, 415 Geary St. (at Mason St.). ☎ 415/749-2ACT. www.act-sfbay.com.Tickets $11–$65.

Eureka Theatre Company   Eureka produces contemporary plays from September through June, and performances are usually Wednesday to Sunday. 215 Jackson St. (between Battery and Front sts.). ☎ 415/788-7469. www.eurekatheatre.org. Tickets $16–$22; discounts for students and seniors.

Lorraine Hansberry Theatre   San Francisco's top African-American theater group performs in a 300-seat theater off the lobby of the Sheehan Hotel, near Mason Street. It mounts special adaptations from literature along with contemporary dramas, classics, and music such as a recent performance of "Underground Jazz Cabaret." Phone for dates and programs. Performing at 620 Sutter St. ☎ 415/474-8800. Tickets $15–$26.

The Magic Theatre   The highly acclaimed Magic Theatre is a major West Coast company dedicated to presenting the works of new playwrights; over the years it has nurtured the talents of such luminaries as Sam Shepard and Jon Robin Baitz. Shepard's Pulitzer Prize–winning play *Buried Child* had its premiere here and a more recent production included Shepard's *The Late Henry Moss* starring Nick Nolte, Sean Penn, and Woody Harrelson. The season usually runs from September through July; performances are Wednesday to Sunday. Performing at Building D, Fort Mason Center, Marina Blvd. (at Buchanan St.). ☎ 415/441-8822. www.magictheater.org. Tickets $8–$30; discounts for students and seniors.

Theatre Rhinoceros   Founded in 1977, this was America's first (and remains its foremost) theater ensemble devoted solely to works addressing gay and lesbian issues. The company presents five main-stage shows and a dozen studio productions of new and classic works each year. The theater is 1 block east of the 16th Street/Mission BART station. 2926 16th St. (☎ 415/861-5079. www.therhino.org. Tickets $15–$25.

DANCE

In addition to the local companies, top traveling troupes like the Joffrey Ballet and the American Ballet Theatre make regular appearances. Primary modern dance spaces include the **Theatre Artaud,** 450 Florida St., at 17th Street (☎ 415/621-7797); the **Cowell Theater,** at Fort Mason Center, Marina Boulevard, at Buchanan Street (☎ 415/441-3400); and the **ODC Theatre,** 3153 17th St., at Shotwell in the Mission District (☎ 415/863-9834). Check the local papers for schedules or contact the theater box offices.

San Francisco Ballet   Founded in 1933, the San Francisco Ballet is the oldest professional ballet company in the United States and is regarded as one of the country's finest. It performs an eclectic repertoire of full-length, neoclassical, and contemporary ballets. Even the *New York Times* proclaimed, "The San Francisco Ballet under Helgi Tomasson's leadership is one of the spectacular success stories of the arts in America." The 2002 Repertory Season runs from February through April; the company performs *The Nutcracker* each December. The San Francisco Ballet Orchestra accompanies all performances. War Memorial Opera House, 301 Van Ness Ave. (at Grove St.). ✆ 415/865-2000 for tickets and information. www.sfballet.org. Tickets $10–$110.

2 Comedy & Cabaret

Bay Area Theatresports (BATS) *Finds*   Combining improvisation with competition, BATS operates an improvisational tournament, in which four-actor teams compete against each other, taking on hilarious challenges from the audience. Judges flash scorecards good-naturedly or honk a horn for scenes that just aren't working. Shows are on Monday only. Phone for reservations. Performing at Center for Improvisational Theatre at the Fort Mason Center, Building B, 3rd floor. ✆ 415/ 474-8935. www.improv.org. Tickets $5–$15.

Beach Blanket Babylon *Moments*   A San Francisco tradition, Beach Blanket Babylon evolved from Steve Silver's Rent-a-Freak service—a group of party-givers extraordinaire who hired themselves out as a "cast of characters" to entertain, complete with fabulous costumes and sets, props, and gags. After their act caught on, it moved into the Savoy-Tivoli, a North Beach bar. By 1974, the audience had grown too large for the facility, and Beach Blanket has been at the 400-seat Club Fugazi ever since. The show is a comedic musical send-up that is best known for outrageous costumes and oversized headdresses. It's been playing for almost 27 years, and almost every performance sells out. The show is updated often enough that locals still attend. Those under 21 are welcome at Sunday matinees at 3pm, when no alcohol is served; photo ID is required for evening performances. Write for weekend tickets at least 3 weeks in advance, or get them through Tix (see "Tickets," above). *Note:* Tickets are within a specific section depending on price; seating is first-come, first-seated within that section. Performances are Wednesday and Thursday at 8pm, Friday and Saturday at 7:30pm, Sunday at 3 and 7pm. At Club Fugazi, Beach Blanket Babylon Blvd., 678 Green St. (between Powell St. and Columbus Ave.). ✆ 415/421-4222. www.beachblanketbabylon.com. Tickets $20–$55.

Cobb's Comedy Club   Located in the Cannery at Fisherman's Wharf, Cobb's may not be much to look at (ceilings are low and decor is seriously lacking), but it does feature such national headliners as Pam Stone, Brian Regan, and Jake Johannsen. There is comedy every night, including a 15-comedian All-Pro Monday showcase (a 3-hour marathon). Cobb's is open to those 18 and over, and occasionally to kids 16 and 17 when accompanied by a parent or legal guardian (call ahead). Cajun-Creole food is served from adjoining Belle Roux Louisiana Kitchen (main courses $12.50–$18.50). Shows are Monday through Wednesday at 8pm, Thursday and Sunday at 9pm, Friday and Saturday at 8 and 10pm. The Cannery, 2801 Leavenworth St. (at Beach St.). ✆ 415/928-4320. Cover Mon–Wed $10, Thurs and Sun $10–$13, Fri–Sat , $13–$15. 2-beverage minimum nightly. Validated parking at Anchorage Shopping Center Garage.

Punch Line   Adjacent to the Embarcadero One office building, this is the largest comedy nightclub in the city. Three-person shows with top national and local talent are featured Tuesday to Saturday. Showcase night is Sunday, when 15 to 20 rising stars take the mike. There's an all-star showcase or a special event on Monday. If you don't want to wait in line, buy tickets in advance from **BASS Ticketmaster** outlets see "Tickets," above). Shows are Tuesday to Thursday and

Sunday at 9pm, Friday and Saturday at 9 and 11pm. 444 Battery St. (between Washington and Clay sts.), plaza level. ℂ **415/397-4337,** or 415/397-7573 for recorded information. www.punchlinecomedyclub.com. Cover $5 Sun, $8–$15 Tues–Sat. 2-drink minimum nightly.

3 The Club & Music Scene

The greatest legacy from the 1960s is the city's continued tradition of live entertainment and music, which explains the great variety of clubs and music. The hippest dance places are South of Market Street (SoMa), in former warehouses; the artsy bohemian scene centers on the Mission; and most popular cafe culture is still in North Beach.

Note: The club and music scene is always changing, often outdating recommendations before the ink can dry on a page. Most of the venues below are promoted as different clubs on various nights of the week, each with its own look, sound, and style. Discount passes and club announcements are often available at clothing stores and other shops along upper Haight Street.

Drink prices at most bars, clubs, and cafes range from about $3.50 to $9, unless otherwise noted.

ROCK & BLUES CLUBS

In addition to the following listings, see "Dance Clubs," below, for (usually) live, danceable rock.

Biscuits and Blues   With a crisp, blow-your-eardrums-out sound system, New Orleans–speakeasy (albeit commercial) appeal, and a nightly line-up of live entertainment, there's no better place to muse the blues than at this basement-cum-nightclub. During performances, prices range, but entrance is free during happy hour (Monday to Friday 5 to 7pm). There's usually recorded music, drink specials, and inexpensive snacks—not to mention the only opportunity to socialize. Once the bands get going, it's so loud you can't even hear yourself holler. *Note:* A full dinner menu is available, but the only notable treat is the moist, flaky biscuits. 401 Mason (at Geary St.). ℂ **415/292-2583.** Cover (during performances) $5–$15.

The Fillmore *(Finds*   Reopened after years of neglect, the Fillmore, made famous by promoter Bill Graham in the 1960s, is attracting big names again. Check listings in magazines, or call the theater for information on upcoming events. And if you make it to a show, check out the fab collection of vintage concert posters, which chronicles the hall's history. 1805 Geary Blvd. (at Fillmore St.). ℂ **415/346-6000.** www.thefillmore.com. Tickets $9–$25.

Grant & Green Saloon   The atmosphere at this historic North Beach dive rockery is not that special, but the local bands are pretty good and the space is an all-around good place to let your hair down. As of 2001 it's also under new ownership, which intends to spruce the place up and add pool tables and big-screen TVs. Live music will continue on weekends. 1371 Grant Ave. (at Green St.). ℂ 415/693-9565. $5 cover on weekends.

Lou's Pier 47 Club   You won't find many locals in the place, but Lou's happens to be good, old-fashioned fun. It's a casual spot where you can let your hair down with Cajun seafood (downstairs) and live blues bands (upstairs). Major happy hour specials (Monday through Friday 4 to 7pm) and a vacation attitude make the place one of the more, um, jovial spots near the Wharf. There's no cover for the first band, which plays nightly from 4 to 8pm, but the second, which comes on at 9pm, will cost you. 300 Jefferson St. (at Jones St.). ℂ **415/771-5687.** Cover $5–$10.

The Saloon   An authentic Gold Rush survivor, this North Beach dive is the oldest bar in the city. Popular with both bikers and daytime pinstripers, it schedules live blues nightly. 1232 Grant Ave. (at Vallejo St.). ℂ **415/989-7666.** Cover $4–$5 Fri–Sat.

Slim's   Co-owned by musician Boz Scaggs, who sometimes takes the stage under the name "Presidio Slim," this glitzy restaurant and bar seats 300, serves California cuisine, and specializes in excellent American music—homegrown rock, jazz, blues, and alternative—almost nightly. Call for a schedule; hot bands sell out in advance. 333 11th St. (at Folsom St.). ℂ **415/522-0333.** www.slims-sf.com. Cover free–$20. 2-drink minimum when seated at a table.

JAZZ & LATIN CLUBS

Cafe du Nord *(Finds)*   Although it's been around since 1907, this basement supper club is rightfully self-proclaimed as the place for a "slightly lurid indie pop scene set in a beautiful old speakeasy." With a younger generation now appreciating the music—swing, jazz, alternative, pop, you name it—the place is often packed from the 40-foot mahogany bar to the back room, where the focus is on live performances. *Note:* If Lavay Smith and the Red Hot Skillet Lickers are in the house, definitely stop by. Du Nord puts out its own great compilation CDs, which you can purchase from the club. 2170 Market St. (at Sanchez St.). ℂ **415/861-5016.** Cover $3–$10.

Jazz at Pearl's   This is one of the best jazz venues in the city. The live jams last until 2am nightly. Ribs and chicken are served, too; prices run $4 to $12. 256 Columbus Ave. (at Broadway). ℂ **415/291-8255.** No cover. 2-drink minimum.

Rasselas   Large, casual, and comfortable, with couches and small tables, this is a favorite spot for local jazz and R&B combos. The adjacent restaurant serves Ethiopian cuisine under an elegant Bedouin tent. Menu items range from $3 to $11. 2801 California St. (at Divisadero St.). ℂ **415/567-5010.** No cover. 2-drink minimum.

Up & Down Club   One of the original homes for SoMa's now-familiar new-jazz scene, the Up & Down supper club attracts a trendy crowd to its restaurant

---

Tips Club-Hopping Tour

If you prefer to let someone else take the lead (and the driver's seat) for a night out, call **3 Babes and a Bus** (ℂ 866/552-2582). The nightclub tour company (the head babe is a stockbroker by day) will take you and a gaggle of 20- to 40-something partiers (mostly single women) out on the town, skipping lines and cover charges, for $35 per person.

Tips Dial-A-Scene

The local newspapers won't direct you to the city's underground club scene, nor will they advise you which of the dozens of clubs are truly hot. To get dialed in, do what the locals do—turn to the **Be-At Line** (© **415/ 626-4087**) for its daily recorded update on the town's most hoppin' hip-hop, acid-jazz, and house clubs. The scene is reported by one of its coolest residents, Mayor Brown's street-suave son, Michael. The far more commercial **Club Line** (© **415/339-8686;** www.sfclubs.com) offers up-to-date schedules for the city's larger dance venues.

---

and dance floor, where singles gyrate to house and hip-hop grooves. Dinner's at 8pm (reservations required), music starts at 9:30, and dancing begins at 10. 1151 Folsom St. (between 7th and 8th sts.). © **415/626-2388**. Cover $5–$10.

DANCE CLUBS

Although a lot of clubs allow dancing, the following are the places to go if all you want to do is shake your groove thang.

The Endup   This unique party space with a huge heated outdoor deck (with waterfall and fountain), indoor fireplace, and eclectic clientele has always thrown some of the most kickin' parties in town. There's a different theme every night: Thursday sets swinging singles loose at the Kit Kat Club; Fag Friday is just what it sounds like, plus lots of throw-down dancing; and Sunday is ever-popular with the sleepless dance-all-day crowd that comes here after the other clubs close (it opens at 6am). Call to confirm nights—offerings change from time to time. 401 Sixth St. (at Harrison St.). © **415/357-0827**. www.theendup.com. Cover free–$10.

Nickie's Bar-be-cue   Don't show up here for dinner—the only hot thing you'll find is the small, crowded dance floor. But don't let that stop you from checking it out—Nickie's is a sure thing. Every time we come here, the old-school disco hits are in full force, casually dressed dancers lose all their inhibitions, and the crowd consists of all types of friendly San Franciscans. This place is perpetually hot, so dress accordingly; you can always cool down with a pint from the wine-and-beer bar. Keep in mind that lower Haight is on the periphery of a shady neighborhood, so don't make your rental car look tempting, and stay alert as you walk through the area. 460 Haight St. (between Fillmore and Webster sts.). © **415/621-6508**. www.nickies.com. Cover $3–$5.

Paradise Lounge   Labyrinthine Paradise features three dance floors simultaneously vibrating to different beats. Smaller, auxiliary spaces include a pool room with a half-dozen tables. Poetry readings are fairly common here and the crowd ranges from everyday party people to grungy-alternative types. 1501 Folsom St. (at 11th St.). © **415/861-6906**. Cover $3–$15.

Rawhide II   Gay or straight, this was one of the city's top country-western dance bars until it recently changed to feature alternative music. It's still patronized by both men and women and can be a darned good time. It's also delightfully casual. 280 Seventh St. (at Folsom St.). © **415/621-1197**. Weekend cover charge $5; includes 1 drink.

Sound Factory   Late great columnist Herb Caen dubbed this disco theme park the "mother of all discos." The maze of rooms and nonstop barrage of house, funk, lounge vibes, and club classics attracts swarms of young urbanites (read: college-age kids) looking to rave it up, sometimes until as late as 6am. Management tries to eliminate the riffraff by enforcing a dress code (no sneakers, hooded sweatshirts, or sports caps). 525 Harrison St. (at First St.). *C* **415/339-6868.** Cover $10 Fri, $15 Sat; free with college ID.

Ten 15 Get decked out and plan for a late night if you're headed to this enormous party warehouse. Three levels, a full-color laser system, and a gigantic dance floor make for an extensive variety of dancing venues, complete with a 20- and 30-something gyrating mass who live for the DJs' pounding house, disco, and acid-jazz music. Each night is a different club that attracts its own crowd ranging from yuppie to hip-hop. A recent $1.5 million renovation added 6,000 square feet of dance floor and a VIP area. This place just keeps getting wilder. Call ahead for a complete schedule of events. 1015 Folsom St. (at Sixth St.). *C* **415/ 431-1200.** www.1015.com. Cover $5–$15.

SUPPER CLUBS

If you can eat dinner, listen to live music, and dance (or at least wiggle in your chair) in the same room, it's a supper club—those are our criteria here.

Blue Bar Whether you're passing by North Beach or finishing a night at Reed Hearon's Black Cat Cafe, drop into this chic-cozy live jazz and blues venue with cushy couches and a laid-back atmosphere. The restaurant's full menu is available here—a plus for late-night eaters and a bummer for those who come exclusively for the music. Below the Black Cat Cafe, 501 Broadway (at Kearny St.). *C* **415/ 981-2233.** Cover $5 Wed–Sun.

Harry Denton's Starlight Room *Moments* Come dressed to the nines or in casual attire to this celestial high-rise cocktail lounge and nightclub, where tourists and locals watch the sunset at dusk and boogie down to live swing and big-band or DJ's tunes after dark. The room is classic 1930s San Francisco, with red-velvet banquettes, chandeliers, and fabulous views. But what really attracts flocks of all ages is a night of Harry Denton–style fun, which usually includes plenty of drinking and unrestrained dancing. The full bar stocks a decent collection of single-malt scotches and champagnes, and you can snack from the pricey Starlight appetizer menu (make a reservation to guarantee a table and you'll also have a place to rest your weary dancing-dogs). Early evening is more relaxed, but come the weekend, this place gets loose. *Tip:* Come dressed for success (no jeans or sneakers), or you'll be turned away at the door. Atop the Sir Francis Drake Hotel, 450 Powell St., 21st floor. *C* **415/395-8595.** Cover $5 Wed after 7pm and Thurs after 8pm, $10 Fri–Sat after 8pm.

Julie's Supper Club Julie's is a longtime standby for cocktails and late dining in a groovy setting. The vibe in both rooms is very 1950s cartoon, with a space-age Jetsons appeal and good-looking singles on the prowl. The food is hit-and-miss, but the atmosphere is definitely a winner—casual and playful and it comes with a little interesting history: This building is one location where the Symbionese Liberation Army held Patty Hearst hostage in the 1970s. Menu items range from $9 to $20. 1123 Folsom St. (at Seventh St.). *C* **415/861-0707.** $5 cover on weekends.

RETRO CLUBS

Club Deluxe *Finds* Before the recent 1940s trend hit the city, Deluxe and its fedora-wearing clientele had been celebrating the bygone era for years. Fortunately, even with all the retro hype, the vibe here hasn't changed. Expect an eclectic mix of throwbacks and generic San Franciscans in the intimate bar and adjoining lounge, and live jazz or blues most nights. Although many regulars dress the part, there's no attitude here, so come as you like. 1511 Haight St. (at Ashbury St.). ✆ 415/552-6949. Cover $2–$10.

HiBall Lounge Retro jazz is no longer full swing in the city, but it's still a delightfully dizzying experience at this North Beach joint. Harking back to Broadway at its best, the vibe is full-on 1940s and '50s, from the red banquettes and stage curtains to the small, dark room. Live bands perform nightly to a young, swingin' crowd. There's also a swing-dance class Wednesday through Sunday. The kitschy-fun adjoining Bamboo Hut lounge celebrates classic tiki cocktails. The dress code: no baseball caps, tennis shoes, T-shirts, or ripped jeans. 473 Broadway (between Kearny and Montgomery sts.). ✆ 415/397-9464. Cover $2–$8.

4 The Bar Scene

Finding your idea of a comfortable bar has a lot to do with picking a neighborhood filled with your kind of people and investigating that area. There are hundreds of bars throughout San Francisco, and although many are obscurely located and can't be classified by their neighborhood, the following is a general description of what you'll find and where:

- **Chestnut and Union Street** bars attract a postcollegiate crowd.
- Young alternatives frequent **Mission District** haunts.
- **Upper Haight** caters to eclectic neighborhood cocktailers.
- **Lower Haight** is skate- and snowboarder grungy.
- Tourists mix with theatergoers and thirsty businesspeople in **downtown** pubs.
- **North Beach** serves all types.
- **The Castro** caters to gay locals and tourists.
- **SoMa** offers an eclectic mix.

The following is a list of a few of San Francisco's most interesting bars. Unless otherwise noted, these bars do not have cover charges.

Backflip Adjoining the funky Phoenix Hotel, this shimmering aqua-blue cocktail lounge—designed to induce the illusion that you're carousing in the deep end—serves tapas and Caribbean-style appetizers to a mostly young, fashionable crowd (so please don't order a Cosmopolitan). While the scene continues to change, Thursday the crowd seems to be young and gay/alternative; weekends, wanna-be-cool yuppies tend to pack the place. Regardless, if you're headed here, you can expect the unexpected, kick back with a martini, and enjoy the city's varied eye candy. 601 Eddy St. (at Larkin St.). ✆ 415/771-FLIP.

Bottom of the Hill *Value* Voted one of the best places to hear live rock in the city by the *San Francisco Bay Guardian,* this popular neighborhood club attracts an eclectic crowd ranging from rockers to real-estate salespeople. The main attraction is live music every night, but it also offers pretty good burgers and kebabs, outdoor seating on the back patio, and an awesome $4 all-you-can-eat barbecue on Sunday from 4 to 7pm. Happy hour runs Monday to Friday from 4 to 7pm. 1233 17th St. (at Missouri St.). ✆ 415/621-4455. Cover $4–$10.

Chalkers Billiard Club Pool hall meets men's smoking club at this enormous billiards joint. Food and drinks are delivered to the 30 cherrywood tables (29 billiard and one 12-food snooker), which you can rent by the hour. Pool sharks especially appreciate the custom cue shop, where savvy sticks can go for up to

$25,000. Happy hour (weekdays 5 to 7pm) offers more beer for your buck. One Rincon Center, 101 Spear St. (at Mission St.). ☎ 415/512-0450. www.chalkers.com.

Edinburgh Castle   Since 1958, this legendary Scottish pub has been known for unusual British ales on tap and the best selection of single-malt scotches in the city. The huge pub is decorated with Royal Air Force mementos, horse brasses, steel helmets, and an authentic Ballantine caber (a long wooden pole) used in the annual Scottish games. Fish-and-chips and other traditional foods are available until 11pm. 950 Geary St. (between Polk and Larkin sts.). ☎ 415/885-4074.

The Great Entertainer   This is a glorified pool hall, with 50 tables, five private billiard suites, snooker, shuffleboard, darts, table tennis, and a video arcade. Drinks, pizza, and other dishes accompany the games. Menu items run $2 to $20. 975 Bryant (at Eighth St.). ☎ 415/861-8833.

Li Po Cocktail Lounge   A divey Chinese bar, Li Po stands out for its clutter of dusty Asian furnishings and mementos. They include an unbelievably huge rice-paper lantern hanging from the ceiling and a glittery golden shrine to Buddha behind the bar. 916 Grant Ave. (between Washington and Jackson sts.). ☎ 415/982-0072.

Perry's   If you read *Tales of the City*, you already know that this bar and restaurant has a colorful history as a pickup place for Pacific Heights and Marina singles. Although the times are not as wild today, locals still come to casually check out the happenings at the dark mahogany bar. A separate dining room offers breakfast, lunch, dinner, and weekend brunch. It's a good place for hamburgers, simple fish dishes, and pasta. Menu items range from $7 to $22. 1944 Union St. (at Laguna St.). ☎ 415/922-9022.

Pied Piper Bar   The huge Pied Piper mural by Edwardian illustrator Maxfield Parrish steals the show at this historic mahogany bar, where high stakes were once won and lost on the roll of the dice. In the Palace Hotel, 2 New Montgomery (at Market St.). ☎ 415/512-1111.

The Red Room   Ultramodern, small, and deliciously dim, this lounge reflects no other color but ruby red. It's a sexy place to sip the latest cocktail. In the Commodore Hotel, 827 Sutter St. (at Jones St.). ☎ 415/346-7666.

The Redwood Room   A true Art Deco beauty, this ground-floor lounge was one of San Francisco's most comfortable and nostalgic piano bars until Ian Schrager got his hands on it. The room was revamped in 2001, and though it retains its gorgeous redwood interior made from a single 2,000-year-old tree, the vibe and clientele promise to be more of a stomping ground for the tragically hip than return guests who have frequented the historic room for over 50 years. Drinks go for $6 to $9. In the Clift Hotel, 495 Geary St. ☎ 415/775-4700.

The Savoy-Tivoli   Euro-trash and wanna-bes crowd the few pool tables and indoor and patio seating, smoking cigarettes and looking cool, at this popular, trendy bar. Tourists and newcomers dominate, because posing gets tiring after a while, and there are far more authentic bars in town. But a sidewalk-facing table in the heart of North Beach allows for great people-watching, and the high-profile clientele does create an entertaining atmosphere. Drinks range from $3.50 to $8. 1434 Grant Ave. (between Green and Union sts.). ☎ 415/362-7023.

Spec's *Finds*   The location of Spec's—Saroyan Place, a tiny alley at 250 Columbus Avenue—makes it less of a walk-in bar and more of a lively local hangout. Its funky decor—maritime flags hang from the ceiling; posters, photos, and various oddities line the exposed-brick walls—gives it character that intrigues every visitor. A "museum," displayed under glass, contains memorabilia and items brought back by seamen who drop in between voyages, and the clientele is funky enough to keep you preoccupied while you drink a beer. 12 Saroyan Place (at 250 Columbus Ave.). ℂ 415/421-4112.

Toronado   Lower Haight isn't exactly a charming street, but there's plenty of nightlife here, catering to an artistic/grungy/skateboarding 20-something crowd. While Toronado definitely draws in the young'uns, its 40-plus microbrews on tap and 60 bottled beers also entice a more eclectic clientele in search of beer heaven. The brooding atmosphere matches the surroundings: an aluminum bar, a few tall tables, dark lighting, and a back room packed with tables and chairs. A DJ picks up the pace on Friday and Saturday nights. 547 Haight St. (at Fillmore St.). ℂ 415/863-2276.

Tosca *Finds*   Open daily from 5pm to 2am, Tosca is a low-key and large popular watering hole for local politicos, writers, media types, incognito visiting celebrities such as Johnny Depp or Nicholas Cage, and similar cognoscenti of unassuming classics. Equipped with dim lights, red leather booths, high ceilings, and the requisite vintage jukebox spilling out Italian arias, it's everything you'd expect an old North Beach legend to be. 242 Columbus Ave. (between Broadway and Pacific Ave.). ℂ 415/986-9651.

Vesuvio   Situated along Jack Kerouac Alley across from the famed City Lights Bookstore, this renowned literary beatnik hangout is packed to the second-floor rafters with neighborhood writers, artists, songsters, wanna-bes, and everyone else ranging from longshoremen and cab drivers to businesspeople all of whom come for the laid-back atmosphere. The convivial space is two stories of cocktail tables, complemented by a changing exhibition of local art and on Friday from 4pm to 7pm live music. In addition to drinks, Vesuvio features an espresso machine. 255 Columbus Ave. (at Broadway). ℂ 415/362-3370. www.vesuvio.com. No credit cards.

BREW PUBS

Gordon Biersch Brewery Restaurant   Gordon Biersch Brewery is San Francisco's largest brew restaurant, serving decent food and tasty beer to an attractive crowd of mingling professionals. There are always several beers to choose from, ranging from light to dark. Menu items run $9.50 to $20. (See chapter 6 for more information.) 2 Harrison St. (on the Embarcadero). ℂ 415/243-8246.

San Francisco Brewing Company   Surprisingly low-key for an alehouse, this cozy brew pub serves its creations along with burgers, fries, grilled chicken breast, and the like. The bar is one of the city's few remaining old saloons (circa 1907), aglow with stained-glass windows, tile floors, skylit ceiling, beveled glass, and mahogany bar. A massive overhead fan runs the full length of the bar—a bizarre contraption crafted from brass and palm fronds. The handmade copper brew kettle is visible from the street. Most evenings the place is packed with everyday folks enjoying music or comedy, darts, chess, backgammon, cards, and dice, and, of course, beer. Menu items range from $3.70 (curiously, for edamame) to $20 for a full rack of baby back ribs with all the fixings. The happy-hour special, a dollar per 10-ounce microbrew beer (or $1.75 a pint), runs daily from 4 to 6pm and midnight to 1am. 155 Columbus Ave. (at Pacific St.). ℂ 415/434-3344. www.sfbrewing.com.

Thirsty Bear Brewing Company   Seven superb, handcrafted varieties of brew, ranging from fruit-flavored Strawberry Ale to a steak-in-a-cup stout, are always on

---

Finds   Midnight (or Midday) Mochas

If you happen to be wandering around North Beach past your bedtime and need your caffeine fix, seek out these two cafes. They offer not only excellent espresso, but also a glimpse into what it must have been like back in the days of the beatniks, when nothing was as crucial as a strong cup of coffee, a good smoke, and a stimulating environment.

Doing the North Beach thing is little more than hanging out in a sophisticated but relaxed atmosphere over a well-made cappuccino. You can do it at **Caffè Greco,** 423 Columbus Ave., between Green and Vallejo streets (© **415/397-6261**), and grab a bite, too. The affordable cafe fare includes beer, wine, a good selection of coffees, focaccia sandwiches, and desserts (try the gelato or homemade tiramisu).

Caffè Trieste, 601 Vallejo St., at Grant Avenue (© **415/392-6739**), is one of San Francisco's most beloved cafes—very down-home Italian, with only espresso drinks, pastries, and indoor and outdoor seating. Opera is always on the jukebox, unless it's Saturday afternoon, when the family and their friends break out in arias from 2 to 5pm.

---

tap at this stylish high-ceilinged brick edifice. Good Spanish food is served here, too (see chapter 6 for more information). Pool tables and dartboards are upstairs, and live music (jazz, flamenco, blues, alternative, and classical) can be heard most nights. 661 Howard St. (1 block east of the Moscone Center). © **415/974-0905.**

COCKTAILS WITH A VIEW

See "Supper Clubs," above, for a full review of **Harry Denton's Starlight Room.** Unless otherwise noted, these establishments have no cover charge.

The Carnelian Room   On the 52nd floor of the Bank of America Building, the Carnelian Room offers uninterrupted views of the city. From a window-front table you feel as though you can reach out, pluck up the TransAmerica Pyramid, and stir your martini with it. In addition to cocktails, it serves "Discovery Dinners" ($48 per person). Jackets and ties are optional, but encouraged, for men. *Note:* The restaurant has the most extensive wine list in the city—1,275 selections, to be exact. 555 California St., in the Bank of America Building (between Kearny and Montgomery sts.). © **415/433-7500.**

Cityscape   When you sit under the glass roof and sip a drink here, it's as though you're sitting out under the stars and enjoying views of the bay. Dinner, focusing on steak and seafood, is available, and there's dancing to a DJ's picks nightly from 10pm. The mirrored columns and floor-to-ceiling draperies help create an elegant and romantic ambience. Hilton San Francisco, Tower I, 333 O'Farrell St. (at Mason St.), 46th floor. © **415/923-5002.**

Equinox   Though locals don't frequent this Fi-Di (Financial District) place, it's very popular with tourists. The hook? The Hyatt's 17-story rooftop restaurant, has a revolving floor that gives each table a 360-degree panoramic view of the city every 45 minutes. In addition to cocktails, it serves dinner daily. In the Hyatt Regency Hotel, 5 Embarcadero Center. © **415/788-1234.**

Top of the Mark *(Finds)* *(Moments)*   This is one of the most famous cocktail lounges in the world, and for good reason—the spectacular glass-walled room features an unparalleled 19th-floor view. During World War II, Pacific-bound servicemen toasted their good-bye to the States here. While less dramatic today than they were back then, evenings spent here are still sentimental, thanks to romantic atmosphere and live entertainment (think swing band) starts at 8:30 nightly. There are free dance lessons on Tuesday nights. Afternoon tea runs from 3 to 5pm Monday to Friday. A recently added price-fixed dinner is served Thursday through Saturday. Sunday brunch, served from 10am to 2pm, costs $44 without Champagne ($22 for children 5 to 14). Drinks are also pricey, ranging from $6 to $8. In the Mark Hopkins Intercontinental, 1 Nob Hill (California and Mason sts.). © 415/616-6916. Cover $6–$10.

SPORTS BARS

Greens Sports Bar   If you think San Francisco sports fans aren't as enthusiastic as those on the East Coast, try to get a seat at Green's during a 49ers game. It's a classic old sports bar, with lots of polished dark wood and windows that open onto Polk Street, but it's loaded with modern appliances, (including a large-screen television and 10 smaller ones) and modern partiers (read: dot-commers and the mid-20s and -30s set). With 18 beers on tap, a pool table, and a late-night happy hour on Sunday to Wednesday from 10pm to 2am, there are reasons to cheer even when the home team's got a day off. 2239 Polk St. (at Green St.). © 415/775-4287.

WINE & CHAMPAGNE BARS

The Bubble Lounge   San Francisco nightlife is in full swing, and toasting the town is a nightly event at this two-level Champagne bar. With 300 Champagnes, around 30 by the glass, brick walls, couches, velvet curtains, and a pool table, there's plenty of pop in this fizzy lounge. 714 Montgomery St. (at Columbus Ave.). © 415/434-4204.

Eos   If you're downtown, head for the London Wine Bar. If you're around the Civic Center, make it Hayes and Vine. For anything west of these two, your top choice is Eos, a fairly new, highly successful restaurant and wine bar in Cole Valley (near the Haight). Around the corner from the restaurant is this chic, lively wine bar filled mostly with young patrons who dabble among the 400 vintages from around the world. (See chapter 6 for more information.) 101 Carl St. (at Cole St.). © 415/566-3063.

Hayes and Vine   You'll find 750 wines (with more than 50 by the glass!) from around the world at this unpretentious wine bar staffed by true cognoscenti of fine wine. (It's a good thing, too, because you have probably never heard of 90% of these wines.) Be sure to ask about taking a "flight," which allows you to try several different wines for a fixed price. Cheese, breads, antipasti, charcuterie, and desserts are also served. 377 Hayes St. (at Gough St.). © 415/626-5301.

London Wine Bar   This British-style wine bar and store is a popular after-work hangout for Financial District suits. It's more of a place to drink and chat than to admire fine wines. Usually two to three dozen wines, mostly from California, are open at any given time. It's a great venue for sampling local Napa Valley wines before you buy. 415 Sansome St. (between Sacramento and Clay sts.). © 415/788-4811.

5 Gay & Lesbian Bars & Clubs

Just like straight establishments, gay and lesbian bars and clubs target varied clienteles. Whether you're into leather or Lycra, business or bondage, there's gay nightlife just for you.

Check the free weeklies, the *San Francisco Bay Guardian* and *San Francisco Weekly*, for listings of events and happenings. The *Bay Area Reporter* is a gay paper with comprehensive listings, including a weekly community calendar. All these papers are free and distributed weekly on Wednesday or Thursday. They can be found stacked at the corner of 18th and Castro streets and Ninth and Harrison streets, as well as in bars, bookshops, and other stores around town. To find out what's up with lesbian events in San Francisco, ranging from women's golf to nightlife, call **Girl Spot** (© 415/337-4962). There are also a number of gay and lesbian guides to San Francisco. See "For Gays & Lesbians," in chapter 2 for further details.

Listed below are some of the city's most established, mainstream gay hangouts.

The Café *Finds* When this place first got jumping, it was the only predominantly lesbian dance club on Saturday nights in the city. Once the guys found out how much fun the girls were having, they joined the party. Today, it's a happening mixed gay and lesbian scene with two bars, a steamy, free-spirited dance floor, and a small patio. 2367 Market St. (at Castro St.). © 415/861-3846. No cover.

The Cinch Saloon Among the popular attributes of this cruisey neighborhood bar are the outdoor patio, Sunday barbecue or buffet, and progressive music and videos. 49er fans also gather here for televised games. Decorated in a Southwestern theme ("down home in Arizona"), the bar attracts a mixed crowd of gays, lesbians (now that there are almost no exclusively lesbian bars left in San Francisco), and gay-friendly straights. There are "beer busts" or theme drink nights weekly. The nominal charge for barbecues and buffets is donated entirely to various AIDS organizations. 1723 Polk St. (near Washington St.). © 415/776-4162. No cover.

Detour Right in the heart of gay San Francisco, this bar attracts a young, often hot crowd of boys, with its low lighting and throbbing house music. Chain-link fences seem to hold in the action while a live DJ spins a web of popular hits. Special events, including Saturday go-go dancers, keep this place jumping. 2348 Market St. (near Castro St.). © 415/861-6053. No cover.

The Eagle One of the city's most traditional Levi's–leather bars, The Eagle boasts a heated outdoor patio, a happy hour (Monday to Friday 4 to 8pm), and a popular Sunday-afternoon beer fest from 3 to 6pm. 398 12th St. (at Harrison St.). © 415/626-0880. www.sfeagle.com. No cover.

The Endup It's a different nightclub every night of the week, but regardless of who's throwing the party, the place is always jumping with the DJ's blasting tunes. There are two pool tables, a flaming fireplace, outdoor patio, and a mob of gyrating souls on the dance floor. Some nights are straight, so call ahead. (See "Dance Clubs" above for more information.) 401 Sixth St. (at Harrison St.). © 415/357-0827. www.theendup.com. Cover free–$10.

Giraffe Lounge Favored by a young, action-seeking crowd, this video bar, with its 15 ceiling-mounted monitors, is a good place for cruising or shooting pool. It's a friendly neighborhood hangout during the week and livens up on weekends. 1131 Polk St. (near Sutter St.). © 415/474-1702. No cover.

Kimo's   This neighborhood bar in the seedier gay section of town is a friendly oasis, decorated with plants, pictures, and "gay banners." The bar provides a relaxing venue for chatting, drinking, and quiet cruising, and things occasionally liven up during drag shows. 1351 Polk St. (at Pine St.). © 415/885-4535. Free to nominal cover.

Lone Star Saloon   Expect lesbians and a heavier, furrier motorcycle crowd (both men and women) most every night. The Sunday-afternoon beer bust on the patio is especially popular. 1354 Harrison St. (between Ninth and Tenth sts.). © 415/863-9999. No cover.

Metro   With modern art on the walls and much use of terra cotta, the Metro provides the gay community with high-energy dance music and the best view of The Castro District from its large balcony. The bar seems to attract people of all ages who enjoy the friendly bartenders and the highly charged, cruising atmosphere. There's a Chinese restaurant on the premises if you get hungry. 3600 16th St. (at Market St.). © 415/703-9750. No cover.

The Mint Karaoke Lounge   Come out of the shower and into the Mint, a gay and lesbian karaoke bar where you can sing show tunes every night. Along with song, you'll encounter a mixed 20- to 40-something crowd that combines cocktails with do-it-yourself cabaret. 1942 Market St. (at Laguna St.). © 415/626-4726. No cover.

The Stud   The Stud, which has been around for more than 30 years, is one of the most successful gay establishments in town. The interior has an antique-shop look and a miniature train circling over the bar and dance floor. Music is a balanced mix of old and new, and nights vary from cabaret and oldies to disco. Call in advance for the evening's offerings. Drink prices range from $2 to $6. Happy hour runs daily from 5 to 9pm. 399 Ninth St. (at Harrison St.). © 415/863-6623 or event info line 415/252-STUD. Cover $3–$10.

Twin Peaks Tavern   Right at the intersection of Castro, 17th, and Market streets is one of The Castro's most famous gay hangouts, which caters to an older crowd and claims to be the first gay bar in America. Because of its relatively small size and desirable location, the place becomes fairly crowded and convivial by 8pm, earlier than many neighboring bars. 401 Castro St. (at 17th and Market sts.). © 415/864-9470. No cover.

6 Film

The **San Francisco International Film Festival** (© 415/931-FILM; www.sfiff. org), held in March, is one of America's oldest film festivals. Tickets are relatively inexpensive. Entries include new films by beginning and established directors. Call or surf ahead for a schedule or information. You can charge tickets by phone through **BASS Ticketmaster** (© 415/478-2277).

Even if you're not here in time for the festival, don't despair. The classic, independent, and mainstream cinemas in San Francisco are every bit as good as the city's other cultural offerings.

REPERTORY CINEMAS

Castro Theatre *(Finds)*   Built in 1922, the beautiful Castro Theatre is known for its screenings of classics and for its Wurlitzer organ, which is played before each show. There's a different feature almost nightly, and more often than not it's a double feature. Bargain matinees are usually offered on Wednesday, Saturday, Sunday, and holidays. Phone for schedules, prices, and show times. 429 Castro St. (near Market St.). ☎ 415/621-6120.

Roxie   The Roxie consistently screens the best new alternative films anywhere. The low-budget contemporary features are largely devoid of Hollywood candy coating; many are West Coast premieres. Films change weekly and sometimes more often. Phone for schedules, prices, and show times. 3117 16th St. (at Valencia St.). ☎ 415/863-1087.

11

Side Trips from San Francisco

The Bay City is, without question, captivating, but don't let it ensnare you to the point of ignoring its environs. The area contains a multitude of natural spectacles like Mount Tamalpais and Muir Woods; scenic communities like Tiburon and Sausalito; and cities like up-and-coming Oakland and its youth-oriented next-door neighbor, Berkeley. To the southwest lies Half Moon Bay, an adorable little coastal town perched on a wide expanse of golden beach.

From San Francisco you can reach any of these points in an hour or less by car. Another option is to hitch a ride with **Tower Tours** (© **415/ 434-8687;** www.towertours.com), which runs regularly scheduled microbus tours to neighboring towns and the countryside. Half- and full-day trips to Muir Woods, Sausalito, Napa, and Sonoma are available, as are excursions to Yosemite and the Monterey Peninsula. Phone for prices and schedules.

1 Berkeley

10 miles NE of San Francisco

Berkeley is famous as the home of the University of California at Berkeley, which is world-renowned for its academic standards, 17 Nobel Prize winners (7 are active staff), and protests that led to the most famous student riots in U.S. history. Today, there's still hippie idealism in the air, but the radicals have aged; the 60s are present only in tie-dye and paraphernalia shops, and the students have less angst. The biggest change the town is facing is yuppification; as San Francisco's rent and property prices soar, everyone with less than a small fortune is seeking shelter elsewhere, and Berkeley is one of the top picks. It's a charming town teeming with all types of people, a beautiful campus, vast parks, great shopping, and some incredible restaurants.

BERKELEY ESSENTIALS

The Berkeley **Bay Area Rapid Transit (BART)** station is 2 blocks from the university. The fare from San Francisco is less than $3.

If you are coming **by car** from San Francisco, take the Bay Bridge (go during the evening commute, and you'll think Los Angeles traffic is a breeze). Follow I-80 east to the University Avenue exit, and follow University until you hit the campus. Parking is tight, so either leave your car at the Sather Gate parking lot on Telegraph and Durant, or expect to fight for a spot.

Phone the **Visitor Hot Line** (© **510/549-8710**) for automated information on events and happenings in Berkeley.

WHAT TO SEE & DO IN BERKELEY

Hanging out is the preferred Berkeley pastime, and the best place to do it is on **Telegraph Avenue,** the street that leads to the campus's southern entrance. Most

The Bay Area

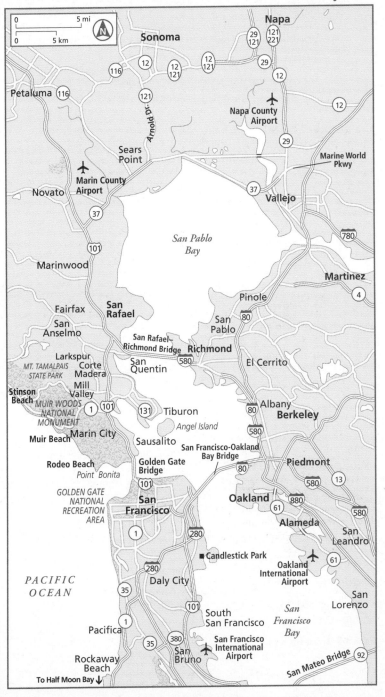

of the action lies between Bancroft Way and Ashby Avenue, where coffeehouses, restaurants, shops, great book and record stores, and craft booths swarm with life. Pretend you're local: Plant yourself at a cafe, sip a latte, and ponder something intellectual or survey the town's unique residents.

Bibliophiles must stop at **Cody's Books,** 2454 Telegraph Ave. (℗ **510/ 845-7852**), to peruse its gargantuan selection of titles, independent-press books, and magazines. Vendors selling everything from T-shirts and jewelry to I Ching and tarot-card readings pack the avenue.

UC BERKELEY CAMPUS

The University of California at Berkeley (www.berkeley.edu) campus is worth a stroll. It's a beautiful old place with plenty of woodsy paths, architecturally noteworthy buildings, and, of course, 31,000 students, many of them scurrying to and from classes. Among the architectural highlights of the campus are a number of buildings by Bernard Maybeck, Bakewell and Brown, and John Galen Howard.

Contact the **Visitor Information Center,** 101 University Hall, 2200 University Ave., at Oxford Street (℗ **510/642-5215**), to join a free, regularly scheduled campus tour. They start Monday through Saturday at 10am and 1pm, Sunday at 1pm; no tours from mid-December to mid-January. Or stop by the office and pick up a self-guided walking-tour brochure.

The university's southern entrance is at the northern end of Telegraph Avenue, at Bancroft Way. Walk through the main entrance into Sproul Plaza, and when school is in session, you'll encounter the gamut of Berkeley's inhabitants: colorful street people, rambling political zealots, chanting Hare Krishnas, and ambitious students. You'll also find the Student Union, complete with a bookstore, cafes, and an information desk on the second floor where you can pick up a free map of Berkeley and the student newspaper (also found in dispensers throughout campus).

You might be lucky enough to stumble upon some impromptu musicians or a heated, and possibly absurd, debate. There's always something going on, so stretch out on the grass for a few minutes and take in the Berkeley vibe.

For viewing more traditional art forms, there are some noteworthy museums, too. The **Lawrence Hall of Science** ⭐ (℗ **510/642-5132;** www.lawrencehallof science.org), offers hands-on science exploration, is open 10am to 5pm daily and is a wonderful place to watch the sunset. Admission is $7 for adults; $5 for seniors, students, and children 7 to 18; $3 for children 3 to 6; free for kids under 3. The **University Art Museum** ⭐ (℗ **510/642-0808**) is open 11am to 5pm on Wednesday and Friday through Sunday, and Thursday 11am to 9pm. Admission is $6 for adults; $4 for seniors, students, and children 12 to 17; free for kids under 12 and U.C. students. This museum contains a substantial collection of Hans Hofmann paintings, a sculpture garden, and the Pacific Film Archive.

If you're interested in notable off-campus buildings, contact the **Berkeley Convention and Visitors Bureau** (℗ **510/549-7040**) for an architectural walking-tour brochure.

PARKS IN BERKELEY

Unbeknownst to many travelers, Berkeley has some of the most extensive and beautiful parks around. If you want to wear out the kids or enjoy hiking, swimming, or just getting a breath of California air and sniffing a few roses, jump in your car and make your way to **Tilden Park** ⭐. On the way, stop at the colorful

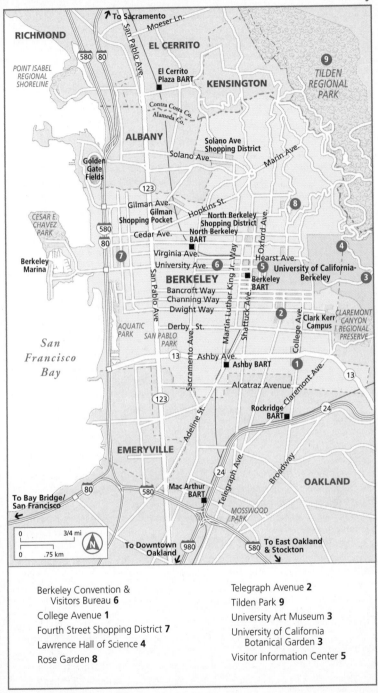

Berkeley

RICHMOND

To Sacramento

Moeser Ln.

POINT ISABEL
REGIONAL
SHORELINE

EL CERRITO

El Cerrito
Plaza BART

KENSINGTON

TILDEN
REGIONAL
PARK

Contra Costa Co.
Alameda Co.

ALBANY

Golden
Gate
Fields

Solano Ave
Shopping District

Solano Ave.

Marin Ave.

CESAR E.
CHAVEZ
PARK

Gilman Ave.
Gilman
Shopping Pocket

Hopkins St.

North Berkeley
Shopping District

Cedar Ave.

North Berkeley
BART

Oxford Ave.

Berkeley
Marina

Virginia Ave.

University Ave.

Hearst Ave.

University of California-
Berkeley

San
Francisco
Bay

BERKELEY

Bancroft Way
Channing Way
Dwight Way

Berkeley
BART

Martin Luther King Jr. Way

Shattuck Ave.

CLAREMONT
CANYON
REGIONAL
PRESERVE

AQUATIC
PARK

SAN PABLO
PARK

Derby St.

College Ave.

Clark Kerr
Campus

Ashby Ave.

Ashby BART

Alcatraz Avenue

Rockridge
BART

Claremont Ave.

EMERYVILLE

Adeline St.

To Bay Bridge/
San Francisco

Mac Arthur
BART

Telegraph Ave.

Broadway

OAKLAND

MOSSWOOD
PARK

0   3/4 mi
0   .75 km

To Downtown
Oakland

To East Oakland
& Stockton

Berkeley Convention &
  Visitors Bureau **6**

College Avenue **1**

Fourth Street Shopping District **7**

Lawrence Hall of Science **4**

Rose Garden **8**

Telegraph Avenue **2**

Tilden Park **9**

University Art Museum **3**

University of California
  Botanical Garden **3**

Visitor Information Center **5**

People's Park/People's Power

In late 1967, the university demolished an entire block of buildings north of Telegraph Avenue. The destruction, which forced hippies and other "undesirables" from the slum housing that stood there, was done under the guise of university expansion and urban renewal—good liberal causes. But after the lot lay vacant for almost 2 years, a group of Berkeley radicals, whose names read like a who's who of 1960s leftists, including Jerry Rubin, Bobby Seale, and Tom Hayden, decided to take the land for "the people."

On April 29, 1969, hundreds of activists invaded the vacant lot with gardening tools and tamed the muddy ground into a park. One month later, Berkeley's Republican mayor sent 250 police officers into the park, and 4,000 demonstrators materialized to challenge them. A riot ensued, and the police fired buckshot at the crowd. One rioter was killed and another blinded. Gov. Ronald Reagan sent in the National Guard, and for the next 17 days, the guardsmen repeatedly gassed innocent students, faculty, and passersby. Berkeley was a war zone, and People's Park became the decade's most important symbol of "people power."

People's Park again sparked controversy in 1992, when university officials decided to build volleyball courts there. In August, a park activist broke into the campus home of the university's chancellor. When a police officer arrived, the activist lunged at him with a machete and was shot dead. On the victim's body was a note with the message: "We are willing to die for this land. Are you?" On news of the contemporary radical's death, more than 150 of her supporters rioted.

Postscript: The volleyball courts didn't get much use, and now basketball courts have taken their place.

terraced **Rose Garden** ✿, in north Berkeley on Euclid Avenue between Bay View and Eunice Street. Then head high into the Berkeley hills to Tilden, where you'll find plenty of flora and fauna, hiking trails, an old steam train and merry-go-round, a farm and nature area for kids, and a chilly tree-encircled lake. By public transit, line no. 67 goes to the north end of the park, and no. 8 skirts the edge of the park. Call ℂ **510/562-PARK** for further information.

Another worthy nature excursion is the **University of California Botanical Garden** (ℂ **510/642-3343**), which features a vast collection of herbage ranging from cacti to redwoods. It's on campus in Strawberry Canyon on Centennial Drive; line no. 8 from the Berkeley BART station runs there.

SHOPPING IN BERKELEY

If you're itching to exercise your credit cards, head to one of two places. **College Avenue** from Dwight to the Oakland border overflows with eclectic boutiques, antique shops, and restaurants. The other option is **Fourth Street,** in west Berkeley, 2 blocks north of the University Avenue exit. This 2-block expanse is the perfect place to go on a sunny morning. Grab a cup of java, read the paper at a patio table, then hit the **Crate and Barrel Outlet,** 1785 Fourth St., between

Hearst and Virginia (© **510/528-5500**). Prices are 30% to 70% off retail. It's open Monday to Saturday 10am to 6pm, Sunday 11am to 6pm. This area also boasts small, wonderful stores crammed with imported and locally made housewares. Nearby is **REI,** the Bay Area's favorite outdoor outfitter, 1338 San Pablo Ave., near Gilman Street (© **510/527-4140**).

WHERE TO STAY IN BERKELEY

Bed and Breakfast California, 12711 McCartysville Place, Saratoga, CA 95070 (© **800/872-4500** or 408/867-9662; fax 408/867-0907; www.bbintl.com), accommodates visitors in more than 150 private homes and apartments in the San Francisco–Berkeley area. The cost ranges from $95 to $300 per night, and there's a 2-night minimum. The **Berkeley Convention and Visitors Bureau,** 2015 Center St., Berkeley, CA 94704 (© **800/847-4823** or 510/549-7040), can find accommodations and supply free visitor guides, maps, and area literature. It's staffed Monday to Friday 9am to 5pm.

WHERE TO DINE IN BERKELEY

East Bay dining is a relaxed alternative to the city's gourmet scene. There are plenty of ambitious Berkeley restaurants and, unlike San Francisco, plenty of parking.

If you want to dine student style, eat on campus Monday to Friday. Buy something at a sidewalk stand or in the building directly behind the Student Union. The least expensive food is available downstairs in the **Cafeteria,** on Lower Sproul Plaza. There's also the **Bear's Lair Pub and Coffee House,** the **Terrace,** and the **Golden Bear Restaurant.** All the university eateries have both indoor and outdoor seating.

Telegraph Avenue has an array of small, ethnic restaurants, cafes, and sandwich shops. Follow the students: If the place is crowded, it's good, super cheap, or both.

EXPENSIVE

Chez Panisse ★★★ CALIFORNIA   California cuisine is so much a product of Alice Waters's genius that all other restaurants following in her wake should be dated "AAW" (After Alice Waters). Read the menus posted outside, and you'll understand why. Most of the produce and meat comes from local farms and is organically produced, and after all these years, Alice still attends to her restaurant with great integrity and innovation.

Chez Panisse is a delightful redwood and stucco cottage with a brick terrace filled with flowering potted plants. The two dining areas, the cafe and the restaurant, both serve Mediterranean-inspired cuisine.

Pricing Guide

In this chapter, restaurants are organized by location, then price range for a complete dinner (appetizer, entrée, and dessert) as follows: **Expensive,** more than $50 per person; **Moderate,** $35 to $50 per person; and **Inexpensive,** less than $35 per person.

Hotels are organized by location, then price range as follows: **Very Expensive,** more than $250 per night; **Expensive,** $200 to $250 per night; **Moderate,** $150 to $200 per night; and **Inexpensive,** less than $150 per night.

In the upstairs cafe are displays of pastries and fruit, and large bouquets of fresh flowers adorn an oak bar. At lunch or dinner, the menu might feature delicately smoked gravlax or roasted eggplant soup with pesto, followed by lamb ragout garnished with apricots, onions, and spices served with couscous.

The cozy downstairs restaurant, strewn with blossoming floral bouquets, is an appropriately warm environment to indulge in the fixed-price four-course gourmet dinner, which is served Tuesday to Thursday. Friday and Saturday, it's four courses plus an aperitif, and Monday is bargain night, with a three-course dinner for $39.

The restaurant posts the menu, which changes daily, each Saturday for the following week. There's an excellent wine list, with bottles ranging from $20 to $200.

1517 Shattuck Ave. (between Cedar and Vine). © 510/548-5525; cafe reservations 415/548-5049. Fax 510/548-0140. www.chezpanisse.com. Reservations essential. Restaurant fixed-price menu $45–$75; cafe main courses $15–$25. AE, DC, DISC, MC, V. Restaurant seatings Mon–Sat 6–6:30pm and 8:30–9:30pm. Cafe Mon–Thurs 11:30am–3pm and 5–10:30pm; Fri–Sat 11:30am–3:30pm and 5–11:30pm. From I-80 north, take the University Ave. exit and turn left onto Shattuck Ave. BART: Berkeley.

MODERATE

Cafe Rouge ★★ MEDITERRANEAN   After cooking at San Francisco's renowned Zuni Cafe for 10 years, chef-owner Marsha McBride launched her own restaurant, a sort of Zuni East. She brought former staff members and some of the restaurant's flavor with her, and now her sparse, loftlike dining room serves salads, rotisserie chicken with oil and thyme, grilled lamb chops, steaks, and homemade sausages. East Bay carnivores are especially happy with the burger; like Zuni's, it's top-notch.

1782 Fourth St. (between Delaware and Hearst). © 510/525-1440. Reservations recommended. Main courses $9.50–$24. AE, MC, V. Mon–Sat 11:30am–3pm; Tues–Sat 3–5pm (interim menu); Tues–Thurs 5:30–9:30pm; Fri–Sat 5:30–10:30pm; Sun 5–9pm. BISTRO.

O Chamé ★★ JAPANESE   Spare and plain in its decor, with ochre-colored walls marked with etched patterns, this spot has a meditative air to complement the traditional and experimental Japanese-inspired cuisine. The menu, which changes daily, offers meal-in-a-bowl dishes ($9 to $12.50) that allow a choice of soba or udon noodles in a clear soup with a variety of toppings—from shrimp and wakame seaweed to beef with burdock root and carrot. Appetizers include a flavorful melding of grilled shiitake mushrooms, and portabello mushrooms, watercress, and green-onion pancakes. There are also specials ($10 to $17.50), which always include delicious roasted salmon.

1830 Fourth St. (near Hearst). © 510/841-8783. Reservations recommended Fri–Sat. Main courses $9–$18.50. AE, DC, MC, V. Mon–Sat 11:30am–3pm; Mon–Thurs 5:30–9pm; Fri–Sat 5:30–9:30pm.

Rivoli ★★★ *Finds* CALIFORNIA   One of the favored dinner destinations in the East Bay, Rivoli offers top-notch food at amazingly reasonable prices. In an otherwise uninteresting space, the owners have created a warm, intimate dining room, which overlooks a sweet little garden with visiting raccoons and possums and a wine bar near the entrance. Aside from a few house favorites, the menu changes entirely every 3 weeks to feature whatever's freshest and in season; the wine list follows suit with around a dozen by-the-glass options hand-picked to match the food. While many love it, I'm not a fan of the portabello-mushroom fritter, a gourmet variation of the fried zucchini stick. However, plenty of dishes shine, including chicken cooked with prosciutto di Parma, potato and scallion souffle, marsala jus, snap peas, and baby carrots; artichoke lasagne with ricotta,

Finds Sweet Sensations at Berkeley's New Chocolate Factory

If you haven't had chocolate nibs, you haven't lived—at least that's what chocoholics are likely to discover upon visiting **Scharffen Berger Chocolate Maker,** California's runaway-success chocolatier that opened its factory and retail shop doors in Berkeley in mid-2001. Within the brick building visitors can not only taste the nibs (crunchy roasted and shelled cocoa beans), but also see how the famous chocolate company uses vintage European equipment during regularly scheduled tours (call for details). And let's not forget there are plenty of tasty products, from candy bars to cocoa powder to chocolate sauce, available in the retail shop. The factory is located at 914 Heinz Ave, Berkeley. (© **510/981-4050;** www.scharffenberger.com). From I-80 East take the Ashby Ave exit, turn left on 7th St, and turn right on Heinz.

mint salsa, and tomato sauce; and braised lamb shank with green garlic risotto, sauteed spinach, and oven-dried tomatoes. Finish the evening with an assortment of cheeses or a warm chocolate truffle torte with hazelnut ice cream, orange crème anglaise, and chocolate sauce.

1539 Solano Ave. © 510/526-2542. www.rivolirestaurant.com. Reservations recommended. Main courses $14–$17. AE, DISC, MC, V. Mon–Thurs 5:30–9:30pm; Fri 5:30–10pm; Sat 5–10pm; Sun 5–9pm.

INEXPENSIVE

Cambodiana's ⚘ CAMBODIAN   For those who relish the spicy cuisine of Cambodia, this is quite a find. The decor is as colorful as the fare—brilliant blue, yellow, and green walls with Breuer-style chairs. Especially tasty choices include curry (chicken, beef, and so on), and Naga dishes with a sauce of tamarind, turmeric, lemongrass, shrimp paste, coconut-milk galinga, shallot, lemon leaf, sugar, and green chili. This sauce may smother salmon, prawns, chicken, or steak. Another tempting dish is chicken *chaktomuk,* prepared with pineapple, red peppers, and zucchini in soy and oyster sauce. There are plenty of vegetarian and low-cal options.

2156 University Ave. (between Shattuck and Oxford). © 510/843-4630. Reservations recommended. Main courses $6.50–$15. AE, DC, MC, V. Tues–Fri 11:30am–9pm; Sat–Sun 5–9:30pm.

2 Oakland

10 miles E of San Francisco

Although it's less than a dozen miles from San Francisco, Oakland is worlds apart from its sister city across the bay. Originally little more than a cluster of ranches and farms, Oakland exploded in size and stature practically overnight, when the last mile of transcontinental railroad track was laid down. Major shipping ports soon followed, and to this day, Oakland remains one of the busiest industrial ports on the West Coast.

The price for economic success, however, is Oakland's lowbrow reputation for being a predominantly working-class city; it is forever in the shadow of chic San Francisco. However, as the City by the Bay has become so crowded and expensive in the past few years, Oakland has experienced a rush of new residents and businesses. As a result, Oak-town is in a renaissance, and its future continues to look brighter and brighter.

Rent a sailboat on Lake Merritt, stroll along the waterfront, explore the fantastic Oakland Museum: They're all great reasons to hop the bay and spend a fog-free day exploring one of California's largest and most ethnically diversified cities.

OAKLAND ESSENTIALS

BART connects San Francisco and Oakland through one of the longest underwater transit tunnels in the world. Fares range from $1 to $4, depending on your station of origin; children under 5 ride free. BART trains operate Monday to Friday from 4am to midnight, Saturday 6am to midnight, Sunday 8am to midnight. Exit at the 12th Street station for downtown Oakland.

By car from San Francisco, take I-80 across the San Francisco–Oakland Bay Bridge and follow signs to downtown Oakland. Exit at Grand Avenue South for the Lake Merritt area.

Downtown Oakland lies between Grand Avenue on the north, I-980 on the west, Inner Harbor on the south, and Lake Merritt on the east. Between these landmarks are three BART stations (12th Street, 19th Street, and Lake Merritt), City Hall, the Oakland Museum, Jack London Square, and several other sights.

WHAT TO SEE & DO IN OAKLAND

Lake Merritt is Oakland's primary tourist attraction, along with Jack London Square (see below). Three and a half miles in circumference, the tidal lagoon was bridged and dammed in the 1860s and is now a wildlife refuge that is home to flocks of migrating ducks, herons, and geese. The 122-acre **Lakeside Park,** a popular place to picnic, feed the ducks, and escape the fog, surrounds the lake on three sides. At the **Sailboat House** ⚜ (☏ **510/444-3807**), in Lakeside Park along the north shore, you can rent sailboats, rowboats, pedal boats, or canoes for $6 to $12 per hour.

Another site worth visiting is Oakland's **Paramount Theatre** ⚜, 2025 Broadway (☏ **510/893-2300**), an outstanding example of Art Deco architecture and decor. Built in 1931 and authentically restored in 1973, it's the city's main performing-arts center. Guided tours of the 3,000-seat theater are given the first and third Saturday of each month, excluding holidays. No reservations are necessary; just show up at 10am at the box office entrance on 21st Street at Broadway. Cameras are allowed, and admission is $1.

If you take pleasure in strolling sailboat-filled wharves or are a die-hard fan of Jack London, you might enjoy a visit to **Jack London Square** ⚜. Oakland's only patently tourist area, this low-key version of San Francisco's Fisherman's Wharf shamelessly plays up the fact that Jack London spent most of his youth along the waterfront. The square fronts the harbor, housing a tourist-tacky complex of boutiques and eateries that are about as far from the "call of the wild" as you can get. Most are open Monday to Saturday 10am to 7pm (some restaurants stay open later). One of the best options is live jazz at **Yoshi's** ⚜ restaurant and club, 510 Embarcadero West (☏ **510/238-9200**). In the center of the square is a small, reconstructed Yukon cabin in which Jack London lived while prospecting in the Klondike during the gold rush of 1897.

In the middle of Jack London Square you'll find a more authentic memorial, **Heinold's First and Last Chance Saloon**—a funky, friendly little bar and historic landmark that's worth a visit. This is where London did some of his writing and most of his drinking; the corner table he used has remained exactly as it was nearly a century ago. Also in the square are the mast and nameplate from USS *Oakland,* a ship that saw extensive action in the Pacific during World War II, and a wonderful museum filled with interesting London memorabilia.

The square is at Broadway and Embarcadero. Take I-880 to Broadway, turn south, and go to the end. Ride BART to 12th Street station, then walk south along Broadway (about half a mile); a free shuttle runs Monday through Friday 11am to 2pm. Or take bus no. 51A to the foot of Broadway.

Oakland Museum of California ⭐   Two blocks south of the lake, the Oakland Museum of California incorporates just about everything you'd want to know about the state and its people, history, culture, geology, art, environment, and ecology. Inside a low, modern building set among sweeping gardens and terraces, it's actually three museums in one: exhibitions of works by California artists from Bierstadt to Diebenkorn; collections of historic artifacts, from Pomo Indian basketry to Country Joe McDonald's guitar; and re-creations of California habitats from the coast to the White Mountains. The museum holds major shows of California artists and exhibitions dedicated to major California movements. A recent photography exhibition included three exhibits: "Capturing Light," masterpieces of California photography from 1860 to 2000, Bob Walker's "The Art of Environmental Photography," and "Every Worker is An Organizer," which took a look at California's farm labor and the resurgence of the united farm workers. The museum also frequently shows photography from its huge collections.

Forty-five-minute guided tours leave from the gallery information desks on request or by appointment. There is a fine cafe, a **gallery** (✆ **510/834-2296**) that sells works by California artists, and a book and gift shop. The cafe is open Wednesday to Saturday 10am to 4pm, Sunday noon to 4pm.

1000 Oak St. (at 10th St.) ✆ **888/625-6873,** or 510/238-2200 for recorded information. Admission $6 adults, $4 students and seniors, free for children under 6; second Sunday of the month is free. Wed–Sat 10am–5pm; Sun noon–5pm, open until 9pm the first Thursday of the month. Closed Jan 1, July 4, Thanksgiving, Dec 25. From I-880 north, take the Oak St. exit; the museum is 5 blocks east. Or take I-580 to I-980 and exit at the Jackson St. ramp. BART: Lake Merritt station; walk 1 block north.

WHERE TO DINE IN OAKLAND
EXPENSIVE
Citron ⭐⭐   FRENCH/MEDITERRANEAN   This petite, adorable French bistro was an instant smash when it opened in 1992, and it continues to earn raves for its small yet enticingly eclectic menu. Chef Chris Rossi draws the flavors of France, Italy, and Spain together with fresh California produce for Chez Panisse–like results. The menu changes every few weeks; dishes range from succulent Sonoma rack of lamb, which is grilled and then baked with an aioli-breadcrumb crust and served atop grilled ratatouille, Provencal with waffle-cut potato chips or spicy bayou seafood stew brimming with fried oysters, shrimp, snapper, and bell pepper and tomato sauce, to breast of pheasant with wild rice croquette, spinach, and apple brandy sauce. Whatever you do, save room for dessert as you won't be able to resist the devilish double-chocolate souffle and Meyer lemon pudding cake with huckleberry sauce and white chocolate glaze.

5484 College Ave. (off the northeast end of Broadway between Taft and Lawton sts.). ✆ **510/653-5484.** Reservations recommended. Main courses $18–$28; 3-course fixed-price menu (Sun–Wed only) $26–$32. AE, DC, DISC, MC, V. Mon–Thurs 5:30–9:30pm; Fri 5:30–10pm; Sat 5–10pm; Sun 5–9pm.

Oliveto Cafe & Restaurant ⭐⭐   ITALIAN   Paul Bertolli, former chef at the world-renowned Chez Panisse restaurant, jumped ship to open one of the top

Italian restaurants in the Bay Area (and certainly the best in Oakland). During the week it's a madhouse at lunchtime, when local workers pile in for the wood-fired pizzas and tapas served in the lower-level cafe. The upstairs restaurant—with suave neo-Florentine decor and a partial open kitchen—is slightly more civil, packed nightly with fans of Bertolli's house-made pastas, sausages, and prosciutto. Oliveto has a wood-burning oven, flame-broiled rotisserie, and high-end liquor cabinet (that is, hard alcohol, but no mixed drinks). An assortment of pricey grills, braises, and roasts anchor the daily changing menu, but it's the reasonably priced pastas, pizzetas, and awesome salads that offer the most tang for your buck. Still, his Arista (classic Italian pork with garlic and rosemary and pork jus) is insanely good, and no one does fried calamari, onion rings, and lemon slices better than Oliveto. *Tip:* There's free parking in the lot at the rear of the Market Hall building.

Rockridge Market Hall, 5655 College Ave. (off the northeast end of Broadway at Shafter/Keith St., across from the Rockridge BART station). ℂ 510/547-5356. Reservations recommended for restaurant. Main courses lunch $9–$15, main courses dinner $16–$30. AE, DC, MC, V. Mon–Fri 11:30am–2pm; Mon–Wed 5:30–9pm; Thurs–Sat 5:30–10pm; Sun 5–9pm.

MODERATE
Bay Wolf ✮✮✮ CALIFORNIA   The life span of most Bay Area restaurants is about a year; Bay Wolf, one of Oakland's most revered restaurants, has been going strong for more than 2 decades. The converted brown Victorian is a comfortably familiar sight for most East Bay diners, who have come here for years to let chef-owner Michael Wilds do the cooking. Bay Wolf enjoys a reputation for simple yet sagacious preparations using only fresh ingredients. Main courses include highly regarded Liberty Ranch duck with blood oranges, braised endive, and lentils; flavorful seafood stew seasoned with saffron and brimful of cracked Dungeness crab, prawns, rockfish, and mussels; and tender braised osso bucco with creamy polenta and gremolata. Informal service means you can leave the tie at home. The front deck has heat lamps, allowing for open-air evening dining—a treat that San Franciscans rarely experience.

3853 Piedmont Ave. (off Broadway between 40th St. and MacArthur Blvd.). ℂ 510/655-6004. www.baywolf.com. Reservations recommended. Main courses lunch $8.50–$16, main courses dinner $16.75–$22. AE, MC, V. Mon–Fri 11:30am–2pm and 6–9pm; Sat–Sun 5:30–9:30pm.

3 Angel Island & Tiburon
8 miles N of San Francisco

A federal and state wildlife refuge, Angel Island is the largest of San Francisco Bay's three islets (the others are Alcatraz and Yerba Buena). The island has been, at various times, a prison, a quarantine station for immigrants, a missile base, and even a favorite site for duels. Nowadays, most visitors are content with picnicking on the large green lawn that fronts the docking area; loaded with the appropriate recreational supplies, they claim a barbecue, plop their fannies down on the lush green grass, and while away an afternoon free of phones, televisions, and traffic. Hiking, mountain biking, and guided tram tours are other popular activities.

Tiburon, situated on a peninsula of the same name, looks like a cross between a fishing village and a Hollywood western set—imagine San Francisco reduced to toy dimensions. The seacoast town rambles over a series of green hills and ends up at a spindly, multicolored pier on the waterfront, like a Fisherman's

Marin County

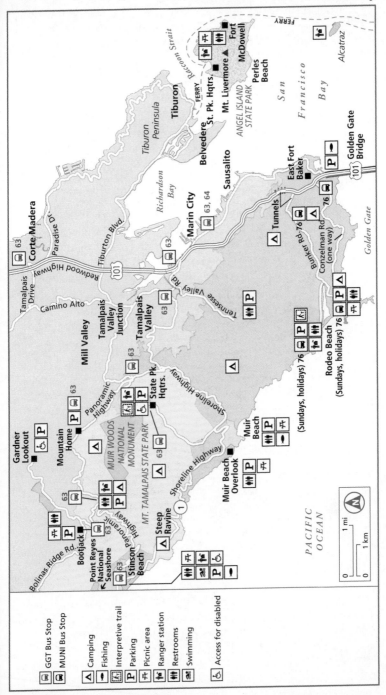

Legend:
- GGT Bus Stop
- MUNI Bus Stop
- Camping
- Fishing
- Interpretive trail
- Parking
- Picnic area
- Ranger station
- Restrooms
- Swimming
- Access for disabled

Wharf in miniature. But in reality it's an extremely plush patch of yacht-club suburbia, as you'll see by the marine craft and the homes of their owners. Ramshackle, color-splashed old frame houses line Main Street, sheltering chic boutiques, souvenir stores, antique shops, and art galleries. Other roads are narrow, winding, and hilly, and lead up to dramatically situated homes. The view of San Francisco's skyline and the islands in the bay is a good enough reason to pay the precious price to live here.

ANGEL ISLAND & TIBURON ESSENTIALS

Ferries of the **Blue & Gold Fleet** (② 415/705-5555) from Pier 41 (Fisherman's Wharf) travel to both Angel Island and Tiburon. Boats run on a seasonal schedule; phone for departure information. The round-trip fare is $10.50 to Angel Island or Tiburon, half-price for kids 5 to 11, and free for kids under 5.

By car from San Francisco, take U.S. 101 to the Tiburon/Highway 131 exit, then follow Tiburon Boulevard all the way into downtown, a 40-minute drive from San Francisco. Catch the **Tiburon–Angel Island Ferry** (② 415/435-2131) to Angel Island from the dock at Tiburon Boulevard and Main Street. The 15-minute round-trip, which runs only on weekends, costs $5.50 for adults, $4.50 for children 5 to 11, $1 for bikes. One child under 5 is free with each paying adult.

WHAT TO SEE & DO ON ANGEL ISLAND

Passengers disembark from the ferry at **Ayala Cove,** a small marina abutting a huge lawn area equipped with tables, benches, barbecue pits, and restrooms. Also at Ayala Cove are a small store, gift shop, cafe (with surprisingly good grub), and overpriced mountain-bike rental shop.

Angel Island's 12 miles of hiking and mountain-bike trails include the **Perimeter Road,** a partly paved path that circles the island. It winds past disused troop barracks, former gun emplacements, and other military buildings; several turnoffs lead to the top of Mount Livermore, 776 feet above the bay. Sometimes referred to as the "Ellis Island of the West," Angel Island was used as a holding area for Chinese immigrants awaiting their citizenship papers from 1910 to 1940. You can still see some faded Chinese characters on the walls of the barracks where the immigrants were held. During the warmer months you can camp at a limited number of sites; reservations are required. For reservations call Reserve America at ② 800/444-7275 and ask about environmental campgrounds at Angel Island. For more information about the island, call Angel Island at ② 415/435-5390 or visit www.angelisland.org.

Guided **sea-kayak tours** ⚓ are also available. The all-day trips, which include a catered lunch, combine the thrill of paddling stable two- or three-person kayaks with an informative, naturalist-led tour around the island (conditions permitting). All equipment is provided, kids are welcome, and no experience is necessary. Rates run about $110 per person. A shorter trip takes 2½ hours and costs $75 per person. For more information, call **Sea Trek** (② 415/332-8494).

The 1-hour **Angel Island Tram Tour** (② 925/426-3058; www.angelisland.com) costs $11.50 for adults, $10.50 for seniors, $7.50 for children 6 to 12; children under 6 are free; schedules vary depending on the time of year.

For recorded information about **Angel Island State Park,** call ② 415/435-1915.

WHAT TO SEE & DO IN TIBURON

The main thing to do in touristy, but pretty, Tiburon is stroll along the waterfront, pop into the stores, and spend an easy $50 on drinks and appetizers before heading back to the city. For a taste of the wine country, stop in at **Windsor Vineyards,** 72 Main St. (© **800/214-9463** or 415/435-3113)—its Victorian tasting room dates from 1888. Thirty-five choices are available for a free tasting with a wine purchase. Wine accessories and gifts—glasses, cork pullers, carry packs (which hold six bottles), gourmet sauces, posters, and maps—are also available. Ask about personalized labels for your selections. The shop is open Sunday to Thursday 10am to 6pm, Friday and Saturday 10am to 7pm.

WHERE TO DINE IN TIBURON

Guaymas MEXICAN   Guaymas offers authentic Mexican regional cuisine and a spectacular panoramic view of San Francisco and the bay. In good weather, the two outdoor patios are almost always packed with diners soaking in the sun and scene. Inside, colorful Mexican artwork brightens the beige walls. Should you feel chilled, to the rear of the dining room is a beehive-shaped adobe fireplace.

Guaymas is named after a fishing village on Mexico's Sea of Cortez, and both the town and the restaurant are famous for their *camarones* (giant shrimp). The restaurant also features ceviche, handmade tamales, and charcoal-grilled beef, seafood, and fowl. Save room for dessert, especially the outrageously scrumptious fritter with "drunken" bananas and ice cream. In addition to a good selection of California wines, the restaurant offers an exceptional variety of tequilas, Mexican beers, and mineral waters flavored with flowers, grains, and fruits.

5 Main St. © 415/435-6300. Reservations recommended. Main courses lunch and dinner $12–$29. AE, DC, DISC, MC, V. Mon–Thurs 11:30am–10pm; Fri–Sat 11:30am–11pm; Sun 10:30am–10pm. Ferry: Walk about 10 paces from the landing. From U.S. 101, exit at Tiburon/Hwy. 131; follow Tiburon Blvd. 5 miles and turn right onto Main St. Restaurant is behind the bakery.

Sam's Anchor Café ⭐ *Finds* SEAFOOD   Summer Sundays are liveliest in Tiburon, when weekend boaters tie up at the docks of waterside restaurants like this one. Sam's is the kind of place where you and your cronies can take off your shoes and have a fun, relaxing time eating burgers and drinking margaritas outside on the pier. The fare is typical—sandwiches, salads, and seafood such as deep-fried oysters—but the quality and selection is inconsequential: beers, burgers, and a designated driver are all you really need.

27 Main St. © **415/435-4527.** www.samscafe.com. Main courses brunch $9–$13; main courses lunch $9–$21; main courses dinner $9–$24. AE, DC, DISC, MC, V. Mon–Thurs 11am–10pm; Fri 11am–10:30pm; Sat 10am–10:30pm; Sun 9:30am–10pm. Ferry: Walk from the landing. From U.S. 101, exit at Tiburon/Hwy. 131, follow Tiburon Blvd. 4 miles, and turn right onto Main St.

4 Sausalito

5 miles N of San Francisco

Just off the northern end of the Golden Gate Bridge is the eclectic little town of Sausalito, a slightly bohemian, nonchalant, studiedly quaint adjunct to San Francisco. With fewer than 8,000 residents, Sausalito feels rather like St. Tropez on the French Riviera—minus the starlets and the social rat race. It has its quota of paper millionaires, but they rub their permanently suntanned shoulders with a good number of hard-up artists, struggling authors, shipyard workers, and fishers. Next to the swank restaurants, plush bars, and antique shops and galleries, you'll see hamburger joints, beer parlors, and secondhand bookstores. Sausalito's main strip is Bridgeway, which runs along the water. Those in the know make a quick detour to Caledonia Street, 1 block inland; not only is it less congested, but there's a far better selection of cafes and shops.

SAUSALITO ESSENTIALS

The **Golden Gate Ferry Service** fleet, Ferry Building (© **415/923-2000**), operates between the San Francisco Ferry Building, at the foot of Market Street, and downtown Sausalito. Service is frequent, departing at reasonable intervals every day of the year except January 1, Thanksgiving, and December 25. Phone for an exact schedule. The ride takes a half hour, and one-way fares are $5 for adults and $3.75 for kids 6 to 12. Seniors and passengers with disabilities ride for $2.50; children 5 and under ride free. Family rates are available on weekends.

Ferries of the **Blue & Gold Fleet** (© **415/705-5555**) leave from Pier 41 (Fisherman's Wharf) and cost $12 round-trip; half-price for kids 5 to 11. Boats run on a seasonal schedule; phone for departure information.

By car from San Francisco, take U.S. 101 north, then the first right after the Golden Gate Bridge (Alexander exit). Alexander becomes Bridgeway in Sausalito.

WHAT TO SEE & DO IN SAUSALITO

Above all else, Sausalito has scenery and sunshine, for once you cross the Golden Gate Bridge you're out of the San Francisco fog patch and under blue California sky (we hope). Houses cover the town's steep hills, overlooking a forest of masts on the waters below. Most of the tourist action, which is almost singularly limited to window shopping and eating, takes place at sea level on Bridgeway.

Sausalito is a mecca for shoppers seeking handmade, original, and offbeat clothes and footwear, as well as arts and crafts. The town's best shops are in the alleys, malls, and second-floor boutiques reached by steep, narrow staircases on and off Bridgeway. Caledonia Street, which runs parallel to Bridgeway 1 block inland, is home to more shops.

Bay Model Visitors Center *(Kids)*   The U.S. Army Corps of Engineers uses this high-tech, 1½-acre model of San Francisco's bay and delta to resolve problems and observe the impact changes in water flow will have. The model reproduces (in scale) the rise and fall of tides, the flows and currents of water, and the mixing of freshwater and saltwater, and indicates trends in sediment movement. There's a 10-minute film and a tour, but the most interesting time to visit is when it's in use, so call ahead.

2100 Bridgeway. © 415/332-3871. www.spn.usace.army.mil/bmvc. Free admission. Labor Day–Memorial Day Tues–Sat 9am–4pm; Memorial Day–Labor Day Tues–Fri 9am–4pm, Sat–Sun and holidays 10am–5pm.

WHERE TO STAY IN SAUSALITO
VERY EXPENSIVE

The Inn Above Tide *(★★)*   Perched directly over the bay atop well-grounded pilings, this former luxury apartment complex underwent a $4 million transformation into one of Sausalito's—if not the Bay Area's—finest accommodations. The view clinches it: Every room affords an unparalleled panorama of the San Francisco Bay, including a postcard-quality vista of the city glimmering in the distance. Should you manage to tear yourself away from your private deck, you'll find that 22 of the sumptuously appointed rooms sport romantic little fireplaces. Some have vast sunken tubs with Jacuzzi jets, remote-control air-conditioning, and wondrously comfortable queen- or king-sized beds. Soothing shades of pale green and blue highlight the decor, which blends in well with the bayscape outside. Be sure to request that your breakfast and newspaper be delivered to your deck, and then cancel your early appointments: On sunny mornings, nobody checks out early.

30 El Portal (next to the Sausalito Ferry Landing), Sausalito, CA 94965. ⓒ 800/893-8433 or 415/332-9535. Fax 415/332-6714. www.innabovetide.com. 30 units. $235–$600 double. Rates include continental breakfast and evening wine and cheese. 2-night minimum stay on weekends. AE, DC, MC, V. Valet parking $12. **Amenities:** Limited concierge; in-room massage; same-day laundry service and dry cleaning. *In room:* A/C, TV, dataport, minibar, fridge, hair dryer, iron.

EXPENSIVE

Casa Madrona ★★   Sooner or later most visitors to Sausalito look up and wonder at the ornate mansion on the hill. It's part of Casa Madrona, a hideaway by the bay built in 1885 by a wealthy lumber baron. The epitome of luxury in its day, the mansion had slipped into decay when Henri Deschamps converted it into a hotel and restaurant. Successive renovations and extensions have added a rambling, New England–style building to the hillside below the main house. Now a certified historic landmark, the hotel offers whimsically decorated rooms, suites, and cottages, which are accessed by steep, gorgeously landscaped pathways. Local designers have uniquely decorated 16 units. The "1,000 Cranes" is Asian in theme, with lots of ash wood and lacquer. "Artist's Loft" is reminiscent of a rustic Parisian artist's studio, complete with an easel and paints. "Summer House" is decked out in white wicker. Other rooms in the mansion are decorated in a variety of styles; some have Jacuzzis, and others have fireplaces. Newer rooms overlook the water, with panoramic views of the San Francisco skyline and bay, and all include a full buffet breakfast. The romantic restaurant Mikayla serves great West Coast cuisine with equally impressive bay views. In late 2001 the hotel is to complete an addition of 31 new rooms and a full-service spa, as well as an additional restaurant.

801 Bridgeway, Sausalito, CA 94965. ⓒ 800/567-9524 or 415/332-0502. Fax 415/332-2537. www.casamadrona.com. 34 units. $188–$275 double; $340 Madrona Villa suite. Rates include breakfast (served 7:30–9:30am). 2-night minimum stay on weekends; Oct–Mar, 3-night minimum anytime from Apr–Sept. AE, MC, V. Valet parking $12. Ferry: Walk across the street from the landing. From U.S. 101 north, take the first right after the Golden Gate Bridge (Alexander exit); Alexander becomes Bridgeway. **Amenities:** 1 restaurant; Jacuzzi; concierge; room service (breakfast and dinner); babysitting; laundry service; dry cleaning. *In room:* TV, dataport, minibar, coffeemaker, hair dryer.

WHERE TO DINE IN SAUSALITO
EXPENSIVE

Ondine ★ ASIAN/FRENCH   Sausalito's best restaurant entered the scene in 1999, delighting Marin diners—and legions of fans crossing the bridge. It offers the ultimate in bayfront views, elegance, service, and the East-meets-West delights of Japanese-trained chef Seiji Wakabayashi, who hails from Wolfgang Puck's Spago. Along with a panoramic vista of the Alcatraz, Angel Island, Bay Bridge, and Tiburon and the wildly colorful room itself, the view on the plate is worth extra attention. Chef "Waka" takes kung-pao cooking to new heights: His luxurious version includes lobster, shrimp, and squid sausage with peanuts, Thai basil, and chiles. Grilled tuna and rock shrimp risotto goes exotic, with coconut-banana curry sauce. Salmon? Perhaps sesame-crusted and served with ginger-sake beurre blanc. Desserts, also whipped up by Waka, are almost as sweet and decadent as the view.

558 Bridgeway. ⓒ 415/331-1133. www.ondinerestaurant.com. Reservations recommended. Main courses $24–$35. AE, DC, MC, V. Mon–Fri 5:30–10pm; Sat–Sun 5pm–10pm. Valet parking $4 for the first 2 hours.

MODERATE

Guernica ★ FRENCH/BASQUE   Established in 1976, Guernica is one of those funky old restaurants that you'd probably pass up for something more chic and modern down the street if you didn't know better. What? You don't know about Guernica's legendary Paella Valenciana? Well, now you do. Be sure to call ahead and order it in advance, and bring a partner, 'cause it's served for two but will feed three. Begin with an appetizer of artichoke hearts or escargots. Other main courses range from pork loin "New Orleans style" to hearty rack of lamb Guernica. Rich desserts include such in-season specialties as strawberry tart, peach Melba, and Basque-style rice pudding.

2009 Bridgeway. ℂ 415/332-1512. Reservations recommended. Main courses $11.75–$22. AE, MC, V. Tues–Sun 5–10pm. From U.S. 101 north, take the first right after the Golden Gate Bridge (Alexander exit); Alexander becomes Bridgeway in Sausalito.

Sushi Ran ★★ SUSHI/JAPANESE   San Francisco isn't exactly stellar in its Japanese selection, but right across from the Golden Gate Bridge is a compact, but fashionable, destination for seriously delicious sushi and cooked dishes. All walks of sushi-loving life cram into the bar, window seats, and more roomy back dining area for standard rolls (yellowtail, unagi, maguro, and the like) and specialty rolls (crab, avocado, and beyond). You'll also find a slew of creative dishes such as generously sized and unbelievably moist and buttery miso-glazed sea bass (a must have), oysters on the half shell with ponzu sauce and tobiko, and a Hawaiian-style ahi poke salad with seaweed dressing that's authentic enough to make you want to hula. Pay the extra $5 or so for fresh wasabi, select from the fine sake and wine list, and don't miss dessert; desserts here are more creative and delicious than those served at most Japanese restaurants.

107 Caledonia St. ℂ 415/332-3620. Reservations recommended. Sushi $5–$13.50; main courses $8.50–$15. AE, DC, MC, V. Mon–Fri 11:45am–2:30pm and 5:30–11pm; Sun 5:30–10:30pm. From U.S. 101 north, take the first right after the Golden Gate Bridge (Alexander exit); Alexander becomes Bridgeway in Sausalito. At Johnson Street turn left, then right onto Caledonia.

PICNIC, ANYONE?

Even Sausalito's naysayers have to admit that it's hard not to enjoy eating your way down Bridgeway on a warm, sunny day. If the crowds are too much or the prices too steep at the bayside restaurants, grab a bite to go for an impromptu picnic in the park fronting the marina.

Hamburgers BURGERS   Like the name says, the specialty at this tiny, narrow cafe is juicy flame-broiled hamburgers, arguably Marin County's best. Look for the rotating grill in the window off Bridgeway, then stand in line and salivate with the rest. Chicken burgers are a slightly healthier option. Order a side of fries, grab a bunch of napkins, and head to the park across the street.

737 Bridgeway. ℂ 415/332-9471. Sandwiches $4.50–$6.25. No credit cards. Daily 11am–5pm. From U.S. 101 north, take the first right after the Golden Gate Bridge (Alexander exit); Alexander becomes Bridgeway in Sausalito.

5 Muir Woods & Mount Tamalpais

12 miles N of the Golden Gate Bridge

While the rest of Marin County's redwood forests were being devoured to feed San Francisco's turn-of-the-century building spree, Muir Woods, in a remote ravine on the flanks of Mount Tamalpais, escaped destruction in favor of easier pickings.

MUIR WOODS

Although the magnificent California redwoods have been successfully transplanted to five continents, their homeland is a 500-mile strip along the mountainous coast of southwestern Oregon and northern California. The coast redwood, or *Sequoia sempervirens,* is the tallest tree in the immediate region; the largest known specimen in the Redwood National Forest towers 367.8 feet. It has an even larger relative, the *Sequoiadendron giganteum* of the California Sierra Nevada, but the coastal variety is stunning enough. Soaring toward the sky like a wooden cathedral, Muir Woods is unlike any other forest in the world and an experience you won't soon forget.

Granted, Muir Woods is tiny compared to the Redwood National Forest farther north, but you can still get a pretty good idea of what it must have been like when these giants dominated the entire coastal region. What is truly amazing is that they exist a mere 6 miles (as the crow flies) from San Francisco—close enough, unfortunately, that tour buses arrive in droves on the weekends. You can avoid the masses by hiking up the **Ocean View Trail** and returning on the **Fern Creek Trail.** The moderately challenging hike shows off the woods' best sides and leaves the lazy-butts behind.

To reach Muir Woods from San Francisco, cross the Golden Gate Bridge heading north on Highway 101, take the Stinson Beach/Highway 1 exit heading west, and follow the signs (and the traffic). The park is open daily 8am to sunset, and the admission fee is $2 per person over 16. There's also a small gift shop, educational displays, and docent-led tours that you're welcome to stand in on. For more information, call the **Muir Woods information line** (☎ **415/388-2595**).

If you don't have a car, you can book a bus trip with the **Red & White Fleet** (☎ **877/855-5506** or 415/447-0597), which takes you straight to Muir Woods and makes a short stop in Sausalito on the way back. The 3½-hour tours run several times daily and cost $33 for adults, $16 for children 5 though 11, and kids under 5 are free. Call for information and departure times.

MOUNT TAMALPAIS

The birthplace of mountain biking, Mount Tam—as the locals call it—is the Bay Area's favorite outdoor playground and the most dominant mountain in the region. Most every local has his or her secret trail and scenic overlook, as well as an opinion on the raging debate between mountain bikers and hikers (a touchy subject). The main trails—mostly fire roads—see a lot of foot and bicycle traffic on weekends, particularly on clear, sunny days when you can see a hundred miles in all directions, from the foothills of the Sierra to the western horizon. It's a great place to escape from the city for a leisurely hike and to soak in breathtaking views of the bay.

To get to Mount Tamalpais **by car,** cross the Golden Gate Bridge heading north on Highway 101, and take the Stinson Beach/Highway 1 exit. Follow the shoreline highway about 2½ miles, turn into Pantoll Road, and continue for about a mile to Ridgecrest Boulevard. Ridgecrest winds to a parking lot below East Peak. From there, it's a 15-minute hike up to the top.

6 Point Reyes National Seashore

35 miles N of San Francisco

The National Seashore system was created to protect rural and undeveloped stretches of the coast from the pressures brought on by soaring real-estate values and increasing population. Nowhere is the success of the system more evident than at Point Reyes. Residents of the surrounding towns—Inverness, Point Reyes Station, and Olema—have steadfastly resisted runaway development. You won't find any strip malls or fast-food joints here, just a laid-back coastal town with cafes and country inns, where gentle living prevails.

Although the peninsula's people and wildlife live in harmony above the ground, the situation beneath the soil is much more volatile. The infamous San Andreas Fault separates Point Reyes—the northernmost land mass on the Pacific Plate—from the rest of California, which rests on the North American Plate. Point Reyes is making its way toward Alaska at a rate of about 2 inches per year, but at times, it has moved much faster. In 1906, Point Reyes jumped north almost 20 feet in an instant, leveling San Francisco and jolting the rest of the state. The half-mile Earthquake Trail, near the Bear Valley Visitor Center, illustrates this geological drama with a loop through an area torn by the slipping fault. Shattered fences, rifts in the ground, and a barn knocked off its foundation by the quake illustrate how alive the earth is. If that doesn't convince you, a seismograph in the visitor center will.

POINT REYES ESSENTIALS

Point Reyes is only 30 miles northwest of San Francisco, but it takes at least 90 minutes to reach **by car** (it's all the small towns, not the topography, that slow you down). The easiest route is Sir Francis Drake Boulevard from Highway 101 south of San Rafael; it takes its bloody time getting to Point Reyes, but does so without any detours. For a much longer but more scenic route, take the Stinson Beach/Highway 1 exit off Highway 101 just south of Sausalito and follow Highway 1 north.

As soon as you arrive at Point Reyes, stop at the **Bear Valley Visitor Center** (© 415/464-5100) on Bear Valley Road (look for the small sign just north of Olema on Highway 1) and pick up a free Point Reyes trail map. The rangers are extremely friendly and helpful and can answer any questions about the National Seashore. Be sure to check out the great natural-history and cultural displays. The center is open weekdays from 9am to 5pm, weekends from 8am to 5pm.

Entrance to the park is free. **Camping** is $10 per site per night, and permits are required. Reservations can be made up to 3 months in advance by calling © 415/464-5149 Monday to Friday 9am to 2pm.

WHAT TO SEE & DO ALONG POINT REYES NATIONAL SEASHORE

When headed to any part of the Point Reyes coast, expect to spend the day surrounded by nature at its finest; however, bear in mind that as beautiful as the wilderness can be, it's also untamable. The bone-chilling waters in these areas are not only home to a vast array of sea life, including sharks, but are also unpredictable and dangerous. There are no lifeguards on duty, and swimming is strongly discouraged because of the waves and rip tides. Pets are not permitted on any of the area's trails.

By far the most popular—and crowded—attraction at Point Reyes National Seashore is the venerable **Point Reyes Lighthouse** ♠ (© 415/669-1534) at the westernmost tip of Point Reyes. Even if you plan to forgo the 308 steps to the

---

Tips Whale Sightings

Rangers suggest that during southern migration (January), you should go to the lighthouse for the best view, and during the northern migration (March) you can see 'em from any of the area's beaches.

Finds   **Johnson's Oyster Farm**

If you want to escape the crowds and enjoy some stinky man-made entertainment, head to **Johnson's Oyster Farm.** Located on the edge of Drakes Estero (a large saltwater lagoon on the Point Reyes peninsula that produces nearly 20% of California's commercial oyster yield), Johnson's might look and smell like a dump, but those tasty bivalves don't come any fresher or cheaper. Granted, it doesn't look like much—a cluster of trailer homes, shacks, and oyster tanks surrounded by huge piles of oyster shells—but that certainly doesn't detract from the taste of fresh-out-of-the-water oysters dipped in Johnson's special sauce. The popular modus operandi is 1) buy a couple of dozen, 2) head for an empty campsite along the bay, 3) fire up the barbecue pit (don't forget the charcoal), 4) split and 'cue the little guys, 5) slather them in Johnson's special sauce, and 6) slurp 'em down. Johnson's (✆ **415/669-1149**) is off Sir Francis Drake Boulevard, about 6 miles west(ish) of Inverness. Open Tuesday to Saturday 8am to 4:30pm, Sunday 9am to 4:30pm.

lighthouse itself, the area is still worth a visit. The dramatic scenery includes thousands of common murres and prides of sea lions that bask on the rock far below (binoculars come in handy).

The lighthouse is also the top spot on the California coast to observe **gray whales** as they make their southward and northward migration along the coast from January through April. The annual round trip is 10,000 miles—one of the longest mammal migrations known. The whales head south in December and January and return north in March. *Note:* If you plan to drive to the lighthouse to whale watch, arrive early because parking is limited. If possible, come on a weekday. On a weekend or holiday from December through April, it's wise to park at the Drake's Beach Visitor Center and take the shuttle bus (weather permitting) to the lighthouse and on to Chimney Rock to watch elephant seals; the shuttle bus runs from around New Year's to the beginning of April. The shuttle bus fare is $3.50 for adults, free for children under 13. Dress warmly—it's often quite cold and windy—and bring binoculars.

Whale watching is far from the only activity at the Point Reyes National Seashore. On weekends, rangers conduct many different tours: You can walk along the Bear Valley Trail, spotting the wildlife at the ocean's edge; see the waterfowl at Fivebrooks Pond; explore tide pools; view some of North America's most beautiful ducks in the wetlands of Limantour; hike to the promontory overlooking Chimney Rock to see the sea lions, harbor seals, elephant seals, and seabirds; or take a guided walk along the San Andreas Fault to observe the site of the epicenter of the 1906 earthquake and learn about the regional geology. And this is just a sampling. Tours vary seasonally; call the **Bear Valley Visitors Center** (✆ **415/464-5100**) or request a copy of *Park Paper,* which includes a schedule of activities and other useful information. Many tours are suitable for travelers with disabilities.

Some of the park's best—and least crowded—highlights can be approached only on foot. They include **Alamere Falls,** a freshwater stream that cascades down a 40-foot bluff onto Wildcat Beach, and **Tomales Point Trail,** which passes through the Tule Elk Reserve, a protected haven for roaming herds of tule elk that once numbered in the thousands. Hiking most of the trails usually ends up being an all-day outing, however, so it's best to split a 2-day trip into a "by car" day and a "by foot" day.

If you're into bird watching, you'll definitely want to visit the **Point Reyes Bird Observatory** (© 415/868-1221), one of the few full-time ornithological research stations in the United States. It's at the southeast end of the park on Mesa Road. This is where ornithologists keep an eye on more than 400 feathered species. Admission to the visitor center and nature trail is free, and visitors are welcome to observe the tricky process of catching and banding the birds. The observatory is open daily from 15 minutes after sunrise to sunset. Banding hours vary; call (© **415-868-0655**) for exact times.

One of my favorite things to do in Point Reyes is paddle through placid Tomales Bay, a haven for migrating birds and marine mammals. **Tamal Saka Tomales Bay Kayaking** ⚓ (© 415/663-1743; www.tamalsaka.com) organizes kayak trips, including 3-hour sunset outings, 3½-hour full-moon paddles, yoga tours, day trips, and longer excursions. Instruction, clinics, and boat delivery are available, and all ages and levels are welcome. Prices for tours start at $65. Rentals begin at $35 for one person, $50 for two. Don't worry—the kayaks are very stable, and there are no waves to contend with. The launching point is on Highway 1 at the Marshall Boatworks in Marshall, 8 miles north of Point Reyes Station. Open daily 9am to 5pm and by appointment.

WHERE TO STAY ALONG POINT REYES NATIONAL SEASHORE

Inns of Marin, P.O. Box 547, Point Reyes Station, CA 94956 (© 800/ 887-2880 or 415/663-2000), is a free service that can help you find accommodations ranging from one-room cottages to inns to complete vacation homes. Many places have a 2-night minimum, but at slow times they might make an exception. They can also refer you to restaurants, hiking, and area attractions.

EXPENSIVE

Manka's Inverness Lodge & Restaurant ★★★ *Finds*   If there was ever a reason to pack your bags and leave San Francisco for a day or two, this is it. A former hunting and fishing lodge, Manka's looks like something out of a Hans Christian Andersen fairy tale, right down to the tree-limb bed stands and the cook's roasted venison sausage in front of the hearth. It's all terribly romantic in a Jack London–ish sort of way, and tastefully done. The lodge consists of a superb restaurant on the first floor, four rooms upstairs (*Tip:* Rooms 1 and 2 have large private decks), and four rooms in the Redwood Annex. Two spacious one-bedroom cabins, behind the lodge and on the water, have living rooms and kitchenettes. For the ultimate romantic splurge, inquire about the three secluded guesthouses: Grizzly Lodge, Boat House, and Chicken Ranch. The lodge's reputation was built on its rustic and romantic restaurant, which dominates the bottom floor and continues to make visitors swoon with house specialties of game and fish and a fixed-price menu ranging from $48 to $68. The limited menu might feature pheasant with Madeira jus, mashed potatoes, and wild-huckleberry jam; black-buck antelope chops with sweet-corn salsa; or, everybody's favorite, pan-seared elk tenderloin. It's open for dinner Thursday to Monday, and the entire property is closed January through March.

30 Callendar St. (at Argyle St. off Sir Francis Drake Blvd., 3 blocks north of downtown Inverness), P.O. Box 1110, Inverness, CA 94937. © **800/58-LODGE** or 415/669-1034. Fax 415/669-1598. www.mankas.com.

14 units, 2 cabins. $185–$335 double; $265–$465 cabin. MC, V. **Amenities:** 1 restaurant; limited room service; in-room massage.

MODERATE
An English Oak Inn ★ *Value*   This venerable two-story 1899 house has survived everything from a major earthquake to a forest fire, which is lucky for you because you'll be hard pressed to find a better B&B for the price in Point Reyes. New owners added private baths to their existing three rooms and added a private cottage complete with a queen and double bed, TV (the only one on the property), and kitchen. Granted, it's not perfect—the main highway is a tad too close—but it's loaded with turn-of-the-19th-century English country farmhouse charm, right down to the profusion of flowers and vines outside and comfy chairs fronting a toasty-warm woodstove inside. An extra bonus to the already reasonable price: a full breakfast, which might include scrambled eggs and muffins or waffles with fruit. It's in a great location, too, with three good restaurants only a block away, and the entire National Seashore at your doorstep.

88 Bear Valley Rd., Olema, CA 94950. © **415/663-1777.** www.anenglishoak.com. 4 units. $120 double; from $160 cottage. Rates include breakfast. MC, V.

INEXPENSIVE
Motel Inverness *Kids*   Finding an inexpensive place to stay in Point Reyes is next to impossible, because hoity-toity B&Bs reign supreme. There is, however, one exception—Motel Inverness, a homey, well-maintained lodging fronting Tomales Bay. For the outdoor adventurer who plans on spending as little time indoors as possible, it's the perfect place to hole up. (Those seeking a little romance should dig a little deeper into their pockets and opt for Manka's; see above.) All the guest rooms were completely renovated and refurnished in 1998, and each has a queen-size bed, skylight, and new mattresses. Attached to the hotel is a giant great room, complete with pool table to distract the kids; parents can relax on the back lawn overlooking the bay, bird sanctuary, and rolling green hills beyond. No smoking. The two-bedroom suite with a kitchenette is ideal for families.

12718 Sir Francis Drake Blvd., Inverness, CA 94937. © **415/669-1081.** 7 units. $99–$175 double; $250–275 suite. AE, DISC, MC, V. *In room:* TV.

WHERE TO DINE ALONG POINT REYES NATIONAL SEASHORE
See "Where to Stay Along Point Reyes National Seashore," above, for details on the highly recommended **Manka's Inverness Lodge and Restaurant.**

MODERATE
Station House Café ★★ AMERICAN   For more than 2 decades the Station House Café has been a favorite pit stop for Bay Areans headed to and from Point Reyes. It's a friendly, low-key place with an open kitchen, an outdoor garden dining area (key on sunny days), and live music on weekends. Breakfast dishes include a Hangtown fry with local oysters and bacon, and eggs with creamed spinach and mashed-potato pancakes. Lunch and dinner specials might include fettuccine with fresh local mussels steamed in white wine and butter sauce, two-cheese polenta served with fresh spinach sautee and grilled garlic-buttered tomato, or a daily fresh salmon special—all made from local produce, seafood, and organically raised Niman Ranch beef. The cafe has an extensive list of fine California wines and local imported beers.

Main St., Point Reyes Station. © **415/663-1515.** Reservations recommended. Breakfast $4.50–$8.50; lunch main courses $7–$10.50; dinner main courses $9–$20. DISC, MC, V. Sun–Tues andThurs 8am–9pm; Fri–Sat 8am–10pm; closed Wed.

INEXPENSIVE

The Gray Whale ⊛ *Value* ITALIAN   For more than a decade, the Gray Whale has been another popular stop for visitors to the lighthouse at Point Reyes. Why so popular? First, it's cheap: Sandwiches—such as roasted eggplant with pesto and mozzarella—are only $7, as are most salads and pastas. Second, it's pretty good. Personal favorites are the specialty pizzas, such as the Californian (artichoke hearts, fresh basil, and tomatoes) and the vegetarian (baked eggplant, roasted onions and romas, broccoli, and piles of freshly grated Parmesan cheese). Veteran hikers and mountain bikers stop by for an espresso booster, sipped on the small patio overlooking the block-long town of Inverness.

12781 Sir Francis Drake Blvd., Inverness. ℂ 415/669-1244. Main courses $6–$12. MC, V. Sun–Thurs 11am–8pm; Fri–Sat 11am–9pm; hours vary in winter.

Taqueria La Quinta ⊛ MEXICAN   Fresh, good, fast, and cheap: What more could you ask for in a restaurant? Taqueria La Quinta has been a favorite lunch stop in downtown Point Reyes for years and years. A huge selection of Mexican-American standards is posted above the counter, but those in the know inquire about the seafood specials. It's all self-serve. Watch out for the salsa—that sucker's hot.

11285 Hwy. 1 (at Third and Main sts.), Point Reyes Station. ℂ 415/663-8868. Main courses $4–$9. No credit cards. Wed–Mon 11:30am–7pm.

7 Half Moon Bay

28 miles SW of San Francisco

A mere 45-minute drive from the teeming streets of San Francisco lies a heavenly little seaside hamlet called Half Moon Bay, one of the finest—and friendliest—small towns on the California coast. Other coastal communities, like Bolinas, make tourists unwelcome, but Half Moon Bay residents are disarmingly amicable, bestowing greetings on anyone and everyone who stops for a visit.

Only in the past decade has Half Moon Bay begun to capitalize on its golden beaches, mild climate, and proximity to San Francisco, so you won't find the ultra-touristy machinations that result in gaudy theme parks and time-share condos. What you will find is a peaceful, unfettered slice of textbook California: pristine beaches, redwood forests, nature preserves, rustic fishing harbors, horse ranches, organic farms, and a host of superb inns and restaurants—everything you need for the perfect weekend getaway.

HALF MOON BAY ESSENTIALS

GETTING THERE   There is no public transportation from San Francisco to Half Moon Bay. There are two ways to get here: the fast way and the scenic way. To save time, take Highway 92 west from Highway 280 or Highway 101 out of San Francisco, which takes you over a small mountain range and drops you directly into Half Moon Bay. A better—and far prettier—route is Highway 1, which technically starts at the south end of the Golden Gate Bridge and veers southwest to the shoreline a few miles south of Daly City. Both routes to Half Moon Bay are clearly marked with numerous signs.

Downtown Half Moon Bay is easy to miss, because it is not on Highway 1. It's a few hundred yards inland; head 2 blocks up Highway 92 from the Highway 1 intersection, then turn south at the Shell gas station onto Main Street until you cross a small bridge.

Tips **Packing Tip**

Temperatures rarely venture into the 70s in Half Moon Bay, so be sure to pack for cool (and often wet) weather.

VISITOR INFORMATION   For more information, contact the **Half Moon Bay Coastside Chamber of Commerce,** 520 Kelly Ave., Half Moon Bay, CA 94019 (© **650/726-8380;** www.halfmoonbaychamber.org).

WHAT TO SEE & DO IN HALF MOON BAY

The best things to do in Half Moon Bay are the same things the locals do. For example, there's a wonderful paved beach trail that winds 3 miles from Half Moon Bay to Pillar Point Harbor. Walking, biking, jogging, and skating are all kosher, and be sure to keep a lookout for dolphins and whales. Bicycles can be rented from the **Bicyclery,** 101A & B Main St. (© **650/726-6000**), in downtown Half Moon Bay. Prices range from $8 to $12 an hour to $25 to $30 per day.

Half Moon Bay is also known for its organically grown produce. The best place to stock up on fruits and vegetables is the **Andreotti Family Farm,** 329 Kelly Ave., off Highway 1 (© **650/726-9461**). Every Friday, Saturday, and Sunday a member of the family slides open the door to the weathered old barn at 10am sharp to reveal a cornucopia of strawberries, artichokes, cucumbers, and the like. It's a terribly charming old-fashioned outfit that's been in business since 1926. To get there, head toward the beach and you'll see it on your right-hand side. Open until 6pm year-round.

A few miles up Highway 92 is the **Obester Winery,** 12341 San Mateo Rd. (© **650/726-9463**), a small wooden shack filled with award-winning wines that are free for the tasting. It's open daily from 10am to 5pm. Exactly 3 miles up Highway 92 from the winery is **Half Moon Bay Nursery,** 11691 San Mateo Rd. (© **650/726-5392**), a wonderful family-owned nursery where the county's serious green thumbs go for prized perennials. It's open daily from 9am to 5pm.

If you're the adventurous type, you might want to consider a day of deep-sea fishing with **Captain John's Fishing Trips** (© **800/391-8787** or 650/726-2913) or **Huck Finn Sportfishing** (© **800/572-2934** or 650/726-7133). Either outfit will take you out for a full day for about $50. You don't need experience, tackle, or even a fishing license; they provide everything, and will clean, fillet, and bag your catch. January through March they also offer whale-watching trips for $30 per adult, $20 per child (reservations recommended). Both charters depart from picturesque Pillar Point Harbor, a full-service harbor that houses over 350 commercial fishing vessels and recreational boats. Whether you plan to go fishing or not, it's worth a gander to watch the trawlers unload their daily catch.

One of the most popular activities in Half Moon Bay is horseback riding along the beach. **Sea Horse Ranch,** a.k.a. Friendly Acres Horse Ranch, Highway 1, 1 mile north of Half Moon Bay (© **650/726-2362** or 650/726-8550), offers guided or unguided (assuming you know how to ride) excursions along the beach or on well-worn trails for about $40. Pony rides delight the kids. Early-bird special rates apply before 10am. Open daily from 8am to 6pm.

And, of course, there's the requisite golf course, **Half Moon Bay Golf Links,** 2000 Fairway Dr., at the south end of Half Moon Bay adjacent to the Half Moon Bay Lodge (© **650/726-4438;** www.halfmoonbaygolf.com). Designed by Arnold Palmer, the oceanside 18-hole layout has been rated among the top 100 courses in the country, as well as no. 1 in the Bay Area. It ain't cheap, though, with greens fees ranging from $132.50 to $153.70. Make reservations as far in advance as possible.

BEACHES & PRESERVES IN HALF MOON BAY

The 4-mile arc of golden-colored sand that rings Half Moon Bay consists of three state-run beaches (Dunes, Venice, and Francis), all part of **Half Moon Bay State Beach.** A $5 per-vehicle entrance fee gets you into all three beaches, but unless you plan on camping or using the restroom often, you're better off saving your lunch money and entering the beach farther north, at Mirada Road. Although surfing is allowed, swimming isn't a good idea unless you happen to be cold-blooded.

When the surf is really up, be sure to check out the banzai surfers at **Maverick Beach,** just south of the radar-tracking station past Pillar Point Harbor. To get there, take Westpoint Road to the West Shoreline Access parking lot and follow the trail to the beach. While you're there, keep a lookout for sea lions basking on the offshore rocks. Also adjacent to the parking lot is tiny **Pillar Point Marsh,** a unique fresh- and saltwater marsh that's home and way station to nearly 20% of all North American bird species—from great blue herons to snowy egrets to red-winged black birds.

A few miles farther north on Highway 1 is the **Fitzgerald Marine Reserve** ⋆ (© **650/728-3584),** a 35-acre tidal reef housing more than 200 species of marine animals, including starfish, snails, urchins, sponges, sea anemones, and hermit and rock crabs. In fact, it's one of the most diverse tidal basins on the West Coast, as well as one of the safest, thanks to a wave-buffering rock terrace 50 yards from the beach. Call before coming to find out when it's low tide (everything's hidden at high tide) and about the docent-led tour schedules (usually offered on Sunday). No dogs are allowed, and rubber-soled shoes are recommended. It's at the west end of California Avenue off Highway 1 in Moss Beach.

Sixteen miles south of Half Moon Bay on Highway 1 (at the turnoff to Pescadero) is the **Pescadero Marsh Natural Preserve,** one of the few remaining natural marshes on the central California coast. Part of the Pacific flyway, it's a resting stop for nearly 200 bird species, including great blue herons that nest in the northern row of eucalyptus trees. Passing through the marsh is the mile-long **Sequoia Audubon Trail,** accessible from the parking lot at Pescadero State Beach on Highway 1 (the trail starts below the Pescadero Creek Bridge).

Starting in December and continuing through March, the **Año Nuevo State Reserve** is home to one of California's most amazing animal attractions—the hallowed breeding grounds of the **northern elephant seal.** Every winter people reserve tickets months in advance for a chance to witness a fearsome clash between the 2½-ton bulls over mating privileges among the harems of females. Reservations are required for 2½-hour naturalist-led tours (held rain or shine December 15 to March 31). For tickets and tour information, call © **800/ 444-4445.** Even if it's not mating season, you can still see the elephant seals lolling around the shore almost year-round, particularly between April and August when they come ashore to molt.

WHERE TO SHOP IN HALF MOON BAY

Half Moon Bay's Main Street is a shopper's paradise. Dozens of small stores and boutiques—ranging from chic to shit-kickin'—line the half-mile strip; you'll find everything from feed and tack stores (should you be on the lookout for a used saddle) to custom furniture and camping gear. Must-see stores (from north to south) include the **Buffalo Shirt Company,** 315 Main St. (© **650/ 726-3194**), which carries a fine selection of casual wear, Indian rugs, and outdoor gear; **Cartwheels,** 330 Main St. (© **650/726-6060**), a nifty store specializing in rustic wood furniture, rugs, and toys; and **Half Moon Bay Feed & Fuel,** 331 Main St. (© **650/726-4814**), a great place to pick up a treat for your pet.

No country boy can survive without **Cunha's Country Store,** 448 Main St. (© **650/726-4071**), the town's beloved grocery and general store that's a mandatory stop for regular visitors from the Bay Area. And, of course, what would Half Moon Bay be without a good bookstore? **Coastside Books,** 432 Main St. (© **650/726-5889**), also carries a fair selection of children's books and postcards.

End your shopping spree with a stop at **Cottage Industries,** 621 Main St. (© **650/712-8078**), to marvel at the high-quality handcrafted furniture.

WHERE TO STAY IN HALF MOON BAY

Beach House Inn 🏵 Although the facade has a rather unimaginative Cape Cod look, the rooms are surprisingly well designed with modern prints, stylish furnishings, and spectacular views of the bay and harbor. Every room comes fully loaded with a wood-burning fireplace, king-sized bed and sleeper sofa, large bathroom, stereo with CD player, private patio or deck access, two color TVs, four telephones with dataports and voicemail, microwave, and refrigerator. *Tip:* Opt for one of the corner rooms, which offer a more expansive view for the same price.

4100 N. Cabrillo Hwy. (Hwy. 1), Half Moon Bay, CA 94019. © **800/315-9366** or 650/712-0220. Fax 650/ 712-0693. www.beach-house.com. 54 units. $199–$350 double. Rates include continental breakfast and Friday and Saturday evening wine tasting. AE, DC, DISC, MC, V. From Half Moon Bay, go 3 miles north on Hwy. 1. **Amenities:** heated outdoor pool; exercise room; ocean-view whirlpool; concierge; room service (lunch and dinner); same-day laundry and dry-cleaning; in-room massage. *In room:* TV, stereo, minibar, dataport, kitchenette, fridge, coffeemaker; hair dryer.

Cypress Inn on Miramar Beach 🏵🏵 A favorite place to stay in Half Moon Bay, the Cypress Inn is blissfully free of Victorian charm (nary a lace curtain in this joint). It's a modern, artistically designed and decorated building with colorful native folk art and rustic furniture made of pine and heavy wicker. Each room has a billowy feather bed, private balcony, gas fireplace, and unobstructed ocean view. Adjacent to the inn are four Beach House rooms equipped with built-in stereo systems and hidden TVs, but they lack the Santa Fe–meets–California effect that I adore in the main house. The ace in the hole is that it's the only B&B perched right on the beach.

407 Mirada Rd., Half Moon Bay, CA 94019. © **800/83-BEACH** or 650/726-6002. Fax 650/712-0380. www. innatdepothill.com. 12 units. $215–$365 double. Rates include breakfast; tea, wine, and hors d'oeuvres; after-dinner treats. AE, DISC, MC, V. From the junction of Hwys. 92 and 1, go 3 miles north, then turn west and follow Medio to the end; hotel is at Medio and Mirada. **Amenities:** Room service (breakfast only); in-room massage. *In room:* TV, coffeemakers in some rooms, hair dryer, iron/ironing board on request.

Mill Rose Inn 🏵 Fashioned after an English country house, the Mill Rose Inn looks as if it were pulled from the cover of a Harlequin romance. The elaborate gardens abound with flowers (literally thousands of them), and the rooms are equally gussied up, with a profusion of brass, porcelain, antiques, and lace—a textbook antithesis to the Cypress Inn. The spacious rooms are loaded with comforts, such as private entrances, king- or queen-sized feather beds, fireplaces (with the exception of the Baroque Rose room), well-stocked refrigerators, cable TV, VCRs, and access to a Jacuzzi that's tucked inside a frosted-glass gazebo. It's in a good spot, too, just off Main Street in a quiet neighborhood.

615 Mill St. (1 block west of Main St.), Half Moon Bay, CA 94019. ℂ 650/726-9794. Fax 650/726-3031. www.millroseinn.com. 6 units. $190–$360 double. Rates include breakfast and afternoon tea, wine, and hors d'oeuvres. AE, DC, DISC, MC, V. **Amenities:** Jacuzzi, which is by reservation for optimum privacy; limited room service; in-room massage; laundry and dry cleaning. *In room:* TV/VCR; minibar stocked with complimentary drinks; coffeemaker, hair dryer, iron.

Seal Cove Inn ⭐⭐ Before Karen Herbert and her husband, Rick, opened this top-notch B&B, she was the writer and publisher of Karen Brown's Country Inns Series, so you can bet she knows what it takes to create and run a superior bed-and-breakfast. The result is a stately, sophisticated B&B that harmoniously blends California, New England, and European influences in a spectacular setting. All rooms have wood-burning fireplaces, country antiques, original watercolors, grandfather clocks, hidden televisions with VCRs, and refrigerators stocked with free beverages. They overlook distant cypress trees and a colorful half-acre wildflower garden dotted with birdhouses. You'll find coffee and a newspaper outside your door in the morning, brandy and sherry by the living-room fireplace in the evening, and chocolates beside your turned-down bed at night. The ocean is just a short walk away.

221 Cypress Ave. (6 miles north of Half Moon Bay off Hwy. 1; follow signs to Moss Beach Distillery), Half Moon Bay, CA 94038. ℂ 650/728-4114. Fax 650/728-4116. www.sealcoveinn.com. 10 units. $200–$300 double. Rates include breakfast, wine, and sherry. AE, DISC, MC, V. **Amenities:** Concierge. *In room:* TV, fax, minibar, hair dryer.

WHERE TO DINE IN HALF MOON BAY

Moss Beach Distillery ⭐ CALIFORNIA/CONTINENTAL   Ever since its bootlegging days during Prohibition almost a century ago, this old stucco distillery on a cliff above Moss Beach has been a wildly popular hangout for both locals and city folk. In the 1920s, silent-film stars and San Francisco politicos frequented the distillery for drinks and the bordello next door for . . . other pastimes. Time and weather have aged it considerably, but a recent renovation spiffed things up. The food—pasta primavera, grilled pork chops, Dungeness crab cakes, chicken Marsala—has never been the main draw; rather, it's the phenomenal view of the rugged coast from almost every window. Your best bet is to come at sunset, order off the appetizer menu (the oysters are always fresh), and snuggle with your partner in the cocktail lounge.

Beach St. (at Ocean St.), Moss Beach (6 miles north of Half Moon Bay off Hwy. 1). ℂ 650/728-5595. Reservations recommended. Main courses brunch $10–$19; main courses dinner $14–$26. AE, DC, DISC, MC, V. Mon–Sat noon–10pm (closing hours vary); Sun brunch 10am–3pm (closing hours vary).

Pasta Moon ⭐⭐ ITALIAN   When visitors ask, "Where is the best place to eat around here?" the inevitable answer is Pasta Moon, a handsome nouveau Italian restaurant in downtown Half Moon Bay. It specializes in making everything from scratch and using only the freshest ingredients. Pasta dishes, which are always freshly made and perfectly cooked, earn the highest recommendations. They include house-made linguine with diver sea scallops, anchovies, garlic, chili flakes, and olive oil and penne with spicy lamb sausage with Swiss chard tomato sauce and fresh ricotta cheese. For dessert, try the wonderful tiramisu, with its layers of Marsala-and-espresso–soaked ladyfingers and creamy mascarpone.

315 Main St., Half Moon Bay. © **650/726-5125.** Reservations recommended. Main courses brunch $9–$13; main courses dinner $15–$25. AE, DISC, MC, V. Mon–Fri 11:30am–2:30pm, Sat noon–3pm, Sun brunch 11am–2:30pm; Sun–Thurs 5:30–9:30pm; Fri–Sat 5:30–10pm.

Sushi Main Street ★ JAPANESE   Chef-owner Hirohito Shigeta started out over a decade ago in a tiny space on Main Street and kept the old name when he moved into larger digs down the street. His wife, Karolynne—an interior designer with impeccable taste—decorated the new space with her collection of museum-quality Balinese artifacts, and the result is sweet, if not a little run down after lots of diner traffic. But even if it looked like the inside of a trailer home, it would still be worth a visit for the fine sushi, tempura, and soba. Adventurous sushi warriors will want to try the New Zealand roll (mussels, radish, sprouts, avocado, and teriyaki), unagi papaya, and marinated salmon roll with cream cheese and spinach. For a traditional shoeless Japanese meal, request the knee-high table in the corner.

696 Mill St., Half Moon Bay. © **650/726-6336.** Main courses $5–$10. MC, V. Mon–Sat 11:30am–2:30pm and 5–9pm; Sun 5–9pm.

12

The Wine Country

Even if you're having the time of your life in downtown San Francisco, I highly recommend that you consider at least a quick jaunt to the Wine Country, an hour or so north by car. Amid the mountains dipping into a grapevine-trellised valley, you'll experience an entirely different northern California: fresh country air, mustard-flower-draped hillsides in spring, hot weather (during summer), some of the world's finest wineries, incredible restaurants, green pastures, and virtually nothing to do but overindulge. With eating, drinking, and lounging the encouraged attractions, there's virtually no better definition of a vacation than a few days here.

To decide which of the Wine Country's two distinct valleys (Napa and Sonoma) you prefer to visit, you need to consider their differences. The most obvious is size—Napa Valley dwarfs Sonoma Valley in population, number of wineries, and sheer volume of tourism (and traffic). Napa is definitely the more commercial of the two, with many more wineries to visit, spas (at far cheaper rates) to choose from, and a superior selection of fine restaurants, hotels, and quintessential Wine Country activities, like hot-air ballooning. Further, if your goal is to really learn about the wonderful world of winemaking, Napa Valley is your choice. World-class wineries such as Sterling and Robert Mondavi offer the most interesting and edifying wine tours in North America, if not the world (although Sonoma's Benziger Winery gives them a run for their money).

If you're planning a more extensive trip to the area, consult *Frommer's Portable California Wine Country.*

1 Napa Valley

Just 55 miles north of San Francisco, the city of Napa and its neighboring towns have an overall tourist and big-business feel. You'll see plenty of rolling hills, flora and fauna, and vast stretches of vineyards, but they come hand-in-hand with upscale restaurants, designer discount outlets, rows of hotels, and, in summer, plenty of traffic. Even with hordes of visitors year-round, Napa is still pretty sleepy, focusing on daytime attractions (wine, outdoor activities, and spas) and, of course, food. Nightlife is very limited, but after indulging all day, most visitors are ready to turn in early anyway.

Although "Napa Valley" seems ominous on a map, it's actually relatively condensed and only 25 miles long. You can venture from the town of Napa all the way to Calistoga in less than half an hour (traffic permitting).

ESSENTIALS

GETTING THERE From San Francisco, cross the Golden Gate Bridge and continue north on U.S. 101. Turn east on California Highway 37 (the fastest way is to skip the 12/121 turnoff and continue to Vallejo), then north on Highway 29, the main road through the Wine Country.

The Wine Country

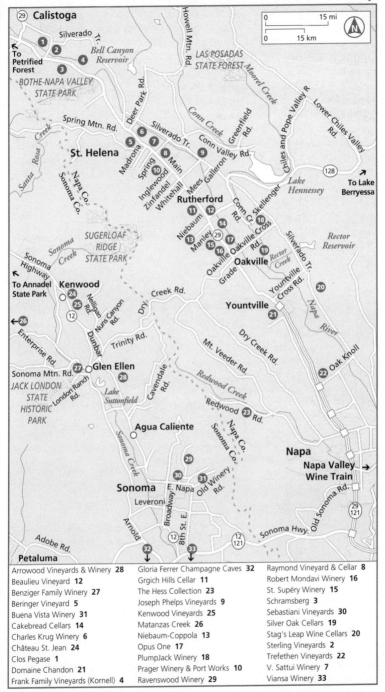

Map labels and features:

- ㉙ **Calistoga**
- Silverado Tr.
- ① ②
- *Bell Canyon Reservoir*
- To Petrified Forest
- ④
- ③
- *BOTHE-NAPA VALLEY STATE PARK*
- *Creek*
- *Santa Rosa*
- Spring Mtn. Rd.
- *Deer Park Rd.*
- *Howell Mtn. Rd.*
- *LAS POSADAS STATE FOREST*
- *Moorel Creek*
- *Conn Creek*
- *Greenfield Rd.*
- *Chiles and Pope Valley R*
- *Lower Chiles Valley Rd.*
- **St. Helena**
- ⑥ ⑦
- ⑤
- Silverado Tr.
- ⑧
- Conn Valley Rd.
- ⑨
- *Napa Co.*
- *Sonoma Co.*
- Madrona
- Spring
- ⑩
- Main
- Inglewood
- Zinfandel
- Whitehall
- Mees
- Galleron
- ㉘ To Lake Berryessa
- *Lake Hennessey*
- **Rutherford**
- ⑪ ⑫
- Niebaum
- ⑭
- ⑬
- Manley
- ㉙
- ⑰
- ⑮
- ⑯
- Oakville Oakville Cross
- Conn. Cr.
- Skellenger
- ⑱
- Rd.
- ⑲
- *Rector Reservoir*
- Silverado Tr.
- *Rector Creek*
- **Oakville**
- Grade
- *SUGERLOAF RIDGE STATE PARK*
- *Sonoma Creek*
- Sonoma Highway
- To Annadel State Park
- **Kenwood**
- ㉔
- ㉕
- Nelligan Rd.
- Nuns Canyon Rd.
- Dunbar
- ⑫
- ㉖
- *Enterprise Rd.*
- Trinity Rd.
- Dry Creek Rd.
- Mt. Veeder Rd.
- Dry Creek Rd.
- **Yountville**
- ㉑
- Yountville Cross Rd.
- ⑳
- *Napa River*
- Oak Knoll
- ㉒
- ㉗ **Glen Ellen**
- ㉘
- Sonoma Mtn. Rd.
- *JACK LONDON STATE HISTORIC PARK*
- London Ranch Rd.
- *Lake Suttonfield*
- Cavendale Rd.
- *Redwood Creek*
- Redwood Rd.
- ㉓
- *Napa Co.*
- **Agua Caliente**
- *Sonoma Creek*
- *Sonoma Co.*
- **Napa**
- **Napa Valley Wine Train**
- ㉙
- ㉚
- ㉛
- **Sonoma**
- E. Napa
- Old Winery Rd.
- Leveroni
- Broadway
- 8th St. E.
- Arnold
- ⑫
- ㉙
- ㉑㉑
- Sonoma Hwy.
- Old Sonoma Rd.
- ㉙ ㉑
- *Adobe Rd.*
- **Petaluma**
- ㉜
- ㉝

Legend (listed alphabetically):

Arrowood Vineyards & Winery **28**	Gloria Ferrer Champagne Caves **32**	Raymond Vineyard & Cellar **8**
Beaulieu Vineyard **12**	Grgich Hills Cellar **11**	Robert Mondavi Winery **16**
Benziger Family Winery **27**	The Hess Collection **23**	St. Supéry Winery **15**
Beringer Vineyard **5**	Joseph Phelps Vineyards **9**	Schramsberg **3**
Buena Vista Winery **31**	Kenwood Vineyards **25**	Sebastiani Vineyards **30**
Cakebread Cellars **14**	Matanzas Creek **26**	Silver Oak Cellars **19**
Charles Krug Winery **6**	Niebaum-Coppola **13**	Stag's Leap Wine Cellars **20**
Château St. Jean **24**	Opus One **17**	Sterling Vineyards **2**
Clos Pegase **1**	PlumpJack Winery **18**	Trefethen Vineyards **22**
Domaine Chandon **21**	Prager Winery & Port Works **10**	V. Sattui Winery **7**
Frank Family Vineyards (Kornell) **4**	Ravenswood Winery **29**	Viansa Winery **33**

261

Highway 29 (the St. Helena Highway) runs the length of Napa Valley. You really can't get lost—there's just one north–south road, on which most of the wineries, hotels, shops, and restaurants are located.

VISITOR INFORMATION   The **Wine Institute,** 425 Market St., Suite 1000, San Francisco, CA 94105 (*©* **415/512-0151**), distributes maps and brochures. Once you're in Napa Valley, stop first at the **Napa Valley Conference and Visitors Bureau,** 1310 Town Center Mall, Napa, CA 94559 (*©* **707/ 226-7459;** www.napavalley.com/nvcvb.html). It offers a $10 package that includes *The Napa Valley Guide,* a bunch of brochures, a map, *Four Perfect Days in The Wine Country Itinerary,* and hot-air balloon discount coupons. If you want less to recycle, call **Vintage Publications,** 2929 Conifer Court, Napa, CA 94558 (*©* **800/651-8953**), to mail order just the guide ($5.95, plus $3.50 for shipping within the U.S.). The website dispenses lots of the same information free.

TOURING THE NAPA VALLEY & WINERIES

Napa Valley claims 34,000 acres of vineyards, making it the most densely planted wine-growing region in the United States. It's an easy venture from one end to the other; you can drive it in around half an hour (but expect it to be closer to 50 minutes during high season, April to November). With around 280 wineries tucked into the nooks and crannies surrounding Highway 29 and the Silverado Trail—almost all of which offer tastings and sales—it's worth researching which wineries you'd like to visit before hitting the wine trails. If you'd like more detailed information on the region's wineries, grab a map from the Visitors Center or purchase *Frommer's Portable California Wine Country.*

Conveniently, most of the large wineries—as well as most of the hotels, shops, and restaurants—are along a single road, Highway 29. It starts at the mouth of the Napa River, near the north end of San Francisco Bay, and continues north to Calistoga and the top of the growing region. When planning your tour, keep in mind that most wineries are closed on major holidays.

All the Napa Valley establishments in this chapter—every town, winery, hotel, and restaurant—is organized below from south to north, beginning in the village of Napa, and can be reached from this main thoroughfare.

NAPA
55 miles from San Francisco

The city of Napa serves as the commercial center of the Wine Country and the gateway to Napa Valley—hence the high-speed freeway that whips you right past it and on to the "tourist" towns of St. Helena and Calistoga. However, if you veer off the highway, you'll be surprised to discover a small but burgeoning community of 63,000 residents with the most cosmopolitan (if you can call it that) atmosphere in the county—and some of the most affordable

---

Tips Reservations at Wineries

Plenty of wineries' doors are open to everyone between 10am and 4:30pm. Most wineries that require reservations to visit do so because of local permitting laws. In many cases they'll be just as happy to see you if you arrive unannounced, but it's always best to call ahead if you have your heart set on visiting a winery that requests that you make reservations.

Tips **Napa Valley Traffic**

Travel the Silverado Trail as often as possible to avoid California Highway 29's traffic. The Silverado Trail runs parallel to and about 2 miles east of Highway 29. You get there from the city of Napa or by taking any of the "cross roads" from Highway 29. Cross roads are not well signposted, but they're clearly defined on most maps. Avoid passing through Main Street in St. Helena during high season. While a wintertime cruise from Napa to Calistoga can take 30 minutes, in summer you can expect the trek to take closer to 50 minutes.

accommodations in the valley. Unfortunately, any charm Napa may exude is all but squelched by the used-car lots and warehouse superstores surrounding the quaint neighborhoods. Head even a few minutes north of Napa, and the real Wine Country atmosphere begins instantly, with wineries, vineyards, and wide-open country views.

The Hess Collection ★★ *Finds*   No place in the valley brings together art and wine better than this winery and art gallery on the side of Mount Veeder. While others strive to pair wine with food, Swiss art collector Donald has gone a different route: After acquiring the old Christian Brothers winery in 1978, he continued to produce wine while funding a huge restoration and expansion project that would honor both wine and the fine arts. The result is a working winery interspersed with gloriously lit rooms that exhibit his stunning art collection; the free self-guided tour takes you through the galleries as it introduces you to the winemaking process.

For a $3 fee, you can sample the winery's current cabernet and chardonnay and one other featured wine. If you want, you can take some with you; prices start at $9.95 for a bottle of the second-label Hess select brand; most other selections range from $15 to $35.

4411 Redwood Rd., Napa. ℭ **707/255-1144**. www.hesscollection.com. Daily 10am–4pm. Closed first week of January. From Hwy. 29 north, exit at Redwood Rd. west, and follow Redwood Rd. for 6½ miles.

Trefethen Vineyards   Listed on the National Register of Historic Places, the vineyard's main building was built in 1886 and is Napa's only wooden, gravity-flow winery. Although Trefethen is one of the valley's oldest wineries, it didn't produce its first chardonnay until 1973—but thank goodness it did. The award-winning whites and reds are a pleasure to the palate. Tastings are free, but if you want to sample a reserve wine, it'll cost you $5.

1160 Oak Knoll Ave. (east of Hwy. 29), Napa. ℭ **707/255-7700**. www.trefethen.com. Daily 10am–4:30pm. Tours by appointment only.

Stag's Leap Wine Cellars   Founded in 1972, Stag's Leap shocked the oenological world in 1976 when its 1973 cabernet won first place over French wines in a Parisian blind tasting. Visit the pretty, unfussy winery and for $5 per person, you can be the judge of the five current releases (with a keepsake glass), or you can fork over up to $35 for estate tastings. The 1-hour tour runs through everything from the vineyard to production facilities and new $5 million caves, which premiered in mid-2001, and ends with a tasting.

5766 Silverado Trail, Napa. ℭ **707/944-2020**. www.cask23.com. Daily 10am–4:30pm. Tours by appointment only. From Hwy. 29, go east on Trancas St. or Oak Knoll Ave., then north to the cellars.

YOUNTVILLE

70 miles from San Francisco

Yountville (pop. 3,700) was founded by the first white American to settle in the valley, George Calvert Yount. While it has lacked the small-town charm of neighboring St. Helena and Calistoga—primarily because its main street, though filling up with hotels, restaurants, and shops, doesn't feel like a center— it's still a great starting point for valley exploration. It's home to a handful of excellent wineries, inns, and a small stretch of fab restaurants, including the world-renowned The French Laundry.

Domaine Chandon ★★ *(Finds)*   French champagne house Moët et Chandon founded the valley's most renowned sparkling winery in 1973. The grounds suit Domaine Chandon's reputation perfectly—this is the kind of place where the world's wealthy might stroll the beautifully manicured gardens under the shade of a delicate parasol, stop at the outdoor patio for sips of the famous sparkling wine, then glide into the dining room for a luncheon.

If you can pull yourself away from the bubbly (sold in tastings for $8 to $12 and served with complimentary bread and spread), the comprehensive tour of the facilities is worth the time. There's a shop, and a small gallery housing artifacts from Moët et Chandon that depict the history of champagnes, revolving art exhibits (available for purchase), which in 2001 included watercolor works of French artist Guy Buffet, and an impressive and formal French-inspired restaurant, which tends to require reservations.

1 California Dr. (at Hwy. 29), Yountville. ℂ 707/944-2280. www.chandonusa.com. Jan–Mar Wed–Sun 10am–6pm; Apr–Dec daily 10am–6pm. Free tours every hour on the hour from 11am to 5pm; no reservations necessary.

OAKVILLE

68 miles from San Francisco

Driving farther north on Highway 29 brings you to Oakville, most easily recognized by Oakville Cross Road.

Silver Oak Cellars   Twenty-five years ago, an oil man from Colorado, Ray Duncan, and a former Christian Brothers monk, Justin Meyer, formed a partnership and launched a mission to create the finest cabernet sauvignon in the world. "We still haven't produced the best bottle of cabernet sauvignon of which Silver Oak is capable," admits Meyer, but this small winery is one of Wine Country's undisputed kings of cabernets.

A narrow tree-lined road leads to the handsome Mediterranean-style winery, which produces roughly 40,000 cases of 100% varietal cab annually. (The partners' Alexander Valley winery in Geyserville produces an additional 10,000 cases annually.) The elegant tasting room is refreshingly quiet and soothing, adorned with redwood panels stripped from old wine tanks and warmed by a wood fire. Tastings and tours are $10, which includes a beautiful German-made burgundy glass. At press time, only two wines were released: a 1996 Alexander Valley and a 1996 Napa Valley. If the $50 and $80 per-bottle price tags are a bit much, for half the price you can take home one of the winery's noncab releases—a velvety Meyer Family Port. No picnic facilities are available.

915 Oakville Cross Rd. (at Money Rd.), Oakville. ℂ 707/944-8808. www.silveroak.com. Tasting room Mon–Sat 9am–4pm. Tours Mon–Fri at 1:30pm, by appointment only.

PlumpJack Winery   If most wineries are like a Brooks Brothers suit, Plump-Jack stands out as the Todd Oldham of wine tasting: chic, colorful, a little wild, and popular with a young, hip crowd. Like the franchise's PlumpJack restaurant and wine shop in San Francisco and its resort in Tahoe, this playfully medieval winery is a welcome diversion from the same old same old. With Getty bucks behind what was once Villa Mt. Eden winery, the budget covers far more than just atmosphere: There's some serious winemaking going on here, too. For $5 you can sample the cabernet, sangiovese, and chardonnay—each an impressive product from a winery that's only been open to the public since mid-1997. The few vintages for sale currently cost $28 to $50. A reserve cab goes for a stiff $150. There are no tours or picnic spots, but this refreshingly stylized, friendly facility will make you want to hang out for a while nonetheless.

620 Oakville Cross Rd. (just west of the Silverado Trail), Oakville. © 707/945-1220. www.plumpjack.com. Daily 10am–4pm.

Robert Mondavi Winery ⊛ *Finds*   If you continue on Highway 29 to Oakville, you'll arrive at the ultimate high-tech Napa Valley winery, housed in a magnificent Mission-style facility. At Mondavi, computers control almost every variable in the winemaking process—it's fascinating to watch. After the tour, you can taste the results of all this attention to detail in selected current wines (free). If you're really into learning more about wine, find out about the additional tours, which range from an "essence" tasting where fruits, spices, nuts, and more are put into glasses so you can smell them and then see if you can detect the same scents in the wine, to an appellation tour and picnic lunch in the vineyards. You can also taste without taking a tour, but it will cost you: Tastings are offered in the Appellation Room (an outdoor tasting area open in summer) and ToKalon Room and start at $5 for a 3-ounce taste to $30 for a rare library wine.

Fridays feature an "Art of Wine and Food" program. It includes a slide presentation on the history of wine, a tour of the winery, and a three-course luncheon with wine pairing; the cost is around $65, and you must reserve in advance. Although you can't bring your own picnic to enjoy on the grounds, Mondavi does offer gourmet picnic lunches from time to time. The Vineyard Room usually features an art show, and you'll find some exceptional antiques in the reception hall. In summer, the winery also schedules some great outdoor jazz concerts. Call to learn about upcoming events.

7801 St. Helena Hwy. (Hwy. 29), Oakville. © 800/MONDAVI or 707/226-1395. www.robertmondavi winery.com. May–Oct daily 9:30am–5:30pm; Nov–Apr daily 9:30am–4:30pm. Reservations recommended for guided tour; book 1 week ahead, especially for weekend tours.

Opus One   Unlike most other vineyard experiences, a visit to Opus One is a serious and stately affair that takes after its wine and its owners: Robert Mondavi and Baroness Phillipe de Rothschild, who, after years of discussion, embarked on this state-of-the-art collaboration. Architecture buffs in particular will appreciate the tour, which takes in both the impressive Greco-Roman-meets-20th-century building and the no-holds-barred ultra-high-tech production and aging facilities. Take note: Newcomers to wine tasting might not appreciate the haute attitude here.

The entire facility caters to one ultra-premium wine, which is offered here for a whopping $25 per 4-ounce taste (and a painful $140 per bottle). But wine lovers should happily fork over the cash: It's likely to be one of the more memorable reds you'll ever sample. Grab your glass and head to the redwood rooftop deck to enjoy the view.

7900 St. Helena Hwy. (Hwy. 29), Oakville. © 707/944-9442. www.opusonewinery.com. Daily 10:30am–3:30pm. Tours by appointment only; in high season, book a month in advance.

RUTHERFORD
3 miles from Oakville

If you so much as blink after Oakville, you're likely to overlook Rutherford, the next small town that borders on St. Helena. Each town has its share of spectacular wineries, but you won't see most of them while driving along Highway 29.

St. Supéry Winery (Kids)   The outside may look like a modern corporate office building, but inside you'll find a functional, welcoming winery that encourages first-time tasters to learn more about oenology. On the self-guided tour, you can wander through the demonstration vineyard, where you'll learn about growing techniques. Inside, kids gravitate toward "SmellaVision," an interactive display that teaches you how to identify different wine ingredients. Adjoining is the Atkinson House, which chronicles more than 100 years of winemaking history. For $5 you'll get lifetime tasting privileges, which includes samples of delicious sauvignon blanc, chardonnay, cab, and more. Even the prices make visitors feel at home: Many bottles go for around $15, although the tag on the 1997 Dollarhide Ranch cabernet says $70.

8440 St. Helena Hwy. (Hwy. 29), Rutherford. (C) **800/942-0809** or 707/963-4507. www.stsupery.com. Daily 9:30am–5pm (until 6pm during summer). Tours 3 times daily.

Cakebread Cellars   This winery's moniker is actually the owners' surname, but it suits the wines produced here—the focus is on making wine that pairs well with food. The owners have done such a good job that a good portion of their 85,000 annual cases go directly to restaurants. Even if you've found the label in your local wine store, your choice has been limited: Just three varieties are distributed nationally. Here you can sample the sauvignon blanc, chardonnay, cabernet, and merlot, most of which are made from Napa Valley grapes. Prices range from an affordable $15.25 for a bottle of 1999 sauvignon blanc to a pricey $85 for the 1997 reserve cab, but the average bottle sells for just a little more than $20. In the tasting room, a large barnlike space, the hospitable hosts pour a $5 or $10 sampling; both include a keepsake wineglass.

8300 St. Helena Hwy. (Hwy. 29), Rutherford. (C) **800/588-0298** or 707/963-5221. www.cakebread.com. Daily 10am–4:30pm. Tours by appointment only.

Niebaum-Coppola (★) (Finds)   In March 1995, Hollywood met Napa Valley when Francis Ford Coppola bought historic Inglenook Vineyards. Although the renowned film director has long dabbled in wine production—he's had a home in the valley for over 25 years—Niebaum-Coppola (pronounced *Nee*-bomb *Coh*-pa-la) is his biggest endeavor yet. He plunked down millions to renovate the beautiful 1880s ivy-draped stone winery and restore the surrounding property to its historic dimensions, gilding it with the glitz and glamour you'd expect from Tinseltown. On display are Academy Awards and memorabilia from such Coppola films as *The Godfather* and *Bram Stoker's Dracula;* the Centennial Museum chronicles the history of the estate and its winemaking as well as Coppola's filmmaking.

In all the Hollywood hullabaloo, wine is not forgotten. Available for tasting are a Rubicon (a blend of estate-grown cabernet, cabernet franc, and merlot, aged for more than 5 years), cabernet franc, merlot, chardonnay, zinfandel, and others. All are made from organically grown grapes and cost from around $10 to more than $80. There's also a variety of expensive and affordable gift items. Speaking of expensive, the steep $7.50-per-person tasting fee might make you wonder whether a movie is included in the price—it's not, but at least you'll get to keep the souvenir glass. And at $20 a pop for the château and garden tour, you've gotta wonder whether you're *funding* his next film. But the grounds are indeed spectacular, and the 1½-hour journey includes a private tasting and a glass. Don't let the prices deter you; if nothing else, at least visit the stunning grounds—it costs nothing to stroll. You're welcome to picnic at any of the designated garden sites.

1991 St. Helena Hwy. (Hwy. 29), Rutherford. ✆ **707/968-1100.** www.niebaum-coppola.com. Daily 10am–5pm (until 6pm Memorial Day–Labor Day). Tours daily at 10:30am and 2:30pm.

Beaulieu Vineyard   Bordeaux native Georges de Latour founded the third-oldest continuously operating winery in Napa Valley in 1900. With the help of legendary oenologist André Tchelistcheff, he has produced world-class, award-winning wines that have been served by every president of the United States since Franklin D. Roosevelt. The brick-and-redwood tasting room isn't much to look at, but with Beaulieu's (pronounced *Bowl*-you) stellar reputation, it has no need to visually impress. Tastings cost $5, and a variety of bottles sell for under $20. The Private Reserve Tasting Room offers a "flight" of five reserve wines to taste for $25, but if you want to take a bottle to go, it may cost as much as $130. A free tour explains the winemaking process and the vineyard's history. No reservation is necessary.

1960 St. Helena Hwy. (Hwy. 29), Rutherford. ✆ **707/967-5230.** www.bvwine.com. Daily 10am–5pm. Tours daily 11am–4pm.

Grgich Hills Cellar   Yugoslavian émigré Miljenko (Mike) Grgich (pronounced *Grr*-gitch) made his presence known to the world when his Château Montelena chardonnay bested the top French white burgundies at the famous 1976 Paris tasting. Since then, the master vintner has teamed up with Austin Hills (of the Hills Brothers coffee fortune) and started this extremely successful and respected winery.

The ivy-covered stucco building isn't much to behold, and the tasting room is even less appealing, but people don't come here for the scenery: As you might expect, Grgich's chardonnays are legendary—and priced accordingly. The smart buys are the outstanding zinfandel and cabernet sauvignon, which cost around $23 and $50, respectively. The winery also produces a fantastic fumé blanc for as little as $18 a bottle. Before you leave, be sure to poke your head into the barrel-aging room and inhale the divine aroma. Tastings cost $5 (which includes the glass) on weekends. No picnic facilities are available.

1829 St. Helena Hwy. (Hwy. 29), north of Rutherford Cross Rd., Rutherford. ✆ **707/963-2784.** www.grgich.com. Daily 9:30am–4:30pm. Free tours by appointment only, Mon–Fri 11am and 2pm, Sat–Sun 11am and 1:30pm.

ST. HELENA
73 miles from San Francisco

Located 17 miles north of Napa on Highway 29, this former Seventh-Day Adventist village maintains a pseudo Old West feel while simultaneously catering to upscale shoppers with deep pockets—hence Vanderbilt and Company, purveyor of fine housewares, at 1429 Main St. It's a quiet, attractive little town, where you'll find a slew of beautiful old homes and first-rate restaurants and accommodations.

Prager Winery & Port Works   If you want a real down-home, off-the-beaten-track experience, Prager's can't be beaten. Turn the corner from Sutter Home and roll into the small gravel parking lot; you're on the right track, but when you pull open the creaky old wooden door to this shack of a wine-tasting room, you'll begin to wonder. Don't turn back! Pass the oak barrels, and you'll quickly come upon the clapboard tasting room, made homey with a big Oriental rug, a cat, and, during winter, a small space heater. Most days, your host will be Jim Prager himself, a sort of modern Santa Claus in both looks and demeanor. But you won't have to sit on his lap for your wish to come true: Just fork over $5 (refundable with purchase), and he'll pour you samples of his delicious $25 Sweet Claire dessert wine, a late-harvest Johannesburg Riesling, and the recently released 10-year-old port (which costs $45 per bottle and has won various awards). Other yummy selections include a cab, which retails for $65. Also available is "Prager Chocolate Drizzle," a chocolate liqueur that tops ice creams and other desserts.

I recommend tasting here, even if you can't afford to purchase; if you do want to buy, this is the only place to do it because Prager doesn't distribute. If you're looking for a special gift, see Jim's daughter, who custom-etches bottles for around $100 in the design of your choice, plus the cost of the wine.

1281 Lewelling Lane (just west of Hwy. 29, behind Sutter Home), St. Helena. ✆ **800/969-PORT** or 707/963-7678. www.pragerport.com. Daily 10:30am–4:30pm.

Joseph Phelps Vineyards ⚐ Visitors interested in intimate, comprehensive tours and a knockout tasting should schedule a tour at this stellar winery. A quick turn off the Silverado Trail in Spring Valley (there's no sign—watch for Taplin Road, or you'll blast right by), Joseph Phelps was founded in 1973 and is a major player in both the region and the worldwide wine market. Phelps himself accomplished a long list of valley firsts, including launching the syrah varietal in the valley and extending the 1970s Berkeley food revolution (led by Alice Waters) to the Wine Country at his store, the Oakville Grocery (see p. 285).

Joseph Phelps is a favorite stop for serious wine lovers. The modern, state-of-the-art winery and big-city vibe are proof that Phelps's annual 100,000 cases prove fruitful in more ways than one. When you pass through the wisteria-covered trellis to the entrance of the redwood building, you'll encounter an air of seriousness that hangs heavier than harvest grapes. Fortunately, the mood lightens as the well-educated tour guide explains the details of what you're tasting while pouring samples of five to six wines, which may include Riesling, sauvignon blanc, gewürztraminer, syrah, merlot, zin, and cab. (Unfortunately, some wines are so popular that they sell out quickly; come late in the season, and you may not be able to taste or buy them.) The three excellently located picnic tables, on the terrace overlooking the valley, are available by reservation.

Taplin Rd. (off the Silverado Trail), P.O. Box 1031, St. Helena. ✆ **800/707-5789**. www.jpvwines.com. Mon–Sat 9am–5pm; Sun 9am–4pm. Tours and tastings by appointment only; tastings $5 per person, $10 per person for reserve tastings.

Raymond Vineyard & Cellar As fourth-generation vintners from Napa Valley and relations of the Beringers, brothers Walter and Roy Raymond have had plenty of time to develop terrific wines—and an excellent wine-tasting experience. The short drive through vineyards to reach the friendly, unintimidating cellar is a case in point: Passing the heavy-hanging grapes makes you feel like you're really in the thick of things before you even get in the door. The spacious, warm room, complete with dining table and chairs, is a perfect setting for sampling the four tiers of wines. Most are free for the tasting and well priced to appeal to all levels of wine drinkers: The Amber Hill label starts at $8 a bottle for chardonnay and $11 for cab; the reserves are priced in the low $30s, and the Generations cab costs $60.

Along with the overall experience, there's a great gift selection, which includes barbecue sauces, mustard, a chocolate wine syrup, and a gooey hazelnut merlot fudge sauce. Private reserve tastings cost $2.50. There are no picnic facilities.

849 Zinfandel Lane (off Hwy. 29 or the Silverado Trail), St. Helena. (℃ **800/525-2659** or 707/963-3141. www.raymondwine.com. Daily 10am–4pm. Tours by appointment only.

V. Sattui Winery ⭐ *Finds* *Kids*　This winery, enormous gourmet deli, and picnic area is a favorite for beginner wine tasters and families. Why? You can fill up on wine, pâté, and cheese samples without ever reaching for your pocketbook, and you can let the kids romp over the grounds while you enjoy your just-bought booty under the shade of a tree. The gourmet store stocks more than 200 cheeses, sandwich meats, pâtés, breads, exotic salads, and delicious desserts such as white-chocolate cheesecake. (It would be an easy place to graze were it not for the continuous mob scene at the counter.)

The long wine bar in the back offers everything from chardonnay, sauvignon blanc, Riesling, cabernet, and zinfandel to a tasty Madeira and a muscat dessert wine. The wines aren't distributed, so if you taste something you simply must have, buy it. (If you buy a case, ask to talk with a manager, who'll give you access to the less crowded, more exclusive private tasting room.) Wine prices start at around $9, with many in the $13 neighborhood; reserves top out at around $75.

This is one of the most popular stops along Highway 29, so prepare for an enormous picnic party and you won't be disappointed. *Note:* To use the picnic area, you must buy food and wine here.

1111 White Lane (at Hwy. 29), St. Helena. (℃ **707/963-7774**. www.vsattui.com. Winter daily 9am–5pm; summer daily 9am–6pm.

Beringer Vineyards ⭐ *Finds*　Follow the line of cars just north of St. Helena's business district to Beringer Vineyards, where everyone stops at the remarkable Rhine House to taste wine and view the hand-dug tunnels carved out of the mountainside. Founded in 1876 by brothers Jacob and Frederick, this is the oldest continuously operating winery in Napa Valley—it was open even during Prohibition, when Beringer stayed afloat by making "sacramental" wines. White zinfandel is the winery's most popular nationwide seller, but plenty of other varietals are available to enjoy. Tastings of current vintages ($3) are soon to be conducted in new facilities, but for now are conducted in the gift shop, where there's also a large selection of bottles for less than $20. Reserve wines are available on the second floor of the Rhine House for a fee of $2 to $10 per taste.

2000 Main St. (Hwy. 29), St. Helena. (℃ **707/963-7115**. www.beringervineyards.com. Off-season daily 9:30am–5pm (last tour 4pm, last tasting 4:30pm); summer 9:30am–6pm (last tour 5pm, last tasting 5:30pm). $5 45-min. tours every 30 min (free for anyone under 21 and accompanied by an adult).; no reservations necessary.

Charles Krug Winery　Founded in 1861, Krug was the first winery built in the valley. The family of Peter Mondavi (yes, Robert is his brother) owns it today. It's worth paying your respects here. A $3 tour takes just under an hour and encompasses a walk through the redwood Italianate wine cellar, built in 1874, as well as the vineyards, where you'll learn more about grapes and varietals. The tour ends with a tasting in the retail center. But you don't have to tour to taste: Just stop by and fork over $3 to sip current releases, $5 to sample reserves; you'll also get a souvenir glass. On the grounds are picnic facilities with

Tips **The Ins & Outs of Shipping Wine Home**

Perhaps the only thing more complex than that $400 case of cabernet you just purchased are the rules and regulations about shipping it home. Because of absurd and forever fluctuating "reciprocity laws"—which supposedly protect the business of the country's wine distributors—wine shipping is limited by regulations that vary in each of the 50 states. Shipping rules also vary from winery to winery. To make matters more confusing, according to at least one shipping company, the list of reciprocal states (those having agreements with California that make it no problem to ship wine there) changes almost daily! Depending on which state you live in, sending even a single bottle of wine can be a truly Kafkaesque experience.

If you happen to live in a reciprocal state and the winery you're buying from offers shipping, you're in luck. You buy and pay the postage, and the winery sends your purchase for you. It's as simple as that. If that winery doesn't ship, it can most likely give you an easy solution.

If you live in a nonreciprocal state, the winery might still have shipping advice for you, so definitely ask! Some refuse to ship at all; others are more than accommodating. Be cautious of wineries that tell you they can ship to nonreciprocal states, and make sure you get a firm commitment: When one of my New York–based editors visited Napa, a winery promised to ship her purchase; when she got home, the winery reneged, leaving her with no way to get the wine and no potable memories of the trip.

You may face the challenge of finding a shipping company yourself. If that's the case, keep in mind that it's technically illegal to box your own wine and send it to a nonreciprocal state; the shipper could lose its license, and you could lose your wine. If you do get stuck shipping illegally (not that we're recommending you do that), you might want to package your wine in an unassuming box and head to a post office,

umbrella-shaded tables overlooking vineyards or the wine cellar. At press time tours were not being given due to renovations, so call to confirm before arriving for a tour.

2800 St. Helena Hwy. (just north of the tunnel of trees at the northern end of St. Helena), St. Helena. © 707/963-5057. www.charleskrugwinery.com. Daily 10:30am–5pm. Tours daily at 11:30am, 1:30, and 3:30pm.

CALISTOGA

81 miles from San Francisco

Calistoga, the last tourist town in Napa Valley, got its name from Sam Brannan, entrepreneur extraordinaire and California's first millionaire. After making a bundle supplying miners during the gold rush, he went on to take advantage of the natural geothermal springs at the north end of the valley by building a hotel and spa in 1859. Flubbing up a speech, in which he compared this natural California wonder to New York State's Saratoga Springs resort town, he serendipitously coined the name "Calistoga," and it stuck. Today, this small, simple resort town,

UPS, or other shipping company outside the Wine Country area. It's less obvious that you're shipping wine from Vallejo or San Francisco than from Napa Valley.

Napa Valley Shipping Companies
Aero Packing, 122 Dodd Court, American Canyon (south of the city of Napa (© 707/554-2088), will pack and ship wine and insures the first $50 (it's 50¢ extra per $100 beyond the first $50). Ground shipping of one case to Los Angeles is $22.50; to Florida, $54. Currently does not ship to a handful of states, including Kentucky and Utah.

The **St. Helena Mailing Center,** 1241 Adams St., at Highway 29, St. Helena (© 707/963-2686), tells me that they will pack and ship anywhere in the United States. Rates are around $21 per case for ground delivery to Los Angeles, $66 to New York. While those who live in reciprocal states get their package insured for up to $100, the Mailing Center does not insure packages shipped to nonreciprocal states. However, it's no big deal; each bottle is packed in styrofoam and should make it home without a problem.

Sonoma Valley Shipping Companies
Mail Boxes, Etc., 19229 Sonoma Hwy., at Verano Street, Sonoma (© 707/935-3438), has a lot of experience with shipping wine. It claims it will ship your wine to any state, via UPS (which currently ships to only a dozen states) or Federal Express. Prices vary from $22 to L.A. (UPS) to as much as $85 to the East Coast (FedEx).

The **Wine Exchange of Sonoma,** 452 First St. E., between East Napa and East Spain streets, Sonoma (© 707/938-1794), will ship your wine, but there's a catch: You must buy an equal amount of the same wine at the store (which they assured me would be in stock, and probably at a better rate). Shipping rates range from $20 to L.A. to $45 to the East Coast.

with 4,713 residents and an old-time main street (no building along the 6-block stretch is more than two stories high), is popular with city folk who come here to unwind. Calistoga is a great place to relax and indulge in mineral waters, mud baths, Jacuzzis, massages, and, of course, wine. The vibe is more casual—and a little groovier—than you find in neighboring towns to the south.

Frank Family Vineyards (a.k.a. Kornell) ⊛ (Finds You've gotta love this place. "Wine dudes" Bob, Danny, Dennis, and Rich will do practically anything to maintain their self-proclaimed reputation as the "friendliest winery in the valley." They'll serve you all the bubbly you want (four to six varieties: Brut, blanc de blanc, blanc de noir, and extra-dry reserve, ranging from $20 to $70 a bottle) and try to ensure that you'll never wait more than 10 minutes to take the 20-minute tour of the oldest champagne cellar in the region.

Former Disney president Richard Frank owns the winery, which used to be Kornell Champagne Cellars. As one employee pointed out, it's not surprising that the unpretentious place is a "celebrity stopover." While the tasting room is so casual you may find yourself kicking back on a case of wine, the stone cellar (listed on the National Register of Historic Places) captures the essence of Wine Country history. Be sure to meander into the Back Room, where chardonnay, zinfandel, sangiovese, and cabernet are poured. The winery makes fewer than 900 cases of still wines a year (versus 10,000 cases of sparkling wine), which means that if you don't try and buy the wine here, you may never get another chance. Behind the tasting room is a choice picnic area, situated under the oaks and overlooking the vineyards.

1091 Larkmead Lane (just off the Silverado Trail), Calistoga. ℂ 707/942-0859. Daily 10am–5pm; tours by appointment.

Schramsberg ✶ *(Finds)*   This 200-acre champagne estate, a landmark once frequented by Robert Louis Stevenson, has a wonderful Old World feel that is one of my all-time favorite places to explore. Schramsberg is the label that presidents serve when toasting dignitaries from around the globe, and there's plenty of historic memorabilia in the front room to prove it. But the real mystique begins when you enter the champagne caves, which wind 2½ miles (reputedly the longest in North America) and were partly hand-carved by Chinese laborers in the 1800s. The caves have an authentic Tom Sawyer ambience, complete with dangling cobwebs and seemingly endless passageways; you can't help but feel you're on an adventure. The comprehensive, unintimidating tour ends in a charming tasting room, where you'll sit around a big table and sample several surprisingly varied selections of bubbly. Tastings are a bit dear ($10 per person), but it's money well spent. Note, however, that tastings are offered only to those who take the free tour, and you must reserve in advance.

1400 Schramsberg Rd. (off Hwy. 29), Calistoga. ℂ 707/942-2414. www.schramsberg.com. Daily 10am–4pm. Tours and tastings by appointment only.

SAY Sterling Vineyards ✶ *(Finds)* *(Kids)*   No, you don't need climbing shoes to reach this dazzling white Mediterranean-style winery, perched 300 feet up on a rocky knoll. Just fork over $6 and take the aerial tram, which offers dazzling bucolic views along the way. If you've been here before, even before embarking, you'll notice major changes due to a complete renovation in 2001. Once you're back on land, follow the self-guided tour (one of the most comprehensive in the Wine Country) of the winemaking process. Currently owned by the Seagram company, the winery produces more than 200,000 cases per year. If you're not into taking the tram or you have kids in tow, visit anyway; there's an elevator that can take you to the tasting room and kids get a goodie bag and a hearty welcome (a rarity at wineries). Samples at the panoramic tasting room are included in the tram fare. Expect to pay anywhere from $10 to $60 for a souvenir bottle ($20 is the average).

1111 Dunaweal Lane (off Hwy. 29, just south of Calistoga), Calistoga. ℂ 707/942-3344. www.sterling vineyards.com. Daily 10:30am–4:30pm.

Clos Pegase ✶ *(Finds)*   What happens when a man falls in love with art and winemaking, purchases more than 450 acres of prime growing property, and sponsors a competition commissioned by the San Francisco Museum of Modern Art to create a "temple to wine"? You'll find out when you visit this magnificent winery. Renowned architect Michael Graves designed this incredible oasis, which integrates art, 20,000 square feet of aging caves, and a luxurious hilltop private home. Viewing the art is as much the point as tasting the wines—which, by the way, don't come cheap: Prices range from $13 for the 2000 Vin Gris

Merlot to as much as $75 for the 1997 Hommage Artist Series Reserve, an extremely limited blend of the winery's finest lots of cabernet sauvignon and merlot. Tasting current releases costs $5 for samples of three premium wines. The grounds at Clos Pegase (pronounced Clo Pay-*goss*) feature an impressive sculpture garden as well as scenic picnic spots.

1060 Dunaweal Lane (off Hwy. 29 or the Silverado Trail), Calistoga. © 707/942-4981. www.clospegase.com. Daily 10:30am–5pm. Tours daily at 11am and 2pm with no reservation necessary.

BEYOND THE WINERIES: WHAT TO SEE & DO IN NAPA VALLEY

NAPA/ST. HELENA

If you have plenty of time and a penchant for Victorian architecture, seek out the **Napa Valley Conference and Visitors Bureau,** 1310 Napa Town Center Mall, off First Street (© 707/226-7459; www.napavalley.com), which offers self-guided walking tours of the town's historic buildings.

SHOPPING   Plan to spend at least an hour if you visit **Red Hen's** co-op collection of antiques. You'll find everything from baseball cards to living-room sets, and prices are remarkably affordable. You can't miss the enormous red barn-style building at 5091 St. Helena Hwy. (Highway 29) at Oak Knoll Avenue West (© 707/257-0822). Its sister property in central Napa is the **Riverfront Antique Center,** 705 Soscol Ave., at Third Street (© 707/253-1966). Here, 70 antique-art dealers exhibit their collections in stalls throughout a mazelike warehouse. During winter, bring a scarf and mittens—there's no indoor heating. Both locations are open daily from 10am to 5:30pm.

St. Helena's Main Street is the best place to go if you're suffering serious retail withdrawal. Take, for example, **Vanderbilt and Company** ⋆, 1429 Main St., between Adams and Pine streets (© 707/963-1010). It offers the crème de la crème of cookware, hand-painted Italian dishes, and everything else you could possibly convince yourself you need for your gourmet kitchen and dining room. Open daily from 9:30am to 5:30pm.

Shopaholics won't be able to avoid at least one sharp turn off Highway 29 for a stop at the **St. Helena Premium Outlets,** 2 miles north of downtown St. Helena (© 707/963-7282). Featured designers include Donna Karan, Coach, Movado, and London Fog. The stores are open daily from 10am to 6pm.

One last favorite stop: **Napa Valley Olive Oil Manufacturing Company,** 835 Charter Oak Rd., at the end of the road behind Tra Vigne restaurant (© 707/963-4173). The tiny market presses and bottles its own oils and sells them at a fraction of the price you'll pay elsewhere. In addition, it has an extensive selection of Italian cooking ingredients, imported snacks, and the best deals on exotic mushrooms. You'll also love the age-old method for totaling the bill, which you simply must find out for yourself.

SPA-ING IT   If the Wine Country's slow pace and tranquil vistas aren't soothing enough for you, the region's diverse selection of spas can massage, bathe, wrap, and steam you into an overly pampered pulp. Should you choose to indulge, do so toward the end of your stay—when you've wined and dined to the point where you have only enough energy left to make it to and from the spa.

Compared to the cosmopolitan-chic day spas of Sonoma Mission Inn (Sonoma) and Health Spa Napa Valley (St. Helena), **White Sulphur Springs Retreat & Spa** ⋆, 3100 White Sulphur Springs Rd. (© 707/963-4361), offers a more spiritual day of cleansing and pampering. Yes, you will encounter

Finds **Enjoying Art & Nature**

Anyone with an appreciation for art absolutely must visit the **di Rosa Preserve**, which until recently was closed to the public. Rene and Veronica di Rosa, who have collected contemporary American art for more than 40 years, converted their 88 acres of prime property into a monument to northern California's regional art and nature. Their world-renowned collection features 1,500 works in all media, by more than 600 greater Bay Area artists. Their treasures are on display practically everywhere—along the shores of their 30-acre lake and in each nook and cranny of their 110-year-old winery-turned-residence, adjoining building, two new galleries, and gardens. With hundreds of surrounding acres of rolling hills (protected under the Napa County Land Trust), this place is a must-see for both art and nature lovers. It's at 5200 Sonoma Hwy. (Highway 121/12); look for the blue gate. Visits are by appointment only. Each tour lasts 2 to 2½ hours, has a maximum of 25 guests, and costs $10 per person. Call © **707/226-5991** to make reservations.

massages, aromatherapy treatments, seaweed or mineral mud wraps, and a pool and Jacuzzi for guests' use. But the most blissful benefits are not the product of some well-known architect or fancy new massage oil. Mother Nature takes the credit for the magic here: acres of redwoods, streams, grassy fields, and wooded groves. The spa treatments in the newly renovated spa make the experience that much more relaxing. The resident spotted owls, woodpeckers, raccoon, deer, and fox don't take advantage of the natural outdoor hot sulfur spring, pool, Jacuzzi, or sauna (free for spa-goers), but you might catch a glimpse of them as you bathe. Massages ($80 to $95 per hour) are given in the homey spa building or outside, amid the redwoods. A day of peaceful pampering doesn't come any cheaper, but take note: This is a casual place, rather than an upscale resort with a formal atmosphere.

BIKING   The quieter northern end of the valley is an ideal place to rent a bicycle and ride the Silverado Trail. **St. Helena Cyclery,** 1156 Main St. (© **707/ 963-7736**), rents bikes for $7 per hour or $25 a day, including rear rack, helmet, lock, and bag in which you can pack a picnic.

CALISTOGA
BICYCLING   Cycling enthusiasts can rent bikes from **Getaway Adventures BHK,** 1117 Lincoln Ave. (© **800/499-BIKE** or 707/763-3040; www.getaway adventures.com). Full-day tours cost $105 and include lunch and a visit to four or five wineries; downhill cruises are available for people who hate to pedal. Bike rental without a tour costs $9 an hour, $20 per half-day, or $28 per day.

HORSEBACK RIDES   If you like horses and venturing through cool, misty forests, then $50 will seem like a bargain for a 1½-hour ride with a friendly tour guide from **Napa Valley Trail Rides,** P.O. Box 877, Glen Ellen, CA 95442 (© **707/996-8566;** www.napasonomatrailrides.com). After a lesson in the basics of horse handling at the stable, you'll be led on a leisurely stroll, with the occasional trot thrown in for excitement. The ride goes through beautiful Bothe-Napa Valley State Park, off Highway 29 near Calistoga.

MUD BATHS   The one thing you should do while you're in Calistoga is what people have been doing here for the past 150 years: Take a mud bath. The natural baths contain local volcanic ash, imported peat, and naturally boiling mineral hot-springs water, mulled together to produce a thick mud that simmers at a temperature of about 104°F.

Indulge yourself at any of these Calistoga spas: **Dr. Wilkinson's Hot Springs,** 1507 Lincoln Ave. (© **707/942-4102**); **Golden Haven Hot Springs Spa,** 1713 Lake St. (© **707/942-6793**); **Calistoga Spa Hot Springs,** 1006 Washington St. (© **707/942-6269**), **Calistoga Village Inn & Spa,** 1880 Lincoln Ave. (© **707/ 942-0991**); **Indian Springs Resort,** 1712 Lincoln Ave. (© **707/942-4913**); **Nance's Hot Springs,** 1614 Lincoln Ave. (© **707/942-6211**); or **Roman Spa Motel,** 1300 Washington St. (© **707/942-4441**).

NATURAL WONDERS   **Old Faithful Geyser of California,** 1299 Tubbs Lane (© **707/942-6463**), is one of only three "old faithful" geysers in the world. It's been blowing off steam at regular intervals for as long as anyone can remember. The 350°F water spews at a height of about 60 feet every 40 minutes, day and night. The performance lasts about a minute, and you can bring a picnic lunch to munch on between spews. An exhibit hall, gift shop, and snack bar are open every day. Admission is $6 for adults, $5 for seniors, $2 for children 6 to 12, free for children under 6. Open daily from 9am to 6pm (to 5pm in winter). To get there, follow the signs from downtown Calistoga; it's between Highway 29 and Calif. 128.

You won't see thousands of trees turned into stone, but you'll still find many interesting petrified specimens at the **Petrified Forest,** 4100 Petrified Forest Rd. (© **707/942-6667**). Volcanic ash blanketed this area after the eruption of Mount St. Helena 3 million years ago. You'll find redwoods that have turned to rock through the slow infiltration of silicas and other minerals, as well as petrified seashells, clams, and marine life indicating that water covered this area before the redwood forest appeared. Admission is $5 for adults, $4 for seniors and youths 12 to 17, $2 for children 6 to 11, free for children under 4. Open daily 10am to 5:30pm (to 4:30pm in winter). Heading north from Calistoga on Calif. 128, turn left onto Petrified Forest Road, just past Lincoln Street.

WHERE TO STAY IN NAPA VALLEY

Accommodations in Napa Valley run the gamut—from motels and B&Bs to world-class luxury retreats—and all are easily accessible from the main highway. While I recommend shacking up in the more romantically pastoral areas such as St. Helena, there's no question you're going to find better deals in the towns of Napa or laid-back Calistoga.

The listings below are arranged first by area, then by price, using the following categories: **Very Expensive,** more than $250 per night; **Expensive,** $200 to $250 per night; **Moderate,** $150 to $200 per night; and **Inexpensive,** less than $150 per night.

When planning your trip, keep in mind that during the high season—April to November—most hotels charge peak rates and sell out completely on weekends; many have a 2-night minimum. If you need help organizing your Wine Country vacation, contact an agency. **Accommodation Referral Bed & Breakfast Exchange** (© **800/240-8466,** 800/499-8466 in CA, or 707/965-3400), which also represents hotels and inns, will ask for dates, price range, and what kind of accommodation you're looking for before coming up with ecommendations. **Bed & Breakfast Inns of Napa Valley** (© **707/944-4444**), an association of B&Bs, provides descriptions and makes reservations. **Napa Valley Reservations Unlimited** (© 800/251-NAPA or 707/252-1985) is also a source for everything from hot-air balloon and glider rides to wine-tasting tours by limousine.

NAPA

Wherever tourist dollars are to be had, you're sure to find big hotels with familiar names, catering to independent vacationers, business travelers, and groups. **Embassy Suites,** 1075 California Blvd., Napa, CA 94559 (© 800/362-2779 or 707/253-9540; www.embassysuites.com), offers 205 of its usual two-room suites. Each has a kitchenette, coffeemaker, modem capability, and two TVs; there are indoor and outdoor pools and a restaurant. Rates range from $190 to $280 and include cooked-to-order breakfast. The 191-room **Napa Valley Marriott,** 3425 Solano Ave., Napa, CA 94558 (© 800/228-9290 or 707/253-7433; www.marriott.com), has lighted tennis courts, an exercise room, a heated outdoor pool and spa, and two restaurants; rates range from $154 to $320.

Moderate

Cedar Gables Inn *(★★ (Finds)* Innkeepers Margaret and Craig Snasdell have developed quite a following with their grand, romantic B&B in Old Town Napa. The Victorian was built in 1892, and rooms reflect the era, with rich tapestries and stunning gilded antiques. Five rooms have fireplaces, five have whirlpool tubs, and all feature queen-size brass, wood, or iron beds. Guests meet each evening in front of the roaring fireplace in the family room for wine and cheese. At other times, it's a perfect place to cuddle up and watch the large-screen TV. Added bonuses include a full breakfast each morning, port in every room, and VIP treatment at many local wineries.

486 Coombs St., Napa, CA 94559. © 800/309-7969 or 707/224-7969. Fax 707/224-4838. www.cedargables inn.com. 9 units. $169–$279 double; winter $129–$249 double. Rates include full breakfast and port. AE, DISC, MC, V. From Hwy. 29 north, exit onto First St. and follow signs to downtown; turn right onto Coombs St.; the house is at the corner of Oak St. *In room:* A/C, TV, dataport, hair dryer, iron.

Napa River Inn *(★★)* Downtown Napa's newest and most luxurious hotel manages an old-world boutique feel through most of its three buildings, which house 66 rooms. The main building, part of the newly renovated Napa Mill and Hatt Market, is a 1884 historic landmark. Each of the fantastically appointed rooms is exceedingly romantic, with burgundy-colored walls, original brick, wood furnishings, plush fabrics, and seats in front of the gas fireplace. A gilded claw-foot tub beckons in the luxurious bathroom. The newest addition is a brand-new building with bright and airy accommodations overlooking the Napa River. Less luxurious, but equally well-appointed, are the mustard-and-brown rooms that also overlook the riverfront, but have a nautical theme and less daylight. Extra perks abound and include complimentary vouchers to a full breakfast and evening cocktails at one of the adjoining restaurants. A small but excellent spa is located in the hotel's parking lot.

500 Main St., Napa, CA 94599. © 877/251-8500 or 707/251-8500. Fax 707-251-8504. www. napariverinn.com. 66 units. $149–$300 double. Rates include vouchers to a full breakfast and evening cocktails at one of the adjoining restaurants. AE, DC, DISC, MC, V. **Amenities:** 1 American restaurant; concierge; business services; same-day laundry service and dry cleaning. *In room:* A/C, TV, CD clock radio, dataport, coffeemaker, hair dryer, iron, safe.

Inexpensive

Chablis Inn *(★)* There's no way around it: If you want to sleep cheaply in a town where the *average* room rate tops $200 per night in high season, you're destined for a motel. But look on the bright side: Because your room is likely to be little more than a crash pad after a day of eating and drinking, a clean bed and a remote control are all you'll really need anyway. And Chablis offers much more than that. Each of the superclean motel-style rooms has a new mattress, and some even boast kitchenettes, whirlpool tubs, or both. Guests have access to an outdoor heated pool and hot tub, plus a basic continental breakfast. Friendly owner Ken Patel is on hand most of the time and is constantly upgrading his tidy highway-side hostelry; his most recent project: replacing all furniture in July 1999.

3360 Solano Ave., Napa, CA 94558. ©707/257-1944. Fax 707/226-6862. www.chablisinn.com. 34 units. Apr to mid-Nov $80–$150 double; mid-Nov to Mar $70–$120 double. Rates include continental breakfast. AE, DC, DISC, MC, V. **Amenities:** Heated outdoor pool; hot tub. *In room:* A/C, TV, dataports in some rooms, kitchenettes in some rooms, fridge, coffeemaker, hair dryer.

Wine Valley Lodge ★ *Value*   Dollar for dollar, the Wine Valley Lodge offers the most for the least in all of Wine Country. At the south end of town in a quiet residential neighborhood, the Mission-style motel is extremely well kept and accessible, just a short drive from Highway 29 and the wineries to the north. The reasonably priced deluxe rooms, which hold two bedrooms connected by a bathroom, are great for families. A $500,000 room renovation, completed in 2000, resulted in new furnishings in most rooms.

200 S. Coombs St. (between First and Imola sts.), Napa, CA 94559. © 800/696-7911 or 707/224-7911. www.winevalleylodge.com. 54 units. $69–$119 double; $120–$165 deluxe. AE, DC, DISC, MC, V. **Amenities:** Heated outdoor pool. *In room:* A/C, TV.

YOUNTVILLE
Very Expensive
Napa Valley Lodge ★★ *Finds*   Many frequent visitors compare this contemporary hotel to the nearby, upscale Vintage Inn, noting that it's even more personable and accommodating. The lodge is just off Highway 29, beyond a wall that does a good job of disguising the road. Guest rooms, which were upgraded in 1999, are large, ultraclean, and better appointed than many in the area. Many have vaulted ceilings, and 33 have fireplaces. Each comes with a king- or queen-size bed, wicker furnishings, robes, and a private balcony or a patio. In 1997, all the bathrooms were upgraded to include a vanity area and nice tile work. The least expensive units, at ground level, are smaller and get less sunlight than those on the second floor. Extras include concierge, afternoon tea and cookies in the lobby, Friday-evening wine tasting in the library, and a full champagne breakfast—with all this, it's no wonder AAA gave the Napa Valley Lodge the four-diamond award for excellence. Ask about winter discounts, which can be as high as 30%.

2230 Madison St., Yountville, CA 94599. © 800/368-2468 or 707/944-2468. Fax 707/944-9362. www.woodsidehotels.com. 55 units. $282–$585 double. Rates include champagne breakfast buffet, afternoon tea and cookies, and Friday-evening wine tasting. AE, DC, DISC, MC, V. **Amenities:** Heated outdoor pool; hot tub; redwood sauna; small exercise room. *In room:* A/C, TV w/pay movies, dataport, minibar, coffeemaker, hair dryer, iron.

Inexpensive
Maison Fleurie ★★   Maison Fleurie, one of the prettiest hotels in the Wine Country, is a trio of beautiful 1873 brick-and-fieldstone buildings overlaid with ivy. The main house—a charming Provençal replica with thick brick walls, terra-cotta tile, and paned windows—holds seven rooms; the rest are in the old bakery building and the carriage house. Some feature private balconies, patios,

sitting areas, Jacuzzi tubs, and fireplaces. Breakfast is served in the quaint little dining room; afterward, you're welcome to wander the landscaped grounds or hit the wine-tasting trail, returning in time for afternoon hors d'oeuvres. It's impossible not to enjoy your stay at Maison Fleurie.

6529 Yount St. (between Washington St and Yountville Cross Rd.), Yountville, CA 94599. © 800/788-0369 or 707/944-2056. Fax 707/944-9342. www.foursisters.com. 13 units. $110–$260 double. Rates include full breakfast and afternoon hors d'oeuvres. AE, DC, MC, V. **Amenities:** Heated outdoor pool; Jacuzzi; free bikes. *In room:* A/C, TV, dataport, hair dryer, iron.

Napa Valley Railway Inn 🎿   This is a favorite place to stay in the Wine Country. Why? Because it's inexpensive and it's cute as all get-out. Looking hokey as heck from the outside, the Railway Inn consists of two rows of sun-bleached cabooses and rail cars sitting on a stretch of Yountville's original track and connected by a covered wooden walkway. Things get considerably better when you enter your private caboose or car. They're sumptuously appointed, with comfy love seats, queen-size brass beds, and tiled baths. The coups de grâce are the bay windows and skylights, which let in plenty of California sunshine. The cars are all suites, so if you're looking to save your pennies, opt for a caboose. Adjacent to the inn is Yountville's main shopping complex, which offers wine tastings and contains some good low-priced restaurants.

6503 Washington St. (adjacent to the Vintage 1870 shopping complex), Yountville, CA 94599. © 707/ 944-2000. 9 units. $75–$140 double. MC, V. *In room:* A/C, TV (no cable); coffeemaker, hair dryer upon request.

OAKVILLE & RUTHERFORD
Very Expensive

Auberge du Soleil ⭐⭐⭐ *Moments*   This spectacular Relais & Châteaux member is the kind of place you'd imagine movie stars frequenting for clandestine affairs or weekend retreats. Set high above Napa Valley in a 33-acre olive grove, it's quiet, indulgent, and luxuriously romantic. The Mediterranean-style rooms are large enough to get lost in, and you might want to once you discover all the amenities. The bathtub alone—an enormous hot tub with a skylight overhead—will entice you to grab a glass of California red and settle in for a while. Oversized, cushy furniture surrounds a wood-burning fireplace—the ideal place to relax and listen to CDs (the stereo comes with a few selections, and there's also a VCR). Fresh flowers, original art, terra-cotta floors, and wood and leather furnishings whisk you out of the Wine Country and into the Southwest. Each sun-washed private deck has views of the valley that are nothing less than spectacular. Those with money to burn should opt for the $2,000-per-night cottage suite; the 1,800-square-foot hideaway has two fireplaces, two full baths, a den, and a patio Jacuzzi. Now that's living. All guests have access to a celestial swimming pool, new exercise room, and the most fabulous (and new) spa in Wine Country, which opened in 2001. Only guests can use the spa, but if you want to get all the romantic grandeur of Auberge, have lunch on the patio at the wonderful restaurant overlooking the valley (see "Where to Dine in Napa Valley," below, for more information). Overall, this is one of my favorite Wine Country places. *Parents take note:* This is not the kind of place you take the kids.

180 Rutherford Hill Rd., Rutherford, CA 94573. © 800/348-5406 or 707/963-1211. Fax 707/963-8764. www.aubergedusoleil.com. 50 units. $350–$600 double. AE, DC, DISC, MC, V. From Hwy 29 in Rutherford, turn right on California 128 and go 3 miles to the Silverado Trail; turn left and head north about 200 yd. To Rutherford Hill Rd.; turn right. **Amenities:** 1 restaurant; 3 outdoor pools ranging from hot to cold; 3 tennis courts; health club & full-service spa; salon; sauna; steam; bikes; concierge; secretarial services; 24-hour room service; massage; same-day laundry service and dry cleaning. *In room:* A/C, TV/VCR w/pay movies, dataport, kitchenette, minibar, fridge, coffeemaker, hair dryer, iron.

Moderate

Rancho Caymus Inn ✷ This Spanish-style hacienda, with two floors opening onto wisteria-covered balconies, was the creation of sculptor Mary Tilden Morton (of Morton Salt). Morton wanted each room in the hacienda to be a work of art, and she hired the most skilled craftspeople she could find. She designed the adobe fireplaces herself, and she wandered through Mexico and South America purchasing artifacts for the property, which was completed in 1985.

Guest rooms surround a whimsical garden courtyard with an enormous outdoor fireplace. The mix-and-match decor is on the funky side, with overly varnished dark-wood furnishings and braided rugs. The inn is cozy, however, and rooms are decent-sized, split-level suites with queen beds, wet bars, sofa beds in the sitting areas, and small private patios. Most of the suites have fireplaces, and five have kitchenettes and whirlpool tubs. Breakfast, which includes fresh fruit, granola, orange juice, and breads, is served in the inn's dining room. Since chef Ken Frank's La Toque opened here, this funky inn has also become a dining destination (see "Where to Dine in Napa Valley," below, for complete details).

1140 Rutherford Rd. (P.O. Box 78), Rutherford, CA 94573. ✆ **800/845-1777** or 707/963-1777. Fax 707/963-5387. www.ranchocaymus.com. 26 suites. $155–$255 double; from $285 master suite; $385 2-bedroom suite. Rates include continental breakfast. AE, DC, MC, V. From Hwy. 29 north, turn right onto Rutherford Rd./Calif. 128 E.; the hotel is on your left. **Amenities:** 1 restaurant. *In room:* A/C, TV, dataport, kitchenettes in some rooms, minibar, fridges in some rooms, hair dryer, iron.

ST. HELENA
Very Expensive

The Inn at Southbridge ✷✷ Eschewing the lace-and-latticework theme that plagues most Wine Country inns, the Inn at Southbridge takes an unswervingly modern, pragmatic approach. Instead of stuffed teddy bears, you'll find terry robes, fireplaces, bathroom skylights, down comforters, private balconies, and a host of other little luxuries. The decor is upscale Pottery Barn trendy, and for some it's a welcome departure from quaintly traditional hotel-style stuff. Functional touches include voicemail and fax modems. One notable bummer: The inn is along the highway, so it lacks that reclusive feel many other upscale hotels offer. The hotel is not ideal for families (especially considering the high price tag), but the adjoining casual and cheap Italian restaurant with games, TV, and pizzas is ideal for kids.

1020 Main St., St. Helena, CA 94574. ✆ **800/520-6800** or 707/967-9400. Fax 707/967-9486. $290–$445 double. AE, DC. MC, V. **Amenities:** 1 restaurant; large heated outdoor pool; excellent health club & full-service spa; Jacuzzi; concierge; limited room service; massage; same-day laundry service and dry cleaning. *In room:* A/C, TV, dataport, minibar, coffeemaker, hair dryer, iron.

Meadowood Napa Valley ✷✷✷ *Finds* This ultra-luxurious resort, tucked away on 256 acres of pristine mountainside in a forest of madrone and oak trees, is quiet and secluded enough to make you forget that the busy wineries are just 10 minutes away. Originally a private country club for Napa's well-to-do families, Meadowood is one of California's top-ranked privately owned resorts, a favorite retreat for celebrities, CEOs, and me. Rooms, which vary in size tremendously depending on the price, are furnished with American country classics and have beamed ceilings, private patios, stone fireplaces, and views of the forest. Many are individual suite-lodges so far removed from the common areas that you must drive to get to them. Lazier folks can opt for more centrally located accommodations.

The resort offers a wealth of activities: golf on a challenging 9-hole course, tennis on seven championship courts, and croquet (yes, croquet) on two international regulation lawns. There are private hiking trails, a health spa, heated pools, and a whirlpool. Those who might actually want to leave and do some wine tasting can check in with John Thoreen, the hotel's wine tutor, whose sole purpose is to help guests better understand and enjoy Napa Valley wines.

900 Meadowood Lane, St. Helena, CA 94574. ℂ **800/458-8080** or 707/963-3646. Fax 707/963-3532. www.meadowood.com. 85 units. $360–$590 double; 1-bedroom suite from $580; 2-bedroom from $910; 3-bedroom from $1,265; 4-bedroom from $1,620. Ask about promotional offers and off-season rates. 2-night minimum stay on weekends. AE, DISC, DC, MC, V. **Amenities:** 2 restaurants; 2 large, heated outdoor pools; golf course; 7 tennis courts; 2 croquet lawns; health club & full-service spa; Jacuzzi; sauna; concierge; secretarial services; room service; same-day laundry service and dry cleaning. *In room:* A/C, TV, dataport, minibar, kitchenettes in some rooms; coffeemaker, hair dryer, iron.

Moderate

Wine Country Inn 🐾🐾   Just off the highway behind Freemark Abbey vineyard, this attractive wood-and-stone inn, complete with a French-style mansard roof and turret, overlooks a pastoral landscape of vineyards. The individually decorated rooms contain iron or brass beds, antique furnishings, and handmade quilts; most have fireplaces and private terraces overlooking the valley, and others have private hot tubs. One of the inn's best features (besides the absence of TVs) is the heated outdoor pool, which is attractively landscaped into the hillside. Another favorite is the selection of suites, which come with stereos, plenty of space, and lots of privacy. The family that runs this place puts personal touches everywhere and makes every guest feel welcome. They serve wine and plenty of appetizers nightly, along with a big dash of hotel-staff hospitality in the inviting living room. A full buffet breakfast is served there, too. Ongoing renovations ensure updated rooms, and new luxury cottages are slated to open in 2002.

1152 Lodi Lane, St. Helena, CA 94574. ℂ **707/963-7077.** Fax 707/963-9018. www.wine-country-inn. com. 24 units (12 with shower only). $130–$345 double. Rates include breakfast and appetizers. MC, V. **Amenities:** Heated outdoor pool; Jacuzzi; concierge. *In room:* A/C, stereo, hair dryer.

Inexpensive

El Bonita Motel 🐾 *Value* *Kids*   This 1930s Art Deco motel is a bit too close to Highway 29 for comfort, but the 2½ acres of beautifully landscaped gardens behind the building (away from the road) help even the score. The rooms, while small and nothing fancy, are spotlessly clean (and sometimes smell strongly of air freshener). They are decorated with new furnishings, and some have kitchens or whirlpool baths. Many families, attracted to the larger bungalows with kitchenettes, consider El Bonita one of the best values in Napa Valley—especially considering the pool, Jacuzzi, sauna, and new massage facility.

195 Main St. (at El Bonita Ave.), St. Helena, CA 94574. ℂ **800/541-3284** or 707/963-3216. Fax 707/963-8838. www.elbonita.com. 41 units. $89–$259 double. Rates include continental breakfast. AE, DC, DISC, MC, V. **Amenities:** Heated outdoor pool; spa; Jacuzzi. *In room:* A/C, TV, fridge, coffeemaker, microwave, hair dryer, iron.

White Sulphur Springs Retreat & Spa 🐾🐾 *Value*   If your idea of the ultimate vacation is a cozy cabin on 330 acres, paradise is a short, winding drive away from downtown St. Helena. Established in 1852, Sulphur Springs claims to be the oldest resort in California. The property holds creeks, waterfalls, hot springs, hiking trails, and redwood, madrone, and fir trees. Guests stay in small and large creekside cabins, which were renovated in 1998 and 1999, or at the inn. The cabins are decorated with simple but homey furnishings; some have a fireplace or wood-burning stove, some have a kitchenette, and some have both. From here you can venture off on a hike; take a dip in the natural hot sulphur spring; lounge by the pool; sit under a tree and watch for deer, fox, raccoon, spotted owl, or woodpecker; or schedule a day of massage, aromatherapy, and other spa treatments in their newly renovated spa, which was completed in early 2001. *Note:* No RVs are allowed without advance notice.

3100 White Sulphur Springs Rd., St. Helena, CA 94574. © 800/593-8873 in CA or 707/963-8588. Fax 707/963-2890. www.whitesulphursprings.com. 28 units, 14 with bathroom; 9 cottages. Carriage House (shared bathroom) $90–$110 double; Inn $115–$155 double; Creekside Cottages $155–$245. Extra person $15. Off-season and midweek discounts available. 2-night minimum stay on weekends Apr–Oct and all holidays. MC, V. **Amenities:** Heated outdoor pool; spa. *In room:* A/C, TV, hair dryer.

CALISTOGA
Expensive
Cottage Grove Inn 🌟🌟   Standing in two parallel rows at the end of the main strip in Calistoga is the perfect retreat—adorable cottages that, though on a residential street (with a paved road running between two rows of accommodations), seem removed from the action once you've stepped across the threshold. Each compact guesthouse has a wood-burning fireplace, homey furnishings, cozy quilts, and an enormous bathroom with a skylight and a deep, two-person Jacuzzi tub. Guests enjoy such niceties as gourmet coffee, a stereo with CD player, VCR (the inn has a video library), wet bar, and fridge. Several major spas are within walking distance. This is a top pick if you want to do the Calistoga spa scene in comfort and style. Smoking is allowed only on the small front porch.

1711 Lincoln Ave., Calistoga, CA 94515. © 800/799-2284 or 707/942-8400. Fax 707/942-2653. www.cottagegrove.com. 16 cottages. $235–$295 double. Rates include continental breakfast and evening wine and cheese. AE, DC, DISC, MC, V. *In room:* A/C, TV/VCR, stereo, dataport, fridge, coffeemaker, hair dryer.

Moderate
Euro Spa & Inn 🌟🌟   In a quiet residential section of Calistoga, this small European-style inn and spa provides a level of solitude and privacy that few other spas can match. The horseshoe-shaped inn consists of a dozen stucco bungalows, a spa center, and an outdoor patio, where a light breakfast and snacks are served. The rooms, although small, are pleasantly decorated in Pottery Barn decor that was implemented in 2000; a few have whirlpool tubs. Spa treatments range from Fango Naturium mud baths to honey-almond body scrubs, seaweed body wraps, and de-stress massage.

1202 Pine St. (between Myrtle and Cedar sts.), Calistoga, CA 94515. © 707/942-6829. Fax 707/942-1138. www.eurospa.com. 13 units. $129–$229 double. Rates include continental breakfast. Weekend packages $369; off-season and midweek package discounts available. AE, DC, DISC, MC, V. **Amenities:** Outdoor heated pool; Jacuzzi. *In room:* A/C, TV, dataport, fridge, hair dryer, iron.

Inexpensive
Calistoga Spa Hot Springs 🌟 *Value* *Kids*   Very few hotels in the Wine Country cater specifically to families with children, which is why I recommend Calistoga Spa Hot Springs if you're bringing the little ones. In any case, it's a great bargain, offering unpretentious yet comfortable rooms, as well as a plethora of spa facilities. All of Calistoga's best shops and restaurants are within easy walking distance, and you can even whip up your own grub at the barbecues near the large pool and patio area.

1006 Washington St. (at Gerrard St.), Calistoga, CA 94515. © 707/942-6269. www.calistogaspa.com. 57 units, 1 family unit. Winter $90 double, $110 family unit; summer $110 double, $130 family unit. MC, V. **Amenities:** 3 heated outdoor pools, kids' wading pool; exercise room; spa. *In room:* A/C, TV, kitchenette, fridge, coffeemaker, hair dryer on request; iron.

WHERE TO DINE IN NAPA VALLEY

Recently, Napa Valley's restaurants have drawn as much attention to the valley as its award-winning wineries. Nowhere else in the state are kitchens as deft at mixing fresh seasonal, local, organic produce into edible magic, which means that menus change constantly to reflect the best available ingredients. Add that to a great bottle of wine and stunning views, and you have one heck of an eating experience.

To best enjoy Napa's restaurant scene, keep one thing in mind: Reserve—especially for a seat in a famous room.

The restaurants listed below are classified first by town, then by price, using the following categories: **Expensive,** dinner from $50 per person; **Moderate,** dinner from $35 per person; and **Inexpensive,** dinner from $20 per person. These categories reflect prices for an appetizer, a main course, a dessert, and a glass of wine.

NAPA
Moderate

Bistro Don Giovanni ★★★ *Value* REGIONAL ITALIAN   Donna and Giovanni Scala—who also run Scala's Bistro in San Francisco—own this bright, bustling, and cheery Italian restaurant, which also happens to be one of my favorite restaurants in Napa Valley. Fare prepared with quality ingredients and California flair never disappoints, especially when it comes to salads and house-made pastas. Every time I grab a menu, I can't get past the beet and haricots verte salad and pasta with duck Bolognese. On the rare occasion that I do, I am equally smitten with outstanding thin-crust pizzas fresh from the wood-burning oven, seared salmon filet perched atop a tower of buttermilk mashed potatoes, and steak frites. Even though portions are generous, there's always room for tiramisu! Alfresco dining in the vineyards is available—and highly recommended on a warm, sunny day. Midwinter, I'm a fan of ordering a bottle of Rafanelli Zin and dining at the bar.

4110 St. Helena Hwy. (Hwy. 29, just north of Salvador Ave.), Napa. ℂ 707/224-3300. Reservations recommended. Main courses $12–$23.50. AE, DC, DIS, MC, V. Sun–Thurs 11:30am–10pm; Fri–Sat 11:30am–11pm.

Inexpensive

Alexis Baking Company ★ BAKERY/CAFE   Alexis (a.k.a. ABC) is a quaint, casual stop for residents and in-the-know tourists. On weekend mornings, the line stretches out the door. But once you order from the counter and find a seat in the sunny room, you can relax, enjoy the coffeehouse atmosphere, and start your day with spectacular pastries, coffee drinks, and breakfast goodies like pumpkin pancakes with sautéed pears. Lunch also bustles with locals who come for daily specials like fusilli pasta with roasted pumpkin, white beans, ham, and Parmesan in cream sauce; grilled-chicken Caesar salad; roast-lamb sandwich with minted mayo and roasted shallots on rosemary bread; and lentil bulgar orzo salad. Desserts run the gamut; during the holidays, they include a moist and magical steamed persimmon pudding.

1517 Third St. (between Main and Jefferson Sts.), Napa. ℂ 707/258-1827. Main courses $3.25–$8 at breakfast, $7–$10 at lunch, $6.75–$13 at dinner. Mon–Fri 6:30am–6pm; Sat 7:30am–3pm; Sun 8am–2pm.

OAKVILLE & RUTHERFORD
Expensive

Auberge du Soleil ★ *Finds* WINE COUNTRY CUISINE   There is no better restaurant view than that at Auberge du Soliel. Perched on a hillside overlooking the valley, alfresco dining rises to an entirely new level here, particularly on warm summer afternoons at sunset. In fact, I recommend coming during the day (request terrace seating) to join the wealthy patrons, many of whom have emerged from their uberluxury guest rooms and are slinking to a table to dine above the vines. The kitchen, which welcomed a new chef in late 2000, is turning out seasonal dishes such as well-prepared sautéed sweetbreads, venison loin with butternut squash, stuffed squab, and roasted saddle of lamb—nothing mind-blowing, but certainly good. While the interior is warm, bustling, and formal enough that some folks wear ties, personally, come dinnertime I'd rather drop big bucks at La Toque, where the food is more creative and even.

180 Rutherford Hill Rd., Rutherford. © 707/963-1211. Reservations recommended. Main courses lunch $17–$20, main courses dinner $25–$30. AE, DISC, MC, V. Daily 7–11am, 11:30am–2:30pm, and 6–9:30pm.

La Toque ✹✹✹ FRENCH   Renowned chef Ken Frank left Los Angeles's fenix at the Argyle Hotel to open one of the Wine Country's most formal dining rooms, which features a beautifully presented five-course extravaganza. Each table at the elegant restaurant adjoining Rancho Caymus Inn is well spaced, making plenty of room to showcase the chef-owner's memorable and innovative French-inspired cuisine. Service is almost too laid back with conversational attitude, but simultaneously it is very professional, ensuring that you never want for anything. If you're lucky, the menu will feature an incredible Indian spice–rubbed foie gras with Madras carrot purée (one of the best I've had), melt-in-your-mouth yellowfin tuna with braised daikon, red wine, and sautéed pea sprouts; knock-out Maine lobster with creamy orzo and lobster cabernet sauce; and Niman Ranch beef tenderloin with roasted root vegetables and red wine. But the menu changes so frequently that you're likely to find a completely different, but equally delicious menu. (Check the website for menus!) Should you find room and the extra few bucks for the cheese course, try a few delicious selections, served with walnut bread. For an additional $32 per person, my party drank splendid, well-paired wines with each course. Alas, we did not have room for desserts of chocolate panna cotta with vanilla Anglaise and toasted pineapple fritter with vanilla bean ice cream—but we ate it anyway.

1140 Rutherford Cross Rd., Rutherford. © 707/963-9770. www.latoque.com. Reservations recommended. Fixed-price menu $72. Wed–Sun 5:30–10pm; Closed Mon–Tues.

YOUNTVILLE
Expensive
The French Laundry ✹✹✹ CLASSIC AMERICAN/FRENCH   It's almost futile to include this restaurant, because you're about as likely to secure a reservation—or get through on the reservation line, for that matter—as you are to drive Highway 29 without passing a winery. Several years after renowned chef-owner Thomas Keller bought the place and caught the attention of epicureans worldwide (including the judges of the James Beard Awards, who named him "Chef of the Nation" in 1997), the discreet restaurant is the hottest dinner ticket *in the world*. At least you can read about it.

The atmosphere is as somber and serious as the oh-so-privileged diners who quietly swoon over the ongoing parade of bite-size delights delivered to the table. Technically, the prix-fixe menu offers a choice of five or nine courses (including a vegetarian menu), but after a slew of cameo appearances from the kitchen, everyone starts to lose count. Signature dishes include Keller's "tongue in cheek" (a marinated and braised round of sliced lamb tongue and tender beef cheeks) and "macaroni and cheese" (sweet butter-poached Maine lobster with creamy lobster broth and orzo with mascarpone cheese). Portions are small, but only because Keller wants his guests to taste as many things as possible. Nobody leaves hungry. The excellent staff is well acquainted with the wide selection of regional wines; there's a $30 corkage fee if you bring your own bottle. On warm summer nights, request a table in the flower-filled garden. *Hint:* If you can't get a reservation, try walking in—on occasion folks don't make their reservation and tables open up, especially during lunch on rainy days.

6640 Washington St. (at Creek St.), Yountville. ✆ 707/944-2380. Reservations required. Vegetarian menu $80; 5-course menu $90; chef's 9-course tasting menu $105. AE, MC, V. Fri–Sun 11am–1pm; daily 5:30–9:30pm.

Moderate

Bistro Jeanty ★★★ FRENCH BISTRO   This casual, warm bistro, with muted buttercup walls, two dining rooms divided by the bar, and patio seats is where chef Phillipe Jeanty creates outstanding French comfort food for legions of fans. A few years back, the highly regarded chef left his 18-year post at Domaine Chandon to open this well-known and affordably priced gem. Jeanty was previously known for formal French cooking, but his cheery bistro is far more laid-back—and equally outstanding. The all-day menu includes legendary tomato soup in puff pastry; foie gras pâté; steak tartare; and house-smoked trout with potato slices. No meal should start without a paper cone filled with fried smelt, and none should end without the most insanely good crème brulée, which comes with a thin layer of chocolate cream between classic vanilla custard and caramelized sugar top. In between, I vote for decadent fall-off-the-bone coq au vin with earthy, smoky red wine sauce or a juicy thick-cut pork chop with jus, spinach, and mashed potatoes. I'm not as excited by the cassoulet of white beans, fennel sausage, pork, and duck leg, which tends to be overwhelming, with an overly dry breadcrumb crust. That said, it's hard not to love this place.

6510 Washington St., Yountville. ✆ 707/944-0103. www.bistrojeanty.com. Reservations recommended. Appetizers $4.50–$7.50, most main courses $13.75–$18.50. MC, V. Daily 11:30am–10:30pm. Closed Thanksgiving and Dec 25.

Bouchon ★ FRENCH BISTRO   Perhaps to appease the crowds who never get a reservation at French Laundry, Thomas Keller teamed up with his brother Joseph to open this far more casual, but still delicious, French brasserie. Adam Tihany, who also conceptualized New York's Le Cirque 2000, designed the dining room. Along with a raw bar, expect superb renditions of steak frites, mussels marinières, grilled-cheese sandwiches, and other heavenly French classics. Prices and atmosphere are far more down-to-earth than at French Laundry. I do like this place, but far prefer Bistro Jeanty. A bonus, especially for restless residents, is the late hours.

6534 Washington St. (at Humbolt), Yountville. ✆ 707/944-8037. Reservations recommended. Main courses $12–$17. AE, DC, MC, V. Daily 11:30am–2pm and 5:30–10:45pm.

Mustards Grill ★★ CALIFORNIA   Mustards is one of those standby restaurants that everyone seems to love because it's dependable and its menu has something that suits any food craving. Housed in a convivial, barn-style space, it offers an 11-page wine list and an ambitious chalkboard list of specials. My party started out with wonderfully light seared ahi tuna that melted in the mouth the way ahi should. Although the tea-smoked Peking duck with almond onion sauce and grilled rabbit with potatoes, fennel, and saffron broth were tempting, we opted for a moist, perfectly flavored grilled chicken breast with mashed potatoes

(Tips) Where to Stock Up for a Gourmet Picnic

You could easily plan your whole trip around restaurant reservations, but put together one of the world's best gourmet picnics, and the valley's your oyster.

One of the finest gourmet-food stores in the Wine Country, if not all of California, is the **Oakville Grocery Co.,** 7856 St. Helena Hwy., at Oakville Cross Road, Oakville (✆ **707/944-8802**). You can put together the provisions for a memorable picnic, or, with at least 24 hours' notice, the staff can prepare a picnic basket for you. The store, with its small-town vibe and claustrophobia-inducing crowds, can be quite an experience. You'll find shelves crammed with the best breads and choicest cheeses in the northern Bay Area, as well as pâtés, cold cuts, crackers, top-quality olive oils, fresh foie gras (domestic and French, seasonally), smoked Norwegian salmon, fresh caviar (Beluga, Sevruga, Osetra), and, of course, an exceptional selection of California wines. Open daily 9am to 6pm. The espresso bar tucked in the corner (open daily from 7am to 3pm), offers breakfast and lunch items, house-baked pastries, and 15 wines by the glass or for tasting.

Another of my favorite places to fill a picnic basket is New York City's version of a swank European marketplace, **Dean & DeLuca,** 607 S. Main St. (Highway 29), north of Zinfandel Lane and south of Sulphur Springs Road, St. Helena (✆ **707/967-9980**). The ultimate gourmet grocery store is more like a world's fair of foods, where everything is beautifully displayed and often painfully pricey. As you pace the barn-wood plank floors, you'll stumble upon more high-end edibles than you've ever seen under one roof. They include local organic produce (delivered daily); 200 domestic and imported cheeses (with an on-site aging room to ensure proper ripeness); shelves and shelves of tapenades, pastas, oils, hand-packed dried herbs and spices, chocolates, sauces, and cookware; an espresso bar; one hell of a bakery section; and more. Along the back wall, you can watch the professional chefs prepare gourmet takeout. Try fresh seared salmon with chanterelle mushrooms ($7.50 for a 6-ounce serving), rotisserie meats, salads, and sautéed vegetables. Or order the to-go fireside dinner, a four-course meal that costs $7.50 to $9.50 per person and may include a Caesar salad, rotisserie pork loin with mustard and apricot glaze, French green lentils, sun-dried tomatoes, and root veggies (two-person minimum). Wine master John Hardesty presides over the 1,200-label collection. Adjoining the wine room is a walk-in cedar humidor that holds more than 200 cigars. Open Monday to Saturday 10am to 7pm (the espresso bar opens at 8am); Sunday 10am to 6pm.

and fresh herbs. The menu includes something for everyone, from vegetarians to good old burger lovers.

7399 St. Helena Hwy. (Hwy. 29), Yountville. ✆ **707/944-2424.** Reservations recommended. Main courses $11–$27. DC, DISC, MC, V. Mon–Thurs 11:30am–9:30pm, Fri 11:30am–10pm, Sat 11am–10pm, Sun 11am–9:30pm.

Piatti 🐾 *(Kids)* ITALIAN   This local favorite—the first (and best) of a swiftly growing northern California chain—is known for serving good, fresh, and reasonably priced food in a rustic Italian-style setting. On the menu the classics are covered—from antipasti and insalata to pasta, oven-baked pizza, and nightly house specialties. For the perfect meal, start with a salad of morning-cut field greens mixed with white corn and Napa Valley strawberry crostini, accompanied by a bowl of spaghetti squash and sweet-potato soup. Although there's a wide array of superb pastas and pizzas, it's the wood-oven-roasted duck—basted with sweet huckleberry sauce and served with grilled polenta and braised greens—that brings back the regulars. Far fancier and more intimate restaurants can be found in the valley, but none where you can fill up on such outstanding fare at these prices. Piatti also offers patio dining year-round, weather permitting.

6480 Washington St. (between Washington and Oak sts.), Yountville. © **707/944-2070.** Reservations recommended. Main courses $10–$19. AE, DC, MC, V. Sun–Thurs 11:30am–10pm; Fri–Sat 11:30am–11pm.

ST. HELENA
Expensive

Terra 🐾🐾🐾 CONTEMPORARY AMERICAN   Terra is one of my favorite restaurants because it manages to be humble even though it serves some of the most extraordinary food in northern California. The creation of Lissa Doumani and her husband, Hiro Sone, a master chef who hails from Japan, is a culmination of talents brought together over 10 years ago, after the duo worked at L.A.'s Spago. Today, the menu reflects Sone's full use of the region's bounty and his formal training in classic European and Japanese cuisine. Dishes—all of which are incredible and are served in the rustic-romantic dining room—range from understated and refined (peeky toe crab salad or the famous broiled sake-marinated sea bass) to rock-your-world flavorful (petit ragout of sweetbreads, proscuitto, mushroom, and white truffle oil or grilled squab with leek and bacon bread pudding with roasted garlic foie gras sauce). I cannot express the importance of saving room for dessert (or forcing it even if you didn't). Doumani's recipes, which include tiramisu and an out-of-this-world-heavenly orange risotto in brandy snap with passion fruit sauce, are some of the best I've tasted.

1345 Railroad Ave. (between Adams and Hunt sts.), St. Helena. © **707/963-8931.** www.terrarestaurant. com. Reservations recommended. Main courses $18.50–$26. DC, MC, V. Sun–Mon and Wed–Thurs 6–9:30pm; Fri–Sat 6–10pm. Closed for 2 weeks in early January.

Moderate

Tra Vigne Restaurant 🐾🐾 ITALIAN   Tra Vigne's combination of good ultra-fresh food, high-energy atmosphere, gorgeous patio seating, and "reasonable" prices makes this restaurant a long-standing favorite among visitors and locals. Add to that plenty of seating and service running from lunch through dinner, and it's no wonder the enormous dining room packs 'em in. Whether guests are in the Tuscany-evoking courtyard (heated on cold nights) or in the center of the bustling scene, they're usually thrilled just to have a seat. Even though the wonderful bread (served with house-made flavored olive oils) is tempting, save room for the robust California dishes, cooked Italian-style by passionate partner/executive chef Carmen Quagliata, who's bent on making as much of your meal after you order as possible. The menu features about one daily oven-roasted pizza special, tried-and-true standbys like shortribs, frito misto, irresistible oven-roasted polenta with cheese, mushroons, and balsamic reduction, and outstanding whole roasted fish. If you're lucky, my favorite will be on the menu: Angry Sand Dab, a spicy celebration of chili oil, crisp and crunchy fried basil, lemon zest, baby jalapenos, garlic slivers, and white beans. Equally tempting are the fresh pastas—such as spaghettini with cuttlefish bolognese and spring onions—and delicious desserts.

The adjoining **Cantinetta** (see below) offers a small selection of sandwiches, pizzas, and lighter meals, and an exciting new wine program, which features 100 by-the-glass selections.

1050 Charter Oak Ave., St. Helena. ℂ **707/963-4444**. Reservations recommended. Main courses $12.50–$22. DC, DISC, MC, V. Daily 11:30am–10pm.

Wine Spectator Greystone Restaurant ⚜ WINE COUNTRY CUISINE

This place offers a visual and culinary feast that's unparalleled in the area, if not the state. The room is an enormous stone-walled former winery, but the festive decor and heavenly aromas warm the space up. Cooking islands—complete with scurrying chefs, steaming pots, and rotating chicken—provide edible entertainment. New head chef Todd Humphries (formerly of Campton Place in San Francisco) has put his own mark on the cuisine. The tastings (appetizer) menu features dishes inspired by fresh ingredients. They include perfect calamari sautéed with paprika, garlic, and rosemary (wonderful every time I come, regardless of the preparation!), a fine seafood and white bean salad, and an unimpressive mushroom piroshki with caramelized onions. Portions are small but affordable; pastas and salads are a bit heftier. Main courses, such as crispy fried lamb shank with cranberry beans, cherry tomatoes, and spinach, are well portioned and darn good, but I recommend that you opt for a barrage of appetizers for your table to share. You should also order the "Flights of Fancy"—for $14 to $20, you can sample three 3-ounce pours of local wines such as white rhone, pinot, or zinfandel. (Wines by the glass are from the same selection, which, annoyingly, does not list by-the-glass prices.) While the food is serious, the atmosphere is playful—casual enough that you'll feel comfortable in jeans or shorts. If you want to ensure a meal here, reserve far in advance. I prefer to stop by, have a snack at the bar, and eat big meals elsewhere.

At the Culinary Institute of America at Greystone, 2555 Main St., St. Helena. ℂ **707/967-1010**. Reservations recommended. Tastings $5–$8; main courses $14–$24. AE, DC, MC, V. Daily 11:30am–10pm.

Inexpensive

The Cantinetta ⚜⚜⚜ WINE BAR/ITALIAN DELI   Regardless of where

else I dine while in the valley, I always make a point of stopping at the Cantinetta for an espresso and a snack. Part cafe, part shop, it's a casual place with a few tables and a counter. The focaccias, pasta salads, and pastries are outstanding. There's a selection of cookies and other wonderful treats, flavored oils (free tastings), wines, and an array of gourmet items, many of which were created here. You can also get great picnic grub to go.

At Tra Vigne Restaurant, 1050 Charter Oak Ave., St. Helena. ℂ **707/963-8888**. Main courses $4–$7. DC, DISC, MC, V. Daily 11:30am–6pm.

Tomatina ⚜ *Value* *Kids* ITALIAN   After spending a week in Wine Country, I

usually can't stand the thought of another decadent wine and foie-gras meal. That's when I race to Tomatina for a $3.50 chopped salad, a welcome respite from gluttonous excess. Families and locals come here for another reason: Although the menu is limited, it's a total winner for anyone in search of freshly prepared, wholesome food at atypically cheap Wine Country prices. A Caesar salad, for example, costs a mere $4.50. "Apizzas"—pizzas folded like a soft taco—are the house specialty, and come filled with such delights as fresh Maine clams and oregano. Pizzas are of the build-your-own variety, with gourmet toppings like sautéed mushrooms, fennel sausage, baby spinach, sun-dried tomatoes, and homemade pepperoni. The 26 respectable local wines come by the glass at a toast-worthy $3.75, or $18 per bottle. Dessert, at less than $4 a pop for gelato, biscotti, or pound cake, is an overall sweet deal. Everything is ordered at the counter and brought to the small or family-style tables in the very casual dining area or the outdoor patio. Kids especially like the pool table and big-screen TV.

At The Inn at Southbridge, 1016 Main St., St. Helena. © 707/967-9999. Pastas $6–$8; pizzas $8–$19. DC, DISC, MC, V. Daily 11:30am–10pm.

CALISTOGA
Moderate
All Seasons Café ★★ CALIFORNIA   Wine Country devotees wend their way to the All Seasons Café in downtown Calistoga because of its extensive wine list and knowledgeable staff. The trick is to buy a bottle of wine from the cafe's wine shop, then bring it to your table; the cafe adds a corkage fee of around $10 instead of tripling the price of the bottle (as most restaurants do). The diverse menu ranges from pizzas and pastas to such main courses as braised lamb shank osso bucco in an orange, Madeira, and tomato sauce. Anything with house-smoked salmon or spiced sausages is also a safe bet. Chef John Coss saves his guests from any major *faux pas* by matching wines to dishes on the menu, so you know just what's right for smoked salmon and Crescenza cheese pizza.

1400 Lincoln Ave. (at Washington St.), Calistoga. © 707/942-9111. Reservations recommended on weekends. Main courses $7.50–$13 at lunch, $10.25–$19 at dinner. MC, V. Mon–Tues and Thurs–Fri 11am–3pm; daily 5:30–9pm. Wine shop Thurs–Tues 11am–7pm.

Catahoula ★ AMERICAN/SOUTHERN   The domain of affable chef Jan Birnbaum, formerly of New York's Quilted Giraffe and San Francisco's Campton Place, this restaurant is a town favorite for good reason: It's the only place in Napa Valley where you can get decent rooster gumbo. And you'd have to travel all over Louisiana to find a crispy-fried catfish with lemon jalapeño Meuiere catfish like this one. Catahoula is funky and fun, with a good sense of humor. The menu offers something for everyone, with a few spicy specialties from the wood-burning oven (roasted porterhouse with grits and pickled cabbage or oven roasted chicken with brown butter Armagnac sauce), lots of flavorful salads and a couple of pizzas, and festive side dishes like potato onion pie and meyer lemon whipped potatoes.

1457 Lincoln Ave. (between Washington and Fairway sts.), Calistoga. © 707/942-2275. Reservations recommended. Main courses $11–$22. DISC, MC, V. Sat–Sun 10am–3:30pm; daily 5:30–10:30pm.

Inexpensive
Smokehouse Café ★★ Kids AMERICAN/SOUTHERN/BBQ   Who would have guessed that some of the best spareribs and house-smoked meats in northern California would come from this little kitchen in Calistoga? Here's the winning game plan: Start with Sacramento delta crawfish cakes and husk-roasted Cheyenne corn. Move on to the slow pig sandwich (slow-smoked), a half slab of ribs, or homemade sausages—all of which take up to a week to prepare (not while you wait, luckily). The clincher is the fluffy all-you-can-eat cornbread dipped in pure cane syrup, which comes with every full-plate dinner. Kids are especially welcome—a rarity in these parts—and patio dining is available in summer.

1458 Lincoln Ave., Calistoga. © 707/942-6060. Main courses $8–$21. MC, V. Daily 8:30am–9pm (closed for dinner Tues–Wed Jan–Feb).

Wappo Bar & Bistro ✦✦ GLOBAL   One of the best alfresco dining experiences in the Wine Country is under Wappo's honeysuckle-and-vine-covered arbor, but you'll also be comfortable at one of the well-spaced, well-polished tables inside the small bistro. The menu offers a wide range of choices, from Chilean sea bass with mint chutney to roast rabbit with oven tomato tagliarini. Desserts of choice are black-bottom coconut cream pie and strawberry rhubarb pie.

1226B Washington St. (off Lincoln Ave.), Calistoga. (✆ **707/942-4712.** Main courses $13.50–$19.75. AE, MC, V. Wed–Mon 11:30am–2:30pm and 6–9:30pm.

2 Sonoma Valley

A pastoral contrast to Napa, Sonoma manages to maintain a backcountry ambience, thanks to its far lower density of wineries, restaurants, and hotels. Small, family-owned wineries are Sonoma's mainstay; tastings are low-key, and they come with plenty of friendly banter with the winemakers (who often do the pouring). Basically, this is the valley to target if your ideal vacation includes visiting a handful of wineries along quiet, woodsy roads, avoiding shopping outlets and Napa's high-end glitz, and simply enjoying the laid-back country atmosphere.

The valley is some 17 miles long and 7 miles wide, and it's bordered by two mountain ranges: the Mayacamas to the east and Sonoma Mountains to the west. Unlike in Napa Valley, you won't find palatial wineries with million-dollar art collections, aerial trams, and Hollywood ego trips (read: Niebaum-Coppola). Rather, the Sonoma Valley offers a refreshing dose of reality, where modestly sized wineries are integrated into the community. If Napa Valley feels like a fantasyland, where everything exists to service the almighty grape and the visitors it attracts, then the Sonoma Valley is its antithesis, an unpretentious gaggle of ordinary towns, ranches, and wineries that welcome tourists but don't necessarily rely on them. The result is a chance to experience what Napa Valley must have been like long before the Seagrams and Moët et Chandons of the world turned the Wine Country into a major tourist destination.

As in Napa, you can also pick up *Wine Country Review* throughout Sonoma. It gives you the most up-to-date information on wineries and related area events.

ESSENTIALS
GETTING THERE   From San Francisco, cross the Golden Gate Bridge and stay on U.S. 101 north. Exit at Highway 37; after 10 miles, turn north onto Highway 121. After another 10 miles, turn north onto Highway 12 (Broadway), which takes you directly into the town of Sonoma.

VISITOR INFORMATION   While you're in Sonoma, stop by the **Sonoma Valley Visitors Bureau,** 453 First St. E. (✆ **707/996-1090;** www.sonomavalley. com). It's open daily from 9am to 7pm in summer and from 9am to 5pm in winter. An additional **Visitors Bureau** is a few miles south of the square at 25200 Arnold Dr. (Highway 121), at the entrance to Viansa Winery (✆ **707/ 996-5793**); it keeps the same hours.

If you prefer some advance information, you can contact the Sonoma Valley Visitors Bureau to order the $2 *Sonoma Valley Visitors Guide,* which lists most every lodge, winery, and restaurant in the valley.

TOURING THE SONOMA VALLEY & WINERIES
Sonoma Valley is currently home to about 35 wineries (including California's first winery, Buena Vista, founded in 1857) and 13,000 acres of vineyards. It produces roughly 25 types of wines, totaling more than 5 million cases a year.

Cabernet is the varietal for which Sonoma is most noted. Unlike the rigidly structured tours at many of Napa Valley's corporate-owned wineries, tastings and tours on the Sonoma side of the Mayacamas Mountains are usually free and low-key.

The towns and wineries covered below are organized geographically from south to north, starting at the intersection of Highway 37 and Highway 121 in the Carneros District and ending in Kenwood. The wineries tend to be a little more spread out here than they are in Napa Valley, but they're easy to find. Still, it's best to decide which wineries you're most interested in and devise a touring strategy before you set out, so you don't do too much backtracking.

I've reviewed some favorite Sonoma Valley wineries here—more than enough to keep you busy tasting wine for a long weekend. If you'd like a complete list of local wineries, be sure to pick up one of the free guides to the valley that's available at the Sonoma Valley Visitors Bureau (see "Visitor Information," above).

THE CARNEROS DISTRICT

As you approach the Wine Country from the south, you must first pass through the Carneros District, a cool, windswept region that borders the San Pablo Bay and marks the entrance to both Napa and Sonoma valleys. Until the latter part of the 20th century, this mixture of marsh, sloughs, and rolling hills was mainly used as sheep pasture (*carneros* means "sheep" in Spanish). After experimental plantings yielded slow-growing, high-quality grapes—particularly chardonnay and pinot noir—several Napa and Sonoma wineries expanded their plantings here. They eventually established the Carneros District as an American Viticultural Appellation. Although about a dozen wineries are spread throughout the region, there are no major towns or attractions—just plenty of gorgeous scenery as you cruise along Highway 121, the major junction between Napa and Sonoma.

Viansa Winery and Italian Marketplace *Finds*   The first major winery you'll encounter as you enter Sonoma Valley from the south, this sprawling Tuscan-style villa perches atop a knoll overlooking the entire lower valley. Viansa is the brainchild of Sam and Vicki Sebastiani, who left the family dynasty to create their own temple to food and wine. (*Viansa* is a contraction of "Vicki and Sam.") While Sam, a third-generation winemaker, runs the winery, Vicky manages the marketplace, a large room crammed with a cornucopia of high-quality preserves, mustards, olive oils, pastas, salads, breads, desserts, Italian tableware, cookbooks, and wine-related gifts.

The winery, which does an extensive mail-order business through its Tuscany Club, has established a favorable reputation for its cabernet, sauvignon blanc, and chardonnay. Blended from premium Napa and Sonoma grapes, they're sold in the sexiest-shaped bottles in Sonoma. Sam is also experimenting with Italian grape varieties such as muscat canelli, sangiovese, and nebbiolo, most of which are sold exclusively at the winery. $5 tastings are poured at the east end of the marketplace, and the self-guided tour includes a trip through the underground barrel-aging cellar adorned with colorful hand-painted murals.

Viansa is also one of the few wineries in Sonoma Valley that sells deli items—the focaccia sandwiches are delicious. You can dine alfresco under the grape trellis while you admire the bucolic view.

25200 Arnold Dr. (Calif. 121), Sonoma. (C) **800/995-4740** or 707/935-4700. www.viansa.com. Daily 10am–5pm; summer 9am–5:30pm. Daily self-guided tours.

Gloria Ferrer Champagne Caves ⭐ *Finds*   When you have had it up to here with chardonnays and pinots, it's time to pay a visit to Gloria Ferrer, the grande dame of the Wine Country's sparkling-wine producers. Who's Gloria? She's the wife of José Ferrer, whose family has made sparkling wine for 5 centuries. The family business, Freixenet, is the largest producer of sparkling wine in the world; Cordon Negro is its most popular brand. That equals big bucks, and certainly a good chunk went into building this palatial estate. Glimmering like Oz high atop a gently sloping hill, it overlooks the verdant Carneros District. On a sunny day, enjoying a glass of dry brut while soaking in the magnificent views is a must.

If you're unfamiliar with the term *méthode champenoise*, be sure to take the free 30-minute tour of the fermenting tanks, bottling line, and caves brimming with racks of yeast-laden bottles. Afterward, retire to the elegant tasting room for a flute of brut or cuvée ($3.50 to $6 a glass, $16 and up per bottle), find an empty chair on the veranda, and say, "Ahhh. *This* is the life." There are picnic tables, but it's usually too windy for comfort, and you must buy a bottle of sparkling wine to reserve a table.

23555 Carneros Hwy. (Calif. 121), Sonoma. 📞 **707/996-7256**. www.gloriaferrer.com. Daily 10am–5:30pm. Tours daily 11am–4pm.

SONOMA

At the northern boundary of the Carneros District along Highway 12 is the centerpiece of Sonoma Valley. The midsized town of Sonoma owes much of its appeal to Mexican General Mariano Guadalupe Vallejo, who fashioned this pleasant, slow-paced community after a typical Mexican village—right down to its central plaza, Sonoma's geographical and commercial center. The plaza sits at the top of a T formed by Broadway (Highway 12) and Napa Street. Most of the surrounding streets form a grid pattern around this axis, making Sonoma easy to negotiate. The plaza's Bear Flag Monument marks the spot where the crude Bear Flag was raised in 1846, signaling the end of Mexican rule; the symbol was later adopted by the state of California and placed on its flag. The 8-acre park at the center of the plaza, complete with two ponds populated by ducks and geese, is perfect for an afternoon siesta in the cool shade. A favorite attraction, however, is the gaggle of brilliantly feathered chickens that roam unfettered through the streets of Sonoma—a sight you'll definitely never see in Napa.

Buena Vista Winery   Count Agoston Haraszthy, the Hungarian émigré who is universally regarded as the father of California's wine industry, founded this historic winery in 1857. A close friend of General Vallejo, Haraszthy returned from Europe in 1861 with 100,000 of the finest vine cuttings, which he made available to all growers. Although Buena Vista's winemaking now takes place at an ultramodern facility in the Carneros District, the winery maintains a tasting room inside the restored 1862 Press House. The beautiful stone-crafted room brims with wines, wine-related gifts, and accessories (as well as a small art gallery along the inner balcony).

Tastings are free for most wines, $3 for the really good stuff. You can take the self-guided tour any time during operating hours; a "Historical Presentation," offered daily at 2pm, details the life and times of the Count. After tasting, grab your favorite bottle, a selection of cheeses from the Sonoma Cheese Factory, salami, bread, and pâté (all available in the tasting room), and plant yourself at one of the many picnic tables in the lush, verdant setting.

18000 Old Winery Rd. (off E. Napa St., slightly northeast of downtown), Sonoma. 📞 **800/926-1266** or 707/938-1266. www.buenavistawinery.com. Daily 10am–5pm. Self-guided tours only.

Sebastiani Vineyards Winery   The name Sebastiani is practically synonymous with Sonoma. What started in 1904, when Samuele Sebastiani began producing his first wines, has in three generations grown into a small empire and
Sonoma County's largest winery, producing some 6 million cases a year. The
winery's setting and structure aren't the most scenic in Sonoma Valley, yet its
place in the history and development of the region is unparalleled.

The 25-minute tour is interesting, informative, and well worth the time. You
can see the winery's original turn-of-the-century crusher and press, as well as the
world's largest collection of oak-barrel carvings, crafted by local artist Earle
Brown. If you don't want to take the tour, head straight for the charmingly rustic tasting room, where you can sample an extensive selection of wines free. Bottle prices are reasonable, ranging from $8 to $60. A picnic area adjoins the
cellars, but a far more scenic spot is across the parking lot in Sebastiani's Cherry-
block Vineyards.

389 Fourth St. E., Sonoma. ✆ **800/888-5532** or 707/938-5532. www.sebastiani.com. Daily 10am–5pm.
Tours 10:30am–4pm, every 30 min. in summer, every 45–60 min. in winter; no reservations necessary.

Ravenswood Winery   Compared to old heavies like Sebastiani and Buena
Vista, Ravenswood is a relative newcomer to the Sonoma wine scene. It has
quickly established itself as the sine qua non of zinfandel, the versatile grape
that's quickly gaining ground on the rapacious cabernet sauvignon. In fact,
Ravenswood is the first winery in the United States to focus primarily on zins,
which make up about three-quarters of its 150,000-case production; it also produces merlot, cabernet sauvignon, and a small amount of chardonnay.

The winery is smartly designed—recessed into the hillside to protect its treasures from the simmering summers. Tours follow the winemaking process from
grape to glass, and include a visit into the aromatic oak-barrel aging rooms. A
gourmet "Barbecue Overlooking the Vineyards" runs from 11am to 4:40pm on
weekends from Memorial Day through September; call for details and reservations). You're also welcome to bring your own picnic basket to any of the tables.
Tastings are free and generous.

18701 Gehricke Rd. (off Lovall Valley Rd.), Sonoma. ✆ **800/NO-WIMPY** or 707/938-1960. www.
ravenswood-wine.com. Daily 10am–4:30pm. Tours by reservation only.

GLEN ELLEN

About 7 miles north of Sonoma on Highway 12 is the town of Glen Ellen.
Although just a fraction of the size of Sonoma, Glen Ellen is home to several of
the valley's finest wineries, restaurants, and inns. Aside from the addition of a
few new restaurants, this charming town hasn't changed much since the days
when Jack London settled on his Beauty Ranch, about a mile west. Other than
the wineries, you'll find few real signs of commercialism; the shops and restaurants, along one main winding lane, cater to a small, local clientele—that is,
until the summer tourist season begins and traffic nearly triples on the weekends. If you haven't decided where you want to set up camp during your visit to
the Wine Country, I highly recommend this lovable little town.

Arrowood Vineyards & Winery   Richard Arrowood had already established
a reputation as a master winemaker at Château St. Jean when he and his wife,
Alis Demers Arrowood, set out on their own in 1986. Their picturesque winery
stands on a gently rising hillside lined with perfectly manicured vineyards. Tastings take place in the Hospitality House, the newer of Arrowood's two stately
gray-and-white buildings. They're fashioned after New England farmhouses,
complete with wraparound porches. Richard's focus is on making world-class

> *Moments* **Touring the Sonoma Valley by Bike**
>
> Sonoma and its neighboring towns are so small, close together, and relatively flat that it's not difficult to get around on two wheels. In fact, if you're in no great hurry, there's no better way to tour the Sonoma Valley than by bicycle. You can rent a bike at the **Goodtime Bicycle Company** ⭐, 18503 Sonoma Hwy. (Calif. 12), Sonoma (② **888/ 525-0453** or **707/938-0453**). The staff will happily point you to easy bike trails, or you can take an organized excursion to Kenwood-area wineries or south Sonoma wineries. Goodtime provides a gourmet lunch featuring local Sonoma products. If you purchase wine along the way, Goodtimes will carry it for you and help with shipping arrangements. Lunch rides start at 10:30am and end around 3pm. The cost, including food and equipment, is $65 per person (that's a darn good deal). Rentals cost $25 a day or $5 per hour, and include helmets, locks, and everything else you'll need. Bikes are also available for rent from **Sonoma Valley Cyclery**, 20093 Broadway, Sonoma (② **707/935-3377**), for $25 a day.

wine with minimal intervention, and his results are impressive: More than one of his current releases has scored over 90 points. Mind you, excellence doesn't come cheap. Prices start at $26 for a 1997 chardonnay and quickly climb to the mid- to high 30s. Arrowood is one of the few wineries in Sonoma that charge for tastings ($3), but if you're curious about what near-perfection tastes like, it's well worth it. No picnic facilities are available.

14347 Sonoma Hwy. (Calif. 12), Glen Ellen. ② **707/938-5170**. www.arrowoodvineyards.com. Daily 10am–4:30pm. Tours by appointment only, daily at 10:30am and 2:30pm.

Benziger Family Winery ⭐ *Finds*   A visit here confirms that you are indeed visiting a family winery. At any given time, three generations of Benzigers (pronounced *Ben*-zigger) may be running around tending to chores, and they instantly make you feel as if you're part of the clan. The pastoral, user-friendly property features an exceptional self-guided tour ("The most comprehensive tour in the wine industry," according to *Wine Spectator*), gardens, a spacious tasting room staffed by amiable folks, and an art gallery. The free 40-minute tram tour, pulled by a beefy tractor, is both informative and fun. It winds through the estate vineyards before making a champagne-tasting pit stop on a scenic bluff. *Tip:* Tram tickets—a hot item in the summer—are available on a first-come, first-served basis, so either arrive early or stop by in the morning to pick up afternoon tickets.

Tastings of the standard-release wines are free, and the winery offers several scenic picnic spots.

1883 London Ranch Rd. (off Arnold Dr., on the way to Jack London State Historic Park), Glen Ellen. ② **800/989-8890** or **707/935-3000**. www.benziger.com. Tasting room daily 10am–5pm. $5 tram tours daily (weather permitting) at 11:30am, 12:30, 2, and 3:30pm.

KENWOOD

A few miles north of Glen Ellen along Highway 12 is the tiny town of Kenwood, the valley's northernmost outpost. Although Kenwood Vineyards's wines are well known throughout the United States, the town itself consists of little more than a few restaurants, wineries, and modest homes on the wooded hillsides. The nearest lodging, the luxurious Kenwood Inn & Spa, is about a mile south of the vineyards. Kenwood makes for a pleasant day trip—a tour of Château St. Jean, dinner at Kenwood Restaurant—from Glen Ellen or Sonoma.

Kenwood Vineyards   Kenwood's history dates to 1906, when the Pagani brothers made their living selling wine straight from the barrel and into the jug. In 1970 the Lee family bought the property and dumped a ton of money into converting the aging winery into a modern, high-production facility (most of it cleverly concealed in the original barnlike buildings). Since then, Kenwood has earned a solid reputation for consistent quality with each of its varietals: cabernet sauvignon, chardonnay, zinfandel, pinot noir, merlot, and, most popular, sauvignon blanc—a crisp, light wine with hints of melon.

Although the winery looks rather modest in size, its output is staggering: Over 400,000 cases of ultra-premium wines fermented in steel tanks and French and American oak barrels. Popular with collectors is winemaker Michael Lee's Artist Series cabernet sauvignon, a limited production from the winery's best vineyards, featuring labels with original artwork by renowned artists. The tasting room, housed in one of the old barns, offers free tastings of most varieties and sells gift items.

9592 Sonoma Hwy. (Calif. 12), Kenwood. (© 707/833-5891. www.kenwoodvineyards.com. Daily 10am–4:30pm. Tours at 11:30am and 2:30pm daily.

Château St. Jean ★ *Finds*   Château St. Jean is notable for its exceptionally beautiful buildings, landscaped grounds, and elegant tasting room. Among California wineries, it's a pioneer in vineyard designation—the procedure of making wine from, and naming it for, a single vineyard. A private drive takes you to what was once a 250-acre country retreat built in 1920; a well-manicured lawn overlooking the meticulously maintained vineyards is now a picnic area, complete with a fountain and picnic tables. There's a self-guided tour with detailed and photographic descriptions of the winemaking process. When you're done, be sure to walk to the top of the faux medieval tower for a magnificent view of the valley.

Back in the elegant tasting room—split into three areas to better handle the traffic—you can sample Château St. Jean's wide array of wines. They range from chardonnays and cabernet sauvignon to fumé blanc, merlot, Johannesburg Riesling, and Gewürztraminer. (Don't miss a rare tasting of late-harvest wines—you'll be amazed what a little more time on the vine can do.) Tastings are $5 per person.

8555 Sonoma Hwy. (Calif. 12), Kenwood. (© 800/543-7572 or 707/833-4134. www.chateaustjean.com. Tasting daily 10am–6pm. At the foot of Sugarloaf Ridge, just north of Kenwood and east of Hwy. 12.

JUST UP FROM THE SONOMA VALLEY: SANTA ROSA

Matanzas Creek ★ *Finds*   It's not technically in Sonoma Valley, but if there's one winery that's worth a detour, it's Matanzas (pronounced Mah-*tan*-zas) Creek. After a scenic 20-minute drive, you'll arrive at one of the prettiest wineries in California, blanketed by fields of lavender (usually in bloom near the end of June), and surrounded by rolling hills of well-tended vineyards.

The winery has a rather unorthodox history. In 1978, Sandra and Bill MacIver, neither of whom had any previous experience in winemaking or business, set out with one goal in mind: to create the finest wines in the country. Actually, they overshot the mark. With the release of their Journey 1990 chardonnay, they were hailed by wine critics as the proud parents of the finest chardonnay ever produced in the United States, comparable to the finest white wines in the world.

This state-of-the-art, environmentally conscious winery produces chardonnay, sauvignon blanc, and cabernet, all of which are available for tasting free. Prices for current releases are, as you would imagine, at the higher end. Also available for purchase is culinary lavender from Matanzas Creek's own lavender field, the largest outside Provence. Purchase a full glass of wine and bring it outside to savor as you wander through these wonderfully aromatic gardens. Picnic tables hidden under groves of oak have pleasant views of the surrounding vineyards. On the return trip, be sure to take the Sonoma Mountain Road detour for a real backcountry experience.

6097 Bennett Valley Rd. (off Warm Springs Rd.), Santa Rosa. © 800/590-6464 or 707/528-6464. www.matanzascreek.com. Daily 10am–4:30pm. Tours daily, by appointment only, at 10:30am, 1, and 3pm. From Hwy. 12 in Kenwood or Glen Ellen, take Warm Springs Rd. turnoff to Bennett Valley Rd.; the drive takes 15–20 min.

WHERE TO STAY IN SONOMA VALLEY

Hotel listings are arranged below first by area, then by price, using the following categories: **Very Expensive,** more than $250 per night; **Expensive,** $200 to $250 per night; **Moderate,** $150 to $200 per night; and **Inexpensive,** less than $150 per night. Keep in mind that during the peak season and on weekends, most B&Bs and hotels require a minimum 2-night stay. Of course, that's assuming you can find a vacancy; make reservations as far in advance as possible.

If you are having trouble finding a room, try calling the **Sonoma Valley Visitors Bureau** (© 707/996-1090). The staff will try to refer you to a lodging that has a room to spare, but won't make reservations for you. Another option is the **Bed and Breakfast Association of Sonoma Valley** (© 800/969-4667), which can refer you to a B&B that belongs to the association and make reservations for you, too.

SONOMA
Very Expensive

Sonoma Mission Inn, Spa & Country Club ★★★   As you drive through Boyes Hot Springs, you may wonder why someone decided to build a multi-million-dollar spa resort in this ordinary little town. There's no view to speak of, and it certainly isn't within walking distance of any wineries or fancy restaurants. So what's the deal? It's the naturally heated artesian mineral water, piped from directly underneath the spa into the temperature-controlled pools and whirlpools. Set on 12 meticulously groomed acres, the Sonoma Mission Inn consists of a massive three-story replica of a Spanish mission (well, aside from the pink paint job) built in 1927, an array of satellite wings housing numerous super-luxury suites, and, of course, world-class spa facilities. It's a popular retreat for the wealthy and well-known, so don't be surprised if you see Barbra Streisand or Harrison Ford strolling around in skivvies. Big changes have occurred since the resort changed ownership a few years ago. It has gained 70 guest rooms and suites, a $20 million spa facility (you won't even recognize the old one), and the Sonoma Golf Club.

The modern rooms have plantation-style shutters, ceiling fans, down comforters, bathroom scales, hair dryers, and oversized bath towels. The Wine Country rooms feature king-size beds, desks, refrigerators, and huge limestone and marble bathrooms; some offer wood-burning fireplaces, and many have balconies. The older, slightly smaller Historic Inn rooms are sweetly appointed with homey furnishings; most have queen-size beds. For the ultimate in luxury, the opulently appointed (and brand-new) Mission Suites are the way to go.

18140 Sonoma Hwy. (Calif. 12), P.O. Box 1447, Sonoma, CA 94576. ℂ 800/862-4945 or 707/938-9000. Fax 707/935-1205. www.sonomamissioninn.com. 230 units. $299–$1,200 double. AE, DC, MC, V. From central Sonoma, drive 3 miles north on Highway 12 and turn left on Boyes Blvd. **Amenities:** 2 restaurants (American and California/Spa Cuisine); 2 large, heated outdoor pools; golf course; tennis courts; health club & spa (see box, "The Super Spa," on p. 297 for the complete rundown); Jacuzzi; sauna; bike rental; concierge; business center; salon; room service (6am–11pm); babysitting; same-day laundry service and dry cleaning. *In room:* A/C, TV, dataport, minibar, hair dryer, iron; safe.

Moderate

El Dorado Hotel ✪✪   This 1843 Mission-revival building may look like a 19th-century Wild West relic from the outside, but inside it's all 20th-century deluxe. Each modern, handsomely appointed guest room—designed by the same folks who put together the ultra-exclusive Auberge du Soleil resort in Rutherford—has French windows and tiny terraces. Some offer lovely views of the plaza; others overlook the private courtyard and heated lap pool. All rooms (except those for guests with disabilities) are on the second floor, contain four-poster beds, plush towels, and hair dryers, and were upgraded in 2001. The two rooms on the ground floor are off the private courtyard, and each has a partially enclosed patio. Though prices reflect its prime location on Sonoma Square, this is still one of the more charming options within its price range. Breakfast, served inside or out in the courtyard, includes coffee, fruits, and freshly baked breads and pastries. The Italian-influenced restaurant Patti, is described below, in "Where to Dine in Sonoma Valley."

405 First St. W., Sonoma, CA 95476. ℂ 800/289-3031 or 707/996-3030. Fax 707/996-3148. www.hoteleldorado.com. 27 units. Summer $220–$265 double; winter $195–$235 double. Rates include continental breakfast and bottle of wine. AE, MC, V. **Amenities:** 1 restaurant; heated outdoor pool; access to nearby health club; bike rental; concierge; room service (11:30am–10pm); laundry service, dry cleaning. *In room:* A/C, TV, dataport, hair dryer.

Inexpensive

Sonoma Valley Inn (Kids   There are just two reasons to stay at the Sonoma Valley Inn: 1) It's the only place left with a vacancy or 2) you're bringing the kids. Otherwise, unless you don't mind staying in a rather drab room with thin walls and a small bathroom, you're probably going to be a little disappointed. Kids, on the other hand, love the place: There's plenty of room to run around, plus a large pool and gazebo-covered spa to play in. The rooms *do* come with a lot of perks, such as continental breakfast delivered to your room, a gift bottle of white table wine (chilling in the fridge), cable TV with HBO, and a balcony or deck overlooking the inner courtyard. It's also in a good location, just a block from Sonoma's plaza.

550 Second St. W. (1 block from the plaza), Sonoma, CA 95476. ℂ 800/334-5784 or 707/938-9200. Fax 707/938-0935. www.sonomavalleyinn.com. 82 units. $89–$379 double. Rates include continental breakfast. AE, DC, MC, V. **Amenities:** Heated outdoor pool; outdoor hot tub; exercise room; coin-operated washers and dryers, same-day dry cleaning. *In room:* A/C, TV w/pay movies, dataport, kitchenettes in some rooms, fridge, coffeemaker, hair dryer, iron.

Sonoma Hotel ✪✪   This cute little historic hotel on Sonoma's tree-lined town plaza emphasizes 19th-century elegance and comfort. Built in 1880 by German immigrant Henry Weyl, it has attractive guest rooms decorated in early California style, with French country furnishings, antique beds, and period decorations. In a bow to modern luxuries, recent additions include private

Finds The Super Spa

The **Sonoma Mission Inn, Spa & Country Club,** 18140 Sonoma Hwy. (© **800/862-4945** or 707/938-9000; www.sonomamissioninn.com), has always been the most complete—and the most luxurious—spa in the whole Wine Country. With its new $20 million, 27,000-square-foot facility, this super spa is now one of the best in the country. The Spanish Mission–style retreat offers more than 50 spa treatments, ever-popular natural mineral baths, and virtually every facility and activity imaginable. You can pamper yourself silly: Soak in mineral baths, have a facial set to music, indulge in a grape-seed body wrap, relax with a massage, take a sauna or herbal steam, go for a dip in the pool—the list goes on and on (and, alas, so will the bill). You can also work off those wicked Wine Country meals with aerobics, weights, and cardio machines; get loose in a yoga class; play tennis; or just lounge and lunch by the pool. Or you can opt for a personal favorite—the $200 Rejuvenator, a 1-hour, 45-minute mega-treatment that includes an "oil drip" onto your hair and scalp, a scalp massage, a hair mask that smells so much like cookie dough you'll be tempted to nibble on it, a face mask, and a glorious massage. After the treatment, work out in the exercise room, take a sauna, steam, and mineral plunge, then relax poolside with a good book. Now that's living.

Of course, they have to pay for this fancy upgrade somehow, and here's how:

• Weekend day-use fee for guests: $35
• Weekday day-use fee for guests: $35
• Weekend day-use fee for nonguests: $45
• Weekday day-use fee for nonguests: $45

Steep, yes, but access to the spa facilities is free if you opt for one of the treatments, so you might as well splurge. Either way, a day at the Sonoma Mission Inn Spa is one of my favorite ways to unwind in the Wine Country.

bathrooms, cable TV, phones with dataports, and (and this is crucial) air-conditioning. Perks include fresh coffee and pastries in the morning and wine and cheese in the evening. The new fantastic restaurant, The Girl & the Fig (see "Where to Dine in Sonoma Valley"), serves California-French cuisine.

110 W. Spain St., Sonoma, CA 95476. © **800/468-6016** or 707/996-2996. Fax 707/996-7014. www.sonoma hotel.com. 16 units. Summer $110–$245 double. Winter Sun–Thurs $95–$170 double; Fri–Sat $115–$195 double. Rates include continental breakfast and evening wine and cheese. AE, DC, MC, V. *In room:* A/C, TV, dataport.

Victorian Garden Inn 🌀 Proprietor Donna Lewis runs what is easily the cutest B&B in Sonoma Valley. A small picket fence and a wall of trees enclose an adorable Victorian garden brimming with violets, roses, camellias, and peonies, all shaded under flowering fruit trees. It's truly a marvelous sight in the springtime. The guest rooms—three in the century-old water tower and one in the main building, an 1870s Greek Revival farmhouse—continue the Victorian theme, with white wicker furniture, floral prints, padded armchairs, and claw-foot tubs. The most popular rooms are the Top o' the Tower and the Wood-cutter's Cottage. Each has its own entrance and a garden view; the cottage boasts a sofa and armchairs set in front of the fireplace. After a hard day's wine tasting, spend the afternoon cooling off in the pool or on the shaded wraparound porch, enjoying a mellow merlot while soaking in the sweet garden smells.

316 E. Napa St., Sonoma, CA 95476. ⓒ **800/543-5339** or 707/996-5339. Fax 707/996-1689. www.victorian gardeninn.com. 4 units. $125–$240 double. Rates include continental breakfast. AE, DC, MC, V. **Amenities:** Outdoor pool; business center; concierge; room service (8am–5pm); laundry service, dry cleaning. *In room:* A/C.

GLEN ELLEN
Expensive

Gaige House Inn ⭐⭐⭐ *(Finds* Owners Ken Burnet, Jr., and Greg Nemrow have managed to turn what was already a fine B&B into *the* finest in the Wine Country. They've done it by offering a level of service, amenities, and decor normally associated with outrageously expensive resorts—but without the snobbery. Every nook and cranny of the 1890 Queen Anne-Italianate building and Garden Annex is swathed with fashionable articles found during the owners' world travels. Spacious rooms offer everything one could want—firm mattresses, wondrously silk-soft linens, and premium down comforters grace the beds, and even the furniture and artwork are the kind you'd like to take home with you. Breakfast is a momentous event, accented with herbs from the inn's garden and prepared by a chef who cooked at the James Beard House in 2001. Bathrooms are equally luxe, range in size, and are stocked with Aveda products. Attention to detail means you'll be treated to the best robe I've ever worn and evening appetizers at wine hour that might include freshly shucked oysters or a sautéed scallop served ready-to-slurp on a Chinese soup spoon.

But wait, it gets better. Behind the inn is a 1.5-acre oasis with perfectly manicured lawns, a 40-foot-long pool, and an achingly inviting creek-side hammock shaded by a majestic Heritage oak. All 15 rooms, each artistically decorated in a plantation theme with Asian and Indonesian influences (trust me, they're beautiful), have king- or queen-size beds; two rooms have Jacuzzi tubs, and several have fireplaces. For the ultimate retreat reserve one of the suites, which have patios overlooking a stream. On sunny days, breakfast is served at individual tables on the large terrace. Evenings are best spent in the reading parlor, sipping premium wines.

13540 Arnold Dr., Glen Ellen, CA 95442. ⓒ **800/935-0237** or 707/935-0237. Fax 707/935-6411. www.gaige.com. 15 units. Summer $250–$325 double, $375–$550 suite; winter $150–$325 double, $325–$550 suite. Rates include full breakfast and evening wines. AE, DC, DISC, MC, V. **Amenities:** Large heated pool; in-room massage. *In room:* A/C, TV, fax, dataport, hair dryer, iron, safe.

Inexpensive

Beltane Ranch ⭐ *(Finds* The word *ranch* conjures up a big ol' two-story house in the middle of hundreds of rolling acres, the kind of place where you laze away the day in a hammock watching the grass grow or pitching horseshoes in the garden. Well, friend, you can have all that and more at the Beltane Ranch, a century-old buttercup-yellow manor that's been everything from a bunkhouse to a brothel to a turkey farm. You simply can't help but feel your tensions ease away as you prop your feet up on the shady wraparound porch overlooking the vineyards, sipping a cool, fruity chardonnay while reading *Lonesome Dove* for the third time. Each room is uniquely decorated with American and European antiques; all have sitting areas and separate entrances. Innkeeper Deborah Mahoney serves a big country breakfast in the garden or on the porch overlooking the vineyards. For exercise, you can play tennis on the private court or hike the trails meandering through the 1,600-acre estate. *Tip:* Request one of the upstairs rooms, which have the best views.

11775 Sonoma Hwy. (Hwy. 12), Glen Ellen, CA 95442. ☎ **707/996-6501.** www.beltaneranch.com. 5 units, 1 cottage. $130–$180 double; cottage $220. Rates include full breakfast. No credit cards; personal checks accepted. **Amenities:** Tennis court. *In room:* No phone.

Glenelly Inn ★★   The Glenelly Inn is one of my favorite places to stay in the Wine Country. First off, the rates are reasonable, particularly when you factor in breakfast and afternoon snacks. More important, this former railroad inn, built in 1916, is positively drenched in serenity. Located well off the main highway on an oak-studded hillside, the peach-and-cream inn comes with everything you would expect from a country retreat. Long verandas offer comfy wicker chairs and views of the verdant Sonoma hillsides; a hearty country breakfast is served beside a large cobblestone fireplace; and bright, immaculate rooms contain old-fashioned claw-foot tubs, Scandinavian down comforters, and ceiling fans. The staff understands that it's the little things that make the difference. Hence the firm mattresses, good reading lights, and a simmering hot tub in a grapevine-and rose-covered arbor. All rooms, decorated with antiques and country furnishings, have queen beds, terry robes, and private entrances. Top picks are the Vallejo and Jack London cottages, both with large private patios, although I also like the rooms on the upper veranda—particularly in the spring, when the terraced gardens below are in full bloom.

5131 Warm Springs Rd. (off Arnold Dr.), Glen Ellen, CA 95442. ☎ **707/996-6720.** Fax 707/996-5227. www.glenelly.com. 8 units. $135–$190 double. Rates include full breakfast. MC, V.

KENWOOD
Very Expensive
Kenwood Inn & Spa ★★   Inspired by the villas of Tuscany, the Kenwood Inn's honey-colored Italian-style buildings, flower-filled flagstone courtyard, and pastoral views of vineyard-covered hills are enough to make any northern Italian homesick. But the friendly staff and luxuriously restful surrounds made this California girl feel right at home. What's not to like about a spacious room lavishly and exquisitely decorated with imported tapestries, velvets, and antiques plus a fireplace, balcony (except on the ground floor), feather bed, CD player, and down comforter? With no phone or TV in the rooms, relaxation is inevitable—especially if you book treatments at the spa, which gets creative with its rejuvinative program. A minor caveat is road noise, which you're unlikely to hear from your room, but can be slightly audible over the tranquil pumped-in music around the courtyard and decent-size pool.

An impressive two-course gourmet breakfast is served poolside or in the Mediterranean-style dining room. Mine consisted of a poached egg accompanied by light, flavorful potatoes, red bell peppers, and other roasted vegetables, all artfully arranged, followed by a delicious homemade scone with fresh berries, and a small lemon tart.

10400 Sonoma Hwy., Kenwood, CA 95452. ☎ **800/353-6966** or 707/833-1293. Fax 707/833-1247. www.kenwoodinn.com. 12 units. Apr–Oct $295–$475 double; Nov–Mar $265–$425 double. Rates include gourmet breakfast and bottle of wine. 2-night minimum on weekends Apr–Oct. AE, MC, V. **Amenities:** Heated outdoor pool; full-service spa; concierge. *In room:* CD player, hair dryer, iron, no phone.

WHERE TO DINE IN SONOMA VALLEY

The restaurants listed below are classified first by town, then by price, using the following categories: **Expensive,** dinner from $50 per person; **Moderate,** dinner from $35 per person; and **Inexpensive,** dinner from $20 per person. These categories reflect prices for an appetizer, a main course, a dessert, and a glass of wine.

SONOMA
Expensive

The Grill 𝒦𝒦 CALIFORNIA/SPA   The Mission Grill, one of the best-known restaurants in the Wine Country, has long suffered from a solid reputation for serving high-caliber spa cuisine. The problem, of course, is the word *spa,* which conjures up visions of blue-haired ladies eating boiled vegetables and soybean salads. Fortunately, the restaurant has found a solution: award-winning chef Toni Robertson. The former executive chef at the five-star Pan Pacific Hotel in Singapore has also done stints in South Africa, Maui, Beverly Hills, and Chicago. Her emphasis is on healthy, uncomplicated cuisine that relies on fresh ingredients and natural flavors. Typical selections from the seasonally changing menu range from lean medallions of ostrich served with a ragout of fingerling potatoes, artichokes, and dried tomatoes, to roasted sea bass with saffron fettuccine, to grilled Liberty duck breast in roasted plum sauce. Service is professional yet friendly, and the wine list is extensive and expensive.

At Sonoma Mission Inn, 18140 Sonoma Hwy., Sonoma. ✆ 707/938-9000. Reservations recommended. Main courses $22.50–$27. AE, DC, MC, V. Daily 6–9:30pm.

Moderate

Cafe La Haye 𝒦𝒦𝒦 ECLECTIC   Well-prepared, wholesome food, an experienced waitstaff, friendly owners, soothing atmosphere, and reasonable prices—including a modestly priced wine list—make La Haye a favorite. In truth, everything about this cafelike restaurant is charming. The atmosphere within the small split-level dining room pleasantly decorated with hardwood floors, an exposed-beam ceiling, and revolving contemporary artwork, is smart and intimate. The vibe is small-business—a welcome departure from Napa Valley's big-business restaurants. The straightforward seasonally inspired cuisine, which chefs bring forth from the tiny open kitchen, is delicious and wonderfully well priced. Although the menu is small, it offers just enough options. Expect a risotto special, pasta such as fresh tagliarini with butternut squash, proscuitto, sage, and garlic cream and pan-roasted chicken breast, perhaps with goat cheese-herb stuffing caramelized shallot jus and fennel mashed potatoes. Meat eaters are sure to be pleased with filet of beef seared with black pepper-lavender sauce and served with gorgonzola-potato gratin, and no one can resist the creative salads. Sunday brunch includes a handful of creative breakfast dishes, such as white cheddar grits with grilled ham, poached egg, and cracked pepper hollandaise, as well as salads and sandwiches.

140 E. Napa St., Sonoma. ✆ 707/935-5994. Reservations recommended. Main courses $12–$20. MC, V. Tues–Sat 5:30–9pm; Sun brunch 9:30am–2pm.

Depot Hotel—Cucina Rustica Restaurant 𝒦 NORTHERN ITALIAN
Michael Ghilarducci has been the chef and owner here for 14 years, which means he's either independently wealthy or a darn good cook. Fortunately, it's the latter. A block north of the plaza in a handsome 1870 stone building, the Depot Hotel offers pleasant outdoor dining in an Italian garden complete with

a reflecting pool and cascading Roman fountain. The menu is unwaveringly Italian, featuring classic dishes such as spaghetti bolognese and veal alla parmigiana. Start with the bounteous antipasto misto, and end the feast with a dish of Michael's handmade Italian ice cream and fresh-fruit sorbets.

241 First St. W. (off Spain St.), Sonoma. ✆ 707/938-2980. www.depothotel.com. Reservations recommended. Main courses $17–$20. AE, DISC, MC, V. Wed–Fri 11:30am–5pm; Wed–Sun 5–close.

The Girl & The Fig ★★ COUNTRY FRENCH   Already well established in its new downtown Sonoma digs (it used to be in Glen Ellen), this modern, attractive, and cozy eatery, with lovely patio seating, is the new home for Sondra Bernstein's (The Girl) beloved restaurant. Here the cuisine is nouveau country with French nuances, and yes, figs are sure to be on the menu in one form or another. The wonderful winter fig salad contains arugula, pecans, dried figs, Laura Chenel goat cheese, and fig-and-port vinaigrette. Toulze uses garden-fresh produce and local meats, poultry, and fish whenever possible, in dishes such as pork tenderloin with a potato-leek pancake and roasted beets, and sea scallops with lobster-scented risotto. For dessert, try the warm pear galette topped with gingered crème fraîche, a glass of Quady Essensia Orange Muscat, and a sliver of raclette from the cheese cart. Sondra knows her wines, and will be happy to choose the best accompaniment to your meal.

110 West Spain St. ✆ 707/938-3634. www.thegirlandthefig.com. Reservations recommended. Main courses $12–$19. AE, MC, V. Daily 11:30am–11pm.

Maya ★★ MEXICAN   Gourmet Mexican might be the best way to describe the food at this lively grill-and-rotisserie restaurant on the southeast corner of Sonoma's plaza. We're not talking top-shelf enchiladas here—rather, it's a winning combination of traditional Yucatán dishes prepared with ultra-fresh ingredients. Take salmon for instance: a thick cut of fresh salmon, perfectly cooked with pasilla pesto, chervil and tarragon risotto, and a medley of root vegetables. The commendable Maya pollo rostizado—a spit-roasted half chicken with a Yucatán spice rub—could easily feed two. Other menu items I considered seriously included smoked duck salad with goat cheese, seasoned walnuts, and blood orange vinaigrette and grilled pork loin with apple chutney, chive potato cake, and Swiss chard. Yes, you're probably going to pay a bit more than you planned to pay for Mexican food, but it's worth the extra few dollars. You are likely to enjoy the faux Mayan village ambience as well: desert earth tones with bright splashes of colorful art and thick, hand-carved wood furnishings. The only caveat is the *muy fuerte* noise level, but a couple of fantastic margaritas on the rocks, and you'll soon be in fiesta mode yourself.

101 E. Napa St., Sonoma. ✆ 707/935-3500. Reservations recommended. Main courses $10.50–$19.50. MC, V. Mon–Sat 11:45am–9:45pm; Sun 4–9pm; closed Monday Jan–Apr.

Meritage ★★ SOUTHERN FRENCH/NORTHERN ITALIAN   Learning from the previous occupants' mistakes—that Sonoma ain't New York City and shouldn't treat its customers that way—chef-owner Carlo Cavallo has eliminated the big-city attitude and prices at his new restaurant without diminishing style, service, and quality. The former executive chef for Giorgio Armani, Cavallo combines the best of southern French and northern Italian cuisines (hence "Meritage," after a blend made with traditional Bordeaux varieties), giving Sonomans yet another reason to eat out. The menu, which changes twice daily, is a good read: handmade roasted pumpkin tortellini in Parmesan cheese sauce; napoleon of escargot in Champagne and wild thyme sauce; organic greens, strawberries, corn, and French feta salad; wild boar chops in white truffle sauce with mashed potatoes. New additions include an oyster raw bar, lovely garden patio, breakfast, and a soon-to-launch take-out deli and marketplace. Such edible enticement—combined with reasonable prices, excellent service, a stellar wine list, cozy booth seating, a handsome dining room, and Carlo's practiced charm—make Meritage one of the most exciting new restaurants in the Wine Country.

522 Broadway, Sonoma. (℃ 707/938-9430. www.sonomameritage.com. Reservations recommended. Main courses $13–$19. AE, MC, V. Wed–Mon 7:30am–9pm.

Piatti ✿ ITALIAN   Part of a northern California chain that originated in Napa, Piatti built a steadfast clientele by consistently serving large portions of good Italian food at fair prices in a festive setting. The restaurant occupies the ground floor of the El Dorado Hotel at the northwest corner of Sonoma Plaza (just follow your nose). Good pizzas and braised meats—such as fine lamb shank flavored with rich port-wine sauce and fresh mint—emerge from a wood-burning oven. A favorite in the array of satisfying pastas is cannelloni stuffed with roasted veal, spinach, porcini mushrooms, and ricotta. Other recom-mended dishes include a wonderful roast-vegetable appetizer, a pile of fresh mussels in tomato-and-herb broth, rotisserie chicken with garlic mashed pota-toes, and veal scaloppini. Granted, there are fancier and more intimate restau-rants in the valley, but none that combine quality and value this deftly. If the sun is out, ask for a courtyard table.

405 First St. W., Sonoma. (℃ 707/996-2351. Reservations recommended. Main courses $10–$19. AE, DC, MC, V. Sun–Thurs 11:30am–10pm; Fri–Sat 11:30am–11pm.

Inexpensive

Cucina Viansa ✿✿ ITALIAN DELI   When it comes to picnic fare, Cucina Viansa is the sexiest thing going in Sonoma. Sam and Vicki Sebastiani, who also run Viansa Winery, own the suave deli and wine bar. This Mecca for to-go goods is a visual masterpiece, with shiny black-and-white-checked flooring, long coun-ters of Italian marble, and track lighting. Start by sampling the preserves and jams near the entrance, then choose from the cured meats, cheese, fruit, pastas, salads, and breads lining the deli. Popular choices are hefty sandwiches on herbed focaccia bread and herb-marinated rotisserie chickens served by the half with your choice of pasta or salad. Roasted turkey, duck, pork, lamb, and rabbit also are available. Opposite the deli is the wine bar, featuring all of Viansa's current releases for both tasting and purchase, as well as a small selection of microbrewed beers on tap. On your way out, stop at the gelateria and treat your-self to some intense Italian ice cream. *Note:* Cucina Viansa schedules live jazz bands every Friday and Saturday from 6 to 11pm.

400 First St. E., Sonoma. (℃ 707/935-5656. Deli items $5–$9. AE, DISC, MC, V. Sun–Thurs 10am–6pm; Fri–Sat 10am–11pm.

Della Santina's ✿✿ ITALIAN   Those of you who just can't swallow another expensive, chi-chi California meal should follow the locals to this friendly, tra-ditional Italian restaurant. How traditional? Just ask father-and-son team Dan and Robert: When I last dined here, they pointed out Signora Santina's hand-embroidered linen doilies as they proudly told me about her Tuscan recipes. (Heck, even the dining room looks like an old-fashioned, elegant Italian living room.) And their pride is merited: Every dish my party tried was refreshingly authentic and well flavored, without overbearing sauces or one *hint* of Califor-nia pretentiousness. Be sure to start with traditional antipasti, especially sliced mozzarella and tomatoes, or delicious white beans. The nine pasta dishes are, again, wonderfully authentic (gnocchi lovers, rejoice!). The spit-roasted meat dishes are a local favorite (although I found them a bit overcooked); for those who can't choose between chicken, pork, turkey, rabbit, or duck, there's a selection that offers a choice of three. Don't worry about breaking your bank on a bottle of wine, because most of the choices go for under $25. Portions are huge, but save room for a wonderful dessert.

133 E. Napa St. (just east of the square), Sonoma. ℂ 707/935-0576. Reservations recommended. Main courses $9–$15. AE, DISC, MC, V. Daily 11:30am–3pm and 5pm–9:30pm.

GLEN ELLEN

Glen Ellen Inn Restaurant ⊛ CALIFORNIA   Christian and Karen
Bertrand have made this room so quaint and cozy that you feel as if you're dining in their home, and that's exactly the place's charm. Garden seating is the favored choice on sunny days, but the covered, heated patio is always welcoming. First courses from Christian's open kitchen might include a wild-mushroom-and-sausage purse served in brandy cream sauce, or warm goat-cheese croquettes. Main courses, which change with the seasons, range from linguine with artichoke hearts and feta to stellar late-harvest ravioli stuffed with pumpkin, walnuts, and sun-dried cranberries on a bed of butternut squash. Other favorites include marinated pork tenderloin on smoked mozzarella polenta, topped with roasted pepper–onion compote, and utterly tender Nebraska corn-fed filet mignon in a foie gras–brandy reduction sauce. On my last visit, the Sonoma Valley mixed green salad, seared ahi tuna, and homemade French vanilla ice cream floating in bittersweet caramel sauce made a lovely meal. The 350-selection wine list offers numerous bottles from Sonoma, as well as more than a dozen wines by the glass. *Tip:* There's a small parking lot behind the restaurant.

13670 Arnold Dr., Glen Ellen. ℂ 707/996-6409. www.glenelleninn.com. Reservations recommended. Main courses $12–$22. AE, MC, V. From 5:30–9:30pm. Closed Mon–Thur last week in Jan.

KENWOOD

Kenwood Restaurant & Bar ⊛⊛ CALIFORNIA/CONTINENTAL   This is
what Wine Country dining should be—but often, disappointingly, is not. From the terrace of the Kenwood Restaurant, diners enjoy a view of the vineyards set against Sugarloaf Ridge as they imbibe Sonoma's finest at umbrella-covered tables. On nippy days, you can retreat inside to the Sonoma-style roadhouse, with shiny wood floors, pine ceiling, vibrant artwork, and cushioned rattan chairs at white-cloth–covered tables. Regardless of where you pull up a chair, expect first-rate cuisine, perfectly balanced between tradition and innovation, and comple-mented by a reasonably priced wine list. Great starters are Dungeness crab cake with herb mayonnaise; superfresh sashimi with ginger, soy, and wasabi; and wonderful Caesar salad. Main-dish choices might include poached salmon in creamy caper sauce, prawns with saffron Pernod sauce, or braised Sonoma rabbit with grilled polenta. But the Kenwood doesn't take itself too seriously: Great sandwiches and burgers are available.

9900 Sonoma Hwy., Kenwood. ℂ 707/833-6326. Reservations recommended. Main courses $13–$26. MC, V. Tues–Sun 11:30am–9pm.

Appendix A:
San Francisco in Depth

Born as an out-of-the-way backwater of colonial Spain and blessed with a harbor that would have been the envy of any of the great cities of Europe, San Francisco boasts a story as varied as the millions of people who have passed through its "Golden Gate," a strait linking the San Francisco Bay to the Pacific Ocean. It was not named for the gold rush; rather, Col. John C. Fremont named it in 1848 after "Chrysoceras" or "Golden Horn," in Constantinople.

THE AGE OF DISCOVERY

After Columbus "discovered" the New World in 1492, legends of the fertile land of California were discussed in the universities and taverns of Europe, even though no one really understood where the mythical land was. (Some evidence of arrivals in California by Chinese merchants hundreds of years before Columbus's landing has been unearthed, although few scholars are willing to draw definite conclusions.) The first documented visit by a European to northern California was by the Portuguese explorer Juan Rodriguez Cabrillo, who circumnavigated the southern tip of South America as far north as the Russian River in 1542. Nearly 40 years later, in 1579, Sir Francis Drake landed on the northern California coast, stopping for a time to repair his ships and to claim the territory for Queen Elizabeth of England. Another Portuguese, Sebastian Cermeño, "discovered" Punta de los Reyes (King's Point) in the mid-1590s. All three adventurers completely missed the narrow entrance to San Francisco Bay, either because it was enshrouded in fog or, more likely, because they simply weren't looking for it. Believe it or not, the bay's entrance is nearly impossible to see from the open ocean.

Two more centuries passed before a European actually saw the bay that would later extend Spain's influence

Dateline

- 1542 Juan Rodriguez Cabrillo sails up the California coast.
- 1579 Sir Francis Drake lands near San Francisco, missing the entrance to the bay.
- 1769 Members of the Spanish expedition led by Gaspar de Portolá become the first Europeans to see San Francisco Bay.
- 1775 The *San Carlos* is the first European ship to sail into San Francisco Bay.
- 1776 Captain Juan Bautista de Anza establishes a presidio (military fort); San Francisco de Asis Mission opens.
- 1821 Mexico wins independence from Spain and annexes California.
- 1835 The town of Yerba Buena develops around the port; the United States tries unsuccessfully to purchase San Francisco Bay from Mexico.
- 1846–1848 War between the United States and Mexico.
- 1847 Americans annex Yerba Buena and rename it San Francisco.
- 1848 Gold is discovered in Coloma, near Sacramento. San Francisco's population swells from about 900 to 26,000.
- 1851 Lawlessness becomes acute before attempts to curb it.
- 1869 The transcontinental railroad reaches San Francisco.
- 1873 Andrew S. Hallidie invents the cable car.
- 1906 The Great Earthquake strikes, and the resulting fire levels the city.

continues

over much of the American West. Gaspar de Portolá, a soldier sent from Spain to meddle in a rather ugly conflict between the Jesuits and the Franciscans, accidentally stumbled upon the bay in 1769, en route to somewhere else. He stoically plodded on to his original destination, Monterey Bay, more than 100 miles to the south. Six years later, Juan Ayala actually sailed into San Francisco Bay while on a mapping expedition for the Spanish and immediately realized the enormous strategic importance of his find.

Colonization quickly followed. Juan Bautista de Anza and around 30 Spanish-speaking families marched through the deserts from Sonora, Mexico, arriving after many hardships at the northern tip of modern-day San Francisco in June 1776. They immediately claimed the peninsula for Spain. (Their claim of allegiance to Spain occurred only about a week before the 13 English-speaking colonies of North America's Eastern seaboard, a continent away, declared their independence from Britain.) Their headquarters was an adobe fortress, the Presidio, built on the site of today's park with the same name. The settlers' church, a mile to the south, was the first of five Spanish missions later developed around the edges of San Francisco Bay. Although the name of the church was officially *Nuestra Señora de Dolores,* it was dedicated to St. Francis of Assisi and nicknamed San Francisco by the Franciscan priests. Later, the name applied to the entire bay.

In 1821, Mexico broke away from Spain, secularized the Spanish missions, and abandoned all interest in the natives. Freed of Spanish restrictions, California's ports suddenly opened to trade. The region around San Francisco Bay supplied large amounts of hides and tallow for transport around Cape Horn to the tanneries and factories of New England and New York. The prospects for prosperity persuaded an English-born sailor, William Richardson, to jump ship in 1822 and settle on the site of what is now San Francisco. To impress the commandant of the Presidio, whose daughter he loved, Richardson converted to

- **1915** The Panama-Pacific International Exposition celebrates San Francisco's restoration and the completion of the Panama Canal.
- **1936** The Bay Bridge is completed.
- **1937** The Golden Gate Bridge is completed.
- **1945** The United Nations Charter is drafted in San Francisco and adopted by the representatives of 50 countries.
- **1950** The Beat Generation moves into the bars and cafes of North Beach.
- **1967** A free concert in Golden Gate Park attracts 20,000 people, ushering in the Summer of Love and the hippie era.
- **1974** BART's high-speed transit system opens the tunnel linking San Francisco with the East Bay.
- **1978** Harvey Milk, a city supervisor and America's first openly gay politician, is assassinated, along with Mayor George Moscone, by political rival Dan White.
- **1989** An earthquake registering 7.1 on the Richter scale hits San Francisco just before a World Series baseball game, as 100 million watch on TV; the city quickly rebuilds.
- **1991** Fire rages through the Berkeley and Oakland hills, destroying 2,800 homes.
- **1993** Yerba Buena Center for the Arts opens.
- **1995** The new San Francisco MOMA opens.
- **1996** Former Assembly Speaker Willie Brown is elected mayor of San Francisco.
- **1998** El Niño deluges San Francisco with its second-highest rainfall in history.
- **2000** Pacific Bell Park opens as the new home of the San Francisco Giants baseball team with an exhibition against the Milwaukee Brewers.

Catholicism and established the beginnings of what would soon became a thriving trading post and colony. Richard named his trading post Yerba Buena (or "good herb") because of a species of wild mint that grew there, near the site of today's Montgomery Street. (The city's original name was recalled with endless mirth 120 years later, during San Francisco's hippie era.) He conducted a profitable hide-trading business and eventually became harbormaster and the city's first merchant prince. By 1839, the place was a veritable town, with a mostly English-speaking populace and a saloon of dubious virtue.

Throughout the 19th century, armed hostilities between English-speaking settlers from the Eastern seaboard and the Spanish-speaking colonies of Spain and Mexico erupted in places as widely scattered as Texas, Puerto Rico, and along the frequently shifting U.S.–Mexico border. In 1846, a group of U.S. Marines from the warship *Portsmouth* seized the sleepy main plaza of Yerba Buena, ran the U.S. flag up a pole, and declared California an American territory. The Presidio (occupied by about a dozen unmotivated Mexican soldiers) surrendered without a fuss. The first move the new, mostly Yankee citizenry made was to officially adopt the name of the bay as the name of their town.

THE GOLD RUSH

The year 1848 was one of the most pivotal in European history, with unrest sweeping through Europe, horrendous poverty in Ireland, and widespread disillusionment about hopes for prosperity throughout Europe and the East Coast of the United States. Stories about the golden port of San Francisco and the agrarian wealth of the American West filtered slowly east, attracting slow-moving groups of settlers. Ex-sailor Richard Henry Dana extolled the virtues of California in his best-selling novel, *Two Years Before the Mast,* and helped fire the public's imagination about the territory's bounty, particularly that of the Bay Area.

The first overland party crossed the Sierra and arrived in California in 1841. San Francisco grew steadily, reaching a population of approximately 900 by April 1848, but nothing hinted at the population explosion that was to follow. Historian Barry Parr has referred to the California gold rush as the most extraordinary event to ever befall an American city in peacetime. Even without the lure of gold, San Francisco's winning combination of raw materials, healthful climate, and freedom would eventually have attracted thousands of settlers. But the gleam of the soft metal is said to have compressed 50 years of normal growth into less than six months. In 1848, the year gold was discovered, the population of San Francisco jumped from under 1,000 to 26,000. As many as 100,000 more passed through San Francisco in the space of less than a year on their way to the rocky hinterlands where the gold was rumored to be.

If not for the discovery of some small particles of gold at a sawmill that he owned, Swiss-born John Augustus Sutter would have left a far less flamboyant legacy. Despite Sutter's wish to keep the discovery quiet, his employee, John Marshall, leaked word of the discovery to friends. It eventually appeared in local papers, and smart investors on the East Coast took immediate heed. The rush did not start, however, until Sam Brannan, a Mormon preacher and famous charlatan, ran through the streets of San Francisco shouting, "Gold! Gold in the American River!" (Brannan, incidentally, bought up all the harborfront real estate he could and cornered the market on shovels, pickaxes, and canned food just before making the announcement that was heard around the world.)

A world on the brink of change responded almost frantically. The gold rush was on. Shop owners hung GONE TO THE DIGGINGS signs in their windows. Flotillas of ships set sail from ports throughout Europe, South America, Australia, and the East Coast, sometimes nearly sinking with the weight of mining equipment. Townspeople from the Midwest headed overland, and the sociology of a nation was transformed almost overnight. Not since the Crusades of the Middle Ages had so many people mobilized in so short a time. Daily business stopped; ships arrived in San Francisco, and their crews almost immediately deserted. News of the gold strike spread like a plague through every discontented hamlet in the known world.

Although other settlements were closer to the gold strike, San Francisco was the famous name and, therefore, where the gold-diggers disembarked. Tent cities sprang up, and demand for virtually everything skyrocketed. Although some miners actually found gold, smart merchants quickly discovered more enduring business in servicing the needs of the thousands of miners who arrived ill-equipped and ignorant of the lay of the land. Prices soared. Miners, faced with staggeringly inflated prices for goods and services, barely turned a profit after expenses. Most prospectors failed, many died of hardship, and others committed suicide, at the alarming rate of 1,000 a year. Yet despite the tragedies, graft, and vice associated with the gold rush, within mere months, San Francisco was forever transformed from a tranquil Spanish settlement into a roaring, boisterous boomtown.

BOOMTOWN FEVER

By 1855, most of California's surface gold had already been panned out, leaving only the richer but deeper veins of ore, which individual miners couldn't retrieve without massive capital investments. Despite that, San Francisco had evolved into a vast commercial magnet, sucking into its warehouses and banks the staggering riches that overworked newcomers had dragged, ripped, and distilled from the rocks, fields, and forests of western North America.

Investment funds poured into more than mining, however. Speculation on the newly established San Francisco stock exchange could make or destroy an investor in a single day, and several noteworthy writers (including Mark Twain) were among the young men forever influenced by the boomtown spirit. The American Civil War left California firmly in the Union camp, ready, willing, and able to receive hordes of disillusioned soldiers fed up with the internecine warmongering of the Eastern seaboard. In 1869, the transcontinental railway linked the Eastern and Western seaboards of the United States, ensuring the fortunes of the barons who controlled it. The railways shifted economic power bases, however, as cheap manufactured goods from the East undercut the costly articles that sailed or steamed around the tip of South America. The "Big Four"—iron-willed capitalists Leland Stanford, Mark Hopkins, Collis P. Huntington, and Charles Crocker—almost completely controlled ownership of the newly formed Central Pacific and Southern Pacific railroads, and their ruthlessness was legendary. (Much of the bone-crushing railway labor was done by low-paid Chinese newcomers, most of whom arrived in overcrowded ships at San Francisco ports.) As the 19th century came to a close, civil unrest became more frequent as the monopolistic grip of the railways and robber barons became more obvious. Adding to the discontent were the uncounted thousands of Chinese immigrants who fled starvation and unrest in Asia at rates rivaling those of the Italians, Poles, Irish, and British.

During the 1870s, the flood of profits from the Comstock Lode in western Nevada diminished to a trickle, a cycle of droughts wiped out part of California's agricultural bounty, and local industry struggled to survive against the flood of manufactured goods coming by rail from well-established East Coast and Midwestern factories. Often, discontented workers blamed their woes on the now-unwanted hordes of Chinese workers, who by preference and for mutual protection had congregated in teeming all-Asian communities.

Despite these downward cycles, the city enjoyed other bouts of prosperity around the turn of the century, thanks to the Klondike gold rush in Alaska and the Spanish-American War. Long accustomed to making a buck off gold fever, San Francisco managed to position itself as a point of embarkation for supplies bound for Alaska. Also during this time, the Bank of America emerged; it eventually grew into the largest bank in the world. Founded in North Beach in 1904, the bank was the brainchild of Italian-born A. P. Giannini, who later funded part of the construction for a bridge that many critics said was preposterous: the Golden Gate.

THE GREAT FIRE

On the morning of April 18, 1906, San Francisco changed for all time. The city has never experienced an earthquake as destructive as the one that hit at 5:13am; scientists estimate its strength at 8.1 on the Richter scale. All but a handful of the city's 400,000 inhabitants lay fast asleep when the ground went into a series of convulsions. As one eyewitness put it, "The earth was shaking . . . it was undulating, rolling like an ocean breaker." The quake ruptured every water main in the city and simultaneously started a chain of fires that rapidly fused into one gigantic conflagration. The fire brigades were helpless, and for 3 days San Francisco burned.

Militia troops finally stopped the flames from advancing by dynamiting entire city blocks, but not before more than 28,000 buildings lay in ruins. Minor tremors lasted another 3 days. The final damage stretched across a path of destruction 450 miles long and 50 miles wide. In all, 497 city blocks, or about one-third of the city, were razed. As Jack London wrote in a heartrending newspaper dispatch, "The city of San Francisco is no more." The earthquake and subsequent fire so decisively changed the city that post-1906 San Francisco bears little resemblance to the town before the quake. Out of the ashes rose a bigger, healthier, and more beautiful town, although latter-day urbanologists regret that the rebuilding that followed the San Francisco earthquake did not follow a more enlightened plan. So eager was the city to rebuild that the old, somewhat unimaginative gridiron plan was reinstated, despite the opportunities for more daring visions that the quake's aftermath afforded.

In 1915, in celebration of the opening of the Panama Canal and to prove to the world that San Francisco was restored to its full glory, the city was host to the Panama-Pacific International Exhibition, a world's fair that exposed hundreds of thousands of visitors to the city's unique charms. The frenzy of boosterism, however, reached its peak during the years just before World War I, when investments and civic pride might have reached an all-time high. Despite Prohibition, speakeasies in and around the city did a thriving business, and building sprees were as high-blown and lavish as the profits on the San Francisco stock exchange.

THE GREAT DEPRESSION & WORLD WAR II

The Great Depression hit San Francisco as it did the rest of the country. To alleviate some of the sting was the federal government's Works Progress Administration (WPA) program, which in the late 1930s provided work for artists during lean years. It not only supplied local artists with funds to create public murals, many of which still exist today and can be viewed at Coit Tower and Golden Gate Park's Beach Chalet, but also documented San Francisco culture and landscape as well as provided citizens with at least a few pictures that were prettier than the then-current state of affairs.

The Japanese attack on Pearl Harbor on December 7, 1941, mobilized the United States into a massive war machine, with many shipyards strategically positioned along the Pacific Coast, including San Francisco. Within less than a year, several shipyards were producing up to one new warship per day, employing hundreds of thousands of people working around the clock. (The largest, Kaiser Shipyards in Richmond, employed more than 100,000 workers.) In search of work and the excitement of life away from their villages and cornfields, workers flooded into the city from virtually everywhere, forcing an enormous boom in housing. Hundreds found themselves separated from their small towns for the first time in their lives and reveled in their newfound freedom.

After the hostilities ended, many soldiers remembered San Francisco as the site of their finest hours and returned to live there permanently. The economic prosperity of the postwar years enabled massive enlargements of the city, including freeways, housing developments, a booming financial district, and pockets of counterculture enthusiasts, such as the beatniks, gays, and hippies.

THE 1950S: THE BEATS

San Francisco's reputation as a rollicking place where anything goes dates from the Barbary Coast days when gang warfare, prostitution, gambling, and drinking were major pursuits, and citizens took law and order into their own hands. Its more modern role as a catalyst for social change and the avant-garde began in the 1950s. A group of young writers, philosophers, and poets challenged the materialism and conformity of American society by embracing anarchy and Eastern philosophy, expressing their notions in poetry. They adopted a uniform of jeans, sweater, sandals, and beret, called themselves "Beats," and hung out in North Beach, where rents were low and cheap wine was plentiful. *San Francisco Chronicle* columnist Herb Caen, to whom they were totally alien, dubbed them "beatniks" in his column.

Allen Ginsberg, Gregory Corso, and Jack Kerouac had begun writing at Columbia University in New York, but it wasn't until they came west and hooked up with Lawrence Ferlinghetti, Kenneth Rexroth, Gary Snyder, and others that the movement gained national attention. The bible of the Beats was Ginsberg's "Howl," which he first read at the Six Gallery on October 13, 1955. By the time he finished reading, Ginsberg was crying, the audience was chanting, and his fellow poets were announcing the arrival of an epic bard. Ferlinghetti published "Howl," which was deemed obscene, in 1956. A trial followed, but the court found that the poem had redeeming social value, reaffirming the right of free expression. Another major Beat work, Kerouac's *On the Road*, was published in 1957 and instantly became a best seller. (He had written it as one long paragraph in 20 days in 1951.) The freedom and sense of possibility the book conveyed became the bellwether for a generation.

While the Beats gave poetry readings and generated controversy, two clubs in North Beach were making waves, notably the hungry i and the Purple Onion, where everyone who was anyone or became anyone on the entertainment scene appeared. Mort Sahl, Dick Gregory, Lenny Bruce, Barbra Streisand, and Woody

Allen all worked there. Maya Angelou appeared as a singer and dancer at the Purple Onion. The cafes of North Beach—the Black Cat, Vesuvio's, Caffè Trieste, Caffè Tosca, and Enrico's Sidewalk Cafe—were the center of bohemian life in the '50s. When the tour buses started rolling in, rents went up, and Broadway became a sex-club strip in the early 1960s. Thus ended an era, and the Beats moved on. The alternative scene shifted to Berkeley and the Haight.

THE 1960S: THE HAIGHT

The torch of freedom passed from the Beats and North Beach to the hippies and Haight-Ashbury, but it was a radically different torch. The hippies replaced the Beats' angst, anarchy, negativism, nihilism, alcohol, and poetry with love, communalism, openness, drugs, rock music, and a back-to-nature philosophy. Although the scent of marijuana wafted everywhere—on the streets, in the cafes, in Golden Gate Park—the real drugs of choice were LSD (a tab of good acid cost $5) and other hallucinogenics. Timothy Leary experimented with its effects and exhorted youth to "turn on, tune in, and drop out." Instead of hanging out in coffeehouses, the hippies went to concerts at the Fillmore or the Avalon Ballroom to dance. The first Family Dog Rock 'n' Roll Dance and Concert, "A Tribute to Dr. Strange," was at the Longshoreman's Hall in 1965. It featured Jefferson Airplane, the Marbles, the Great Society, and the Charlatans. At the event, the first major happening of the 1960s, Ginsberg led a snake dance through the crowd. In January 1966, Longshoreman's Hall was the site of the 3-day Trips Festival, organized by rock promoter Bill Graham. The climax came with Ken Kesey and the Merry Pranksters Acid Test show, which used five movie screens, psychedelic visions, and the sounds of the Grateful Dead and Big Brother and the Holding Company. The "be-in" followed in the summer of 1966 at the polo grounds in Golden Gate Park, when an estimated 20,000 heard Jefferson Airplane perform and Ginsberg chant, while the Hell's Angels acted as unofficial police. During the Summer of Love, in 1967, thousands of young people streamed into the city in search of drugs and sex.

The '60s Haight scene was very different from the '50s Beat scene. The hippies were much younger than the Beats had been, constituting the first youth movement to take over the nation. (They also became the first generation of young, independent, and moneyed consumers to be courted by corporations.) Ultimately, the Haight and the hippie movement deteriorated from love and flowers into drugs and crime, drawing a fringe of crazies like Charles Manson and leaving only a legacy of sex, drugs, violence, and consumerism. As early as October 1967, the "Diggers," who had opened a free shop and soup kitchen in the Haight, symbolically buried the dream in a clay casket in Buena Vista Park.

The end of the Vietnam War and the resignation of President Nixon took the edge off politics. The last fling of the mentality that had driven the 1960s occurred in 1974, when the Symbionese Liberation Army kidnapped newspaper heiress Patty Hearst from her Berkeley apartment and took her on a bank-robbing spree before surrendering in San Francisco.

THE 1970S & 1980S: GAY RIGHTS

The homosexual community in San Francisco developed at the end of World War II, when thousands of military personnel returned to the United States via San Francisco. A substantial number of those men were homosexual and decided to stay in the city. A gay community grew up along Polk Street between Sutter and California. Later, the larger community moved into The Castro, where it remains today.

The gay political-protest movement is usually dated from the 1969 Stonewall raid in Greenwich Village. Although the political movement started in New York, California had already given birth to two major organizations for gay rights: the Mattachine Society, founded in 1951 by Henry Hay in Los Angeles, and the Daughters of Bilitis, a lesbian organization founded in 1955 in San Francisco.

After Stonewall, the Committee for Homosexual Freedom was created in the spring of 1969 in San Francisco; a Gay Liberation Front chapter was organized at Berkeley. In the fall of 1969, Robert Patterson, a columnist for the *San Francisco Examiner,* referred to homosexuals as "semi males," "drag darlings," and "women who aren't exactly women." On October 31 at noon, a group began a peaceful picket of the *Examiner.* Peace reigned until someone threw a bag of printer's ink from an *Examiner* window. Someone wrote "Fuck the Examiner" on the wall, and the police moved in to clear the crowd, clubbing as they went. The remaining picketers retreated to Glide Methodist Church, then marched on city hall. Unfortunately, the mayor was away. Unable to air their grievances, they started a sit-in that lasted until 5pm, when they were ordered to leave. Most did, but three remained and were arrested.

Later that year at an anti-Thanksgiving rally, gays protested against several national and local businesses: Western and Delta airlines (the former for firing lesbian stewardesses, the latter for refusing to sell a ticket to a young man wearing a Gay Power button); radio station KFOG, for its anti-homosexual broadcasting; and some local gay bars for exploitation. On May 14, 1970, a group of gay and women's liberationists invaded the convention of the American Psychiatric Association in San Francisco to protest the reading of a paper on aversion therapy for homosexuals, forcing the meeting to adjourn.

The rage against intolerance was appearing on all fronts. At the National Gay Liberation conference in August 1970 in the city, Charles Thorp, chairman of the San Francisco State Liberation Front, called for militancy and issued a challenge to come out with a rallying cry of "Blatant is beautiful." He also argued for the use of what he felt was the more positive, celebratory term *gay* instead of *homosexual,* and decried the fact that homosexuals were kept in their place at the three Bs: the bars, the beaches, and the baths. As the movement grew in size and power, debates on strategy and tactics occurred, most dramatically between those who wanted to withdraw into separate ghettos and those who wanted to enter mainstream society. The most extreme proposal was made in California by Don Jackson, who suggested establishing a gay territory in California's Alpine County, about 10 miles south of Lake Tahoe. It would have had a totally gay administration, civil service, university, museum—everything. The residents of Alpine County were not pleased with the proposal. But before the situation turned really ugly, Jackson's idea was abandoned because of lack of support in the gay community. In the end, the movement concentrated on integration and civil rights, not separatism. Gays would elect politicians who were sympathetic to their cause and celebrate their new identity by establishing National Gay Celebration Day and Gay Pride Week, the first of which was celebrated in June 1970, when 1,000 to 2,000 marched in New York, 1,000 in Los Angeles, and a few hundred in San Francisco.

By the mid-1970s, the gay community craved a more central role in city politics. Harvey Milk, owner of a camera store in The Castro, decided to run for the board of supervisors. He won, becoming the first openly gay person to hold a major public office. He and liberal Mayor George Moscone developed a gay rights agenda, but in 1978 they were both shot and killed by former Supervisor Dan White, after Moscone refused his request for reinstatement. White, a former police officer, had consistently opposed Milk's and Moscone's more liberal policies. At his trial, White successfully pleaded temporary insanity caused by additives in his fast-food diet. The media dubbed it the "Twinkie defense," but the murder charges against White were reduced to manslaughter. On that day, angry and grieving, the gay community rioted, overturning and burning police cars in a night of rage. To this day, a candlelight memorial parade is held on November 27. Milk's martyrdom was both a political and a practical inspiration to gay candidates across the country.

The emphasis in the gay movement shifted abruptly in the 1980s, when the AIDS epidemic struck the community. AIDS has had a dramatic impact on the Castro. While it's still a thriving and lively community, it's no longer the constant party it once was. The hedonistic lifestyle that had played out in the discos, bars, baths, and streets changed as the seriousness of the epidemic sunk in and the number of deaths increased. Political efforts have shifted away from enfranchisement and toward demanding money for social services and research money to deal with the AIDS crisis. The gay community has developed its own organizations, such as Project Inform and Gay Men's Health Crisis, to publicize information about the disease, available treatments, and safe sex.

THE BIG ONE, PART TWO

Compared to previous decades, the 1980s may have arrived in San Francisco with a whimper, but they went out with quite a bang. At 5:04pm on Tuesday, October 17, 1989, as more than 62,000 fans filled Candlestick Park for the third game of the World Series—and the Bay Area commute moved into its heaviest flow—an earthquake of magnitude 7.1 struck. Within the next 20 seconds, 63 lives were lost, $10 billion in damage occurred, and the entire Bay Area community was reminded of its humble insignificance. Centered about 60 miles south of San Francisco in the Forest of Nisene Marks, the deadly temblor was felt as far away as San Diego and Nevada.

Although scientists had predicted an earthquake would hit on this section of the San Andreas Fault, certain structures built to withstand such an earthquake failed miserably. The most catastrophic event was the collapse of the elevated Cypress Street section of Interstate 880 in Oakland, where the upper level of the freeway pancaked the lower level, crushing everything with such force that cars were reduced to inches. Other heavily damaged structures included the San Francisco–Oakland Bay Bridge, shut down for months when a section of the roadbed collapsed; San Francisco's Marina District, where several multimillion-dollar homes collapsed on their weak, shifting bases of landfill and sand; and the Pacific Garden Mall in Santa Cruz, which was devastated.

President Bush declared the seven hardest-hit counties a disaster area; at least 3,700 people were reported injured and more than 12,000 were displaced. More than 18,000 homes were damaged and 963 others destroyed. Although fire raged in the city and water supply systems were damaged, the major fires in the Marina District were brought under control within 3 hours, mostly through the heroic efforts of San Francisco's firefighters.

After the rubble finally settled, it was unanimously agreed that San Francisco and the Bay Area had pulled through miraculously well—particularly compared with the recent earthquake in Kobe, Japan, which had killed thousands and displaced an entire city. After the quake, a feeling of esprit de corps swept the city as neighbors helped each other rebuild and donations poured in from all over the world. Although over a decade has passed, San Francisco is still feeling the effects of the quake, most noticeably during rush hour as commuters take a variety of detours to circumvent freeways that were damaged or destroyed and are still under construction.

THE 1990S: THE NEW GOLD RUSH

During the early 1990s, nothing earth-shattering took place. The nationwide recession influenced the beginning of the decade, and the quiet rumblings of the new frontier in Silicon Valley escaped much notice. By the middle of the decade, San Francisco and the surrounding areas had discovered a new kind of gold rush—the Internet industry.

Not unlike the gold fever of the 1800s, people flocked to the western shores to strike it rich—and they did. In 1999, local media reported that every day 64 Bay Area residents were gaining millionaire status. Long before the last year of the millennium, real estate prices went into the stratosphere, and the city's gentrification financially squeezed out many of those residents who didn't mean big business (read: many of the alternative types, elderly, and minorities who made the city colorful). New businesses popped up everywhere—especially in the SoMa area, where startup companies jam warehouse spaces to the rafters.

As the most popular posteducation destination for MBAs and the leader in the media of the future, San Francisco no longer opened its Golden Gate to everyone looking for the legendary alternative lifestyle—unless they could afford a $1,000 studio apartment and $20-per-day fees to park their car.

The new millennium was christened with bubbly in hand, foie gras and caviar in mouth, and seemingly everyone in the money. New restaurants charging $35 per entrée were all the rage, hotels were renovated, the new bayfront ballpark was packed, and stock market tips were as plentiful as new million-dollar SoMa condos and high rises. Though there were whispers of a stock market correction, San Franciscans were too busy raking in the dough and working and playing hard to heed the writing on the wall.

2001: A REALITY CHECK

The new millennium started off well enough. The initial fallout in the market and the stability of previously well-funded companies was expected; everyone cashing in on the new economy knew the situation was too good to be true. Venture capitalists began holding on to their funding with both hands, rather than doling it out freely to anyone with an idea and a ".com" suffix. The business community figured the scale was finally balancing, with sound companies outweighing the less-concrete ideas on the bandwidth-bandwagon.

But by mid-2000 investors began to shy from companies with high valuations and no profits. The billions of dollars of funding that poured into the Bay Area had dried up thanks to expensive Superbowl TV advertising spots, pricey operating systems, foolish budgeting practices, and the realization that acquiring customers in many cases cost more than the price of doing business. Dot-com obituaries and layoff notifications grew longer and grimmer, and as this book goes to press, hundreds of Bay Area employees from all walks of high-tech life are getting laid off weekly. Fancier dining rooms are bracing themselves, while on the bright side there is finally no shortage of restaurant staff. Whereas apartments have been scarce for the past five years, they're now becoming available. SoMa is now SloMa and boasts nearly as many commercial for-rent signs as it does surviving dot-coms. And many of those newly arrived gold-diggers are going back to where they came from. The City by the Bay may be perched on prime coastal real estate, but by no means is it out of the financial woods. But that's not to say San Francisco isn't in great shape these days. The city was too crowded, too successful, too rich, and becoming too ruthless. The year 2001 is giving us a much needed reality check and an opportunity to step back, look at where we've come from, and move forward at a more thoughtful and reasonable speed to where we'd like to go.

Appendix B:
Useful Toll-Free Numbers & Websites

AIRLINES

Air Canada
℘ 888/247-2262
www.aircanada.ca

Alaska Airlines
℘ 800/426-0333
www.alaskaair.com

American Airlines
℘ 800/433-7300
www.im.aa.com

America West Airlines
℘ 800/235-9292
www.americawest.com

British Airways
℘ 800/247-9297
℘ 0345/222-111 in Britain
www.british-airways.com

Continental Airlines
℘ 800/525-0280
www.continental.com

Delta Air Lines
℘ 800/221-1212
www.delta.com

Hawaiian Airlines
℘ 800/367-5320
www.hawaiianair.com

Northwest Airlines
℘ 800/225-2525
www.nwa.com

Southwest Airlines
℘ 800/435-9792
www.southwest.com

Trans World Airlines (TWA)
℘ 800/221-2000
www.twa.com

United Airlines
℘ 800/241-6522
www.united.com

US Airways
℘ 800/428-4322
www.usairways.com

Virgin Atlantic Airways
℘ 800/862-8621 in Continental U.S.
℘ 0293/747-747 in Britain
www.virgin-atlantic.com

CAR-RENTAL AGENCIES

Alamo
℘ 800/327-9633
www.goalamo.com

Avis
℘ 800/331-1212 in the
  Continental U.S.
℘ 800/TRY-AVIS in Canada
www.avis.com

Budget
℘ 800/527-0700
www.drivebudget.com

Dollar
℘ 800/800-4000
www.dollar.com

Enterprise
℘ 800/325-8007
www.enterprise.com

Hertz
℘ 800/654-3131
www.hertz.com

National
© 800/CAR-RENT
www.nationalcar.com

Payless
© 800/PAYLESS
www.paylesscarrental.com

Rent-A-Wreck
© 800/535-1391
www.rent-a-wreck.com

Thrifty
© 800/367-2277
www.thrifty.com

MAJOR HOTEL & MOTEL CHAINS

Best Western International
© 800/528-1234
www.bestwestern.com

Clarion Hotels
© 800/CLARION
www.clarioninns.com

Comfort Inns
© 800/228-5150
www.comfortinns.com

Courtyard by Marriott
© 800/321-2211
www.courtyard.com

Days Inn
© 800/325-2525
www.daysinn.com

Doubletree Hotels
© 800/222-TREE
www.doubletree.com

Econo Lodges
© 800/55-ECONO
www.econolodge.com

Hilton Hotels
© 800/HILTONS
www.hilton.com

Holiday Inn
© 800/HOLIDAY
www.basshotels.com

Howard Johnson
© 800/654-2000
www.hojo.com

Hyatt Hotels & Resorts
© 800/228-9000
www.hyatt.com

ITT Sheraton
© 800/325-3535
www.starwood.com

La Quinta Motor Inns
© 800/531-5900
www.laquinta.com

Marriott Hotels
© 800/228-9290
www.marriott.com

Motel 6
© 800/4-MOTEL6
www.motel6.com

Quality Inns
© 800/228-5151
www.qualityinns.com

Radisson Hotels International
© 800/333-3333
www.radisson.com

Ramada Inns
© 800/2-RAMADA
www.ramada.com

Rodeway Inns
© 800/228-2000
www.rodewayinn.com

Super 8 Motels
© 800/800-8000
www.super8.com

Travelodge
© 800/255-3050
www.travelodge.com

Vagabond Inns
© 800/522-1555
www.vagabondinn.com

Wyndham Hotels and Resorts
© 800/822-4200 in Continental U.S.
and Canada
www.wyndham.com

Index

See also Accommodations and Restaurant indexes, below.

GENERAL INDEX

A AA (American Automobile Association), 21–22, 32
Aardvark's, 213
AARP (American Association of Retired Persons), 18
Accommodations, 55–96
  in Berkeley, 237
  best, 5–8
  with free parking, 80
  Napa Valley, 275–281
  price categories, 55
  reservations, 56
  Sonoma Valley, 295–299
  what's new, 1
Addresses, finding, 39
AIDS Memorial Quilt, 180
Airfares, 22–23
Airlines, 21, 22, 31
Airport, accommodations near, 95–96
Airports, 19–20
Alabaster, 208
A La Carte, A La Park, 15
Alamere Falls (Point Reyes National Seashore), 251–252
Alamo Square Historic District, 174–175

Alcatraz Island, 4, 149, 152
Alessi, 208
All American Boy, 205
Alma (ship), 159
American Association of Retired Persons (AARP), 18
American Automobile Association (AAA), 21–22, 32
American Conservatory Theater (A.C.T.), 218
American Express, 51
  traveler's checks, 11
Amtrak, 18, 21
Anchorage, the, 211
Andreotti Family Farm (Half Moon Bay), 255
Angel Island, 242, 244
  ferries to/from, 51
Año Nuevo State Reserve, 256
Antiques, 199, 202
  Napa Valley, 273
Aquarium, Steinhart, 168
Aquarium of the Bay, 153–154
Aquatic Park, 172, 181
Architectural highlights, 174–177
Area codes, 51
Arrowood Vineyards & Winery (Glen Ellen), 292–293

Art festivals, 13, 15
Art galleries, 202–203
  Napa Valley, 274
Arthur Frommer's Budget Travel Online, 23, 25
Artisan Cheese, 206
Art of China, 207
Arts and crafts, 204
Asian Art Museum, 168
Atelier Dore, 202
ATMs (automated teller machines), 10, 30
  online ATM locators, 26
Ayala Cove (Angel Island), 244

B abushka, 207
Baby-sitters, 51
Backflip, 224
Baker Beach, 173, 181
Balclutha (ship), 159
Ballet, 16, 218
Ballooning, 180–181
Bank of America, 188
Bank of America World Headquarters, 176
Bank of Canton, 188
Bars, 224–231
  brew pubs, 226–227
  cocktails with a view, 227–228
  gay and lesbian, 229–230

Bars (*cont.*)
　　sports, 228
　　wine & champagne,
　　　228
BART (Bay Area
　　Rapid Transit), 48
　　Berkeley, 232
　　Oakland, 240
　　tour, 178
Baseball, 184
Basketball, 184
Bay Area Theatres-
　　ports (BATS), 219
Bay Area Women's
　　and Children's
　　Center, 18
Bay Guardian, 38
Bay Meadows, 185
Bayporter Express,
　　20
Bay to Breakers Foot
　　Race, 13, 183
*Beach Blanket
　　Babylon,* 196, 219
Beaches, 181
　　Half Moon Bay, 256
Bear Valley Visitor
　　Center, 250
Be-At Line, 222
Beats (beatniks),
　　191, 195, 226, 227,
　　309–310
Beaulieu Vineyard
　　(Rutherford), 267
Belden Place, restau-
　　rants on, 111
Belli Annex, 192
Benziger Family
　　Winery (Glen Ellen),
　　293
Beringer Vineyards
　　(St. Helena), 269
Berkeley, 232–239
　　what's new, 2
Bicycling
　　Half Moon Bay, 255
　　Napa Valley, 274
　　Sonoma Valley, 293
Biking, 181
Biordi Art Imports,
　　195, 208

Bird-watching, Point
　　Reyes Bird Obser-
　　vatory, 252
Birkenstock, 210
Biscuits and Blues,
　　220
Blue Bar, 223
Blues, 220–221
Blues Festival, San
　　Francisco, 15
Boating, 181
Boat tours, 178
Booksmith, The, 203
Bookstores, 203
　　Berkeley, 234
　　City Lights, 195,
　　　203
　　Half Moon Bay, 257
Borders Books &
　　Music, 203
Botanical Gardens,
　　Strybing Arboretum
　　&, 169
Bottom of the Hill,
　　224
Boulangerie, 206
Brennan, Pam and
　　Bruce, 179
Brew pubs, 226–227
British travelers, 29
Brooks Brothers, 206
Bubble Lounge, The,
　　228
Bucket shops, 22
Buddhist Church of
　　San Francisco, 163
Buena Vista Park,
　　183
Buena Vista Winery
　　(Sonoma), 291
Buffalo Exchange,
　　213
Bulo, 210
Buses, to/from
　　airports, 19–20
Business hours, 51
Bus tours, 178–179
Bus travel, 32, 45
Butterfield &
　　Butterfield, 202

Cabaret, 219–220
Cable Car Barn
　　Museum, 157
Cable Car Clothiers,
　　206
Cable cars, 5, 44–45,
　　154
Caen, Herb, 222, 309
Cafe du Nord, 221
Cafes, 227
　　in North Beach, 3
Café, The, 229
Caffè Greco, 227
Caffè Trieste, 195,
　　227
Cakebread Cellars
　　(Rutherford), 266
Calendar of events,
　　12–16
California Academy
　　of Sciences, 168
California Historical
　　Society, 160
California Palace of
　　the Legion of
　　Honor, 157–158
California Street
　　cable car line, 45
Calistoga
　　restaurants,
　　　288–289
　　sights and activities,
　　　274, 275
　　spas, 275
　　wineries, 270–273
CalTrain, 21
Cameron House, 189
Camping, Point
　　Reyes National
　　Seashore, 250
Cannery, the, 154,
　　156, 211
Canton Bazaar, 188,
　　204
Carnelian Room, The,
　　227
Carneros District,
　　290–291
Carnival, 13

Car rentals, 21, 32, 48–50
Car travel, 21–22, 32, 48
  to Angel Island and Tiburon, 244
  to Berkeley, 232
  Highway 29 (St. Helena Highway), 262, 263
  to Mount Tamalpais, 249
  to Muir Woods, 249
  to Oakland, 240
  safe driving tips, 30, 49
  to Sausalito, 246
Cass Marina, 181
Castro, the, 4–5, 44, 311, 312
  accommodations, 93–94
  restaurants, 142–144
  sightseeing, 164
  tour, 179
Castro Street Fair, 15
Castro Theatre, 230–231
Catharine Clark Gallery, 202
C.A. Thayer (ship), 159
Cathedral
  Grace, 174
  Old St. Mary's, 188
Chalkers Billiard Club, 224
Chanel Boutique, 206
Charles Krug Winery (St. Helena), 269–270
Château St. Jean (Kenwood), 294
Cherry Blossom Festival, 12
Chestnut Street, shopping on, 198
Children's Zoo, 171, 172

China, 203–204
China Beach, 173, 181
Chinatown, 4, 38, 40
  restaurants, 116–117
  shopping, 198
  sightseeing, 162–163
  tour, 179
  walking tour, 186–191
Chinatown Gateway Arch, 186
Chinatown Kite Shop, 188, 212
Chinese Cultural Center, 191
Chinese Historical Society of America Museum, 189–190
Chinese New Year, 12
Churches and other religious buildings, 173–174
  in Chinatown, 188, 190
  Japantown, 163
Cinch Saloon, The, 229
Cinco de Mayo Celebration, 13
Cinemas, repertory, 230–231
Circle Gallery, 175–176
Citizen Clothing, 206
City Box Office, 214, 215
City Hall, 175
City Lights Booksellers & Publishers, 195, 203
City Pass, 45
Cityscape, 227
Civic Center, 41
  accommodations, 90–91
  restaurants, 131–132
  sightseeing, 175

Classical music, 215
Clean, Well-Lighted Place for Books, A, 203
Cliff House, 173
Climate, 12
Clos Pegase (Calistoga), 272–273
Clothing (fashions), 205–206
  vintage, 213
Club Deluxe, 223–224
Club Fugazi, 196
Club Line, 222
Clubs, 220–224
  dance, 222–223
  gay and lesbian, 229–230
  live-music, 220–221
  retro, 223–224
  supper, 223
Coastal Trail, 3–4, 173
Cobb's Comedy Club, 219
Cody's Books (Berkeley), 234
Coit Tower, 156
Columbus Avenue, No. 140, 194
Columbus Tower, 194
Comedy clubs, 219
Condor Club, former site of the, 194–195
Conservatory of Flowers, 169
Consolidators, 22
Cost Plus Imports, 207
Cowell Theater, 218
Cow Hollow, 41
  accommodations, 85–88
  restaurants, 125–131
Cow Hollow Playground, 177
Crafts, 204

Credit cards, 11, 29
Crocker Galleria, 211
Cruisin' the Castro
  tour, 179
Culture Pass, 168
Currency, 29
Currency and
  currency exchange,
  32–33
Customs regulations,
  28

D ance clubs,
  222–223
Dance companies
  and performances,
  218–219
Dandelion, 207
Dean & DeLuca
  (St. Helena), 285
Dentists, 52
Department stores,
  204
Detour, 229
De Vera Galleries,
  209
De Young Memorial
  Museum, 45, 158,
  166
Dianne's Old & New
  Estates, 209
DiMaggio, Joe, 197
Disabilities, travelers
  with, 16
Discount shopping,
  204–205
Disney Store, 212
Distractions &
  Euphoria, 207
Doctors, 52
Doda, Carol,
  194–195
Domaine Chandon
  (Yountville), 264
Drinking laws, 33
Drugstores, 52
Dutch windmill, 166

E agle, The, 229
Earthquake
  1989, 312–313
  and fire of 1906,
    161, 192, 251,
    308
Earthquakes, 52
Edinburgh Castle,
  225
Electricity, 33
Eleonore Austerer
  Gallery, 202
Elephant seals, 168,
  251, 256
Embarcadero, 39
Embarcadero
  promenade, 183
Embassies and
  consulates, 33
Emergencies, 33, 52
  medical, 34
Endup, The, 222, 229
Entry requirements,
  27–28
Eos, 228
Eppleton Hall (ship),
  159
Equinox, 227
E-Savers, 23, 24
Esprit Outlet Store,
  205
Eureka (ship), 159
Eureka Theatre
  Company, 218
Exotic Erotic
  Halloween Ball, 15
Expedia, 24
Exploratorium, 158

F abrics, 205
Factory-outlet stores,
  204–205
  St. Helena, 273
Families with
  children, 19
  restaurants for, 117
FAO Schwarz, 212
Farmers' Market, 156

Fashions (clothing),
  205–206
  vintage, 213
Fax facilities, 36
Ferlinghetti,
  Lawrence, 195, 196,
  203, 309
Fern Creek Trail
  (Muir Woods), 249
Ferries, 50–51
  Angel Island and
    Tiburon, 244
  Sausalito, 246
Ferry Building, 176
Festivals and special
  events, 12–16
Filbert Street Steps,
  182
Fillamento, 208
Fillmore, the, 220
Fillmore Street,
  shopping on,
  198–199
Film Festival, San
  Francisco Inter-
  national, 13, 230
Financial District, 40
  accommodations,
    75–77
  restaurants,
    108–113
Fire of 1906, 161,
  192, 251, 308
Fisherman's Wharf,
  40, 124–125, 152,
  153
  accommodations,
    81–84
  shopping in, 199
Fishing, 182
  Half Moon Bay, 255
Fitzgerald Marine
  Reserve, 256
Flax, 208
Flood Mansion, 176
Fong-Torres, Shirley,
  179–180
Food stores, 206–207
Football, 184–185

Foreign visitors, 27–37

Fort Mason Center, 172

Fort Point, 173

Fourth of July Celebration and Fireworks, 14

Fraenkel Gallery, 202

Frank Family Vineyards (a.k.a. Kornell) (Calistoga), 271

Fumiki Fine Asian Arts, 202

Furnishings, 208–209

G asoline (petrol), 34

Gays and lesbians
in the 1970s and 1980s, 310–312
bars & clubs, 229–230
the Castro, 164
San Francisco Lesbian, Gay, Bisexual, Transgender Pride Parade & Celebration, 14
tips and resources, 17–18

Geary Theater, 218

Ghirardelli Square, 152, 211

Gifford, Jay, 180

Gifts, 207

Gimme Shoes, 211

Ginsberg, Allen, 191, 194, 195, 309, 310

Giraffe Lounge, 229

Gira Polli, 197

Girl Spot, 229

Glass, 203–204

Glen Ellen
restaurant, 303
wineries, 292–293

Glide Memorial United Methodist Church, 5, 174

Gloria Ferrer Champagne Caves (Sonoma), 291

Golden Era Building, 192

Golden Gate Bridge, 156–157
walking across, 4

Golden Gate Fields, 185

Golden Gate Fortune Cookie Company, 189, 207

Golden Gate National Recreation Area, 170, 172–173
walking & hiking, 183–184

Golden Gate Park, 5, 166–169, 177
information on, 166
museums inside, 168–169
restaurants near, 147
special events, 13, 15
tennis, 183

Golden Gate Park Boat House, 181

Golden Gate Park Course, 182

Golden Gate Promenade, 173

Golden State Warriors, 184

Gold rush, 190, 306–307

Golf, 182
Half Moon Bay, 255–256

Good Byes, 213

Good Vibrations, 208

Gordon Biersch Brewery Restaurant, 226

Grace Cathedral, 174

Grand Women's Boutique, 205

Grant Avenue, 186

Grant & Green Saloon, 220–221

Grateful Dead, 179, 310

Great China Herb Co., 190

Great Depression, 308–309

Great Entertainer, The, 225

Green Apple Books, 203

Greens Sports Bar, 228

Grgich Hills Cellar (Rutherford), 267

Gucci America, 205

Gump's, 203–204

H aas-Lilienthal House, 158

Haight-Ashbury, 4, 44
in the 1960s, 310
accommodations, 94–95
restaurants, 144–145
sightseeing, 164
walking tour, 179

Haight Street, shopping on, 199

Haight Street Fair, 14

Hailey, Trevor, 179

Half Moon Bay, 254–259
accommodations, 257–258
restaurants, 258–259
shopping, 256–257
sights and attractions, 255–256
traveling to, 254
visitor information, 255

Half Moon Bay Nursery (Half Moon Bay), 255

Half Moon Bay State Beach, 256
Hallidie Building, 176
Halloween, 16
Halloween Ball, Exotic Erotic, 15
Handball, 182
Harbor seals, 251
Harry Denton's Starlight Room, 223
Harte, Bret, 192
Hayes and Vine, 228
Hayes Valley, shopping in, 199
Health, 18
Heinold's First and Last Chance Saloon (Oakland), 240–241
Hercules (ship), 159
Hess Collection (Napa), 263
HiBall Lounge, 224
Highway 29 (St. Helena Highway), 262, 263
Hiking, 183–184
History of San Francisco, 304–314
HIV-positive visitors, 28
Holidays, 34
Horseback riding
    Half Moon Bay, 255
    Napa Valley, 274
Horse racing, 185
Hot springs, in Calistoga, 275
Housewares, 208–209
Hungry i, 194
Huntington Park, 162, 177

I Can't Believe I Ate My Way Through Chinatown tour, 180
Images of the North, 202

Ina Coolbrith Park, 183
Information sources, 10, 38–39
In-line skating, 183
Insect Zoo, 172
Insurance, 28–29
International Film Festival, San Francisco, 13, 230
International Gay & Lesbian Travel Association (IGLTA), 17
Internet access, 52–53
Internet Travel Network, 23
Interstate 5, 21
Inverness, 249, 251, 252, 253, 254
Italian Heritage Parade, 15

J ack London Square (Oakland), 240
Jackson Square
    400 block of, 192
    antiques dealers on, 199, 202
Japan Center, 163
Japanese Tea Garden, 169
Japantown, 41
    accommodations, 88–90
    sightseeing, 163–164
Javawalk, 179
Jazz, 14, 221–222
    Oakland, 240
Jazz and All That Art on Fillmore, 14
Jazz at Pearl's, 221
Jazz Festival, San Francisco, 16
Jeremy's, 205
Jerusalem Shoppe, 209

Jewelry, 209–210
Johnson's Oyster Farm (near Inverness), 251
Joseph Phelps Vineyards (St. Helena), 268
Joseph Schmidt Confections, 207
Julie's Supper Club, 223
Julius Kahn Playground, 177

K abuki Springs & Spa, 163, 164
Kayaking. *See* Sea kayaking
Kenneth Cole, 211
Kenwood
    restaurant, 303
    wineries, 293–294
Kenwood Vineyards, 294
Kerouac, Jack, 191, 194, 195, 309
Key, 53
Kids. *See* Families with children
Kimo's, 230
Kite Flight, 212
Konko Church of San Francisco, 163

L akeside Park (Oakland), 240
Lands End, 173
Larkspur, ferries to/from, 50–51
La Rosa, 213
Lawrence Hall of Science (Berkeley), 234
Life in California murals, 156
Limn, 209
Lincoln Park, 173, 183

Lincoln Park Golf
Course, 182
Li Po Cocktail
Lounge, 225
Liquor laws, 53
Live-music clubs,
220–221
Lombard Street, 157
London, Jack, 240
London Wine Bar,
228
Lone Star Saloon,
230
Lorraine Hansberry
Theatre, 218
Lou's Pier 47 Club,
221
Lyon Street Steps,
182

MAC, 206
McLaren, John, 166,
169
McLaren Lodge and
Park Headquarters,
166
McLaren Memorial
Rhododendron
Dell, 166
Macy's, 204
Magical Trinket, 210
Magic Theatre, 218
Mail and post
offices, 34, 53
Marathon, San
Francisco, 14, 183
Marina District, 40
accommodations,
85–88
restaurants,
125–131
Marina Green, 173
Marin Headlands, 4
Mario's Bohemian
Cigar Store, 196
Market Street, 39
Matanzas Creek
(Santa Rosa),
294–295
Maverick Beach, 256

Maxwell Galleries,
203
Medical Dental
Building, 176
Medical emergencies,
34
Medic Alert Identifi-
cation Tag, 18
Medical require-
ments for entry, 27
Merritt, Lake
(Oakland), 240
Métier, 206
Metreon Entertain-
ment Center, 160
Metro, 230
Metro streetcar
lines, 45, 48
Mexican Museum,
160
Meyerovich Gallery,
203
M. H. De Young
Memorial Museum,
45, 158, 166
Milk, Harvey, 179,
312
Minis, 206
Mint Karaoke
Lounge, The, 230
Mission Bay Golf
Center, 182
Mission District, 41
restaurants,
138–142
sightseeing,
164–166
Mission Dolores
(Mission San
Francisco de
Assisi), 41, 166,
174
Molinari Deli-
catessen, 195–196
MOMA (San
Francisco Museum
of Modern Art), 5,
159–160
MuseumStore, 208
Mondavi Winery
(Oakville), 265

Money, 10–11, 29
Monroe, Marilyn, 197
Montgomery Block,
192
Montgomery Street,
No. 1010, 194
Morrison
Planetarium, 168
Moscone, George,
312
Mud baths, in
Calistoga, 275
Muir Woods, 4,
248–249
Muni (San Francisco
Municipal Railway),
44, 45
Murals, 156, 165,
176, 195, 196, 225,
290, 309
Musée Mecanique,
173
Museum of Modern
Art, San Francisco
(MOMA), 5,
159–160
MuseumStore, 208
MuseumStore,
SFMOMA, 208
Music
classical, 215
live, 220–224
Music festivals, 14,
15, 16
Music stores, 210

NAMES Project,
180
Napa
accommodations, 2,
276–277
restaurants, 282
sights and activities,
273
wineries, 262–263
Napa Valley, 260–289
accommodations,
275–281
restaurants,
282–289

Napa Valley (*cont.*)
sights and activities, 273–275
touring, 262–273
traveling to, 260, 262
visitor information, 262
wineries, 262
Beaulieu Vineyard (Rutherford), 267
Beringer Vineyards (St. Helena), 269
Cakebread Cellars (Rutherford), 266
Charles Krug Winery (St. Helena), 269
Clos Pegase (Calistoga), 272–273
Domaine Chandon (Yountville), 264
Frank Family Vineyards (a.k.a. Kornell) (Calistoga), 271–272
Grgich Hills Cellar (Rutherford), 267
Hess Collection (Napa), 263
Joseph Phelps Vineyards (St. Helena), 268
Niebaum-Coppola (Rutherford), 266–267

Opus One (Oakville), 265
Plump-Jack Winery (Oakville), 264–265
Prager Winery & Port Works (St. Helena), 267–268
Raymond Vineyard & Cellar (St. Helena), 268–269
Robert Mondavi Winery (Oakville), 265
St. Supéry Winery (Rutherford), 266
SAY Sterling Vineyards (Calistoga), 272
Schramsberg (Calistoga), 272
Silver Oak Cellars (Oakville), 264
Stag's Leap Wine Cellars (Napa), 263
Trefethen Vineyards (Napa), 263
V. Sattui Winery (St. Helena), 269
Napa Valley Olive Oil Manufacturing Company (St. Helena), 273
Natural History Museum, 168–169
Neighborhoods, 39–44
sightseeing, 161–166

Neiman Marcus, 204
Nest, 209
Newspapers and magazines, 34, 53
New Unique Company, 204
Nickie's Bar-be-cue, 222
Niebaum-Coppola (Rutherford), 266–267
Nightlife, 214–231. *See also* **Bars; Cabaret; Clubs; Comedy clubs; Music; Performing arts; Theater**
current listings, 214
tickets, 214
what's new, 2
Nihonmachi Mall, 163
Niketown, 205
Nob Hill, 40
accommodations, 77–81
restaurants, 113–116
sightseeing, 161–162
Nordstrom, 204
North Beach, 40
accommodations, 81–84
cafes, 3, 195, 227
Italian Heritage Parade, 15
Javawalk tour, 179
restaurants, 117–123
shopping, 205
sightseeing, 162
walking tour, 191–197
North Beach Festival, 14
North Beach Museum, 196
North Face, 205

O akland, 239–242
Oakland Athletics, 184
Oakland International Airport, 20
Oakland Museum of California, 241
Oakland Raiders, 184
Oakville, wineries, 264–265
Oakville Grocery Co., 285
Obester Winery (Half Moon Bay), 255
Ocean Beach, 181
Ocean View Trail (Muir Woods), 249
Octagon House, 158–159
ODC Theatre, 218
Old Faithful Geyser of California, 275
Old St. Mary's Cathedral, 188
On the Road Again, 212
Opera, 215
Opera in the Park, 15
Opus One (Oakville), 265
Orbitz, 24
Our World, 17
Out & About, 17
Outdoor activities, 180–184

P acific Bell Park, 184
Pacific Heights, 41
    accommodations, 85–88
    restaurants, 125–131
Package deals, 22–23
Painted Ladies, 174–175
Palace of Fine Arts, 158

Pampanito, USS, 153
Paradise Lounge, 222
Paramount Theatre (Oakland), 240
Parking, 50
Parks, 183
    in Berkeley, 234–236
Passports, 27
Passports (Muni discount passes), 45
Peace Pagoda, 163
Pearl & Jade Empire, 210
People's Park (Berkeley), 236
Performing arts, 214–219
Perimeter Road (Angel Island), 244
Perry's, 225
Pescadero, 259
Pescadero Marsh Natural Preserve, 256
Petrified Forest, 275
Petrol (gasoline), 34
Philharmonia Baroque Orchestra, 215
Phipps Ranch (Pescadero), 259
Picnic and take-out fare, 2, 197
    Napa Valley, 285
    Sausalito, 248
Pied Piper Bar, 225
Pier 39, 152, 211–212
Pillar Point Marsh, 256
Planetarium, Morrison, 168
Plump-Jack Winery (Oakville), 264–265
Pocket Opera, 215
Point Lobos, 173
Point Reyes Bird Observatory, 252

Point Reyes Lighthouse, 250–251
Point Reyes National Seashore, 4, 249–254
Police, 53
Politics, 6–7
Portsmouth Square, 190–191
Post offices, 34, 53
Powell-Hyde cable car line, 44
Powell-Mason cable car line, 44
Prager Winery & Port Works (St. Helena), 267–268
Precita Eyes Mural Arts Center, 165–166
Presidio, the, 169–173
Presidio Golf Course, 182
Presidio Museum, 171
Punch Line, 219
Puppets on the Pier, 212

Q ixo, 25
Quantity Postcards, 208

R adio and television, 34
Rainfall, average, 12
Rasselas, 221
Ravenswood Winery (Sonoma), 292
Rawhide II, 222
Raymond Vineyard & Cellar (St. Helena), 268–269
Recycled Records, 210
Red Room, The, 225

Redwood Room, The, 225

Reggae in the Park, 15

Renaissance Pleasure Faire, 14

Repertory cinemas, 230–231

Restaurants, 97–148
  in Berkeley, 237
  best, 8–9
  by cuisine, 98–101
  family-friendly, 117
  Napa Valley, 282–289
  online reservations, 97
  Sonoma Valley, 300–303
  what's new, 1

Retro clubs, 223–224

Richmond district, 44
  restaurants, 145–148

Rincon Center, 176

Ripley's Believe It or Not! Museum, 153

Robert Mondavi Winery (Oakville), 265

Rock music, 220–221

Rose Garden, 166

Rose Garden (Berkeley), 236

Ross Alley, 189

Roxie, 231

Running, 183

Russian Hill, 40
  restaurants, 113–116

Rutherford
  restaurants, 282–283
  wineries, 266–267

Safety, 30, 53

Sailboat House (Oakland), 240

Sailing, 181

St. Helena
  restaurants, 286–288
  sights and activities, 273, 274
  wineries, 267–270

St. Helena Highway (Highway 29), 262, 263

St. Mary's Square, 188

St. Patrick's Day Parade, 12

Saints Peter and Paul Church, 196

St. Supéry Winery (Rutherford), 266

Sales tax, 199

Saloon, The, 221

SamTrans, 20

San Francisco 49ers, 184

San Francisco Ballet, 16, 218–219

San Francisco Bay Guardian, 53, 214

San Francisco Blues Festival, 15

San Francisco Brewing Company, 226

San Francisco Chronicle, 53, 214

San Francisco Contemporary Music Players, 215

San Francisco Convention and Visitors Bureau, 10

San Francisco Examiner, 13, 53, 214

San Francisco Gallery Guide, The, 202

San Francisco Giants, 184

San Francisco Guide, 53

San Francisco International Airport, 19–20

San Francisco International Film Festival, 13, 230

San Francisco Jazz Festival, 16

San Francisco Lesbian, Gay, Bisexual, Transgender Pride Parade & Celebration, 14

San Francisco Marathon, 14, 183

San Francisco Maritime National Historical Park, 159

San Francisco Museum of Modern Art (MOMA), 5, 159–160

San Francisco-Oakland Bay Bridge, 176

San Francisco Opera, 215

San Francisco Performances, 214–215

San Francisco Shopping Centre, 212

San Francisco Sports and Boat Show, 12

San Francisco Symphony, 215

San Francisco Weekly, 214

San Francisco Zoo & Children's Zoo, 171–172

Sausalito, 245–248
  ferries, 50

Sausalito Art Festival, 15

Savoy-Tivoli, The, 225

SAY Sterling Vineyards (Calistoga), 272
Scenic drives, 4
49-mile, 177–178
Scharffen Berger Chocolate Maker (Berkeley), 2, 239
Schramsberg (Calistoga), 272
Sea kayaking
Tomales Bay (Point Reyes National Seashore), 252
tours from Angel Island, 244
Sea lions, 40, 152, 181, 212, 251, 256
Seals
elephant, 168, 251, 256
harbor, 251
Seasons, 11
Sebastiani Vineyards Winery (Sonoma), 292
Seniors, 18–19
Sequoia Audubon Trail, 256
SFMOMA Museum-Store, 208
SFO Airporter buses, 19–20
Shipping, 199
wine, 270–271
Shoes, 210–211
Shopping, 198–213
in Berkeley, 236–237
discount, 204–205
Half Moon Bay, 256–257
major shopping areas, 198–199
Napa Valley, 273
what's new, 1–2
Shopping centers and complexes, 211–212

Sightseeing, 149–180
49-mile scenic drive, 177–178
Culture Pass, 168
for kids, 177
Sigmund Stern Grove, 183
Silicon Valley, 313
Silkroute International, 204
Silver, 203–204
Silverado Trail, 263
Silver Oak Cellars (Oakville), 264
Skating, 183
Slim's, 221
Smile, 208
Smoking, 35, 53–54, 220
Society for the Advancement of Travel for the Handicapped (SATH), 16
Sokoji-Soto Zen Buddhist Temple, 163
SoMa
accommodations, 91–93
restaurants, 133–138
shopping, 199
SoMa (South of Market), sightseeing, 162
SoMa No, 41
Sonoma
restaurants, 300–303
wineries, 291–292
Sonoma Valley, 289–303
accommodations, 295–299
bike tours, 293
restaurants, 300–303
traveling to, 289

visitor information, 289
wineries, 289–295
Arrowood Vineyards & Winery (Glen Ellen), 292–293
Benziger Family Winery (Glen Ellen), 293
Buena Vista Winery (Sonoma), 291
Château St. Jean (Kenwood), 294
Gloria Ferrer Champagne Caves (Sonoma), 291
Kenwood Vineyards, 294
Matanzas Creek (Santa Rosa), 294–295
Ravenswood Winery (Sonoma), 292
Sebastiani Vineyards Winery (Sonoma), 292
Viansa Winery and Italian Marketplace (Sonoma), 290
Sony's Metreon Entertainment Center, 160
Sosa, Elaine, 179
Sound Factory, 222–223
Spa Radiance, 164
Spas
in Napa Valley, 273–274
Sonoma Mission Inn, Spa & Country Club (Sonoma), 297

Special events and festivals, 12–16

Spec's, 225–226

Spec's Adler Museum Café, 195

Spectator sports, 184–197

Sports bars, 228

Spreckels Mansion, 176

Stag's Leap Wine Cellars (Napa), 263

Stair climbing, 182

Steinhart Aquarium, 168

Stern Grove Midsummer Music Festival, 14

Stevenson, Robert Louis, 191

Stinson Beach, 4

Stockton Street, 163, 189

Store hours, 199

Stow Lake, 169, 181

Strawberry Hill, 169

Streetcar lines, 45, 48

Streetlight Records, 210

Strybing Arboretum, 166

Strybing Arboretum & Botanical Gardens, 169

Stud, The, 230

Sue Fisher King, 209

Sunset district, 44
    restaurants, 145–148

SuperShuttle, 20

Supper clubs, 223

Surfing, Maverick Beach, 256

Sutro Baths, 173

Sweeney Ridge, 173

Sweeny, Tom, 67

Tamalpais, Mount, 249

Taxes, 35, 54

Taxis, 48
    for travelers in wheelchairs, 16

Telegraph Avenue (Berkeley), 232

Telegraph Hill, 40
    restaurants, 117–123

Telegraph services, 36

Telephone, 35–36
    area codes, 51
    useful numbers, 54

Telephone directories, 36

Television, 54

Temperatures, average, 12

Ten 15, 223

Tenderloin, 39–40

Tennis, 183

Ten Ren Tea Co., 188–189, 207

Theater, 218

Theater District, 40

Theatre Artaud, 218

Theatre Rhinoceros, 218

Therien & Co., 202

Thirsty Bear Brewing Company, 226

Thomas Bros. Maps & Books, 212

3 Babes and a Bus, 221

Three Bags Full, 205

Tiburon, 51, 242, 244–245

Tiburon-Angel Island Ferry, 244

Tiffany & Co., 210

Tilden Park (Berkeley), 234

Time zones, 36, 54

Tin How Temple, 190

Tipping, 36–37

Tix Bay Area, 214

Toilets, 37

Tomales Point Trail (Point Reyes National Seashore), 252

Top of the Mark, 228

Toronado, 226

Tosca, 226

Tourist information, 10, 38–39

Tourist visas, 27

Tours. See also Scenic drives
    Angel Island, 244
    BART, 178
    boat, 178
    bus, 178–179
    club-hopping, 221
    sea-kayak (from Angel Island), 244
    for travelers with disabilities, 16
    walking, 179–180

Tower Tours, 232

Toys, 212

Train travel, 18, 21
    for foreign visitors, 31–32

TransAmerica Building, original, 192

TransAmerica Pyramid, 176, 191–192

Transit information, 54

Transportation, 44–51
    information, 54

Travel agencies, gay-friendly, 17

Traveler's checks, 11, 29

Travel goods, 212–213

Traveling to San Francisco, 19–23
    from overseas, 31

Travelocity, 24

Trefethen Vineyards (Napa), 263
Twain, Mark, 192, 307
Twin Peaks, 184
Twin Peaks Tavern, 230

Union Square, 39
accommodations, 56–74
restaurants, 101–108
shopping, 198
Union Street, shopping on, 198
Union Street Art Festival, 13
Union Street Goldsmith, 210
University Art Museum (Berkeley), 234
University of California at Berkeley, 234
University of California Botanical Garden (Berkeley), 236
University of California Golden Bears, 184–185
Up & Down Club, 221

Van Ness Avenue, 39
Vesuvio, 195, 226
Viansa Winery and Italian Marketplace (Sonoma), 290
Victorian Homes Historical Walking Tour, 180
Victorian Interiors, 209
Vintage clothing, 213
Virgin Megastore, 210

Visas, 27
Vision-impaired travelers, 16
Visitor information, 10, 38–39
V. Sattui Winery (St. Helena), 269

Walking, 183–184
Walking tours, 179–180, 186–197
self-guided, 192
Walk & Wok tour, 180
Washington Square, 196
Waverly Place, 190
Wax Museum, 153
Weather, information, 54
Websites, 10
travel-planning resources, 23–26
Wells Fargo History Museum, 160
Whale watching, in Point Reyes National Seashore, 250, 251
Wheelchairs, travelers in, 16
Where, 214
White Sulphur Springs Retreat & Spa, 273–274
Wilkes Bashford, 205
William Stout Architectural Books, 203
Windsor Vineyards (Tiburon), 245
Wine, 213
shipping, 270–271
Wine & champagne bars, 228
Wine Club San Francisco, 213
Wine Country, 260–303. *See also* Napa Valley; Sonoma Valley

Wine country, 2
Wine Institute, 262
Wineries
Half Moon Bay, 255
Napa Valley, 262
Beaulieu Vineyard (Rutherford), 267
Beringer Vineyards (St. Helena), 269
Cakebread Cellars (Rutherford), 266
Charles Krug Winery (St. Helena), 269
Clos Pegase (Calistoga), 272–273
Domaine Chandon (Yountville), 264
Frank Family Vineyards (a.k.a. Kornell) (Calistoga), 271–272
Grgich Hills Cellar (Rutherford), 267
Hess Collection (Napa), 263
Joseph Phelps Vineyards (St. Helena), 268
Niebaum-Coppola (Rutherford), 266–267
Opus One (Oakville), 265
Plump-Jack Winery

Wineries (*cont.*)
(Oakville),
264–265
Prager Winery &
Port Works
(St. Helena),
267–268
Raymond
Vineyard &
Cellar
(St. Helena),
268–269
Robert Mondavi
Winery
(Oakville), 265
St. Supéry Winery
(Rutherford),
266
SAY Sterling
Vineyards
(Calistoga),
272
Schramsberg
(Calistoga),
272
Silver Oak Cellars
(Oakville), 264
Stag's Leap
Wine Cellars
(Napa), 263
Trefethen
Vineyards
(Napa), 263
V. Sattui Winery
(St. Helena),
269
Sonoma Valley,
289–295
Arrowood
Vineyards &
Winery (Glen
Ellen),
292–293
Benziger Family
Winery (Glen
Ellen), 293
Buena Vista
Winery
(Sonoma), 291
Château St. Jean
(Kenwood),
294

Gloria Ferrer
Champagne
Caves
(Sonoma), 291
Kenwood
Vineyards, 294
Matanzas Creek
(Santa Rosa),
294–295
Ravenswood
Winery
(Sonoma), 292
Sebastiani
Vineyards
Winery
(Sonoma), 292
Viansa Winery
and Italian
Marketplace
(Sonoma), 290
Tiburon, 245
Wok Shop, The, 188,
209
**Wok Wiz Chinatown
Walking Tours &
Cooking Center,**
179
**Women's Philhar-
monic,** 215
Women travelers, 18
World War II, 309
**WPA (Works Progress
Administration)
murals,** 156, 176,
309
Wright, Frank Lloyd,
175

Yerba Buena
Center for the Arts,
160
Yerba Buena Gardens,
5, 160, 161
Yountville
restaurants,
283–284
wineries, 264

Z eum, 160
Zinc Details, 209
Zoo, Children's, 172
Zoo, San Francisco,
171–172

ACCOMMODATIONS

24 Henry, 93–94
Abigail Hotel, The,
90–91
Adelaide Inn, The, 73
Andrews Hotel, The,
68
An English Oak Inn
(Olema), 253
Archbishop's Man-
sion, 5, The, 88–89
Argent Hotel, The, 91
Auberge du Soleil
(Rutherford), 278
Beach House Inn
(Half Moon Bay),
257
Beck's Motor Lodge,
80, 94
Bed & Breakfast Inn,
86
Beltane Ranch (Glen
Ellen), 298–299
Calistoga Spa Hot
Springs, 281
Campton Place
Hotel, 1, 8, 56–57
Cartwright Hotel,
The, 68
Casa Madrona
(Sausalito), 247
Castillo Inn, The, 94
Cedar Gables Inn
(Napa), 276
Chablis Inn (Napa),
276–277
Clarion Bedford,
Hotel, The, 1, 68–69
Clift Hotel, 1
Clift Hotel, The, 57
Comfort Suites, 95

Commodore Hotel, The, 69

Cornell Hotel de France, The, 69

Cottage Grove Inn (Calistoga), 281

Cow Hollow Motor Inn & Suites, 80, 87

Cypress Inn on Miramar Beach (Half Moon Bay), 257

Donatello, The, 57, 60

Edward II Inn & Suites, 87–88

El Bonita Motel (St. Helena), 280

El Dorado Hotel (Sonoma), 296

El Drisco, 85

Embassy Suites, 95

Embassy Suites (Napa), 276

Euro Spa & Inn (Calistoga), 281

Fairmont Hotel & Tower, The, 1, 6, 77

Fifth Floor Restaurant, 8

Fitzgerald, The, 69–70

Fort Mason Youth Hostel, 80

Gaige House Inn (Glen Ellen), 298

Glenelly Inn (Glen Ellen), 299

Golden Gate Hotel, The, 74

Grand Hyatt San Francisco on Union Square, 60

Grant Plaza Hotel, 74

Handlery Union Square Hotel, 63

Harbor Court, The, 91

Hilton San Francisco, 63–64

Holiday Inn, 68, 95

Hostelling International San Francisco-Downtown, 73–74

Hostelling International San Francisco-Fisherman's Wharf, 88

Hotel Beresford, 70

Hotel Beresford Arms, 70

Hotel Bohème, The, 5, 81, 84

Hotel Del Sol, 1, 86

Hotel Diva, 64

Hotel Griffon, The, 91–92

Hotel Majestic, The, 1, 5, 89

Hotel Milano, 65

Hotel Monaco, 60

Hotel Nikko, 61

Hotel Palomar, 8, 92

Hotel Rex, 61

Hotel Triton, 61–62

Hotel Vintage Court, 65

Huntington Hotel, The, 1, 6, 77–78

Hyatt Regency San Francisco, 1, 75

Inn Above Tide (Sausalito), The, 246–247

Inn at Southbridge (St. Helena), The, 279

Inn at Union Square, The, 65

Inn on Castro, 93

Jackson Court, 86–87

Joie de Vivre, 68

Juliana Hotel, The, 1, 66

Kensington Park Hotel, The, 66

Kenwood Inn & Spa, 299

King George Hotel, 70–71

Laurel, The, 6, 80, 87

Maison Fleurie (Yountville), 277–278

Mandarin Oriental, 8

Mandarin Oriental, The, 7–8, 75

Manka's Inverness Lodge & Restaurant, 252

Marina Inn, The, 6, 88

Mark Hopkins Inter-continental, The, 78

Maxwell, The, 66–67

Meadowood Napa Valley (St. Helena), 279–280

Mill Rose Inn (Half Moon Bay), 257–258

Monticello Inn, The, 71

Motel Inverness, 253

Napa River Inn (Napa), 2, 276

Napa Valley Lodge (Yountville), 277

Napa Valley Marriott (Napa), 276

Napa Valley Railway Inn (Yountville), 278

Nob Hill Inn, The, 80–81

Nob Hill Lambourne, 79–80

Palace Hotel, The, 5–6, 75–76

Pan Pacific, The, 62

Parker House, The, 93

Park Hyatt San Francisco, The, 76–77

Personality Hotels, 68

Petite Auberge, 71

Phoenix Hotel, The, 7, 80, 90

Prescott Hotel, 62
Queen Anne Hotel, The, 90
Radisson Miyako Hotel, The, 1, 89
Rancho Caymus Inn (Rutherford), 279
Renaissance Stanford Court Hotel, 78–79
Ritz-Carlton, The, 8, 79
San Francisco Airport North Travelodge, 96
San Francisco Marriott, 92–93
San Remo Hotel, 6, The, 84
Savoy Hotel, The, 71–72
Seal Cove Inn (Half Moon Bay), 258
Seal Rock Inn, 76
Serrano Hotel, 67
Sheehan Hotel, The, 74
Sheraton Fisherman's Wharf Hotel, 81
Sherman House, 5, 85–86
Sir Francis Drake, 67
Sonoma Hotel (Sonoma), 296–297
Sonoma Mission Inn, Spa & Country Club (Sonoma), 295–296
Sonoma Valley Inn (Sonoma), 296
Stanyan Park Hotel, 94–95
Tuscan Inn, The, 81
Union Street Inn, 7, 86
Victorian Garden Inn (Sonoma), 297–298
Villa Florence, 72
Warwick Regis, The, 72
Washington Square Inn, The, 84

Westin St. Francis, 5, 62–63
Wharf Inn, The, 80, 84
White Sulphur Springs Retreat & Spa (St. Helena), 280–281
White Swan Inn, The, 7, 72–73
Willows Inn, The, 94
Wine Country Inn (St. Helena), 280
Wine Valley Lodge (Napa), 277
W San Francisco Hotel, 7, 92

RESTAURANTS
Absinthe, 8, 131
Ace Wasabi's Rock 'n' Roll Sushi, 126–127
Alexis Baking Company (Napa), 282
Alioto's, 124
All Seasons Café (Calistoga), 288
Ana Mandara, 1, 125
Andalé Taqueria, 129–130
Aqua, 8, 108
A. Sabella's, 124
AsiaSF, 137
Auberge du Soleil (Rutherford), 282–283
Avenue 9, 147
Azie, 133
bacar, 1, 133
Bay Wolf (Oakland), 242
Beach Chalet Brewery & Restaurant, 145–146
Belden Place, 111
The Big Four, 113
Bistro Don Giovanni (Napa), 282

Bistro Jeanty (Yountville), 284
Bix, 117–118
Bouchon (Yountville), 284
Boulevard, 8, 133
Brandy Ho's Hunan Food, 116
Brasserie Savoy, 105–106
Butterfly, 1, 138
Cafe Bastille, 111
Café Claude, 107
Cafe Kati, 125–126
Cafe La Haye (Sonoma), 300
Cafe Pescatore, 125
Cafe Rouge (Berkeley), 238
Cafe Tiramisu, 111
Caffé Luna Piena, 142–143
Caffè Macaroni, 121–122
CafféMuseo, 160
Caffè Sport, 118
Cambodiana's (Berkeley), 239
The Cantinetta (St. Helena), 287
Capp's Corner, 122
Carnelian Room, 109
Catahoula (Calistoga), 288
Cha Cha Cha, 9, 144–145
Chez Panisse (Berkeley), 237–238
Chow, 143
Citron (Oakland), 241
Cliff House, 117, 146
Cucina Viansa (Sonoma), 302
Delfina, 8, 140–141
Della Santina's (Sonoma), 302–303
Depot Hotel-Cucina Rustica Restaurant (Sonoma), 300–301
Doidge's, 127

Dottie's True Blue Café, 107–108
Duarte's Tavern (Pescadero), 259
Ebisu, 147
The Elite Café, 127
Eliza's, 117, 130
Ella's, 1, 127
Emporio Armani Cafe, 108
Enrico's, 118, 120
Eos, 144
Farallon, 8, 101, 104
Fifth Floor Restaurant, 134
Firewood Café, 143–144
Fleur de Lys, 8, 104
Florio, 127–128
Flying Saucer, 138
Fog City Diner, 120
Foreign Cinema, 138–139
42 Degrees, 139
The French Laundry (Yountville), 283–284
Fringale Restaurant, 9, 135
The Girl & The Fig (Sonoma), 301
Glen Ellen Inn Restaurant, 303
The Golden Turtle, 116
Gordon Biersch Brewery Restaurant, 135
Gordon's House of Fine Eats, 8, 139–140
Grand Café, 104–105
The Gray Whale (Inverness), 254
Greens Restaurant, 9
Greens Restaurant, Fort Mason, 128
The Grill (Sonoma), 300

Guaymas (Tiburon), 245
Guernica (Sausalito), 247–248
Hamburgers (Sausalito), 248
Harbor Village, 109
Hard Rock Cafe, 113, 116, 117
Harris', 126
Hawthorne Lane, 134–135
Hayes Street Grill, 132
House of Dim Sum, 189
House of Nanking, 116
Il Fornaio, 120
Il Pollaio, 122
Jardinière, 131
Johnfrank, 143
Kabuto Sushi, 146
Kenwood Restaurant & Bar, 303
Khan Toke Thai House, 146–147
Kokkari, 111
Kuleto's, 106
Kyo-Ya, 109
La Folie, 126
La Toque (Rutherford), 283
Le Colonial, 106
Long Life Noodle Company & Jook Joint, 137
L'Osteria del Forno, 122
The Mandarin, 124
Manora's, 137
Marcello's Pizza, 144
Mario's Bohemian Cigar Store, 9, 122
Masa's, 105
Maya (Sonoma), 301
Maykedah, 120–121
Mecca, 142
Mel's Diner, 117, 130

Meritage (Sonoma), 301–302
Millennium, 132
MoMo's, 1, 135
Montage, 160
Moose's, 118
Mo's Gourmet Burgers, 117, 123
Moss Beach Distillery (Half Moon Bay), 258
Mustards Grill (Yountville), 284–285
O Chamé (Berkeley), 238
Oliveto Cafe & Restaurant (Oakland), 241–242
Ondine (Sausalito), 247
One Market, 109–110
O'Reilly's Irish Pub, 196
Oritalia, 106–107
Pane e Vino, 128
Park Chow, 143
Pasta Moon (Half Moon Bay), 258–259
Pasta Pomodoro, 8, 117, 123
Pauline's, 8, 141
Phineas T. Barnacle, 146
Piatti (Sonoma), 302
Piatti (Yountville), 286
Plouf, 111
PlumpJack Café, 128–129
Pluto's, 130
Postrio, 105
Prego, 129
Restaurant Gary Danko, 8, 124–125
Restaurant Lulu, 136
R&G Lounge, 116

Rivoli (Berkeley), 238–239

Rose Pistola, 121

Rubicon, 8, 110

Sam's Anchor Café (Tiburon), 245

Sam's Grill & Seafood Restaurant, 111–112

Scala's Bistro, 107

Seafood and Beverage Co., 146

Sears Fine Foods, 108

The Slanted Door, 9, 140

Smokehouse Café (Calistoga), 288

South Park Café, 136

Station House Café (Point Reyes Station), 253

The Stinking Rose, 121

Straits Café, 147

Sushi Main Street (Half Moon Bay), 259

Sushi Ran (Sausalito), 248

Swan Oyster Depot, 113

Sweet Heat, 145

Tadich Grill, 112

Taqueria La Quinta (Point Reyes Station), 254

Taquerias La Cumbre, 141

Terra (St. Helena), 286

Terrace Restaurant, 9

Thep Phanom, 145

Thirsty Bear Brewing Company, 136–137

Ti Couz, 141–142

Tomatina (St. Helena), 287–288

Tommaso's, 123

Tommy Toy's, 110

Ton Kiang, 9, 147

Tra Vigne Restaurant (St. Helena), 286–287

Tú Lan, 137–138

2223 Restaurant & Bar, 142

Universal Café, 140

Upstairs at the Cliff House, 146

Wappo Bar & Bistro (Calistoga), 289

Washington Bakery & Restaurant, 189

The Waterfront Restaurant & Cafe, 112

Wine Spectator Greystone Restaurant (St. Helena), 287

World Wrapps, 130–131

Yank Sing, 112–113

Yoshi's (Oakland), 240

Zinzino, 129

Zona Rosa, 145

Zuni Café, 132

FROMMER'S® COMPLETE TRAVEL GUIDES

Alaska
Amsterdam
Argentina & Chile
Arizona
Atlanta
Australia
Austria
Bahamas
Barcelona, Madrid & Seville
Beijing
Belgium, Holland & Luxembourg
Bermuda
Boston
British Columbia & the Canadian Rockies
Budapest & the Best of Hungary
California
Canada
Cancún, Cozumel & the Yucatán
Cape Cod, Nantucket & Martha's Vineyard
Caribbean
Caribbean Cruises & Ports of Call
Caribbean Ports of Call
Carolinas & Georgia
Chicago
China
Colorado
Costa Rica
Denmark
Denver, Boulder & Colorado Springs
England
Europe
European Cruises & Ports of Call
Florida
France
Germany
Greece
Greek Islands
Hawaii
Hong Kong
Honolulu, Waikiki & Oahu
Ireland
Israel
Italy
Jamaica
Japan
Las Vegas
London
Los Angeles
Maryland & Delaware
Maui
Mexico
Montana & Wyoming
Montréal & Québec City
Munich & the Bavarian Alps
Nashville & Memphis
Nepal
New England
New Mexico
New Orleans
New York City
New Zealand
Nova Scotia, New Brunswick & Prince Edward Island
Oregon
Paris
Philadelphia & the Amish Country
Portugal
Prague & the Best of the Czech Republic
Provence & the Riviera
Puerto Rico
Rome
San Antonio & Austin
San Diego
San Francisco
Santa Fe, Taos & Albuquerque
Scandinavia
Scotland
Seattle & Portland
Shanghai
Singapore & Malaysia
South Africa
Southeast Asia
South Florida
South Pacific
Spain
Sweden
Switzerland
Texas
Thailand
Tokyo
Toronto
Tuscany & Umbria
USA
Utah
Vancouver & Victoria
Vermont, New Hampshire & Maine
Vienna & the Danube Valley
Virgin Islands
Virginia
Walt Disney World & Orlando
Washington, D.C.
Washington State

FROMMER'S® DOLLAR-A-DAY GUIDES

Australia from $50 a Day
California from $70 a Day
Caribbean from $70 a Day
England from $70 a Day
Europe from $70 a Day
Florida from $70 a Day
Hawaii from $70 a Day
Ireland from $60 a Day
Italy from $70 a Day
London from $85 a Day
New York from $80 a Day
Paris from $80 a Day
San Francisco from $60 a Day
Washington, D.C., from $70 a Day

FROMMER'S® PORTABLE GUIDES

Acapulco, Ixtapa & Zihuatanejo
Alaska Cruises & Ports of Call
Amsterdam
Australia's Great Barrier Reef
Bahamas
Baja & Los Cabos
Berlin
Boston
California Wine Country
Charleston & Savannah
Chicago
Dublin
Hawaii: The Big Island
Hong Kong
Houston
Las Vegas
London
Los Angeles
Maine Coast
Maui
Miami
New Orleans
New York City
Paris
Phoenix & Scottsdale
Portland
Puerto Rico
Puerto Vallarta, Manzanillo & Guadalajara
San Diego
San Francisco
Seattle
Sydney
Tampa & St. Petersburg
Vancouver
Venice
Washington, D.C.

FROMMER'S® NATIONAL PARK GUIDES

Family Vacations in the National Parks
Grand Canyon
National Parks of the American West
Rocky Mountain
Yellowstone & Grand Teton
Yosemite & Sequoia/ Kings Canyon
Zion & Bryce Canyon

FROMMER'S® MEMORABLE WALKS

Chicago	New York	San Francisco
London	Paris	Washington, D.C.

FROMMER'S® GREAT OUTDOOR GUIDES

Arizona & New Mexico	Northern California	Southern New England
New England	Southern California & Baja	Vermont & New Hampshire

FROMMER'S® BORN TO SHOP GUIDES

Born to Shop: France	Born to Shop: Italy	Born to Shop: New York
Born to Shop: Hong Kong, Shanghai & Beijing	Born to Shop: London	Born to Shop: Paris

FROMMER'S® IRREVERENT GUIDES

Amsterdam	Los Angeles	Seattle & Portland
Boston	Manhattan	Vancouver
Chicago	New Orleans	Walt Disney World
Las Vegas	Paris	Washington, D.C.
London	San Francisco	

FROMMER'S® BEST-LOVED DRIVING TOURS

America	France	New England
Britain	Germany	Scotland
California	Ireland	Spain
Florida	Italy	Western Europe

THE UNOFFICIAL GUIDES®

Bed & Breakfasts in California	Golf Vacations in the Eastern U.S.	New Orleans
Bed & Breakfasts in New England	The Great Smokey & Blue Ridge Mountains	New York City
Bed & Breakfasts in the Northwest	Inside Disney	Paris
Bed & Breakfasts in Southeast	Hawaii	San Francisco
Beyond Disney	Las Vegas	Skiing in the West
Branson, Missouri	London	Southeast with Kids
California with Kids	Mid-Atlantic with Kids	Walt Disney World
Chicago	Mini Las Vegas	Walt Disney World for Grown-ups
Cruises	Mini-Mickey	Walt Disney World for Kids
Disneyland	New England with Kids	Washington, D.C.
Florida with Kids		World's Best Diving Vacations

SPECIAL-INTEREST TITLES

Frommer's Britain's Best Bed & Breakfasts and Country Inns

Frommer's France's Best Bed & Breakfasts and Country Inns

Frommer's Italy's Best Bed & Breakfasts and Country Inns

Frommer's Caribbean Hideaways

Frommer's Adventure Guide to Australia & New Zealand

Frommer's Adventure Guide to Central America

Frommer's Adventure Guide to India & Pakistan

Frommer's Adventure Guide to South America

Frommer's Adventure Guide to Southeast Asia

Frommer's Adventure Guide to Southern Africa

Frommer's Gay & Lesbian Europe

Frommer's Exploring America by RV

Hanging Out in England

Hanging Out in Europe

Hanging Out in France

Hanging Out in Ireland

Hanging Out in Italy

Hanging Out in Spain

Israel Past & Present

Frommer's The Moon

Frommer's New York City with Kids

The New York Times' Guide to Unforgettable Weekends

Places Rated Almanac

Retirement Places Rated

Frommer's Road Atlas Britain

Frommer's Road Atlas Europe

Frommer's Washington, D.C., with Kids

Frommer's What the Airlines Never Tell You

Let Us Hear From You!

Dear Frommer's Reader,

You are our greatest resource in keeping our guides relevant, timely, and lively. We'd love to hear from you about your travel experiences—good or bad. Want to recommend a great restaurant or a hotel off the beaten path—or register a complaint? Any thoughts on how to improve the guide itself?

Please use this page to share your thoughts with me and mail it to the address below. Or if you like, send a FAX or e-mail me at frommersfeedback@hungryminds.com. And so that we can thank you—and keep you up on the latest developments in travel—we invite you to sign up for a free daily Frommer's e-mail travel update. Just write your e-mail address on the back of this page. Also, if you'd like to take a moment to answer a few questions about yourself to help us improve our guides, please complete the following quick survey. (We'll keep that information confidential.)

Thanks for your insights.

Yours sincerely,

Michael Spring

Michael Spring, *Publisher*

Name (Optional) _____

Address _____

_____

City _____ State _____ ZIP _____

Name of Frommer's Travel Guide _____

Comments _____

_____

_____

_____

_____

_____

_____

_____

_____

_____

_____

Please tell us a little about yourself so that we can serve you and the Frommer's community better. We will keep this information confidential.

Age: ( )18-24; ( )25-39; ( )40-49; ( )50-55; ( )Over 55

Income: ( )Under $25,000; ( )$25,000-$50,000; ( )$50,000-$100,000; ( )Over $100,000

I am: ( )Single, never married; ( )Married, with children; ( )Married, without children; ( )Divorced; ( )Widowed

Number of people in my household: ( )1; ( )2; ( )3; ( )4; ( )5 or more

Number of people in my household under 18: ( )1; ( )2; ( )3; ( )4; ( )5 or more

I am ( )a student; ( )employed full-time; ( )employed part-time; ( )not employed at this tim ( )retired; ( )other

I took ( )0; ( )1; ( )2; ( )3; ( )4 or more leisure trips in the past 12 months

My last vacation was ( )a weekend; ( )1 week; ( )2 weeks; ( )3 or more weeks

My last vacation was to ( )the U.S.; ( )Canada; ( )Mexico; ( )Europe; ( )Asia; ( )South America; ( )Central America; ( )The Caribbean; ( )Africa; ( )Middle East; ( )Australia/New Zealand

( )I would; ( )would not buy a Frommer's Travel Guide for business travel

I access the Internet ( )at home; ( )at work; ( )both; ( )I do not use the Internet

I used the Internet to do research for my last trip. ( )Yes; ( )No

I used the Internet to book accommodations or air travel on my last trip. ( )Yes; ( )No

My favorite travel site is ( )frommers.com; ( )travelocity.com; ( )expedia.com;

other _____

I use Frommer's Travel Guides ( )always; ( )sometimes; ( )seldom

I usually buy ( )1; ( )2; ( )more than 2 guides when I travel

Other guides I use include _____

What's the most important thing we could do to improve Frommer's Travel Guides?

_____

_____

_____

_____

Yes, please send me a daily e-mail travel update. My e-mail address is

_____

Mail to: Michael Spring, Publisher and Vice President, Frommer's Travel Guides
909 Third Ave., New York, NY 10022   FAX: 212.884.5432

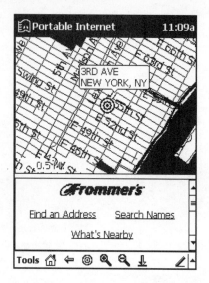